VOICES FROM THE DUST

NEW INSIGHTS INTO ANCIENT AMERICA

Voices From The Dust

New Insights Into Ancient America

A Comparative Evaluation of
Early Spanish and Portuguese Chronicles
Archaeology and Art History
The Book of Mormon

With a Foreword by
Robert E. Wells
1st Quorum of the Seventy (Emeritus)

David G. Calderwood

Copyright ©2005 by David G. Calderwood

All rights reserved.

No part of this book may be reproduced or utilized in any form whatsoever, by photography or xerography or by any other means, by broadcast or transmission, by translation into any kind of language, nor by recording electronically or otherwise, without permission from the publisher except for brief excerpts used in reviews.

This work is not an official publication of The Church of Jesus Christ of Latter-day Saints. The views expressed herein are the responsibility of the author and do not necessarily represent the position of the Church or of Historical Publications, Inc.

Published by:
Historical Publications, Inc.
8205 Racine Trail
Austin, Texas 78717
1-800-880-6789

Library of Congress Cataloging-in-Publication Data

Calderwood, David G., 1937-
  Voices from the dust : new insights into ancient America : a comparative evaluation of early Spanish and Portuguese chronicles, archaeology and art history, the Book of Mormon / David G. Calderwood ; with a foreword by Robert E. Wells.
    p. cm.
  Summary: "A comparative evaluation of early Spanish and Portuguese chronicles, sixteenth and seventeenth century New World conquistadores and colonizers, the Book of Mormon, and Latin American archaeology and art history"--Provided by publisher.
  Includes bibliographical references and index.
  ISBN 1-881825-50-7 (alk. paper)
  1. Book of Mormon--Evidences, authority, etc. 2. Indians--Origin. 3. Lost tribes of Israel. 4. America--Antiquities. I. Title.
  BX8627.C28 2005
  289.3'22--dc22
                               2005009568

Printed in the United States of America
Print and Bind Direct!
Books@PrintAndBind.com

10 9 8 7 6 5 4 3 2

And thou shalt be brought down, and shalt speak out of the ground, and thy speech shall be low out of the dust, and thy voice shall be, as of one that hath a familiar spirit, out of the ground, and thy speech shall whisper out of the dust.

Isaiah 29:4

DEDICATED TO . . .

The hundreds of Spanish and Portuguese soldiers, Catholic priests, and government officials who devoted their time, energy and resources to preserve for posterity the folklore, legends, accounts and observations of the native Americans at the time of the conquest and colonization.

Preface

While living in Lima, Peru, in the early 1970's, I came across Pedro de Cieza de León's second book, *El Señorio de los Incas* (*The Lordship of the Incas*),¹ and was struck by the similarities between Pre-Columbian Indian legends and accounts contained in the *Book of Mormon*, a book that has long been a center of controversy. *El Señorio de los Incas* was written in 1553, but was not published until 1880, fifty years after the *Book of Mormon* was published. This discovery led me to investigate whether other early conquistador writings also contained similar accounts. During the ensuing years, I collected more than seventy books written by Spaniards or Portuguese in early America. The original manuscripts date between 1500 and 1650 A.D.

In addition to my own collection, I augmented my research material with access to early chronicle writings held in the Nettie Lee Benson Library at the University of Texas at Austin, where I obtained a Master of Art's Degree in 1999. The Benson Library has arguably the finest collection of early chronicle writings in the Western Hemisphere. Through subsequent research, it soon became evident to me that many of these other early

---

¹Pedro de Cieza de León, *El Señorio de los Incas*. Madrid Circa 1553. Original manuscript was lost until 1880 when it was published by Marcos Jimenez de la Espada, Madrid. (Republished by the Instituto de Estudios Peruanos, Lima, 1967.)

chronicles also contain information that appears similar to *Book of Mormon* accounts.

Joseph Smith claimed to have translated the *Book of Mormon*, purportedly a record of early American inhabitants, from gold plates that Moroni, an ancient warrior and prophet, hid by burying them in 421 A.D. This is more than one thousand years before the 1492 voyage of Columbus. The Spanish and Portuguese chroniclers obviously knew nothing about the gold plates buried by Moroni. These early writers obtained valuable folklore, legends, and significant minutiae of the Pre-Columbian natives which they included in their writings. When their manuscripts arrived in Spain or Portugal, most of them were lost for more than 300 years and were unknown to the uneducated Joseph Smith in the 1820's when he claims to have acquired and translated the gold plates. He published this translation as the *Book of Mormon* in 1830.

Notwithstanding the numerous similarities and parallel accounts contained in the chronicles and the *Book of Mormon*, no secular historian or Mormon historian has ever made any significant comparative evaluation between the *Book of Mormon* and these early records. Most of the chronicles were printed in old Spanish or Portuguese and are relatively unknown even today within the United States. Only a few of these books have been translated into English.

As I pursued my studies of the Spanish and Portuguese chronicle writings, I also took classes in Andean and Mesoamerican art history, iconography, and archaeology to ascertain whether scientific investigations would complement the information contained in the chronicles and the *Book of Mormon*. Although I have only scratched the surface of art history and archaeology, I have become increasingly convinced that greater insights can be obtained about Pre-Columbia America and particularly the Formative Period (2500 B.C. to 400 B.C.)

and the Classical Period (400 B.C. to 600 A.D.) by blending the information and ideas obtained from archaeological discoveries with information gleaned from the *Book of Mormon* and from the chronicles.

In Peru, for example, the Moche artists (100 B.C. to 600 A.D.), who lived along the northern coast near the modern-day city of Trujillo, depicted on some of their ceramic vessels a glorious, powerful "Rayed Deity," who, according to one series of iconographic presentations, quelled a "revolt of the objects" or upheaval of nature. Who was this majestic Rayed Deity, who was shown wearing elaborate military accouterments?

For their part, the chroniclers recorded legends of a White God who appeared in the New World during approximately the same time frame as the Moche civilization. This White God healed the sick, the blind and the lame and performed other miracles.[2] In Peru he was known as Ticci Viracocha or Pachacamac and in Mexico as Quetzalcoatl or Huitzilopochtli.

The *Book of Mormon* contains an account of a miraculous appearance of the resurrected Jesus Christ in the Americas where he performed many miracles such as healing the sick, the blind, and the lame. His appearance was heralded by a period of earthquakes and overwhelming destruction in the Americas. His appearance coincided with the return of calm to the area.

The intent of my book is to bring together the folklore, legends, and accounts collected by the early chroniclers and compare them with accounts recorded in the *Book of Mormon*. Whenever possible, I will compare my findings with scientific evidence, discovered and reported by archaeologists and art historians.

As a fifth-generation Mormon, I have always studied the *Book of Mormon* and considered it to be a faithful account of some ancient American inhabitants. Because of my faith in the

---

[2]Ibid., 9.

Book of Mormon narrative, I served a two and a half year mission from 1957 to 1959 for The Church of Jesus Christ of Latter-day Saints in Uruguay and Paraguay. During the ensuing years, I have visited many archaeological sites in Bolivia, Peru and Mexico which seemed relevant to the *Book of Mormon* history. Since discovering these Spanish and Portuguese chronicles and comparing their legends and accounts with *Book of Mormon* narrative, I have been able to augment and balance my initial faith with additional information and insights.

Archaeologists and art historians generally discover their artifacts by digging into the ground. As they reveal ancient cultures, it is as if the ancients were speaking out of the dust. Coincidentally, most of the manuscripts of the early chroniclers were lost or forgotten and lay on library or museum shelves for centuries gathering their own kind of dust. Joseph Smith claimed that the last *Book of Mormon* prophet, Moroni, hid the gold plates in the ground where they remained for fourteen hundred years before Moroni retrieved them and passed them to Smith for translation.

The accounts and histories of these three totally unrelated sources, passed down through the ages, could be interpreted as if their speech or histories whispered out of the dust.

Perhaps the ancient Israelite prophet Isaiah, who claimed to have seen far into the future, was privileged to see our day and he recognized that ancient truths about pre-Columbian America would be revealed out of the dust.

> *And thou shalt be brought down, and shalt speak out of the ground, and thy speech shall be low out of the dust, and thy voice shall be, as of one that hath a familiar spirit, out of the ground, and thy speech shall whisper out of the dust.*
> Isaiah 29:4

Foreword

VOICES FROM THE DUST is a "must read" book for the serious student of the *Book of Mormon* as well as for anyone curious about the remarkable parallels between the beliefs and practices of both North and South American Indians and the three different groups of people whose migrations from the Old World to the New World are covered in the pages of the *Book of Mormon*. The cover explains the subject matter by calling it "New Insights Into Ancient America" and "A Comparative Evaluation of Early Spanish and Portuguese Chronicles, Archaeology, Art History and the *Book of Mormon*."

The author has gathered in this book, through serious scholarship and a lot of hard work over many years, the best collection I have yet seen to date of information about the culture and religion of the ancient inhabitants of the Americas relative to comparable information in the *Book of Mormon*. The amazing thing is that none of this material could possibly have been available prior to 1829/1830 when the *Book of Mormon* was published.

David Calderwood, because of his personal linguistic and research ability, has brought together for the reader new and detailed information coming from the "Chroniclers" of the Spanish and Portuguese Conquistadores. These "Chroniclers" or "Historians" wrote about what the Conquistadores found among the Pre-Columbian inhabitants. Much of their work was never translated into English, nor was it ever published even in the original language, and much of their work was destroyed or hidden by higher authorities for various reasons, political as well as religious. Bits and pieces of material have come to light over the centuries but none of it was available to Joseph Smith when he presented the *Book of Mormon* to the world. Joseph never pretended to have written the *Book of Mormon* himself, which is fortunate because no one of his time could possibly have known all the details about the civilizations, cultures, religions, political maneuvering, strategies of aggressive and defensive war-making, origins and migrations, etc. Now, in one volume, the whole scope of what is known today is available, and the hope is that there will be a great deal of additional information come forth in the future. The author's command of both old Spanish and old Portuguese as well as his listing of his sources will greatly help others do further research in the future.

The author does not resolve nor get into the discussion of two Hill Cumorahs nor a narrow neck of land nor anything about the exact geography of the *Book of Mormon*. Part of the appeal of this new book to me is that here is a non-judgmental portrayal of patterns and parallels coming from the Guarani/Amazon basin as well as the Andean area of South America that fits in with the information found in Central America, (Mesoamerica), Mexico, and North America. Rather than defend a theory or position, Calderwood just lays it out for us to read and digest ourselves. Yet it is a solid defense of the fact that the *Book of Mormon* fits into all of these geographical areas and into the cultures and beliefs of virtually all the "Indian Nations" found by the invading Spaniards and Portuguese.

There is strong evidence throughout this book of ancient apostasy from once lofty religious concepts related to the Israelite/Christian traditions. The success of the conquerors in subduing the natives has always been attributed largely to the natives' almost universal belief in the past visit of a "white God" who said He would return, as well as visits of others who seem to have echoes of similarity with Christian Apostles of old. This information has never been as well documented in one volume as is now presented in this book. And again, this is a subject covered in the *Book of Mormon*; yet Joseph Smith could not have known that such a tradition was so wide spread throughout all of Latin America.

My association with David Calderwood comes from having worked together in Paraguay some 45 years ago when I had been sent there to open a branch office of an international bank. Over the years since then our paths have crossed many times in business and church assignments as well as being neighbors in Argentina for a few years. Our children still stay in touch because of close ties between us dating from that time. Thirty-five years of my life have been spent living in Latin America and another twenty years, while residing in the USA, my trips to Latin America averaged two or more weeks per month. Aside from 19 years in international banking, I also was called into full-time Church service which resulted in a second career lasting 35 years as mission president, Regional Representative, First Quorum of the Seventy, and temple president. At one time or another I was assigned to supervise Church affairs in every country south of the Rio Grande for The Church of Jesus Christ of Latter-day Saints.

David spent a similar number of years in Diplomatic service, business affairs, and Church callings, mostly in Latin America, so our paths crossed inevitably and often. I congratulate David on his scholarship and diligence in gathering so much material and weaving it together in a meaningful way of great value to all who are interested in the *Book of Mormon* and the remarkable story behind it.

My own "expeditions" into remote areas of Latin America have allowed me to be exposed to local stories about "white Indians in the jungle," navigation instruments similar to the "Liahona," reports from people who say they have seen "gold plates with an ancient religious history sacred to the Indians," legends of races of Indians who descended from brothers who had crossed the ocean, etc. The stories abound even today. But David has not used hearsay and oral legend. He has done the research, kept the notes, bought the old books, visited the libraries, and his work is now available for all to read.

The author is also to be congratulated for weaving together his chapters in an interesting manner using quotes from his wide range of sources, from the original "Chroniclers" with quotes from the Book of Mormon itself, to the Old Testament and the New Testament and even the Pearl of Great Price. He points out where doctrinal drift and outright apostasy has occurred just as spoken of in the *Book of Mormon*.

The whole purpose of David Calderwood's research and writing is a careful defense of the inspiration of Joseph Smith and the *Book of Mormon* as being from the Lord and not a book any living person could possibly have written without the gift from the Lord. David quotes Dr. Hugh Nibley as saying: "There is no point at all to the question: Who wrote the *Book of Mormon*? It would have been quite as impossible for the most learned man alive in 1830 as it was for Joseph Smith." Then David adds, "The new archaeological discoveries in recent years as well as the discovery and publication of numerous sixteenth and seventeenth century chronicles in the last 150 years highlight what a remarkable book the *Book of Mormon* is." (Page 499 of the manuscript.)

I also appreciated the author's tribute to his ancient sources. "A study of chroniclers, whether they were Catholic Priests, soldiers, or government officials, suggests that they were guided by an honest effort to inform their fellow Europeans about the New World and the Native Americans. Most wrote at considerable sacrifice of time, money, and comfort. They were often highly dedicated and highly motivated individuals who gathered their information and wrote under difficult circumstances...... With few exceptions, they wanted future generations to know and understand what they discovered after arriving in the New World." ..... "They were not without flaws and they struggled with language difficulties, political problems, and inadequate information.....They faithfully recorded the legends, teachings and accounts passed down over hundreds of years by native historians......." (page 503 of the manuscript)

David Calderwood editorializes in one of the last pages of the book an important point. He says, "I believe that many of the New World writers received divine guidance in pursuing their investigations and in recording their findings. Several chroniclers.....declared that they felt God's influence compelling them to pursue their lofty activities. It is noteworthy that most of these sixteenth and seventeenth century manuscripts were not published shortly after they were written and disappeared for three and four hundred years, only to be discovered and published many years after the publication of the *Book of Mormon*. I believe that this was no accident. If the libraries of the 1820's had been replete with these early American chronicles, the critics of the *Book of Mormon* could have argued that Joseph Smith simply used these early chronicle accounts to write an historical fiction novel." (Page 504 of the manuscript)

The title of this book, <u>Voices From The Dust</u>, refers to three separate sources of material that speak from the dust: (1) The *Book of Mormon*, whose gold plate source was buried for hundreds of years and then brought forth out of the ground/dust by Divine power; (2) The "Chroniclers", who included in their histories the legends, folklore, stories, beliefs, etc. of the natives, but which manuscripts were lost or hidden under centuries of library and archival dust; and (3) the archaeologists and art historians who discover their artefacts and art by digging in the dust of old ruins.

The author, David Calderwood, in writing the last paragraph of the last page of this book (page 522), ties it all together with these thoughts: "The *Book of Mormon* (is) this "Second Witness of Jesus Christ" (second to the Holy Bible). The primary role of the early-American chroniclers and the findings of the archaeologists and art historians, the other two" Voices From The Dust", is to testify of the *Book of Mormon*." David puts all three together in a very informative and readable volume which accomplishes his purpose in great style.

        Robert E. Wells
        1st Quorum of the Seventy (Emeritus)
        The Church of Jesus Christ of Latter-day Saints

ACKNOWLEDGMENTS

Many people all over the world generously gave me access to their rare chronicle writings and encouraged me to continue in the pursuit of this comparative evaluation. Dr. Mario Castro Arenas, the former Peruvian Ambassador to Panama, and Fabio Satizabel, a Colombian student of ancient America, are two of whom particular mention should be made. I am deeply indebted to those members of the University of Texas at Austin faculty who are closely associated with the Institute of Latin American Studies (ILAS) and particularly to Dr. Henry Selby, the former Senior Faculty Advisor at ILAS who kindly read my numerous reports describing the histories and antecedents of the early chroniclers; to Drs. Susan Deans-Smith and Virginia Garrard Burnett for their guidance and numerous suggestions which helped mold my Master's thesis into an acceptable paper; to Dr. Terrence Grieder, who provided insights into the Art History world of pre-Columbian America; to Dr. Steve Bourget, who introduced me to the Moche culture; and to Dr. Orlando Kelm, who unselfishly gave of his time to ensure that my Master's thesis, which has served as the basic structure for this book, maintained a balance in the religious content. Also I am indebted to Daryl Gibson who proofread the manuscript and provided valuable suggestions. I thank my wife, Della, who designed the dust cover for my book and for frequently bailing me out of numerous computer glitches. Lastly I thank my children, siblings, and close friends, who patiently listened to my oral presentations of chronicle and *Book of Mormon* stories and accounts. They always encouraged me to continue with my research.

Illustrations and Photographs

Front Dust Cover
The sketch of Francisco Pizarro's encounter with the Lord Inca Atahualpa was drawn by Felipe Guaman Poma de Ayala in the early 1600's. His sketches have been used by Historians and Art Historians since their discovery in 1908 by Richard Pietschmann.

"Moroni Burying the Plates" by Tom Lovell
© by Intellectual Reserve, Inc.
Courtesy of the Museum of Church History and Art

A statue of an apparently ancient Mayan leader with a strikingly Egyptian appearance in the head wear, pectoral and facial features that was encountered in the jungle near the Maya ruins at Chichen Itzá, Yucatán, Mexico. Picture taken by Author in 1959.

Back Dust Cover
Photograph shows the Southeast corner of the 3000 year old structure of the New Temple at Chavín de Huántar, Peru. Picture taken by the Author in 1973.

Photographs and Illustrations in the Text
The photographs of the Mural located in the Temple of the Huaca de la Luna and the Huaca de la Luna archaeological site near Trujillo, Peru, were taken by Dr. Steven Bourget, who graciously provided the pictures. (Page 141.)

Figure 1 (page 142), Figure 2 (page 143), and Figure 3 (Page 144) were graciously provided by Drs. Jeffrey Quiltar and Donna McClelland.

The photographs of human sacrifice at the Huaca de la Luna (Page 217) were taken by Dr. Steven Bourget, who graciously provided the pictures.

The Combat scenes on page 311 of dark and light-skinned warriors comes from Moche ceramic vessels and is portrayed in Federico Kauffmann Doig's book, *Manual de Arqueología Peruana*. Ediciones Peisa, Lima, Peru. 1969.

The photograph of the reed boat on Lake Titicaca shown on page 375 from Victor Wolfgang Von Hagen's book, *The Incas*. Picture is courtesy of the University of Oklahoma Press.

The photographs on pages 405 and 406 of Tiwanaku, Bolivia, were taken by Rodney Dial during his Church mission to the Titicaca region of Bolivia in 1980.

The war scenes at Cerro Sechín, Peru, depicting Chavín war scenes were initially shown in Richard L. Burger's book, *Chavín and the Origins of Andean Civilization*. Permission to use these scenes was granted by Dr. Burger and the publisher, Thames and Hudson, Ltd., London. (Pages 437-439.)

All other photographs were taken by the Author during various excursions into archaeological sites in South America and Mexico.

TABLE OF CONTENTS

Chapter .... Page

    Dedication vii

    Preface ix

    Foreword xiii

    Acknowledgements xix

1 Origin Theories of the Indians 1

2 Introduction to the Chronicles 17

3 Overview of New World Discoveries 41

4 Introduction to the *Book of Mormon* 71

5 Native American Origins According to the *Book of Mormon* ... 99

6 Period "When They Did Not See the Sun" 121

7 A Period of Great Natural Upheavals 139

8 Immortality of the Soul and the Resurrection 155

9 Christian and Jewish Ethic and Morality in the

   New World 187

10 Sacrifice, Sacrament and the Atonement 211
11 Ten Commandments and Other Israelite Teachings 233
12 Prosperity and Degeneration During America's
    Formative Years 2500 B.C. to 400 B.C. 269
13 Prosperity and Degeneration During Pre-Classic and Classic
    period 600 B.C. to 400 A.D. 293
14 White Indians in the New World 315
15 Fatalism or Prophecies Among The Indians 343
16 Pre-Columbian Technical Skills 365
17 Warfare and Weaponry 433
18 Messiah Ben Joseph 463
19 A Marvellous Work and a Wonder 493
   Appendix A 523
   Appendix B 527
   Bibliography 551
   Index 565

1

ORIGIN THEORIES OF THE INDIANS

When the adventurous, expansion-minded Europeans first heard the exciting news of Christopher Columbus's discovery and exploration of the New World, many were enticed by the possibilities of opportunities. But they were also beset by questions about the native tribes that Columbus had found. Who were these people? Where did they originate? When and how did they arrive in the Americas? While writing in his journal on 17 October 1492, Columbus mistakenly referred to the newly discovered natives as "Indians."[1] This misnomer has been applied to the native Americans for the last 500 years. The *conquistadores*, colonizers, Catholic priests, and many subsequent explorers encountered a wide variety of

---

[1]Cristobal Colón, *Diario de a Bordo* (Transcribed by Friar Bartolomé de las Casas, who had access to many papers written by Columbus. Las Casas finished his manuscript entitled *Historia de las Indias* in 1551, in which Las Casas included Columbus's narrative of his first voyage. Las Casas's manuscript was also lost and not published until 1875 in Madrid. Las Casas left intact Columbus's Prologue and letter to the Spanish monarchy; all of which has been extracted into his *Diario a Bordo*.) Edition, introduction, notes and appendix—Vicente Muñoz Puelles. (This edition printed by Grupo Anaya, S.A., Madrid, 1985.) 76.

natives, scattered throughout the Americas who showed marked differences in terms of skin coloring, cultures, religions, traditions, and languages.

The initial discovery of the New World by Columbus on behalf of the Spanish royalty was quickly followed by other explorers sailing mainly from Spain and Portugal; however, the French, English, Dutch, Italians and Germans also mounted their own exploratory expeditions and attempted to lay claim on the Americas.

Among the thousands of Europeans pouring into the New World, a few of the conquistadores, colonizers, government administrators, priests, and eventually native Americans as well, took the time to write accounts of conquest, discovery, and adventure in the New World. Their accounts provided information about the topography, the natural resources, and the people they encountered. Their reports, in the form of diaries, official documents, and historical manuscripts, contributed eyewitness descriptions of the conquest as well as extensive background information on many of the native groups. These early writings became collectively known as the "Chronicles of the Indies" and the writers were generally referred to as "New World chroniclers."

Conscientious writers, who recorded their contacts with the natives, provided insights into the native cultures and religious beliefs. These early explorers and priests had the advantage of hearing the first uncorrupted versions of the native legends and other stories which had been passed down in songs, tales, or through devices such as the *quipos* in Peru,[2] and paintings and

---

[2] The quipos, also spelled quipus, was a mechanical system involving the knotting of multi-colored strings in such a fashion that it enabled the Inca and Andean Indians to record numerical and historical data. Those who could read this system were called quipocamayocs. Many of the chroniclers obtained valuable historical information from the quipocamayocs who were still actively plying their trade until the seventeenth century.

books in Mesoamerica, by which the natives remembered their cultural legacy.³ In Mesoamerica, the Spaniards encountered libraries of written and painted materials (codices) by the Mayas and Aztecs, but, unfortunately, the invaders soon destroyed most of the native books and paintings, generally, in an effort to destroy the native religions which the Spanish looked upon as satanic-inspired idolatry.

After the early explorers realized that the newly discovered Western Hemisphere was, in reality, a New World, many of them attempted to ferret out the origins of the natives and to ascertain how they arrived on a continent so far away from Europe, Africa and Asia. Since these early writers were mainly Catholics who unquestioningly embraced the Biblical creation narrative contained in Genesis, they also accepted the idea that Adam and Eve were our first parents. They believed there was a universal flood and that all human beings were descendants of Noah. They reasoned that the animals discovered in the New World must have been carried in Noah's ark through the flood and somehow managed to migrate to the Americas after the waters subsided. These early investigators supplemented their Bible studies with some of the Biblical apocryphal writings. Schooled in Europe, they also researched classical writers such as Aristotle, Plato, Pliny, Ptolemy, and Strabon to augment their theories.

Numerous theories about the origins of the Indians began to surface in the mid-1500's. According to the 16th Century historian and priest, Pedro Mártir de Angleria, Columbus himself suggested the theory that the Indians were descendants of the

---

[3] Both the Maya and the Nahuatl speaking Indians of Mesoamerica were gifted in hieroglyphic writings and elaborate paintings which contained a history of the most noted events, native rulers, and deities. Iconographers and art historians are becoming increasingly adept at reading the ancient Maya and Nahuatl symbols.

ancient inhabitants of the land of Ophir where Solomon sent his ships to retrieve rare building materials for the Israelite temple.[4] Ophir is identified in Genesis 10:29 as a son of Joktan and grandson of Heber, who lived around the time of the Tower of Babel. After the voyage of Ferdinand Magellan (1519-1522) revealed the great distance from the Americas to Asia, many chroniclers discounted the Ophir theory. One of the strongest proponents of the Ophir theory, however, was Friar Miguel Cabello Valboa, who wrote his *Miscelánea Antártica, Una Historia del Peru Antiguo* (*Miscellaneous Antarctic, A History of Ancient Peru*) in 1586.[5]

As these early writers delved into the origin of the native Americans, different hypotheses were introduced. One school advanced the theory that they were descendants from the legendary lost city of Atlantis which was believed to have bridged the gap between southern Europe/northern Africa and the Americas. With the alleged sinking of Atlantis about 1320 B.C., those Atlantians in the New World were trapped and remained there. Other chroniclers advocated a Carthaginian or Phoenician source. A few writers believed the Indians were Spaniards who sailed from Spain during the reign of Hespéro, a mythical king of Spain who allegedly ruled circa 1600 B.C. and supposedly discovered the Hespérides Islands, believed by some theorists to be the West Indies.

Many chroniclers supported a theory that the native Americans were descendants of the Lost Ten Tribes of Israel.

---

[4]Pedro Mártir de Anglería, *Décadas del Nuevo Mundo* (First published in partial form in 1511, First complete edition in Latin in 1530. The first Spanish Edition published in 1892.) Published in Buenos Aires, Argentina by Editorial Bajel with the Latin translated to Spanish by Dr. Joaquín Torres Asensio in 1944. Republished in Mexico City, with Introduction and Notes from Edmundo O'Gorman, by Jose Porrua e Hijos in 1964. 29.

[5]Miguel Cabello Valboa, *Miscelánea Antártica, Una Historia del Peru Antiguo*. Written in manuscript form in 1586. (Introduction and Notes by Luis E. Valcarcel. First published by the Universidad Nacional Mayor de San Marcos, Facultad de Letras, Instituto de Etnología, Lima 1951.)

The northern Ten Tribes of Israel were captured by the Assyrian King Shalmaneser IV in 721 B.C., and, according to Apocryphal accounts, they were taken north and eventually disappeared. This theory gained popularity when a few writers allegedly identified some of the New World religious rites and customs as being of Hebrew or Israelite origin. The chroniclers encountered legends of a flood in Mesoamerica as well as in South America. Some of the chroniclers reported that many natives adhered strictly to various aspects of the Ten Commandments.

Other writers advanced a theory that the natives were Jews who fled Israel at the time of the siege of Jerusalem by the Romans circa 70 A.D. The Augustinian cleric Jerónimo Román y Zamora and other priests thought they saw evidence of Christian ceremonies and teachings among the Indians. They found tribes of Indians where the natives seemed to practice confession and had baptismal rites. There were accounts of "saintly preachers" who appeared to follow an apostolic role. Some chroniclers dismissed these accounts as the efforts of the devil to deceive the Indians to keep them from accepting the "true Catholic religion." Modern historians tend to discredit these early accounts by suggesting that the priests had the tendency to view and distort native religions through their Catholic eyes.

Compounding the question of the native American origins was the puzzle of how they arrived in the New World and how and when the animals arrived. The conquistadores observed that although many animals were similar to those found in the Old World, there were others that were obviously unique to the Americas. Once later investigators considered the immensity of the Atlantic and Pacific Oceans, the idea of passage by ship was soon discarded. They realized how difficult it would be to cross either ocean without the aid of a compass. Before the invention of the compass, most sailors are believed to have traveled during daylight hours and within sight of land. Few ventured into the open seas. The chroniclers theorized that even if a ship had been blown off course to the New World by a great storm, the ship would not be carrying animals, especially carnivores, and probably not women either. Consequently, they discarded the idea of an accidental migration as the source of native populations. Many New World writers suggested a land route or a narrow water passage in the far north or the far south over which both men and animals could cross. Magellan's voyage of 1521 seemed to rule out a southern land connection, which left only the mysterious regions of Anian in the far north.[6]

In 1590, the erudite Jesuit priest, Joseph de Acosta, published his manuscript *Historia Natural y Moral de las Indias*, (*Natural and Moral History of the Indies*)[7] in which he emphasized the importance of experience or research and logical deduction to gain insights into the origin of the Indians. Acosta, dismissing the idea of an Atlantis connection or a Jewish origin, concluded "that the New World was not completely divided and separated from the Old World."[8] He suspected that there was either a land connection or a narrow strait in the far north that had not yet been explored. He accepted the idea of a gradual migration over this land connection or strait. Subsequent investigators were greatly influenced by the Acosta theory.

In 1607, the Dominican friar, Father Gregorio García, wrote a book entitled *Orígen de los Indios de el Nuevo Mundo e Indias Occidentales* (*Origin of the Indians of the New World and West*

---

[6]Anian was a vague location which was thought to exist in the far northeastern corner of Siberia or the far northwestern part of the Americas, in what is roughly the Siberian-Alaska area. The Straits of Anian were subsequently named the Bering Straits after their discovery by Vitus Bering, a Danish captain who sailed into the straits in 1728.

[7]Father Joseph de Acosta, *Historia Natural y Moral de las Indias,* initially written and published in 1590 in Seville. (Edition prepared by Edmundo O'Gorman, professor in the College of Letters and Sciences in the National Autonomous University of Mexico. Mexico D.F. 1940.)

[8]Ibid., 77.

Indies) in which he investigated and recorded all the known theories that had surfaced to his day concerning the origin of the American Indians.⁹ García proposed that there were four ways in which information about the origin of the Indians could be obtained. The first was an appeal to *Science*, the second to *Divine Faith*, the third to *Human Faith* (or *Tradition*), and the fourth to *Opinion*. He rejected the *Scientific* approach of his day because "there is no demonstration nor reason which engenders in our understanding, true and certain knowledge from whence the Indians came." He also rejected *Divine Faith* because the scriptures do not reveal their origin.¹⁰ García discounted *Human Faith* because until Columbus discovered the Americas, no one ever mentioned anything about them or gave any reports of the New World. García concluded that *Opinion* was their only recourse and for 336 pages of text he analyzed the opinions, pro and con, of every theory that had been advocated to his day. Finally, he concluded that one man's opinion was as good as another's.

Although reluctant to provide his own opinion, García conceded that there were probably several migrations over time from several areas and by different routes. The Indians were not just one homogeneous family. Unknowingly, he was probably the first investigator to offer the *Diffusionist* theory of the origins of the Indians.¹¹

During the first one hundred fifty years after the discovery of America, most of the origin theories were advanced by the

---

⁹Fray Gregorio García, *Origen de los Indios de el Nuevo Mundo e Indias Occidentales*, (First Edition 1607, Valencia). Preliminary study and notes by Franklin Pease, G. Y., Reedited by Fondo de Cultura Económica, México, 1981.

¹⁰Ibid., 9.

¹¹*Diffusionists* generally accept the idea that skills, customs, and ideas were transmitted from one group to another through human contact. Individuals separated by great distances did not automatically invent the same skills, customs or ideas, but those things were transmitted or diffused by human contact. Conversely there are those who believe that similar skills, customs and ideas were developed or invented independently by dispersed groups. The latter became known as *Independent Inventionists*.

Spaniards and to a lesser extent the Portuguese. During the next two hundred years, however, the northern Europeans, mainly the English and the Dutch, took a more active role in proposing origin theories.

The northern Europeans paid little attention to the Ophir, Carthaginian, or Lost Tribes theories and adhered more closely to Acosta's theory of a land bridge or strait which, in their view, provided a more logical hypothesis that would account for the migration of both humans and animals. Several English writers theorized that the Indians were descendants of Tatars (also spelled Tartars) or Mongols of northern Asia.

In the mid-1600's the Dutch became embroiled in a literary controversy between Hugo Grotius, the father of international law, and Joannes de Laet, an early director of the Dutch West India Company. Grotius proposed that the Indians of North America were probably Norse descendants. The Indians of the Yucatán, who practiced circumcision, were probably Ethiopians. And the Peruvian Indians, who had "highly refined minds," were probably Chinese. He rejected a land route to the New World and specifically the Tatar theory because the Tatars would have brought horses with them. De Laet was drawn to the Acosta theory of a land route and argued for a Tatar connection, suggesting that perhaps they came prior to the domestication of the horse by the Tatars.[12]

The lack of a cohesive, provable hypothesis led to other less orthodox theories. For example, Paracelsus (1493-1541) suggested that perhaps God had created a second Adam for America. In this vein, Isaac de la Peyrère, a French Huguenot, wrote *Prae-*

---

[12]For more information on the Grotius/de Laet controversy see Lee Eldridge Huddleston's essay entitled *Origins of the American Indians, European Concepts, 1492-1729*. Published for the Institute of Latin American Studies by the University of Texas Press, Austin and London, 1967. Chapter IV.

[13]Isaac de la Peyrère, *A Theological System upon that Presupposition that Men were before Adam*. London. Published first in Latin in 1655. (Information taken from Huddleston's 1967 Essay.)

Adamitae (*Men Before Adam*)[13] in which he claimed that historical and Biblical evidence showed that men probably existed before Adam. Adam was placed on earth during the second creation and became the father of the "Jews." The flood destroyed only the Hebrews. In La Peyrère's view this helped explain why Egypt and Mesopotamia seemed more ancient than Israel, and why men could have been in America before the flood.[14]

Although many Europeans believed the Indians were God's children and merited the saving grace of the gospel, many others viewed them as nothing more than "barbarians," suggesting they were subhuman; consequently, they were hunted and killed like wild beasts. The Indians were viewed by some as wild men of the literary imagination, those creatures who were thought to live in the woods and the mountains far removed from the activities of rational men. These wild men belonged to a clearly defined group, the *similitudines hominis*, a class of half-men/half-beast creatures. Some writers suggested that the wild men, including the American Indians, might be soulless men descended from another Adam or perhaps created spontaneously from the earth.

Unlike the Spaniards who produced dozens of chronicles about the New World, there were few North American historians during the early years of the colonization period who were interested in Indian origins. This may stem from the fact that the settlers in the United States and Canada generally pushed the Indians towards the west or isolated them in enclaves or reservations. There was little direct contact and certainly far fewer intermarriages between the settlers of North America and the Indians than occurred between the Spaniards and the Indians which, in the latter case, gave rise to the mestizo class.

In 1721, Cotton Mather, one of the leading Puritan ministers of the day, rejected both Paracelsus and La Peyrère, asserting that the Indians were descendants of Noah. Elias Boudinot, who

---

[14]Huddleston, 139.

served as a delegate from New Jersey to the Continental Congress from 1777 to 1778 and from 1781 to 1784 and was the founder and first president of the American Bible Society, published a book in Boston in 1816 entitled *Star in the West, or, a Humble Attempt to Discover the Long Lost Ten Tribes of Israel*. Boudinot drew heavily upon the writings of James Adair, an Irishman who lived among the Chickasaw, Choctaw, and Cherokee Indians for forty years (1735-1775) before returning to England. Adair published a book in 1775 entitled *The History of the American Indians*. Boudinot, like Adair, strongly defended the idea that the Indians were Israelites.[15] In 1823, Ethan Smith, a Congregational Minister, published, *View of the Hebrews, or The Tribes of Israel in America*.[16] Ethan Smith also extensively quotes Adair in formulating his *View*.

Although North America did not have the great Indian urban areas like those built by the Mayans, Aztecs, or Incas, there were numerous areas east of the Mississippi containing remnants of fortifications and cities that had been built by a group known simply as the Mound Builders. There were various books written in the late 1700's and early 1800's which speculated about the origins of the Mound Builders. While many of these authors referred to origin theories published by the early Spaniards, most of their ideas were borrowed from northern Europeans. Again there was no common consensus among North American theorists concerning the origin of the Indians or how they came to be in the New World.

In March of 1830, Joseph Smith, Jr., an unschooled twenty four-year-old farmer living near Palmyra, a small village not far from Rochester, New York, published the *Book of Mormon*.

---

[15] Elias Boudinot, *A Star in the West, or a humble Attempt to Discover the Long Lost Tribes of Israel* (Trenton, New Jersey, 1816.) The reference cited and Bibliography came from Dan Vogel's *Indian Origins and the Book of Mormon* (Signature Books, Inc. United States of America, 1986.)

[16] Ethan Smith, *View of the Hebrews or Tribes of Israel in America* (Second Edition, Published and Printed in Poultney, Vt. 1825.)

Joseph Smith claimed that he had translated the book from gold plates which had been entrusted to him by an angel. The *Book of Mormon* allegedly contains, "the Fullness of the Everlasting Gospel" as delivered through ancient prophets living in the New World. The book describes three boat migrations to the Americas from several areas in the Old World. The first migration left the Middle East at the time of the Tower of Babel, perhaps around 2500 B.C. The second migration led by a Hebrew prophet, contemporaneous with Jeremiah, left Jerusalem in 600 B.C. The third group left Jerusalem when the city was overthrown by the Babylonian armies under King Nebuchadnezzar, circa 588 B.C. The *Book of Mormon* does not rule out the migration of other groups to the New World. However, it makes no mention of any other inhabitants in the Americas except these three groups.

Although the book provides an abbreviated chronology and history of each group, the main thrust of the *Book of Mormon* is religious. Reportedly a compilation of ancient writers, the focus of each *Book of Mormon* writer was to teach about Jesus Christ. The most significant account within the *Book of Mormon* is the alleged personal appearance of the resurrected Jesus Christ in the Americas shortly after his resurrection and appearance in Jerusalem. After the publication of the *Book of Mormon*, Joseph Smith and five other men formally organized The Church of Jesus Christ of Latter-day Saints on 6 April 1830. His unwavering affirmation of the truthfulness of the *Book of Mormon* and of his own role as a modern prophet ultimately led to Smith's assassination in 1844.

A few early chroniclers like Father Acosta attempted to use a logical and a scientific approach to find answers to the origin and cultures of the native Americas. Unfortunately, modern archaeology, anthropology, and ethnology did not begin in earnest until the mid-1800's. In 1839, the President of the United States,

Martin Van Buren, appointed John Lloyd Stephens, a lawyer who had gained fame writing about his travels in Egypt and other middle eastern countries, as a Special Ambassador to Central America to negotiate a treaty with that region.

During this assignment, Stephens and Frederick Catherwood, a celebrated artist, traveled into the Yucatán to explore the ancient ruins discovered there. On his return to the United States, Stephens wrote *Incidents of Travel in Central America, Chiapas and Yucatan*, which was published in June 1841. In his book, Stephens described the Maya ruins and featured Catherwood's vivid artist renditions which captured the flavor and essence of these ancient buildings and Mayan art works. Intrigued by the possibilities of exploring these ancient ruins, other explorers interested in archaeology followed Stephens's footsteps into Mexico. Peru also attracted numerous archaeologists and art historians who have explored a variety of early civilizations.

With the development of ever more sophisticated techniques for interpreting and understanding ancient civilizations, scientists began to formulate new, and continually evolving, theories concerning the origins and cultures of the pre-Columbian Americans. These later scientists were greatly influenced by the writings of Charles Darwin (1809-1882) and Thomas Henry Huxley (1825-1895). Darwin, one of the more controversial scientists of his day, published his classic, *The Origin of Species by Means of Natural Selection*, in 1859. Although not directly related to Indian-origin theories, Darwin's book helped promote the theory of *evolution*, which in turn has had great impact upon scientific thinking concerning the origin of the native Americans.

In 1863, Huxley published his own book, *Evidence on Man's Place in Nature*, a comprehensive review of what was known at the time about primate and human paleontology. Huxley's book was the first attempt to apply evolution explicitly to the human race. As modern scientists embraced the theory of evolution and gained greater understanding of the earth's age, most of them discredited a literal Judeo-Christian interpretation of the Biblical narrative of the creation.

Many scientists support the Acosta theory that men and animals must have crossed the Bering Straits, but they propose a much earlier date than did Acosta. Scientists, who adhere to the *Independent Inventionist* theories, insist that it was at the end of the last Ice Age, or approximately 15,000 to 20,000 years ago, and that the migrants were Tatars or Mongols. Still, not even the scientists can agree among themselves. The *Diffusionists* argue that Old World inhabitants had intentional contact across both the Atlantic and the Pacific Oceans, beginning in the late Stone Age (7000-3000 B.C.) Their theories have enraged the *Independent Inventionists*, who contend that the Pre-Columbian Americans were essentially free from outside contact, after their initial migration, until the arrival of Columbus in 1492.

In this war of hypotheses, the *Inventionists* seem to have gained the upper hand. University and high school text books generally reflect this Mongol-Ice Age invasion theory. Richard A. Diehl and Michael D. Coe summarized the general *Independent Inventionist* thinking in their joint essay entitled "Olmec Archaeology."

> Biologically, the Olmec were Native Americans whose Ice Age ancestors entered the New World from northern Asia via the Bering Strait land bridge. This may come as a surprise to readers familiar with recent sensationalistic claims that the Olmec were Egyptians, Phoenicians, West Africans, Chinese, or even refugees from sunken continents. Scholars rightly dismiss such ideas as outlandish fairy tales and will continue to do so until archaeologists uncover at least one Old World artifact or human skeleton in an Olmec archaeological site.[17]

---

[17] Harry N. Abrams, *The Olmec World*, Published by the Art Museum, Princeton University with essays by Michael D. Coe, Richard A. Diehl, David A. Freidel, Peter T. Furst, F. Kent Reilly, III, Linda Schele, Carolyn E. Tate, Karl A. Taube. Foreword and Acknowledgments by Allen Rosenbaum, Princeton, 1995, 11.

Diehl and Coe were not the first to articulate such a hypothesis. Many others like John Hemming, Director of the Royal Geographic Society in London,[18] contended that all of the early Chronicler theories and ideas were made before the application of serious archaeology, anthropology or paleontology to the problem. In Hemming's view, the most plausible theories placed the origin of the Americans in eastern Asia, the result of migrations of Mongols, Tartars, Chinese, or Polynesians. Hemming saw obvious similarities in the skin coloring and facial appearance of the American Indians and the Mongolian inhabitants of central Asia. He also opined that the application of scientific methods to the problem vindicated those scientists who support the East Asian origin theories.

Aleš Hrdlička of the National Museum of Washington elaborated a theory that American Indians form a single race, both in the fossil remains and in the surviving Indians. He suggested that they traveled to America not more than 10,000 or 20,000 years ago across the Bering Straits.[19]

Independent Inventionists appear to have accepted unquestioningly two hypotheses from which they established the "normative paradigm" or model upon which they base all of their findings and conclusions. First, they implicitly assume that the world as we observe it today is a direct result of evolutionary processes. Second, they also teach that the ancestors of all native Americans were Tatars or Mongols who came into the New World 15,000-20,000 years ago from northeast Asia across the Bering Strait and migrated south in spite of the fact that the oldest ruins and skeletons, found in the New World, have been found in South America not North America. They believe that

---

[18]John Hemming was Director of the Royal Geographic Society in London and went on many expeditions to the Amazon. He probably visited more Indian tribes than any other non-Brazilian. Among several books he authored is *Red Gold, The Conquest of the Brazilian Indians* (first published by Macmillan London, 1978).

[19]Ibid., 49.

there was no other significant contact or migration into the New World until the arrival of Columbus.

The scientists reject the theories of the chroniclers concerning the origins of the Indians. Scientists and historians view the chronicle writers as well-meaning Catholics who put a Catholic spin on everything they discovered, but did not have the advantages that modern scientists enjoy, were not trained historians, and did not utilize "scientific methodology." They refer to these writings only occasionally; generally when the chronicle writings support a point of archaeology or iconography.

In rejecting the Chronicler theories, however, the scientists generally reject or undervalue the eye-witness accounts of these early New World writers who spent years among the Indians. Scientists who have focused their efforts upon Pre-Columbia America apparently do not take into account what the Indians have related about themselves as they recite their folklore and legends that have been handed down for centuries. Dr. Vine Deloria, Jr., a member of the Standing Rock Sioux tribe of North Dakota, repeatedly expressed his frustration that the scientists and historians have made no effort to ask the tribes what they know of their own history. He also disagrees with the idea that the Indians are Tartars or Mongols who migrated from Siberia.[20]

Over the past century, archaeologists, art historians, and iconographers have made great advances in delving into the cultures of these ancient Americans. Hundreds of archaeologists and art historians have literally dug into the pre-Columbian ruins throughout the New World. They have been able to categorize the various sites of ancient ruins by type and time periods, and they have added a wealth of information about each group.

---

[20]Dr. Vine Deloria, Jr. is a professor of history at the University of Colorado at Boulder. His numerous books include *Custer died for Your Sins* (1969), *God Is Red* (1973), and *Red Earth, White Lies* (1995).

They have analyzed thousands of hieroglyphs, artifacts, pottery shards, and ruins.

As the scientists became more adept at gathering and analyzing information, they also became more convinced that the scientific method would provide all of the answers concerning the origin and cultures of these early Americans. Archaeological findings in the New World are generally presented in such a way that they conform with the two scientifically-accepted theories of evolution and the East Asian origin; even though there are numerous accounts and data that point to other possibilities.

The purpose of my research is to move outside of the "normative paradigm" and create a new model designed to enhance our understanding of the origins, cultures, and religions of the pre-Columbian inhabitants discovered in the New World. This new model will demonstrate how a greater understanding of ancient America can be obtained by combining and harmonizing scientific data with religious traditions, specifically the sixteenth and seventeen century chronicle accounts and the *Book of Mormon*. Misunderstandings and prejudice have isolated these important pieces of the pre-Columbian puzzle for too long.

2

Introduction to the Chronicles

Unlike historical reporting of the 21st Century wherein a book frequently comes out within months after the event transpires, the first reports of the New World were not published immediately. In fact, the first book of the New World discoveries was not printed until 1511.

When Columbus arrived back in Spain on 15 March 1493, after his first voyage, he immediately left for Barcelona, where Fernando [Ferdinand] and Isabella [Isabel] had temporarily located their court, to render his report of his trip. Although Columbus kept a diary of each of his four voyages, he died on 20 May 1506 before he was able to published his writings. News of the discoveries by Columbus and other early explorers were initially transmitted by letters and personal accounts to a limited European audience.

The Catholic priest Bartolomé de las Casas, who spent years at the Spanish Court and apparently had access to many of Columbus's original documents, wrote his *Historia de las Indias* (*History of the Indies*) in 1551. His book included material from

Columbus's diary as well as an extensive biography of Columbus. Las Casas's *Historia*, like so many other Chronicles, became lost. It was not published until 1875 in Madrid. Modern historians extracted the information pertaining to Columbus's diary from Las Casas's book and published Columbus's accounts separately in a book entitled *Diario de a Bordo* (Diary on Board).[1]

Because of the limited writings or publication of Columbus's findings, his discoveries were relatively unknown outside of Spain and Portugal. The proclamation to the rest of Europe that the islands and apparent mainland, discovered several thousand miles to the west, were part of a new continent was left up to other explorers. The Florentine explorer, Amérigo Vespucci, who accompanied at least three exploratory expeditions to the Americas, is reportedly the first to publically declare that the explorers had discovered a New World.

Pero de Magalhães de Gandavo, who is accredited with writing the first book describing Brazil, began his *Historia Da Provincia Sācta Cruz* (*History of Santa Cruz Province*) by relating the discovery of Brazil.[2] He explained how Pedro Alvarez de Gouvea Cabral as commander of a fleet, organized by the Portuguese King Dom Manuel, sailed from Lisbon on 9 March 1500 with the intention of rounding the Cape of Good Hope and heading towards the Orient. The armada sailed far out into the Atlantic to avoid what was termed the Guinea calms and after weeks sailing in this exaggerated circuitous route they discovered the coast of Brazil which they assumed to be an uncharted island. After sailing along the coast for more than a day, Cabral anchored his fleet just off the coast and soon sighted numerous natives along the shore.

[1] Cristobal Colón, 359.
[2] Pero de Magalhães de Gandavo, *Historia da Provincia Sācta Cruz* and *Tratado da Terra do Brasil*. *Historia* was finished and published circa 1576; however, *Tratado* was never published until 1827. (Published from the unabridged edition of 1922 by Longwood Press Ltd, Boston, 1978.) An English copy of these two rare books is found in the Nettie Lee Benson Library at the University of Texas at Austin.

The following day, reportedly Easter Sunday, Cabral and most of the sailors went ashore where they erected an altar, a cross, and held mass. The Portuguese were soon surrounded by natives who observed the mass and even tried to imitate the Portuguese by also kneeling down and beating their breasts as if they had the light of faith. In a letter written by Pero Vaz de Caminha, secretary to the fleet, subsequently dispatched to Portugal by Cabral, Vaz de Caminha stated that the natives appeared disposed to accept Christianity. In this same letter, Vaz de Caminha described what they observed in the land. Cabral and his men also named the new land Sancta Cruz (often written as Sācta Cruz) and since it was considered as a province of Portugal, the original name was given as the Provincia da Sancta Cruz. Magalhães mentioned that it was also called Brazil after the Brazil wood found there.[3]

Magalhães alleged that when King Dom Manuel received news of this new land he was delighted and from that time on he began to send more ships to the New World in an effort to establish a Portuguese foothold in the Americas. Duarte Coelho and Amérigo Vespucci arrived in the New World in 1501. Vespucci traveled to the New World again in 1502 and details of his voyages were contained in five letters that he wrote. Two of the letters, "Mundus Novus" [*New World*], and "Lettera di Amérigo Vespucci delle isole nuovamente ritrovate in quatto suoi viaggi," are what brought Vespucci his fame as an explorer of these regions. The second letter ended up in the hands of the German Martin Waldseemüller, writer and map maker for the court of Duke René II of Loraine. Waldseemüller was the first to suggest that the continent should be named America after Amérigo Vespucci.[4] Waldseemüller made a map showing the recently dis-

---

[3]Ibid., 22-23. (Stetson included in his notes a lengthy treatise of how the word Brazil or Brasil evolved. One thing is certain the name came from the Brazil wood, which is red and resembles hot coals and is coveted for the extraction of the red dye.)
[4]Ibid., 194.

covered islands and mainland completely separate from Asia. His usage of the name of America on his map was copied by other map makers and the name America came into common usage.

The Italian born Pietro Martire D'Anghiera, more commonly known in Spanish as Pedro Mártir de Anglería and in English as Peter Martyr of Angleria, has the fame of being the first New World chronicler.[5] Beginning in 1494, Peter Martyr wrote about the initial discoveries and early explorations. He included the events that occurred during the four voyages by Columbus. He obtained information on the establishment of Spanish fortresses in the New World, the discovery of the Pacific Ocean by Vasco Nuñez de Balboa in 1513, and the subsequent establishment of a Spanish colony in Darién, later known as Panama, under Governor Pedro Arias de Avila. Martyr also described the explorations around the Yucatán peninsula and into the Bahamas, Florida and Georgia. He mentioned the 1513 voyage of Juan Ponce de León in which he discovered Florida and the 1526 voyage of Lucas Vázquez de Ayllón, who also explored along the coast of South Carolina and Georgia and attempted unsuccessfully to establish a colony in what is now South Carolina.

Martyr's record covered more than thirty years of exploration and depending upon the language was given various titles. The Spanish generally refer to Martyr's books under the title, *Décadas del Nuevo Mundo*. In 1555, Richard Eden translated the Latin edition into English under the title, *The Decades of the New World or West Indies*.

Born in Italy on 2 February 1457 or 1459, Martyr studied medicine and became the private doctor to King Louis XI in France. He later relocated to Spain in 1487 and fought in the last battles against the Moors. He was ordained to the priesthood in 1492 and was named the personal chaplain to Queen Isabella. He remained close to the Spanish Royal Court and personally

---

[5]Martyr, 13.

met with Columbus from whom he obtained the details concerning Columbus's adventures in the New World.[6]

By 1494, he had already written the first two books of Decade I,[7] describing Columbus's voyages. In 1511, Decade I was published apparently without Martyr's knowledge. Between 1514 and 1516, Martyr wrote Decade II and Decade III. He authorized the publication of all three Decades in 1516. In all he wrote eight Decades, ending his work with the events surrounding Hernán Cortés's conquest of Mexico.

In 1524, Martyr was appointed a member of the Supreme Council of the Indies. Interestingly, Martyr never traveled to the New World, but his writings reflect a style as if he personally witnessed everything that he narrated. Martyr stated that he never wrote anything that he did not carefully verify with knowledgeable individuals. Because of his exalted position at the Spanish Court, all of the important conquistadores met with him during visits back to Spain or they sent him letters describing their adventures.

The lure of fame and fortune beckoned the vast majority of Spaniards and Portuguese to the Americas. The opportunity to proselytize and convert millions of "God's children" was another drawing point. Within a few days after Columbus sighted land, he wrote in his diary that he believed that the Indians could all be converted to the Church. When Columbus returned to Spain after his first trip, he urged Fernando and Isabella, the Catholic monarchs, to prepare other exploratory expeditions and one of his selling points was the opportunity to teach the gospel to the Indians.

---

[6]Ibid., 9.

[7]Martyr broke the exploration of the New World into periods covering several years, hence Decade I covered the first years after Columbus discovered America. Although in modern terminology a "decade" is considered ten years, Martyr did not adhere to this rule. What Martyr called a book is more like a short chapter in a book written today.

Hernán Cortés was another conquistador who saw the opportunity to teach religion to the inhabitants of the New World. In his *Cartas de la Relación* (*Letters of the Account*), Cortés stated that he set out to explore, christianize, and to colonize.[8] The Spanish conquistadores always took Catholic priests with them. Although not considered as a chronicler per se, no study of the New World would be complete without considering the five letters sent by the conquistador and colonizer Hernán Cortés to King Charles V describing Cortés's overthrow of the Aztec empire. These were much more than just letters from a soldier back to his king, but were an official account of the actions taken by Cortés during this most dramatic period of the expansion of Spain into the New World. He included in each letter sufficient narrative of the events to attempt to persuade Charles V that Cortés had acted prudently and that he had the sole interest of Spain and the Crown in mind.

Mario Hernandez Sanchez-Barba, Professor of Contemporary History at the Universidad Complutense de Madrid, who wrote the introduction to *Cartas de la Relación* stated that there were only nineteen writers who are considered by modern historians as "chroniclers of the conquest (1492-1541);"[9] however, many New World writers during the initial one hundred and fifty years of the conquest, exploration, and colonization period (1492-1650) provided valuable, and frequently unique, informa-

---

[8] Hernan Cortés, *Cartas de la Relación*, (Written between 1519 and 1526), Edition of Mario Hernandez Sanchez-Barba, Professor of Contemporary History at the Universidad Complutense de Madrid, Printed by NILO, Industria Gráfica, Madrid, 1985. (A *"Relación"*– is the name given to an official report, witnessed and authenticated by a notary, which every royal officer in the Indies was expected to provide of his activities. Bartolomé de Las Casas used this term to begin his denouncement of the treatment of the Indians by the Spaniards in his book entitled *Brevísima Relación de la Destrucción de las Indias*. The intent of those who used the term "Relación" was to convey the impression that their report, story or account was true in every sense and their aim was to have their documents considered to possess all the accuracy of a legal document.)

[9] Cortés, 9.

tion and insights on the initial conquest and colonization period, as well as about the Indians. In fact, several of the post-1541 chroniclers provided some of the best information available today concerning the cultures, legends, and religious beliefs of the natives.

Another conquistador writer was Bernal Díaz del Castillo, who personally lived the high adventure of the conquest of Mexico and outlived all of the other Conquistadores of his time. Although in his seventies when he wrote his classic, *La Verdadera Historia de la Conquista de Nueva España* (*The True History of the Conquest of New Spain.*)[10] Díaz del Castillo relied upon an incredible memory in which the day-to-day events of the conquest were so ingrained in his mind that he was able to recall them over forty years after they occurred. His classic became a companion book to Hernán Cortés's *Cartas de la Relación*.

Díaz del Castillo joined the 1514 expedition organized by Pedro Arias de Avila, the newly appointed Governor of Tierra Firme [Panama, Darién and northern Colombia]. Díaz del Castillo joined up full of zeal and high hopes; however, on his arrival at the Isthmus of Panama, reality fell dismally short of expectations. When the expedition reached Nombre de Dios, an Atlantic port on the Isthmus of Panama, it remained there for three or four months, until an unknown epidemic broke out. There were also serious disputes between Arias de Avila and his new son-in-law, Vasco Nuñez de Balboa, who had discovered the Pacific Ocean. Arias de Avila ordered that his son-in-law be decapitated and Nuñez de Balboa was executed at that time. Díaz del Castillo stated that he and the other Spaniards who had joined the expedition were witnesses to these events and, in dismay, many of the Spaniards decided to try their luck in Cuba and left Panama.

---

[10]Bernal Díaz del Castillo, *The Conquest of New Spain*, Written in the 1560's, but not published until 1632. Translated with an Introduction by J. M. Cohen, Penguin Books, Great Britain, 1963.

After three fruitless years in Panama and Cuba, Díaz del Castillo joined an expedition organized by Captain Francisco Hernández de Córdoba to discover unknown lands to the west. After twenty one days of sailing, they eventually sighted a heavily populated land, Cape Catoche on the Yucatán Peninsula. Cordoba explored along the west side of the Yucatán Peninsula, but after several disastrous battles with the Indians, the company returned to Cuba.

The Spanish governor of Cuba, Diego Velázquez insisted that Díaz del Castillo serve in the next expedition which Velázquez organized in the year 1518 under the direction of Juan de Grijalva. Grijalva retraced the route sailed by Hernández de Cordoba, but continued farther along the coast until he reached what is now Veracruz, Mexico. This time two hundred and forty soldiers and settlers volunteered to accompany the Grijalva expedition. Díaz del Castillo was commissioned as an ensign for this voyage. Consequently, when he joined Cortés in 1519, Díaz del Castillo had already become very familiar with the terrain. He accompanied Cortés throughout the conquest of Mexico and was an eye-witness to the events of the conquest. He remained in the New World for the rest of his life and provided excellent descriptions of its people and geography. He provided some of the best descriptions of Tenochtitlan, Cholula, Tlaxcala and other pre-conquest sites in New Spain [now Mexico].

Fray Diego Durán, a Catholic priest of the Dominican Order, is considered by many modern scholars to be the foremost Sixteenth Century historian and ethnographer of the Aztec Indians and their pre-conquest history. Durán wrote three books about the Aztecs, also frequently called Mexicános, that provided insights to their history, religion, and ancient calendars. His works were the *Book of the Gods and Rites*, believed to have been written between 1574 and 1576; the *Ancient Calendar*, written in 1579; and *The History of the Indies of New Spain*, written in

1581.¹¹ His command of Nahuatl, the native tongue of the Aztecs, gave him access to Aztec legends, Aztec writings, and other pre-conquest histories that were not shared with other chronicle writers.

When Durán began his writings, there were Indians still living in the areas he frequented who had witnessed the conquest period and were able to remember the histories, folklore, and legends of their ancestors. During the conquest of Mexico and shortly after Spanish takeover, the Spaniards and particularly the Catholic priests destroyed most of the Aztec books and historical paintings in hieroglyph. With the destruction of the Aztec libraries by the Spaniards, historians have been forced to rely upon the writings of these sixteenth-century chroniclers such as Father Durán to piece together a pre-conquest history of these fascinating New World early residents. It is not known when or how Durán sent his manuscripts back to Spain for publication or safe keeping, but none of his manuscripts were published during his lifetime and they disappeared into the Spanish library repositories for three hundred years.

Another important early chronicler on the religion of the natives of highland Mexico was Fray Bernardino de Sahagún, the Catholic Priest who spent over 30 years from 1547 to 1577 working with Aztec religious leaders compiling information on the rites, ceremonies and teachings of the ancient highland Mexican Indians. He wrote his findings in twelve volumes entitled, *Historia General de las Cosas de Nueva España* (Published in English with the title *A History of Ancient Mexico, The Religion*

---

¹¹Diego Durán, *The History of the Indies of New Spain*, originally written in 1581. It was not until the 1850s that José Fernando Ramírez, discovered Durán's manuscript of *La Historia de las Indias de Nueva España y Islas de Tierra Firme* in the Biblioteca Nacional de Madrid. (Translated, Annotated, and with an Introduction by Doris Heyden. Published by University of Oklahoma Press. 1994.)

and the Ceremonies of the Aztec Indians, 1547-1577).[12] Sahagún's books are probably the most oft-cited works on ancient Mexico.

Fray Bernardino spent over a quarter century gathering the materials for the *Historia General de las Cosas de Nueva España*. While he was teaching Spanish and Latin to the Indians, he was also learning from them and continued studying their history, customs, and language. He eventually assembled twelve Indians who were well versed in their native lore. These informants were highly qualified to aid Sahagún since they had previously been recorders of pre-Conquest history and several were trilingual in Spanish, Latin and Nahuatl.

Once his team was assembled, Sahagún introduced a method of research never utilized anywhere previously. He realized that the ancient Mexican history was contained in hieroglyphic signs, many of which had been destroyed by the Spaniards. The Indians recreated the glyphs, while the Spanish speaking Indians of his advisory board explained the glyphs to him.[13] There was little doubt in the mind of Sahagún that the material was authentic because it was composed by the Indians, who had drawn the pictures and had translated the meaning into Spanish and Nahuatl.

The Mexican historian, Carlos Maria de Bustamante, made the first publication of Sahagún's twelve-volume manuscript in Mexico in 1840. Bustamante claimed that the *Historia General de las Cosas de Nueva España* by Sahagún is one of the most complete sources of information concerning the ancient Mexican Indians and that Fray Bernardino was one of the most learned figures of Spanish American history.[14]

Father Diego de Landa, a priest of the Catholic Order of Saint Francis, is widely considered to be the foremost early

---

[12]Fray Bernardino de Sahagún, *1547 — 1577, A History of Ancient Mexico, The Religion and the Ceremonies of the Aztec Indians,* translated by Fanny R. Bandelier from the Spanish Version of Carlos Maria de Bustamante. (The Rio Grande Press, Inc., Glorieta, New Mexico 87535.)

[13]Ibid., 8.

[14]Ibid., 17.

chronicler on the Maya Indians and the Yucatán Peninsula. His book, *Relación de las Cosas de Yucatán* (*Account of the Things of Yucatán*), revealed many customs and legends of the Mayas.[15] He initially finished his manuscript in Spain in 1566, but the manuscript was not published until 1864.

The conquest of Peru also produced a rich assortment of chroniclers. The renowned nineteenth century Spanish historian, Marcos Jiménez de la Espada,[16] referred to Pedro de Cieza de León as the "Prince of Chroniclers." Cieza de León was born in Llerena, Spain, in 1520. At the remarkably young age of 13, he left his family behind and traveled to Colombia. Cieza de León began taking notes of the things that he saw from the time he arrived. He had a great thirst for knowledge and his writings provide the first excellent descriptions of central Colombia and the extensive Inca Empire which stretched from Pasto, Colombia, to the Maule River, south of Santiago, Chile [a distance of over 3,250 miles], as well as extraordinary insights into the pre-Inca world. He began writing in 1541 while living in Colombia and finished writing when he left Peru to return to Seville, Spain, in 1550. In all, he gathered sufficient material to write eight books. His first book, *La Crónica del Perú* (*The Chronicles of Peru*), was published in 1553.[17] His second volume, *El Señorio de los Incas* (*The Lordship of the Incas*) and his other books were not published for more than three hundred years.

Victor Wolfgang Von Hagen combined into one volume the first two books of Cieza de León–*La Crónica del Peru* and *El*

---

[15]Father Diego de Landa, *Relación de las Cosas de Yucatan*, originally written in 1566. Manuscript discovered in 1864 by Abbé Brasseur de Bourbourg in the Academia de la Historia de Madrid. First published in 1864. (Eighth Edition, translated and edited with notes by Alfred M. Tozzer. Published by the Peabody Museum of American Archaeology and Ethnology, Harvard University. 1941.)

[16]Marcos Jiménez de la Espada, *Prólogo a Pedro de Cieza de León, Tercero Libro de las Guerras Civiles del Perú, el cual se llama la Guerra de Quito*, Madrid, 1877

[17]Cieza de León, *La Crónica del Perú*, Madrid, 1553. (Edition published by Promoción Editorial Inca S.A. 1973.)

Señorío de los Incas and wrote an introduction in a book which was published in 1959 in English under the title *The Incas*. Von Hagen noted with amazement that Cieza de León took notes of everything he saw and heard and instead of killing time, he made time "to turn aside, to observe, and to record."[18]

Cieza de León recorded that "Everywhere I turned aside to see what I could of the regions in order to learn and set down what they contained." What made him decide to write? He provided his own answer in the following comments:

> As I saw the strange and wonderful things that exist in this New World of the Indies, there came to me a great desire to write certain of them, those which I had seen with my own eyes, and also what I had heard from highly trustworthy persons. But when I considered my small learning, I cast this desire from me, holding it vain, because it has been the province of great and learned minds to write histories, and for the unlearned, even to think of such a thing was folly. For that reason, time elapsed without my drawing on my scant powers until God, favoring me with grace, aroused in me once more what I had forgotten. And taking heart, with mounting confidence, I determined to devote a part of my life to writing history. And I was moved to this by the following reasons: The first, because I had taken notice wherever I went that nobody concerned himself with writing aught of what was happening. And time so destroys the memory of things that only by clues and inference can the future ages know what really took place. The second, because considering that we and these Indians all have our origin in our common parents, it is just that the world should know how so great a multitude as these Indians were brought into the lap of the Church by the efforts of the Spaniards, an undertaking so great that no other nation of all the universe could have accomplished it."[19]

---

[18]Pedro de Cieza de León, *La Crónica del Peru*, published in Spain in 1553 and *El Señorío de los Incas,* discovered and published in Spain in 1880. (The English translation was done by Harriet de Onis and was published by the University of Oklahoma Press, Norman, Oklahoma, 1959.) xxxix

[19]Cieza de León, 17. Von Hagen in *The Incas*, 3.

Cieza de León stated that "the things that I deal with in this history I have observed with great care and diligence."[20] The scarcity of paper and ink in the New World only added to his problems. He mentioned that a sheet of paper cost him 30 pesos in Cali, Colombia. The eight books written by Cieza de León required nearly 8,000 sheets of foolscap. He bought paper when he could have been buying a horse! He carried books and manuscripts when he could have been carrying gold!

Another chronicler who experienced first hand the conquest of Peru was Pedro Pizarro, a first cousin of Francisco Pizarro and Francisco's three brothers, Juan, Hernando, and Gonzalo. In January 1530, as a fifteen year old, Pedro Pizarro joined the expedition of Francisco Pizarro, initially as a page and subsequently as a soldier. He was an eye-witness and participant of the conquest of Peru and the post-conquest colonization period. He wrote his *Relación del Descubrimiento y Conquista de los Reinos del Peru* (*Account of the Discovery and Conquest of the Kingdoms of Peru*) in 1571 while living in Arequipa, Peru, where he served as mayor for a time.[21]

Felipe Guaman Poma de Ayala, an Andean native with close ties to Inca nobility, was one of the first Native Americans to write extensively about his ancestors. In addition to his written narrative, Poma de Ayala was a very talented sketch artist and he sprinkled drawings of daily life and important Inca personalities throughout his book entitled *Nueva Córonica y Buen Gobierno* (*A New Crown and Good Government*).[22] These sketches have fre-

---

[20] Von Hagen in *The Incas*, xlii

[21] Pedro Pizarro, *Relation of the Discovery and Conquest of the Kingdoms of Peru*, (originally written in 1571 in manuscript form, but not published until at least 1844 in Martin Fernandez de Navarrete's *Colección de documentos para la historia de España*, Volume V, pages 201-388, Madrid 1844.) Translated into English and annotated by Philip Ainsworth Means, The Cortes Society, New York, 1921.

[22] Felipe Guaman Poma de Ayala, *Nueva Corónica y Buen Gobierno*, original manuscript finished circa 1615. Transcription, Prologue, Notes y Chronology by Franklin Pease. (This edition published by Biblioteca Ayacucho, Apartado Postal 14413, Caracas 101, Venezuela. 1978)

quently been used by other chroniclers and twentieth century writers to depict pre-Columbian life in Peru.

Poma de Ayala stated that his grandfather was an important Inca historian or quipocamayoc (one who records history and administrative affairs on the *quipos* and can also read the *quipos*). Poma de Ayala obtained much of his information for his book from the quipos that still existed in his day. He stated:

> I decided that I would write the history and tell about the descendants as well as the more notable activities of the first kings, lords, captains, and forefathers from the time of the first Indians who were called Vari Viracocha Runa, who lived in the days of Adam, and Vari Runa, who was a descendant of Noah.[23]

He spent more than 30 years writing his book and was 80 years old when he finished his history in approximately 1615. His manuscript remained unpublished until 1936.

A contemporary and distant relative of Poma de Ayala, Inca Garcilaso de la Vega, also brought a unique native perspective to his accounts of Inca and pre-Inca society, culture and religion. He spent his first 20 years living in an Inca household in Cuzco where he learned from his mother and her illustrious family of Inca nobles about Inca heritage.[24] Garcilaso de la Vega was born in Cuzco on 12 April 1539. He was the illegitimate son of the Spanish captain Sebastian Garcilaso de la Vega Vargas and an Inca princess. Although Inca Garcilaso de la Vega was an illegitimate son, he was recognized by his father and received an inheritance from his father so that he could continue his studies in Spain.[25]

Concerning his massive work *Comentarios Reales* (*Royal Commentaries*), Garcilaso de la Vega began to write his book, or

---

[23]Poma de Ayala, 8.
[24]Inca Garcilaso de la Vega, *Comentarios Reales*. Volumes I, II, and III. Printed in Portugal in 1609. (Printed by Editorial Litografica, La Confianza S.A. Lima, Peru.)
[25]Ibid., *25*

at least gather material for it, as early as 1586. In a letter which he sent to King Phillip II, he mentioned that he was putting together a book about the history, rites, customs, and habits of the people living in Peru. He said he would give priority to the social culture of the Inca civilization. He subsequently sent the manuscript of *Comentarios Reales* to Lisbon where it was published in 1609. In *Comentarios Reales,* Garcilaso de la Vega included a five hundred year (1000 AD to 1532 AD) history of the reign of the Incas.

Another one of the more controversial of the early Conquistador writers was Fernando de Montesinos, who finished his manuscript for the book, *Memorias Antiguas Historiales y Políticas del Perú (Ancient Political and Historical Memories of Peru),* in 1642.[26] Montesinos's manuscript was lost for several hundred years and was not published until 1909. Horacio H. Urteaga, who wrote the preamble to *Memorias,* stated that until recently Montesinos's book was considered to be one of the most artificial and ludicrous books written by the chroniclers of the old Peruvian empires, and Montesinos was expunged from any list of truthful, conscientious historians of his day. Urteaga observed that, in spite of the scathing attacks on Montesinos's pre-Columbian history, the patient labor of modern day archaeologists and more impartial critics is beginning to lend more credibility to his works.[27]

Although most of the early chroniclers tended to live in Mexico or Peru, a few writers were based in other countries. No study of early chroniclers would be complete without including some writings of the early Jesuit Priests who helped establish the

---

[26]Fernando de Montesinos, *Memorias Antiguas Historiales y Políticas del Perú. Crónica del Siglo XVII,* Notes and reconciliation with other Chronicles of the Indies by Horacio H. Urteaga, written 6 March 1930, Lima. Biography of the Historian Montesinos by Domingo Angulo, written 1 March 1930, Lima. Appendix of the Monarchs of Montesinos by Guinaldo M. Vasquez, written April 1912, Lima. (Published by Libreria e Imprenta Gil in Lima, 1930).

[27]Ibid., iv.

Indian Missions in Paraguay, Argentina and Brazil. The Jesuit priests began to teach the Guaraní Indians as early as 1611. One of the most notable of these early Jesuit Priests was Father Antonio Ruiz de Montoya, who wrote the book, *La Conquista Espiritual del Paraguay* (*The Spiritual Conquest of Paraguay*), which was published in Madrid in 1639.[28] The biographer, Dr. Ernesto J. A. Maeder claimed that Ruiz de Montoya, in his time, earned the reputation as an apostle to the Guaraní Indians, who inhabited most of Paraguay and southern Brazil.

The evangelization of the Guaraní Indians in South America was one of the largest evangelization efforts undertaken by the Catholic Church in the Spanish Colonies of the New World. This enormous task was carried out by a few Jesuit missionaries, who attempted to create a model of American Christianity in which the members would be able to live religious principles according to their faith and in harmony with the rest of the colonial society. Ruiz de Montoya played a special role in this undertaking by virtue of his pastoral activities between 1613 and 1652.

An early chronicler who wrote about his experiences in Chile was Alonso de Ercilla y Zuñiga, who was born on 11 August 1533 in Madrid of aristocratic Spaniards.[29] In 1548, King Charles V granted a position for young Alonso, to serve as page to Prince Phillip. Alonso remained in that position for the next seven years. In July 1554, Ercilla y Zuñiga accompanied Phillip to England for Phillip's marriage to Mary Tudor, daughter of Henry VIII. During this trip Alonso met up with Gerónimo de

---

[28] Antonio Ruiz de Montoya, *La Conquista Espiritual del Paraguay, Hecho por los Religiosos de la Compañia de Jesus en las Provincias de Paraguay, Paraná, Uruguay y Tape.* (First edition in printed in Madrid in1639.) The biography, preliminary study and notes of the 1989 re-edition of Ruiz de Montoya's book was done by Dr. Ernesto J. A. Maeder. Reprinted by Equipo Difusor de Estudios de Historia Iberoamericana, Rosario, Argentina 1989.

[29] Alonso de Ercilla y Zuñiga, *La Araucana*, published in parts between 1569 and 1589. Introduction by Ofelia Garza de Del Castillo. (Published by Editorial Porrua, S.A. in Mexico City, 1968.) x.

Alderete, the newly appointed Spanish Governor of Chile, who had returned from Peru bringing news of the revolt of the Araucano Indians in Chile. The Araucano Indians opposed the Spanish attempts to establish a colony on their lands.[30]

Alonso enlisted as a captain under Alderete and they left Spain on 15 October 1555. The new Spanish Viceroy to Peru, Andrés Hurtado de Mendoza with his two sons, Don García and Don Felipe, sailed on this same voyage. During the crossing, Alderete became seriously ill and died near Panama City.

Mendoza, in his capacity as Viceroy of Peru, named his young son, Don García Hurtado de Mendoza, as the new governor of the Province of Chile. The Spaniards in Lima quickly organized an expeditionary force to punish the "rebellious" Araucanos. Ercilla y Zuñiga was one of the newcomers to enlist along with many *encomenderos* (wealthy land owners), soldiers, and Catholic priests.[31]

Don García Hurtado de Mendoza began his trip south on 21 June 1557 with only two ships and one hundred and fifty men. After arriving in Chile at the area of conflict, the Spaniards engaged the Araucano Indians in numerous bloody battles. Ercilla y Zuñiga wrote that the undermanned Spaniards frequently felt that they only survived the Indian attacks because of divine intervention. These battles and a description of the Araucano Indians were immortalized by Ercilla y Zuñiga in his epic poem, *La Araucana*.

Many of the chroniclers seemed intent on learning everything possible about the Indians and went to great lengths to gather valuable information on the pre-Columbian cultures. A significant bi-product of this New World adventure is the vast

---

[30]Ibid., xi. (According to Garza, Valdivia had established in the south of Chile, three Spanish forts: Arauco, Purén, and Tucapel. Tucapel was attacked by the Araucanos, under the direction of Lautaro, one of the Araucano chiefs, and Valdivia was killed on 25 December 1553.)

[31]Ibid, xii.

wealth of letters and books written by soldiers, clergymen, and government administrators about their discoveries. In addition to the chroniclers already named, there were at least fifty or sixty other writers who made significant contributions concerning the conquest and more particularly about the pre-Columbian natives they discovered.

Many of their original manuscripts, written in Latin or Spanish, were lost and not discovered until centuries later. The few manuscripts which were published during the 1500's and early 1600's soon became rare books themselves. John B. Stetson, a collector of rare books, declared that all the books printed in the Iberian Peninsula of that period were published in small editions, rarely exceeding three hundred copies and often as few as one hundred copies. He maintained that unless a book was popular enough to be republished, it soon disappeared from circulation.[32] Published versions of these rare books did not appear in the United States until the last half of the nineteenth century.

Victor Wolfgang Von Hagen gave one explanation for the disappearance of these early manuscripts in the introduction to his book *The Incas*.[33] Von Hagen commented that prior to and during the time of the conquest any manuscript presented for publication in Spain had to be reviewed and approved by three separate councils: the King's Council; the Holy Office of the Inquisition; and the Council of the Indies. Cieza de León's first book, *La Crónica del Perú*, initially published in 1553, received the direct approval of Prince Phillip.

In this book as well as in his second manuscript, Cieza de León occasionally upbraided the Spaniards for their treatment of

---

[32]Magalhães de Gandavo, 19.

[33]Victor Wolfgang Von Hagen was born in 1908 in St. Louis, Missouri, and became a world-famous explorer, naturalist, and ethnographer. He is the author of more than 50 books including *Ecuador the Unknown* (1939), *The Aztec and Maya Papermakers* (1943), *The Desert Kingdoms of Peru* (1965), and *The Ancient Sun Kingdoms of the Americas* (1962).

the Indians. To a certain degree he defended the unpopular position of the infamous Fray Bartolomé de Las Casas, the Bishop of Chiapas, who at that time was berating the Spaniards for their efforts to enslave and exploit the Indians.[34] Unfortunately, Cieza de León's other manuscripts as well as many manuscripts by other chroniclers in the 1550's were caught up in the power struggles between Spain, England, and France.

Las Casas was not the only one castigating the Spaniards for their treatment of the Indians. Many of the other European powers were attempting to undermine Spain's power and large holdings within the New World. In his attempt to mend international fences, King Charles V decided to have his son Prince Phillip wed Mary Tudor.

Las Casas, who resided at the Spanish Court, lobbied that the "New Laws" governing the treatment of the Indians by the Spaniards to be fully carried out. Although Phillip had been very sympathetic to the plight of the Indians and, in fact, had helped set down the "New Laws," Las Casas had become so vociferous in his denunciations of the Spaniards that the enemies of Spain began to use these same complaints against Charles V and later against Phillip II after he became King in 1556. This put Phillip II under great pressure at home and abroad. On 2 September 1556, Phillip II issued a Royal Decree in which he tried to further control the creation and circulation of works pertaining to the Indies.[35]

Von Hagen claims that Las Casas not only brought down himself, but most of the other chroniclers as well. One by one, as new manuscripts were submitted to the Council of the Indies for

---

[34] Bartolomé de Las Casas, *Brevísima Relación de la Destrucción de las Indias*, (Originally published in Madrid in 1552.) Republished in 1992 by Información y Revistas, S.A. - CAMBIOS 16, Barcelona, Spain.

[35] Irving A. Leonard's book, *Books of the Brave*. (Originally published by Harvard University Press, 1949.) Republished in 1992 with an introduction by Rolena Adorno by the University of California Press. xxv.

review and to receive the necessary license for publication, they were confiscated and placed in "security." Many of them never came to light again for more than three hundred years.[36]

In spite of Phillip II's efforts to stop the printing of books that might portray the Spaniards in a negative light, some books were still printed in Spain and more frequently in Portugal or Italy. On 22 April 1577, Phillip II sent an edict to the Spanish viceroy in Mexico prohibiting all writings referring to "superstitions and the way of life of the Indians" in any language and specifically ordered the confiscation of the works of Friar Bernardino de Sahagún.[37]

John B. Stetson, in the introduction to his publication of Magalhães's book, suggested another factor that brought about a scarcity of books of this genre. He argued that these manuscripts were also suppressed because of the trade rivalry which existed at that time among all the European countries. Spain and Portugal had acquired vast colonies outside of Europe, exciting jealousy on the part of the French, English and Dutch, who wanted their share of this lucrative overseas trade and resource base. The Spaniards and Portuguese went to great efforts to prevent other countries from obtaining exact information concerning the wealth of the New World. Books, which provided too much information on the natural resources of a territory, were frequently suppressed.[38]

As these early chronicles have come to light during the last 150 years, they have been received with mixed reactions by contemporary historians. Some modern historians have pointed out that the chroniclers were not trained historians and did not follow established evidentiary procedures. In her book, *The Armature of Conquest*, Beatriz Pastor Bodmer was particularly

---

[36]Cieza de León, The Incas, lxxii–lxxiv.
[37]Leonard, xxxii.
[38]Magallães de Gandavo, 20.

critical of the writings of Christopher Columbus and, in many ways, her writings reflect the attitude of many historians towards the newly discovered writings. Bodmer described the writings of Columbus as mainly fictionalized fantasy and that he held onto old pre-conceptions long after evidence would have dictated otherwise.[39] She anguished over Columbus's vision of himself as a man of God, divinely guided and protected by Deity. She believed that Columbus was overly influenced by the writings of Marco Polo; consequently, when she read the account of Columbus's third voyage to the Americas and his remarks about the light skinned natives who wore silky clothing, Bodmer theorized that Columbus naively imbued them with physical characteristics similar to the oriental people previously described by Polo.[40]

In 1992 as part of the Quincentennial celebrations of the discovery of America by Columbus, Dr. De Lamar Jensen, emeritus professor of history at Brigham Young University, wrote an article about Columbus, the myths and counter myths.[41] He pointed out that at one time, there seemed no limit to the fantasies of Columbian mythology. Many of these myths have been debunked over the years. He added, however, that some of the debunkers, have become overenthusiastic, even slanderous, in their attempts to demythologize Columbus. Jensen noted that "their approach often serves to bolster a political cause rather than promote a search for truth. They attempt to replace the heroic myth with an equally false myth of Columbus as a villain."

---

[39] Beatriz Pastor Bodmer, *The Armature of Conquest, Spanish Accounts of the Discovery of America, 1492-1589*. Originally published in Spanish in 1983 under the title *El discurso narrativo de la conquista de América*, Colección Premio Casa de las Américas, Havana, Cuba. (Subsequently translated by Lydia Longsteth Hunt, and published by Stanford University Press, California in 1992.) 20.

[40] Ibid., 33.

[41] De Lamar Jensen, *Columbus and the Hand of God*, printed in the October 1992 *ENSIGN*, a magazine printed by The Church of Jesus Christ of Latter-day Saints.

It is true that Columbus felt that he was inspired by God which partly explains his tenacity and stubbornness in the face of great odds. He wrote, "I could sense God's hand upon me, so that it became clear to me that it was feasible to navigate from here to the Indies, and he gave me the will to do it."[42] During his fourth voyage, Columbus stated that he received another divine assurance during a perilous moment when he was about to abandon all hope. Columbus wrote:

> Exhausted, I fell asleep, groaning, when I heard a very compassionate voice, saying: *"O fool and slow to believe and to serve thy God, the God of all! . . . Thou criest for help, doubting. Answer, who has afflicted thee so greatly and so often, God or the world? . . . Not one jot of his word fails; all that He promises, He performs with interest; is this the manner of men? I have said that which thy Creator has done for thee He does for all men. Now in part He shows thee the reward for the anguish and danger which thou hast endured in the service of others."* I heard all of this as if I were in a trance, but I had no answer to give to words so true, but could only weep for my errors. He, whoever he was, who spoke to me, ended saying: *"Fear not; have trust; all these tribulations are written upon marble and are not without cause."*[43]

Beatriz Pastor Bodmer frequently sites Irving A. Leonard's book, *Books of the Brave*, in which Leonard strongly suggests that the "Romances of Chivalry" novels of the 15th and 16th centuries strongly influenced the conquistadores and their subsequent chronicles. Leonard mentioned a few romantic novels of that time which priests and moralists of the day denounced as "lying histories."[44] Leonard believed that these "lying histories" may have greatly influenced the conquistadores to desecrate the tem-

---

[42] Jensen, quoting from Columbus to Doña Juana de la Torre, *Raccolta di documenti e studi pubblicati della R. Commissione Colombiana*, pt. I, vol. Ii; I *Scriti di Cristoforo Colombo*, ed. Cesare de Lollis (Rome 1894), 79.

[43] Ibid., "Letter of Columbus on the Fourth Voyage," in *The four voyages of Columbus*, tr. Cecil Jane, 2:90-92.

[44] Irving A. Leonard, 32-33.

ples and tombs found in the New World; to perform "superhuman" feats of endurance, and to commit acts of barbarism as they pushed along unknown trails and across unheard-of realms.[45]

Unlike Pastor Bodmer, however, Leonard viewed the early conquistador as a product of his time and circumstance. He wrote,

> The Spanish Conquistador, like all other human elements before and after him, was the creature of his own age, molded and conditioned by the contemporary influences of his environment. If, in retrospect, he appears excessively primitive, fanatic, proud, cruel, and romantic, it is only because he reflected more conspicuously than did other Europeans of his age the dominant traits of his own time and of his Western European culture, and only in this light can he be rightly judged.[46]

Historian Rolena Adorno pointed out in the introduction to her publication of Leonard's work that the challenge for the conquistador-reporters was to convince their readers that the experiences they described were real, not invented and that the fiction contained in the romantic novels of the time paled in comparison to what they witnessed. The historical deeds and experiences they described exceeded the only possible models (the romantic novels) for comparison that existed in their readers's imaginations.[47]

Some modern historians view the chronicles as misguided efforts on the part of early Spanish writers to justify their terrible excesses in the New World or, conversely, as over-zealous efforts on the part of a few chroniclers to excoriate the behavior of the conquistadores. That being said, perhaps the greatest contribution of the early chroniclers may not necessarily be their accounts or evaluations of the conquest per se, but the information they acquired from the Indians concerning the folklore and

---

[45]Ibid., 35.
[46]Ibid., 2.
[47]Ibid., xxiv.

legends that provided insights to their origins, cultures, and religions prior to the arrival of the Spaniards and the subsequent massive proselyting efforts of the Catholic Priests. Unfortunately later writings were frequently contaminated through the process of synergism in which the Indians combined their own religious beliefs with Catholic teachings, thus causing the original Indian beliefs to become obscured or distorted.

Although the chroniclers may not have been trained historians and their writings may not qualify as a good historiography of pre-Columbia America or even of the colonial period, they still merit serious consideration. Their writings represent the only eye witness accounts of the events during the Conquest period. Perhaps Cieza de León said it best when he noted that without a written account "time so destroys the memory of things that only by clues and inference can the future ages know what really took place."[48]

Rolena Adorno also observed that:

> The magnificent works produced during the viceregal period in Latin America have been too long overlooked by exegetes seeking a more conventional history of belles lettres in Latin America. The problem was not a failure in intellectual and creative endeavors during those centuries, but rather the much more recent failure to appreciate the learned and original contributions of early New World writers.[49]

---

[48] Cieza de León from The Incas, 3.
[49] Leonard, xxvii.

3

OVERVIEW OF
NEW WORLD DISCOVERIES

As the early conquistadores extended their explorations into the vast lands of the Americas, they were astonished at the variety of natives they found in the New World. Even during the four voyages of Columbus, the Spaniards discovered at least two different groups of Indians. The Tainos were described as being "as naked as the day they were born . . . with beautiful bodies, good faces, and long black hair. . .dark skin, not black."[1] However, on Columbus's third voyage when he discovered the island which he named Trinidad, Peter Martyr described the natives who approached Columbus's ship in large canoes thus "these people of the Iland of Trinidad are whyte, with longe heare, and of yellow colour."[2] Columbus

---
[1] Colon, 65.
[2] (Pietro Martire de Anghiera, "The Syxte Booke of the Fyrste Decade, to Cardinall of Aragonie" as taken from the Third English Book on America.) First printed in 1511 later translated by Richard Eden in June 1555.

also wrote about the white Indians that he encountered on the Venezuelan mainland during this same voyage.

As the conquistadores, accompanied by the Catholic priests, extended their conquests and explorations deeper into the New World, they discovered vast native kingdoms such as the Aztec, Maya and Inca empires with demonstrated evidence of advanced engineering skills. They also discovered small and medium size tribes which were quite primitive. The conquistadores encountered nomadic groups that lived mainly by hunting and fishing, while other more sedentary communities were deeply involved in agriculture and displayed well-tended gardens and orchards.

In general, most native groups demonstrated strong religious orientation with a wide variety of religious practices that included human sacrifice and cannibalism. Conquistador writers throughout the Americas soon discovered that most of the natives believed in the immortality of the soul and many also believed in a form of resurrection. Many built elaborate structures which the Spaniards referred to as temples while others maintained secret shrines and sacred places with idol gods. Although the Spaniards noted that some of the tribes reportedly worshiped the Sun, the Moon, or diverse gods of nature, others worshiped a heavenly deity, who vaguely resembled the Biblical Jehovah or Jesus Christ. This deity was known as Ticci Viracocha or Pachacamac in the Andes, Quetzalcoatl or Huitzilopochtli in Mesoamerica, or Botchia in Colombia.

Since many of the early chronicles identified some of the folklore and legends that existed among the Indians of pre-Columbia America, a study of the folklore and legends might provide a clue to what the natives believed about their own origins, customs and religions. The near universality of the legends such as a general belief in the immortality of the soul, a story about a universal flood, a similar remembrance of a time when the sun was darkened, tends to point to a central or common origin for many such beliefs. Changes and variations within the legends might be attributed to time and distance. As time passed and as the groups spread out from a central point, the legends began to vary and take on distinct flavors. Consequently, it is not surprising that there existed confusion concerning the origin of these legends. Most of the Indians did not have the benefit of writing and relied upon the transmission of oral histories, artist renditions on paper or ceramic vessels, or the quipos (the Andean system of using multi-colored strings and knots) to transmit their basic religious beliefs and customs.

Most of the conquistador writings have accounts of a universal flood, however, considering the millennia that had passed since the traditionally accepted date of Noah's flood, it is not surprising that concrete details were lacking. Cieza de León wrote:

> Many of these Indians tell that they heard from their forebears that in remote times a great flood occurred as I have already written. . . And they imply that the antiquity of their origins is very great and in this connection they relate so many tales and fables, if they are that, that I shall not waste time setting them down.[3]

In his writing, Father Joseph de Acosta confirmed the idea that the Indians believed in a flood, but made the following observation:

> Frequently among them [Indians], there is great notice and many discussions of a flood; however, it cannot be determined whether the flood to which the Indians refer is the "universal flood" mentioned in the scriptures or whether it was a local flood.[4]

Concerning the flood, Inca Garcilaso de la Vega wrote the following:

---

[3]Cieza de León, 272-273.
[4]Acosta, 63.

> The common people in Peru relate another fable about the origin of their Inca Kings.... They say that after the flood—of which they are not able to provide more information other than to say it happened. They do not understand whether it was the one that took place at the time of Noah, or at some other time; therefore, we will not pursue what they say about it or other similar things. They appear to be more like dreams or poorly organized fables than historical events–and after the waters ceased, a man appeared in Tiahuanaco [also spelled Tiwanaku] who was so powerful that he divided the world into four parts and turned these parts over to four men whom he called kings: the first was called Manco Cápac, the second Colla, the third Tocay and the fourth Pinahua.[5]

A Mercedarian friar, Father Martín de Murúa, who finished his manuscript, entitled *Historia General del Perú* (*General History of Peru*), about 1611, lived in Peru for more than fifty years. He spent many years in the environs of Lake Titicaca and apparently learned both Quechua and Aymara.[6] He observed that the Indians related numerous diverse tales and fables about the origin of the Incas. He said that the most common account is that the first Inca was named Manco Capac. Murúa said that all the Indians that he encountered tied the beginning of the Incas to a time of a flood.

> The Indians state that when the people were killed off by the flood, four brothers came out of the window of a cave some five leagues from Pacaritambo. From these four brothers came the Incas. The oldest brother was Manco Capac, and after him came Ayarcache, Ayarauca and Ayarhuchu. They also brought out four sisters...The old Indians state that the brothers saw a rainbow in the sky. Manco Capac told his brothers that the rainbow was a good sign and the world would not be destroyed again by water.[7]

---

[5]Inca Garcilaso de la Vega, *Comentarios Reales* (Tomo I, Impreso en Editorial Litográfica "LA CONFIANZA" S.A. —R.I. 8610, Lima, Peru.) 40. (Garcilaso de la Vega sent the manuscript of *Comentarios Reales* to Lisbon for publication. It was published in 1609 by Diego de Silva.)

[6]Martín de Murúa, *Historia General del Perú de los Orígenes al Último Inca*. Originally written in 1611. (Published by Informaciòn y Revistas, S.A., Hermanos García Noblejas, 41 - 28037 Madrid. Historia 16, 1986.)

[7]Ibid., 49-50.

Stories of a flood were not confined to the Andes. In Mexico, the chroniclers also discovered similar accounts. Fernando de Alva Ixtlilxochitl, one of the early mestizo writers who was born in either 1568 or 1578 in Mexico and died 1650, wrote several books including *Historia de la Nación Chichimeca* (*History of the Chichimeca Nation*).[8] Alva Ixtlilxochitl began his narrative by describing four creations or destructions of the world. He wrote the following:

> The most serious historical authors of ancient America were Quetzalcóatl, The First, and Nezahualcoyotzin, King of Tetzcuco.... These historians declared that God, Creator of all Things, after he had created the world, created the first parents from whom all others descend. They were given the earth to be their habitat. The earth has four ages: The first age was called, in their language, "sun of water" because the first world or creation was destroyed by a great flood which drowned all men. The second age was called "sun of earth" because the earth was devastated by earthquakes. The earth opened up in many parts and swallowed many people, or mountains and hills fell down upon the earth and destroyed most of the people. The third age was called "sun of air" because great winds destroyed the buildings and trees which also killed many people. The fourth age is the one in which we live and the earth will be destroyed by fire.[9]

Peter Martyr wrote that during an exploratory excursion in early 1522, Gil González and a group of Catholic priests baptized thousands in an area known as Nicoragua, named after King Nicoragua, who was also baptized. King Nicoragua asked Gil González whether the king of Spain had any information concerning an ancient catastrophe in which the people and the

---

[8] Fernando de Alva Ixtlilxochitl, *Historia de la Nación Chichimeca*, (Original manuscript completed by 1640, but not published.) Lord Kingsborough published Alva's *Historia* in 1948 in London. Edmundo O'Gorman discovered and published *Historia* in 1977 in Mexico. Re-published with Notes by Germán Vázquez for Historia 16 in Madrid, 1985.

[9] Ibid., 49, 50.

animals were drowned in a great flood. Gil González confirmed that they believed in such a flood as well.[10]

Another book that has become somewhat controversial is the *Popol Vuh* which was written by anonymous members of the K´iche´-Maya nobility in Guatemala in the mid-1500's. During the conquest period, Pedro Alvarado and the Spaniards devastated the K´iche´-Maya people which brought severe condemnation from Bartolomé de las Casas. Allen J. Christenson, who translated and edited a recent English edition of *Popol Vuh*, pointed out that in the preamble to the *Popol Vuh*, the K´iche´ authors wrote that its contents were based on an ancient book that contained "light that had come from across the sea."[11] Unfortunately the ancient text of the *Popol Vuh* was lost.

In the 1988 Spanish version, Carmelo Saenz de Santa Maria stated that the *Popol Vuh* manuscript, created by the anonymous K'iche'-Mayas in the sixteenth century, was also lost until a Dominican Friar Francisco Ximénez discovered it in Guatemala in the early 1700's. Ximénez made a copy of the badly faded manuscript, but his manuscript was also lost until it turned up in the library of the University of San Carlos in Guatemala City where it was discovered by an Austrian Carl Scherzer in 1854. He made a copy of Ximénez's translation and published it in Spanish in 1857.

Concerning the *Popol Vuh*, Christenson observed:

> The authors of the *Popol Vuh* were traditionalists, in the sense that they recorded the history and theology of the ancient highland Maya people without adding material from European sources and, consequently, the *Popol Vuh* contains very little direct Christian influence. By its own account, it is a faithful record of the contents of the ancient version of the *Popol Vuh*, which could no longer be seen.

---

[10]Martyr, 481.

[11]*Popol Vuh*, (translated and edited by Allen J. Christenson.) Published by The Foundation for Ancient Research and Mormon Studies (FARMS), Provo, Utah, 2000. 4.

Although the traditions of the book were compiled after the Conquest, "within the voice of God and Christianity," the ancient Maya gods were nevertheless venerated as luminous, wise beings who brought life and light to the world through their creative works. The statement that the *Popol Vuh* was composed within Christianity immediately follows a declaration that the Maya gods "expressed and accomplished all things in the brightness of their being" long before the arrival of the Christian God. Thus the *Popol Vuh* contrasts its "ancient word," which contains light and life, with that of the more recent voice of Christianity. In highland Maya society, antiquity denotes authority.[12]

In Christenson's view such unapologetic reverence for the Mayan pagan gods would have been offensive to the early Spanish missionaries. During the first decades of the Spanish conquest, the most obvious expressions of Maya religion and literature were either destroyed or hidden. Old hieroglyphic books were singled out as dangerous hindrances to the conversion of the people and were actively sought out and destroyed. Those found in possession of such books were persecuted and even killed. Several hundred years later, the K´iche´ still kept some of their books hidden from the priests.[13]

Supposedly, the *Popol Vuh* contains the K´iche´s understanding of the creation of the world and its inhabitants prior to the first dawning of the sun. It narrates in poetic form five creative attempts. Each attempt was carried out with the intention of giving form to beings who could speak intelligently, remember their creators, and offer them appropriate words of reverence. In the *Popol Vuh*, each creative attempt that failed to accomplish this purpose was destroyed. In one of the initial attempts to create man, the gods created and shaped men from wood, but when they discovered that the "images of carved wood" did not possess hearts nor minds and they did not remember their "Framer or

---

[12]Christenson, 6.
[13]Ibid., 8.

their Shaper," they were destroyed in a flood. Consequently the Maya also have an account of a flood that destroyed men anciently. Those scientists who have accepted an evolutionary beginning of the earth and mankind discredit the *Popol Vuh* as a mixture of pagan myths and distorted Christianity.

Because many of the native American kingdoms believed in some kind of flood, many trace their origins to a post-diluvial period. One of the most interesting of the early chroniclers who supported the theory of a post-diluvial migration was a Catholic priest, Miguel Cabello Valboa, a great nephew of Vasco Nuñez de Balboa. In his book *Miscelánea Antártica: Una Historia del Peru Antiguo*, initially written in 1586, but not published until 1951, Cabello Valboa wrote that he came to the Americas with the "obsession of discovering the origin of the Americans."[14]

Cabello Valboa believed that the fathers of these Indians separated themselves from the grandchildren and great grandchildren of Noah at the time of the Tower of Babel when God punished the tower-builders by confounding their language. Cabello Valboa not only identified the time of this migration to America, but claimed that Ophir, the son of Joktan and grandson of Heber, and a great, great grandson of Shem, who was the son of Noah, was the leader of the group.[15] In formulating his theory, Cabello Valboa cited writings from Josephus, Ptolemy, and I Kings 10:11, which record that King Solomon sent Hiram, King of Tyre, to Ophir to obtain gold. He also cited the writing of Saint Jerome, who upon discussing the whereabouts of the sons of Joktan, wrote that he had no further information about them as they disappeared at the time of the confounding of tongues.[16]

---

[14]Cabello Valboa, xxxv.

[15]Ibid., 5-6.

[16]Note: Joktan was one of two known sons of Heber; the other son was Peleg in whose days the earth "was divided" (Genesis 10:25). Heber was considered an exceptional man, was the father of the Hebrews, and the language spoken by Heber (Hebrew) was also spoken by Abraham, Isaac, and Jacob (Israel). Abraham was a descendent of Peleg. Nothing further is known about Joktan.

Overview of New World Discoveries 49

Cabello Valboa contended that Ophir and his group traveled east from Babylon (located on the Euphrates River in what is now present day Iraq) towards India and the islands of South East Asia where they spent considerable time until they lost their fear of the sea and acquired knowledge of boat making and navigation. Subsequently, they sailed east until they arrived in "our Indies."[17] According to Cabello Valboa, Ophir and his followers were led to the Americas by God, who gave them commandments, directed them to build temples, and taught them about agriculture.[18] He argued that these descendants of Heber kept the commandments of God, continued to worship Him, and did not have their language confounded.[19]

He also identified numerous words employed by the Indians that appear to be a form of Hebrew. He believed the name Peru to be a derivation of the name Ophir in which Ophir became Opiri, then Piru and eventually Peru. He also believed the name of the Yucatán Peninsula in Mesoamerica was named after Father Joktan.[20]

Cabello Valboa was not the only chronicler to provide considerable detail concerning a post-flood migration to the Americas. As mentioned previously, one of the more controversial of the early Conquistador writers was Fernando de Montesinos. By 1628, Montesinos had received the "sacred orders" within the Catholic Church and had transferred to the New World. After 1640, Montesinos was appointed the Bishop of Quito, Ecuador. Apparently Montesinos finished his book *Memorias Antiguas Historiales y Políticas del Perú*, in 1642, while

---

[17]Cabello Valboa, 6.
[18]Ibid., 74.
[19]Ibid., 78.
[20]Ibid., 104-105, 106, 108, 110. (Alfred M. Tozzer, who wrote the Notes in Diego de Landa's *Relación de las Cosas de Yucatán*, claimed that Gaspar Antonio Chi, a native Mayan in the 1500s who was educated in Spanish, said that he found in some ancient writings of the Indians that "they called this country of theirs '*Iuquitan*' and the word, having been corrupted, is now generally called Yucatán.")

living in Ecuador. As happened with most of the manuscripts written by the early chroniclers, Montesinos's manuscript was lost for several hundred years and was not published until 1909.

Montesinos also maintained that God led Ophir, grandson of Heber, and his descendants to the New World and gave them strict commandments to live by. These descendants lived for a few years in peace and harmony, obeying the commandments of God, but later war broke out over greed for land and material possessions. Montesinos asserted that the people became very greedy. Montesinos did not specify the route Ophir and his group followed in leaving the Old World, but indicated that, after arriving in the New World, they mainly populated Peru and Chile.[21]

Another chronicler who stipulated that the native Americans came to the New World shortly after the universal flood was Indian chronicler Felipe Guaman Poma de Ayala. He provided supporting information to Cabello Valboa and Montesinos's theses, in his book, *Nueva Corónica y Buen Gobierno*. He believed that God brought one of the descendants of Noah to the "Indies," who initially kept the commandments of God. These early American inhabitants whom Poma de Ayala identified as Vari Viracocha Runa [Men of the god Viracocha] eventually lost their faith and hope in God, his writings, and commandments, but did retain a faint recollection of a creator of man and a creator of the world. They adored and worshiped a God known as Runacamac Viracocha.[22] According to Poma de Ayala, they retained a vague knowledge of the flood and a belief that the flood was a punishment sent by their god.[23]

---

[21]Montesinos, 5.

[22]Poma de Ayala frequently sprinkled Quechua words in his narrative because they apparently were more descriptive to him; however, he did not always provide the Spanish equivalent. He did not provide the meaning of Runacamac Viracocha, but *Viracocha* is their equivalent for god, creator of the world, and *runa* is man. The modifier *cámac* is the unknown element, but it also appears in the Quechua term *Pacha Cámac*, which also means creator of the world.

[23] Ibid., 40.

Poma de Ayala further explained that although the initial Indians were obedient and worshiped Pacha Cámac, the creator of the world, later generations which he identified as "pacarimoc runa" were not as capable as the earlier inhabitants. Poma de Ayala implied that as the people drifted away from worshiping their deity, they also became more primitive in their standard of living. Montesinos also observed that the ancient people of Cuzco, mainly the *amautas* or wise men, knew how to read and write and they frequently wrote on dried banana leaves. He pointed out that centuries later the descendants of these people lost the ability to read and write and had to resort to the system of strings and knots known as the quipos.[24]

It is interesting to note that Poma de Ayala and Montesinos viewed the earlier inhabitants as having a superior civilization and that it was later generations who lost contact and faith with God and showed inferior capabilities.

Most of the chronicle writers who went into Peru recorded an account of the three or four brothers who suddenly appeared near Cuzco with three or four women. Some chroniclers claim that the women were sisters to the men, others claim that they were sisters to each other. Some of the chroniclers have the group appearing as early as the period shortly after Noah and the great flood, others have them arriving shortly before the birth of Jesus Christ. Still others indicate that they arrived about 600 A.D. From the various accounts already cited, it is evident that the site of Cuzco was inhabited by other groups prior to the arrival of the brothers. Setting aside the unresolved issue of the timing of their arrival, the overriding narrative in the different accounts is the conflict between the brothers.

In Cieza de León's narrative, there were only three brothers and their wives:

---

[24]Montesinos, 21.

The men who appeared there, according to their account, were Ayar Oco, Ayar Cachi Awga, and Ayar Manco. . . .They say that Ayar Cachi was so brave and strong that with the sling he brought, dealing blows or hurling stones, he leveled the hills, and at times when he shot straight up, the stones almost attained the clouds. To the other brothers this seemed an affront, for they felt themselves humiliated at not being able to match his feats. And so, galled by envy, they begged him with fair words, which were full of guile, to return to the cave where they had their treasures and bring them a goblet of gold they had forgotten, and to beg the sun, their father, to prosper them so they could rule the earth. Ayar Cachi, unaware of the deceit in what his brothers asked, went joyfully to do their bidding, and no sooner was he in the cave that the other two buried him under such a weight of stones that he was nevermore seen. When this was done, they tell that the earth shook in such a manner that many mountains fell down upon the valleys.[25]

In Fernando de Montesinos's account, he claimed that four brothers, Ayar Manco Tupac, Ayar Cachi Tupac, Ayar Auca Tupac, and Ayar Uchu, and their wives settled at Cuzco. The youngest of the four brothers, Ayar Uchu, also known as Pirua Pacari Manco, deceived the other three and eventually took over control of the family. Montesinos claimed that Peru received its name from Pirua Pacari Manco.[26] He was the first one to reign in Cuzco and he was not an idol or sun worshiper, but worshiped the God of Noah, the Creator of the World, whom they called Illatici Huira Cocha (also called Ticci Viracocha). Montesinos said that when the four brothers arrived they encountered remnants of earlier inhabitants whom they finally convinced to give loyalty to Pirua Pacari Manco.

According to legend, the older inhabitants inquired of their gods concerning Pirua Pacari Manco and his son Manco Cápac and were told that these new kings of Cuzco would prevail over

---

[25]Cieza de León, 31-34.
[26]Montesinos, 8.

all adversity and the land would be a blessing to their descendants.[27] With this news, the former inhabitants made a peace treaty with Pirua Pacari Manco.

A study of the Pre-Columbian ruins show that some of the largest and best constructed ruins discovered by the archaeologists date back over 4,000 years.[28] Twentieth century archaeologists and art historians have discovered several distinct groups who anciently inhabited the New World, beginning as early as 2500 B.C. The two earliest civilizations were the Chavín civilization in Peru and Ecuador and the Olmec civilization in Mesoamerica. Throughout this book, I will occasionally refer to one or more of these different groups or nations. There are numerous other tribes and families scattered throughout North, Central and South America that are not mentioned mainly because their archaeology and art history is not as well defined nor understood. The dates provided are only approximations. Even the archaeologists have difficulty agreeing among themselves and there are ongoing studies of the various civilizations which produce new information and new theories each year.

ANCIENT ANDEAN AND MEXICAN CIVILIZATIONS

ANDES

Chavín: Dates from approximately 2500 B. C. to 400 B.C. The Chavín civilization was located from southern Ecuador to south of Lima, Peru, mainly along the Pacific coast but extending up and over the Andes onto the Eastern slopes.

---

[27]Montesinos, 22.
[28]Richard L. Burger, *Chavín and the Origins of Andean Civilization*, (Thames and Hudson Ltd., London.1992.)

Moche (Mochica): Dates from approximately 200 B.C. to 600 A.D. The Moche were located along the north Peruvian coast from just south of modern Trujillo to near modern Chiclayo.

Tiwanaku (Tiahuanaco): Dates from approximately 200 B.C. to 600 A.D. The Tiwanakans were situated around Lake Titicaca between Peru and Bolivia. The most famous ruins are located between Lake Titicaca and the modern city of La Paz, Bolivia.

Nazca and Paracas: Date from approximately 200 B.C. to 600 A.D. These two centers appear to have been part of the Tiwanaku civilization. Both are located along the coast of southern Peru, beginning about 50 miles south of Lima and extending for about 300 miles south.

Inca: Dates from approximately 1100 A.D. to 1535 A.D. The Incas eventually extended their control from Pasto, Colombia, to south of Santiago, Chile (approximately 3,250 miles). They controlled from the Pacific Ocean to the eastern slopes of the Andes including the Cochabamba area of Bolivia and south to Tucuman, Argentina, on the eastern side of the Andes.

MEXICO AND MESOAMERICA

Olmec: Dates from approximately 1500 B.C. to 400 B.C. The Olmec were located mainly in the Mexican states from just north of Mexico City to Guatemala. They occupied lands from the Gulf of Mexico to the Pacific Ocean, mainly in that narrow portion of Mexico known as the Isthmus of Tehuantepec.

Pre-Classic and Classic Maya: Dates from approximately 300 B.C. to 600 A.D. The Maya occupied the Yucatán Peninsula, the Mexican state of Chiapas, Guatemala, Belize, parts of Honduras and El Salvador. Post-classic Maya continued in the same areas even after the Spanish conquest.

Teotihuacán: Dates from approximately 150 B.C. to 600 A.D. The great pyramid of Teotihuacán is located about 35 miles northeast of modern Mexico City. The Teotihuacán influence has been discovered throughout the Mesoamerican area including Yucatán. The city of Teotihuacán was burned about 700 A.D.

Toltec: Dates from approximately 900 A.D. to 1150 A.D. The capital of the Toltecs was Tula or Tollan. Archaeologists have never ascertained the location of Tula, but many theorize that it was Tula Hidalgo, located just north of modern Mexico City. The Toltecs dominated northern and central Mexico during this period as well as the Guatemalan highlands and most of the Yucatán Peninsula.

Aztec: Dates from approximately 1150 A.D. to 1521 A.D. The Aztec coalition controlled all of central Mexico from just north of Mexico City to the southeast nearly to the Isthmus of Tehuantepec and the Maya frontier. It also extended from the Gulf of Mexico to the Pacific Ocean.[29]

---

[29]The Aztecs were only one of seven Nahuatl-speaking tribes that lived somewhere in the north in a land of seven caves. The first of these tribes began migrating south perhaps as early as 800 A.D. Father Diego Durán claimed that the Aztecs were the last to leave the seven-cave area and were late-comers to central Mexico (now the Mexico City area).

Richard L. Burger, in his study on Chavín, argues that of the six independent centers of civilization in world prehistory, probably the least well known is that which developed in the central Andes.[30] The earliest evidence of the Chavín society has been dated back to 2300-2700 B.C., but may go back as far as 3000 B.C. when cotton supposedly appeared along the pacific coast. Peruvian archaeologist, Julio C. Tello spent years investigating numerous excavations that displayed the distinctive Chavín architecture and style. He discovered Chavín de Huántar in 1930.[31]

Chavín de Huántar is not the oldest of the Chavín sites, but it is the site whose name was expanded out to include all of the other sites demonstrating the same culture. What struck Julio C. Tello and many later scholars as remarkable about the cultures of the Early Horizon (2000 B.C. - 0 A.D.) was the quality of the religious art, the sophisticated and innovative technologies used to produce it, and the unprecedented degree of homogeneity that characterized the assemblages from previously unrelated regions.[32]

In his book, Cabello Valboa mentioned that God instructed Ophir and his followers after they arrived in the New World how to build and use temples. One of the most significant aspects of the Chavín culture was the construction of special buildings which art historians and archaeologists believed were "temples." John H. Rowe suggested that the great temple at Chavín de Huántar is one of the most remarkable surviving structures of Pre-Columbian architecture.[33]

---

[30]Burger, 9. (Burger called these ancient civilizations "pristine civilizations" because they apparently developed from purely internal or autochthonous factors. The other five world "pristine civilizations" were those that developed in Mesopotamia, China, the Indus Valley, Egypt, and Mesoamerica.)

[31]Ibid., 11.

[32]Ibid., 183.

[33]John H. Rowe, *Chavín Art—An Inquiry into Its Form and Meaning*, The Museum of Primitive Art, New York. (University Publishers Inc., New York. 1962)

This temple was often referred to as "El Lanzón" because of the enormous sculptured white granite shaft, 14 feet 10 inches in height, located in one of the rooms inside the Old Temple.[34] According to Burger and other archaeologists, this stone is carved with the image of a fanged-deity in the form of a man. The sculpture's location, along with its size, artistry and iconography indicate that this was the principal cult image of the Old Temple. The image on the granite shaft was carved in such a fashion to show the right arm being raised with the open palm of the hand exposed, and its left arm hangs to the side of the image with the back of the hand visible.[35]

Although there has been much speculation as to what or whom the image was meant to represent, Julio C. Tello identified the Lanzón icon with "Wira Kocha," the creator God worshiped by the Incas.[36] [Undoubtably, when he saw the raised hand on the Lanzón icon, it reminded him of the gold statue of Ticci Viracocha.] Many of the early Chroniclers who wrote about the Peruvian conquest have provided information about Wira Kocha (more commonly spelled as Viracocha.) In a footnote in his book, *The Incas*, Victor Wolfgang Von Hagen referred to an explanation of Ticci-Viracocha as recorded by Leonardo Villar in his book, *Lexicologia Keshua Uiracocha* (Lima, 1887) as follows:

> Ticci-Viracocha was the Incas' creator-god. He created both natural and supernatural beings, and according to one of the three Spaniards who saw Cuzco before its rape [plunder by the Spaniards], Viracocha was represented as man, in an effigy of solid gold, with his right arm raised "as in command." He generally lived in the sky, but did appear to the people in time of grave crisis. Like

---

[34]Luis Guillermo Lumbreras, *Los Templos de Chavín*, (Publication of the Proyecto Chavín de Investigaciones Arqueológicas. Sponsored by the Corporación Peruana del Santa, Primera Edición, Lima, Peru. 1970)
[35]Burger, 135, 136.
[36]Ibid., 150.

the Mexican god Quetzalcóatl he was a cultural-hero, and was thought to have taught all peoples the arts of civilization... If the myth has substance, there must be some connection between Quetzalcóatl (Mexico), Botchia (Colombia), and Viracocha (Peru).[37]

On several occasions, Cieza de León referred to Ticci Viracocha and each time he was described as the creator or maker of all created things.[38]

The history of the settlement of Mexico and Central America is equally as convoluted. According to art historians Richard Diehl and Michael Coe, the Olmec culture in Mexico and Mesoamerica rose and fell during what archaeologists call the Early and Middle Formative or Pre-classic periods (about 1500 B.C. to 400 B.C.). Although there was evidence of farming as early as 2200 B.C., the earliest evidence of human occupation in the Olmec heartland, dating from about 1500 B.C. to 1200 B.C., appeared at La Venta in Tabasco and then later at San Lorenzo which flourished and collapsed during the Initial Olmec Period. Evidence of the Olmec culture appeared as far north as Mexico City and as far south as Guatemala and Honduras. Dietl and Coe are convinced that true Olmec culture drew to a close by 300 B.C.

Diego Durán provided probably what is the best history of the Nahuatl speaking tribes, including the Aztecs, who moved into central and southern Mexico. He stated that the only information that he acquired about the origins of the Aztecs is that they came from the north where they lived in an area called Seven Caves. In the Seven Caves area, there lived seven great families. One by one each family abandoned its cave area and moved south. The Aztecs were the last family to leave the Seven Caves area, a place also known as the "Place of Reeds" which the

---

[37]Von Hagen as recorded in *The Incas*, 29.
[38]Ibid., 181.

Indians claimed was in the north near the region of La Florida.[39] Durán noted that the Indians did not have any recollection or history of what transpired prior to the time when they lived in the Seven Caves area nor how long they lived there. Their accounts were limited to claiming their ancestors were born in the caves.

According to the Aztec calenders, these tribes, one by one, began to abandon the caves in 820 A.D. Durán wrote that the initial six tribes left the Seven Caves area in the following order: the Xochimilcas, the Chalcas, the Tepanecs, the Colhuas, the Tlalhuicas, and the Tlaxcalans. The Aztecs were reluctant to leave and remained at Seven Caves for another 300 years. In the case of the Aztecs, it took them approximately 80 years to reach the valley of Mexico because of the many delays they encountered.[40] They claimed to have built cities and other settlements along the way where they left behind the elderly, the sick or the exhausted, who in turn peopled the area. They also planted and harvested crops along the way. The Aztecs claimed to have left Seven Caves because their god Huitzilopochtli promised to guide them to a "promised land."

When the Xochimilcas arrived in the vicinity of Lake Tenochtitlan [which no longer exists], they selected as their place to live a mountain ridge which is an area directly south of Lake Tenochtitlan.[41] The next group to arrive were the Chalca lineage, who joined the Xochimilca on the east and adjusted their common boundaries peacefully. The next group to arrive were the

---

[39] Durán, 10. (Heyden clarifies that in early Spanish colonial times, La Florida referred not only to what is now the State of Florida, but to the region north of Tamaulipas, which would include northeastern Mexico and southeastern Texas. Aztlan is considered the original home of the Aztecs and gave them their name, which means "People of Aztlan.")

[40] Ibid., 12.

[41] Heyden noted that many of the towns built by the Xochimilcas are located in the modern state of Morelos as well as Mexico D.F.

Tepanecs who settled the area around Tacuba, just west of the Lake Tenochtitlan.

The fourth group to arrive in the Valley of Mexico were the Tezcocan tribe.[42] Durán obviously takes pride in the fact that he grew up in Tezcoco and learned his Nahuatl in that refined center. He mentioned that among the Tezcocans were many illustrious and courageous men who constructed a city of great order and fine planning. He added that there are beautiful towns and the inhabitants are educated and courteous, clever, sagacious, of fine speech, elegant, and polished.[43] Tezcoco is almost directly east of Lake Tenochtitlan. Durán mentioned that the areas occupied by these four groups completely circled Lake Tenochtitlan. Consequently, when the fifth group, the Tlalhuicas arrived, they moved much further south into the Oaxaca area, described as one of the most beautiful and pleasant lands in the world, and if it were not for the great heat there, it would be another Garden of Eden.

When the Tlaxcalans arrived, they could not find any lands where they could establish themselves near Lake Tenochtitlan; therefore, they moved over the Sierra Nevada mountain range and chose lands to the east. (Durán noted that the Tlaxcalans never had to pay tribute to the Spaniards after the conquest because of their close support during the conquest. Without their Tlaxcalan allies, the Spaniards would have been quickly destroyed by the Aztec armies.)

Durán stated that 300 years after the first of the six tribes arrived in the vicinity of Lake Tenochtitlan, the Aztec finally arrived. The Aztecs or Mexicános believed that their prophets

---

[42] Durán did not clarify whether the Tezcocan tribe was the same as the Colhuas which he had identified as one of the seven tribes in the Seven Caves area.

[43] Heyden observed that the Nahuatl language was spoken all the way from Jalisco to Central America. It was also known as Mexica or Mexicáno and was divided into a number of dialects. Several chroniclers commented on the superior linguistic capability of the Tezcocans.

and gods had promised to lead them to a land of plenty. They brought with them an idol called Huitzilopochtli.[44] In his book, *Book of the Gods and Rites*, Durán claimed that Huitzilopochtli was the most revered of all the gods and was the only one the Nahuatl-speaking Indians referred to as the Lord of All Created Things and The Almighty. Huitzilopochtli was a wooden statue carved in the image of a man seated upon a wooden bench in the fashion of a litter. The Indians painted the bench blue indicating that Huitzilopochtli's abode was the heavens. Thousands of men were sacrificed to this god each year. During the sacrificial ceremonies, the victims' chests were opened up with a stone knife and the heart ripped out and offered to the god.

The Nahuatl speaking tribes were not the first to live near Lake Tenochtitlan. Fernando de Alva Ixtlilxochitl claimed that before the Nahuatl speaking tribes arrived the land was occupied by the Olmecs [not to be confused with the Olmecs that lived between 1,500 B.C. and 400 B.C.] and the Xicalancas, who according to their histories arrived in ships from the east. They arrived during the third age[45] and landed near Potonchan, located south of modern Veracruz, where they began to settle and spread out.

During the fourth age, the Toltec nation arrived. According to their historians, they were exiled from their homelands and after navigating along the Pacific coast past several land areas, they landed near Huitlapalan in the Oaxaca region. Alva

---

[44]Heyden noted that Huitzilopochtli, the god-hero of the Aztecs, is presented as an idol or as a human being, a chieftain who led the Aztecs during their migration to find the promised land. Later in Durán's narration he is represented by the idol in the main temple in the city of Mexico-Tenochtitlan.

[45]Chronicle writers frequently referred to different ages. They did not follow a set pattern. Some times they referred to an age as being a thousand year period at other times, the age may refer to a period of time marked by a natural disaster such as the flood, or a "time when the sun died" and there were great earthquakes, or a time when great winds destroyed the buildings. It is unclear what age Alva Ixtlilxochitl was referring to in his narrative.

Ixtlilxochitl claimed that the date of the arrival of the Toltecs was 387 A.D.[46] The Toltecs then crossed Mexico to the Atlantic side where they settled several cities. They eventually settled the city of Tollan (also spelled Tula) which became their principal center.

Alva Ixtlilxochitl named various kings who ruled over the Toltecs and provided the years in which each king reigned. He mentioned that in 882 A.D., the great king Topiltzin, whom others also called Quetzalcoatl, which in Nahuatl means "feathered Serpent," came to reign. Alva Ixtlilxochitl claimed that the Toltec nation lasted for 572 years before a great drought and internal struggles brought about its collapse. Topiltzin or Quetzalcoatl fled east towards the Yucatán peninsula. Among the Mayas, he was known as Kukulcan, which in the Maya language also means "feathered serpent." He reportedly promised that he would return and retake his kingdom.

In his book on the history of Yucatán, Diego de Landa claimed that some of the older Maya inhabitants of Yucatán in the 1500s state that they heard from their ancestors that Yucatán was occupied by a race of people, who came from the East, whom God had delivered by opening twelve paths through the sea. Landa saw this as an indication that the Indians were descendants of the Jews (meaning Israelites).

Menasseh Ben Israel, a Jewish Rabbi who was born in Lisbon in 1605, provided an entirely new perspective on the origins of the native Americans. He spent most of his life in Holland where he learned the Hebrew tongue and was instructed in the *Talmud*. Although he never set foot in the New World, his book *Esto Es Esperança de Israel, Sobre el Origen de Los Americanos* (*This Is the Hope of Israel, about the Origin of the Americans*), initially pub-

---

[46] Alva Ixtlilxochitl, 53. (This date is several centuries earlier than the date assigned by art historians.)

lished in Amsterdam in 1650, contains far reaching implications concerning the origins of the Native Americans.[47]

Ben Israel wrote that he personally believed that the Indians were Israelites. The nucleus for Ben Israel's ideas came from an Israelite visitor to the New World, Aharon Levi, who spent some time in Colombia in the 1600s, and subsequently returned to Holland on 18 December 1644 to report that he had discovered a colony of white Indians hidden in the jungle who revealed to him their Israelite background. Aharon Levi claimed to be a *marrano* Jew[48] and member of the Tribe of Levi. He also used the Spanish name of Antonio Montezinos in his attempt to pass himself off as Catholic and avoid the Inquisition.

Levi reported to Ben Israel and a group of Portuguese Jews that some two and a half years earlier, he left the West Indies to travel to Quito, Ecuador. He obtained a pack of mules and hired several Indians under the leadership of Francisco, a local Indian chief, to help him make the trip. Levi stated that some time after this trip, he was in the city of Cartagena, Colombia, where he was placed under arrest by the Inquisition. While in jail, entrusting himself to God, he offered the following prayer "Blessed be the name of the Lord, that did not make me idolatrous, barbarian, black, or Indian." Levi claimed that upon saying "Indian," it suddenly came to him that these Indians were Hebrews."[49] The thought so startled him that he decided that he must be losing his mind. Every day during the following week he offered the

---

[47] Menasseh Ben Israel, *Esto Es Esperança de Israel, Sobre El Origen de los Americanos*, published in Amsterdam, 1650 by Semuel Ben Israel Soeiro. (Reprinted in Madrid, 1881. Editorial Plata S.A. 1974.)

[48] A *marrano* Jew is a Jew who changed his name and adopted Catholicism to avoid the Inquisition. Many rose to prominent positions within the Catholic Church while practicing their Jewish religion in the secrecy of their own homes. It appears from Ben Israel's writing that there was no attempt on the part of the inquisition forces to differentiate between a member of the Tribe of Judah and the Tribe of Levi. All known Israelites were called Jews, which was the predominant tribe living in Jerusalem and scattered throughout the world.

[49] Ben Israel, 3

same prayer and every day he received the same strong impression that the Indians were Hebrews.[50]

As soon as he obtained his freedom, he sought out Francisco with whom he had established a good relationship in order to find out whether there might be any truth to the idea that the Indians were Hebrews. During the ensuing conversation, Levi revealed to Francisco that he, Aharon Levi, was an Israelite from the Tribe of Levi and that his God was Adonay.[51]

Francisco told Levi that if he would obey Francisco in everything, he would take him to a place where Levi could find out the answers to his questions concerning Israelites in the Americas. The following day, Francisco arrived at Levi's hut and instructed him to leave his sword and cape behind and take only some food and a walking stick. The two men walked for eight days into the interior of Colombia until they finally came to a wide river. Taking a large handkerchief from around his waist, Francisco signaled to the other side of the river. Shortly thereafter three men and one woman crossed the river by canoe. The four strangers left the canoe and approached Levi and Francisco. When the men approached Francisco, he immediately bowed down in a sign of great respect. With a demonstration of considerable kindness, the men lifted Francisco up, spoke briefly with him and then approached Levi. Using Francisco as an interpreter, they began to speak to Levi.

The men began their discourse by citing a scripture which Levi recognized was from the Book of Deuteronomy 6:4 which states "Hear, O Israel: The Lord our God is one Lord." The

---

[50] Israelites and Jews frequently use the term Hebrews when referring to themselves, but they should not be confused with the Hebrews who were descendants through Joktan as mentioned by Cabello Valboa, but to those Hebrews who were descendants through the linage of Peleg, Joktan's brother, and, subsequently, through Abraham, Isaac, and Jacob.

[51] Adonay is a Hebrew word or title meaning "Lord" and was often used by Hebrew-speaking groups to refer to "Jehovah."

men, still using Francisco as an interpreter, made the following additional declarations:

> First: Our Father is Abraham, Isaac, Jacob, Israel, and holding up three fingers mentioned these four. Then adding Ruben, they held up four fingers.
> Second: Those who want to live with us, we will give them lands.
> Third: Joseph lives in the middle of the ocean (holding up two fingers together and then opening them) in two parts.[52]
> Fourth: In the near future, we will come out to look around and to walk around. (Upon saying that they made signs with their eyes and stomped with their feet.)
> Fifth: Some day we will all speak, and we shall come out as if the earth gave us birth.[53]
> Sixth: A messenger will go forth.
> Seventh: Francisco will later tell you a little more. (They held up their fingers showing a little.)
> Eighth: Give us a place where we can prepare ourselves and do not delay. (They moved their hands from one place to another.)
> Ninth: Twelve men will be sent who can write. (Each man made a sign that the twelve men would have beards.)[54]

Levi informed his Jewish audience in Holland that for three days the men and women kept repeating the same words and would not answer any of his questions about themselves. At one point he slipped away from the group, grabbed a canoe and tried to cross the river to see their homes and villages, but they caught him and dumped him in the river. When they saw that he could not swim, they quickly jumped in and pulled him out. They angrily told him that he would not be allowed to cross the river. Levi added that for three days the canoe did not stop bringing

---

[52]This statement assumes additional importance in light of Book of Mormon claims that will be noted later.

[53]Their prediction sounds very similar to the words of Isaiah 29:4 "...and thy voice shall be, as of one that hath a familiar spirit, out of the ground, and thy speech shall whisper out of the dust."

[54]Ben Israel, 9.

people over to greet him and he calculated that he must have met over 300 people. He described them as follows:

> These people were lightly tanned by the sun, some wore their hair almost to their knees, but others wore their hair much shorter, others commonly wore it evenly cut. They were all good size, had pleasant faces, and had well-shaped feet and legs. They wore a cloth band around their head.

Before he and Francisco departed the area, the Israelites brought them food and many gifts. He noticed that these people seemed to enjoy all of the comforts that the Spaniards enjoyed in the New World. They had plenty to eat, good clothing to wear, cattle, seeds, and other basic essentials.[55]

During the trip back to Cartagena, Francisco provided the following additional information about the people with whom they had just met:

> Your brothers, the sons of Israel, were brought by God to this land. He did wonderful things for them, so many astonishing things that if I were to tell you about all of them, you would not believe me. These things have been told to me by my fathers. When we Indians arrived in this land, we made war on them and we treated them worse than the Spaniards have treated us.[56]

Francisco claimed that their Indian *Mohanes* (priests) taught his people the following prophecy which they claimed to be true:

> The God of these Sons of Israel is the true God. All that is written on their stones is true. At the end of time, they will be Lords over all the people in the world. There will come into this land a people who will bring with them many things and, after this land is com-

---

[55] Ibid., 10.

[56] Ibid., 12 (Obviously Francisco, who was an Indian, differentiated between his people and these light skinned "Israelites." When Francisco refers to "arriving in this land" it would appear that "this land" refers to where these "Israelites" lived.)

pletely filled up, these Sons of Israel will come out from where they are, and will dominate the whole land as they did before. Those of you who wish to be venturesome, remain close to them.[57]

When Francisco finished relating the prophecy of the Mohanes, he mentioned that his parents were chiefs and, along with several other chiefs who believed that the Mohanes's prophecies were true, moved as close to the Israelites as they could in hope that someday they could learn more about them. Francisco said that the Israelites promised to reveal any important prophecy or new event that might occur among them. Francisco said that, according to his Israelite friends, the three most notable events which the Israelites had observed, and which caused great celebration, had been the arrival of the Spaniards, the arrival of ships in the South Sea (Pacific), and finally the visit of Aharon Levi. According to Francisco, these Israelites claim that these three events were in fulfilment of their prophesies.[58]

It would appear that Aharon Levi believed that he had discovered a group of Israelites secreted away in the jungles of Colombia. It is unclear why these Israelites, who had been hidden for so many years, agreed to meet with Francisco nor after meeting with him, why they refused to provide additional information about themselves nor allow Levi to travel into their village.

After meeting with these American "Israelites," Levi traveled as fast as he could back to Amsterdam to inform the Jewish Synagogue about what he had found. Ben Israel spent six months questioning Levi in detail about his adventure. He stated that Levi later went to Pernambuco, Brazil, where he lived for only two years more and swore on his deathbed that the story he

---

[57]Ibid., 13. (In this case, it appears that "this land" refers to the Americas.)
[58]Ibid., 14-15.

related was true.⁵⁹ Ben Israel affirmed in his book that he believed Levi's *Relación*; however, he admitted that this account could not be proven by science nor even through a study of the Holy Scriptures because the Holy Scriptures do not mention any event in which people left the Old World to inhabit the New World.

Francisco's comment that "All that is written on their stones is true," reinforces later findings about written records in ancient America. During the last 100 years, art historians have discovered a very complex writing system engraved upon rocks as well as in books among the Indians especially among the Maya and Aztec Indians in Mexico. In their book, *The Code of Kings*, Drs. Linda Schele and Peter Mathews stated that "The past four decades have seen the decipherment of the Maya hieroglyphic writing system and the reading of the history of one of the great civilizations of the world."⁶⁰

As Ben Israel investigated the accounts of the early Spanish and Portuguese explorers to the New World, he encountered evidence that the Indians had news of the creation of the world and the universal flood, which indicated to him that at some time in the past Israelites must have lived in those areas and the Indians learned these things from them. He observed that the Indians were brown without beards; however, he had received information about cases where white natives with beards had been seen, who, in his opinion, were Israelites.

Ben Israel mentioned the expedition of General Diego Vaca de Viega who set out to explore new lands. In 1622, the Spaniards entered into the Province of Yarguarsongo [not fur-

---

⁵⁹ Ibid., 42.

⁶⁰Linda Schele and Peter Mathews, *The Code of Kings, the Language of Seven Sacred Maya Temples and Tombs*, (Scribner, New York, 1998.) Although it is unclear when the New World natives began to write, the work book for the XXII Maya Hieroglyphic Forum at Texas, March, 1998, states: "The lowland Maya did not invent writing in Mesoamerica; rather, they inherited the idea of writing from an earlier cultural period between 600 B.C. and 50 A.D."

ther identified except that the word is Quechua and would likely place the Province along the coast of Peru or Ecuador] and crossed the Andes to where they came upon the Marañon River [Amazon River] which they followed east for some 1500 miles. They finally arrived at the Guariaga River and met up with the Guariaga Indians. These Indians told the Spaniards that four or five days journey down river lived a group of white men, tall and well built. These Indians said the white natives also had beards similar to the Spaniards.[61]

Ben Israel cited another case in which bearded white Indians were discovered. He mentioned that in the early 1600's, eight Tabajares [not further identified, but probably Portuguese] left Pernambuco, Brazil, to explore the interior of Brazil and discover whether there were inhabited areas in the interior. They walked almost directly west and after four months they came upon some high mountains. After crossing the mountains, they came upon a lovely plain that was watered by a peaceful river. Along the river banks, they discovered a white people with beards. After nine months, five of the Tabares returned to Pernambuco with the news of their discovery. Three of the men died during the journey.[62] Other examples cited by Ben Israel are included in Chapter 15.

In addition to the writings of Ben Israel, other conquistadors have pointed out numerous customs among the native Americans that appear to have similarities with Israelite practices. During his travels and investigations, Cabello Valboa came across the story of what appears to be a Passover ritual in the Americas. He wrote the following comments:

> Some new islands were discovered and, upon arriving at one of them, we encountered where the natives had build a solemn temple and they gathered every day at the temple to celebrate their holidays

---

[61]Ben Israel, 35.
[62]Ibid., 36.

and in the first quarter of the new moon, they looked for a male lamb without spot or blemish and they sacrificed it. They then sprinkled the blood of this lamb around the frames of their doors.[63]

Cabello Valboa stated that from this practice, his group judged that these people were descendants of the Jews.

It would appear from an analysis of the various types of people encountered by the Spanish and Portuguese that there was a wide variety of native cultures, customs, dress, skin colorings, and religions. There are indications that some of the civilizations were very old and disappeared over time. Others came on the scene more recently which would suggest that there may have been several migrations into the New World at different times and from different areas of the Old World. Additional evidences of Israelite and Christian teachings, ceremonies and religious rites will be recounted in Chapters 8 through 11.

---

[63] Cabello Valboa, 195.

4

INTRODUCTION TO THE
BOOK OF MORMON

Perhaps the most detailed theory of the origin of ancient Americans comes not from the chronicles, but from the writings of a poor 19th Century farm boy in upstate New York who produced one of the most controversial books of the last two hundred years–the *Book of Mormon*. For some time before the *Book of Mormon* was published in Palmyra, New York, in early 1830, Joseph Smith was the center of an intense religious controversy. It is not possible to analyze the *Book of Mormon* without first investigating the background of Joseph Smith and his religious claims. Even today, believer and non-believer alike inexorably link together Joseph Smith and the *Book of Mormon*. Those who accept the *Book of Mormon* as scripture and as a true record of some of the ancient Americans, also accept Joseph Smith as a "prophet, seer, and revelator."[1] Conversely, those who

---

[1] Joseph Smith was first called a "Prophet, Seer and Revelator" on 6 April 1830 at the time of the establishment of The Church of Jesus Christ of Latter-day Saints. Doctrine and Covenants 21:1. (Abbreviated D&C in future references.)

believe that Joseph was an imposter and a charlatan, are equally convinced that the *Book of Mormon* is not only "fiction, but monstrous fiction filled to overflowing with heresy."[2]

It is difficult to find objective critiques about Joseph Smith and the *Book of Mormon*. Believers and non-believers alike are more likely to be subjective—highly influenced by their feelings and passions—than objective reviewers of historical events. Most of the early followers of Joseph Smith were those who were closest to him, knew him best, and were intimately involved in the publication of the *Book of Mormon* and the subsequent establishment of The Church of Jesus Christ of Latter-day Saints. His critics were generally those who had little contact with Joseph, but in someway felt threatened by him and his "new religion." Others who had been close to him and then became disaffected joined the ranks of critics. The latter were often the most virulent in their criticisms or attacks upon Smith.

The following brief history of Joseph Smith and the *Book of Mormon* is provided mainly by Smith himself or by his mother Lucy Mack Smith, who recorded her memories shortly after Joseph's assassination in 1844.

Joseph Smith, Jr. was born on 23 December 1805, in Sharon, Windsor County, Vermont. He was the fifth child of Joseph Smith, Sr. and Lucy Mack Smith. Lucy Mack and Joseph, Sr. began married life somewhat prosperously, having received a 100-acre farm and a $1000 wedding gift. By the time, Joseph, Jr. was born, they had lost their farm and dowery in order to pay off some unfortunate debts.

Joseph, Sr., like other New England merchants of that time, had purchased and shipped a load of ginseng to China on con-

---

[2]Jan Shipps, *Mormonism, The Story of a New Religious Tradition*, (University of Illinois Press,1987.) 26. Shipps wrote that an early example of the charge that the *Book of Mormon* was heresy is found in the writing of the Rev. Diedrich Willers. See D. Michael Quinn, trans. and ed., "The First Months of Mormonism: A Contemporary (1830) View by Rev. Diedrich Willers," New York History 54 (July 1973): 331.

Introduction to the *Book of Mormon*   73

signment. Another merchant named Stevens, who accompanied his own load of ginseng to China, subsequently informed Joseph, Sr. that the sale of their merchandise in China had been a failure. Joseph, Sr. later learned that the ginseng had sold well, but when he went to confront Stevens, he discovered that Stevens had absconded to Canada with the money, leaving Joseph, Sr. with heavy debts to pay. Joseph and Lucy sold their farm and used her $1000 dowry to pay those debts. Joseph was reduced to renting land for farming and hiring out as a wage laborer.[3]

Historian Jan Shipps described this fall from status as a landowner as having a serious impact upon the Smith family. It carried them away from the solid center of respectability towards the fringes of polite society.[4]

In 1816, the Smith family moved to Manchester, New York, near Palmyra where they procured some land of their own. Both Joseph, Sr. and Lucy were described as persons of considerable education and Joseph, Sr. taught school for a time in Sharon, Vermont. But there is no indication that Joseph, Jr. ever attended public school or received any formal education. Whatever education he received as a child apparently came from his parents. The Smith family habitually read from the Bible. Joseph, Jr. frequently acknowledged his lack of formal education and particularly his poor spelling. In later years, he generally used a scribe to record his books and pronouncements.

His mother remembered him as a "remarkably quiet, well-disposed child, much less inclined to the perusal of books than

---

[3] Richard L. Bushman in his book, *Joseph Smith and the Beginnings of Mormonism,* (Published in 1984 by the University of Illinois) provides extensive historical background on the ancestors of Lucy Mack and Joseph Smith, Sr. Bushman quotes extensively from an 1844 Historical book written by Lucy Mack Smith after the martyrdom of Joseph Smith, Jr. and his brother, Hyrum Smith entitled *Biographic Sketches of Joseph Smith, the Prophet, and His Progenitors for Many Generations.* (London and Liverpool: Published for Orson Pratt by S. W. Richards, 1853); reprinted ed., New York: Arno Press and the New York Times, 1969.

[4] Shipps, 6.

any of the rest of our children, but far more given to meditation and deep study."⁵ The lack of formal education was an accusation commonly used by non-believers to discredit Smith and the *Book of Mormon*.

Although the Smith family did not belong to any organized religion, they considered themselves as "believers in an All Mighty." Religious revivals were a common occurrence along the frontier in the early 1800s and that spirit of revival reached the Palmyra area in 1816 and 1817. The Smiths, along with the other residents of Manchester and Palmyra, became caught up in the upsurge in religion. Young Joseph attended a number of revivals, spent considerable time with professors of religion and joined a juvenile debating club to discuss the existence of God.⁶ In his subsequent history, Smith described his state of mind in 1820 in these words:

> I was at this time in my fifteenth year. My father's family was proselyted to the Presbyterian faith, and four of them joined that church, namely, my mother, Lucy; my brothers Hyrum and Samuel Harrison; and my sister Sophronia.
>
> During this time of great excitement my mind was called up to serious reflection and great uneasiness; but though my feelings were deep and often poignant, still I kept myself aloof from all these parties, though I attended their several meetings as often as occasion would permit. In the process of time my mind became somewhat partial to the Methodist sect, and I felt some desire to be united with them; but so great were the confusion and strife among the different denominations, that it was impossible for a person young as I was, and so unacquainted with men and things, to come to any certain conclusion who was right and who was wrong.⁷

---

⁵Lucy Mack Smith. *History of Joseph Smith by His Mother*, was dictated to Martha Jane Knowlton Coray, who acted as her amanuensis. It was first published by Mormon Apostle Orson Pratt in Liverpool, England 1853 without the consent of Brigham Young, Smith's successor. The original was revised somewhat and then republished in Salt Lake City in 1901 by her grandson, Joseph F. Smith (Joseph Smith, Jr.'s nephew and the sixth President of The Church of Jesus Christ of Latter-day Saints.) A re-edited edition was published in 1996 by Bookcraft, Salt Lake City. 111.

⁶Ibid., 55.

⁷Pearl of Great Price: Joseph Smith – History. Chapter 1:7-8.

Introduction to the Book of Mormon · 75

Smith stated that while meditating on the subject of religion and the religious confusion that he had observed, he was impressed by the counsel of James as recorded in the *Bible*, James 1:5, which states "*If any of you lack wisdom, let him ask of God, that giveth to all men liberally, and upbraideth not; and it shall be given him.*" Smith decided to pray vocally in a nearby grove of trees. Although only fourteen at the time, when he emerged from that grove of trees, he proclaimed that while praying, he had received a vision in which he saw God and Jesus Christ. He further claimed that Jesus Christ told him to join none of the churches "for they were all wrong..."[8] Joseph Smith's declaration, which he never retracted the rest of his life, set into motion an expanding circle of animosity and persecution that twenty four years later culminated in his assassination and the assassination of his brother Hyrum.

In Church history this episode became known as the "First Vision." In addition to relating the events of that encounter to his parents, young Joseph related the First Vision to a Methodist preacher, who "treated my communication not only lightly, but with great contempt, saying it was all of the devil, that there were no such things as visions or revelations in these days; that all such things had ceased with the apostles and that there would never be any more of them."[9] Joseph soon found that his story fomented a great deal of prejudice against him, especially among the professors of religion, which continued unabated throughout his life.

In her book, *Joseph Smith, the First Mormon*, Donna Hill found it puzzling that Smith's claim of such a religious experience in his youth should arouse such skepticism and hostility.[10]

---

[8]Ibid., 1:19. (Joseph's account of what transpired in the grove of trees can be found in verses 14-20 or in Chapter 18 of this book.)

[9]Ibid., 1:21.

[10]Donna Hill, *Joseph Smith, The First Mormon*. (Doubleday & company, Garden City, New York. 1977.)

She remarked that an intense conversion experience is not uncommon during adolescence and this was recognized in Smith's day. Hill pointed out what Joshua Bradley said of similar revivals in Delaware and Connecticut between 1811 and 1818 that, like most awakenings, the work was mainly among young people.[11] Even the more vivid claims of manifestations of religious experience, such as dreams, visions and revelations, were common in Smith's day, and they were not generally viewed with scorn. Nevertheless, Joseph's visions, in particular his first, have received the special attention of historians, theologians and psychologists who have called them hallucination, delusion, fabrication, imagination and hoax.[12]

The First Vision was not the last of the visions or revelations that Smith claimed to have received. He asserted that on 21 September 1823 while praying in the confines of his bedroom for guidance and forgiveness, he received a personal visitation from another heavenly being. Smith related the initial words of his visitor thus:

> He called me by name, and said unto me that he was a messenger sent from the presence of God to me, and that his name was Moroni; that God had a work for me to do; *and that my name should be had for good and evil among all nations, kindreds, and tongues, or that it should be both good and evil spoken of among all people* [emphasis added].
>
> He said there was a book deposited, written upon gold plates, giving an account of the former inhabitants of this continent, and the source from whence they sprang. He also said that the fulness of the everlasting Gospel was contained in it, as delivered by the Savior to the ancient inhabitants.
>
> Again, he told me, that when I got those plates of which he had spoken–for the time that they should be obtained was not yet ful-

---

[11] Joshua Bradley, *Accounts of Religious Revivals in Many Parts of the United States from 1815 to 1818* (Albany, N.Y.; G. J. Loomis & Company 1819.) As quoted in Donna Hill's *Joseph Smith, The First Mormon*. 54.

[12] Hill, 55.

Introduction to the Book of Mormon   77

filled—I should not show them to any person; neither the breastplate with the Urim and Thummim; only to those to whom I should be commanded to show them; if I did I should be destroyed. While he was conversing with me about the plates, the vision was opened to my mind that I could see the place where the plates were deposited, and that so clearly and distinctly that I knew the place again when I visited it.[13]

Smith wrote that Moroni appeared to him three times during that night and again the following day in a field near his home. During the repeat visits, Joseph claimed that Moroni spoke almost verbatim the instructions provided during the initial visit plus added new instructions and admonitions with each additional appearance. Moroni instructed him to tell his father about the previous night's experience and then to meet Moroni at the indicated burial site of the gold plates on a hill called Cumorah near the Smith home. Joseph claimed that he was allowed to view the plates and other artifacts in the deposit, but was not allowed to retrieve them. Furthermore, he was instructed to return to the same site every September 22 for the next four years to receive additional instructions.

During the following four years, Joseph Smith, Jr. continued to hire himself out to contribute financially to his family. He worked at a variety of jobs including digging ditches and clearing land. At one point, he was hired by Josiah Stowell from Colesville, New York, to dig around a hill for an old silver mine that was rumored to exist in the area. Smith's critics frequently interweave his digging for a silver mine into his account of eventually finding the gold plates.[14]

In January 1827, Joseph Smith married Emma Hales from Harmony, Pennsylvania, whom he had met while boarding with

---

[13]Joseph Smith–History 1:33-34, 42. A more complete description of this Heavenly Being is found in verses 30-32.

[14]See Bushman, 67-72, and Shipps, 10-11, for additional information concerning Joseph's treasure digging activities and the perception of these activities by his critics.

her family. Emma declared that she believed his claims to revelation and she was very supportive of him the rest of her life, even though she endured great hardships and sacrifices.

With the arrival of 22 September 1827, Joseph declared that he received the gold plates along with an instrument he called a Urim and Thummim.[15] By this time the opposition to Smith's claims in the Palmyra area was so strong that he was unable to begin the work of translating the language of the plates into English. Joseph and Emma finally decided to move back to Harmony where they could live with Emma's parents and find the tranquility to begin translating.

In January 1928, Smith claimed that he translated some of the characters inscribed on the plates. Martin Harris, a wealthy Palmyra farmer and close supporter, served Smith as a scribe. Joseph also copied some of the characters from the plates which he attached to his English translation. Harris took a copy of these characters with a partial translation to New York City where he showed them to Professor Charles Anthon, a professor of classical studies at Columbia College. Anthon professed familiarity with the most eminent authorities on Egypt as well as hieroglyphics of Egypt. According to Bushman, Anthon was probably the most qualified man in New York to validate Smith's translation.[16]

Martin Harris related the events of that encounter:

> I went to the city of New York, and presented the characters which had been translated, with the translation thereof, to Professor Charles Anthon, a gentleman celebrated for his literary attainments.

---

[15]The Bible dictionary published by The Church of Jesus Christ of Latter-day Saints in connection with the authorized King James Version states that Urim and Thummim is a Hebrew term that means "lights and perfections." It is described as an instrument prepared of God to assist man in obtaining revelations from the Lord and in translating languages. Using a Urim and Thummim is the special prerogative of a seer. It may have been used from as early as the time of Adam. It is first mentioned in the Bible in Exodus 28:30.

[16]Bushman, 87.

Professor Anthon stated that the translation was correct, more so than any he had before seen translated from the Egyptian. I then showed him those which were not yet translated, and he said that they were Egyptian, Chaldaic, Assyriac, and Arabic; and he said they were true characters. He gave me a certificate, certifying to the people of Palmyra that they were true characters, and that the translation of such of them as had been translated was also correct. I took the certificate and put it into my pocket, and was just leaving the house, when Mr. Anthon called me back and asked me how the young man found out that there were gold plates in the place where he found them. I answered that an angel of God had revealed it unto him.

He then said to me, "Let me see that certificate." I accordingly took it out of my pocket and gave it to him, when he took it and tore it to pieces, saying that there was no such thing now as ministering of angels, and that if I would bring the plates to him he would translate them. I informed him that part of the plates were sealed, and that I was forbidden to bring them.[17] He replied, "I cannot read a sealed book." I left him and went to Dr. Mitchell, who sanctioned what Professor Anthon had said respecting both the characters and the translation.[18]

Bushman pointed out that Anthon and Harris differed drastically in their accounts of what happened. According to Bushman, Anthon wrote letters in 1834 and 1841 to critics of the Mormons, denying that he had verified Smith's translation or the authenticity of the characters. Anthon claimed that "he saw through the hoax at once, feared that Martin was about to be cheated out of his money, and warned the 'simple-hearted

---

[17] According to Joseph Smith's account, when he received the gold plates, he was instructed to translate only a portion of the plates. He was forbidden to translate a portion of the plates that were described as being sealed.

[18] Joseph Smith–History 1:64-65. Believers are quick to notice the similarity between Professors Anthon's comments about not being able to "read a sealed book" and a prophecy of the last days as found in Isaiah 29:11-12 which states: "And the vision of all is become unto you as the words of a book that is sealed, which men deliver to one that is learned, saying Read this, I pray thee: and he saith, I cannot; for it is sealed: And the book is delivered to him that is not learned, saying, Read this, I pray thee: and he saith, I am not learned."

farmer' to beware of rogues."[19] Nevertheless, after Harris's trip to New York, he seemed all the more eager to help Smith with the translation work. From 2 April 1828 to 14 June 1828, he served as scribe while Smith translated 116 pages from the plates–a segment which Joseph called the *Book of Lehi*.[20]

Harris, who had become a strong benefactor to Joseph Smith, both in terms of time and money, begged Joseph to let him take the 116 page manuscript back to Palmyra to show to his wife, who was extremely skeptical of Harris's activities. Smith was reluctant, but finally relented on condition that Harris promise to show the manuscript to only five family members.[21] These 116 pages disappeared while in Harris's possession and were never found again.

Lucy Mack Smith surmised in her history that Martin's wife, Lucy, had taken the manuscript with the view of retaining it until Smith made another translation of the same material. She then planned to alter the original translation for the purpose of showing a discrepancy between the two versions, and thus make the whole appear to be a deception.[22] Whatever the reason, the manuscript was gone and Smith felt personally responsible. He announced that the Angel Moroni had appeared again and told him to return the plates and the Urim and Thummim to Moroni temporarily and that Harris was not allowed to serve as scribe again. In late July 1828, Joseph claimed that he received the

---

[19]Bushman, 87-88.

[20]Ibid., 90.

[21]Lucy Mack Smith, Chapter 24: 160-166. (An editorial footnote states, "One can only imagine the pressure Joseph was feeling at this time to gratify Martin Harris. Martin was twenty-two years older than Joseph. He had liquidated Joseph and Emma's debts. He had financed the move from Manchester to Harmony. He was spending all of his time as a scribe on the work. He was risking his good reputation to continue to associate with Joseph. He was losing his wife's confidence and affections and potentially losing his own place in his home. All these considerations must have weighed heavily on Joseph's mind and heart."

[22]Ibid., 171

Urim and Thummim from Moroni but was instructed not to retranslate that portion which had been lost.[23]

On 22 September 1828, Smith received the plates again, but little translation was performed during the next several months until a school teacher named Oliver Cowdery arrived in Harmony. Cowdery had stayed with the Smith family in Palmyra for a time and became so intrigued with the story of Joseph that he decided to travel to Harmony to meet him. Cowdery told Joseph Smith that he too had received a revelation and that he had been sent to help Joseph. Beginning on 7 April 1829, with Oliver serving as scribe, translation resumed at a rapid pace. During translation none of the scribes were allowed to see the plates themselves. The scribe and Smith sat on opposite sides of a blanket partition so the plates were not in view of the scribe. From 7 April 1829 until late June 1829, Smith translated approximately 600 pages, the entire *Book of Mormon*.

It was also during this three month period that Smith lost the support of his in-laws. That and the persecution around Harmony forced him to seek another location for his work. Oliver wrote to an acquaintance, David Whitmer, in Fayette, New York, and obtained permission for himself, Emma and Joseph to stay in the home of David's father, Peter Whitmer. The Whitmers took great interest in the translation. Martin Harris joined the group as well.

While staying with the Whitmers, Smith stated that he received a revelation of the Lord in which Oliver Cowdery, Martin Harris, and David Whitmer were to be given the opportunity to see the gold plates; subsequently, these three accompanied Joseph into a grove of trees where they said they saw the Angel Moroni who showed them the gold plates and

---

[23] See D&C, Section 3.

the Urim and Thummim and allowed each of the three men to handle the plates.[24]

In early July 1829, Joseph Smith, in the company of Oliver Cowdery, four of Peter Whitmer's sons (Christian, Jacob, Peter Jr., and John), a Whitmer son-in-law, Hiram Page, plus Joseph's father and his brothers Hyrum and Samuel, traveled to Palmyra to see about printing the *Book of Mormon* for which Joseph had already secured a copyright. These eight men testified that on this trip Smith showed them the gold plates which they examined thus making twelve men who affirmed to have seen the gold plates.[25]

Even before finishing the translation, Joseph had begun negotiating with Egbert B. Grandin, a Palmyra bookseller, printer and publisher of the *Wayne Sentinel*, to print the book. Grandin agreed providing he was given adequate guarantee of payment. Martin Harris mortgaged his farm for $3,000 as security.[26] On 26 March 1830, the printing of the first 5000 copies of the *Book of Mormon* was completed.[27] Opposition to Joseph Smith and the *Book of Mormon* continued to grow in Palmyra. However, Joseph Smith, Jr. and five other men officially organ-

---

[24] D&C 17. The full declaration of Oliver Cowdery, Martin Harris and David Whitmer is found in the front of the *Book of Mormon*. Eventually these three witnesses left the Church, but years later after the Church had migrated to Utah, Cowdery and Harris requested permission from Brigham Young to be rebaptized and Harris subsequently moved to Utah as well.

[25] The testimony of the eight men is also included in the front of the *Book of Mormon*. Over time, three of the eight, Jacob and John Whitmer and Hiram Page left the Church, but none ever denied his testimony. (Christian and Peter Whitmer, Jr. had died earlier in full fellowship.) Those who left the Church apparently convinced themselves that Joseph Smith eventually became a "fallen prophet."

[26] Bushman, 108. (Bushman pointed out that Mrs. Harris refused to co-sign the mortgage papers and he noted "In a sense she was right about the [financial] consequences of Martin's involvement with Joseph. Joseph never profited personally from the *Book of Mormon*, but Martin did sell his farm on April 7, 1831.")

[27] Church records indicate that by the beginning of the year 2000 over 100 million copies of the *Book of Mormon* had been printed in 90 different languages.

Introduction to the Book of Mormon

ized, under New York State law, the Church of Jesus Christ on 6 April 1830 at the Whitmer home in Fayette, New York.[28]

Bushman stated that the publication of the *Book of Mormon* made Joseph a minor national figure. The newspapers of the region quickly characterized the *Book of Mormon* as the "gold bible" and the phrase "Mormonism" was soon coined. Bushman observed that for all the effort and trouble Joseph put into the translation and subsequent publication, he took little credit for his efforts to translate and publish the book. The first edition conveyed virtually nothing about Joseph himself. The preface contained only one sentence about his part in the work; there was no effort of self-promotion. Joseph presented his handiwork to the public and turned his attention to running the newly organized Church. The book thenceforth had a life of its own.[29]

The historian Jan Shipps, in her book *Mormonism, The Story of a New Religious Tradition*, commented:

> This curious book seemed to some of its readers to be a harmless romance, as historical novels were then quaintly called. Upon reading it (or even just hearing about it), others also concluded that it was not only fiction, but a monstrous fiction filled to the overflowing with heresy. The Book convinced a select number of readers, however, that it was not ordinary—or even extraordinary—fiction. To them the *Book of Mormon* was precisely what it said it was: a translation of ancient records that had been written, sealed up, and hidden in the earth for more than fourteen centuries.[30]

Shipps opined that making judgments about whether the book was interesting, informative, or worthwhile was not enough. The issue was much more fundamental:

---

[28]In a revelation given to Joseph Smith on 26 April 1838, he was instructed that the Church should be called *The Church of Jesus Christ of Latter-day Saints*. See Doctrine and Covenants Section 115.
[29]Bushman, 112-113.
[30]Shipps, 26-27.

Was this a Hebraic record once "hid up," but now "brought forth" to show the Indians that they were a "remnant of the House of Israel" and brought forth, too, in order to demonstrate to "Jew and Gentile that Jesus is the Christ, the Eternal God manifesting Himself to all nations"? In other words, was this a "second witness"; was it "another testament of Jesus Christ"?[31]

The citizens of Palmyra soon rose up against the *Book of Mormon*. Even before it was printed, Abner Cole, editor of the Palmyra *Reflector*, wrote derogatory satires about Joseph Smith and the *Book of Mormon*.[32] Interestingly, Cole never questioned whether Smith was connected with the *Book of Mormon* because during the printing, he pirated pages of the text from the Grandin Press, where he also printed the Palmyra *Reflector*, and ran these pages in his newspapers until Joseph threatened him with copyright laws. Cole's views were sent throughout New York and into neighboring states and others soon took up the attacks.

The scene of the attacks against Joseph and the *Book of Mormon* soon shifted from Palmyra to Painesville, Ohio, after Oliver Cowdery and Peter Whitmer traveled there in October 1830 and began to convert en masse members of the Campbellite Church including one of the pastors, Sidney Rigdon. Both Thomas Campbell and Alexander Campbell argued that Joseph was a magician or bogus worker and that Mormons were one more example of human gullibility.[33]

---

[31]Ibid., 27.

[32]Bushman, 120. (Bushman states that Francis W. Kirkham compiled a great many of the news articles on Mormonism in his book, *New Witness for Christ in America*. Salt Lake City, Utah Printing Co., 1967.)

[33]Bushman refers to Kirkham's *New Witness* 2:60-62, 65-66, 70, 93, 95; and Alexander Campbell's, *Delusions: An Analysis of the Book of Mormon* (Boston: Benjamin H. Greene, 1832), pp 5-6.

One critic with whom Smith had serious problems was an excommunicated Mormon named Philastus Hurlburt.[34] In the fall of 1833, Hurlburt discovered a work of fiction that was penned in 1813 by the Reverend Solomon Spalding, a former resident of Conneaut, Ohio. Hurlburt claimed that Spalding's work of fiction appeared to be similar to the *Book of Mormon*. When Hurlburt questioned the residents of the town of Conneaut, they vowed that Spalding's novel told about lost tribes of Israel moving from Jerusalem to the Americas and his manuscript included names such as Lehi, Nephi, Mormon and Moroni, names that are prominent in the text of the *Book of Mormon*. Hurlburt shared information of his findings with the editor of the Painesville Telegraph, Eder D. Howe. The two men agreed to write an exposé of Joseph Smith and the *Book of Mormon*.

To add authenticity to their exposé, Hurlburt began a search for the missing Spalding novel. Hurlburt eventually found Spalding's widow (Spalding died in 1816), living in New York, and discovered a 135 page manuscript in a trunk in her attic which he supposed was the original. But upon examination Hurlburt found that, although vaguely familiar to some aspects of the *Book of Mormon*, the novel told a story of a group of Romans who became lost anciently and ended up in the New World where they encountered the Indians. They supposedly wrote their history in Latin and hid it in a cave. Spalding began

---

[34]Philastus Hurlburt had been ordained an elder in the Church in March 1833 but was excommunicated from the Church for adultery and indecent behavior towards women in June of that same year. He publically threatened the life of Joseph Smith and was taken to trial in Chardon, Ohio, on 2 April 1834 where he was found guilty of threatening Smith. Hurlburt was fined $300.00, ordered to keep the peace for six months, and required to pay all court costs. Joseph referred to him as a wicked man. Joseph Smith's *History of The Church of Jesus Christ of Latter-day Saints*. (A six volume work dictated by Joseph Smith to scribes from 1838 to 1844.) Copyrighted by George Albert Smith for The Church of Jesus Christ of Latter-day Saints 1951. An Introduction and Notes by B. H. Roberts. Second Edition Revised and Published by the Deseret Book Company, Salt Lake City, Utah 1973. For ordination and excommunication, see Vol. I, pp 334, 353-355. For Court trial, see Vol II, pp 46-49.

his novel with the "discovery" of the Roman manuscript. Spalding entitled his novel "*Manuscript Found.*"[35]

The Spalding manuscript found by Hurlburt did not contain any names found in the *Book of Mormon*. When he shared this with Howe, they decided that there must have been a second manuscript and they both spent years looking for it. They also concluded that anyone as uneducated as Joseph Smith could not have turned the Spalding manuscript into the *Book of Mormon*; consequently, they conjectured that the real author of the *Book of Mormon* was the well-educated, former Campbellite preacher, Sidney Rigdon.

The Spalding manuscript theory was the mainstay of *Book of Mormon* critics throughout the rest of the Nineteenth Century and appeared in numerous books including Howe's *Mormonism Unvailed (SIC).*[36] Bushman points out, however, that the purveyors of this theory have never been able to connect Sidney Rigdon, who joined the Church in Kirtland, Ohio, in October 1830, seven months after the *Book of Mormon* was printed, with Joseph Smith, who, up to that time, had not traveled west of Rochester, New York.[37]

For many years, the Spalding manuscript, initially obtained and signed by Hurlburt, was lost and a second manuscript was never discovered. The Spalding manuscript signed by Hurlburt turned up in Hawaii in 1884 among some papers belonging to L. L. Rice, who in turned passed them to James Fairchild, President of Oberlin College. Fairchild published the results of his study of the manuscript and concluded that there was no similarity in

---

[35]See Bushman 126-127, and Lester E. Bush, Jr's, *The Spalding Theory Then and Now* as Printed in *Dialogue: A Journal of Mormon Thought*, Vol. X, No. 4 Autumn 1977.

[36]Eder D. Howe, *Mormonism unvailed: or A Faithful Account of That Singular Imposition and Delusion*. . . .(Painesville, Ohio: Printed and Published by the Author, 1834.)

[37]See Bushman 119-127 for extensive details of maneuvering by the various critics.

Introduction to the Book of Mormon

style, names or incidents between the manuscript and the *Book of Mormon* and he concluded that the Spalding theory "will probably have to be relinquished."[38]

Even after the Spalding manuscript was discovered to bear no resemblance whatsoever to the *Book of Mormon*, its critics continued to search for new arguments to deride Joseph Smith and to debunk the book. In 1945, Fawn McKay Brodie, the niece of the ninth president of the Latter-day Saint Church, David O. McKay, became disaffected with the Church and wrote *No Man Knows My History, The Life of Joseph Smith*.[39] Brodie attacked both Joseph Smith and the *Book of Mormon*. Concerning the latter, Brodie wrote:

> The *Book of Mormon* was a mutation in the evolution of American literature, a curious sport, at once sterile and potent. Although it bred no imitators outside Mormonism and was ignored by literary critics, it brought several hundred thousand immigrants to America in the nineteenth century. The twentieth century sees the distribution of thousands of copies each year. For more than a hundred years missionaries have heralded it throughout the world as religious history second only to the Bible.
> Scholars of American literary history have remained persistently uninterested in the *Book of Mormon*. Their indifference is the more surprising since the book is one of the earliest examples of frontier fiction, the first long Yankee narrative that owes nothing to English literary fashions. Except for the borrowings from the King James Bible, its sources are absolutely American. No sociologist has troubled to draw parallels between the *Book of Mormon* and other sacred books, like the *Koran* and *Science and Health* [Mary Baker Eddy and the Christian Science Church], though all are ostensibly divinely inspired and all are an obscure compound of folklore, moral platitude, mysticism, and millennialism.

---

[38] Lester E. Bush, Jr. *The Spalding Theory Then and Now*, Dialogue: A Journal of Mormon Thought. Vol. X, No. 4 Autumn 1977. (Mormon Miscellaneous, Reprint Series, Utah, June 1984.) 15.

[39] Fawn M. Brodie, *No Man Knows My History, The Life of Joseph Smith*, (Copyright and published by Adolph A. Knopf, Inc., New York, 1945) Revised and published by Adolph A. Knopf, Inc. in New York, 1971.

Every creed perhaps must have its sacred books. And among such books the Mormon Bible is one of the most remarkable for sheer pretension. It is easy enough to deride its style, and painstaking research can uncover the sources of all its ideas. But nothing can detract from the fact that many people have found it convincing history. Henry A. Wallace recognized this when he said in 1937: "Of all the American religious books of the nineteenth century, it seems probable that the *Book of Mormon* was the most powerful. It reached perhaps only one per cent of the people of the United States, but it affected this one per cent so powerfully and lastingly that all the people of the United States have been affected, especially by its contribution to opening up one of our great frontiers."[40]

Brodie's reference to the *Book of Mormon* as a work of fiction is a clear indication that she never accepted the idea that Joseph Smith had access to or the capability to translate any gold plates. She described many of the numerous myths and accounts of the gold plates, but placed greater reliance on the accounts of those who claimed that they never saw the plates. She suggested the theory that the idea of the existence of gold plates was spun out of Joseph Smith's wild imagination. She theorized that "perhaps in the beginning Joseph never intended his stories of the golden plates to be taken so seriously, but once the masquerade had begun, there was no point at which he could call a halt."[41]

Convinced that the *Book of Mormon* was "frontier fiction," Brodie never bothered to explain away the testimonies of the twelve witnesses who claimed to have seen and handled the plates. She appears to follow the tack that if the plates never existed, then they could not have been seen by anyone. Although she does not address the issue, she implies that twelve supposedly honest men entered into a plot to deceive the world. Even though six of these witnesses later became disaffected with Joseph Smith and left the Church, there is no record that any of

---

[40]Ibid., 67. (Brodie's quote of Henry A. Wallace was given at an address before the New York Times National Book Fair, *New York Times*, November 5, 1937.)
[41]Ibid., 41.

INTRODUCTION TO THE BOOK OF MORMON

the six who left the Church ever disavowed his affidavit that he had seen the gold plates.

The disaffected witnesses included Oliver Cowdery, David Whitmer and Martin Harris–the three who not only claimed to have seen and handled the plates, but also to have seen the Angel Moroni. The other three who left the Church were Jacob and John Whitmer and their brother-in-law, Hiram Page. Brodie was unswayed by the fact that both Martin Harris and Oliver Cowdery, in later years, requested permission to be rebaptized into the Church even though they both realized that they would never again enjoy the positions of authority that they occupied in the early 1830's.

Before he died in 1888, David Whitmer wrote a letter to the "Richmond Conservator" in Richmond, Missouri, in which he reaffirmed that he had seen the gold plates and the Angel Moroni. Whitmer wrote:

> It having been represented by one John Murphy, of Polo, Caldwell County, Mo., that I, in a conversation with him last summer, denied my testimony as one of the three witnesses to the 'Book of Mormon.'
>
> To the end, therefore, that he may understand me now, if he did not then; and that the world may know the truth, I wish now, standing as it were, in the very sunset of life, and in fear of God, once for all to make this public statement:
>
> That I have never at any time denied that testimony or any part thereof, which has so long since been published with that Book, as one of the three witnesses. Those who know me best, well know that I have always adhered to that testimony. And that no man may be misled or doubt my present views in regard to the same, I do again affirm the truth of all my statements, as then made and published.[42]

---

[42] Keith W. Perkins, *True to the Book of Mormon, The Whitmers*, printed in the February 1989 *ENSIGN*, a magazine printed by The Church of Jesus Christ of Latter Day Saints. (Taken from David Whitmer, *An Address to All Believers, in Christ*, Richmond, Missouri: David Whitmer, 1887, 30-56.)

Brodie does not address the difficulties that Joseph Smith would have encountered in trying to get eleven men to enter into a conspiracy with him to deceive the world, especially as the conspirators began, one by one, to leave the Church. There existed newspapers and a vociferous opposition that would have been willing to pay large sums of money to get even one man out of the twelve to retract his testimony.

Brigham Young University Professor of ancient scripture, Hugh W. Nibley, published a lengthy response to Brodie's work in pamphlet form called, *No, Ma'am, That's Not History*.[43] Nibley wrote the following preface in his pamphlet:

> When the writer first read Mrs. Brodie's book thirteen years ago he was struck by the brazen inconsistencies that swarm in its pages, and so wrote this hasty review. At that time he had no means of knowing that inconsistency was the least of the author's vices, and assumed with other reviewers that when she cited a work in her footnotes, she had actually read it, that when she quoted she was quoting correctly, and that she was familiar with the works in her bibliography. Only when other investigations led the reviewer to the same sources in ensuing years did the extent of Mrs. Brodie's irresponsibility become apparent. While a large book could (and probably should) be devoted to this remarkable monument of biographical mendacity, more than a decade of research abetted by correspondence with Mrs. Brodie's defenders has failed to discredit a single observation made in our 1946 review, which is printed here with only a few typographical errors corrected.[44]

Discounting the "gold plates" theory, Brodie was faced with the problem of how to explain where the uneducated Joseph Smith obtained the skill and information that he used to write

---

[43]Hugh W. Nibley, *No, Ma'am, That's Not History*, Published by Bookcraft, Salt Lake City, Utah, 1946.

[44]Hugh W. Nibley, *No, Ma'am, That's Not History*, Published by Bookcraft, Salt Lake City, Utah, 1946. (Reprinted by Permission from *Tinkling Cymbals and Sounding Brass*, Vol. 11 of *The Collected Works of Hugh Nibley* (Salt Lake City: Deseret Books and FARMS, 1991). 3.

the *Book of Mormon*. She had already claimed "that painstaking research can uncover the sources of all its ideas." Brodie suggested that "Joseph's familiarity with the theory of the Hebraic origin of the Indians seems, however, to have come chiefly from a popular book by Ethan Smith, pastor of a church in Poultney, Vermont. This book, *View of the Hebrews; or the Ten Tribes of Israel in America*, was published in 1823." Brodie wrote that "it may, in fact, have been *View of the Hebrews* that gave Joseph Smith the idea of writing an Indian history in the first place."[45] Because none of Joseph Smith's critics in the 1830's ever linked Joseph with Ethan Smith's book, Brodie added the following disclaimer, "It may never be proved that Joseph saw *View of the Hebrews* before writing the *Book of Mormon*, but the striking parallelism between the two books hardly leave a case for mere coincidence.[46]

Fawn McKay Brodie was not the only writer to suggest that Joseph Smith resorted to the *View of the Hebrews* and other eighteenth and nineteenth century writings to obtain the background that he needed to write the *Book of Mormon*. In 1986, Dan Vogel published a book entitled *Indian Origins and the Book of Mormon*.[47] Both Vogel and Ethan Smith quote extensively from James Adair, an Irishman who spent forty years living among and trading with the Chickasaw, Catawba and Cherokee Indians in the American South when it was a British colony.

Adair arrived in South Carolina about 1735 and was an important figure during the French and Indian wars in the south. Adair felt a kindred spirit among the Chickasaws and was able to instill within them a dislike for the French. He was instrumental in helping the British save the Mississippi Valley from

---

[45]Brodie, 46.
[46]Ibid., 47.
[47]Dan Vogel, *Indian Origins and the Book of Mormon* (Signature Books, Inc. United States of America, 1986.) At the time, Vogel was a senior in history at California State University at Long Beach.

falling into the hands of the French. Adair wrote most of his *History of the American Indian* while living among the Chickasaws between 1761 and 1768. He returned to England in 1775 and published his findings.[48] Williams stated that Adair's *History* has been regarded and treated by ethnologists and historians as a reliable authority on the southern Indians as well as on southern history.

The main thrust of Adair's book is that the native Americans "were of one descent and there was strong similarity of religious rites, and of civil and martial customs."[49] He discounted the idea that they were Chinese, Mongols or Tatars. He suggested that the remaining traces of their religious ceremonies, and civil and martial customs, are quite opposite to similarities of these far eastern inhabitants. Adair stated that

> From the most exact observations I could make in the long time I traded among the Indian Americans, I was forced to believe them lineally descended from the Israelites, either while they were a maritime power, or soon after the general captivity; the latter however is the most probable.[50]

For the next 500 pages, Adair attempted to show that the Indians were Hebrew and part of the Lost Ten Tribes. He set forth a series of twenty two arguments in which he evaluated the similarities between the Indians and the Israelites.

Brodie and Vogel strongly argue that Joseph Smith must have used one of these books for his inspiration or the basis for his accounts in the *Book of Mormon*. It appears to me that these two scholarly critics do not understand the basic thrust of the

---

[48]James Adair, *History of the American Indian*, London, 1775. (Re-published in the United States by The National Society of Colonial Dames of Tennessee with Introduction and Notes by Samuel Cole Williams under the title, *Adair's History of the American Indians*, Promontory Press, New York, 1930.)

[49]Adair, 11.

[50]Ibid., 13-14.

Introduction to the *Book of Mormon*

Book of Mormon. In their critiques, they appear to deliberately overlook the fact that the core message in the *Book of Mormon* is centered on Jesus Christ not the Mosaic Law or ancient Jewish traditions as suggested by Adair and Ethan Smith. Neither Adair nor Ethan Smith attempted to demonstrate in their writings that Christianity thrived in pre-Columbian America. Early in the *Book of Mormon*, Nephi wrote:

> And, notwithstanding we believe in Christ, we keep the law of Moses, and look forward with steadfastness unto Christ, until the law shall be fulfilled.
>
> For, for this end was the law given; wherefore the law hath become dead unto us, and we are made alive in Christ because of our faith; yet we keep the law because of the commandments.
>
> And we talk of Christ, we rejoice in Christ, we preach of Christ, we prophesy of Christ, and we write according to our prophecies, that our children may know to what source they may look for a remission on their sins (2 Nephi 25: 24-26).

What Brodie terms as "the striking parallelism between the two books hardly leave a case for mere coincidence" could be best described as a slight overlap between the two books, but insufficient material out of which the uneducated Joseph Smith could have written a book with the internal complexities contained in the *Book of Mormon*. Vogel unintentionally called attention to the difficulties of writing any book. Vogel acknowledged in the Preface to his own 73 page book the extensive support he received from others in gathering the material and writing his book:

> My debt to American and British libraries and institutions is such that I can offer appreciation only in a general way. I would especially like to thank the Librarians at California State University at Long Beach for their courteous and prompt assistance in securing books and other materials through interlibrary loan. The library's microfiche, microfilm, and microtext collections proved invaluable,

as did materials at the library at the University of California at Irvine. My thanks also to the Library of Congress, the Historical Department of The Church of Jesus Christ of Latter-day Saints, the archives of the Reorganized Church of Jesus Christ of Latter Day Saints, the Utah State Historical Society, the British Museum, and the American Antiquarian Society.[51]

Vogel did not state how long it took him to write 73 pages, but he probably spent a year or more just gathering the materials. I have spoken with university professors who have spent years putting together a book that is not nearly as complex as the *Book of Mormon*. In my own case, I began gathering these early chronicles more than thirty years ago, spent three years in graduate school and took a full year to write a 155 page Master's thesis. I was aided at every step by professors reading my thesis and making suggestions. My job was also made easier with the invention of computers and computer software that enabled me to make corrections, move material and add and delete material at will.

Joseph Smith had no computers, inter-library loan services, microfiche or any materials that today's historians utilize to write a book; however, he was able to produce approximately 600 pages in less than 67 days. There is no evidence that he resorted to any outside research and he made no changes in the text. He could take up the thread of the narrative after a lapse of several days without even having his last dictation read back to him.

Whereas Bushman pointed out that the critics failed to ground their views in the actual contents of the *Book of Mormon* and did not do justice to the work's complexity, believers, on the other hand, have gone to great lengths to analyze every chapter and verse of the *Book of Mormon*. Hugh Nibley, who is an authority on ancient Near Eastern studies and has written numerous books and articles on the subject, made the following emphatic comment:

---

[51] Vogel, 1.

Introduction to the *Book of Mormon*

There is no point at all to the question: Who wrote the *Book of Mormon*? It would have been quite as impossible for the most learned man alive in 1830 as it was for Joseph Smith. And whoever would account for the *Book of Mormon* by any theory suggested so far–save one–must completely rule out the first forty pages.

To write a history of what could have happened at the very beginning of recorded history would have been as far beyond the scope of any scholar living in 1830 as the construction of an atom bomb would have been.[52]

Nibley's comments concerning the first forty pages of the *Book of Mormon* refer to the migrations. Nephi described their travel from Jerusalem south along the Red Sea and then almost directly east to a point probably in modern Oman where the travelers reached the ocean and built a ship to cross "the great waters." Nibley argues that only in the last one hundred years have archaeologists discovered enough about this remote area to properly evaluate the setting described by Nephi. Nibley has analyzed every facet of Nephi's description to ensure that it conforms with what is known today about what the area was like 2500 years ago. Nibley has studied the personal names and place names of the period, mode of transportation, routes, hazards and idiosyncracies of the Bedouins and other nomads who have inhabited that area for thousands of years. He concludes that no one in the world and particularly no one in 1830 America could have written the first forty pages of the Book of Mormon and been in such close conformity with the ancient period described by Joseph Smith.[53]

From my research over the last 30 years, I believe it would have been as equally difficult for Joseph Smith to write a book on the earliest civilizations in the Americas based upon informa-

---

[52] Hugh W. Nibley, *Lehi in the Desert; The World of the Jaredites; There Were Jaredites.* (Published in 1988 by Deseret Book Company, Salt Lake City, Utah.) xiv.

[53] Nibley's *Lehi in the Desert* plus accompanying of footnotes. (Please see Appendix A for additional information on Lehi's route.)

tion that was available in the United States in 1830. What was known in Joseph Smith's day about customs, rituals, military warfare and weaponry, and technical skills that were in use four thousand years ago in the New World? How could Smith have been so accurate in his chronology of major civilizations and prehistoric events? There was not yet any scientific knowledge available in the early 19th Century describing archaeological and iconographic discoveries of ancient times. How could he have described so accurately the major religious beliefs, customs, and historical accounts that have been revealed during the last one hundred years? No record of these details had reached the United States by the 1820's.

Concerning man's ability to know the truthfulness of the *Book of Mormon*, the historian Jan Shipps wrote:

> It has never lent itself to the same process of verification that historians use to verify ordinary accounts of what happened in the past. The historicity of the *Book of Mormon* has been asserted through demonstrations that ancient concepts, practices, doctrines, and rituals are present in the work; that the nineteenth century's overwhelming concern with liberty and the working of the political process is absent from it; that from the standpoint of archaeology, its account of settlement and peoples "makes sense" and could have happened; that the pre-Columbian compilers of the various books within the *Book of Mormon* had distinct literary styles, and so on. But such demonstrations point, finally, only to plausibility. Proof is a different matter.[54]

I submit that a careful examination of the early chronicles, coupled with findings of archaeologists and iconographers, as will be seen in the following chapters, enhances the "plausibility

---

[54]Shipps, 28. (In her footnote, she cites the efforts of Dr. Hugh Nibley and particularly two of his books *Lehi in the Deseret and the World of the Jaredites* ((Salt Lake City: Deseret Book, 1952)) and *Since Cumorah: The Book of Mormon in the Modern World* ((Salt Lake City: Deseret Book, 1967)), plus numerous other students of the Book of Mormon including Richard L. Bushman.)

of the veracity" of the *Book of Mormon* and comes extremely close to the long hoped for "material proof."

In 1842, Joseph Smith wrote:

> We can not but think the Lord has a hand in bringing to pass his strange act, and proving the *Book of Mormon* true in the eyes of all the people. . . . It will be as it ever has been, the world will prove Joseph Smith a true prophet by circumstantial evidence, in experiments, as they did Moses and Elijah.[55]

---

[55] Joseph Smith, *Teachings of the Prophet Joseph Smith*, Comp. Joseph Fielding Smith (Salt Lake City, Deseret Book, 1976), 267. Excerpt first printed in *Times and Seasons* 3 (15 Sep 1842): 922.

5

NATIVE AMERICAN ORIGINS ACCORDING TO THE BOOK OF MORMON

The *Book of Mormon*, published in Palmyra, New York in 1830, narrates a brief, but complex history of three different groups of people who migrated to the New World thousands of years ago. The *Book of Mormon* does not rule out the possibility that other groups may have also migrated to the New World; however, it only provides information about three. The first group, known as Jaredites because their initial leader was a man named Jared, left the Old World at the time of the building of the Tower of Babel and the confounding of tongues (approximately 2200-2500 B.C.), crossed the ocean in specially designed barges, and landed in the Americas.

According to the *Book of Mormon*, the second group left Jerusalem in 600 B.C. This group was led by a man named Lehi, who is described as an Israelite prophet and contemporary of the Old Testament Prophet Jeremiah. Lehi claimed that he received several visions from the Lord and in these visions he foresaw the destruction of Jerusalem if the people did not repent of their wickedness. The book says Lehi went among the inhabitants of Jerusalem telling them the things that he had seen and heard in his visions. Like Jeremiah and other prophets of that time, the denizens of Jerusalem threatened to kill Lehi, the bearer of bad news. After receiving threats on his life, he said that the Lord appeared to him and told him to take his family away from Jerusalem.[1] In addition, Lehi succeeded in convincing a man named Ishmael and his family to join them on the long trek from Jerusalem toward what they believed to be a "promised land." Lehi, his family, and the family of Ishmael crossed the ocean and landed somewhere in the Americas.

According to the *Book of Mormon*, the third group, known as the Mulekites, left Jerusalem about twelve years after Lehi and after the Babylonian armies had sacked Jerusalem and carried away most of the Jews to Babylon. The particulars concerning the departure and route of the Mulekites are not recorded except to indicate that they also crossed the "great waters" and remained in the same area in the New World where they initially landed. The *Book of Mormon* (Helaman 6:10) narrates that Mulek was a son of King Zedekiah, who was the king of the Jews at the time that Nebuchadnezzar and his Babylonian armies destroyed Jerusalem (Jeremiah 52:1-10). The Mulekites were descendants of the Tribe of Judah.

The first two groups reportedly brought a written record with them from the Old World which would have included some of the same prophetic writings as found in the Old Testament up until the time each group left the Middle East. In their hurry to escape, the Mulekites did not bring any written

---

[1] Lehi's narrative of the conditions in Jerusalem in his day is complemented by similar accounts in the Old Testament. See writings of Jeremiah, Chapters 2-9.

records with them and thus, over time, lost the knowledge of their history as well as their language.

The *Book of Mormon* begins with the writings of Nephi, youngest of the four sons of Lehi, who relates the experiences of his father. Nephi wrote that Lehi gathered his family with provisions and headed south into a "wilderness" until they came to the Red Sea. Initially the family consisted of Lehi and Sariah, his wife, plus four sons: Laman, Lemuel, Sam, and Nephi (I Nephi 2:5). Nephi was the youngest and was apparently in his late-teens when the family fled Jerusalem because he remarked that although still young he was large and strong for his age. Lehi and Sariah also had daughters, but they are not named. Lehi apparently was a wealthy man because Nephi poignantly declared that they left behind the "land of their inheritance, their gold, silver and precious things."

In contrast to Nephi's support of his father, Laman and Lemuel did not believe that Lehi had received visions or spoke with the Lord. Neither did they believe that Jerusalem would be destroyed as Lehi and other prophets were prophesying; consequently, they were extremely reluctant to leave their comfortable lifestyle. They complained about the hardships of the journey and repeatedly rebelled against their father. Nevertheless, even though they were adults, they acquiesced to follow him into the desert.

After reaching an isolated region near the Red Sea, Lehi camped for a brief period; however, he soon declared that he had received another vision in which he had been instructed to send the four boys back to Jerusalem to obtain "a record of the Jews which also contained the genealogy of their forefathers." This record was engraved on brass plates and was held by Laban, a Jewish elder and one of the rulers.[2]

---

[2] The brass plates would have contained similar material to the Old Testament down to the time of Jeremiah; consequently it provided very important scriptures and historical background. Furthermore, Lehi would have valued it to preserve his written language.

Nephi explained that this extremely important record was only obtained at great risk to him and his brothers. Laban not only refused to give them the record, but he stole the gold, silver and precious jewels they offered and he attempted to kill them. Nephi later returned to the house by himself and obtained the brass plates with the help of Laban's servant, Zoram, who consented to join Lehi's family (1 Nephi Chapters 3, 4). Nephi also took Laban's sword which he used as a model to make his own weapons.

After the sons had returned to their father's tent with the brass plates, Lehi perused the plates and discovered that they contained five books by Moses, an account of the creation of the world as well as a "record of the Jews" from the beginning, and all the prophecies of the holy prophets from the beginning. Lehi also found the genealogy of his fathers in the writings and learned that he was a direct descendant of Joseph, the son of Jacob, through the lineage of Manasseh (1 Nephi 5:11-16).[3]

After Lehi shared the information on the brass plates with his family, he announced that the Lord had told him to send his sons back to Jerusalem a second time to convince Ishmael, his wife, their two married sons and families plus five unmarried daughters to leave Jerusalem and join them in their trek to the "promised land." Ishmael and his family were also descendants of Joseph.

During this period while camped near the Red Sea, Lehi had several important visions that served as spiritual guides for his people. In one vision, he saw "the tree of life" and described the conditions associated with it. He perceived that all of his immediate family except Laman and Lemuel ate its "precious fruit."

---

[3]Although descendants of Ephraim and Manasseh were among the ten tribes captured and led north by the Assyrians 120 years earlier, it would appear from the *Book of Mormon* that at least a few people from the northern tribes were living south in the land of Jerusalem. In this sense, these native Americans could be considered as part of the Ten Tribes, but they did not refer to themselves as such.

He again predicted the destruction of Jerusalem and the eventual coming of the Messiah among the Jews. He foretold the death and resurrection of the Messiah.

Although Nephi was the youngest son, he, too, claimed to have sought and received spiritual manifestations similar to those his father had enjoyed. Nephi insisted that an angel visited him and showed him in a vision "the land of promise" and he saw his descendants on the land as well as the descendants of his brothers, Laman and Lemuel. Nephi saw that his brothers' descendants became a lazy, slothful people. He claimed to foresee the birth of the Holy Messiah in Jerusalem as well as his crucifixion and resurrection. Nephi viewed a massive geological upheaval in the "promised land" at the time of the crucifixion of the Savior and saw Jesus visit the descendants of Lehi in the "land of promise." He saw Jesus establish a Church among them and pick twelve disciples to lead it.[4]

Nephi asserted that an angel showed him all that would happen to Lehi's descendants in the "land of promise" after they were visited by the Messiah and how they would live in peace for four generations. But that after this time, Nephi saw that his own descendants would become wicked and would be nearly destroyed by the posterity of Laman and Lemuel. Nephi observed that the posterity of his brothers degenerated even further and incurred the wrath of God.

Nephi foresaw that after many years, the Spirit of the Lord would inspire a man whom Nephi called a "gentile" to cross the ocean and find the remnants of his brothers. After this man came to the New World, many other "gentiles" would follow and

---

[4]The principal message of all the *Book of Mormon* prophets has been to look forward to the coming of the Savior and to keep His commandments. Although the descendants of Lehi lived the Law of Moses as contained in the Brass plates (2 Nephi 5:10), they did not believe that salvation came by the Law of Moses, but only that it prepared them to follow Jesus Christ (Alma 25:15-16).

destroy many of the descendants of Laman and Lemuel.[5] Nephi saw that the gentiles prospered in the New World and "obtained the land for their inheritance" and he described the gentiles as being "white, and exceedingly fair and beautiful" (1 Nephi 13:14-15). He noted that those of Lehi's descendants who were left when the gentiles came would eventually receive a record of their history from the Gentiles, a foreshadowing of the publication of the *Book of Mormon* and Joseph Smith's zeal to put it in the hands of the Indians, whom he called "Lamanites."

All of these visions came to Nephi before his family crossed the ocean to the New World. His contribution to the *Book of Mormon* includes a detailed account of their journey. Before leaving the Red Sea area and plunging further into the desert, the four sons of Lehi and Zoram married the five daughters of Ishmael (1 Nephi 16:7). Two of Ishmael's sons, and two of his daughters and their families soon joined Laman and Lemuel in rebellion against Lehi and Nephi.

Nephi indicated that as they camped in the desert, Lehi awoke one morning and discovered a strange instrument in front of his tent. Nephi described this instrument:

> And it came to pass that as my father arose in the morning, and went forth to the tent door, to his great astonishment he beheld upon the ground a round ball of curious workmanship; and it was of fine brass. And with the ball were two spindles; and the one pointed the way whither we should go into the wilderness.
>
> And it came to pass that I, Nephi, beheld the pointers which were in the ball, that they did work according to the faith and diligence and heed which we did give unto them (I Nephi 16:10, 28).

---

[5]Latter-day Saints believe that Nephi saw Christopher Columbus and believe that Columbus was led by God. They also believe that Nephi saw other explorers come after Columbus and witnessed the devastating effects they had upon the Indians.

Five hundred years later, another *Book of Mormon* prophet, Alma, called this ball a "Liahona" and explained that it came from God and had served as a compass to the travelers. Alma taught the descendants of Nephi that the Liahona had been a miracle and that Lehi and his sojourners had been the beneficiaries of many miracles (Alma 37:38-40).[6]

Nephi wrote that, guided by the Liahona, his family headed in a south-southeast direction stopping occasionally for long periods to rest and to replenish their food supplies. After many months in the desert, Ishmael died and was buried in a place Nephi called Nahom. From there the group turned and traveled almost due east, again stopping for months at a time to rest, have children, and replenish their supplies. While in the desert, Lehi and Sariah had two more sons, Jacob and Joseph. Nephi recorded that it took Lehi's group eight years to travel through extremely desolate country.[7] They finally came to a land, near an ocean, which they called Bountiful because of its fruit, wild honey, green vegetation and many trees (See Appendix A).

By the time Lehi and his expanding family reached Bountiful, Nephi had essentially taken over the control of the group's day-to-day activities. The desert, old age, and the infighting in his family had taken their toll on Lehi. Nephi claimed that he frequently was forced to intercede and admonish his brothers and their followers for their rebellion. Sometime after reaching Bountiful, Nephi announced that the Lord had commanded him to "construct a ship after the manner that I will show thee, that I may carry thy people across these many waters" (1 Nephi 17:8).[8]

---

[6] Joseph Smith, Oliver Cowdery, Martin Harris and David Whitmer reported that they saw the Liahona, the sword of Laban, the Brass Plates taken from Laban and the Urim and Thummim, along with the Gold Plates (D&C 17: 1.)

[7] Hugh W. Nibley, professor of ancient Near Eastern Studies at Brigham Young University believes that Lehi and his family traversed approximately 2,500 miles through some of the most desolate country on earth. Nibley, *Lehi in the Desert*, 63.

[8] Bible readers will recall that the Lord also instructed Noah in great detail how to build the ark (Genesis 6:14-16).

After the ship was finished and loaded with provisions, the extended family sailed into the ocean towards "the promised land." Nephi did not indicate in his record the direction they sailed or what ocean they crossed. (One of the arguments against an ocean crossing put forth by scientists is the idea that seafarers would not dare attempt to cross the open seas without a compass. According to the account, Lehi did not have that problem because he had the Liahona.) After "many days" they arrived in the New World, pitched their tents and planted their seeds. Nephi wrote that the Lord had promised them that if they would keep God's commandments, they would prosper in "the land of promise;" but, if they did not keep his commandments, they would not prosper and they would not enjoy the company of the Lord (2 Nephi 1:20).

After the death of Lehi, Laman and Lemuel refused to accept Nephi as their leader and conspired to kill him. Nephi narrated that the Lord warned him of the plot and told him to flee with his followers, which included the families of Nephi, Sam, Nephi's sisters, and Zoram as well as the two younger brothers, Jacob and Joseph. Thus did the two factions of Lehi's clan begin separate lives. Laman, Lemuel and the two sons of Ishmael stayed behind and formed a new alliance. Nephi wrote that from that time his older brothers refused to obey any more the commandments of God and refused to teach their children about God.[9] (Although the descendants of Lehi were aligned into seven families or tribes, the two opposing groups eventually became known as Nephites, or followers of Nephi, and Lamanites, or followers of Laman.)

Shortly after arriving in the New World, Nephi proclaimed that he had been commanded by the Lord to make a set of gold

---

[9]The separation of the sons of Lehi, a descendant of Joseph, into two groups–Nephites and Lamanites–gives credence to the story related by Aharon Levi to Ben Israel when he stated that the "Israelite Indians" told him that "Joseph lives in the middle of the ocean in two parts."

plates to record his family's history from the time they left Jerusalem. Once Nephi finished the initial set of plates, he was instructed to make a second set of plates upon which he was to write the religious and spiritual events of their history. (These two sets of plates are frequently referenced in the *Book of Mormon*. The first set of plates, known as the "large plates of Nephi," contained a secular history and was kept by the Nephite kings, who were believed to have been direct descendants of Nephi. The second set of plates, known as the "small plates of Nephi," contained more of the religious history and after Nephi wrote his part, he passed the small plates to his brother Jacob, who in turn, passed them to his descendants.)[10]

Nephi said he wrote "in the language of my father, which consists of the learning of the Jews and the language of the Egyptians" (1Nephi 1:2). One thousand years later when Moroni, one of the last Nephites, finished the abridgement of the whole of the Nephite record, he provided additional information concerning their written language. His explanation shows his concern about how later readers would perceive the language:

> And now, behold, we have written this record according to our knowledge, in the characters which are called among us the reformed Egyptian, being handed down and altered by us, according to our manner of speech.
> And if our plates had been sufficiently large we should have written in Hebrew; but the Hebrew hath been altered by us also; and if we could have written in Hebrew, behold, ye would have had no imperfections in our record.

---

[10] The 116 pages of manuscript that Martin Harris lost were a translation from part of the large plates of Nephi. When Joseph Smith finished translating the large plates, he discovered the small plates of Nephi which Mormon had included with his abridgement of the large plates. Since Joseph was told to not retranslate the lost portion from the large plates, he used the briefer history recorded on the small plates. The first 143 pages of the current Book of Mormon is taken from the small plates; which focused more upon the spiritual history; consequently, there are gaps in the secular history which Nephi said was written in greater detail upon the large plates.

But the Lord knoweth the things which we have written, and also that none other people knoweth our language; and because that none other people knoweth our language, therefore he hath prepared means for the interpretation thereof (Mormon 9:32-34).

The *Book of Mormon* relates the history of the Nephites, mainly covering the accounts of their dealings with God, their internal conflicts, wars with the Lamanites, and migrations within the New World. Nephi recorded that he taught his people to be industrious and to labor with their hands. He taught them to build buildings and to work in wood, iron, copper, brass, steel, gold, silver, and other precious metals. He also instructed them to build a temple after the fashion of King Solomon's temple. While recording a history of his own people, Nephi wrote that the Lamanites ceased to worship God and became a lazy and indolent people. The Lamanites soon forgot their language and could not read or write.[11]

Nephi and other Book of Mormon writers affirm that when Lehi and his family as well as the family of Ishmael left Jerusalem they were white [light-skinned]; however, after the Lamanites rebelled against God and refused to keep his commandments, the Nephite prophets claim the Lord cursed the Lamanites by withdrawing his spirit from among them. He also put a mark of a dark skin on them to distinguish them from the Nephites and if possible to keep the "righteous Nephites" from marrying with the "idolatrous" Lamanites. Consequently, the *Book of Mormon* claims there were both light-and dark-skinned Israelites living in the New World.[12]

During their one thousand years of recorded history, rebellious Nephites occasionally joined forces with the Lamanites and

---

[11]Guaman Poma de Ayala's description of how some of the people degenerated after they disobeyed God's commandments is very familiar to Nephi's account. See Poma de Ayala 38-40.

[12]See Chapter 14.

some of the Lamanites also joined the Nephites thus bringing about some intermarriages between the two groups. A general theme within the *Book of Mormon* is the ongoing conflict and numerous wars between the Nephites and the Lamanites.

About 150 B.C., under heavy military pressure from the Lamanites, the Nephites moved from the Land of Nephi to a new area where they discovered a new group of people in a land called Zarahemla. The Nephite King Mosiah instructed that all the people of Zarahemla be taught in the language of the Nephites.[13] Subsequently, the Nephites learned from the king of Zarahemla that his forefathers came out of Jerusalem at the time that Zedekiah, the Biblical king of Judah, was captured by the Babylonians.

The Bible tells how all of Zedekiah's sons were killed during the capture of Jerusalem, but the *Book of Mormon* claims that one son, Mulek, escaped and came to the New World. His descendants, the "Mulekites" were the people of Zarahemla. The Mulekites claimed that they originally spoke Hebrew, but over the years their language had become so corrupted that they could not speak or understand it any more. They also revealed that they did not bring any records with them and did not know how to read or write. Once they learned to communicate with each other, Mosiah shared with them the teachings found upon the brass plates. The people of Zarahemla also accepted Mosiah as their king and the Mulekites became known as Nephites as well.

The Mulekites related to the Nephites what brief history and genealogy they could remember and also showed the Nephites a large stone with engravings on it. Mosiah, with the aid of a Urim and Thummim, translated the engravings and discovered an account about a king named Coriantumr and the destruction of his people. Coriantumr had wandered into the Mulekites after

---

[13]Hundreds of years later, the Incas caused that all of the highland Indians in Peru, Ecuador and Bolivia be taught Quechua so they could understand each other.

all of his people were killed in a war and he lived with them until his death. The Mulekites could not provide an accurate time frame when Coriantumr appeared among them.

About 121 B.C., or a few years after discovering the people of Zarahemla, a group of Nephite explorers found the land of Coriantumr's origin–a land covered with human bones, the wreckage of a great war. Among the ruins of this ancient civilization, they encountered twenty four gold plates with strange engravings which they assumed may have been a history of this ancient people. These plates were also taken to King Mosiah for him to translate. His translation revealed the story of Coriantumr's ancestors, the people of Jared or Jaredites who had left the vicinity of the Tower of Babel at the time of the confounding of tongues. Thus three civilizations are accounted for in the *Book of Mormon*–the Nephites, the Mulekites and the Jaredites. There was no written history of the Mulekites. A brief summary of the Jaredite's story will be included later in this chapter.

The dominant theme of the *Book of Mormon* is the Nephites' story–their prophecies and teachings about the life and mission of Jesus Christ. Several chapters cover events that occurred in the Americas at the time of the birth of Christ and also describe a period of total darkness, terrible destruction and loss of life among the wicked that occurred in the Americas at the time of the crucifixion. The event of total darkness and destruction will be analyzed in greater detail in Chapter 6. To many believers, the most important book within the *Book of Mormon* is 3 Nephi, which relates the personal appearance of Jesus Christ in the Americas after his resurrection. He reportedly descended out of the heavens and appeared before 2,500 Nephites and Lamanites congregated at the temple in the land of Bountiful (not to be confused with the Bountiful, located on the Arabian coast, which was discovered by Lehi and his band before setting sail for the New World.)

Jesus Christ reportedly taught the people in the Americas the same principles he taught in Jerusalem. He also performed many miracles including healing the sick, the blind and the lame. He chose twelve of the most righteous men from among those assembled as the leaders of his church. He referred to them as twelve "disciples." Once they had been ordained, he instructed them to preach the gospel and to establish his church in the New World. He invited everyone assembled at the temple that day to approach him and to touch the marks in his hands and in his side, thus providing each with a personal witness that he was Jesus Christ, their Messiah and Savior, and that he had been resurrected.[14]

Jesus Christ provided the survivors with additional information concerning the rest of the House of Israel and he informed those assembled at the temple that they were the "other sheep" about whom he had spoken to the Jews in Jerusalem.[15] The Nephite prophet at that time, also named Nephi, wrote that Jesus called all of the little children to come to him and he blessed each one individually and after this blessing the heavens were opened and the people saw angels descend out of heaven and "minister" to the children. Nephi remarked that they saw and heard things too sacred to be written. Christ instituted the sacrament of bread and wine among the Nephites and the Lamanites and instructed them how to baptize.

He had them bring their historical records to him so that he could review them and ensure they were complete. Jesus also promised the people that their records, engraved upon the gold

---

[14]According to the findings of many chroniclers, most of the native Americans they encountered believed in the immortality of the soul and believed in a form of resurrection or the body coming back to life. See Chapter 8.

[15]John 10:16: "And other sheep I have, which are not of this fold: them also I must bring, and they shall hear my voice; and there shall be one fold, and one shepherd."

plates, would be preserved for the benefit of their descendants. As he was preparing to leave them for the last time, he called the twelve disciples to him and gave them final instructions as well as individual blessings. As he had done with his apostles in Jerusalem before his final ascension (John 21:19-23), Jesus inquired of them concerning their desires. Nine of the twelve said they wanted to be with Christ as soon as they died; however, three of them made no comment. Nephi said that Jesus Christ then turned to them and said:

> Behold, I know your thoughts, and ye have desired the thing which John, my beloved, who was with me in my ministry, before that I was lifted up by the Jews, desired of me.
> Therefore, more blessed are ye, for ye shall never taste of death; but ye shall live to behold all the doings of the Father unto the children of men, even until all things shall be fulfilled according to the will of the Father, when I shall come in my glory with the powers of heaven.
> And ye shall never endure the pains of death; but when I shall come in my glory ye shall be changed in the twinkling of an eye from mortality to immortality; and then shall ye be blessed in the kingdom of my Father (3 Nephi 28:6-8).

As Mormon was compiling his record of this episode four centuries later, he said that as he was about to write the names of those who, like John the apostle, were to live until the Second Coming, the Lord forbade him. Consequently, Mormon did not record their names. Mormon said that he had personally seen the three Nephites and described some of the miracles surrounding their lives:

> And they were cast into prison by them who did not belong to the church. And the prisons could not hold them, for they were rent in twain.
> And they were cast down into the earth; but they did smite the earth with the word of God, insomuch that by his power they were

delivered out of the depths of the earth; and therefore they could not dig pits sufficient to hold them.

And thrice they were cast into a furnace and received no harm.

And thrice were they cast into a den of wild beasts; and behold they did play with the beasts as a child with a suckling lamb, and received no harm (3 Nephi 28:19-22).

A miraculous event similar to these described above was recorded by Pedro de Cieza de León and other chroniclers and will be described in the next chapter.

During the 200 years after Christ's appearance among them, the Nephites and Lamanites lived in a spirit of love and harmony. The twelve disciples preached the gospel throughout all the lands inhabited by the Nephites and the Lamanites and, by 36 A. D., all of the Nephites and the Lamanites were converted to the Church of Jesus Christ. Nephi, the son of the Nephi, who was present for Christ's appearance, wrote:

> And they had all things common among them; therefore there were not rich and poor, bond and free, but they were all made free, and partakers of the heavenly gift (4 Nephi 1:3).
>
> And there were no envyings, nor strifes, nor tumults, nor whoredoms, nor lyings, nor murders, nor any manner of lasciviousness; and surely there could not be a happier people among all the people who had been created by the hand of God.
>
> There were no robbers, nor murderers, neither were there Lamanites, nor any manner of -ites; but they were in one, the children of Christ, and heirs to the kingdom of God (4 Nephi 1:16-17).

Mormon observed, however, that after 200 years, wickedness began to creep back into the Church and the Nephites no longer shared their possessions. After 210 years, there were many churches in the land which professed to know and teach about Jesus Christ, but they had already begun to deny the more important parts of the gospel. Mormon wrote that they had begun to accept every kind of wickedness and had begun to impart that which was sacred to those who were unworthy (4 Nephi 1:25-27).

Mormon recorded that, after many years, pride, selfishness, and other sins crept back in among them and more particularly among those who had previously been identified as Lamanites. The two groups, Nephites and Lamanites, again split into warring adversaries. Their peaceful existence gave way to years of warfare between the two old nemeses; however, as had been predicted by the first Nephi, hundreds of years earlier, this time the Lamanites began a protracted destruction of the Nephite nation. Mormon, in his role as prophet, said that he tried unsuccessfully to get his own people, the Nephites, to repent and live the principles of the gospel. At the age of sixteen, Mormon was made the general of the Nephite armies and led them in battle for many years. Concerning the wars, he wrote:

> And it is impossible for the tongue to describe, or for man to write a perfect description of the horrible scene of the blood and carnage which was among the people, both of the Nephites and of the Lamanites; and every heart was hardened, so that they delighted in the shedding of blood continually.
> And there never had been so great wickedness among all the children of Lehi, nor even among all the house of Israel, according to the words of the Lord, as was among this people. (Mormon 4:11-12).

Mormon wrote that as the Lamanites gained superiority over the Nephites, the Nephites began to retreat; however, they decided to make one last stand against the Lamanites in a land called the Land of Cumorah, described as having many rivers, lakes and fountains. The Nephite warriors were divided into armies of ten thousand men with a commander over each army. Hundreds of thousands of the Nephites including men, women and children were killed by the Lamanites during these final battles.

After the final battle, Mormon's son, Moroni, recorded that his father had been killed and only a few Nephites had managed to survive and escape to the south. Some of the Nephites survived by denying Jesus Christ and deserting over to the Lamanite armies. For many years the Lamanite armies hunted and killed the Nephites who had escaped into the south. Then the Lamanites began to war among themselves. Moroni, living in hiding, observed that "the whole face of this land is one continual round of murder and bloodshed; and no one knoweth the end of the war" (Mormon 8:8).[16]

During Mormon's final years when he had not been leading the Nephite armies in battle, he made a synopsis or abridgement of their thousand year history on gold plates and turned the records over to his son, Moroni, who finished the work and then hid the plates in the earth so that they would not fall into the hands of the Lamanites and be destroyed. Because Mormon abridged the ancient records, the resulting book carries his name.

One of Moroni's last tasks before burying the records was to abridge the account of the Jaredites that had been translated from the twenty four gold plates discovered five hundred years earlier in the land covered with bones. The Jaredite history is found in the section of the *Book of Mormon* called the Book of Ether and was written by Ether, a contemporary of the last survivor, Coriantumr. In Moroni's abridgement of Ether, he mentioned that the twenty four gold plates also contained a history of the creation of the world, the story of Adam and his posterity down to Noah as well as from Noah down to the time of the building of the Tower of Babel, but he chose not to include that information because he supposed that information was already "had among the Jews."[17]

---

[16] See Chapter 13 for greater details on the wars during this period.

[17] All of the *Book of Mormon* prophets refer to Adam and Eve, Noah, the flood and a dispersion and the people after the flood. This is at variance with the commonly accepted scientific theories of evolution and the non existence of a universal flood.

According to the writings of Ether, his ancestor Jared, apparently was the leader of a group of people who wanted to keep the commandments of God at the time of the construction of the Tower of Babel. Jared went to his brother, who is known only as the "brother of Jared," and requested that he pray for God's blessings so their language might not be confounded. Jared also requested that his brother ask the Lord to lead them to a "choice land." The brother, described as a large and mighty man who was "highly favored of the Lord," received instructions from God that he should gather his family and friends along with animals of every kind and seeds of the earth, and that God would lead them to a "land choice above all other lands." Ether recorded the following concerning their route from the Tower of Babel:

> And it came to pass that when they had come down into the valley of Nimrod the Lord came down and talked with the brother of Jared; and he was in a cloud, and the brother of Jared saw him not.
> And it came to pass that the Lord commanded them that they should go forth into the wilderness, yea, into that quarter where there never had man been. And it came to pass that the Lord did go before them, and did talk with them as he stood in a cloud, and gave directions whither they should travel." (Ether 2:4-5)

Moroni, in his abridgement, observed that the Lord had made a similar promise to Lehi and his family, with the proviso that whoever possessed the "promised land" would have to obey the Lord and keep his commandments or they would be "swept off when the fulness of his wrath should come upon them" (Ether 2:7-10).

Ether narrated that the Lord led the Jaredites until they came to the "sea which divides the lands" where they remained for four years. At the end of four years, the Lord told them to build eight "barges" following his directions. Moroni provided a fairly detailed description of the barges which he said were small and rode light on the waters. They were water-tight and peaked at the ends. Their lengths were as long as a tree and when the door was shut it was also water-tight. When the Jaredites had finished the construction, the brother of Jared prayed again to the Lord and expressed two concerns about the barges: first, they had no light inside and, second, they were so tight that there was no way to get fresh air inside.

Ether wrote that the Lord answered the prayer and instructed the brother of Jared to cut a hole in the top and in the bottom of each barge and when they needed fresh air, they could open the hole in the top which they could quickly close if water began to enter. The Lord then reasoned with the brother of Jared concerning the lighting problem. In the exchange, the Lord pointed out that windows and fire were impractical. The Lord said that at times the barges would be buried in the depths of the sea; consequently, windows would be "dashed to pieces" and they could not take a fire with them. He then asked the brother of Jared what he wished the Lord to do under these circumstances.

The brother of Jared decided he would resolve the problem and went up to a high mountain they called Shelem[18] and "did molten out of rock sixteen small stones and they were white and clear, even as transparent glass" (Ether 3:1).[19] He then took these stones up into the very top of mount Shelem and asked the Lord to touch each of the stones with his finger to make them shine. Ether wrote that the Lord touched each one as requested.

---

[18]In a lecture entitled, *The Mountain of the Lord's House*, Professor Hugh W. Nibley pointed out that the original word of Shelem, Shalom, means "peace," but it originally meant "safe" or security because it was a high place. The Shelem was a high place. It is still the word for ladder in Hebrew.

[19]Nibley reasoned that when the Lord instructed Noah to build an ark, he said, "A window shalt thou make to the ark" (Genesis 6:16) that the use of the word "window" is an incorrect translation. The Hebrew version of the Bible uses the word "Tsohar" which some rabbis believe to have been a precious stone that shone in the ark. Nibley argues that the brother of Jared was very familiar with the construction of the ark because the Jaredites had a written record; consequently, he made sixteen "tsohars" which he carried up to the top of the mountain to present to the Lord.

With the lighting problem resolved, the Jaredites set sail. They were pushed along by great winds, but recorded that it still took them 344 days to arrive at the "promised land." Although it is known that their final destination was the Americas, the *Book of Mormon* does not give the route nor the precise landing location.[20] Before leaving the Old World, during the crossing, and upon arrival in the New World, the brother of Jared witnessed many miracles of God. He also saw many future events that would transpire in the earth and was commanded to write all the things that he saw.[21]

The Jaredites were given commandments on how they should live and worship God; however, not many generations passed away after their arrival in the New World before they fell into sin and began fighting among themselves. The Jaredites were warned repeatedly by prophets that if they did not repent and keep God's commandments they would be destroyed and their "promised land" would be given to another people.

Precise geography is not a strong point in the *Book of Mormon*. It mentions the land northward, great bodies of water, a narrow neck of land, lands without trees, the land southward, of people who "went up" or who "went down" which could be interpreted as either altitude or direction. It mentions great topographical changes that took place at the time of the crucifixion of Jesus Christ, but mentions very few topographical features after this event; consequently, the topography of today may be

---

[20] It is generally assumed by members of The Church of Jesus Christ of Latter-day Saints that both the Jaredites and the Lehites crossed the Pacific and landed on the west coast of the Americas; however, the Book of Mormon does not state the direction traveled nor the landing site of any of the groups.

[21] When Moroni added the Book of Ether to his plates, he was told to seal off that portion of the writings of the brother of Jared which contained information of certain future events. Joseph Smith did not translate that portion that was sealed. Martin Harris knew that part of the plates had been sealed and used this as an explanation as to why he could not give Professor Anthon the plates thus leading Anthon to exclaim that he "could not read a sealed book."

quite different than what was described by those living prior to the crucifixion of Christ.

The Book of Ether narrates accounts of wars between the various factions, of plagues and pestilence that God sent to humble them and cause them to repent. One plague mentioned was a plague of poisonous snakes which killed off many of the people and their cattle. The poisonous snakes established themselves in a "narrow neck of land" where they existed for many centuries effectively blocking people from going back and forth (Ether 9:31-34.) The battle against the poisonous snakes was an ongoing battle which lasted for several generations.[22]

Moroni included very little description of daily life in his abridgement of Ether; however, he wrote the following description narrated by Ether during one particular period of peace and prosperity among the Jaredites:

> And they were exceedingly industrious, and they did buy and sell and traffic one with another, that they might get gain.
> And they did work in all manner of ore, and they did make gold and silver, and iron, and brass, and all manner of metals; and they did dig it out of the earth; wherefore, they did cast up mighty heaps of earth to get ore, of gold, and of silver, and of iron, and of copper. And they did work all manner of fine work.[23]
> And they did have silks, and fine-twined linen; and they did work all manner of cloth, that they might clothe themselves from their nakedness.
> And they did make all manner of tools to till the earth, both to plow and to sow, to reap and to hoe, and also to thrash.
> And they did make all manner of tools with which they did work their beasts.
> And they did make all manner of weapons of war. And they did work all manner of work of exceedingly curious workmanship.

---

[22]The country of Panama has always been plagued by a profusion of poisonous snakes. It has several species of pit vipers, 11 species of coral snakes, the fer-de-lance, the bushmaster and several species of sea snakes.

[23]See Chapter 17.

And never could be a people more blessed than were they, and more prospered by the hand of the Lord. And they were in a land that was choice above all lands, for the Lord had spoken it (Ether 10:22-28).

Ether related that towards the end, the Jaredites did not repent and frequently killed their prophets. Their society was plagued by what Ether described as "secret combinations," made up of wicked men who banded together in secret societies with the express purpose of killing and robbing, overthrowing governments, and taking control of every facet of life. They used secret signs and signals to identify one another, but were not known to the populace overall. At times they would hide in the mountains, the deserts or other secluded places and carry out raids upon the people.

For hundreds of years the Jaredites expanded their civilization and they built many cities and temples. Unfortunately, they fell into total apostasy, made war with each other and basically destroyed themselves in a horrible series of fratricidal wars circa 300 - 400 B.C. There is no record that the Nephites ever had any direct contact with the Jaredites; however, they discovered their cities and described the carnage that must have taken place because they found the piles of bones heaped up by a people who were apparently too pressed in fighting to bury their dead.[24]

Moroni wrote that in 421 A.D. he buried the gold plates, containing the valuable history of the ancient Americans. Consequently, their records were not known to the early Catholic priests and other chroniclers when they arrived in the New World over one thousand years later.

---

[24]There is a close time similarity between rise and fall of the Jaredite civilization and the rise and fall of the Chavín civilization.

6

PERIOD WHEN THEY DID NOT SEE THE SUN...

Pedro de Cieza de León had a great thirst for knowledge and avidly wrote detailed descriptions of everything he observed from Colombia to Bolivia, as well as what he saw during numerous side trips along the way. He remained in Colombia from 1535 until 1546, when he joined other Spanish knights in Colombia who were ordered to travel to Peru to put down the rebellion of Gonzalo Pizarro and return the control of Peru back to the Spanish crown.[1] (In 1545, Gonzalo and many of the wealthy land owners, who relied upon Indian slave labor to cultivate their vast land holdings, objected to the "New Laws," designed to free the Indians from servitude, and declared their independence from Spain. Charles V organized an army to put down this rebellion.)

---

[1]Cieza de León, *The Incas*, xlv

The Royalist army traveled through Quito, Ecuador, through mountain passes flanked by high volcanoes, and over the high plateaus of the Andes into the valleys that lead to the ancient Inca city of Tomebamba (near the modern city of Cuenca, in southern Ecuador). From Tomebamba, the Spanish army turned west towards the coastal town of Paita where the Spaniards had first arrived in Peru. Cieza de León provided an excellent description of the plants, animals, and people that he observed along the way. His group followed the coastal road through the Chimor civilization located near the modern Peruvian city of Trujillo. They later traveled across the Rimac River at Lima and onto Pachacamac where they turned east again, following the superbly-engineered road across the Andes to Jauja, located in the central Peruvian highlands.

In 1548, they reached the plains near Cuzco, where the royalist army under the direction of Pedro de la Gasca met and defeated Gonzalo Pizarro's forces. After this battle, Cieza de León was introduced to La Gasca, who read Cieza de León's descriptive accounts of his travels. Cieza de León was taken under La Gasca's wing and returned with him to Lima, where La Gasca appointed him *Cronista de Indias* (Official Chronicler of the Indies).[2]

With letters given him by President La Gasca, certifying his appointment as Official Chronicler, Cieza de León was authorized to travel throughout the Andeans. He immediately began learning all that he could about Peru. He provided the first descriptions of the coca leaf [from which cocaine is made] and described how many Spaniards became exceedingly wealthy marketing the coca leaf as a narcotic in the 1500's. He had access to many of the conquistadores who were still in Peru and also spoke with many of the *Orejones* (literally big ears, the Inca nobility who were still alive) from whom he learned many

---

[2] Ibid., liv.

Period When They Did Not See The Sun 123

things, particularly about the Incas and about other natives who lived in Peru prior to the Inca reign.

With all that Cieza de León observed and learned from the natives, he highlighted the following as the single most significant event:

> Before the Incas came to reign in these kingdoms or were known there, these Indians tell a thing that far exceeds all else they say. They state that a long time went by in which they did not see the sun, and that they suffered great hardships from this lack, and that they made great prayers and vows to those they held to be their gods, imploring of them the light that had failed. When things stood like this, there emerged from the island of Titicaca, which lies in the great lake of the Colla region, the sun in its splendor, at which all rejoiced.
>
> And after this had occurred, they say that out of the regions of the south there came and appeared among them a white man, large of stature, whose air and person aroused great respect and veneration. And this man whom they saw in this guise had great powers, making plains of the hills, and of the plains, high mountains, and bringing forth springs in the living rock. And when they saw his power, they called him the Maker of all things, their Beginning, Father of the sun, for aside from these, they say he did other even greater things, for he called into being men and animals, and, in a word, that great benefits came to them from his hand. And this man, so the Indians say who told me this which they had heard from their forefathers, who, in turn, had heard it in old songs that had come down to them, took his way to the north, working and doing these wonders, by the route of the uplands, and they never saw him again.
>
> They say that in many places he instructed people how they should live, and spoke to them lovingly and meekly, exhorting them to be good and not to do one another harm or injury, but rather to love one another, and use charity toward all. For the most part he is called Ticci Viracocha. Temples were built to him in many places, where statues in his likeness were erected before which they performed sacrifices.[3]

---

[3]Cieza de Leon, *Señorio de los Incas*, 9. (The above version came from Von Hagen's *The Incas* with the English translation by Harriet de Onis. 27.)

From his narrative, Cieza de León appears to be referring to two separate events which were closely connected chronologically: The first was the period when they did not see the sun; and the second was the appearance of a white man who gained great respect because of the miracles he performed and for his teachings. Cieza de León did not provide a historical time frame for these happenings, but it was not part of a creation myth as some historians have suggested because there were already people in the area. Ticci Viracocha had great powers and Cieza de León seemed to indicate that he was able to change the physical topography of the earth, i.e., making plains of the hills and high mountains out of the plains.

Cabello Valboa also wrote of a phenomenon that appeared to be the same event recorded by Cieza de León, but with sufficient differences in the story that it is evident that his account came from a different source. He recorded this incident as follows:

> There is a story, passed down by tradition from fathers to sons, that one day, all of a sudden, the earth shook, and the sun (outside of its normal trajectory) was darkened and the rocks were broken up by smashing some against the others, *and many graves of men dead since many years earlier were seen open* [emphasis added]. Many of the animals were greatly disturbed. By conjecture and numerous indications, this appears to have taken place on the holy day of the crucifixion and death of our Redeemer Christ because it was also said that within a few years there were seen in some areas of Peru certain men of venerable presence and appearance with long beards who dealt justly with everyone. They preached ideas of a new, more saintly way to live. The natives did not remember very much of the message of these preachers, but believed that the event as described in ancient songs took place. The natives claimed that these men taught in many areas and some natives acquired engraved stone images of these preachers.[4]

---

[4] Cabello Valboa, 237.

Father Francisco de Avila, who compiled information while assigned to the Curate at Huarochirí, Peru, in 1598, wrote a book entitled, *Huarochiri Manuscript, A Testament of Ancient and Colonial Andean Religion.* The *Huarochiri Manuscript* contained the following account which also appears to be related to the same event:[5]

> In ancient times the sun died.
> Because of his [the sun's] death it was night for five days.
> Rocks banged against each other.
> Mortars and grinding stones began to eat people.
> Buck llamas started to drive men.

Father Francisco de Avila inserted his opinion of the event when he exclaimed that "Here's what we Christians think about it. We think these stories tell of the darkness following the death of our Lord Jesus Christ. Maybe that is what it was."[6]

There were few Spaniards who had an opportunity to get closer to the Inca nobility than Juan de Betanzos, who married into the royal line of Lord Inca Pachacuti Inca Yupanqui. Betanzos took advantage of his Inca contacts to provide a history of the Incas from a quasi insiders point of view. Betanzos wrote his oft quoted *Suma y Narración de los Incas* (*Narrative of the Incas*) in 1557, but it was not published until 1880.[7]

There is very little information concerning Betanzos's background available to historians. Betanzos dedicated himself to learning Quechua and apparently was considered the best lin-

---

[5] Father Francisco de Avila, The *Huarochiri Manuscript, A Testament of Ancient and Colonial Andean Religion.* This version was translated from Quechua by Frank Salomon and George L. Urioste. (Published by the University of Texas Press, Austin, 1991.)

[6] Ibid., 35.

[7] Juan Díaz de Betanzos, *Suma y Narración de los Incas*, original manuscript completed in 1557, but not published until 1880. (Prologue, transcription, y notes by Maria del Carmen Martin Rubio; preliminary studies by Horacio Villanueva Urteaga, Demetrio Ramos and Maria del Carmen Martin Rubio). Madrid. 1987.

guist in Peru at that time. Betanzos demonstrated such a gift for learning Quechua that he was quickly drawn to the attention of Francisco Pizarro with whom he established a close personal relationship. Taking advantage of Betanzos's command of the language, Pizarro took Betanzos with him in the capacity of "official interpreter" during his numerous trips. Even after Pizarro's death in 1541, Betanzos continued in his capacity as the Spanish colonial government's official translator.

Betanzos began his manuscript by referring to ancient legends of a time when the land and the provinces of Peru were dark and neither firelight nor daylight existed, and Peru was inhabited by people whose name had long been forgotten.[8] The fact that Betanzos started his account with this legend is indicative of the importance the natives placed on this event of total darkness when there was neither sun light nor apparently fire of any kind. Unlike the three accounts sited earlier in which the loss of sun light was reported, Betanzos emphasized that there was no light from any source. Betanzos then relates that during this time of total darkness, the people were visited by a lord whose name was Contiti Viracocha [Ticci Viracocha], who went to the area known at Tiahuanaco.[9]

Betanzos wrote that he was informed that Contiti Viracocha had also emerged another time before and, on that first occasion, he created the sky and the earth. The Indians said that he was called Contiti Viracocha Pacha-yachachic, which in their language means "God, maker of the world."

In his writings, Felipe Guaman Poma de Ayala did not mention the event of the disappearance of the sun, but did write

---

[8]Ibid., 1.
[9]Ibid., 7. (Most of the early chroniclers referred to this great lord as "Ticci Viracocha;" however, because of the language difficulties there were different spellings and even name variations. Thor Heyerdahl obtained the idea for his raft voyage across the Pacific after visiting Tiahuanaco and hearing the legend of Contiti Viracocha which was included in his famous book *Kon Tiki*.)

Period When They Did Not See The Sun 127

about terrible disasters that occurred among the Indians when they were disobedient to God's commandments. Poma de Ayala's description of certain types of disasters closely paralleled similar calamities described in the *Book of Mormon*. He narrated that the disasters took place during the reign of the Lord Inca Sinche Roca Inca. According to Poma de Ayala's calender, Jesus Christ was born during the eightieth year of the reign of Sinche Roca Inca so he dated these destructions to a period close to the death of Jesus Christ.[10]

> God punished them by sending down fire from heaven to burn them, mountains fell upon them and covered them over, some villages were covered with water, other villages were swallowed up by the earth, all as a punishment sent by God....during the time of the Incas, mountains fell down, rocky cliffs and crags were brought down, volcanos erupted and rained fire from hell upon them, sand flattened a city and the surrounding areas, earthquakes killed many, tidal waves hit the coastal regions killing many. God also sent plagues and pestilence, hail storms, and heavy snows killed many people and animals.[11]

The legend of a time when the Indians did not see the sun was not confined to the Andes. In Mexico, Diego Durán discussed in his *History* a ritual that relates to a period when the natives did not see the sun and were also deprived of fire. He mentioned the Aztec calender and its fifty-two year century cycle. As part of the celebration and ritual which accompanied this new cycle, the priests and elders "pretended that the sun and the moon were to be hidden for four days and that everything would be enveloped in darkness." Thus it was ordered that in all the provinces around Mexico-Tenochtitlan all the fires should be put out. No one dared light a fire, even in secret, for four days and

---

[10]Poma de Ayala, 65.
[11]Ibid., 68.

then a great fire was rekindled on the hill of Huixachtlan from which the inhabitants might ignite their own fires.

This New Fire ceremony was celebrated with great solemnity and the priests of all the temples were present. There were offerings and incense, together with human sacrifice on the hill of Huixachtlan. Vessels filled with human blood were sent to smear the lintels of the doors, posts, and altars of the temples, and to sprinkle on the statues of the gods.[12] It is significant that this legend of this period of total darkness appears both in North and in South America, which suggests that natives in both continents were privy to this unusual event.

Book of Mormon Account of Events in Ancient America

The *Book of Mormon* narrates that six years before the birth of Jesus Christ in the Old World, the Nephites in the New World had become very wicked and many prophets and teachers went among them attempting to get them to repent. One such prophet, known only as Samuel the Lamanite, appeared at Zarahemla and began to preach unsuccessfully to the Nephites. As Samuel was leaving Zarahemla, he reported that an angel appeared to him and commanded him to return and prophesy to the people words that the Lord would put in his heart. Samuel returned to Zarahemla, climbed up on a high wall overlooking the city and began preaching again. He prophesied of the coming birth of Jesus Christ and gave the Nephites a sign that would herald the Savior's birth—a 36-hour day with no darkness:

---

[12]Durán, *Historia*, 445. (This legend described by Durán appears to be part of the pre-migration history of the Nahuatl-speaking tribes into Central Mexico. This gives credence to the idea that the Nahuatl-speaking tribes lived in the New World before the Christian era and long before they settled the Valley of Mexico.)

And behold, he said unto them: Behold, I give unto you a sign; for five years more cometh, and behold, then cometh the Son of God to redeem all those who shall believe on his name.

And behold, this will I give unto you for a sign at the time of his coming; for behold, there shall be great lights in heaven, insomuch that in the night before he cometh there shall be no darkness, insomuch that it shall appear unto man as if it was day.

Therefore, there shall be one day and a night and a day, as if it were one day and there were no night; and this shall be unto you for a sign; for ye shall know of the rising of the sun and also of its setting; therefore they shall know of a surety that there shall be two days and a night; nevertheless the night shall not be darkened; and it shall be the night before he is born.

And behold, there shall a new star arise, such an one as ye never have beheld; and this also shall be a sign unto you.

And behold this is not all, there shall be many signs and wonders in heaven (Helaman 14:2-6).

Samuel then told the assembled people that he would also give them a sign of the death of Jesus Christ—three days of total darkness:

But behold, as I said unto you concerning another sign, a sign of his death, behold, in that day that he shall suffer death the sun shall be darkened and refuse to give his light unto you; and also the moon and the stars; and there shall be no light upon the face of this land, even from the time that he shall suffer death, for the space of three days, to the time that he shall rise again from the dead.

Yea, at the time that he shall yield up the ghost there shall be thunderings and lightnings for the space of many hours, and the earth shall shake and tremble; and the rocks which are upon the face of this earth, which are both above the earth and beneath, which ye know at this time are solid, or the more part of it is one solid mass, shall be broken up;

Yea, they shall be rent in twain, and shall ever after be found in seams and in cracks, and in broken fragments upon the face of the whole earth, yea, both above the earth and beneath.

And behold, there shall be great tempests, and there shall be many mountains laid low, like unto a valley, and there shall be many places which are now called valleys which shall become mountains, whose height is great.

And many highways shall be broken up, and many cities shall become desolate.

And many graves shall be opened, and shall yield up many of their dead; and many saints shall appear unto many. [Emphasis added]

And the angel said unto me that many shall see greater things than these, to the intent that they might believe that these signs and these wonders should come to pass upon all the face of this land, to the intent that there should be no cause for unbelief among the children of men (Helaman 14:20-25, 28).

Nephi, the prophet of that day and a descendant of the first Nephi, wrote that many Nephites believed the words of Samuel, but many did not and tried to kill him with their bows and arrows or slings. The spirit of God was so powerful upon him that he could not be killed.

In 1 B.C., Nephi left Zarahemla and turned all the records over to his son, Nephi. This Nephi recorded the events surrounding the birth of Jesus Christ and proclaimed that they occurred just as Samuel the Lamanite had prophesied. Nephi wrote that these were difficult years for both the Nephites and the Lamanites because, in spite of the fact that Samuel's prophecy about Christ's birth came true, both nations increased in wickedness and had many wars between them. The Nephite government was overthrown by an anti-Christ group and the Nephite nation split into several tribes.

Nephi wrote that in the thirty fourth year after the sign of Christ's birth:

. . .there arose a great storm, such an one as never had been known in all the land.

And there was also a great and terrible tempest; and there was terrible thunder, insomuch that it did shake the whole earth as if it was about to divide asunder.

Period When They Did Not See The Sun

And there were exceedingly sharp lightnings, such as never had been known in all the land.

And the city of Zarahemla did take fire.

And the city of Moroni did sink into the depths of the sea, and the inhabitants thereof were drowned.

And the earth was carried up upon the city of Moronihah, that in the place of the city there became a great mountain.

And there was a great and terrible destruction in the land southward.

But behold, there was a more great and terrible destruction in the land northward; for behold, the whole face of the land was changed, because of the tempest and the whirlwinds, and the thunderings and the lightnings, and the exceedingly great quaking of the whole earth.

And the highways were broken up, and the level roads were spoiled, and many smooth places became rough.

And many great and notable cities were sunk, and many were burned, and many were shaken till the buildings thereof had fallen to the earth, and the inhabitants thereof were slain, and the places were left desolate.

And there were some who were carried away in the whirlwind and wither they went no man knoweth, save they know that they were carried away.

And behold, the rocks were rent in twain; they were broken up upon the face of the whole earth, insomuch that they were found in broken fragments, and in seams and in cracks, upon all the face of the land.

And it came to pass that when the thunderings, and the lightnings, and the storm, and the tempest, and quakings of the earth did cease–for behold, they did last for about the space of three hours; and it was said by some that the time was greater; nevertheless, all these great and terrible things were done in about the space of three hours–and then behold, there was darkness upon the face of the land.

And it came to pass that there was thick darkness upon all the face of the land, insomuch that the inhabitants thereof who had not fallen could feel the vapor of darkness;

And there could be no light, because of the darkness, neither candles, neither torches; neither could there be fire kindled with their fine and exceedingly dry wood, so that there could not be any light at all;

And there was not any light seen, neither fire, nor glimmer, neither the sun, nor the moon, nor the stars, for so great were the mists of darkness which were upon the face of the land.

And it came to pass that it did last for the space of three days that there was no light seen; and there was great mourning and howling and weeping among all the people continually; yea, great were the groanings of the people, because of the darkness and the great destruction which had come upon them (3 Nephi 8: 5-23).

From the above graphic description recorded in the *Book of Mormon*, it is understandable why Cieza de León described possibly the same event as "a thing that far exceeds all else they say." It is also easy to see why the Indians were so grateful for the return of the sun that they hastened to build a temple in honor of the occasion. The circumstances surrounding this event were handed down through songs and stories for fifteen hundred years, and the versions of the chroniclers are strikingly similar to the description of the events recorded in the *Book of Mormon*.

Betanzos's opening paragraph in his book, *Narrative of the Incas* states that there was a time "when the land and the provinces of Peru were dark and neither light nor daylight existed."[13] This takes on a new meaning when compared with Nephi's description of how neither fires nor sun light nor star light could be seen. It would appear from Diego Durán's account in *The History of the Indies of New Spain* that the Nahuatl speaking tribes in ancient times had also experienced a period of time when they did not see the sun and could light no fires. It would not be unusual to find that with the passing of the centuries and the distance that separated the different Indian nations and tribes that such universal events acquired a regional flavor. The Aztecs and other Mesoamerican people seemed to couple the loss of the sun and fire light with great sacrifice and another

---

[13]Betanzos, 1.

ancient Israelite custom connected with the Passover of smearing blood around the lintels of the doorways.

As mentioned previously, Cieza de León recorded that shortly after the sun reappeared, a white man, Ticci Viracocha–the creator of the world—appeared among the Indians and performed many miracles. Similarly the *Book of Mormon* records that shortly after the period of destruction, the survivors heard a voice from heaven speaking to them of the terrible destruction that had taken place. The voice then told the survivors that they had been spared because they were more righteous than those who had been destroyed. The voice then proclaimed:

> *Behold, I am Jesus Christ, the Son of God. I created the heavens and the earth, and all things that in them are. I was with the Father from the beginning. I am in the Father, and the Father in me; and in me hath the Father glorified His name* (3 Nephi 9:15).

By this time, many people began to gather at the temple in the land of Bountiful and while assembled there conversing about the great physical changes that had taken place, they again heard a voice from heaven, but they could not understand the words. Three times they heard a voice speak to them, but only on the third time were they able to understand the words.

> *Behold my Beloved Son, in whom I am well pleased, in whom I have glorified my name–hear ye him.*
>
> And it came to pass, as they understood they cast their eyes up again towards heaven; and behold, they saw a Man descending out of heaven; and he was clothed in a white robe; and he came down and stood in the midst of them; and the eyes of the whole multitude were turned upon him, and they durst not open their mouths, even one to another, and wist not what it meant, for they thought it was an angel that had appeared unto them.
>
> And it came to pass that he stretched forth his hand and spake unto the people, saying:

> *Behold, I am Jesus Christ, whom the prophets testified shall come into the world.*
>
> *And behold, I am the light and the life of the world; and I have drunk out of that bitter cup which the Father hath given me, and have glorified the Father in taking upon me the sins of the world, in the which I have suffered the will of the Father in all things from the beginning* (3 Nephi 11:7-11).

The *Book of Mormon* claims that Jesus Christ spent considerable time in the Americas. It would appear from the writings of the chroniclers that a knowledge of these events and the Savior's teachings may have survived in a highly diluted form for 1500 years and were shared with the early chroniclers.

Miguel Cabello Valboa's account, as noted earlier, includes this strange phrase about the time of upheaval: "*y muchos sepulcros de hombres muertos de mucho tiempo atras se vieron abiertos.*" (Author's translation: "*and many graves of men, dead since many years earlier, were seen open.*") If the phrase only referred to cemeteries that had been destroyed by an earthquake or a flood, which happens periodically in the Andes, the memory of the event would not have been passed forward for centuries.

In the *Book of Mormon*, Samuel the Lamanite prophesied that the graves would be opened and yield up their dead at the time of the resurrection of Jesus Christ. Subsequently, when Jesus Christ examined the Nephite records during his brief visit to the New World, he observed that the Nephites had not recorded the fulfilment of this prophecy and questioned Nephi whether any resurrected saints had appeared and administered unto the surviving Nephites and Lamanites. When Nephi affirmed that the event had occurred as prophesied, Jesus Christ commanded that it should be recorded. (See 3 Nephi 23:11, 13). In the Bible, Matthew also recorded a similar event:

And the graves were opened; and many bodies of the saints which slept arose,
And came out of the graves after his resurrection, and went into the holy city, and appeared unto many (Matthew 27:51-52).

There are notable similarities in the wording of the event passed to Cabello Valboa by the Indians and the narrative in the *Book of Mormon*. Cabello Valboa may not have understood the significance of the phrase, but he recorded it anyway because he apparently felt that it was of singular importance to the natives. We will never know whether the Indians told him that some of their dead ancestors had come back to life at the time Ticci Viracocha appeared. If they did, he may have found the idea so hard to believe that he mentioned only open graves, but omitted any reference to resurrection. Numerous chroniclers refer to the fact that the Indians believed in the resurrection and that belief often dictated how they buried their dead (See Chapter 8).

Account of the Appearance of a Saintly Individual

Cieza de León, along with other chroniclers, recorded a legend of a second man in addition to the appearance of Ticci Viracocha. Cieza de León wrote:

> In addition to this they say that after some time had elapsed another man similar to the one described was seen, *whose name they do not state* [emphasis added], and that they heard for a fact from their forebears that wherever he went he healed the sick and restored their sight to the blind with only the words he spoke, and for these kind and helpful deeds he was greatly beloved. And in this manner, working great things with his words, he came to the province of the Canas, where, close to a village called Cacha, over which Captain Bartolomé de Terrazas holds an encomienda [a large ranch], the natives rose up without consideration and advanced on him with the

intention of stoning him. Suiting their acts to their thoughts, as they drew near, they saw him kneeling, with his hands raised to heaven as though imploring divine aid against the danger that threatened.

These Indians go on to say that at that very moment a great fire appeared in the sky, so that they thought they should all be consumed. Filled with fear and trembling, they crowded toward him whom they wanted to kill, and with loud cries they begged him to have mercy and save them, for they recognized that this had been sent them for the sin they had committed in wanting to stone him. They saw that when he ordered the fire to cease, it went out, but the flames had so scorched and consumed the stones that they served as witnesses that this which has been set down took place. . .and they further relate that, leaving that place, he went until he came to the shore of the sea, where, spreading his cloak, he moved on it over the waves, and never again appeared nor did they see him.[14]

A perusal of the chronicles reveal that there is little agreement about the identity of this saintly individual. Poma de Ayala claimed that he was the apostle Saint Bartholomew.[15] Ruiz de Montoya, a native born Peruvian who headed up the Jesuit Missions in Brazil, Argentina and Paraguay for many years, was equally sure that the individual who appeared at Cacha was the apostle Saint Thomas.[16] Cabello Valboa discounted the idea that the man could have been either Thomas or Bartholomew because it was recorded in Catholic tradition that Thomas was killed by the Brahmans in India and Bartholomew was skinned

---

[14]The Incas, 28. (In 1971, while living in Lima, I met a young man who visited the site of this event near Cacha and obtained about a two inch diameter core sample from the place where apparently a fire had scorched the earth. The piece was about five inches long and at the top, it was possible to see where a fire had been so hot that it had melted and fused the rocks for about 3/4 of an inch down from the top. The top looked like it had been one solid piece of rock; however, after the first 3/4 of an inch, it became possible to discern individual pebbles stuck together almost without shape. Lower down the sample where the heat was less intense, the pebbles took on a more definite shape. The young man with the specimen said that the diameter of the burnt area was about 15 meters. Unfortunately I had not read this account of Pedro de Cieza de León when I saw his sample of earth.)

[15]Poma de Ayala, 67.
[16]Ruiz de Montoya, 117.

alive in Armenia, but Cabello Valboa suggested that the individual might be one of Saint Thomas's disciples.[17]

Logic dictates that if Jesus Christ himself appeared in the New World and chose twelve disciples, as described in the *Book of Mormon*, to preach his gospel to the natives in the Western hemisphere, it would not be necessary to send an apostle from the Old World to preach to them. Cieza de León may have unwittingly given us the identity of the preacher who appeared at Cacha. The Indians told Cieza de León that the man who appeared was the man "*whose name they do not state.*"

As previously indicated, when Mormon was writing about the twelve disciples chosen by Jesus Christ to preach the gospel and establish his Church in the Americas, he was prohibited from revealing the names of the three disciples who chose to remain behind and who were seen periodically for hundreds of years. The miracle that occurred to protect the saintly individual's life was certainly similar to the miracles connected with the three disciples described by Mormon. The Indians may have recognized this individual as one of the three Nephites who remained behind and was only known to them as one "*whose name they do not state.*"

Joseph Smith could not have known about the period of time when the sun did not shine, accompanied with massive destruction and the subsequent appearance of the "creator of the earth" to restore calm. He could not have known about the teaching of "saintly preachers" in the New World. None of the chronicles containing these accounts had been published in 1830.

---

[17] Cabello Valboa, 241-243.

7

A Period of Great
Natural Upheavals

As noted earlier, in spite of its rather desolate-looking appearance, the north coast of Peru was inhabited anciently by at least three groups of people. The Chavín civilization from circa 2500 B.C. to 400 B.C., the Moche or Mochica civilization from circa 100 B.C. to 600 A.D., and the Chimor civilization that flourished sometime after the end of the Moche period and was conquered by the Incas circa 1300 A.D. The Moche civilization is of particular interest because of its existence during a critical period within the *Book of Mormon* time frame.

The Moche are renown for their incredible iconography which they painted upon the walls of their temples and public buildings, but more particularly upon their ceramic pottery vessels. During the last fifty years, thousands of these ceramic vessels have been discovered and analyzed. Iconographers, specializing in Moche art, have arranged this pottery according to apparent subject matter or by iconographic themes.

One of the more interesting themes in Moche iconography touches upon the an apparent upheaval in nature which Jeffrey Quilter, the Director of Pre-Columbian Studies in the Dumbarton Oaks Museum in Washington, D. C., linked to a time "when the sun died" in his article entitled *The Moche Revolt of the Objects*.[1] According to Quilter, stories involving the death of the sun and a subsequent revolt of objects against humans are variants of a common and ancient native American myth. This theme is depicted on a number of art works from the Moche Culture, on murals as well as pottery.

In Quilter's paper, he identified the "Revolt of the Objects" theme in three major depictions: a mural (Figure 1) discovered in an upper rear room of the Huaca de la Luna pyramid in the Moche Valley, which is an enormous man-made pyramid situated near the city of Trujillo on the north coast of Peru, and two painted pottery vessels, both now housed in German museums—one in Berlin (Figure 2) and the other in Munich (Figure 3).

The Huaca de la Luna mural was discovered in 1910.[2] Quilter observed that at the time of discovery the painting was so deteriorated that many characters depicted were difficult to discern; however, it was clear that a number of objects including headdresses, clubs, shields, and other regalia were shown having arms and legs. These objects are chasing humans or holding them captive. Although there are four scenes, only the two clearest ones are included here.

Although only partially visible, one of the chief entities is a human in a headdress and long skirt who holds a blood-collection bowl. In 1980, Art Historians Anna Maria Hocquenghem and Patricia J. Lyon identified this figure as being a woman and

---

[1] Jeffrey Quilter, "The Moche Revolt of the Objects." *Latin American Antiquity*, 1(1), 1990. pp. 42-65

[2] A. L. Kroeber, "Archaeological Explorations in Peru, Part II: The Northern Coast." In *Anthropological Memoirs* vol. 2, no. 2, pp. 45-116, 1930. Field Museum of Natural History, Chicago.

A painted and carved mural located in the Temple of the Huaca de la Luna archaelogical site near Trujillo, Peru. Dr. Steven Bourget, who is the main Art Historian working this site, graciously provided the picture.

The Huaca de la Luna archaelogical site near Trujillo, Peru. There are several entrances into the temple and the scene shown in Figure 1 is located in one of the upper rooms. Dr. Steven Bourget, who is the main Art Historian working this site, graciously provided the picture.

Figure 1

an important Moche supernatural entity, who is frequently associated with death and sacrifice.[3]

According to Quilter, the importance of the revolt-theme mural is emphasized by its location in an apparently prestigious and isolated part of the Huaca de la Luna Pyramid. He believed that its location in a rear room on the highest level limited access to the mural to only a few high ranking people. Also since the pyramid site and its companion pyramid, the Huaca del Sol, are known to have been abandoned at approximately 600 A.D., the mural probably dates to approximately 400 to 500 A.D.

Quilter then described the iconography on the Berlin Vase (Figure 2). It shows both land and sea activities. Two naked

---

[3] A. M. Hocquenghem and P. J. Lyon, "A Class of Anthropomorphic Supernaturals Females in Moche Iconography." *Ñawpa Pacha* 1980 18:27-48.

A Period of Great Natural Upheavals

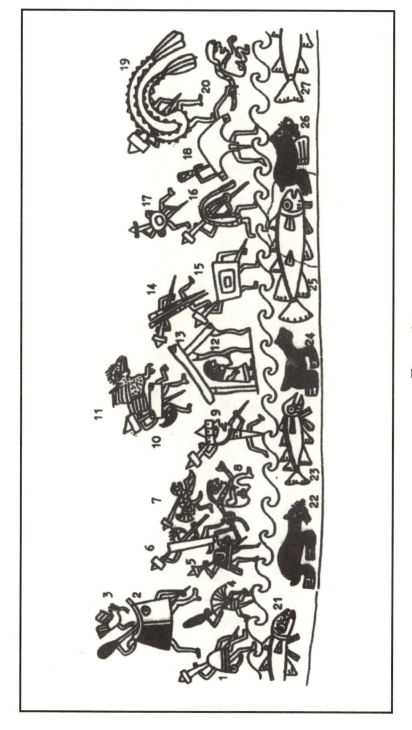

Figure 2

THE MOCHE REVOLT OF THE OBJECTS

Figure 4. Roll-out drawing of the Munich Vase painting. Numbers added by the author (after Kutscher 1983: Abbildung 267). Note some duplication at edges to show overlaps.

Figure 3

humans held captive with ropes by animated objects create a rough symmetry among the animated objects. A human (Number 12) is not engaged actively in the events. Hocquenghem and Lyon, in a 1980 paper, "A Class of Anthropomorphic Supernatural Females in Moche Iconography," claimed that this figure is a woman. The profile of this woman is similar to the profile of the woman identified as an important Moche supernatural being in Figure 1.

Quilter noted that some of the revolting figures are depicted in direct association with the water which suggests to him that the sea is involved with the events on land. Beneath the wave scroll a series of alternating fish and sea lions or seals is shown. The fish are shown to be much larger than their normal relationship with the sea lions/seals.

Quilter suggests that this may be the artists way of showing the fish as predators and the sea lions/seals as victims. He opines that the entire scene suggests one in which the normal order of things has been reversed with objects attacking humans and former prey becoming predators in the natural world, and perhaps even the sea rising up to inundate the land.

The second vase known as the Munich vase is currently in the Museum für Völkerkunde, Munich. It depicts a more elaborate presentation of the Revolt of the Objects theme as can be seen in Figure 3[4] (indicated as Figure 4 in the original article). In the lowest part of the painting the objects are successfully attacking humans who are shown in various stages of defeat and capture, from fully clothed warriors grabbed by the chin or hair to naked and bound prisoners. At the top of the scene, the animated objects are captured by a number of apparently supernatural beings who have halted the revolt. The movement in the lower scene is towards a stepped platform on which an entity described as an Owl Deity (Number 43) stands with a Woman (Number 1) near by.

---

[4]Figure 1 (page 142), Figure 2 (page 143), and Figure 3 (Page 144) were graciously provided by Drs. Jeffrey Quiltar and Donna McClelland.

The action of the upper scene is also centered around two figures. In this case, a human (Number 48) is seated under a tree and is addressing the much larger standing figure, identified as the Rayed Deity (Number 45).[5] The outstretched arms and the position of the hands of the seated figure suggest it is in a role of supplication to the Rayed Deity.

The Owl Deity and Rayed Deity are on opposite sides of the vessel on which they are painted. The Woman (Number 1) found next to the Owl Deity in the lower register appears to be nearly identical with the woman identified in the upper register as a prisoner (Number 49) of one of the apparent aides of the Rayed Deity. Both the Owl and the woman are accompanied by assistants; however, the Owl plays the senior role as evidenced by its domination of the platform summit and its larger size. This scene demonstrates that the Owl, at the very least, has a strong interest in the successful revolt of the objects. The revolt is crushed by the Rayed Deity and the woman is caught by forces of the Rayed Deity, but the Owl escapes immediate capture.

Quilter suggests that the Huaca de la Luna mural scene and the ceramic pottery art relate to the same story or slight variants of it and that the basic tale concerns the rising up of artifacts or nature against humans. In his account, Quilter noted that the "Revolt of the Objects" murals and pottery seem to be connected with the ancient legend recorded in the *Huarochiri Manuscript*. Quilter believes the existence of oral traditions such as the *Popol Vuh* and the *Huarochiri* stories strengthen the account because they demonstrate that the legend is widespread throughout the Americas.

As indicated in Chapter 6, the *Huarochiri Manuscript* contained the following account:

---

[5]Christopher B. Donnan, *Moche Art of Peru*. Museum of Cultural History, University of California, Los Angeles, 1978.

A Period of Great Natural Upheavals

> In ancient times the sun died.
> Because of his death it was night for five days.
> Rocks banged against each other.
> Mortars and grinding stones began to eat people.
> Buck llamas started to drive men.

This legend appears to connect two related incidents, i.e. a time when the inhabitants of the Americas did not see the sun and a time when catastrophic natural events such as an earthquake transpired and animals and natural objects turned on mankind. It would be easy to understand why the Moche and other native Americas viewed this as a revolt of nature. Poma de Ayala's affirmation that tidal waves hit the coastal regions killing many people seems to coincide with Quilter's appraisal that the oceanic scene on the Berlin Vase may have been the Moche attempt to show that the ocean waters in the form of tidal waves inundated the land.

The Moche, who lived from 100 B.C. to 600 A.D., would have been witnesses to the destructive forces of nature mentioned by the chroniclers and the *Book of Mormon* writers and apparently left their own iconographic record of these events several hundred years later.

Additional information gleaned from the chronicles and the *Book of Mormon* might be useful in the interpretation of the iconography described by Quilter. It should also be noted that the mural at Huaca de la Luna and the several pottery scenes were done in the late Phase IV or early Phase V periods or roughly 400 to 600 A.D. If the events apparently portrayed in the Revolt of the Objects took place at the time of the crucifixion as narrated by the chroniclers and the *Book of Mormon*, several hundred years would have passed away before these incidents were recorded in iconographic form by the Moche. It is difficult to know how much distortion of these early episodes transpired during this extended interval.

Quilter observed that the efforts to liken the symbolism of Pre-Columbian art to political and social events is a task fraught with difficulties. Iconographers's understanding of the art is still at an elementary level and knowledge of socio-political events also uncertain. An examination of the available iconography and archaeology provides a snapshot of cultural practices at a particular time and place; nevertheless, Quilter and many other art historians and archaeologists recognize that there are limitations on the information that can be obtained purely from a study of iconography or archaeology alone. David A. Freidel, a professor in the Department of Anthropology at Southern Methodist University, observed, "It is a tricky business back-streaming from later cultures into the past. We are always in danger of imposing without adequate reason later meanings on early examples of symbols or forms."[6]

Art historians and iconographers's understanding would be enhanced if their study of iconography was supplemented by the *Book of Mormon* and the chronicles. For example, if the *Book of Mormon* account that a resurrected Jesus Christ personally appeared in the New World and performed many miracles including healing the sick, blind, and lame—essentially, reversing the role of a destructive nature—is correct, then the Rayed Deity, who halted the revolt of the objects, might be an iconographic portrayal of Jesus Christ. The rays emanating from the body of the Rayed Deity might be the artist's effort to portray a resurrected body (a super-natural body).

Another significant entity in the Revolt of the Objects is the Owl Deity. Elizabeth Benson stated that owls play important roles in Moche art and are among the most commonly portrayed

---

[6]David A. Freidel's Essay on "Preparing the Way," published in *The Olmec World, Ritual and Rulership* (The Art Museum, Princeton University, 1996.) 9.

non-humans. They are depicted in natural as well as anthropomorphized forms. They commonly are associated with ritual and sacrifice and often are garbed in warrior's clothes with weapons.[7] In D. Sharon's 1978 study of modern shamanism on the north coast of Peru, which shows clear ties with Moche iconography, the owl symbolizes corpses, cemeteries, and spirits of the dead.[8] A. M. Mester notes that Poma de Ayala stated that all owls were bad omens signaling the approach of death and were considered noxious animals, set loose in underground prisons for the torment of the worst criminals.[9] As mentioned earlier, the owl could then represent the darkness or evil forces in Moche iconography.

Book of Mormon writers were cognizant of the forces of darkness and constantly warned their followers to beware of Satan and his forces. For example, the prophet Amulek lashed out at the people of the city of Ammonihah and cried,

> O ye wicked and perverse generation, why hath Satan got such a great hold upon your hearts? Why will ye yield yourselves unto him that he may have power over you, to blind your eyes, that ye will not understand the words which are spoken, according to their truth (Alma 10:25)?

Information gained from the chronicles and the *Book of Mormon* might cast a new light upon a study of Figure 3 and potentially offers a different perspective. For example, the woman (identified as Numbers 1 and 49), who also appears in numerous other Moche iconography scenes, is generally associated with death. In this particular Revolt of the Objects theme, death (perhaps represented by the woman) is present in the lower scenes along side of the Owl, who is suggested as representing

---

[7]Benson 1972: 52; Donnan 1976: 124-136

[8]D. Sharon, *Wizard of the Four Winds: A Shaman's Story*, Free Press, New York, 1978.

[9]A.M. Mester, "The Owl in Moche Iconography." Paper presented at the 11th Annual Conference on Andean and Amazonian Archaeology and Ethnohistory, Bloomington, 1983. 14-15

the dark forces, the underworld or perhaps what many religionists refer to as hell.

The Munich vessel (Figure 3) might in fact have a dual significance. During the incident of the Revolt of the Objects, death or capture was a common occurrence as the forces of nature beset most of the inhabitants in the Americas. The Rayed Deity [Jesus Christ] restored calm and brought the elements under control. This appears to be the more superficial explanation; however, it could be argued that the very sophisticated Moche artist might have included a sub-theme within his masterpiece. A common theme throughout Christianity is the belief that through Christ's suffering or atonement and resurrection, he broke the bands of death and hell. If this is true, then perhaps the capture of the woman (Number 49) is an effort by the Moche to represent the power of the Rayed Deity [Jesus Christ] over the lasting effects of death.

The thoughtful observer might notice, as did Quilter in his paper, that the Owl escaped or at least is not shown as being captured. Again a Christian principle might clarify this anomaly. One of the principal teachings within the *Bible* and the *Book of Mormon* is the concept that beginning with Adam, mankind can suffer two kinds of death: the temporal death or death of the body and a spiritual death which is being cast out or cut off from the presence of God (Adam and Eve's expulsion from the Garden of Eden).

The *Book of Mormon* and the *Bible* teach that the resurrection is a free gift to all mankind in that eventually everyone who has lived on earth will resurrect and will not be forever subject to a temporal or physical death; however, in order to overcome the spiritual death, there was a need for an atonement, also a gift of Christ. The Bible explains that Jesus Christ provided the teachings of how mankind can obtain the benefits of the atonement, but it still requires action on the part of humans to be effective.

Mankind was and still is subject to the influence of Satan or the forces of darkness. The Moche artist may have understood this principle and reflected it by demonstrating that the Owl (or forces of darkness) remains at large to tempt mankind.

One of the enigmas of Figure 3 is the role of the human under the tree (Number 48) in an attitude of supplication. What does the tree, with what appears to be fruit hanging down from its branches, have to do with the revolt of the objects or the scenes of destruction? The man in a supplicatory position and the tree with fruit appear to be completely out of context with the revolt of the objects. I would suggest that the inclusion of the tree may have been placed on the pottery vessel by the Moche artist to symbolically identify the man. Who was he? Again the *Book of Mormon* may identify the man and the reason why he is in a supplicatory position before the Rayed Deity.

Six hundred years before the birth of Christ and after Lehi had led his family into the wilderness, he informed them that he had beheld a vision in which he saw a tree loaded with fruit. Nephi's record of Lehi's vision included the following:

> And it came to pass that I beheld a tree, whose fruit was desirable to make one happy, and it came to pass that I did go forth to partake of the fruit thereof; and I beheld that it was most sweet, above all that I ever before tasted. Yea, and I beheld that the fruit thereof was white, to exceed all the whiteness that I had ever seen. And as I partook of the fruit thereof it filled my soul with exceedingly great joy; wherefore, I began to be desirous that my family should partake of it also; for I knew that it was desirable above all other fruit (1 Nephi 8:10-12).

Lehi said that in his vision, his wife Sariah and sons, Nephi and Sam, and others came forward to this Tree of Life and ate the fruit, but the rebellious brothers, Laman and Lemuel, refused to eat. Lehi expressed concern that Laman and Lemuel and their descendants would reject the things of God.

Subsequent to Lehi's account of this vision, Nephi witnessed a similar vision, but received additional information in which he was told that the fruit of the tree was the love of God. Nephi claimed to have also seen in a vision the birth of Jesus Christ in Jerusalem during a period six hundred years from the time Lehi's family left Jerusalem. In the same vision, Nephi saw the crucifixion of Jesus Christ, his subsequent resurrection and his appearance among Lehi's descendants in the "Land of Promise." Nephi associated the "Tree of Life" with the followers of Jesus Christ.[10]

Archaeologists and iconographers have observed evidence of the Tree of Life or World Tree theme throughout the Americas. If the Rayed Deity, drawn by the Moche artist, is a representation of the Creator of the World, as is implied by the early Chroniclers in their descriptions of Ticci Viracocha and Quetzalcoatl or Jesus Christ in *Book of Mormon* terminology, then the man by the tree bearing fruit, who is kneeling before the Rayed Deity, may be the Moche artist's way of identifying the man as a believer in Jesus Christ who is in an attitude of supplication from or rendering thanks to Jesus Christ (the Rayed Deity) for saving him from the destruction being carried out by the revolt of the objects. Several verses in 3 Nephi 19 appear to support this idea of prayer and supplication at the time of Christ's visit to the New World. Nephi recorded:

> And it came to pass that while the angels were ministering unto the disciples, behold, Jesus came and stood in the midst and ministered unto them.
>
> And it came to pass that he spake unto the multitude, and commanded them that they should kneel down again upon the earth, and also that his disciples should kneel down upon the earth.

---

[10]For those desiring additional information on the Tree of Life theme in the *Book of Mormon*, read I Nephi Chapters 8-11.

And it came to pass that when they had all knelt down upon the earth, he commanded his disciples that they should pray.

And behold, they began to pray; and they did pray unto Jesus, calling him their Lord and their god (3 Nephi 19: 15-18).

The solitary human figure may have been placed in this position to represent all of the "followers of Christ" who had been saved by his intervention and atonement.

A careful iconographic study of these ancient New World artifacts has told us much about the native Americans. The Revolt of the Objects Theme fortunately lends itself to a study in which other sources of information about Pre-Columbia America, i.e. the folklore and legends recorded by the early chronicle writers and the *Book of Mormon*, can be exploited. These additional tools could enable the archaeologist or art historian to identify new contexts in which to analyze their findings and form alternate hypotheses concerning these early inhabitants of the "New World."

8

IMMORTALITY OF THE SOUL AND THE RESURRECTION

There are three great questions in life: Where did we come from? Why are we here? And where are we going? In one form or another, Lawrence E. Sullivan discusses these profound questions in his book, *Icanchu's Drum*.[1] He probes these questions by exploring the mythology and the understanding of remote twentieth century South American Indian societies. These Indians, who have been largely untouched by modern religions, reflect, in many ways, the understanding of the pre-Columbian natives.

Sullivan suggests that the way a nation, tribe, group, or family treats its dead is a good indication of its knowledge and understanding of the purpose of life and death. Do they believe in the immortality of the soul? Do they believe that each indi-

---

[1] Lawrence E. Sullivan, *Icanchu's Drum, An Orientation to Meaning in South American Religions*. (Macmillan Publishing Company, New York, 1988.)

vidual has a spirit and does this spirit live after the body has died? Do they believe that the spirit has physical needs or that personal relationships formed in life continue after death? Do they believe in a resurrection of the body? Why do some natives bury food, drink, gold, silver and other possessions including even wives along with the dead husbands?

Sullivan gathered information on numerous remote Indian tribes and described their religious habits and myths. As would be expected, many of the myths and forms of religion appear to outsiders to be primitive; however, they are often very complex. There is frequently a core of Judeo-Christian-like teachings scattered throughout their myths which have not been tainted by contemporary religions and appear to be related more to the Indians Pre-Columbian beliefs. The *Book of Mormon* and the early Spanish and Portuguese chronicles relate ancient historical and religious teachings that might shed light on the myths and beliefs of the numerous twentieth century Indians tribes.

NATURE OF SPIRITS

During a provocative art history graduate seminar on ancient Pre-Columbian mythology, the professor asked his graduate students if they believed that humans possess a spirit and, if so, what is the nature of this spirit. No hands went up. After additional urging from the professor, several students cautiously suggested that man might have a spirit which could be considered as some form of cosmic energy. None of the students was willing to pose the idea that a spirit could be an individual entity with perceivable form which leaves the body and lives on after death.

One of the principal teachings of the *Book of Mormon* is the eternal nature of man. As noted earlier, before the Jaredites departed the Old World, the brother of Jared is recorded to have fashioned sixteen small stones that were as transparent as glass

Immortality of the Soul and the Resurrection

and then prayed to the Lord to have the Lord touch the stones so that, with the power of his touch, they would shine in the darkness and illuminate the interior of the Jaredites' eight barges during their crossing of the "great waters." Ether recorded that because of the brother of Jared's great faith, Jehovah responded to his request and touched each of the sixteen stones. As he did so, the brother of Jared, who to that point had only heard the voice of Jehovah, saw the finger of the Lord and fell to the earth in great fear and astonishment. Jehovah then offered to show himself fully to the brother of Jared. Moroni recorded this unique event in the Book of Ether as follows:

> . . . .Seest thou that ye are created after mine own image? Yea, even all men were created in the beginning after mine own image.
> Behold, this body, which ye now behold, is the body of my spirit; and man have I created after the body of my spirit; and even as I appear unto thee to be in the spirit will I appear unto my people in the flesh.
> And now, as I, Moroni, said I could not make a full account of these things which are written, therefore it sufficeth me to say that Jesus showed himself unto this man in the spirit, even after the manner and in the likeness of the same body even as he showed himself unto the Nephites (Ether 3:15-17).

Two important beliefs of Mormons are confirmed from this account of the brother of Jared. First that Jehovah and Jesus Christ are the same person and that Jesus Christ is the God of the Old Testament as well as the New Testament. The God of the Old Testament, Jehovah, is seldom mentioned by name in the Bible, but out of reverence is translated as "Lord" or "God." This Jehovah is assumed by many Christians to be God, the Father. Mormons believe it was Jesus Christ instead, acting on behalf of the Father. Mormons believe it was Jesus who spoke to Adam and Eve after they were driven from the Garden of Eden as well as the other great antediluvian prophets in the *Bible*. He commanded Noah to build an ark and showed him how to build it. He is the "Great I Am," who appeared to Abraham, and entered into an important covenant with Abraham (Genesis 17). He also appeared to Moses on Mount Horeb and instructed him to deliver the House of Israel from the bondage of the Egyptians. When Moses asked the Lord how he could convince the Israelites that he had spoken with their God, Jehovah identified himself as "*I AM THAT I AM*" and instructed Moses to tell the Israelites that "*I AM*" had sent him (Exodus 3:13-14). After Jesus Christ was born and was teaching the people, he greatly angered the Jews when he proclaimed:

> Your father Abraham rejoiced to see my day: and he saw it, and was glad.
> Then said the Jews unto him, Thou art not yet fifty years old, and hast thou seen Abraham?
> Jesus said unto them, Verily, verily, I say unto you, Before Abraham was, *I Am* [emphasis added] (John 8:56-58).

The second Mormon belief illustrated in the encounter between the brother of Jared and Christ is that a spirit has the form of a human or more importantly that humankind was created in the image of Christ's spirit form. This coincides with the narrative in Genesis:

> And God said, Let us make man in our image, after our likeness: and let them have dominion over the fish of the sea, and over the fowl of the air, and over the cattle, and over all the earth, and over every creeping thing that creepeth upon the earth.
> So God created man in his own image, in the image of God created he him; male and female created he them (Genesis 1:26-27).[2]

---

[2]Joseph Smith claimed to have received a revelation expanding on the Biblical writings of and about Moses. It included a more detailed account of the creation than that found in Genesis. Smith published it as *The Book of Moses* and included it in a larger volume of Latter-day Saint scripture known as *The Pearl of Great Price*.

Immortality of the Soul and the Resurrection 159

The revelation given to Moses concerning the creation of the world as recorded in the Book of Moses in the Mormon scripture *The Pearl of Great Price* provides even greater clarity:

> And I, God, said unto mine Only Begotten, which was with me from the beginning: Let us make man in our image, after our likeness; and it was so. And I, God, said: Let them have dominion over the fishes of the sea, and over the fowl of the air, and over the cattle and over all the earth, and over every creeping thing that creepeth upon the earth.
>
> And I, God, created man in mine own image, in the image of mine Only Begotten created I him; male and female created I them (Moses 2:26-27).

Mormons believe that during this creative period, God the Father had a physical body, but Jesus Christ, who had not yet been born on earth, had not acquired a physical body. The difficulty of distinguishing between a spirit personage and a resurrected body becomes apparent when the resurrected Christ appeared to ten of his apostles, as recorded by Luke:

> And as they thus spake, Jesus himself stood in the midst of them, and saith unto them, Peace be unto you.
>
> But they were terrified and affrighted, and supposed that they had seen a spirit.
>
> And he said unto them, Why are ye troubled? And why do thoughts arise in your hearts?
>
> Behold my hands and my feet, that it is I myself: handle me, and see; for a spirit hath not flesh and bones, as ye see me have.
>
> And when he had thus spoken, he shewed them his hands and his feet (Luke 24:36-41).

Obviously, these early apostles were familiar with the notion that spirits visited with men on earth from time to time generally as heavenly angels.

NATURE OF ANGELS

Concerning the nature and mission of angels, the Old Testament narrates angelic visitations on numerous occasions such as the three men (understood to be angels) who visited with Abraham (Genesis 18) and subsequently met with Lot in the city of Sodom (Genesis 19). Angels attended Hagar and her son, Ishmael, in the desert, an act which is greatly revered in the Moslem world (Genesis 16). The most famous Biblical accounts of angelic visitations are the appearances of the Angel Gabriel to Zacharias to announced the coming birth of John the Baptist; and subsequently, Gabriel's appearance to Mary, the mother of Jesus Christ.[3]

Later at the birth of Jesus Christ, an angel appeared to the shepherds and provided instructions concerning where they should go to find the new-born Christ child. This unidentified angel was accompanied by a choir of heavenly hosts. The Four Gospels contain accounts of Jesus Christ being periodically attended to by angels throughout his ministry. One of the most notable of these is when Jesus Christ was transfigured before Peter, James and John. At that time, two ancient prophets, Moses and Elias (Elijah, the Prophet), two prophets who were taken into heaven without tasting death, appeared and administered to Jesus Christ as well as to the three apostles.

According to all four gospel narratives, during the morning of the resurrection, unnamed angels were seen by Christ's disciples inside or near his tomb. After the resurrected Lord spent

---

[3]The Bible dictionary in the King James Version published by The Church of Jesus Christ of Latter-day Saints states that angels "are messengers of the Lord, and are spoken of in the epistle to the Hebrews as "ministering spirits" (Hebrews 1:14). We learn from latter-day revelation that there are two classes of heavenly beings who minister for the Lord: those who are spirits and those who have bodies of flesh and bone. Spirits are those beings who either have not yet obtained a body of flesh and bones, or who have once had a mortal body and have died, and are awaiting the resurrection."

Immortality of the Soul and the Resurrection

approximately forty days ministering to his apostles, he ascended into heaven. As his apostles watched him ascend, two angels dressed in white appeared to them and said that "this same Jesus, which is taken up from you into heaven, shall so come in like manner as ye have seen him go into heaven" (Acts 1:10-11).

The *Book of Mormon* provides numerous accounts of angels who interceded in the affairs of men. Early in the *Book of Mormon* narrative, Nephi described the adventures that he and his three brothers had when they tried to obtain the extremely important record of the Jews which was written on plates of brass that were in the possession of a Jewish elder, Laban. After being robbed by Laban and chased through the streets of Jerusalem by Laban's servants, Nephi's two older brothers, Laman and Lemuel, in a dramatic response to their fear and frustration, began to beat Nephi and another brother, Sam, with a rod. During the beating, an angel suddenly appeared and asked the rebellious brothers why they were beating Nephi. The angel strongly rebuked the two older brothers and then departed.

Nephi instructed his family that angels speak by the power of the Holy Ghost, and thus, they speak the words of Christ. About 124 B.C., the Nephite King Benjamin taught the people about the future coming of Jesus Christ to the world. He declared that the details of the future birth of the Savior had been communicated to him by an angel from God. Benjamin stated:

> And the things which I shall tell you are made known unto me by an angel from God. And he said unto me: Awake; and I awoke, and behold he stood before me.
> And he said unto me: Awake, and hear the words which I shall tell thee; for behold, I am come to declare unto you the glad tidings of great joy.
> For the Lord hath heard thy prayers, and hath judged of thy righteousness, and hath sent me to declare unto thee that thou mayest rejoice; and that thou mayest declare unto thy people, that they may also be filled with joy.

> For behold, the time cometh, and is not far distant, that with power, the Lord Omnipotent who reigneth, who was, and is from all eternity to all eternity, shall come down from heaven among the children of men, and shall dwell in a tabernacle of clay, and shall go forth amongst men, working mighty miracles, such as healing the sick, raising the dead, causing the lame to walk, the blind to receive their sight, and the deaf to hear, and curing all manner of diseases.
>
> And he shall be called Jesus Christ, the Son of God, the Father of heaven and earth, the Creator of all things from the beginning; and his mother shall be called Mary (Mosiah 3:2-5, 8).

Another case where an angel appeared to men in the *Book of Mormon* involved five rebellious sons of believing fathers—Alma, the son of Alma, and the four sons of King Mosiah. They were actively attempting to destroy the church of God. Mosiah recorded the event in the following narrative:

> And now it came to pass that while he [Alma] was going about to destroy the church of God, for he did go about secretly with the sons of Mosiah seeking to destroy the church, and to lead astray the people of the Lord, contrary to the commandments of God, or even the king—
>
> And as I said unto you, as they were going about rebelling against God, behold, the angel of the Lord appeared unto them; and he descended as it were in a cloud; and he spake as it were with a voice of thunder, which caused the earth to shake upon which they stood; (Mosiah 27:10-11).

Finally about 420 A.D., the great warrior and prophet Moroni, the last keeper of the Nephite records, declared that the angels are subject to Christ and are charged to minister to the faithful according to Christ's instructions. The failure of angels to appear unto men is because of the lack of faith and men's failure to keep the commandments (see Moroni 7).

Angels appear to be an important element in God's communication network with man on earth. Not only were angels operative in the past, but the scriptures record that they also will have an important role in God's future communications with his children. The Apostle John was given a vision of the future which Mormons interpret as a foreshadowing of the restoration of the gospel in modern times. In the Book of Revelations, John declared that "I saw another angel fly in the midst of heaven, having the everlasting gospel to preach unto them that dwell on the earth, and to every nation, and kindred, and tongue, and people," (Revelation 14:6). Mormons believe that "other angel" was Moroni who delivered the *Book of Mormon* records to Joseph Smith.

NATURE OF SATAN

The Chronicle writers often referred to the agents of Satan, the devil, or Lucifer[4] who made their own appearances on earth. The Bible teaches that Lucifer played an important role in the Garden of Eden persuading Eve to eat the forbidden fruit. Moses provided considerable more indepth information about Satan. Initially, Moses wrote about his encounter with God:

> And he saw God face to face, and he talked with him, and the glory of God was upon Moses; therefore Moses could endure his presence.
> And God spake unto Moses, saying: Behold, I am the Lord God Almighty, and Endless is my name; for I am without beginning of days or end of years; and is not this endless?
> And, behold, thou art my son; wherefore look, and I will show thee the workmanship of mine hands; but not all, for my works are without end, and also my words, for they never cease.
> Wherefore, no man can behold all my works, except he behold all my glory; and no man can behold all my glory, and afterwards remain in the flesh on the earth.

---

[4]The Bible Dictionary in the King James version of the Bible, published by The Church of Jesus Christ of Latter-day Saints states that Lucifer means literally the *Shining One* or *Son of the Morning*, identifying him as one of God's children.

And the presence of God withdrew from Moses, that his glory was not upon Moses; and Moses was left unto himself. And as he was left unto himself, he fell unto the earth.

And it came to pass that it was for the space of many hours before Moses did again receive his natural strength like unto man; and he said unto himself: Now, for this cause I know that man is nothing, which thing I never had supposed.

But now mine own eyes have beheld God; but not my natural, but my spiritual eyes, for my natural eyes could not have beheld; for I should have withered and died in his presence; but his glory was upon me; and I beheld his face, for I was transfigured before him (Moses 1:2-5, 9- 11).

After the Lord departed, Moses claimed that Satan appeared unto him and tempted him. Moses recorded his encounter with Lucifer as follows:

And it came to pass that when Moses had said these words, behold, Satan came tempting him, saying: Moses, son of man, worship me.

And it came to pass that Moses looked upon Satan and said: Who art thou? For behold, I am a son of God, in the similitude of his Only Begotten; and where is thy glory, that I should worship thee?

For behold, I could not look upon God, except his glory should come upon me, and I were transfigured before him. But I can look upon thee in the natural man. Is it not so, surely?

Blessed be the name of my God, for his Spirit hath not altogether withdrawn from me, or else where is thy glory, for it is darkness unto me? And I can judge between thee and God; for God said unto me: Worship God, for him only shalt thou serve.

Get thee hence, Satan; deceive me not; for God said unto me: Thou art after the similitude of mine Only Begotten.

And he also gave me commandments when he called unto me out of the burning bush, saying: Call upon God in the name of mine Only Begotten, and worship me.

And again Moses said: I will not cease to call upon God, I have other things to inquire of him: for his glory has been upon me, wherefore I can judge between him and thee. Depart hence, Satan.

Immortality of the Soul and the Resurrection 165

And now, when Moses had said these words, Satan cried with a loud voice, and ranted upon the earth, and commanded, saying: I am the Only Begotten, worship me.

And it came to pass that Moses began to fear exceedingly; and as he began to fear, he saw the bitterness of hell. Nevertheless, calling upon God, he received strength, and he commanded, saying: Depart from me, Satan, for this one God only will I worship, which is the God of glory.

And now Satan began to tremble, and the earth shook; and Moses received strength, and called upon God, saying: In the name of the Only Begotten, depart hence, Satan.

And it came to pass that Satan cried with a loud voice, with weeping, and wailing, and gnashing of teeth; and he departed hence, even from the presence of Moses, that he beheld him not (Moses 1:12 - 22).

After Satan departed, the Lord appeared again to Moses and explained to him how Satan or Lucifer had been cast out of heaven. Again Moses recorded the following conversation that he had with God.

And I, the Lord God, spake unto Moses, saying: That Satan, whom thou hast commanded in the name of mine Only Begotten, is the same which was from the beginning, and he came before me, saying—Behold, here am I, send me, I will be thy son, and I will redeem all mankind, that one soul shall not be lost, and surely I will do it; wherefore give me thine honor.

But, behold, my Beloved Son, which was my Beloved and Chosen from the beginning, said unto me—Father, thy will be done, and the glory be thine forever.

Wherefore, because that Satan rebelled against me, and sought to destroy the agency of man, which I, the Lord God, had given him, and also, that I should give unto him mine own power; by the power of mine Only Begotten, I caused that he should be cast down;

And he became Satan, yea, even the devil, the father of all lies, to deceive and to blind men, and to lead them captive at his will, even as many as would not hearken unto my voice (Moses 4:1 - 4).

In the *Bible*, John provided additional information concerning the role of Satan before the creation and the resultant war between the spirits who followed Satan and those who followed Jesus Christ. In the Book of Revelation, John wrote:

> And there was a war in heaven: Michael and his angels fought against the dragon; and the dragon fought and his angels,
> And prevailed not; neither was their place found any more in heaven.
> And the great dragon was cast out, that old serpent, called the Devil, and Satan, which deceiveth the whole world: he was cast out into the earth, and his angels were cast out with him (Revelations 12:7-9).

Based on their unique books of scripture, Mormons believe that there was a war in heaven during the pre-mortal existence of the spirit children of God. The war was primarily over how their life on earth would be governed. The issues involved such things as freedom of choice, how to gain salvation to return to God, and who should be the Redeemer. Lucifer promised to save every soul by taking away their right to choose between good and evil. In return, he wanted to preempt God's glory. Although Satan and his followers were cast out of heaven, Mormons believe the warfare continues on earth in the conflict between right and wrong.

One result of the expulsion of Lucifer is that neither he nor his followers will ever receive bodies of flesh and bone nor will they ever have offspring. Mormons firmly believe that body and spirit together are superior to spirit alone, and thus Satan is angry at being deprived. His goal is to make men and women as miserable as he is and to destroy man's agency by enslaving him with sin.

Before Lehi died, he taught his children about the efforts of the devil to deceive mankind:

Immortality of the Soul and the Resurrection   167

And now, my sons, I speak unto you these things for your profit and learning; for there is a God, and he hath created all things, both the heavens and the earth, and all things that in them are, both things to act and things to be acted upon.

And to bring about his eternal purposes in the end of man, after he had created our first parents, and the beasts of the field and the fowls of the air, and in fine, all things which are created, it must needs be that there was an opposition; even the forbidden fruit in opposition to the tree of life; the one being sweet and the other bitter.

Wherefore, the Lord God gave unto man that he should act for himself. Wherefore, man could not act for himself save it should be that he was enticed by the one or the other.

And I, Lehi, according to the things which I have read, must needs suppose that an angel of God, according to that which is written, had fallen from heaven; wherefore, he became a devil, having sought that which was evil before God.

And because he had fallen from heaven, and had become miserable forever, he sought also the misery of all mankind. Wherefore, he said unto Eve, yea, even that old serpent, who is the devil, who is the father of all lies, wherefore he said: Partake of the forbidden fruit, and ye shall not die, but ye shall be as God, knowing good and evil (2 Nephi 2:14 - 18).

Nephi also taught the Nephites about the craftiness of Satan and his efforts to deceive men:

For the kingdom of the devil must shake, and they which belong to it must needs be stirred up unto repentance, or the devil will grasp them with his everlasting chains, and they be stirred up to anger, and perish;

For behold, at that day shall he rage in the hearts of the children of men, and stir them up to anger against that which is good.

And others will he pacify, and lull them away into carnal security, that they will say: All is well in Zion; yea, Zion prospereth, all is well—and thus the devil cheateth their souls, and leadeth them away carefully down to hell.

And behold, others he flattereth away, and telleth them there is no hell; and he saith unto them: I am no devil, for there is none—

and thus he whispereth in their ears, until he grasps them with his awful chains, from whence there is no deliverance.

Yea, they are grasped with death, and hell; and death, and hell, and the devil, and all that have been seized therewith must stand before the throne of God, and be judged according to their works, from whence they must go into the place prepared for them, even a lake of fire and brimstone, which is endless torment (2 Nephi 28:19-23).

Throughout the *Book of Mormon*, the prophets warned the people to not allow themselves to become chained by Satan and his followers, but, in the end, both the Nephites and the Lamanites fell prey to the devil. Concerning the Nephites, Mormon wrote:

But now, behold, they are led about by Satan, even as chaff is driven before the wind, or as a vessel is tossed about upon the waves, without sail or anchor, or without anything wherewith to steer her; and even as she is, so are they (Mormon 5:18).

When the Spaniards and the Portuguese arrived in the New World, they found the Indians involved with idolatry, human sacrifice, cannibalism, warfare and murder as well as numerous other vices such as immorality, drunkenness and the use of narcotics. The explorers attributed these customs to the influence that the devil had over the Indians. Cieza de León was quick to blame Satan for many of the customs he observed among the Andean people, such as in the practice of burying living wives with their dead husbands. Cieza de León also narrated that the Indians believed that on certain days the devil was seen by the native priests who talked with the devil and told him their affairs.[5]

In the footnotes to Diego de Landa's book, prepared by Alfred M. Tozzer, who edited and wrote the notes to the 1941

---

[5] Cieza de León, *The Incas*, 95.

edition, Tozzer observed that the Lancandon Indians believed that "below the earth is the abode of *Kisin*, the earthquake and god of the underworld." He is the god of evil. Tozzer also claimed that other Indians gave the name *Xibalba* for the underworld, which is a term that appears in the *Popol Vuh*.[6] Some of the Indians in the Caribbean called the devil *Supay*. Each different tribe or nation appeared to have its own word for devil just as they had a word for god.

IMMORTALITY OF THE SOUL

In addition to teaching the role of angels in God's eternal purposes, the *Book of Mormon* also teaches the immortality of the soul. Approximately 550 B.C., Lehi's son, Jacob, gave a powerful discourse to the small band of Nephites assembled in the New World. As he began his sermon, Jacob reminded the Nephites that he had been called by God, and ordained in the holy priesthood (2 Nephi 6:2). Jacob taught the Nephites about the immortality of the soul and the need for a resurrection. His teachings were passed down to subsequent generations of Nephites and to many of the Lamanites as well. As will be seen, traces of this doctrine of the immortality of the soul appear in the religious beliefs of the Indians encountered by the Europeans. Extracted portions of Jacob's sermon are:

> For I know that ye have searched much, many of you, to know of things to come; wherefore I know that ye know that our flesh must waste away and die; nevertheless in our bodies we shall see God.
> For as death hath passed upon all men, to fulfil the merciful plan of the great Creator, there must needs be a power of resurrection, and the resurrection must needs come unto man by reason of the fall; and the fall came by reason of transgression; and because man became fallen they were cut off from the presence of the Lord.

---

[6]Landa, 132, n617 and n618.

Wherefore, it must needs be an infinite atonement–save it should be an infinite atonement this corruption could not put on incorruption. Wherefore, the first judgment which came upon man must needs have remained to an endless duration. And if so, this flesh must have laid down to rot and to crumble to its mother earth, to rise no more.

And because of the way of deliverance of our God, the Holy One of Israel, this death, of which I have spoken, which is the temporal, shall deliver up its dead; which death is the grave.

And this death of which I have spoken, which is the spiritual death, shall deliver up its dead; which spiritual death is hell; wherefore, death and hell must deliver up their dead, and hell must deliver up its captive spirits, and the grave must deliver up its captive bodies, and the bodies and the spirits of men will be restored one to the other; and it is by the power of the resurrection of the Holy One of Israel.

O how great the plan of our God! For on the other hand, the paradise of God must deliver up the spirits of the righteous, and the grave deliver up the body of the righteous; and the spirit and the body is restored to itself again, and all men become incorruptible, and immortal, and they are living souls, having a perfect knowledge like unto us in the flesh, save it be that our knowledge shall be perfect.

And it shall come to pass that when all men shall have passed from this first death unto life, insomuch as they have become immortal, they must appear before the judgment-seat of the Holy One of Israel; and then cometh the judgment, and then must they be judged according to the holy judgment of God (2 Nephi 9:4, 6-7, 11-13, 15).

The next important discourse on immortality and the resurrection recorded in the *Book of Mormon* was the speech of the Prophet Abinadi to wicked Nephite King Noah and his subjects in about 148 B.C. Abinadi called King Noah and his wicked priests and his followers to repentance. Alma, one of Noah's priests, believed Abinadi and subsequently recorded his sermon. Abinadi revealed that the resurrection came about because of the action of Jesus Christ and that there would be more than

Immortality of the Soul and the Resurrection

one resurrection. The people also learned that the wicked would not resurrect at the same time as the righteous, but would have to wait for a later resurrection. Abinadi became the first recorded martyr in the *Book of Mormon* because he was burned at the stake for his teaching.

About 73 B.C., Alma, the younger, had cause to chastize his son, Corianton, for immoral behavior. During his reprimand, Alma perceived that Corianton did not yet understand the principle of the resurrection. Alma explained that he had asked God specifically about what happens to the spirit during the time that it is separated from the body after death. He wrote:

> Now, concerning the state of the soul between death and the resurrection–Behold, it has been made known unto me by an angel, that the spirits of all men, as soon as they are departed from this mortal body, yea, the spirits of all men, whether they be good or evil, are taken home to that God who gave them life.
>
> And then shall it come to pass, that the spirits of those who are righteous are received into a state of happiness, which is called paradise, a state of rest, a state of peace, where they shall rest from all their troubles and from all care, and sorrow.
>
> And then shall it come to pass, that the spirits of the wicked, yea, who are evil–for behold, they have no part nor portion of the Spirit of the Lord; for behold, they chose evil works rather than good; therefore the spirit of the devil did enter into them, and take possession of their house–and these shall be cast out unto outer darkness; there shall be weeping, and wailing, and gnashing of teeth, and this because of their own iniquity, being led captive by the will of the devil.
>
> Now this is the state of the souls of the wicked, yea, in darkness, and a state of awful, fearful looking for the fiery indignation of the wrath of God upon them; thus they remain in this state, as well as the righteous in paradise, until the time of their resurrection. . . (Alma 40:11-14).

Six years before the birth of Jesus Christ, Samuel, a Lamanite prophet, reminded the wicked Nephites about the resurrection of

Jesus Christ and the impending redemption of all men who repent. The centerpiece of the *Book of Mormon* is the recorded appearance of the resurrected Jesus Christ, to the Nephites and Lamanites in the New World after his resurrection in Jerusalem.

NATIVE BELIEFS IN IMMORTALITY AND THE RESURRECTION

At the time European explorers arrived in the New World, the Indians demonstrated a strong belief in the immortality of the soul and the resurrection of the body. Although some of the early conquistadores recognized vestiges of Christian and Israelite beliefs, these beliefs and practices had been vastly diluted and radically changed during the eleven hundred year interval that corresponds with the end of the *Book of Mormon* narrative.

During Columbus's second voyage to the Americas, he sailed along the southern coast of Cuba in an effort to discover whether Cuba was the mainland he sought. He went ashore in several areas and at one point held a mass upon the shore. Peter Martyr recorded this event as it had been described to him by Columbus:

> While the Admiral heard the mass on the beach, he was approached by a distinguished looking Indian, who appeared to be about 80 years old. Although the leader was completely naked, he was accompanied by a large following. The leader stayed back and respectfully watched Columbus and the Spaniards celebrate mass. After mass, the Indian gave Columbus a basket full of fruit which he carried in his hand. He then sat down and, using Diego Colón as an interpreter, narrated the following:
>
> We have been told that you have traveled with a powerful army through all of these provinces that up to now have been unknown to you and you have caused more than a little fear among the people that inhabit the area. Consequently, I must caution you, and remind you that the souls of men, when they leave the body, follow one of two paths: one dark and gloomy path that has been prepared for

those who bother and hurt others; the other pleasurable and delightful path is for those who in life loved peace and tranquility. If you remember that you are mortal and each individual receives his future rewards according to the works he has done in this life, do not do anyone any harm.[7]

In the Darién region of Panama, Nuñez de Balboa discovered that the natives kept their dead ancestors in the house with them. The Indians took great care of the dead, going so far as to dress them in fine clothing and placing expensive jewels around their necks.[8] On Hispaniola, many of the chiefs had numerous wives. Normally the first and dearest wife was buried alive with her husband when he died. Other wives could also accompany the dead husband in his grave. Peter Martyr recorded that the natives also buried jewelry and other personal effects as well as a large jar of water and yucca flour bread with their dead indicating their belief that the dead may have need of provisions.[9]

Cieza de León observed many times throughout his travels that the natives expressed their belief in the immortality of the soul. Inevitably, he would indicate their burial practices and also their general belief in immortality and in a creator of some sort. The Indians worshiped a creator deity who had his own name. Cieza de León pointed out that after a particularly difficult battle, the Lord Inca Huayna Cápac "recovered those of his men who were still alive, and those who were dead, he had buried with due honors, according to their heathen fashion, for they all recognized the immortality of the soul."[10]

In discussing the natives near the ancient Inca city of Huánaco, Cieza de León wrote:

---

[7]Martyr, 40.
[8]Ibid., 144.
[9] Ibid., 281.
[10]Cieza de León, *The Incas*, 48.

And their temples were located in convenient places for their sacrifices and rites; . . .yet beneath their general blindness, they believed in the immortality of the soul. These Indians are intelligent, and they show it in their answers to questions put to them. The native chieftains of these people were never laid in their graves alone, but accompanied by living women, the most beautiful of them, as was the case with the others. And when these chieftains were dead and their soul had departed their body, these women buried with them in those great vaults which are their tombs await the fearful hour of death to go and join the dead man. They consider it a great good fortune and blessing to leave this world together with their husband or lord, thinking that afterwards they will serve him as they did on earth. And for this reason they believe that the woman who died quickly would the sooner find herself in the other life with her lord or husband. This custom has its root in what I have described on other occasions, which is that they see (so they say) the devil in the fields and lands, pretending to be the dead man, accompanied by his wives and other things that were put into the tomb with him.[11]

Juan Polo de Ondegardo was not one of the more well-known early chroniclers, but he was frequently cited by other early conquistador writers. When Polo de Ondegardo was the Chief Magistrate or mayor of Cuzco in 1571, he wrote numerous documents concerning the Incas, their form of government, origins and religion. Some of these writings were subsequently collected and published in a book entitled *Informaciones Acerca de la Religión y Gobierno de Los Incas* (*Information About the Religion and Government of the Incas.*)[12]

In these documents, Polo de Ondegardo stated that the Indians commonly believed that the spirits or the souls of men lived after this life. Those who had been good received glory and those who had done bad or evil received pain or suffering.

---

[11]Ibid., 110.

[12]El Licenciado Juan Polo de Ondegardo, *Informaciones Acerca de la Religión y Gobierno de los Incas, Volume III*, written in 1571 under instructions from the Council of Lima. Biographic Notes and Concordance of the Text by Horacio H. Urteaga, Dean of The History of Civilization at the University of San Marcos, Lima, Peru. Biography of Polo de Ondegardo by Carlos A. Romero from the Historical Institute of Peru. Printed in Lima, Peru 1916.

Immortality of the Soul and the Resurrection

He noted, however, that the Indians did not understand the idea of a resurrection of the body; therefore, they were very diligent in conserving the bodies, sustaining them and honoring them after death.[13]

Polo de Ondegardo believed that the idea that the dead needed help from the living was a terrible notion that was passed to the Indians by the devil. He commented that this general belief was universal in the New World and could be seen in one form or another in New Spain [Mexico], throughout Peru, in the provinces of the Rio de la Plata, and in Chile. He remarked that all believed in the immortality of the soul. After making an extensive study of this general belief, Polo de Ondegardo held the opinion that this belief placed a heavy burden upon the believers because they had to work so hard to take care of their dead, in some places to sacrifice humans yearly to honor the dead kings or Lord Incas and other men of wealth and influence. He mentioned that the Incas believed that the state of a person in the hereafter life depended greatly upon the way the individual had lived on earth.[14]

In Mexico, Diego Durán stated that the Aztecs also believed in a life after death. In the preparation of the body of a warrior killed in battle, women brought a mantle dyed red which they gave to one of the elders. The women also provided a cloth which could be used as money for the dead and a slave who was sacrificed at the same time to serve the deceased in the afterworld. All these things were called "offerings to those who must die" and were given to mourners.[15] Durán noted that all the orators talked directly to the dead king as if he were still alive. He saw this as a bestial and idolatrous practice.[16]

---

[13] Ibid., 7.
[14] Ibid., 116-119.
[15] Durán, 150.
[16] Ibid., 383. (Heyden noted that in 1967, Garibay expressed his indignation at Durán's criticism and pointed out that Sahagún praised them. Garibay indicated that they represent an elevation of concepts. They also constitute a fine example of prehispanic oral literature.)

Fray Bernardino de Sahagún revealed a slightly different focus in his writings about the Aztec Indians. According to Sahagún, the souls of the dead went to one of three places, depending on how they died, not so much on how they had lived.

One of the places was a hell called Chicunamictla, where a devil or demon lived. It was considered a most somber place which had neither light nor windows and those consigned there never got out. The dead would have neither anxiety nor longing to return from where they had departed. To prepare them for the next life, the bodies were adorned with papers and tied or bound tightly. A little water was poured on the head and a tiny jar of water was placed with the dead to serve them during their wandering. The body, papers and water were then placed in a shroud and again bound tightly. The deceased was then given special papers, placed in an orderly fashion, to enable him to pass by various obstacles. One set of papers enabled him to pass between the two mountain ranges that joined one another. Another set of papers enabled the soul to pass along the road that was guarded by a snake. Still a third set of papers helped the dead individual to pass along the road guarded by a green lizard. Other papers helped the soul to pass over eight sets of moors or swamps and through eight hillocks. Finally, there were papers to enable the soul to pass by the wind of knives.

Because of the severe winds and the cold that the dead had to withstand, the Indians burned all the chests and weapons and all the remains of the captives they had captured in war, as well as all the clothes these had worn, saying that all these things were to go with the deceased to keep him warm in that passage. They did a similar thing when a woman died, burning all the tools with which she wove and spun, as well as all her clothes to keep her warm. The Indians also had the dead take with them a little dog of bright reddish hair, and they put around its neck a loose

Immortality of the Soul and the Resurrection

cotton thread because, according to Sahagún, the dead swam astride a little dog when they crossed a river of hell.

Sahagún learned from his Aztec scholars that the second place where the souls of the departed went was the terrestrial paradise, Tlalocan, where there was much rejoicing and no suffering. They were also dressed in papers and a cane was placed in one hand. In Tlalocan, it was always summer and everything was green with flowers and trees.

The third place where the souls of the departed went was heaven, where the Sun lived. It was believed that in heaven there were forests of different kinds of trees and that the offerings which were made to the dead by the living were received in the forest. After four years in heaven, the souls of the dead were changed into different kinds of birds of rich plumage of fine hues, and they flew off to drink honey from all flowers in heaven and on the earth, as do the hummingbirds.[17]

In Yucatán, Bishop Diego de Landa believed that the Indians in Yucatán had an excessive fear of dying and there were periods of great mourning when someone died. They had the custom of filling the mouth of a dead person with ground maize and some money, so that the individual would not be without something to eat in the next life. The dead were buried inside the house or directly behind it and some of their idols were buried with them. If the dead man was a priest, some of his books were buried with him and if he was a sorcerer, he was buried with some of his stones for witchcraft. As for the nobles and persons of high esteem, their bodies were burned, their ashes placed in great urns and temples were built over them.

Landa wrote that the Mayas believed that they would be rewarded according to how they lived. Landa wrote:

---

[17]Sahagún, 190-194.

This people has always believed in the immortality of the soul. More than many other nations, although they have not reached such a high state of civilization; for they believed that there was another and better life, which the soul enjoyed when it separated from the body. They said that this future life was divided into a good and a bad life—into a painful one and one full of rest. The bad and the painful one was for the vicious people, while the good and the delightful one was for those who had lived well according to their manner of living.

The delights which they said they were to obtain, if they were good, were to go to a delightful place, where nothing would give them pain and where they would have an abundance of foods and drinks of great sweetness, and a tree which they call there *yaxche, very cool and giving great shade, which is the ceiba, under the branches and the shadow of which they would rest and forever cease from labor.*

The penalties of a bad life, which they said that the bad would suffer, were to go to a place lower than the other, which they called *Metnal*, which means "hell," and be tormented in it by the devils and by great extremities of hunger, cold, fatigue and grief. They maintain that there was in this place a devil, the prince of all the devils, whom all obeyed, and they call him in their language *Hunhau*. And they said that these lives, bad and good, had no end for the soul has none.[18]

Father Antonio Ruiz de Montoya, the early Jesuit Priest who helped establish the Guaraní Indian Missions in Paraguay, Argentina and Brazil, wrote about the religious and burial beliefs of those Indians. He narrated that the Guaraní believed that the soul separated from the dead body, but still accompanied it into the grave; consequently, many Indians buried their dead in large earthen jars. The Indians placed a plate in the mouth of the jar so that a small space could be maintained in which the soul would be more comfortable. The earthen jars were not completely buried in the ground so the soul was not trapped with the body.

When the Catholic priests arrived and began to bury the dead completely under the ground, an old man with a strange

---

[18]Landa, 131-132.

Immortality of the Soul and the Resurrection

apparatus that looked like a sieve would visit the grave and go through the motions as if he were removing something from the grave. This act reportedly freed the soul or spirit so that it would not suffer by being trapped with the body.[19]

Although several chroniclers wrote that the Indians did not understand the idea of a resurrection, Inca Garcilaso de la Vega, in his book, *Comentarios Reales*, wrote that the Incas believed in a universal resurrection of the dead. He provided one of the best descriptions of the Inca belief in the resurrection, which was as follows:

> They went to great pains to ensure that all of their fingernail clippings or hair that came out while combing were carefully kept in a crack in the wall so that they would be safe and close at hand. If, over time, some fell out of the crack, any other Indian who saw them would pick them up and put them back. Many times, just to see what they would say, I asked diverse Indians at diverse times why they did that and all responded with the same words saying, "Do you not know that all who have been born on earth will be born in the world again (they did not have a verb for resurrection), and the souls of those who have died will rise again with everything that belonged to their bodies and in order that our souls do not lose time looking for fingernail clippings nor hair, because in that great day there will be a great bustling activity and everyone will be in a hurry, we put these things here together so that they can rise up more quickly."[20]

In Paraguay, the Guaraní also saved the hair and fingernails which they kept together in a small pouch that was buried with the individual.[21]

---

[19] Ruiz de Montoya, 78.

[20] Garcilaso de la Vega, 75.

[21] While teaching a Sunday School class in 1995 in Asuncion, I raised this peculiar habit of some of the native Americans to carefully gather any hair and fingernail clippings and bury them with the body. A Paraguayan in the class stated that his grandmother, a full blooded Guaraní, was still practicing this custom. Compare Alma 40:23 which reads "The soul shall be restored to the body, and the body to the soul; yea, and every limb and joint shall be restored to its body; yea, even a hair of the head shall not be lost; but all things shall be restored to their proper and perfect frame."

Francisco Lopez de Gomara, who wrote about the Indian belief in a resurrection stated the following about the graves of the Inca rulers and other Inca noblemen:

> When the Spaniards opened the graves and scattered the bones around, the Indians begged them not to do that because the bones had to be together for the resurrection; the Indians also believe in the resurrection of the body and the immortality of the souls.[22]

According to Juan de Betanzos, the Incas had a belief that "When this world comes to an end, we will all rise up with life and with this flesh as we are now." Betanzos wrote that someone made them understand this; they know it very well; consequently, the Inca military leaders always attempted to return all of the dead soldiers to Cuzco or their home.[23]

ART HISTORY AND ARCHAEOLOGY DISCOVERIES

In her paper on *Death-Associated Figures on Mochica Pottery* presented at Dunbarton Oaks, Elizabeth P. Benson, described a variety of Mochica (frequently called Moche) pottery paintings or drawings that revealed death-type figures. Benson observed that the Moche believed in and described an afterlife. She stated that many of their pottery representations depicted sacrifice, funeral rites, passage to and life in the afterworld. She explained that the Mochica convention for representing the dead in art was to show socket eyes (if not a skeletal head) and, in some cases, a skeletal ribcage, in an otherwise normal body. The sexual organs of men were usually displayed in art, even when the man in the artwork was dead. Sacrifice and the collection of blood were also present in many pottery scenes depicting death

---

[22]Garcilaso de la Vega, 75
[23]Betanzos, 94.

and afterlife. Women also appear in the preparation-for-death and afterlife scenes, both in elaborate painted and relief pottery and on modeled pots. The woman's role in death ceremonies and the afterlife probably explains the meaning of some of the erotic scenes involving a live woman, or sometimes a dead woman or two women, with a dead man. The Rafael Larco Herrera Museum in Lima has hundreds of pottery examples showing these types of scenes.[24]

Closely related to Benson's description of the Moche belief in the afterlife, is a series of iconographic scenes depicting what Christopher Donnan and Steve Bourget describe as a "transformation" in which individuals in skeletal form pass from an "underworld" into the "world of the ancestors." This "underworld" appears to be more like what Mormons would call the "spirit world." As it makes this transition, the body takes on flesh once again. What the art historians call transformation, the religionists would call a resurrection.

In 1979, Christopher Donnan and Donna McClelland collaborated on an article entitled, *The Burial Theme in Moche Iconography*. They had identified the burial theme as one of the main themes of Moche art mainly from their study of iconographic representations on six ceramic bottles. Each bottle describes the effort to lower a casket into a deep hole by the use of ropes. A variety of grave goods surround the casket and extend above between the ropes. Various kinds of food are shown. In their report, Donnan and McClelland noted that corn and beans have been obtained from some of the better preserved Moche graves. The burial theme in Moche art normally

---

[24]The Rafael Larco Herrera Museum has one of the finest collections of Moche pottery and art in the world. The Museum has a separate section located in the basement of erotic pornographic pottery that portray reproductive and non-reproductive sexual activities, both in life as well as in the hereafter, which indicated that the Mochica believed that sexual relations were possible after death. The Moche artists portrayed only the gods as having reproductive sexual relations in their afterlife scenes. All others were engaged in non-reproductive sexual activities.

contains groupings of human, animal and anthropomorphized figures—non-human things made into human shapes. The scientists are still pondering the meaning and nature of the anthropomorphized figures.[25]

In 1987, looters digging near the pyramids of Sipán, a small village located in the Lambayeque River valley of Peru, discovered a buried tomb of inestimable value. Fortunately one of the looters, perhaps discontent with his allotted plunder, informed the police of the find and turned in his fellow robbers. The Peruvian police arrested several of the looters (called *Huaqueros* in Spanish) and confiscated much of their illegal treasure. The police also notified Walter Alva, director of the Bruning Museum in Lambayeque.

Alva discovered that the exquisite craftsmanship of some of the pieces surpassed anything previously known to have been produced by the Moche. Alva contacted Christopher Donnan at the Fowler Museum of Cultural History in Los Angeles who joined the team in locating and excavating the tomb. During their excavation they discovered several other tombs loaded with immense treasures of gold, silver, and copper objects. Because of the immense wealth, the art historians determined that these tombs had to be the final resting place of Moche royalty. In their book entitled *Royal Tombs of Sipán*, Alva and Donnan described the burial chamber as follows:

> The burial chamber was actually a room, with solid mud-brick benches along its sides and at the head end. Niches had been created in these benches—two in each of the sides and one at the head. The benches reduced the floor space of the burial chamber to an area 2.40 meters north-south by 3.25 meters east-west. The plank coffin had been placed in the center of this area, aligned parallel to the side walls. The contents of the coffin were then placed inside it, and the coffin lid was securely fastened with copper straps. Hundreds of ceramic vessels were subsequently lowered into the burial chamber

---

[25]Christopher B. Donnan and Donna McClelland, *The Burial Theme in Moche Iconography*, Dunbarton Oaks, Washington, D.C. 1979.

and arranged in groups that filled the niches in the side benches... The ceramics were predominantly mold-made jars sculpted in the form of nude prisoners with ropes around their necks, warriors holding warclubs and shields... At about the same time the ceramics were being placed in the burial chamber, two sacrificed llamas were put on the floor–one on each side adjacent to the foot of the coffin. The body of a child was also placed on the floor near the head of the coffin. The child was seated with its back leaning against the southwest corner of the burial chamber, and its legs extended forward along the floor. The child had died at the age of nine or ten.

Once the ceramics, llamas, and child were placed in the funerary chamber, five coffins, each containing one adult, were lowered into position. One of these coffins, containing the body of a well built adult male was placed on the east side of the plank coffin, directly on top of one of the sacrificed llamas. His body was covered with copper objects, including a large crescent-shaped headdress ornament and a circular shield. Along side his body was a large warclub, completely encased in copper sheet. His body had been wrapped in a coarsely woven shroud, and placed inside a rectangular box-like coffin made of cane...On the other side of the plank coffin was another cane coffin, placed on top of the other sacrificed llama. It also contained an adult male lying extended on his back. His age at death has been estimated as between thirty-five and forty-five years. He was wearing a beaded pectoral, and had several unidentified copper objects on top of his body. Inside his coffin was a dog, stretched out with its head near the man's feet.

Three other cane coffins contained adult females. Two of these were stacked one on top of the other at the head of the plank coffin. The lower coffin had been placed over the extended legs of the seated child. Both females were fully extended and the lower individual lay on her back, while the upper one was lying face down. The third cane coffin containing a female was at the foot of the plank coffin. She lay on her side with her head to the west, facing the plank coffin. All three women were between fifteen and twenty years old when they died. Perhaps the flanking males were his bodyguards, or member of his court, and the females were his wives, concubines, or servants. However, concerning the females, further investigation revealed that they had probably been dead quite some time before they were placed in the royal tomb.[26]

---

[26] Walter Alva and Christopher B. Donnan, *Royal Tombs of Sipán*, Fowler Museum of Cultural History, University of California, Los Angeles, 1993. 119-123.

The chronicle writers elaborated extensively upon the Pre-Columbian natives's belief in an afterlife and their efforts to bury important individuals with artifacts, riches, wives and slaves. The discovery of the Royal Tombs at Sipán has provided extensive corroboration to chronicle accounts.

The idea of an after life was equally impressive in the codices and painting of the ancient Maya and Nahuatl speaking peoples of Mesoamerica. In their book, *A Forest of Kings, The Untold Story of the Ancient Maya*, modern art historians Linda Schele and David Freidel observed that there is a remarkable continuity to be seen between modern villagers and their predecessors as described by the Spanish chroniclers. Schele and Freidel wrote that both the powerful and the humble buried their dead under the stones of their courtyards so that their ancestors could remain with them and hear the sounds of their descendants' children playing over their heads.[27]

Schele and Freidel described the expansion of the Maya during the Pre-Christian era and singled out Tikal in Mesoamerica as an important site. Focusing on the burial practices, they wrote:

> The North Acropolis tombs from this era reveal a unique glimpse of the newly emergent Maya ruling elite, who had themselves buried in vaulted chambers set under shrine-like buildings. We find, interred in these chambers, not only the physical remains of these people and the objects they considered of value, but even some pictorial representations of them. In one of these tombs, images of Maya nobles were drawn in black line on the red-painted walls. The paintings, along with the rich burial goods laid around the woman's body, mark the tomb as the "earliest interment of someone of patent consequence" at Tikal. It is interesting that the deceased person in this tomb was a woman, for the Maya of Tikal, like other Maya, gave primacy to males in the reckoning of social status through the principle of patrilineal descent. This tomb, however, shows that status had transcended gender and was now ascribed to both the men and women of noble families.[28]

---

[27]Linda Schele and David Freidel, *A Forest of Kings, The Untold Story of the Ancient Maya*, Published by William Morrow and Cia, Inc. New York 1990. 45.
[28]Ibid., 133.

Immortality of the Soul and the Resurrection

Schele and Freidel are just two of many Mayanologists who have focused on death, burial and sacrifice among the Maya. Their findings as well as the findings of the art historians who have focused mainly on the Moche civilization in Peru highlight how beliefs similar to many of the ancient teachings of the *Book of Mormon* prophets resonated among the Indian groups throughout the Americas.

New World chroniclers, modern anthropologists, archaeologists and art historians have all discovered evidence that the Pre-Columbian Americans had a strong belief in the immortality of the soul and that the individual maintained a separate identify after the death of the body. Although they have a distinct New World flavor, the evidence is overwhelming that these early native Americans had Old World connections. The following chapter explores the evidence of both Hebrew or Israelite as well as Christian teachings in the New World.

9

EVIDENCES OF ISRAELITE AND CHRISTIAN ETHICS, MORALITY AND CUSTOMS IN THE NEW WORLD

The New World chroniclers advanced many theories to explain the evidence of both Hebrew and Christian teachings, rites, and ceremonies among the Pre-Columbian tribes and kingdoms. A few of the chroniclers surfaced theories that the native Americans were all or at least part of the Lost Ten Tribes. Several writers were of the opinion that one of the early Christian apostles had visited the Americas and spread the gospel. Other chroniclers simply attributed their findings to a scheme of Satan, whom they claimed must have taught the "primitive" Americans ceremonies, rituals, and beliefs that resembled the ancient Hebrew religion or Christianity, in a diabolical effort to divert the natives so they would not accept "true" Christianity when it was presented to them. In spite of numerous vestiges of Christianity and Judaism, there did not appear to be an organized church in the Americas when the Portuguese and Spaniards arrived in the New World in the fifteenth and sixteenth centuries.

In the Biographical Notes of Diego Durán's *Book of the Gods and Rites*, Doris Heyden noted that as Durán penetrated into the history and religion of the Aztecs in New Spain, he became increasingly puzzled by similarities to personages, rites, and events in the Old Testament. He observed that both the Hebrews and the Mexicans believed "that in the beginning, God created the heaven and the earth." The Old World had its Tower of Babel, and New Spain had its lofty Pyramid of Cholula, the largest known pyramid in the world. The pagan priests of Huexotzinco kept a chest containing holy relics, a treasure held in as much awe by them as the Ark of the Covenant was by the Jews. There existed a legend in which the Toltec Indian hero, Topiltzin Quetzalcoatl, had touched the sea with his rod and the waters had parted, allowing his persecuted people to pass through the gap unharmed while their pursuers were drowned.

Durán claimed that he saw ancient Aztec paintings describing the hardships of their journey to reach Tenochtitlan. The Indian with whom Durán consulted explained a scene that while the sojourners "were camped on some high hills, a great, frightful earthquake occurred. The earth opened up and swallowed certain evil men who were among them, an occurrence that filled the other people with dread."

Durán related that the same painting showed how sand or very fine hail rained on the people. He was told that "the sand from the sky rained on their forefathers continually during their journey to reach this land." To Durán's way of thinking both the Aztecs and the Israelites had been fed by manna from heaven during extended pilgrimages.[1]

---

[1] Durán, 7-8.

Evidences of Israelite and Christian Ethics　189

Heyden also claimed that Durán searched throughout Mexico for ancient documents, which he thought might include lost "Holy Scripture," written in Hebrew. He suspected, as did many in his day, that the people of Mexico were one of the lost tribes of Israel. He also believed that Topiltzin Quetzalcoatl, the hero-god of the Toltecs, was the apostle Saint Thomas.[2]

Heyden did not attempt to unravel the puzzle repeatedly posed by Durán but simply concluded that Durán was a diffusionist and that his writings only represented the "Catholic thinking of his time." Heyden then dismissed his findings by reminding her readers that:

> Modern-day archaeologists, of course, place no credence in Durán's diffusionist theories. They claim that scientists generally agree that New World Indian cultures were the result of a long evolution of Mongolian peoples who migrated from northeastern Asia many thousands of years before the time of Moses or of Saint Thomas, the Apostle. They do not accept the idea that other people could have arrived in the New World at later times.[3]

This kind or rebuff of early chronicle findings has generally prevailed within the scientific world because any other explanation would be outside the "normative paradigm." Scientists and historians have consistently refused to carry out a systematic analysis of the chroniclers's findings and other sources and they have been dismissive of faith-based resources such as the *Book of Mormon* narrative.

Durán, Bernardino de Sahagún, and Diego de Landa as well as other chroniclers in Mexico and Mesoamerica offered numerous comparisons, other than the *Book of Mormon*, between the ancient Mexican religious beliefs and the teaching of the Old

---

[2]Ibid., xxvii. (Durán was only one of many Catholic priests who suggested that Saint Thomas, the apostle who spent his life teaching the poor, had visited the Americas.)

[3]Durán, *Book of Gods*, 23-31

and the New Testaments. These will be explored in more depth later in this chapter. In the Andes, Pedro de Cieza de León, Miguel Cabello Valboa, Felipe Guaman Poma de Ayala and other writers found similar evidences of Israelite and Christian teachings in South America. The Law of Moses and especially the observance of the Ten Commandments appeared to be similar to religious tenets that were kept in many areas of the New World. The punishment for breaking one of these New World "Ten Commandments" was frequently carried out in a manner similar to the ancient Israelite customs of meting out punishment (See Chapter 11).

Stories of a universal flood have been examined in Chapter 3, however, there are also creation stories among various Indian groups that appear similar to the Biblical account. A brief examination of the *Popol Vuh* creation myth reveals numerous similarities to the creation account in Genesis. These similarities will also be examined later in this chapter.

In 1959, Leon Cadogan, an anthropologist who lived many years among the Mbyá-Guaraní Indians, a group located in remote sections of Paraguay and Brazil, published his findings in a book entitled *Ayvu Rapyta, Textos Míticos de los Mbyá-Guaraní del Guairá* (*Ayvu Rapyta, Mythical Texts of the Mbyá-Guarani of the Guairá*).[4] Cadogan specifically chose the Mbyá-Guaraní because he discovered that the early Catholic priests had little or no contact with that tribe. Cadogan believed their religion and mythology would be less tainted by outside contact. According to Cadogan, the Mbyá-Guaraní possess a very detailed creation story which, upon close examination, is very similar to Genesis.

Modern historians and scientists, who adhere to evolution and East Asian migration theories to explain the origins of the

---

[4] Leon Cadogan, *Ayvu Rapyta—Textos Míticos de los Mbyá Guaraní del Guaira.* Boletim No. 227 - Antropologia, No. 5, São Paulo, Faculdade de Filosofia, Ciencias e Letras, 1959. (Second edition was edited by Bartomeu Meliá and published by the Biblioteca Paraguaya de Antropología, Asunción, 1992.)

Indians, discount books like the *Popol Vuh* as a post-conquest combination of primitive native mythology and Catholic theology. However, as Allen Christenson pointed out in his Introduction to the *Popol Vuh*, the Indian authors of the *Popol Vuh* went to great lengths to keep even the existence of their record a secret from the priests, who were known to mete out severe punishment to those Indians who attempted to retain any evidence of their ancient religion. If the Catholic priests encountered any vestige of pre-conquest Christianity in the native religions, they assumed this was the work of the devil and quickly snuffed it out. Furthermore, the Catholic priests were competing with the native priests for the loyalty of their Indian "converts."

The behavior of Friar Diego de Landa in Yucatán is typical of the zealous efforts of the Catholic priests to destroy any vestige of the ancient religions found in the New World. Landa discovered as early as 1558 that the newly-Christianized Mayas had secretly resumed or had not given up worshiping their hidden idols. By 1562, Landa and his fellow priests decided that simply teaching Christianity to the Mayas was not enough to persuade them to desist in the practice of their former religion. Landa resorted to more drastic measures to eliminate the old religious practices.

Landa, with other Franciscans under his direction, started a preliminary investigation into the Indians's religious activities, which ultimately led to a full scale Inquisition at Mani, Yucatán. Many Indians were thrown into prison and information was reportedly extracted under torture. The friars soon learned that the practice of idolatry was more wide spread than they initially thought and the idolaters included not only the common people and the Indian priests, but also many leading citizens such as chiefs and teachers. Those Indians that the friars suspected of being guilty were fined, flogged or imprisoned.

Tozzer and other writers recorded that although Landa never admitted torturing the Indians, other documentation indicates that many Indians died as a result of the torture they received from the priests, or they committed suicide because of the desperate situation in which they found themselves. Diego Quijada, the mayor of Yucatán at that time, wrote that the number of those severely tortured by the priests was 4,549 men and women.[5] Landa limited his comments of this event to the following brief statement: "The friars made an Inquisition about this and asked the aid of the *alcalde major* (Quijada), and they arrested a great number and put them on trial, after which an *auto de fe* [confession under torture] was celebrated."[6] This took place on 12 July 1562 at Mani.

Landa also caused a great many native books to be burned as another way of inhibiting idolatry and distancing the Mayas from their past. He wrote:

> We found a large number of books of these characters and, as they contained nothing in which there were not to be seen superstition and lies of the devil, we burned them all, which they (the Indians) regretted to an amazing degree and which caused them much affliction.[7]

Bernardo de Lizana[8] was one of the first authors to speak of the burning of books at Mani in 1562. Lizana, after telling of the discovery of some idols in a cave and the subsequent visit of Landa to Mani, wrote:

---

[5]Diego Quijada, the principal mayor of the Yucatán, kept many documents relating to this period. He also sent several letters to the King which surfaced many years later by such investigators as Ralph L. Roys, and Frances V. Scholes, who collaborated on several important books on Yucatán such as *Fray Diego de Landa*, 1938.

[6]Landa, 76.

[7]Ibid.,78, n340.

[8]Bernardo de Lizana, *Historia de Yucatán, Devocionario de Nuestra Señora de Izmal y Conquista Espiritual. Mexico.* 1633. (Parts of Part 1, I-IV with French trans. Brasseur de Bourbourg, 1864, 348-65.)

Thus he collected the books and the ancient writing and he commanded them burned and tied up. They burned many historical books of the ancient Yucatán which told of its beginning and history, which were of much value if, in our writings, they had been translated because today there would be something original. At best there is no great authority for more than the traditions of these Indians.

To better understand why the *Popol Vuh* and *Ayvu Rapyta* appear so similar to ancient Hebrew scripture, it will be helpful to compare the narrative in those two books with the creation narrative in Genesis.

ACCOUNTS OF THE CREATION

In the preamble to the Popol Vuh, the K´iche´-Maya authors wrote that its contents were based on an ancient book that contained "light from across the sea." The sixteenth century authors decided to bring it forth again because there was no longer the means whereby the Popul Vuh, the one that was written anciently, could be read.[9] Allen Christenson pointed out that the *Popol Vuh* is the most important highland Maya text in terms of its historical and mythological content. He characterized it as a sublime work of literature, composed in rich and elegant poetry.[10] It

---

[9]Christenson, 38. (Christenson suggests that the "across the sea" may be referring to Tulan (Dr. Linda Schele states that the Tulan referred to in *Popol Vuh* is perhaps an early Maya city in Yucatán), but the phrase may be referring to a time even more ancient than that and to a place much more distant than Yucatán. The "across the sea" explanation is reminiscent of the *Book of Mormon* account of Lehi bringing with him the religious records of his people called the Brass Plates. In his introduction, Christenson also mentioned that the authors of Popol Vuh referred to it as an *ilbäl*, meaning an instrument of sight, or seeing place. Christenson noted that the word is also used today to refer to quartz crystals that K´iche´ priests use in divinatory ceremonies. It may also refer to magnifying glasses or spectacles, by which things may be seen more clearly. Thus the rulers of the K´iche´s consulted the Popol Vuh in times of national distress as a means of seeing the future. This *ilbal* sounds like an apparatus similar to the Urim and Thummim described by Joseph Smith, which he used in the translation of the Gold Plates.)

[10]Ibid., 12.

is filled with chiasmus, a style of poetic parallelism that has been identified with Hebrew writings.

According to the *Popol Vuh*, the creation was carried out by a number of distinct gods who came together and worked in concert. A better understanding of this concept can be obtained by comparing various similar accounts. In the *Popol Vuh* it states:

> Heart of Sky, who is called Huracán. . . came together with Sovereign and Quetzal Serpent. Together they conceived light and life.

In Genesis it speaks of plural creators:

> And God said, Let us make man in our image, after our likeness . . .(Genesis 1:26)

Christenson provides an excellent comparative analysis of the creation as described in the *Popol Vuh* and in Genesis. In both Genesis and the *Popol Vuh*, the creation is said to have been effected merely by the expression of God's thoughts vocally. It is therefore the divine word alone that causes disorganized elements to take material form. In the New Testament, John apparently understood this when he described Jesus Christ as "the Word" in his role as creator of all things (John 1:1-3).

In Genesis it is recorded:

> And God said, Let there be light: and there was light.
> And God said, Let the waters under the heaven be gathered unto one place, and let the dry land appear.
> And God called the dry land Earth.
> And God said, Let the earth bring forth grass, the herb yielding seed, and the fruit tree yielding fruit after his kind, whose seed is in itself, upon the earth: and it was so (Genesis 1:3, 9-11).

Evidences of Israelite and Christian Ethics 195

The *Popol Vuh* states:

> Together they conceived light and life. (p. 42)
> May the water be taken away, emptied out, so that the level surface of the earth may reveal itself. (P.43)
> Therefore the earth was created by them. Merely their word brought about the creation of it. To create the earth, they said "Earth," and immediately it was created. (P. 43)
> Straightaway were created cypress groves and pine forests to cover the face of the earth. (P. 43)

Christenson observed that both accounts of the creation of animals stress the same three classes–large mammals, birds, and reptiles.

Genesis states:

> And God created great whales, and every living creature that moveth, which the waters brought forth abundantly, after their kind, and every winged fowl after his kind: and God saw that it was good.
> And God said, Let the earth bring forth the living creature after his kind, cattle, and creeping thing, and beast of the earth after his kind: and it was so (Genesis 1:21,24).

The *Popol Vuh* reads:

> Then were conceived the animals of the mountains, the guardians of the forest, and all that populate the mountains–the deer and the birds, the puma and the jaguar, the serpent and the rattlesnake, the cantil viper and the guardians of the bushes. (P.44)

Christenson noted that the *Popol Vuh* differs from the Biblical account in the nature of man's physical body. Genesis states that the first man was formed "of the dust of the ground," dampened by a mist that had risen from the earth (Genesis 2:6-7) The *Popol Vuh* also mentions the creation of a manlike being from "earth and mud," but this attempt turned out to be a dismal failure that soon crumbled and dissolved away. Only later was humankind successfully created from yellow and white corn dough.

Genesis states:

> And God said, let us make man. (Genesis 1:26)
> And God saw everything that he had made, and, behold, it was very good. (Genesis 1:31)
> But there went up a mist from the earth, and watered the whole face of the ground. (Genesis 2:6)

The *Popol Vuh* reads:

> This then is the beginning of the conception of humanity, when that which would become the flesh of mankind was prepared. (P.127)
> Thus Quetzal Serpent rejoiced... "That which we have framed and shaped shall turn out well." (P. 43)
> Just like a cloud, like a mist, was the creation and formation of it. (P.43)

In both accounts, the first men were given life through the bestowal of "breath." Christenson writes that in Hebrew, the word for "breath" also refers to the human spirit or soul. He claims this is true as well of the K´iche´ word *uxilab´*, which is used to refer to the process of breathing, as well as to the soul, or essential being of any living thing.

Genesis reads:

> And the Lord God formed man of the dust of the ground, and breathed into his nostrils the breath of life; and man became a living soul (Genesis 2:7).

The *Popol Vuh* reads:

Evidences of Israelite and Christian Ethics 197

Thus, let us try again to make one who will honor us.... Then was the making, the doing of it. Of earth and mud was its flesh composed. (P. 46)

They had their breath, therefore they became. (P. 131)

Christenson continued in a similar fashion comparing the creation story from Genesis with the *Popol Vuh*. He also focused close attention on the various gods who participated in the creative process. These gods were arranged in pairs and the narrative not only consists of the names of the separate gods, but their titles and secondary names as well. He points out that this use of name, titles and secondary names leads to considerable confusion and makes it extremely difficult to identify how many gods participated in the creation. However, upon close examination it appears that at least three pairs of gods actively participated in the creative process: the Framer and Shaper; Sovereign and Quetzal Serpent; and Xmucane (She Who Has Born Children) and Xpiyacoc (He Who Has Begotten Sons).[11] Without their titles, the same six names appear together planning the creation. Later in the account, yet another god, Heart of Sky, will be named as the presiding deity who oversees the work. Heart of Sky is sometimes referred to as Huracán.[12]

As can be readily seen from the *Popol Vuh*, the native Americans had primary names, secondary names, and titles for many of their gods. It would appear likely that they also added characteristics to these numerous titles. This has been apparent both in North America as well as in South America. Whereas art historians, archaeologists, and anthropologists have accused the Indians of worshiping numerous pagan gods, a closer examination might reveal that they were worshiping the same god under different titles, names, or characteristics.

---

[11] Ibid., 36, n10.
[12] Ibid. (See Christenson's complete Introduction for a more complete understanding of the similarities between Genesis and the *Popol Vuh*.)

Modern Christians are not so different in that we repeatedly confuse ourselves and others with the use of a wide variety of names to identify the different individuals within the Godhead or Trinity. This has led to considerable confusion within the Christian world and has given rise to numerous churches and to a variety of man-made religious creeds. In this vast array of confusion some Christians believe that God, the Father, his son Jesus Christ, and the Holy Ghost are manifestations of the same individual and that God is "a spirit without body, parts or passions." Mormons view the Godhead as three separate individuals with both God, the Father, and Jesus Christ having immortal bodies of flesh and bone, whereas the Holy Ghost does not have a body, but is a Spirit.

Christians apply numerous names to Jesus Christ. He is known as the Savior, the Messiah, the Redeemer of Israel, Alpha and Omega, the First and the Last, the Great I AM, Immanuel, our Mediator with the Father, Endless, the Son of Man, the Only Begotten Son, the Lord of Hosts, the Eternal Father of Heaven and Earth, the Lord, and the Prince of Peace to name just a few. He is described as being all-knowing, all-powerful, perfect, all-caring, all-loving, just, and merciful.

Similarly, when the Indians refer to a rain-god, a wind-god, a fire-god, etc., they may be referring to characteristics or attributes of one god, the creator of those elements. In the Andean region, the natives have identified Ticci Viracocha or Pachacamac as the "creator of the earth." In Mesoamerica, Ehecatl Quetzalcoatl or Huitzilopochtli has, at times, been referred to as the creator of the earth.

Some of the early Spaniards also became convinced, and that conviction as been passed onto many modern scientists, that the native Americans worshiped the sun. However, Cabello Valboa included in his book, *Miscelánea Antártica*, a religious speech attributed to the Lord Inca Viracocha Yupanqui in which

Viracocha Yupanqui told his people that there was a power greater than the sun and this power was the Creator of the Universe as well as creator of the sun. Cabello Valboa discounted the idea that the Incas were sun worshipers.[13] Many of the other chroniclers also observed that the native Americans did not worship the sun, but recognized its important value in their daily lives especially after passing through a period when they did not see the sun.

In *Ayvu Rapyta,* Cadogan observed that according to ancient patriarchs within the Mbyá-Guaraní, the patriarchs kept religious annals that could be divided into two categories: common religious accounts which were accessible to anyone who wanted to study them; and separate sacred accounts, called *"The first Beautiful Words."* Access to the sacred records was limited to tribal members and a few others who had the full and complete confidence of the tribal elders. Cadogan added that they were also only accessible to those who understood the Mbyá-Guaraní language. He mentioned that he lived with the Mbyá for many years in a close friendly, harmonious relationship without even being aware of the existence of the sacred records.

After he helped free one of the tribal members from jail, Cadogan was accepted as a full member of the tribe and was provided information concerning the existence of sacred myths. He had Indians dictate most of their "esoteric" myths which he initially wrote in the Mbyá-Guaraní dialect. Later he translated the narrative into Spanish and added notes explaining word meanings. A translation of Cadogan's Spanish text into English, risks compounding the distortions Cadogan may have made in his translation from Guaraní, but the essential elements of the original text are there. The Mbyá-Guaraní patriarchs dictated to Cadogan the following creation account:

---
[13]Cabello Valboa, 308-309.

> Our very First Absolute Father created himself in the midst of the primeval dark mists. The divine body and the small place of abode were created in the midst of the primeval dark mists during the course of their evolution. The reflection of the divine wisdom, the divine "hear-it-all," the divine hands with the scepter of power were created by Ñamandui during the course of his evolution in the midst of the primeval dark mists. From the divine crown of the head, the flowers were like drops of dew. The primeval bird, the hummingbird, fluttered among the flowers. While our very first Father created, in the course of his evolution, his divine body, there existed in the midst of the primeval winds: even before having conceived his future earthly abode, even before having conceived his future firmament, even before the original idea, the hummingbird refreshed his mouth. It was the hummingbird who sustained Ñamandui with products from paradise.
>
> Even before creating, in the course of his evolution, his future paradise, our First Father Ñamandú did not see the darkness even though the sun did not yet exist. He was illuminated by the reflection of his own heart; his own wisdom contained within his own divinity served as a light. Our first Father Ñamandú existed in the midst of the primeval winds where he stopped to rest. The Owl produced the darkness until night was created. Before our very first Father Ñamandú created his future paradise during the course of his evolution, before having created the first earth, He existed in the midst of the primeval winds.[14]

In his notes, Cadogan points out that the hummingbird appears in Mbyá-Guaraní mythology as the personification of a god. In a manner similar to the K´iche´-Maya, the Mbyá-Guaraní have multiple gods involved in the creation as well as several names for god, such as: *Ñande Ru Papa Tenonde, Ñamanduí, Ñamandu Ru Ete, Ñande Ru Tenonde*.[15] Cadogan explained that according to his Mbyá sources, *Ñande Ru Papa Tenonde* is the creator of the God *Ñamandu Ru Ete* and it is this latter god

---

[14]Cadogan, 25-27.

[15]Ibid., 28. (During my Church mission in Paraguay, the missionaries used *Ñande Yara* when referring to Jesus Christ and this name was well known and accepted by our Guaraní speaking contacts in Paraguay.)

Evidences of Israelite and Christian Ethics 201

who is considered to be the *Creator of the World*. This distinction appears to be in accord with the *Book of Mormon* teaching that Jesus Christ is the creator of the world under the direction of his Father.

In the Mbyá creation myth, the author gives the impression that the Guaraní accepted the idea that there was a spiritual creation before the physical creation. The Genesis account alludes to this first creation but does not specify that it was a spiritual creation. The Genesis account states:

> These are the generations of the heavens and of the earth when they were created, in the day that the Lord God made the earth and the heavens.
> And every plant of the field before it was in the earth, and every herb of the field before it grew: for the Lord God had not caused it to rain upon the earth, and there was not a man to till the ground (Genesis 2:4-5).

The account in the Book of Moses in the Mormon Scripture, the *Pearl of Great Price* provides additional information about this spiritual creation:

> And now, behold, I say unto you, that these are the generations of the heaven and of the earth, when they were created, in the day that I, the Lord God, made the heaven and the earth,
> And every plant of the field before it was in the earth, and every herb of the field before it grew. For I, the Lord God, created all things, of which I have spoken, spiritually, before they were naturally upon the face of the earth. For I, the Lord God, had not caused it to rain upon the face of the earth. And I, the Lord God, had created all the children of men; and not yet a man to till the ground; for in heaven created I them; and there was not yet flesh upon the earth, neither in the water, neither in the air;
> But I, the Lord God, spake, and there went up a mist from the earth and watered the whole face of the ground (Moses 3:4-6).

In Cadogan's notes, he analyzes the meanings of the Guaraní words and provides additional information that he obtained from the patriarchs in the tribe. The Indians explained that when they spoke of the creation of man, it was to be understood that man was made in the same image of God or the same form that Ñande Ru assumed. They knew that in the beginning there was darkness and chaos in that there was unorganized matter. Even though there was not yet a sun, there was light which Cadogan described as the light that emanates from the heart of Ñande Ru. In today's vernacular, Christians have a similar concept—the "Light of Christ." The Mbyá indicated that the "scepter of power" was an emblem of the power of Ñande Ru. It would appear that they are referring to the power of the priesthood.[16] The Mbyá-Guaraní also believed that the First Earth, created by God, was destroyed by a flood.

OTHER ISRAELITE CUSTOMS

Menasseh Ben Israel, the Jewish rabbi in Holland, pointed out that numerous Israelite customs and laws had parallels among the native Americans. For example, he stated that "The Indians of Yucatán and Cozumel are circumcised. The Toltecs and the Mexicános also have the same ritual as testified by Roman y Gómara in the *General History of the Indies*. They also tear their clothing, like the Hebrews, when subjected to some ill-fated event or death"[17] He said that the Mexicános [Aztecs] and

---

[16]In his book *Mormon Doctrine*, Bruce R. McConkie wrote: "As pertaining to eternity, priesthood is the eternal power and authority of Deity by which all things exist; by which they are created, governed, and controlled; by which the universe and worlds without number have come rolling into existence; by which the great plan of creation, redemption, and exaltation operates throughout immensity. It is the power of God. As pertaining to man's existence on this earth, priesthood is the power and authority of God delegated to man on earth to act in all things for the salvation of men."

[17]Ben Israel, 28.

Evidences of Israelite and Christian Ethics

the Peruvians kept an eternal flame in the temples similar to the eternal flame mentioned in the Book of Leviticus. In Nicaragua, the Indians prohibited the women who had recently given birth from entering the temple until they had been purified. On the Island of Hispaniola, it was a sin for a man to have sex with his wife if she had recently given birth. In Peru, Guatemala and Mexico, the man married his sister-in-law if her husband was killed just as was mandated by Israelite law.[18]

EVIDENCE OF ISRAELITE TEACHINGS IN NORTH AMERICA

James Adair, who wrote *History of the American Indians*, published in 1775 in London, described a variety of Israelite customs which he found among the Indians of the southern United States. He took great exception to the idea that the Indians with whom he lived had come from East Asia thousands of years before. He went to considerable effort to study the habits, customs, traditions and religious ideas of these American Indians and to compare them with what was known about customs and traditions among the Mongolians in northeastern Asia. Adair wrote:

> Some have supposed the Americans to be descended from the Chinese; but neither their religion, laws, customs, etc., agree in the least with those of the Chinese: which simply proves they are not of that line. . . . From the most exact observations I could make in the long time I traded among the Indian Americans, I was forced to believe them lineally descended from the Israelites, either while they were a maritime power, or soon after the general captivity; the latter however is the most probable.[19]

---

[18] Ibid., 27-29
[19] Adair, 13-14.

Adair then proceeded to lay out his arguments or proofs that the Indians were Israelites in nearly 200 pages of narrative. The following is a brief synopsis of each of Adair's arguments:

Argument I. The Israelites were divided into Tribes and had chiefs over them. The Indians are divided into Tribes with their own chiefs. The Indians regard their tribal linage as carefully as the Israelites observed their tribal linage.

Argument II. The Israelites worshiped the God, *Jehovah*. The true and living god. The Indians worship *Yohewah*, which signifies Lord or Master. When the Indians go to war, they prepare and sanctify themselves, only by fasting and ablutions, that they may not defile their supposed holy ark (which they carry with them) and thereby incur the resentment of the Deity.

Argument III. The Indians think the Deity to be the immediate head of their state. They are intoxicated with their religious pride. They have contempt for the white people and refer to themselves as "the beloved people," because their ancestors, as they affirm, were under the immediate government of the Deity, who was present with them, in a very particular manner, and directed them by prophets; while the rest of the world were aliens and out-laws to the covenant. They see themselves as the "covenant people."

Argument IV. The Indians believe that there are both good spirits and bad spirits. They believe in God, so they firmly believe that there is a class of higher beings than men, and a future state and existence. Many Indians believe that they have "concomitant holy spirits" [guardian angels] who have forewarned them, as by intuition, of a dangerous ambuscade.

Argument V. The Indian language, and dialects, appear to have the very idiom and genius of the Hebrew. Their words and sentences are expressive, concise, emphatic, sonorous, and bold–and often, both in letters and significance, synonymous with the Hebrew language. There are many common words between the Indian language and Hebrew. There are Hebrew words that appear in many different Indian dialects throughout the Americas.[20] Skillful people conjecture them to be hieroglyphical characters, in imitation of the ancient Egyptian manner of writing their chronicles.

Argument VI. They divide the time after the manner of the Hebrews. They count the year by lunar months like the Israelites, who counted by moons. They also counted their time by weeks or by sevenths, which was an ancient custom, practiced by the Syrians, Egyptians, and most of the oriental nations.

Argument VII. In conformity to, or after the manner of the Jews, the Indian Americans have their prophets, high-priests and other religious order. As the Jews had a *sanctum sanctorum*, or most holy place, so have all the Indian nations; particularly, the Muskogee. Before the Indian *Archi-magus* officiates in making the supposed holy fire, for the yearly atonement of sin, the Sagan clothes him with a white ephod, which is a waistcoat without sleeves. When he enters on that solemn duty, a beloved attendant spreads a white-dressed buck-skin on the white seat, which stands close to the supposed holiest, and then puts some white

---

[20]In the October 1972 Monthly Bulletin of the Israelite Association of Venezuela, Isidoro Aizenberg wrote an article entitled "Jews in Pre-Columbia America?" He wrote out six Quechua words and their meaning and six Hebrew words which sounded like the Quechua words and their meaning: Quechua: chay (person)–Hebrew: chay (living being); Quechua: mayu (cold)–Hebrew: mayim (water); Quechua: hara (hillside)–Hebrew: har (mountain); Quechua: Khata (to cover)–Hebrew: Khasa (to cover); Quechua: zara (grain)–Hebrew: zarah (seed); Quechua: chana (era)–Hebrew: shana (year).

beads on it, that are given him by the people. The Indians are as strict observers of all their set forms, as the Israelites were of those they had from divine appointment.

Argument VIII. The Indian festivals, fasts and religious rites have also a great resemblance to those of the Hebrews. Like the Hebrew, the Indians celebrate the feast of the first harvest. The Indians still retained such sacred words as Aleluiah or Haleluyah and Shiloh. They drink bitter herbs to cleanse their bodies. After cleansing, they go into deep water to wash away their sins. After being sanctified they return to the festivals. During religious festivals, they abstain from having sexual relations or even touching anyone of the opposite sex.

Argument IX. The Indians offer a daily sacrifice such as did the ancient Israelites. The Indian women always throw a small piece of the fattest of the meat into the fire when they are eating, and frequently before they begin to eat. The Indians have among them the resemblance of the Jewish Sin-Offering, and Trespass-Offering. This is done whenever they make a kill of venison. They observe another religious custom of the Hebrews in making a Peace-Offering, or sacrifice of gratitude. Like the Israelites, they believe their sins are the true cause of all their evils, and that the divinity in their ark, will always bless the more religious party with the best success.

Argument X. Similar to the Hebrew custom of anointing themselves and bathing frequently, the Indians practiced purification and ablutions. The women always bathed apart from the men. The Indians also exclude the women from their temples by ancient custom, except six old beloved women, who are admitted to sing, dance, and rejoice, in the time of the annual expiation of sins, and then retire. The Indian priests and prophets are initiated by unction or anointing after going through a rigorous cleansing ceremony. Once the priest is purified, then bear's oil is poured upon his head.

Argument XI. The Indians have customs consonant to the Mosaic Laws of Uncleanness. They oblige their women in their *lunar retreats* [menstrual period], to build small huts, at as considerable a distance from their dwelling-houses as they imagine may be out of the enemies reach; where, during the space of that period, they are obliged to stay at the risk of their lives. When the time of the women's separation is ended, they always purify themselves in deep running water, return home, dress, and anoint themselves.

Argument XII. Like the Jews, the greatest part of the southern Indians abstain from eating things that are considered unclean such as eating birds of prey or animals that died by themselves. The Indians abstain from eating the blood of any animal as it contains the life, and the spirit of the beast.

Argument XIII. The Indian marriages, divorces, and punishments of adultery, still retain a strong likeness to the Jewish laws and customs in these points. Most tribes had severe punishment for adultery and the female is often killed.

Argument XIV. Many of the Indian punishments resemble those of the Jews. The Israelites cut off the hands and feet of murderers (2 Samuel 4:12), strangled false prophets and sometimes burned, stoned, or beheaded those malefactors who were condemned by the two courts of judgment. They also forgave all crimes at the annual atonement of sins; except murder, which is always punished with death.

Argument XV. The Israelites had Cities of Refuge, or places of safety, for those who killed a person unawares, and without design; to shelter them from the blood-thirsty relatives of the deceased. According to the same particular divine law of mercy, each of these Indian nations have either a house or town of refuge, which was an asylum to protect a man-slayer, or the unfortunate captive, if they can once enter into it.

Argument XVI. Before the Indians go to war, they have many preparatory ceremonies of purification and fasting, like what is recorded of the Israelites. As the ancient Israelites moved about with their Ark of the Covenant, the Indians also have their own Indian Ark which contains consecrated vessels. The Indian Ark was carried by the War Chief or a sanctified waiter and is never allowed to touch the ground.

Argument XVII. The Israelites were fond of wearing beads and other ornaments, even as early as the patriarchal age, and their fondness for trinkets increased to such a degree that it became criminal, and was sharply reprehended by the prophets. The Indians also are prone to wear fine jewelry, beads and other ornaments.

Argument XVIII. The Indian manner of curing their sick is very similar to that of the Jews. They always invoke Yo He Wah a considerable space of time before they apply any medicines. The Indians deem the curing of their sick or wounded a very religious duty; and it is chiefly performed by their supposed prophets, and magi because they believe they are inspired with a great portion of the divine fire.

Argument XIX. The Hebrews have at all times been very careful in the burial of their dead—to be deprived of it was considered as one of the greatest of evils. Throughout the Americas, the natives buried the dead with their riches and so make his corpse and the grave heirs of all. Furthermore they never disturb the graves of the dead. The grave proves an asylum, and a sure place of rest to the sleeping person, till at some certain time, according to their opinion, he rises again to inherit his favorite place. If they lose their people at war, they allocate some time to collect the bones of their relatives; which they call bone gathering, or "gathering the bones to their kindred," according to the Hebrew idiom.

Argument XX. The Jewish record states that the Jewish women mourn for the loss of their deceased husbands, and were reckoned vile if they married in the space of ten months after their death. In resemblance to that custom, all the Indian widows, by an established strict penal law, mourn for the loss of their deceased husbands. Every evening, and at the very dawn of day, for the first year of her widowhood, she is obliged through the fear of shame to lament her loss, in very intense audible strains. The husband cannot remarry for at least four months and often does not leave the house.

Argument XXI. In the Mosaic law, the surviving brother was to raise seed to a deceased brother who left a widow childless, to perpetuate his name and family, and inherit his goods and estate. The Indian custom is very similar. Although a widow is bound, by strict law, to mourn the death of her husband for the space of three years; yet, if she be known to lament her loss with a sincere heart, for the space of a year, and her circumstances of living are so strait as to need a change of her station, she is thereby exempted from the law of mourning. If the deceased husband's brother refuses to marry her, she has the liberty to tie up her hair, anoint and paint herself in the same manner as the Hebrew widow and is free to marry whom she pleases.

Argument XXII. When the Israelites gave names to their children or others, they chose such appellatives as suited best with their circumstances, and the times. This custom was as early as the Patriarchal age; for we find Abram was changed into Abraham; Sarai to Sarah, Jacob into Israel, etc. This custom is a standing rule with the Indians. They gave their children names, expressive of their tempers, outward appearances, and other various circumstances.[21]

Many of the customs described by Adair are very similar to customs, folklore and legends of native Americans throughout the Americas. The hundreds of similarities, which have changed somewhat over time and space as the natives scattered and as generations passed by, proclaim a common origin and a set of common religious beliefs. This does not preclude the arrival in the New World of other groups, but would tend to indicate that they either assimilated at least some of the core beliefs held by the majority, or that the newcomers did not make a significant impact upon the central belief system. Adair attributed all of the Indian customs and folklore to a connection with ancient Israel. In his narrative, he presents compelling evidence concerning each of his arguments.

---

[21]Giving a name was very important. Some Indian groups in Latin America changed the name as the child matured. Leon Cadogan revealed that among the Mbyá-Guaraní, the individual received a "new name." The gods proclaimed that "only when they are called by the names that we [the gods] give them will they find joy in their earthly abode and will cease to be rebellious. The priests of the Mbyá also refused to give this "new name" to a child conceived through adultery. Cadogan, 71, 78.

10

SACRIFICE, SACRAMENT, AND THE ATONEMENT

One of the religious rituals initiated by Adam's family was the sacrifice of animals to God. In Genesis, we read:

> And in process of time it came to pass, that Cain brought of the fruit of the ground an offering unto the Lord.
> And Abel, he brought of the firstling of his flock and of the fat thereof. And the Lord had respect unto Abel and to his offering:
> But unto Cain and to his offering he had not respect. And Cain was very wroth, and his countenance fell (Genesis 4:3-5).

The narrative in the Book of Moses clarifies that animal sacrifice was a symbol of Christ's crucifixion, thus Abel's sacrifice of the "firstlings of the flock" was accepted, while Cain's sacrifice of "fruit of the ground" was disrespectful and was rejected. Moses states:

> And he (God) gave unto them commandments, that they should worship the Lord their God, and should offer the firstlings of their flocks, for an offering unto the Lord. And Adam was obedient unto the commandments of the Lord.
>
> And after many days an angel of the Lord appeared unto Adam, saying: Why dost thou offer sacrifices unto the Lord? And Adam said unto him: I know not, save the Lord commanded me.
>
> And then the angel spake, saying: This thing is a similitude of the sacrifice of the Only Begotten of the Father, which is full of grace and truth. (Moses 5:5-7).

After Noah and his family disembarked from the ark, "Noah builded an altar unto the Lord; and took of every clean beast, and of every clean fowl, and offered burnt offerings on the altar" (Genesis 8:20). The meaning of sacrifice as a symbol of the future crucifixion of Jesus Christ was reinforced in the Lord's commandment to Abraham to sacrifice his son Isaac. In Genesis, we read:

> And Isaac spake unto Abraham his father, and said, My father: and he said, Here am I, my son. And he said, Behold the fire and the wood: but where is the lamb for a burnt offering?
>
> And Abraham said, My son, God will provide himself a lamb for a burnt offering: so they went both of them together.
>
> And they came to the place which God had told him of; and Abraham built an altar there, and laid the wood in order, and bound Isaac his son, and laid him on the altar upon the wood.
>
> And Abraham stretched forth his hand, and took the knife to slay his son.
>
> And the angel of the Lord called unto him out of heaven, and said, Abraham, Abraham: and he said, Here am I.
>
> And he said, Lay not thine hand upon the lad, neither do thou any thing unto him: for now I know that thou fearest God, seeing thou hast not withheld thy son, *thine only son from me* (emphasis added) (Genesis 22:7-12).

SACRIFICE, SACRAMENT, AND THE ATONEMENT 213

The Latter-day Saint Bible Dictionary notes that God gave Adam and Eve and all of his true followers, the "law of sacrifice" which included the offering of the best of their flocks. Whenever there have been true believers on the earth, with priesthood authority, sacrifices were offered. This continued until the death of Jesus Christ, which ended the shedding of blood as a gospel practice. Jesus replaced the sacrament of the shedding of blood with a sacrament of bread and wine, in remembrance of his broken body and blood.

In Old Testament times, it was important that the sacrificial animal be without "spot or blemish," in remembrance of the Savior, a perfect man. The blood was frequently collected in a vessel and was poured out or sprinkled over various objects or places to make an atonement or, in other words, to make amends for transgression. Under the Law of Moses, sacrifice became extremely ritualistic. During those periods when ancient Israel fell into apostasy, the ritual of sacrifice was greatly distorted. King David lamented in Psalms that the Israelites had begun to worship false gods and to sacrifice their children to these idols.

> Yea, they sacrificed their sons and their daughters unto devils,
> And shed innocent blood, even the blood of their sons and of their daughters, whom they sacrificed unto the idols of Canaan: and the land was polluted with blood (Psalms 106:37-38).

The prophet Ezekiel complained accusingly.

> Moreover thou hast taken thy sons and thy daughters, whom thou hast borne unto me, and these has thou sacrificed unto them to be devoured. Is this of thy whoredoms a small matter,
> That thou hast slain my children, and delivered them to cause them to pass through the fire for them [referring to the idols] (Ezekiel 16:20-21)?

Even then the ancient Israelites often perverted the ordinance of sacrifice and attempted to cover a multitude of sins by offering sacrifices. This general apostasy of these ancient Israelites and their refusal to keep the commandments of God, in spite of the warnings of many prophets, caused the Lord to withdraw his divine protection which eventually led to the overthrow of the Kingdom of Israel by the Assyrians and, subsequently, the Kingdom of Judah by the Babylonians.

The *Book of Mormon* reveals little concerning the offering of animal sacrifices. Nephi wrote that when he and his brothers returned from Jerusalem with the plates of brass, they all "rejoiced exceedingly, and did offer sacrifice and burnt offerings unto the Lord; and they gave thanks unto the God of Israel" (I Nephi 5:9). Several hundred years later (about 124 B.C.), Mosiah wrote that "They also took of the firstlings of their flocks, that they might offer sacrifice and burnt offerings according to the law of Moses" (Mosiah 2:3). About 74 B.C., Alma wrote the following concerning the termination of blood sacrifice.

> Therefore, it is expedient that there should be a great and last sacrifice, and then shall there be, or it is expedient there should be, a stop to the shedding of blood; then shall the law of Moses be fulfilled; yea, it shall be all fulfilled, every jot and tittle, and none shall have passed away.
>
> And behold, this is the whole meaning of the law, every whit pointing to that great and last sacrifice; and that great and last sacrifice will be the Son of God, yea, infinite and eternal.
>
> And thus he shall bring salvation to all those who shall believe on his name; this being the intent of this last sacrifice, to bring about the bowels of mercy, which overpowereth justice, and bringeth about means unto men that they may have faith unto repentance (Alma 34:13-15).

Sacrifice, Sacrament, and the Atonement   215

In his book, *Chavín and the Origins of Civilization*, Richard L. Burger described the construction of numerous buildings throughout the Chavín area, located in northwest Peru, in which were constructed unique firepits. These firepits were usually set in the middle of the room and were sunk into the floor. Two subfloor flues ensured the complete incineration of the contents, and the firepits were normally found filled with fine ash. Burger believed that the distinctive constructions were created to provide an environment for religious ceremonies, in which the burning of offerings was a critical element.

At unspecified intervals these ceremonial chambers were intentionally filled with dirt and debris and covered to permit the construction of a new series of similar buildings at a higher level. The excellent condition of most of these buried structures, and the care with which they had been covered, led art historians excavating the Chavín ruins to refer to this practice as "temple entombment." The presence of these public complexes in areas of dissimilar environment, economy, and culture caused the archaeologists to suspect several groups of people shared a common set of religious beliefs which entailed similar kinds of ritual activities.[1] As noted earlier, the Chavín civilization flourished in Peru from approximately 2500 B.C. to 400 B.C.

In the Old Temple at Chavín de Huántar, located on the east slope of the Andes, art historians discovered a special gallery which they named the Gallery of Offerings because of the large number of ceramic vessels which apparently had been filled with food. Burger noted that mixed in with the abundant food waste were 233 human bones. Like the animal remains, most were burnt and fragmented. Burger suggests that these bones were part of a cannibalistic ritual.[2]

---

[1] Burger, 45-46.
[2] Ibid., 140.

During the Formative Period (1500 to 400 B.C.) in Mesoamerica, human sacrifice appears to have been a common occurrence. In *Olmec World*, contributors Richard A. Diehl and Michael D. Coe wrote that "a more grisly aspect of Olmec ritual is presented by the bones of children sacrificed as ritual offerings.[3] In his essay in *Olmec World*, F. Kent Reilly, III, pointed out that bloodletting played a significant role in the cosmology of Olmec and Middle Formative ceremonies, as it continued to do in later Mesoamerican cultures. Reilly described blood as a magical substance opening the portal between the natural and supernatural worlds. Though scenes of bloodletting are not as numerous in Olmec art as they seem to be in the art of the classic Maya, strong evidence for bloodletting and human sacrifice exists in Middle Formative period art.[4] Like the Chavín, the Olmec civilization disappeared by approximately 400 B.C.

Archaeologists and art historians have discovered that sacrifice of animals and humans continued in the New World after the disappearance of the Chavín and the Olmec. In an article written by Drs. Steven Bourget and Margaret E. Newman entitled *A Toast to the Ancestors, Ritual Warfare and Sacrificial Blood in Moche Culture*, the writers described the importance of sacrifice to the Moche culture.

> A series of archaeological excavations conducted at sites such as Sipán, San José de Moro, Dos Cabezas, Huaca del Cao Viejo and Huaca de la Luna have made it increasingly apparent that ritualized warfare and sacrificial practices were central to Moche religion and ideology. Impressive murals depicting battle scenes and male prisoners were uncovered at Huaca del Cao Viejo, while evidence of human sacrifice has been found in funerary contexts, and also within the perimeters of all the Moche temples presently under investigation.[5]

---

[3] Abrams, 16.
[4] Ibid., 34.
[5] Steven Bourget, Margaret E. Newman, *A Toast to the Ancestors, Ritual Warfare and Sacrificial Blood in Moche Culture*, Published in Baessler–Archiv. Neue Folge, Band XLVI (1998) 85.

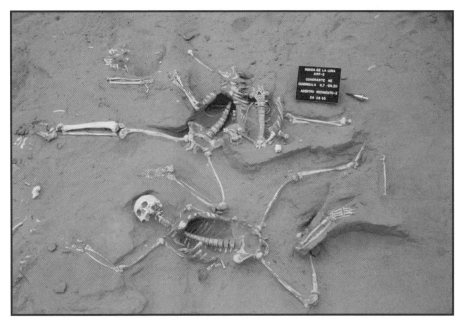

The careful positioning of the bodies indicates that these individuals were victims of human sacrifice at the Huaca de la Luna archaeological site near Trujillo, Peru. Dr. Steven Bourget, who is the main Art Historian working this site, graciously provided the picture.

Another example of human sacrifice discovered at the archaelogical site near Trujillo, Peru. More than 60 sacrificial victims have been discovered at the site. Dr. Steven Bourget, who is the main Art Historian working this site, graciously provided the picture.

At the Huaca de la Luna, Bourget discovered that 60 individuals were sacrificed during at least six rituals. Analyses of the bones indicate that all of the victims were males aged between 15 and 39 years. The bodies revealed numerous well healed fractures. Bourget suggested that the victims had probably been warriors who had recovered from combat injuries. His findings at Huaca de la Luna are supported by hundreds of ceramic vessels showing battle scenes of combat between individuals in which death was not the object, but capture for sacrificial purposes. It is evident that the prisoners in these "wars of capture" were sacrificed in the temples of their captors.

In the early 1990's, Walter Alva and Christopher Donnan discovered in several elaborate tombs, the remains of individuals who were dressed with the same kind of ceremonial garments that have been observed on various ceramic vessels as ceremonial garments worn by individuals involved in sacrificial ceremonies. Bourget noted that the sacrifice ceremony was enacted all over the Moche State, by high-ranking individuals wearing similar regalia and using the same paraphernalia during a period of at least three to four hundred years.[6]

During the wars between the Nephites and the Lamanites in the *Book of Mormon*, there is little mention of human sacrifice; however, during the final days of their intense wars, Mormon wrote that the Lamanites sacrificed many of the captured Nephite women and children. He stated:

> And they (the Lamanites) did also march forward against the city Teancum, and did drive the inhabitants forth out of her, and did take many prisoners both women and children, and did offer them up as sacrifices unto their idol gods.
>
> And it came to pass that in the three hundred and sixty and seventh year, the Nephites being angry because the Lamanites had sacrificed their women and their children, that they did go against the

---

[6]Ibid., 92.

SACRIFICE, SACRAMENT, AND THE ATONEMENT 219

Lamanites with exceedingly great anger, insomuch that they did beat again the Lamanites, and drive them out of their lands.

And when they had come the second time, the Nephites were driven and slaughtered with an exceedingly great slaughter; their women and their children were again sacrificed unto idols (Mormon 4:14-15, 21).

In a letter that Mormon wrote to Moroni, deploring the Nephite situation, Mormon again noted the inhumanity of the opposing sides towards each other. He considered the behavior of the Nephites to be as wicked as that of the Lamanites. Both fed human flesh to their opponents or consumed human flesh. Mormon wrote:

> And now I write somewhat concerning the suffering of this people. For according to the knowledge which I have received from Amoron, behold, the Lamanites have many prisoners, which they took from the tower of Sherrizah; and there were men, women, and children.
>
> And the husbands and fathers of those women and children they have slain; and they feed the women upon the flesh of their husbands, and the children upon the flesh of their fathers; and no water, save a little, do they give unto them.
>
> And notwithstanding this great abomination of the Lamanites, it doth not exceed that of our people in Moriantum. For behold, many of the daughters of the Lamanites have they taken prisoners; and after depriving them of that which was most dear and precious above all things, which is chastity and virtue–
>
> And after they had done this thing, they did murder them in a most cruel manner, torturing their bodies even unto death; and after they have done this, they devour their flesh like unto wild beasts, because of the hardness of their hearts; and they do it for a token of bravery (Moroni 9:8-10).

The time in the Moche culture when human sacrifice was most prevalent coincides with the final days of the Nephites when Mormon decried the sacrifice of humans. It would appear that the sacrifice of humans continued unabated in many areas throughout the Americas until the conquest by the Spaniards and the Portuguese when most of the natives were converted to Christianity. The Spanish and Portuguese chroniclers were shocked by the scenes of human sacrifice that they encountered when they arrived in the New World and particularly in Mexico where it was very prevalent among the Nahuatl speaking tribes (Aztecs, Tlaxcalan, Tezcocans, etc.), and also to a lesser extent among the Maya. In his first letter back to Charles V, Hernán Cortés wrote:

> Before the Indians begin any work, they burn in their mosques incense and sometimes they even sacrifice some of their own people, cutting off the tongues of some, and ears of others, or stabbing the bodies of others with knives. All of the blood that runs out of the victims is offered to their idols, by scattering the blood all around the mosque. Sometimes they throw the blood towards the heavens and they carry out many other kinds of ceremonies. The Indians have an even more horrible and abominable custom, which is worthy of severe punishment. When they petition their idols about something that they really want, they will take children or adults, and in front of their idols, they would cut open their breasts while the individual is still alive and pull out his or her heart and entrails and they burn the entrails and hearts in front of the idols and offer as a sacrifice the resulting smoke. Some of us have witnessed this sacrificial ceremony and everyone of us who have seen it state that it is the most crude and terrible thing that we have ever seen.[7]

Diego Durán noted that in the Biblical Book of Leviticus, the Hebrews sacrificed animals that were without blemish. He also observed that among the Aztecs, the same unblemished quality was required of human victims. On February 3, the natives celebrated the great feast in honor of the god Quetzalcoatl in the following fashion:

---

[7]Cortés, 66-67.

SACRIFICE, SACRAMENT, AND THE ATONEMENT

Forty days before this feast, the merchants bought a man who was flawless of hands and feet, without stain or blemish, nor one-eyed, nor with a cloud in his eye, nor lame, nor lacking one hand, nor crippled, nor with bleary eyes, nor drooling, nor lacking teeth. He was to have no blemish–none whatsoever–the sutures of his skull closed, nor signs of a cleft chin, nor pustules, nor scrofula–he was to be free of all imperfections.

This slave was bought so that, arrayed as a god, he might represent him during those forty days. Before he donned his costume, he was purified by being washed twice in the "divine water." After he had been washed and purified, he was dressed like the idol. . . This living man was bought to represent the god for forty days, and he was served and revered as such. . . .Then they went with him about the city as he sang and danced in order to be recognized as the impersonator of the god. After having honored the youth with incense and music, he was taken away and sacrificed at midnight by having his heart cut out. The heart was offered to the moon and having thrown it to the god in whose presence he had been slain, they let the dead body roll down the steps. The body was then gathered up by the merchants and taken home and cooked up into different dishes so that by dawn this food would be ready for the meal and banquet.[8]

During the New Fire Ceremony at the beginning of a new century, the Indians sacrificed hundreds of captives. The form of sacrifice and the use of the blood are reminiscent of ancient Israelite Passover scenes. Durán wrote the following:

This ceremony was celebrated with great solemnity and the priests of all the temples were present, led by the high priest dressed in his sacerdotal vestments and finery. There were offerings and incense, together with the sacrifice of many human beings on that hill who died as victims to the god of fire. . . This sacrifice began at midnight and lasted most of the next day. Triumphant and joyful, the priests were bathed in blood, and the vessels filled with human blood were sent to smear the lintels of the doors, posts, and altars of the temples, and to sprinkle the statues of the gods. This smearing with blood was always done when there was a sacrifice.[9]

---

[8]Durán, *Book of the Gods and Rites*, 131-133.
[9]Durán, *History of New Spain*, 446.

In the Andean region, the chroniclers noted that the Incas occasionally sacrificed humans, but they generally sacrificed animals. In this regard, Martín de Murúa mentioned the propensity of the Indians to resort to fasting and prayer to obtain favors or to learn about future events. He wrote:

> They seldom resorted to sacrificing humans, but maintained large herds of animals, generally llamas, to be sacrificed for special events, however, during the coronation of the Inca, children were sacrificed to ensure a successful reign of the Inca. The Incas held to the custom of sacrificing animals to their gods and *huacas*. In this regard they maintained a special herd of white llamas that they used for special sacrifices to the sun. Those animals selected were reportedly without spot or blemish. The Incas never used wild animals as a sacrifice, but only animals that they themselves had raised. The animal always had to be a male animal as they never used the female animals for sacrifice. They also sacrificed precious objects which were generally made of gold or silver.[10]

Juan de Betanzos wrote about the preparations that the Lord Inca Pachacuti Inca Yupanqui, king over the Inca nation, made dedicating the temple to the sun:

> Inca Yupanqui ordered the lords of Cuzco to have ready within ten days provisions of maize, sheep (llamas) and lambs along with fine garments and a certain number of boys and girls, all of which was for making a sacrifice to the sun. When everything was gathered, Inca Yupanqui ordered that a big fire be built to which, after having the heads cut off of the sheep and lambs, he ordered them thrown (into the fire) along with the garments and maize as a sacrifice to the sun. The boys and girls whom they had brought together were well dressed and adorned. He ordered them to be buried alive in that temple which was especially made where the statue of the sun was. With the blood which had been taken from the lambs and sheep, he ordered certain lines drawn on the walls of this temple. All of this signified a way of blessing and consecrating this temple.

---

[10]Murua, 420-422

SACRIFICE, SACRAMENT, AND THE ATONEMENT 223

During the sacrifice, Inca Yupanqui and his friends went barefoot and acted with great reverence for this temple of the sun. With the same blood, Inca Yupanqui also drew certain lines on the face of the man who was designated as caretaker of this temple, and he did the same to those three lords, his friends, and to the *mamaconas* or nuns in the service of the sun.[11]

The sacrifice of animals and at times humans appears to have been prevalent throughout the Americas for thousands of years. Although the rituals were more brutal in many areas especially in Mexico, many of the chroniclers recognized elements of ancient Israelite customs in the sacrificial rituals. Other rituals reminded them of Christian ceremonies and particularly the sacrament or the "last supper."

SACRAMENT CEREMONY

Durán wrote that the most solemn and celebrated feast in all Mexico was that for the god Huitzilopochtli. Durán observed that the ceremony and rites seemed to be a mixture of diverse ceremonies. Parts of the ritual resembled Christian rites; other parts resembled elements found in the Old Testament and still other rites appeared to Durán to be diabolical and an invention of the Indians. In the ritual, Huitzilopochtli was represented by a wooden statue carved in the image of a man seated upon a wooden bench in the fashion of a litter. The bench was painted blue, indicating to the Indians that Huitzilopochtli's abode was in the heavens. On his head he wore a rich headdress in the shape of a bird's beak—symbolic of a hummingbird.

Durán described the habits of the hummingbird in which he saw an element of Christian "rebirth." When winter approaches, the hummingbird seeks out a crack in a leafy tree. The bird perches on a twig next to that crack, pushes its beak into the

---

[11]Betanzos, 46.

crack as far as possible, and stays there six months of the year nourishing itself with the essence of the tree. It appears to be dead, but at the advent of spring, when the tree gives forth new leaves, the little bird, with the aid of the tree's life, is reborn. Consequently, the Indians state that the hummingbird dies and is reborn.[12]

In the temple of Huitzilopochtli, there were always young maidens who were required to carry out religious ceremonies and to keep the temple clean. As the time arrived for the celebration of Huitzilopochtli, a large replica of the statue was made of amaranth-seed dough. At the same time, the maidens made large bone-shaped objects also of dough. These "bones" and the "dough idol" were then carried to the top of the pyramid honoring Huitzilopochtli and were placed before the idol of Huitzilopochtli. As the ceremony progressed and the sacrifice of humans began, the blood of the sacrificial victims was sprinkled on both the idol, the dough replica of the idol, and the "bones" that represented the flesh and bones of the god. All of the dough pieces which the Indians called *tzoalli* were then blessed and anointed with human blood, obtained through this great sacrifice of human beings.

On the final day of the feast, it was a solemn rule in all the land that no one, not even small children, could eat or drink anything, except to eat a morsel of *tzoalli* with honey. The *tzoalli* was to be eaten at dawn of that day, but the people could not eat any other thing until the ceremony was finished in the late afternoon.

At the beginning of the ceremonies on the final day, the dough idol and the dough bones were all broken into small pieces which represented the flesh and the bones of their god, who they believed was the creator of the world. Beginning with the elders, everyone—men, women, and children—received

---

[12]Durán, *Rites*, 73.

communion with a piece of dough. Durán noted that all received it with such reverence, awe, and joy, that it was truly a thing of wonder. The people claimed that they had eaten the flesh and the bones of their god. Those who had sick ones at home begged for a piece and carried it away with reverence and veneration.

Durán noted that this ceremony always occurred on 10 April, close to the Christian celebration of Easter. He viewed this as a diabolical scheme of the devil to deceive the Indians by having them imitate a ceremony of the Catholic religion. Although Durán attributed to Satan the instigation of an imitation sacrament, he was equally convinced that an early apostle must have come into the New World to preach Christianity to the natives.

Fray Joseph de Acosta, who wrote about both Peru and Mexico, also mentioned this same sacrament of eating the flesh and bones of Huitzilopochtli, which he claimed were shared by all with great reverence.[13]

The *Book of Mormon* teaches that when Jesus Christ appeared in the Americas and established his church there, he also instituted the ordinance of the sacrament. Nephi recorded:

> And it came to pass that Jesus commanded his disciples that they should bring forth some bread and wine unto him.
> And while they were gone for bread and wine, he commanded the multitude that they should sit themselves down upon the earth.
> And when the disciples had come with bread and wine, he took of the bread and brake and blessed it; and he gave unto the disciples and commanded that they should eat.
> And when they had eaten and were filled, he commanded that they should give unto the multitude.
> And when the multitude had eaten and were filled, he said unto the disciples: Behold there shall one be ordained among you, and to him will I give power that he shall break bread and bless it and give it unto the people of my church, unto all those who shall believe and be baptized in my name.

---

[13] Acosta, 258.

And this shall ye always observe to do, even as I have done, even as I have broken bread and blessed it and given it unto you.

And this shall ye do in remembrance of my body, which I have shown unto you. And it shall be a testimony unto the Father that ye do always remember me. And if ye do always remember me ye shall have my Spirit to be with you.

And it came to pass that when he said these words, he commanded his disciples that they should take of the wine of the cup and drink of it, and that they should also give unto the multitude that they might drink of it.

And it came to pass that they did so, and did drink of it and were filled; and they gave unto the multitude, and they did drink, and they were filled (3 Nephi 18:1-9).

Over the centuries before the arrival of the Spaniards, the Indians had distorted the sacred ordinance of the sacrament. Durán's description of the ceremony honoring Huitzilopochtli, revered as their creator of the world, is one of the best examples, recorded by New World writers in which the remnants of a Christian ordinance apparently had been retained for hundreds of years.

THE ATONEMENT

In addition to the sacrifice and the ordinance of the sacrament in remembrance of Jesus Christ, both ancient and modern scriptures teach about the atonement. The Bible dictionary in the Latter-day Saint 1979 publication of the King James version of the Bible states:

> From the time of Adam to the death of Jesus Christ, true believers were instructed to offer animal sacrifices to the Lord. These sacrifices were symbolic of the forthcoming death of Jesus Christ, and were done by faith in him. Jesus Christ as the Only Begotten Son of God and the only sinless person to live on this earth, was the only one capable of making an atonement for mankind. By his selection

SACRIFICE, SACRAMENT, AND THE ATONEMENT 227

and foreordination in the Grand Council before the world was formed, his divine Sonship, his sinless life, the shedding of his blood in the garden of Gethsemane, his death on the cross and subsequent bodily resurrection from the grave, he made a perfect atonement for all mankind. All are covered unconditionally as pertaining to the fall of Adam. Hence, all shall rise from the dead with immortal bodies, because of Jesus Christ's atonement. "For as in Adam all die, even so in Christ shall all be made alive" (I Corinthians 15:22).[14]

Moses taught the Israelites the doctrine of the atonement and the importance of the blood of Christ that would eventually be shed for them. In Leviticus it states:

> And whatsoever man there be of the house of Israel, or of the strangers that sojourn among you, that eatest any manner of blood; I will even set my face against that soul that eatest blood, and will cut him off from among his people.
> For the life of the flesh is in the blood: and I have given it to you upon the altar to make an atonement for your souls: for it is the blood that maketh an atonement for the soul (Leviticus 17:11-12).

In John's General Epistle, he wrote "But if we walk in the light, as he is in the light, we have fellowship one with another, and the *blood of Jesus Christ* (emphasis added) his son cleanseth us from all sin" (1 John 1:7). Both the Old and the New Testaments are replete with references to the atonement of Jesus Christ and the manner in which he sanctified his true believers. Paul wrote to the Hebrews the following: "Wherefore Jesus also, that he might *sanctify the people with his own blood* (emphasis added), suffered without the gate" (Hebrews 13:12).

On the American continent, the *Book of Mormon* prophets wrote concerning the atonement and the Savior's sanctifying act. Nephi wrote:

---

[14]Bible Dictionary definition as noted in the King James version of the Bible, published by The Church of Jesus Christ of Latter-day Saints, 1979.

> Behold he offereth himself a sacrifice for sin, to answer the ends of the law, unto all those who have a broken heart and a contrite spirit; and unto none else can the ends of the law be answered.
>
> Wherefore, how great the importance to make these things known unto the inhabitants of the earth, that they may know that there is no flesh that can dwell in the presence of God, save it be through the merits, and mercy, and grace of the Holy Messiah, who layeth down his life according to the flesh, and taketh it again by the power of the Spirit, that he may bring to pass the resurrection of the dead, being the first that should rise.
>
> Wherefore, he is the first fruits unto God, inasmuch as he shall make intercession for all the children of men; and they that believe in him shall be saved (2 Nephi 2:7-9).

About 30 B.C., Helaman reminded the Nephites of this important mission of Jesus Christ when he wrote:

> O remember, remember, my sons, the words which King Benjamin spake unto his people; yea, remember that there is no other way nor means whereby man can be saved, only through the atoning blood of Jesus Christ, who shall come; yea, remember that he cometh to redeem the world (Helaman 5:9).

In the *Book of Mormon* account of Christ's appearance in the New World, he invited all to come and touch and see that he was resurrected:

> Arise and come forth unto me, that ye may thrust your hands into my side, and also that ye may feel the prints of the nails in my hands and in my feet, that ye may know that I am the God of Israel, and the God of the whole earth, and have been slain for the sins of the world (3 Nephi 11:14).

In the final windup scenes before sealing up the plates, Moroni urged all mankind to remember the sacrifice of Jesus Christ:

> Yea, come unto Christ, and be perfected in him, and deny yourselves of all ungodliness; and if ye shall deny yourselves of all ungodliness, and love God with all your might, mind and strength, then is his grace sufficient for you, that by his grace ye may be perfect in Christ; and if by the power of God ye are perfect in Christ, ye can in nowise deny the power of God.
>
> And again, if ye by the grace of God are perfect in Christ, and deny not his power, then are ye sanctified in Christ by the grace of God, through the shedding of the blood of Christ, which is in the covenant of the Father unto the remission of your sins, that ye become holy, without spot (Moroni 10:32-33).

In addition to human sacrifice, one of the rites which mystified the early conquistadores was the ritual of drawing one's own blood in an apparent act of purification. Concerning this self-sanctification, Landa wrote:

> They offered sacrifices of their own blood, sometimes cutting themselves around in pieces and they left them in this way as a sign. Other times they pierced their cheeks, at others their lower lips, or cutting the ears. . . .Others slit the superfluous part of the virile member, leaving it as they did their ears, on account of which the general historian of the Indies was deceived saying that they practiced circumcision. They anointed the idol with the blood which flowed from all these parts; and he who did this the most was considered as the bravest; and their sons from the earliest age began to practice it, and it is a horrible thing to see how inclined they were to this ceremony. The women did not practice this shedding of blood, though they were great devotees, but from all things which they could obtain whether they were birds of the sky, or beasts of the land, or fish of the sea, they always smeared the faces of the idols with their blood.[15]

Sahagún also described the act of drawing one's own blood or piercing one's body as part of repentance and penitence. After the Indian had confessed his sins before the priest, the priest would instruct the penitent individual to perform a suitable act.

---

[15]Landa,113-114.

Frequently, that would be to pierce his tongue or his ears or both with a thorn. He was told that this was done as a sign of true repentance of his evil deeds.[16] Throughout Sahagún's book, he described the various kinds of human sacrifice. On nearly every occasion, he made reference to this ceremony of drawing one's own blood as a sign of penitence or as a request to the gods for the bestowal of a blessing.

In the book *The Olmec World*, F. Kent Reilly, III, observed that bloodletting played a significant role in the cosmology of Olmec and Middle Formative ceremonies, as it continued to do in later Mesoamerican cultures. He pointed out that although the art historians did not find as many scenes of bloodletting in the Olmec art as in the art of the Classical Maya, there exists evidence in the form of artifacts such as instruments shaped like ice picks and stingray spines that art historians believe were used for bloodletting rituals during the Olmec era (1500 B.C.-400 B.C.).[17]

Durán also recorded that the Aztec leaders went through a process of bloodletting. When the Aztec king Axayacatl returned from a victory over a neighboring state, he went directly to the temple of Huitzilopochtli to give thanks. In front of the god idol, Axayacatl drew blood from his own ears, calves, and shinbones. He also sacrificed many quail, which he decapitated with his own hands.[18]

If the Incas or other Andean Indians resorted to the ritual of drawing blood from their own bodies, it was not noted by the chroniclers. Human sacrifice was sparse among them and did not reach the magnitude practiced in Mesoamerica. The Andeans were more prone to sacrifice animals.

In the book, *Code of Kings*, Linda Schele and Peter Mathews make several references to the bloodletting ceremony among the Maya Indians. In their chapter on Copan; The Great Plaza of

---

[16] Sahagún, 32.
[17] Abrams, 34.
[18] Durán, 270.

Waxaklahun-Ubah-K'awil, located in Honduras near the Guatemalan border, these two noted art historians described many of the altars as well as the Stela or pillars they found at the ruins. In their description of Stela H, they narrate:

> This magnificent stela depicts Waxaklahun-Ubah-K'awil in the role of the Maise God as he danced at Creation. In the Classic-period story of Creation, the Maize Gods are the central characters in the drama that explains the processes of death and rebirth through confrontation with the Lords of Death in Xibalba. Classic-period imagery shows the Maize Gods being reborn from a snake, growing from infancy to adulthood, and being dressed in full regalia by beautiful young women. Once fully dressed, the Maize Gods danced in the company of dwarves and began the activities that led to the Fourth Creation. Waxaklahun-Ubah-K'awil reenacts this dance on Stela H.
>
> The imagery along the sides, between his body and the feathers of his backrack, reiterate the themes of resurrection and fertility. Twisted cords of the cosmic umbilicus rise from the inside of a hollow glyph reading *sak*, "white," because the umbilicus carries the kind of soul the Maya called *sak nik*, "white flower." The white signs hold *wayob*, "animal-spirit companions," conjured from the Otherworld. Square-nosed serpents with glyphs for "white flower" attached to their noses terminate the twisted cords. These "white flower" signs refer both to the flowers that grow on the branches of the World Tree and to the human soul, because we humans are like the flowers of this tree. Clinging to the twisted cords like monkeys are four Maize Gods, one of whom carries a bloodletter in personified form. Personal bloodletting was the ritual sacred to the Maize Gods and to the process of rebirth.[19]

Schele and Mathews' description ties the bloodletting ceremony to creation, rebirth, and resurrection, all of which are tied to the role of Jesus Christ and his atonement.

---

[19] Schele, 154-155.

11

Ten Commandments and Other Israelite Teachings

The most important material object that Lehi took with him in his journey to the "promised land," according to the *Book of Mormon* narrative, was the plates of brass. Nephi wrote that the plates contained all of the Old Testament history up until the time that Lehi and his family left Jerusalem. Furthermore, Nephi said it contained God's commandments to the ancient Israelites, particularly the rules on how they were to conduct their lives. When the Nephites and the Lamanites separated, the Nephites took the plates of brass with them and adopted the text as their code of conduct. In addition, numerous prophets who lived among the Nephites claimed to have received revelations from God and they taught the people God's will for them. These prophets and teachers wrote that the Nephites lived the same Ten Commandments or the Decalogue that had been given to Moses on Mt. Sinai (Exodus 20:2-17).

The Nephite prophet Abinadi gave great emphasis to the importance of the Ten Commandments during his discourse to wicked King Noah and his priests (Mosiah 13). The Ten Commandments appeared to have survived hundreds of years among the native Americans as the Spanish and Portuguese discovered elements of the Ten Commandments throughout the New World. The Spaniards and Portuguese also discovered other rules or customs that appeared to be very similar to teachings contained in the *Bible* and the *Book of Mormon.*

Over the years, prophets and teachers labored within the Nephite community to teach the gospel. They built many temples and synagogues for their religious and spiritual studies. Jarom, a grandson of Jacob, wrote:

> Wherefore, the prophets, and the priests, and the teachers, did labor diligently, exhorting with all long-suffering the people to diligence; teaching the law of Moses, and the intent for which it was given; persuading them to look forward unto the Messiah, and believe in him to come as though he already was. And after this manner did they teach them (Jarom 1:11).

Book of Mormon writers frequently spoke of the priesthood, and men among both the Jaredites and the Nephites were ordained to offices in the priesthood. Shortly after Lehi's family arrived in the New World, Nephi ordained his brothers, Jacob and Joseph, priests and teachers over the Nephites. When the chroniclers studied the native societies, they invariably discovered that these kingdoms and tribes had a fairly complicated religious structure with priests, shamans, and religious healers. A better understanding of how the priesthood functioned during *Book of Mormon* times will provide insights on how similar beliefs about priesthood were evident in the widely-scattered Indian tribes at the time of the arrival of the Europeans.

In the Book of Moses, the Lord told Moses that the priesthood was given to Adam and to all of his worthy descendants down to the time of Moses. Joseph Smith taught that in the early days this priesthood was called, *the Holy Priesthood after the Order of the Son of God*, but, to avoid the too frequent use of the name of Deity, the name was changed to the Melchizedek Priesthood after an Old Testament prophet. Melchizedek was the King of Salem and a High Priest from whom Abraham received his Priesthood. When the Lord discovered that the Israelites, led out of Egypt by Moses, were not yet ready to function under the Melchizedek Priesthood, they were given a lesser priesthood, the Aaronic or Levitical Priesthood which continued among the Israelites until the coming of Jesus Christ. Moses retained the Melchizedek priesthood as did a few other prophets such as Joshua, Samuel, Isaiah, Jeremiah, and Ezekiel, who attempted to teach and guide Israel.

Jesus Christ reinstated the full order of the Melchizedek Priesthood and ordained his twelve apostles to this higher priesthood. Joseph Smith taught that all the prophets throughout history had the Melchizedek Priesthood and were called and ordained by God himself or one of his Heavenly messengers. Among that number was Lehi, who carried that priesthood to the New World. Occasionally groups of Nephites fell into wickedness and lost the power of the priesthood.

In the Book of Mosiah, there is an account of a Nephite, King Noah, who surrounded himself with men claiming to be priests. Alma recorded an account of their decadent reign in the following language:

> And now it came to pass that Zeniff conferred the kingdom upon Noah, one of his sons; therefore Noah began to reign in his stead; and he did not walk in the ways of his father.
> For behold, he did not keep the commandments of God, but he did walk after the desires of his own heart. And he had many wives

and concubines. And he did cause his people to commit sin, and do that which was abominable in the sight of the Lord. Yea, and they did commit whoredoms and all manner of wickedness.

And he laid a tax of one fifth part of all they possessed, a fifth part of their gold and of their silver, and a fifth part of their ziff, and of their copper, and of their brass and their iron; and a fifth part of their fatlings; and also a fifth part of all their grain.

And all this did he take to support himself, and his wives and his concubines; and also his priests, and their wives and their concubines; thus he had changed the affairs of the kingdom.

For he put down all the priests that had been consecrated by his father, and consecrated new ones in their stead, such as were lifted up in the pride of their hearts.

Yea, and thus they were supported in their laziness, and in their idolatry, and in their whoredoms, by the taxes which king Noah had put upon his people; thus did the people labor exceedingly to support iniquity.

Yea, and they also became idolatrous, because they were deceived by the vain and flattering words of the king and priests; for they did speak flattering things unto them (Mosiah 11:1-2, 4-7).

The Lord sent the prophet Abinadi to straighten out King Noah and his priests. Abinadi gave a powerful discourse on the gospel of Jesus Christ and the atonement of Christ. A priest named Alma was the only one among all of Noah's priests who believed Abinadi. King Noah and his priests subsequently burned Abinadi to death. In the meantime, Alma went quietly among the people testifying of the truthfulness of Abinadi's words and he converted many to the gospel. Alma and these new converts fled the area controlled by Noah and eventually arrived in a land called Zarahemla where they were kindly received by other Nephites led by a king called Mosiah. King Mosiah appointed Alma as the high priest over all the Church.

Before Alma died, he conferred the priesthood upon his son, Alma, who explained the authority, function and power of the Melchizedek Priesthood in the following verses:

And again, my brethren, I would cite your minds forward to the time when the Lord God gave these commandments unto his children; and I would that ye should remember that the Lord God ordained priests, after his holy order, which was after the order of his Son, to teach these things unto the people.

Now, as I said concerning the holy order, of this high priesthood, there were many who were ordained and became high priests of God; and it was on account of their exceeding faith and repentance, and their righteousness before God, they choosing to repent and work righteousness rather than to perish;

Therefore they were called after this holy order, and were sanctified and their garments were washed white through the blood of the Lamb.

Now they, after being sanctified by the Holy Ghost, having their garments made white, being pure and spotless before God, could not look upon sin save it were with abhorrence; and there were many, exceedingly great many, who were made pure and entered into the rest of the Lord their God.

And now, my brethren, I would that ye should humble yourselves before God, and bring forth fruit meet for repentance, that ye may also enter into that rest.

Yea, humble yourselves even as the people in the days of Melchizedek, who was also a high priest after this same order which I have spoken, who also took upon him the high priesthood forever.

And it was this same Melchizedek to whom Abraham paid tithes of one-tenth part of all he possessed.

Now, there were many before him, and also there were many afterwards, but none were greater; therefore, of him they have more particularly made mention (Alma 13:1-3, 6-15, 19).

Alma also indicated that at one time, he was not only the high priest over all the church, but he also held the position of chief judge over the Nephites. When the people became extremely wicked, Alma gave up his position as chief judge and dedicated his full time to preaching. He recorded that he could do the Nephites more good by peaching the gospel than he could in his position as chief judge. From this affirmation, it became apparent that the office of high priest was a position of influence and great power among the people.

These early Americans had great respect for their priests. The importance of the calling of a priest was reinforced in the *Book of Mormon* account when the resurrected Jesus Christ visited the Americas. Shortly after the Savior arrived and began to teach them and to establish his Church, he called twelve Disciples. Nephi recorded this event as follows:

> And it came to pass that he [Jesus] spake unto Nephi (for Nephi was among the multitude) [this Nephi was a descendant of the son of Lehi] and he commanded him that he should come forth.
> And the Lord said unto him: I give unto you power that ye shall baptize this people when I am again ascended into heaven.
> And again the Lord called others, and said unto them likewise; and he gave unto them power to baptize. And he said unto them: On this wise shall ye baptize; and there shall be no disputations among you (3 Nephi 11:18, 21-22).
> And it came to pass that when Jesus had spoken these words unto Nephi, and to those who had been called, (now the number of them who had been called, and received power and authority to baptize was twelve) and behold, he stretched forth his hand unto the multitude, and cried unto them, saying: Blessed are ye if ye shall give heed unto the words of these twelve whom I have chosen from among you to minister unto you, and to be your servants; and unto them I have given power that they may baptize you with water; and after that ye are baptized with water, behold, I will baptize you with fire and with the Holy Ghost; therefore blessed are ye if ye shall believe in me and be baptized, after that ye have seen me and know that I am (3 Nephi 12:1).

These twelve disciples, who were given the same authority as the twelve apostles in Jerusalem, called and ordained other high priests. The priesthood continued in force in the New World for several hundred more years until both the Nephites and the Lamanites became so wicked and the church so perverted that God withdrew his priesthood power and authority. Mormon wrote about 322 A.D. the following:

But wickedness did prevail upon the face of the whole land, insomuch that the Lord did take away his beloved disciples, and the work of miracles and of healing did cease because of the iniquity of the people.

And there were no gifts from the Lord, and the Holy Ghost did not come upon any, because of their wickedness and unbelief.

And it came to pass that there were sorceries, and witchcrafts, and magics; and the power of the evil one was wrought upon all the face of the land, even unto the fulfilling of all the words of Abinadi, and also Samuel the Lamanite (Mormon1:13-14, 19).

Even though God had withheld the priesthood from the survivors of the Nephites and the Lamanites, these two groups recognized that a priestly function was still very important and the numerous tribes attempted to retain the office of priest within the tribe.

CHRONICLE ACCOUNTS OF PRIESTHOOD ORDERS AMONG THE INDIANS

Some of the early chroniclers attempted to gain insights to the New World Priesthood orders and how they functioned. They noticed some similarities with New Testament accounts. One of the leading students of the New World priesthood order was the Catholic priest, Fray Bernardino de Sahagún.[1]

Sahagún provided considerable information about the priesthood organization among the Aztecs. He observed how the Aztec priesthood organization appeared similar to many of the priesthood organizations and functions in the Bible. He described how the priests were trained and prepared within the Aztec priesthood. He noted that the priest who was perfect in the performance of all the customs, exercises and learning as observed by the ministers of the idols, was elected highest pontiff. He had to be virtuous, humble and peace-loving, considerate and discreet.

---

[1] Sahagún, 8.

He had to be zealous in observing the rules, but at the same time, a friend of all, merciful, devout, and in fear of God. He had to pass through several degrees within their priesthood.

The priest started out as a Tlamacazto, which Sahagún believed corresponded to acolyte; then he became Tlamacazqui, which office Sahagún interpreted as a deacon. The third degree was Tlanamacac, that is to say, priest. From among the priests the best qualified were selected as the high pontiffs, who were called Quetzalcoatl, which in this usage meant a successor of Quetzalcoatl. Sahagún wrote that the life of these ministers of the idols was hard:

> ... and in the election no attention was paid to lineage, but rather to the customs, exercises, learning and good (clean) living; (meaning) whether they led this life unalterably (steadfastly); kept all the rules, observed by the priests of the idols. He who was virtuous, humble and peace-loving, considerate and discreet (judicious), not light, but serious and rigorous, zealous in observing the rules; loving compassionate, tender-hearted (merciful), and a friend of all, devout and in fear of god, was the one elected to this highest honor.[2]

A similar standard was imposed on bishops in the New Testament:

> This is a true saying, If a man desires the office of a bishop, he desireth a good work. A bishop then must be blameless, the husband of one wife, vigilant, sober, of good behavior, given to hospitality, apt to teach; Not given to wine, no striker, not greedy of filthy lucre; but patient, not a brawler, not covetous; One that ruleth well his own house, having his children in subjection with all gravity; (For if a man know not how to rule his own house, how shall he take care of the church of God?) Not a novice, lest being lifted up with pride, he fall into the condemnation of the devil. Moreover he must have a good report of them which are without, lest he fall into reproach and the snare of the Devil (I Timothy 3:1-7).

---

[2]Ibid., 202-203.

In Yucatán, Diego de Landa mentioned that the Maya were as attentive to the matters of religion as to those of government, and they had priests and a high priest. The high priest was greatly respected by the Mayas who brought the high priest offerings. One of the high priest's sons or one of his nearest relatives succeeded him in his office.

The high priest taught the other priests in the subject of religion and science. He taught them about the Maya religious festivals and ceremonies, the administration of the sacraments, their prophecies and their "methods of divination." For science, the high priest taught the lesser priests how to compute the years, months and days. He taught them how to cure disease and how to read and write in their hieroglyphic characters. The high priest provided priests for the towns when they were needed.[3] In a footnote to Landa's book, Alfred M. Tozzer observed that, in many cases, the priestly and the political functions had been combined in such a manner that it was difficult, if not impossible, to differentiate them.

Concerning the organization of the priesthood among the Incas, Cieza de León noted that the high priest, called a Villacumu, meaning sorcerer who speaks, held his position for life.[4] The high priest was married and so revered that he competed in authority with the Lord Inca. He had power over all the shrines and temples, and appointed and removed priests. The priests were of noble lineage and powerful families, and this dignity was never conferred on men of low station, however great their merits. Cieza de León also mentioned that the priests were greatly venerated, and even the Inca nobility obeyed them in whatsoever things they ordered.

---

[3]Landa, 27-28.
[4]In a footnote in the book *The Incas*, Von Hagen noted that this exalted high priest was related by blood to the Lord Inca and held this post for life. 183, n2.

Every tribe or nation had some form of a priesthood organization and priestly function. These native priests were frequently called *shamans* or *Mohanes*. Their function was often described by the Spaniards, in a more mundane fashion, as witchdoctors, medicine men (curanderos), or simply priests.

CONFESSION AND BAPTISM

Diego de Landa reported that the Maya went to their priests and confessed their sins and that they also had an elaborate baptismal ceremony. Landa recorded:

> Baptism is not found in any part of the Indies except in Yucatán, where it exists under the Mayan term or name *caput sihil* which means "to be born anew or again." We have not been able to find its origin, more than that it is a custom that has always existed, and for which they had so much devotion that no one failed to receive it; and so much reverence for the rite that those who had sins, if they were capable of knowing they had committed them, were obligated to make a special confession of them to the priest, in order to receive baptism, and they had such great faith in it that they never repeated it in any way. Landa said that the Mayas considered baptism to be a disposition towards being good within their way of living and not to be injured in the temporal affairs by the evil spirits, and by this means and by a well ordered life to attain glory, which they hoped for, in which they were to enjoy eating and drinking.[5]

Landa commented on how crafty the devil was to teach the Indians a form of baptism which resembled the Christian ordinance.

Sahagún also described what he termed a baptismal rite. In his Book II, he wrote:

> The lords and chieftains, the nobles, and the wealthy merchants, were very careful in watching the sign, day and hour, under which a

---

[5]Landa, 102.

Ten Commandments and Other Teachings 243

son or daughter was born to them, and they immediately went to inform the judicial astrologers of it, and to ask them about the good or bad fortune the new-born babe might have. If the sign was propitious, they had the child baptized at once, and if it was adverse, they selected the most prosperous house of that sign where to baptize it. To this baptismal feast, they invited their relatives and friends to be present at the christening, and gave them to eat and drink, and also asked all the children of the district where they lived. Baptism took place at sunrise in the house of the parents, and was performed by the midwife pronouncing many prayers and making a number of ceremonies over the child.[6]

Sahagún also described the formal Aztec ceremony of personal confession of sin. In many respects the ceremony as narrated by Sahagún was similar to the Christian confession in that the sinner appeared before a duly ordained priest who maintained the confession in the strictest of confidence. The priest explained that he was the stand-in representative of the God Almighty called Yoallichccatlostees-Tezcatlipoca and the confessor should understand that he was confessing not to the man, but to God. The priest then prescribed a series of rites that the confessor must perform which usually included fasting for a certain period and some form of personal bloodletting such as piercing the tongue or another body part. Sahagún also said that once the sinner had confessed his sins and after having received his orders for penance, he would go home and try never again to incur in the same sins, because it was said that if these same sins were repeated then there would be no more absolution.

Sahagún explained that long before Christianity was preached to the natives, the Indians already insisted on confessing the most serious and nefarious sins, such as homicide, adultery, etc. The Indians also believed that once they had confessed their sins and done penance, they would not be brought to civil justice for the sin. Sahagún said that it was generally the old men and women

---

[6]Sahagún, 72.

who confessed to major sins, which lead the Catholic priests to suppose that they had committed many sins in their youth, but waited until they were old before making the confession.[7]

In Peru, Martín de Murúa found that the Incas practiced a very structured religion that included confession similar to the Catholic practice in which the priest was obligated to keep confidential the confession. Some of the sins for which the Indians confessed were murder, adultery, poisoning another person, theft, assault, lack of reverence for religious objects and symbols, and dishonor to the Lord Inca. After confession, the penitent individual went down into a fast-flowing river to wash away his sins. He would repeat essentially the following phrase: "I have confessed my sins to my father, the Sun. River, with your currents, take my sins swiftly to the sea from where they will never again appear." They called the ceremony *opacuna*.[8]

Acosta wrote that the Andean Indians had the important ceremony of confession. He, like other chroniclers, blamed the devil for introducing the practice as a mockery of Christianity. The ancient Peruvians were of the opinion that all adversity and sicknesses came upon an individual because of his or her sins. In order to remedy the situation it was necessary to confess sins vocally to an assigned native priest.

Acosta reported that the Indians had numerous ceremonies that appeared to be similar to those practiced under Mosaic Law, but others appeared to be similar to those used by the Moors in Africa, and some of the ceremonies were reminiscent of Christianity. As examples he cited the special wash basins which the natives called *opacuna* where they bathed in water to be "cleaned from their sins."[9]

---

[7] Ibid., 30-33.
[8] Murúa, 413.
[9] Acosta, 265. (Acosta seemed to struggle with the Spanish word to describe the *opacuna*. He used the word *lavatorio*, or wash basin, but *opacuna* sounds more like a baptismal font wherein the individual could be immersed.)

Rules Against Adultery, Fornication and Other Indiscretions

Many native tribes also had what appeared to be a strong Judeo-Christian moral culture that is similar to what is reflected in both the Old and New Testaments. They had stringent rules against murder, adultery, homosexual behavior, theft, lying, or breaking an oath, etc. In most tribes the sanctity of marriage was extremely important and adultery was a grievous crime punishable at times by death.

Landa mentioned that the Mayas had what he considered to be high morals. He said that they had strong codes against adultery or fornication. If a man was guilty of adultery, the tribal chief and the principal men of the village bound him to a post and put his fate in the hands of the husband of the woman who was at fault. If the husband pardoned him, he was free, but if not, the husband killed him by dropping a large stone down from a high place striking him in the head. They usually did not punish the woman. Her disgrace, which was great, was sufficient punishment; furthermore, the husbands usually abandoned their wives for this crime.[10]

Landa maintained that the Maya women prided themselves on being chaste and virtuous. A woman would prefer to give up her life than be defiled by a man. Maya women turned their backs to men whenever they met them in public and stepped aside to let them pass. They taught their young girls to be extremely modest and quickly punished them if they were immodest. It was considered very improper for women to look at men or to laugh at them. At the same time, he said that the Maya women were prudent, polite and sociable with friends and were extremely generous.[11]

---

[10] Landa, 123-124.
[11] Ibid., 125-128.

According to Landa, the penalty for homicide, or even a death caused by accident, was punished by death at the hands of the dead person's relatives; or if not, the latter had to pay the family of the dead man. Those caught stealing were reduced to slavery. If a nobleman was caught stealing, his face was tattooed on both sides from the chin to the forehead, which was regarded as a very great disgrace. Landa observed that when the Spaniards arrived in Yucatán they found no evidence of the practice of homosexuality among the Mayas as in other parts of the New World.[12]

Durán wrote about the strict moral code that existed among the Aztecs. One of the many laws given by the king, Motecuhzoma, the First, who reigned approximately in the early 1400s, was that all of the youth must observe chastity in the strictest way, under pain of death. He also established strict rules against adultery. The adulterer was to be stoned to death and his or her body thrown into the river or left for the buzzards to eat.[13]

In Peru, the native chronicler Felipe Guaman Poma de Ayala wrote that many of the Indians had rules similar to the Ten Commandments and these first Indians kept the laws given them by God through his *amautas* [wise men or judges] and other leaders of that time. Wives were virtuous, did not commit adultery, and did not drink alcohol [chicha]. These Indians watched over the poor and widows. They were not given to idol worshiping, witchcraft, or immoral activities. They abstained from adultery or having sexual relations with a close relative which he enumerated as the mother, sister, cousin, aunt, or niece; they punished thieves and robbers. He wrote extensively about the punishment meted out to sinners and often accompanied his narrative with sketches. For example, the man or woman who committed adultery was stoned to death. A murderer was always

---

[12]Ibid., 124, n576.
[13]Durán, 210.

Ten Commandments and Other Teachings 247

executed. A thief was severely punished, but not killed unless he stole a second time and then he was killed.[14]

Poma de Ayala explained that in the case of adultery, an investigator first determined if both the man and the woman were equally guilty, because if they were, the punishment was equal. The guilty were stoned to death. If the man had forced himself upon the woman, he was killed and the woman was also punished with a certain number of lashes. If the woman had seduced the man, she was stoned to death and he was punished with lashes and put in exile in some remote mountain area. As an additional punishment, those executed for adultery were not buried in the ground, but their bodies were left upon the earth where the vultures and buzzards could eat their flesh.[15]

Poma de Ayala said that the youth were given strict guidance concerning chastity and the importance of remaining clean and pure. This was particularly true for the young women and especially those selected to serve in the temples. To commit fornication was not tolerated and was severely punished. Both the boys and the girls were strung up by their hair and left hanging until they died. It was considered an offense against their gods.

Martín de Murúa wrote that vagabonds who refused to work or learn a trade were treated as minor thieves. Liars and those who spread gossip were accorded the same punishment as meted out to minor thieves. Murúa observed that the Indians were assigned territories where they could live and it was unlawful to move to another place outside of the assigned district. Those Indians who fled their assigned territories were imprisoned or killed. Indians who pastured their llamas and alpacas on other people's lands were punished. Murúa expressed his surprise at the similarities between many of the Inca rules and the ancient Hebrew laws and ordinances.

---

[14] Poma de Ayala, 49-51.
[15] Ibid., 220.

Juan de Betanzos also confirmed the prohibition against adultery. He added that if the testimony against the accused could not be proven, the one who had given it would be stoned. The Lord Inca decreed that if the first husband of a woman died and she wanted another husband, she would be married to the closest relative of her husband. If the first husband left no children, the second husband should be from the first husband's lineage; thus the lineage of the first husband would continue.[16]

Prohibition Against Homosexual Activities

In the writings of many of the chroniclers, there is evidence that homosexuality was practiced in many areas throughout the New World. Most of the chroniclers referred to this practice as sodomy, and from their descriptions it is evident that for them the term was synonymous with same-sex sexual relations in both sexes. The Catholic priests decried the activity and went to great effort to eliminate it among the Indians with whom they worked; however, they noted that the more advanced Indian nations such as the Incas, the Mayas and the Aztecs also attempted to eliminate the practice themselves wherever it was found.

Cieza de León wrote that the Incas went to great efforts to eliminate homosexuality or sodomy encountered among the different tribes they conquered. He wrote:

> In this kingdom of Peru it is notorious among all the natives that in certain settlements in the vicinity of Puerto Viejo [near Guayaquil, Ecuador] the abominable sin of sodomy was practiced, and also in other lands there were no doubt evil-doers, just as in the rest of the world. I must point out a great virtue of these Incas, for being such absolute rulers who had to account to nobody for what

---
[16]Betanzos, 105.

they did, nor was there any among their subjects powerful enough to demand it, and though they spent their nights and days sporting with their women and in other pastimes, yet never was it said of any of them that they were guilty of the aforesaid sin, but, on the contrary, they despised those who used it, looking down on them as vile and contemptible for glorying in such filth. Not only did they themselves not indulge in this, but they did not even allow anyone whom they knew to practice it to enter their homes or palaces.[17]

Fernando de Montesinos wrote that in the ninth year of the reign of Tupac Cauri Pachacuti, the Seventh, this Inca king began to observe the behavior of the natives in some of the cities and provinces outside of his control, and found them to be corrupt in their religious practices and in some customs.[18] The Lord Inca Tupac Cauri Pachacuti decided that he should conquer or, at least change, the behavior of these people. He reasoned that if they had contact with his own citizens, they would infect and corrupt his people with their vices of idolatry and homosexuality. Initially, the king sent messengers throughout the countryside asking the leaders in these outlying cities and provinces to stop their idolatry and the worship of so many different gods and to cease their homosexual activities. According to Montesinos, the natives killed his messengers.

Montesinos also wrote about an invasion from Panama through the Andes to Cuzco.[19] He described the invaders as barbarians who were heavily involved in homosexual activities. The invasion took place during the reign of Cuntar Roca, or approx-

---

[17]Cieza de León, *The Incas*, 179.

[18]Montesinos, 67. (Montesinos time table is difficult to reconstruct. He claimed that Tupac Cauri Pachacuti, the Seventh, reigned about 3,500 years after the great flood. Because of an earlier reference in Montesinos to the birth of Jesus Christ, the reign of this king would have been about 300 or 400 A.D.)

[19]In a footnote concerning an invasion from the north, Horacio H. Urteaga, who wrote the introduction and notes for this edition of Montesinos's book, commented that archaeologists Max Uhle, Jijón Caamaño and Otto Von Buchwald also observed evidence that there had been an invasion from the north into the Andes. See Max Uhle's *Orígenes de las Civilizaciones Peruanas*, Quito 1926.

imately 500 A.D. Cuntar Roca gathered his people together and taught them that the "ancient laws" prohibited the vices of sodomy and cannibalism that were practiced by the invaders. He told them that Ticci Viracocha had forbidden such activities and Ticci Viracocha would always punish those who disobeyed.[20]

Montesinos wrote that as a result of the invasion from the north there existed a general state of wickedness among the inhabitants in the Andes, causing the situation in Peru to became more intolerable for righteous people. The kings were kings in name only because the people had become so wicked they no longer obeyed their leaders. Some men were consumed with homosexuality. The women who had lost their husbands to this vice became so desperate that they would try various remedies to "cure" their husbands including the use of herbs.

Montesinos added that not all the men were involved in homosexual activities and many joined the women in an effort to resolve the problem. One of the leading men in this venture was Inca Roca, the son of Mama Ciuaco. Mama Ciuaco devised a plan in which she would have her son disappear for four days and tell the people that he had been called home to visit the sun. During the four days, Mama Ciuaco and other women secretly covered his body with highly polished sheets of gold. They then staged his return in such a manner that as he stood upon the hill, the rays of the sun brilliantly reflected off the polished gold. They proclaimed him to be the "Son of the Sun."

Inca Roca was accepted as the new ruler and he called together the amautas (wise men or judges) and had them review the quipos to research the ancient laws. Inca Roca reinstated the

---

[20] Ibid., 69-70. (In a footnote, Urteaga pointed out that the customs of these barbaric invaders are the same customs that were observed by Cieza de León, Gutiérrez de Santa Cruz, López de Gomara and Garcilaso de la Vega as being practiced by the ancient inhabitants of Puerto Viejo in Ecuador. Pedro Pizarro described the terrible infections that the Spaniards contracted when they had sexual relations with the women in Puerto Viejo.)

laws which prohibited many vices and slowly he was able to eradicate homosexuality and similar vices from among the Andeans living near Cuzco. According to Montesinos this was the beginning of the reign of the Lord Incas.[21]

In Mexico, Bernal Díaz del Castillo wrote that Hernán Cortés was forever trying to get the natives of that land to give up their immoral practices and idolatry. When he arrived at Cempoala (Cortés eventually established the city of Veracruz, Mexico, in Cempoala), Cortés captured some of Motecuhzoma, the Second's, ambassadors and tax collectors who had arrived in Cempoala from Tenochtitlan [Mexico City] to collect taxes from the Cempoalans. As a sign of appreciation, the Cempoalan chiefs offered the Spaniards seven beautiful Indian girls as a gift. Cortés thanked the chiefs, but told them that before the Spaniards could accept the girls and before the Cempoalans could become their brothers, the natives would have to abandon their idols and quit the sacrifice of humans. He told them that the girls would also have to become Christians before the Spaniards could receive them, and the people must give up sodomy, for they had boys dressed as women who practiced that for profit.[22]

Importance of an Oath

There are innumerable scriptures in both the Old and the New Testament describing the value the ancient Israelites and the early Christians put on making or swearing by oaths which were considered sacred covenants. One of the most important oaths or covenants in the Old Testament is the covenant that God made with Abraham.

---

[21]Ibid., 71-78.
[22]Díaz del Castillo, 121-122.

> And when Abram was ninety years old and nine, the Lord appeared to Abram, and said unto him, *I am* the Almighty God; walk before me, and be thou perfect.
>
> And I will make my covenant between me and thee, and will multiply thee exceedingly.
>
> And Abram fell on his face: and God talked with him, saying,
>
> As for me, behold, my covenant is with thee, and thou shalt be a father of many nations.
>
> And I will establish my covenant between me and thee and thy seed after thee in their generations for an everlasting covenant, to be a God unto thee, and to they seed after thee (Genesis 17:1-4).

Later this same oath or covenant was offered to Abraham's son, Isaac, and to Jacob.

In the Book of Numbers in the Bible, Moses wrote:

> And Moses spake unto the heads of the tribes concerning the children of Israel, saying, This is the thing which the Lord hath commanded.
>
> If a man vow a vow unto the Lord, or swear an oath to bind his soul with a bond; he shall not break his word, he shall do according to all that proceedeth out of his mouth (Numbers 30:1-2).

Early in the *Book of Mormon* narrative, the sacredness of taking an oath became dramatically apparent. When Nephi obtained the brass plates from Laban's house, he had to dress in Laban's clothes and to speak like Laban. Initially Laban's servant, Zoram, accompanied Nephi outside the walls of Jerusalem thinking that he was accompanying his master, Laban. As soon as Zoram discovered that Nephi was not Laban, he tried to flee. Nephi recorded the event in the following language:

> And now I, Nephi, being a man large in stature, and also having received much strength of the Lord, therefore I did seize upon the servant of Laban, and held him, that he should not flee.
>
> And it came to pass that I spake with him, that if he would hearken unto my words, as the Lord liveth, and as I live, even so that if he would hearken unto our words, we would spare his life.

Ten Commandments and Other Teachings 253

And I spake unto him, even with an oath, that he need not fear; that he should be a free man like unto us if he would go down in the wilderness with us.

And it came to pass that Zoram did take courage at the words which I spake. Now Zoram was the name of the servant; and he promised that he would go down into the wilderness unto our father. Yea, and he also made an oath unto us that he would tarry with us from that time forth.

And it came to pass that when Zoram had made an oath unto us, our fears did cease concerning him (1 Nephi 4:31-33, 35, 37).

Many years later, during a period of wars between the Nephites and the Lamanites, Captain Moroni had surrounded and captured the Lamanite armies and he commanded them to lay down their weapons and to swear an oath that they would not come to battle ever again against the Nephites. The Lamanite commander, Zerahemnah handed over his weapons to Moroni, but Zarahemnah refused to make an oath which he claimed the Lamanites would never keep. Moroni returned Zerahemnah's weapons to him and told him that the Lamanites should continue fighting because the Nephites had made an oath that they would not spare any of the Lamanites until they made an oath that they would not invade the Nephite lands again. The battle continued until hundreds of the Lamanites were killed. Finally when the Lamanites realized they would all be killed unless they swore an oath, those who did not want to die made the oath.

In a separate account, the four sons of Mosiah, served for fourteen years as missionaries among a group of Lamanites and they converted thousands of Lamanites to believe in Jesus Christ. These newly converted Lamanites, who had previously been extremely bloodthirsty, swore an oath that they would never again use their weapons to shed the blood of others and, as a sign of this promise, they buried their weapons. Ammon wrote the following account:

> And this they did, it being in their view a testimony to God, and also to men, that they never would use weapons again for the shedding of man's blood; and this they did, vouching and covenanting with God, that rather than shed the blood of their brethren they would give up their own lives; and rather than take away from a brother they would give unto him; and rather than spend their days in idleness they would labor abundantly with their hands (Alma 24-18).

These converted Lamanites were soon put to the test as a large army of their fellow Lamanites attacked them. Hundreds of the peace-loving Lamanites were killed when they simply knelt down in front of the advancing waves of soldiers. Many of the attacking forces were so moved by the unexpected faith of their Lamanite brothers that they also threw down their weapons and made a similar oath. Thus, they essentially became defenseless and Ammon interceded with other Nephites to resettle these Lamanites into an area called Jershon that was under Nephite control. From that time forth, the Nephite armies protected them.

Concerning the solemnity of oaths, many of the chronicle writers discovered that the native Americans had an equally strong belief in the sacredness of making an oath. In Mexico, Sahagún wrote that the Aztecs made oaths in the following fashion:

> It was also their custom to make a solemn oath to fulfill a certain promise, and anyone who made such a promise was exacted a solemn oath, to be certain of his word. This oath was administered as follows: 'For the life of the sun, for the life of our lady (matron) the earth, I shall not forget what I promised, and for greater guaranty I herewith eat this earth,'—and he forthwith touched the soil with his fingers and then raised them to his lips and licked them, thus eating earth (soil or dirt), and making a solemn promise. If, in some need or other, anyone asked his god for help, he made a vow or an oath to do a certain thing in that god's service, and he always kept his oath or promise.[23]

Diego Durán narrated that when the Aztec armies under their commander, Tlacaelel, finally defeated the larger Army of Azcapotzalco, the fledgling Aztec army followed up their bloody victory with rage and fury. Like meat-hungry dogs, they pursued the fleeing Azcapotzalcas into the hills. Durán wrote:

> There they found the Azcapotzalcas prostrated upon the earth. These vanquished men surrendered their weapons, promising the Aztecs lands and service in their homes and fields, and to be their perpetual tributaries. They promised stone, lime, and wood as tribute, as well as foodstuffs such as maize, beans and chiles. At this point the Aztecs took pity on them; therefore, Tlacaelel was merciful and ordered the pursuit to cease and his men to assemble. He made those of Azcapotzalco swear that they would fulfill what they had promised. This they did: they swore they would comply with their promise.[24]

Magalhães de Gandavo wrote that in Brazil many of the native women took an oath of chastity, and hence they did not marry, or have relations with men in any respect. They would rather die than break this oath.[25]

In describing the adventures of Hernando de Soto, who attempted to establish a Spanish colony in Florida in 1538, the Peruvian-born writer, Inca Garcilaso de la Vega narrated an interesting account of an Indian chief in Florida who protected a Spaniard from cruelty and death. The Spaniard, Juan Ortiz, had accompanied the ill-fated Pamphilo de Narváez 1534 expedition along the western Florida coastline. Ortiz and three other Spaniards were captured and tortured by an Indian chief named Hirrihigua. The other three Spaniards were eventually sacrificed, but Hirrihigua kept Ortiz alive for several years as a slave. When

---
[23] Ibid., 168.
[24] Durán, *Historia*, 80.
[25] Magalhães de Gandavo, 173.

it became apparent to Hirrihigua's daughter, who was sympathetic towards the unfortunate Spaniard, that her father Hirrihigua was going to torture Ortiz to death, she sent Ortiz with an emissary to a neighboring Chief Mucozo and begged him to take care of Ortiz. Chief Mucozo took Ortiz into his house and promised to protected him from the angry Hirrihigua, a very powerful chief. Garcilaso de la Vega claimed that even though Mucozo knew he would incur the wrath of Hirrihigua, Mocozo told Ortiz that he would do all possible to save him and that as long as he, Mucozo, lived no one would bother Ortiz. Garcilaso de la Vega wrote that Mucozo treated Ortiz like his own brother and that Mucozo's behavior was much more admirable than that of many Christian princes who had less value for their sworn and promised fidelity.[26]

TEMPORAL CARE OF THE POOR, WIDOWS AND ORPHANS

Soon after Lehi and his family arrived in the "promised land," they were admonished by the Lord to "clothe the naked, and to feed the hungry, and to liberate the captive, and administer relief to the sick and the afflicted (Jacob 2:19)." This became a reoccurring theme throughout the 1,000 years of the Nephite society. The Nephites were frequently admonished by their prophets and leaders to be more generous with the poor and to avoid the pride that frequently accompanies the accumulation of riches. One of the truly great discourses on service to God and God's children was given by the Nephite king Benjamin about

---

[26]Inca Garcilazo de la Vega, *The Florida of the Inca*, initial manuscript finished in 1599 and, subsequently, published in 1605 in Portugal under title *La Florida del Ynca. Historia del Adelantado Hernando de Soto, Governador y capitan general del Reyno de la Florida, y de otros herioicos cavalleros Españoles è Indios.* (Translated and Edited by John Grier Varner and Jeannette Johnson Varner from the 1723 Spanish edition published by Andrés González Barcia Carballido.) University of Texas Press, Austin. 1996. 70-73.

Ten Commandments and Other Teachings 257

124 B.C. King Benjamin called all the Nephites together to speak to them and to inform them that he was turning his kingship over to his son, Mosiah. The following are a few excerpts from his speech:

> I say unto you that as I have been suffered to spend my days in your service, even up to this time, and have not sought gold nor silver nor any manner of riches of you...
>
> And even I, myself, have labored with mine own hands that I might serve you, and that ye should not be laden with taxes, and that there should nothing come upon you which was grievous to be borne–and of all these things which I have spoken, ye yourselves are witnesses this day.
>
> And behold, I tell you these things that ye may learn wisdom; that ye may learn that when ye are in the service of your fellow beings ye are only in the service of your God.
>
> Behold, ye have called me your king; and if I, whom ye call your king, do labor to serve you, then ought not ye to labor to serve one another? (Mosiah Chapter 2)

By comparison, Cieza de León noted that the Lord Inca and his nobles occasionally worked the land as an example to their subjects. He wrote:

> No one who was lazy or tried to live by the work of others was tolerated; everyone had to work. Thus on certain days each lord went to his lands and took the plow in hand and cultivated the earth, and did other things. Even the Incas themselves did this to set an example, for everybody was to know that there should be nobody so rich that, on this account, he might disdain or affront the poor. And under their system there was none such in all the kingdom, for, if he had his health, he worked and lacked for nothing; and if he was ill, he received what he needed from the storehouses. And no rich man could deck himself out in more finery than the poor, or wear different clothing, except the rulers and headmen, who, to maintain their dignity, were allowed great freedom and privilege, as well as the *Orejones* [Inca nobility], who held a place apart among all the peoples.[27]

Continuing with King Benjamin's discourse, he stated:

> And ye will not suffer your children that they go hungry, or naked; neither will ye suffer that they transgress the laws of God, and fight and quarrel one with another, and serve the devil, who is the evil spirit which hath been spoken of by our fathers, he being an enemy to all righteousness.
>
> But ye will teach them to walk in the ways of truth and soberness; ye will teach them to love one another, and to serve one another.
>
> And also, ye yourselves will succor those that stand in need of your succor; ye will administer of your substance unto him that standeth in need; and ye will not suffer that the beggar putteth up his petition to you in vain, and turn him out to perish.
>
> Perhaps thou shalt say: The man has brought upon himself his misery; therefore I will stay my hand, and will not give unto him of my food, nor impart unto him of my substance that he may not suffer, for his punishments are just–
>
> But I say unto you, O man, whosoever doeth this the same hath great cause to repent; and except he repenteth of that which he hath done he perisheth forever, and hath no interest in the kingdom of God.
>
> For behold, are we not all beggars? Do we not all depend upon the same Being, even God, for all the substance which we have, for both food and raiment, and for gold, and for silver, and for all the riches which we have of every kind?
>
> And now, for the sake of these things which I have spoken unto you–that is, for the sake of retaining a remission of your sins from day to day, that ye may walk guiltless before God–I would that ye should impart of your substance to the poor, every man according to that which he hath, such as feeding the hungry, clothing the naked, visiting the sick and administering to their relief, both spiritually and temporally, according to their wants (Mosiah 4:14-19, 26).

This Judeo-Christian idea of caring for the poor, the widowed and the disadvantaged was prevalent among a number of American tribes. Cieza de León gave a clear view of how this was handled within the Inca realm.

---

[27]Cieza de León. *The Incas*, 178.

Ten Commandments and Other Teachings

As this kingdom was so vast, as I have repeatedly mentioned, in each of the many provinces there were many storehouses filled with supplies and other needful things; thus, in times of war, wherever the armies went they drew upon the contents of these storehouses, without ever touching the supplies of their confederates or laying a finger on what they had in their settlements. And when there was no war, all this stock of supplies and food was divided up among the poor and the widows. These poor were the aged, or the lame, crippled, or paralyzed, or those afflicted with some other diseases; if they were in good health, they received nothing. Then the storehouses were filled up once more with the tributes paid the Inca. If there came a lean year, the storehouses were opened and the provinces were lent what they needed in the way of supplies; then, in a year of abundance, they paid back all they had received.[28]

Juan de Betanzos recorded that the Lord Inca would frequently visit the cities and towns under his control. At each place he would order the local leaders to bring him an account of the number of widows and orphans in that area. Then the Lord Inca ordered that they be fed from the storehouses that were in each town.[29]

In Mexico, when the last Aztec ruler, Motecuhzoma, the Second, was chosen by the men who made up the election council, he received the following advice from the king of Tacuba:

> You should keep in mind the old men and the old women, whose youth was spent in doing service for the republic, and now, their hair white, they are unable to work and die of hunger. Remember, too, the poor commoners, who are the wings and feathers, the hands and feet of the cities. Be careful to see that they are not mistreated or oppressed, nor that justice for them dies because there is no one to speak for them.[30]

---

[28] Cieza de Leon, 178.
[29] Betanzos, 169.
[30] Durán., 392.

After Christ appeared in the Americas and established his Church, the newly converted saints became so faithful and so watchful of each other that they had no poor among them. Mormon described the scene in the following narrative:

> And it came to pass in the thirty and sixth year, the people were all converted unto the Lord, upon all the face of the land, both Nephites and Lamanites, and there were no contentions and disputations among them, and every man did deal justly one with another.
>
> And they had all things common among them; therefore there were not rich and poor, bond and free, but they were all made free, and partakers of the heavenly gift (4 Nephi 1:2-3).

Mormon described very briefly the righteous activities of these New World Christians over the next two hundred years. He pointed out how they became rich and spread throughout the land, but accumulation of wealth became their own downfall. Mormon briefly narrated the following:

> And now I, Mormon, would that ye should know that the people had multiplied, insomuch that they were spread upon all the face of the land, and that they had become exceedingly rich, because of their prosperity in Christ.
>
> And now, in this two hundred and first year there began to be among them those who were lifted up in pride, such as the wearing of costly apparel, and all manner of fine pearls, and of the fine things of the world.
>
> And from that time forth they did have their goods and their substance no more common among them.
>
> And they began to be divided into classes; and they began to build up churches unto themselves to get gain, and began to deny the true church of Christ (4 Nephi1:23-25).

When the Spaniards and the Portuguese arrived they encountered, especially among the poorer tribes, a form of communal living. In his writings about pre-Columbia Brazil, Magalhães revealed that the Indians along the Brazilian coast shared their goods and that the daily living was much easier for them than for the Portuguese and other Europeans. They owned no property and they made no effort to acquire property. Magalhães wrote:

> They live free from greed and inordinate desire for riches, which are prevalent among other nations. This is true to such an extent that neither gold nor silver nor precious jewels have any value among them, nor have they need of the use of such or any similar objects . . . They appeared to have no class distinction or ideas of dignities or ceremonies, nor did they need them. They lived in harmony with their surroundings and all lived justly in conformity with the laws of nature.[31]

Magalhães narrated that the Indians lived in villages made up of seven or eight long houses. He observed that in every house all lived together in harmony. The Indians were so friendly with one another that what belonged to one belonged to all, and when one of them had something to eat, no matter how small, all his neighbors shared in it.[32]

The Cuna Indians on the San Blas Islands off the coast of Panama for centuries had no private ownership on the islands and shared with each other their food and lodging. Even to this day, although they now have private ownership of many farms and businesses in Panama proper, they still have "common" responsibilities on each island according to where the individual was born.[33] Similar patterns of communal living are reported in the Bible. Luke wrote in Acts the following account:

---

[31] Magalhães, 92.
[32] Ibid., 87.
[33] From personal observation when I lived in Panama from 1963-1966 and again from 1987-1989. During both periods I worked closely with the San Blas Indians of the Cuna Indian tribe and was told that this is a practice that has been with the Cuna Indians since pre-Hispanic times.)

And all that believed were together, and had all things common; and sold their possessions and goods, and parted them to all men, as every man had need. And they, continuing daily with one accord in the temple and breaking bread from house to house, did eat their meat with gladness and singleness of heart (Acts 2:44-46).

This period of having "all things common" did not last many years in either the New or the Old Worlds. Mormon wrote:

> And it came to pass that two hundred and forty and four years had passed away, and thus were the affairs of the people. And the more wicked part of the people did wax strong, and became exceedingly more numerous than were the people of God.
> And they did still continue to build up churches unto themselves, and adorn them with all manner of precious things. And thus did two hundred and fifty years pass away, and also two hundred and sixty years.
> And also the people who were called the people of Nephi began to be proud in their hearts, because of their exceeding riches, and became vain like unto their brethren, the Lamanites (4 Nephi 1:40-41, 43).

Prophets throughout the thousand year history of the Nephites admonished them repeatedly against loving their riches. As will be elaborated on in Chapter 13, the pride and arrogance of the Nephites when they accumulated gold, silver and fine clothing eventually led to their being chastened by the Lord.

The chroniclers discovered how deeply imbedded this problem, and the attendant differentiation into social classes, had become within the great civilizations they discovered in the New World. Once the Aztecs gained control of the area around Tenochtitlan and they became wealthy, the Aztec kings set up strict rules on how their subjects could dress. Durán noted several of the rules set down by Motecuhzoma, the First:

> 1. The king must never appear in public except when the occasion is extremely important and unavoidable.

2. Only the king may wear a golden diadem in the city, except when at war and the warriors and nobles who represent the king may wear a diadem and royal insignia.

3. Only the king is to wear the fine mantles of cotton brocaded with designs and threads of different colors and adorned with featherwork. The king is to decide which type of cloak is to be used by the royal person and at which times.

4. The great lords, who are twelve, may wear special mantles of certain make and design, and the minor lords, according to their valor and accomplishments, may wear others.

5. The common soldiers are permitted to wear only the simplest type of mantle. They are prohibited from using any special designs that might set them off from the rest.

6. The commoners will not be allowed to wear cotton clothing, under pain of death, but can use only garments of maguey fiber. The mantle must just cover the knee and not be worn longer than this. If anyone allows it to reach the ankle, he will be killed unless he has wounds received in war on his legs.

7. Only the great noblemen and valiant warriors are given license to build a house with a second story; for disobeying this law a person receives the death penalty. No one is to put peaked or flat or round additions upon his house. This privilege has been granted by the gods only to the great.

8. Only the great lords are to wear labrets, ear plugs, and nose plugs of gold and precious stones, except for commoners who are strong men, brave captains, and soldiers, but their labrets, ear plugs and nose plugs must be of bone, wood, or other inferior material of little value.

9. Only the king of Tenochtitlan and sovereigns of the provinces and other great lords are to wear gold armbands, anklets, and golden rattles on their feet at the dances.[34]

The chronicle writers in Peru also noted this shift towards a class society in the Andean region. Martín de Murúa described the clothing worn by the various Lord Incas and their wives which set them apart from the other Indians. For example, Mama Ocllo was described as a beautiful woman, who always dressed in the finest of clothing made from a cloth that could

[34] Durán, 208-210.

only be described as silky in texture with beautiful decorations. She normally changed her dress three times per day and never put on the same dress twice.[35] Whenever Mama Ocllo went out among the people, she was carried on a litter and received the same respect that was accorded to her husband.

Pedro de Cieza de León gave a physical description of the Inca Atahualpa, who was captured by Francisco Pizarro and the Spaniards. Cieza de León described the reverence shown to Atahualpa by his subjects. No man could enter his presence unless the visitor was barefoot and carried a load on his back. Even Atahualpa's army general, Challicuchima, who arrived at Cajamarca on a litter, humbled himself before Atahualpa. Cieza de León mentioned that the Lord Inca, the Inca nobility (Orejones), and their wives wore extremely soft and luxurious clothing, but the common people wore coarse clothing. Atahualpa even had clothing made out of bat skin by the Indians at Puerto Viejo. Cieza de León said that this was the softest, most velvety cloth that he had ever seen.[36]

Principle of Fasting

Fasting is another principle practiced both during the time of the early Christian Church as well as in the New World among the native Americans. In Mexico, Sahagún observed that the Aztec priests "fasted and did penance for forty days prior to the festival to honor their god or gods."[37] Also when an individual had committed a sin and confessed it to the Aztec priest, one of the rites that the penitent was to perform was to fast. According to Sahagún, the priests would choose the penance based on the

---

[35]Murúa, 107.
[36]Cieza de León, *The Incas*, 224.
[37]Sahagún, 148.

Ten Commandments and Other Teachings

type of sin. In some cases, the priest would have the penitent fast for four days to "punish your stomach and your mouth."[38]

During the ceremony to honor the god Huitzilopochtli, everyone including small children were expected to abstain from all food and water and only eat the "flesh and bones" [tzoalli] of Huitzilopochtli. In nearly every feast and religious ceremony in Mexico among all the tribes, fasting was an important part of the ritual.

In Peru, Cieza de León wrote the following concerning fasting before special feasts:

> They call this feast Hátun Raimi, which in our tongue means "very solemn feast," because at it thanks and praises were given to the great god, maker of heaven and earth, whom they called Ticci Viracocha, and to the sun, the moon, and their other gods, for having given them a good year of harvests for their maintenance. And to celebrate this feast with greater devotion and solemnity, it is said that they fasted for ten or twelve days, refraining from eating much and sleeping with their women.[39]

Betanzos noted that at the time that Pachacuti Inca Yupanqui was to "put on the borla" (a fringe that the Lord Inca put on his head when he was anointed), the formal ceremonies, sacrifices, and fasts would begin. The newly appointed Lord Inca was also given a bride at that time. During this ceremony the Lord Inca, his bride and her parents went into a room that was prepared for this ceremony. All of them went on a fast, eating nothing but raw maize and drinking *chicha* (the fermented corn liquor so popular in the Andes) for ten days.[40]

Pedro Pizarro observed that when a boy of nobility [orejones] reached the age of ten, the father dressed him in short shirt and shoes made of straw, and gave him a blanket in preparation for

---

[38]Ibid., 31.
[39]Cieza de León, *The Incas*, 182.
[40]Betanzos, 77.

the ceremony in which his ears would be perforated and small disks inserted. The boy and his father were required to abstain or fast many days during which time they could not eat salt or, hot peppers, or drink any chicha during the important ceremony. This ceremony lasted for thirty days after which the priest perforated the ears and inserted the disks or trusses.[41]

The early Christians also fasted to purify themselves and gain spiritual power. The most famous example is the 40-day fast of Jesus Christ as recorded in the various gospels. It is interesting to note that the Aztec priests engaged in a modified fast for 40 days.

In the *Book of Mormon*, fasting was an important principle and was practiced throughout the history of the Nephites when they were righteous. It is first mentioned by the prophet Amalaki, a descendent of Jacob and the last prophet to write upon the "small plates" of Nephi, who urged the people to "continue in fasting and prayer, and endure to the end" (Omni 1:26). When Alma, the younger, was ordained a high priest and began teaching the people, he wrote:

> Behold, I testify unto you that I do know that these things whereof I have spoken are true. And how do ye suppose that I know of their surety?
> Behold, I say unto you they are made known unto me by the Holy Spirit of God. Behold, I have fasted and prayed many days that I might know these things of myself. And now I do know of myself that they are true; for the Lord God hath made them manifest unto me by his Holy Spirit; and this is the spirit of revelation which is in me (Alma 5:45-46).
> Nevertheless the children of God were commanded that they should gather themselves together oft, and join in fasting and mighty prayer in behalf of the welfare of the souls of those who knew not God (Alma 6:6).

---

[41]Pizarro, 105.

When the four sons of King Mosiah went into the lands of the Lamanites to preach the gospel, it is recorded that they fasted and prayed.

> And it came to pass that they journeyed many days in the wilderness, and they fasted much and prayed much that the Lord would grant unto them a portion of his Spirit to go with them, and abide with them, that they might be an instrument in the hands of God to bring, if it were possible, their brethren, the Lamanites, to the knowledge of the truth, to the knowledge of the baseness of the traditions of their fathers, which were not correct.
>
> And it came to pass that the Lord did visit them with his Spirit, and said unto them: Be comforted. And they were comforted (Alma 17: 2-3, 9-10).

Although the idea of fasting and prayer continued with the New World natives for hundreds of years, the Indian propensity to resort to human sacrifice, cannibalism and the use of drugs greatly distorted the purpose and meaning of the principle of fasting and prayer.

12

THE CYCLE OF PROSPERITY AND DECLINE IN AMERICA'S FORMATIVE YEARS 2500 B.C. TO 400 B.C.

From information recorded by the Spanish and Portuguese chroniclers and accounts in the *Book of Mormon*, as well as more recent discoveries by art historians and archaeologists, it is evident that the pre-Columbian Americans went through great cycles of prosperity and decline in which civilizations, nations, and tribes rose and fell during the pre-Christian era. The clearest portrayal of prosperity and decline, and the reasons behind each cycle, are contained within the *Book of Mormon*; however, the findings of the conquistadores during the sixteenth and seventeenth centuries and the archaeological investigations during the last one hundred years tell the same story.

The *Book of Mormon* record of these very early civilizations began with the instructions given by God to the brother of Jared when he asked the Lord to guide his family and friends to a "choice land for their inheritance" at the time of the Tower of Babel circa 2500 B.C. It is recorded that the Lord gave the following information to the brother of Jared:

> ...And there will I meet thee, and I will go before thee into a land which is choice above all the lands of the earth.
> And then will I bless thee and thy seed, and raise up unto me of thy seed, and of the seed of thy brother, and they who shall go with thee, a great nation. And there shall be none greater than the nation which I will raise up unto me of thy seed, upon all the face of the earth. And this I will do unto thee because this long time ye have cried unto me (Ether 1:42-43).

God also gave additional, very precise instructions on how the Jaredites should live in this new land. They were warned that if they, and any others who settled there, did not obey God's commandments, they would face dire consequences. The Jaredite record keeper Ether recorded the following additional instructions:

> And now, we can behold the decrees of God concerning this land, that it is a land of promise; and whatsoever nation shall possess it shall serve God, or they shall be swept off when the fulness of his wrath shall come upon them. And the fulness of his wrath cometh upon them when they are ripened in iniquity.
> Behold, this is a choice land, and whatsoever nation shall possess it shall be free from bondage, and from captivity, and from all other nations under heaven, if they will but serve the God of the land, who is Jesus Christ, who hath been manifested by the things which we have written (Ether 2:9, 12).

Several times the Lord reminded these, his "other" chosen people, that if they did not keep his commandments they "would be swept off" or destroyed. They were repeatedly promised that they would be free from bondage if they would but serve Jesus Christ. Many hundreds of years later, Nephi clarified this for his own people and for the future inhabitants of the Americas, when he said:

> But behold, this land, said God, shall be a land of thine inheritance, and the Gentiles shall be blessed upon the land.
> And this land shall be a land of liberty unto the Gentiles, and there shall be no kings upon the land, who shall raise up unto the Gentiles.
> And I will fortify this land against all other nations.
> And he that fighteth against Zion shall perish, saith God.
> For he that raiseth up a king against me shall perish, for I, the Lord, the king of heaven, will be their king, and I will be a light unto them forever, that hear my words (2 Nephi 10:10-14).

The *Book of Mormon* says it was Jesus Christ who appeared personally to the brother of Jared and guided the Jaredites to the New World. Before he died, the brother of Jared counseled his people that they should not have a king rule over them. He warned that a monarchy would lead to strife and downfall. Nevertheless, the people selected one of the sons of Jared to serve as king. Ether noted that over the years the Jaredites prospered under good kings and suffered greatly under wicked kings. It was not unusual for the son of a king to overthrow his father and take over the kingship or for a brother to dispose of his brother to reign as king in his stead.

Ether wrote that the Jaredites were not in the Americas for many generations before sin became rampant. The Lord sent prophets among the people who prophesied that the wickedness and idolatry of the people would bring a curse upon the land and they would be destroyed if they did not repent. At times, the Jaredites heeded the prophets, but more often than not they reviled, persecuted and even killed them.

Ether also revealed that, in order to gain power and wealth, a few of the more wicked Jaredites introduced a stratagem to form "secret combinations" or gangs whose purpose was to undermine the government and then take it over. Within these secret combinations, the followers or members took upon themselves solemn oaths to keep secret any wrongdoing, including murder, committed by anyone in the group. He pointed out that the plans or activities of these secret combinations were included within the writings that the Jaredites brought with them from the Old World.[1] He warned against these secret combinations:

> And they were kept up by the power of the devil to administer these oaths unto the people, to keep them in darkness, to help such as sought power to gain power, and to murder, and to plunder, and to lie, and to commit all manner of wickedness and whoredoms.
> And it came to pass that they formed a secret combination, even as they of old; which combination is most abominable and wicked above all, in the sight of God;
> For the Lord worketh not in secret combinations, neither doth he will that man should shed blood, but in all things hath forbidden it, from the beginning of man (Ether 8:16, 18-19).

Unlike the Nephites, who had a formal way of numbering their years, the Jaredites did not record a clear time line except to note that they left the Old World at the time the Lord confounded the languages of the people. Ether wrote that rulership over communities, tribes, or nations passed from one person to another either by descent or intrigue. He also noted that deposed leaders would flee to other areas and set up new kingdoms and that it was not unusual to have regions where the people lived wickedly and other nearby areas where they lived righteously. Those who

---

[1] In the Book of Genesis, chapter four, it describes the efforts of Cain and his son Lamech to conceal their wrongdoings; however, the writings in the Book of Moses, chapter five, provide a more precise picture of how some of the ante-diluvian people entered into a secret pact to murder and to profit from their crimes and anyone within the covenant who revealed the secret was killed.

The Cycle of Prosperity and Decline 273

were righteous prospered and those who lived wickedly were ultimately destroyed. Ether gave an example of this.

> And the Lord began again to take the curse from off the land, and the house of Emer did prosper exceedingly under the reign of Emer; and in the space of sixty and two years they had become exceedingly strong, insomuch that they became exceedingly rich—
> Having all manner of fruit, and of grain, and of silks, and of fine linen, and of gold, and of silver, and of precious things;
> And also all manner of cattle, of oxen, and cows, and of sheep, and of swine, and of goats, and also many other kinds of animals which were useful for the food of man (Ether 9:16-18).

Ether wrote that Emer was such a righteous king that he was privileged to "see the Son of Righteousness, and did rejoice and glory in his day."[2]

Ether recorded that at one point the Jaredites, conversely, became so wicked that the Lord sent a famine and a plague of poisonous snakes which killed most of their cattle and drove the remainder of their animals southward. Some of the Jaredites also fled into the south. Only after the people began to die of starvation did they repent. Later Ether wrote that there could not be a people more blessed by the hand of the Lord than the Jaredites, but this prosperity was short lived. Wars, dissensions and wickedness began to dominate Jaredite life.

Ether also declared that the Jaredites were told that if they did not repent, the land would be given to another people. The precise chronology of these events are not known; however, Ether was born at about this time (approximately 400 B.C.) and he lived to witness the final destruction of the Jaredites. He prophesied that the wars which would occur during King

---

[2] As mentioned in an earlier footnote, the Inca creator-god, Ticci Viracocha, was represented as man, in an effigy of solid gold, with his right arm raised "as in command." He generally lived in the sky, but did appear to the people in time of grave crisis. This would be consistent with the writings of Ether.

Coriantumr's reign would end the Jaredite civilization. It was recorded that these wars were the most destructive ever seen among the *Book of Mormon* peoples in the Americas. Ether described the scene thus:

> And so great and lasting had been the war, and so long had been the scene of bloodshed and carnage, that the whole face of the land was covered with the bodies of the dead.
>
> And so swift and speedy was the war that there was none left to bury the dead, but they did march forth from the shedding of blood to the shedding of blood, leaving the bodies of both men, women and children strewed upon the face of the land, to become a prey to the worms of the flesh.
>
> And the scent thereof went forth upon the face of the land, even upon all the face of the land; wherefore the people became troubled by day and by night, because of the scent thereof (Ether 14:21-23).

Ether related that in the beginning of this series of battles, Coriantumr lost more than two million men plus their wives and their children. Once Coriantumr saw the carnage, he regretted the destruction that he had caused to come upon the people and he attempted to break off the war; however, the contending armies were so consumed with the love of bloodshed that they continued to fight. The armies paused only long enough for the people who were scattered over the land to gather for one final battle. Ether, who witnessed this gathering and subsequent destruction, narrated that it required four years to gather the people into one of the two opposing camps. Ether said that everyone including men, women and children armed themselves with their shields, breastplates, and head-plates. During the war of destruction that ensued, Ether narrated that everyone was killed from both armies except Coriantumr.

ARCHAEOLOGICAL EVIDENCE

Many archaeologists and art historians, through the discoveries at their excavation sites, have been able to provide additional insights into these early American civilizations that parallel the *Book of Mormon* time line. Two of the more notable civilizations in the New World were the Chavín civilization located in northern Peru and the Olmec civilization located in Mesoamerica. Archaeologists have discovered early Chavín sites along the Pacific coastal area in Peru and Ecuador which date from as early as 2500 B.C. Richard L. Burger in his illuminating book, *Chavín and the Origins of Andean Civilization*, reports:

> The best known of the early Peruvian civilizations is Chavín. Its name is taken from Chavín de Huántar, an archaeological site in the northern highlands of Peru which is notable for its monumental architecture, finely carved stone sculpture, and elaborate iconography. The distinctive style utilized on the sculptures of Chavín de Huántar appears elsewhere in Peru on clay friezes, hammered gold, woven and painted cloth, and a host of other materials. The quality of these objects and their relatively early date led Peruvian archaeologist Julio C. Tello to propose in the 1930s that Chavín provided the cultural foundations out of which all later Peruvian civilizations grew. . . .Chavín is frequently presented as the South American counterpart to the Shang civilization in China, the Sumerian civilization in Mesopotamia, and the Olmec civilization in Mesoamerica.[3]

Burger observed that numerous advances, made in radiocarbon dating and other chronometric systems, have aided in determining the age of artifacts and sites, but cautioned that many early Peruvian sites lack enough evidence to adequately date

---

[3]Burger, 11. (I visited Chavín de Huántar in 1973 and spent two days examining the ruins. According to the archaeologist working the site, Chavín de Huántar had been settled more than 1000 years before the birth of Jesus Christ and had lasted for 600 to 800 years before the Chavín people completely disappeared. He also mentioned that it had been settled and abandoned on at least two occasions.)

The Temple complex at Chavín de Huántar, Peru. The Old Temple is on the right and has an entry point into the various rooms located under the Old Temple. One of the rooms contains the 14 ft. high sculptured granite rock, known as the "Lanzon," believed by many art historians to be a representation of Ticci Viracocha. The New Temple is on the left. Picture taken by Author in 1973.

A large 200 meter by 200 meter sunken plaza with accompanying staircases that is located in front of both the Old and the New Temples at Chavín de Huántar. Picture taken by Author in 1973.

them. According to Burger, there is a significant discrepancy between radiocarbon ages and calendar years which is primarily due to past fluctuations in the quantity of unstable Carbon-14 in the atmosphere. He adds that it is necessary to correct or calibrate the radiocarbon measurements to obtain calendar dates, and to compare the antiquity of early Peruvian civilizations with the Old World, where chronologies are based primarily on written records.[4]

According to Burger, the oldest architectural sites in Peru are found along the coast just north of Lima. The radiocarbon measurements from the Huaca de los Sacrificios at Aspero are 2772 B.C. and 2903 B.C. This would make the earliest stone platforms there contemporary with the royal pyramids of Egypt and with the ziggurats of the Sumerians in Mesopotamia. Burger claims that the Pre-ceramic constructions in Peru are the oldest known examples of monumental architecture in the New World. The pyramids of the Olmec and other Pre-classic cultures of Mesoamerica did not appear until more than 1,000 years later.[5]

Concerning the construction of the enormous architectural sites, Burger theorized that religious ideology played an important role. He believed that an organized religion empowered the Chavín leaders to mobilize a sufficiently large labor pool to build the huge archaeological sites encountered in Peru. Large corporate labor projects were characteristic not only of the Late Pre-ceramic, but also of much of Peruvian prehistory.[6]

When Burger discussed the various Pre-ceramic highland architectural sites, he observed the remarkable similarities that existed, despite the distances separating them. He suggested that the similarities were the result of religious ceremonies, in which the burning of offerings was a critical element. It appears that these scattered communities shared a set of religious beliefs

---

[4]Ibid., 12.
[5]Ibid., 28.
[6]Ibid., 37.

which entailed similar kinds of rituals and, consequently, required a similar type of ceremonial building.[7]

One of the early sites that provided an example of military conflict in the area is the site at Cerro Sechín, located near the juncture of the Sechín and Moxeke Rivers north of Lima in the Casma Valley complex. The site yielded more than 400 stone sculptures on granite blocks, some measuring 85 x 70 centimeters and others 3 x 1 meters. The hundreds of individual sculptures were arranged in the platform wall to portray a single mythological or historical scene in which two columns of warriors approach each other from opposing sides amidst the carnage of their adversaries. The iconography of these warriors revealed that they carried weapons and had breastplates. They also wore helmets which Burger called "pill-box" hats. (See Chapter 17 on Weaponry and Warfare.)

Burger notes that Chavín de Huántar was not the earliest of the sites that carried the distinctive Chavín style nor was it the largest, but it was considered to have the most complete collection of artifacts and the most unusual style of architecture, sculpted heads, and interior rooms. He believes that Chavín de Huántar was founded during the late Initial Period or approximately 1000 B.C. Chavín de Huántar is located on the eastern slopes of the Andean Cordillera Blanca range at an altitude of 3,150 meters (10,400 ft.). The location of Chavín de Huántar enabled this center to gain access to commercial exchange networks linking distant production zones between the eastern jungles and the coastal regions. Also, its site controlled the flow of armies or raiding parties through the area.

A few centuries after the initial construction of the "Old Temple" at Chavín de Huántar, the Old Temple was replaced as the principal site of worship when the natives built a new, much

---

[7]Ibid., 46. (The archaeologists generally refer to these ceremonial buildings as temples.)

The back wall of the New Temple at Chavín de Huántar with a sculptured head revealing a distorted face pylon that had been inserted into the rock wall. Picture taken by Author in 1973.

Various sculptured rock heads at Chavín de Huántar, which reveal distorted facial features caused by the effects of psychotropic substances obtained from the narcotic producing vegetation such as the San Pedro cactus. Picture taken by Author in 1973.

larger pyramid/temple to the south. It would appear that the people of Chavín de Huántar may have turned their backs on the deity of the Old Temple, *Wira Kocha* (Ticci Viracocha), and moved their center of worship to this new temple.

A granite shaft found just east of the temple complex, is the Tello Obelisk. Although the Tello Obelisk is smaller than the "Lanzón" granite shaft, located in a room under the Old Temple, it is still very large and elaborately engraved. Burger described the Tello Obelisk as a sculpture in bas-relief with two profile representations of a hybrid monster dominated by cayman attributes.[8] In this late stage of the Chavín culture, they apparently no longer worshiped their "Creator Ticci Viracocha" and had turned to other deities. Coincidently, this is also the period leading up to their final decline and eventual destruction.

Archaeologists who have worked on the various sites containing Chavín ruins have pondered the factors that contributed to the demise of the Chavín culture. Burger focused considerable attention on this period of apparent unrest and warfare. He points out that as early as 900 B.C., the coastal societies had begun to disintegrate, and by 700 B.C. few of them continued to function as they had during the Initial Period. New construction and the renovation of older buildings along the coast ceased. Many of the people began to retreat to more easily defended positions in the mountains with heavily defensible fortresses or citadels.

Burger purports that, with the loss of protection provided by the old social order and disintegration of intergroup alliances, the population in most valleys splintered into smaller units and apparently sought more secure locations for their settlements. The citadels on the north-central coast of this period were the first convincing indications of intersocietal warfare.[9]

---

[8]Ibid., 174-176.
[9]Ibid., 188.

The most dramatic illustrations of abandonment comes from the public buildings of Las Haldas on the shoreline south of Casma, Peru. When archaeologists excavated the central staircase to the pyramid's summit, they found that construction had been halted before the steps were finished. Plastering had been completed on only half of the stairs and wooden survey stakes and cotton cord used to lay out this feature had been left in place. It would appear that the population left in a hurry and never returned.[10]

Burger readily admits that the available evidence does not permit a satisfactory answer to what factors led to these "cataclysmic changes." He believes some answers may lie in internal contradictions and problems. Burger's following comments certainly coincide with the disasters predicted in the Book of Ether:

> In summary, the abandonment of large-scale public constructions in the lower valleys along the coast at the end of the Initial Period can be interpreted as indicative of a serious crisis for many, if not all, of the small-scale societies in this region. Inasmuch as the ceremonial architecture provided a setting for the community rituals and the design of these centers can be interpreted as expressing aspects of religious cosmology, the failure to maintain these centers or reproduce them elsewhere implies a profound cultural change. If the legitimacy of a center's cosmology was called into question, so too would the non-coercive authority of the leaders associated with this sacred knowledge. Ultimately, this would have undermined the very basis of the social relations that underlay the productive systems, and the functioning of these societies as viable units. With the loss of protection provided by the old social order and the disintegration of intergroup alliances, the populations in most valleys splintered into smaller units.[11]

Another factor worth mentioning is the heavy reliance of the Chavín society on the use of hallucinogenic drugs such as the San Pedro cactus. The priests within the Chavín cult believed they could transform themselves into jaguars to contact and

---
[10]Ibid., 185.
[11]Ibid., 189.

affect the behavior of supernatural forces. Hallucinogenic snuffs and beverages apparently catalyzed these changes, and their consumption was an integral part of the rituals of the New Temple at Chavín de Huántar.[12]

The use of hallucinogenic drugs to achieve a "spiritual experience" appears far removed from the powerful visions and revelations received by the Jaredite prophets who practiced fasting and prayer before their revelatory experiences. At no time does the *Book of Mormon* indicate that the prophets who received such powerful revelations from the Lord required any outside stimulants to have spiritual experiences. The heavy dependency of the Chavín society upon psychotropic substances appears to be an effort to bring about pseudo-spiritual experiences and is another indication of how far they appeared to have drifted away from traditional worship of their Creator.

Burger claimed that by approximately 400 B.C., the Chavín sphere of interaction began to disintegrate completely. With this transformation, a cultural pattern was broken that had existed for centuries, and in some cases, millennia.[13] This apparent disintegration of culture lends credence to the chronicle writings of Felipe Guaman Poma de Ayala and Fernando de Montesinos, set forth below, that the earlier peoples enjoyed a more advanced civilization than some of the later groups.

Pedro de Cieza de León mentioned that east of the Province of Huaraz, over the White Mountains (Cordillera Blanca), there was a large fortress or ancient monument. His description sounds like he may have found the ruins at Chavín de Huantar. Most of the Indians believed that it had existed long before the Incas reigned in Peru. These early inhabitants died off and disappeared, without leaving any trace of themselves except the stones and structures Cieza de León encountered.[14]

---

[12]Ibid., 157.
[13]Ibid., 228.
[14]Cieza de León, *The Incas*, 107.

THE CYCLE OF PROSPERITY AND DECLINE

ANDEAN CHRONICLES DESCRIBING THE DECLINE OF CIVILIZATION

As indicated in Chapter 4, Felipe Guaman Poma de Ayala was one of the first native Americans to write extensively about his Inca ancestors. In his book, *Nueva Corónica y Buen Gobierno*, Poma de Ayala narrated that the first native Americans came to the New World shortly after the universal flood. He attributed his knowledge to information contained in their quipos as well as the folk tales of the elderly Indian men and women living during his time.[15] He wrote that these first people, who were called Vari Viracocha Runa (men of the god Viracocha), were brought to this land by God and that they spread out over the New World in pairs. Poma de Ayala further narrated that these people eventually lost their faith and hope in God and they also lost their writings and commandments of God. They retained vague oral traditions of their creator and the heavens. These people did not know from whence they came nor how they arrived. They did not remember whether their ancestors survived the flood with Noah, but they knew of a flood and they considered that it was a punishment sent by God.

Poma de Ayala claimed that these Vari Viracocha Runa worshiped Ticci Viracocha and Pachacamac.[16] From among the

---

[15] Poma de Ayala, 7. (A close relative of Guaman Poma de Ayala, named Guaman Chawa, was a keeper of the quipos (a Quipocamayoc). Poma de Ayala claims to have obtained considerable "historical" information from the quipos.)

[16] Both Ticci Viracocha and Pachacamac were individually described as the *Creator of the World* and were held in great reverence by all the Andean Indians. Generally they are referred to separately, but occasionally their names are linked. The distinction between the two is unclear; however, the famous temple of Pachacamac, south of Lima, was built by an unknown people long before the Incas arrived on the scene. When the Incas wanted to replace the Temple of Pachacamac with a temple of the sun, the Indians of the area objected so strenuously that the Inca left the Temple of Pachacamac intact and built a temple to the sun nearby. Pilgrimages to the Temple of Pachacamac came from as far away as the Colombian border. It may be that Ticci Viracocha was the name that the Incas from Cuzco gave to the Creator of the World and Pachacamac was the name applied to the same Creator by the non-Inca Andeans.

Indians of Vari Viracocha Runa, there came many great men. He had the highest praise for the Vari Viracocha Runa people because "they had a light and a knowledge of the Creator of heaven and earth."[17]

Poma de Ayala wrote that the second generation was called *Pacarimoc Runa* because the people were generally inept. They did not make fine clothing, but covered themselves with animal skins. The *Pacarimoc Runa* greatly multiplied. From Poma de Ayala's description, it appears that the people split into two groups–those who farmed and worshiped God and those who were inept. Poma de Ayala's division of the *Pacarimoc Runa* into two groups appears to be more like the *Book of Mormon* description of the descendants of Lehi into the two groups of Nephites and Lamanites except for Poma de Ayala's timing of the division.

This second generation worked the land and they made irrigation systems from rivers, lakes and wells. For houses, they made small rock buildings that looked like ovens, which Poma de Ayala claimed could still be seen in many areas. Poma de Ayala emphasized that they did not worship idols, but continued to worship Ticci Viracocha. They were obedient to God's commandments that they received when they first arrived in the New World. The first and second generations combined lasted 2,150 years. These people knew that a God existed and that there was a heaven or a hell where they would suffer pain, hunger and punishment.

The third generation was called Purunruna and they were offspring of Vari Viracocha Runa and Vari Runa. Poma de Ayala said that they multiplied greatly. These Indians began to make various kinds of clothing from cloth, some woven and others knitted or twined from yarn.[18] They built rock houses and other

---

[17] Poma de Ayala, 41.

[18] Art historians have found many different kinds of cloth in their excavations. One popular process for making cloth was a form of twining which is similar to a knit. I own a 2,000 year old cotton burial shroud from Paracas, Peru. The colors and design were woven into the fabric and are still very distinct.

buildings. Also, from Poma de Ayala's commentary, it would appear that they had private property which they delineated with stone boundary markers.

Poma de Ayala wrote that initially this third generation observed their laws and religious ordinances. They established a system of justice among them. The Indians of Purunruna began to spread out and farm those areas where they encountered good soil. They also built irrigation ditches. These Purunruna also began to seek for the trappings of wealth. They learned how to weave cloth with streaks of color and began to dye their wool. They raised many herds of animals and they began to mine for silver, gold, copper and other precious metals. They even incorporated silver and gold into their apparel. They began to multiply so fast that cities could easily assemble an army of ten or twenty thousand men.

Poma de Ayala wrote that a few chroniclers believed that some of the Indians were descendants of Jews because many looked like Jews; i.e. they wore beards, were blond and had blue eyes. Poma de Ayala observed that the Indians had what appeared to be the "Law of Moses" and they knew how to read and write.[19] He stated that they eventually began to quarrel over timber, their farms, and water rights. They also began to covet the wealth and riches of each other. Eventually they entered into wars with neighboring towns where they stole fine clothing, gold, silver, and other riches.[20]

As they drifted away from those ancient laws, they also abandoned their villages and moved to high mountains and crags where they built strong fortifications or *Pucarás* to defend themselves during the destructive wars they underwent. They organized their forces and from these fortresses they went out to fight others or to defend themselves. When they defeated their ene-

---

[19]Poma de Ayala, 49.
[20]Ibid., 46.

mies, they captured their women and children, took possession of their lands and fields, and stole their clothes, gold, silver and copper.[21] When they killed an enemy, they would tear his heart out and eat it.[22] He mentioned that after this fourth age, it was the end of the Auca Runa and shortly thereafter the Incas Indians came on the scene.[23]

In Poma de Ayala's chronology, the Andean Indians had kings from the time they first arrived in the New World after the universal flood. Most of the kings were good kings until the end of the fourth age. It was during the beginning of the fifth generation, which was Poma de Ayala's time of the reign of the Lord Inca Runa and corresponded to the time just before the birth of Jesus Christ, that Manco Cápac and the succession of Inca rulers described by all the chroniclers, came on the scene.[24] Poma de Ayala claimed that it was the Inca kings beginning with Manco Cápac who introduced idolatry into the Andes.

Poma de Ayala also asserted that Manco Cápac and his group came from the Lake Titicaca and Tiahuanaco region of present day Bolivia.[25] According to Poma de Ayala, Jesus Christ was born in Jerusalem in the eightieth year of the reign of Inca Roca, the son of Manco Cápac. Poma de Ayala described separate generations of people living in the Andes, but he did not portray these separate generations as people arriving during different migrations. His description of the earlier periods, the generation of the *Vari Viracocha Runa* and *Pacarimoc Runa*, sound similar to the

---

[21]Ibid., 48.

[22]Ibid., 49. (These people sound very much like the secret combinations in the days of the Jaredites or the Gadianton robbers in the days of the Nephites and Lamanites.)

[23]Ibid., 57.

[24]The term Inca means king, but has been given a broader usage because the Spaniards and subsequent historians apply the term to the natives who moved into Cuzco and eventually conquered the territory from Pasto, Columbia, to south of Santiago, Chile. When Poma de Ayala refers to the Incas he is referring to the kings of whatever group.

[25]Ibid., 60

Book of Mormon description of the Jaredite period. Poma de Ayala's description of later people sound more like the people and activities that the *Book of Mormon* narrate took place during the Nephite/Lamanite period. Poma de Ayala did not or could not differentiate between the separate groups who essentially occupied much of the same areas, but at different times and who experienced similar cycles of prosperity and decline.

A review of the table found in Chapter 3 of the archaeological timetable might be helpful. The archaeologists and art historians studying the Andes have established fairly clear time lines. The Chavín civilization lasted from approximately 2500 B.C. to 400 B.C. in northern Peru and southern Ecuador. About 200 B.C., the Mochica civilization appeared along the north coast of Peru with its center near modern Trujillo. At the same time, the Tiwanaku civilization appeared around Lake Titicaca between Peru and Bolivia. The Nazca and Paracas civilization sprang up south of Lima and extended to what is now the Chilean border. The culture of these latter three are so dissimilar to the Chavín civilization that they are not considered as an extension of the Chavín civilization.

Fernando de Montesinos, who finished his manuscript for the book, *Memorias Antiguas Historiales Y Políticas del Perú*, in 1642, tried diligently to discover for himself the ancient story of Pre-Columbian America. He supported the theory that God led Ophir, grandson of Heber, and his descendants to the New World and gave them strict commandments to live by. He did not specify the route Ophir and his group followed, but indicated that they mainly populated Peru and Chile. Their descendants lived for a few years in peace and harmony, obeying the commandments of God, but later war broke out over land and material possessions. Montesinos said that the people became very greedy.

Montesinos said that these ancient people of Cuzco, particularly the *amautas* or wise men, knew how to read and write and they frequently wrote on dried banana leaves. He pointed out that centuries later the descendants of these people lost the ability to read and write and had to resort to the system of strings and knots known as the quipos.

According to Montesinos, these early people frequently lived to be over 100 years old. Montesinos compiled a genealogy of these early kings and provided a very brief history of each ruler. He related that over the centuries the kings and their vassals were involved in numerous wars with outsiders who came into their area normally from the south. Their history was replete with stories of obedience to their god's laws and of periods when they were less obedient. He cited the story of one king, Inti Capac, who tried to bring about order within his kingdom which he found to be in disarray and lacked needful laws. The king commanded that they should recognize the supreme being and creator of the World, Illatici Huira Cocha [Ticci Viracocha].[26]

King Inti Capac also divided his people into more manageable entities and caused them to be broken down into groups of 10,000, 1,000 and 100. He instituted a system using the *amautas* (wise men or judges) to govern at the local levels.[27] According to Montesinos, Inti Cápac instituted a system of *chasquis*, or runners, who kept the king informed with news from the far corners of the empire. Montesinos said that initially these chasquis carried written messages, but later had to rely upon the quipos.

Guinaldo Vasquez pointed out that Montesinos's account of the arrival of the first native Americans is very much like the accounts of several other chroniclers; however, his ability to provide a name for each of the kings is noteworthy. Vasquez said that Montesinos named a total of 105 kings who governed in

---

[26]Montesinos, 32.
[27]Ibid., 34-35

Peru, and he frequently provided information about the chronological period and significant events in the reign of particular kings. Vasquez stated that Valera and another unnamed Jesuit priest, who wrote *Relación Anónima,* also produced a list of names similar to the list of Montesinos.[28]

As with the writings of Poma de Ayala, Montesinos's description of the ancient Americas contains numerous themes that parallel the *Book of Mormon* accounts of both the Jaredites and the descendants of Lehi as will be seen in the next chapter.

ARCHAEOLOGICAL EVIDENCE OF THE OLMEC

In the book *Olmec World,* Richard A. Diehl and Michael D. Coe write that of all the ancient civilizations known, none is more intriguing than the Olmecs in Mesoamerica.[29] The Olmec period dates from approximately 1500 B.C. to 400 B.C. The first Olmec colossal head was discovered at Veracruz, Mexico, in 1862.

Diehl and Coe believe that the Olmecs were not the first inhabitants in Mesoamerica, but the Olmecs evolved into complex, hierarchically arranged societies that anthropologists call chiefdoms. Olmec culture rose and fell during what archaeologists call the Early and Middle Formative or Pre-Classic period.[30] Diehl and Coe noted that the large Olmec capital of San Lorenzo, near the southern border of the current Mexican state of Veracruz, flourished and collapsed during the Initial Olmec period (1200–900 B.C.). The reasons for this decline are unknown to archaeologists.

---

[28]Ibid., 131 - 136.
[29]There is no record of what the culture now known as Olmec was called anciently. Diehl and Coe explained that modern scholars mistakenly applied the name *Olmeca,* the Aztec name for the region's inhabitants during the reign of the Aztecs, to the much older Pre-Aztec culture that art historians are now studying and the misnomer has refused to go away.
[30]Abrams, 12.

Another prominent Olmec site was at La Venta, about 75 miles away from San Lorenzo on the Gulf of Mexico coast. The two art historians suggest that the grandeur of La Venta may have even surpassed that of San Lorenzo; however, by 400 B.C. La Venta had also declined dramatically. The Olmec culture gained prominence and recognition because of the colossal heads and stone monuments that were sculpted during its eleven hundred years of prominence. Art historians have discovered more than seventy stone monuments at San Lorenzo alone, among them some of the finest sculptures ever created in Mesoamerica. The best known feature of La Venta is a one hundred foot high Great Pyramid.

Both Diehl and Coe observed that there were other cultures in Mexico that were contemporary with the Olmecs and that the Olmecs probably did not think of themselves as a unified ethnic group. Concerning the question of the origin of the Olmec, Diehl and Coe claim that they were "native Americans whose Ice Age ancestors entered the New World from northern Asia via the Bering Straits land bridge," the classic Independent Inventionist claim. Nevertheless, an argument can be made that they were remnants of the much older Chavín civilization in Peru. Miguel Covarrubias, in his book *Indian Art of Mexico and Central America*, saw some similarities in Olmec art with Chavín art.[31] Although the Olmec art is much more focused on humans, like the Chavín art, the Olmec art also features numerous artistic poses of the jaguar and the harpy eagle.[32]

Art historians, studying the ancient Chavín, have also encountered colossal heads made of clay that are many centuries older, but not so dissimilar to the more polished heads found in the Olmec culture. Burger also observed that "features once posited as being derived from Mesoamerica, such as pyramid

---

[31]Ibid., 22.
[32]Ibid., 69.

construction, are now known to have emerged in the central Andes centuries before their appearance in Mesoamerica."[33] Another area of Olmec and Chavín similarity is the presence of ceramic figures representing individuals under the influence of psychotropic drugs. Both civilizations were heavily involved with the use of psychotropic drugs and carved grotesque figures showing the effects of those drugs.

Dr. Terrence Grieder, one of the foremost scholars of the Andean Formative Period, has described how textile patterns developed in Peru and Ecuador at approximately 2000 B.C. were gradually moved north into Mesoamerica at a time when the Olmec were predominant there. During my 1973 excursion to Chavín de Huántar, the Peruvian archaeologist on site emphasized the discovery of evidence of commercial intercourse between Chavín de Huántar and the Olmec.

None of the essayists writing for the *Olmec World* described the circumstances leading up to the disappearance of the Olmec society. However, several writers described the increasing influence of drugs, idolatry and human sacrifice which they discovered within the Olmec society. Both the Olmec and the Chavín disappeared in approximately 400 B.C., just about the time that the *Book of Mormon* indicates that the Jaredite civilization disappeared.

The *Book of Mormon* cites an overall general wickedness, killing of the prophets and turning away from God as the reasons for unabated warfare. Burger denotes the role that warfare played in the demise of the Chavín civilization. The evidence of warfare among the Olmecs is not as clear, but the Chavín and Olmecs also became increasingly corrupt as demonstrated by their adherence to human and specifically to child sacrifice and their use of psychotropic drugs in an effort to create the illusion of shamanistic powers.

---
[33]Burger, 221.

13

PROSPERITY AND DECLINE DURING PRE-CLASSIC AND CLASSIC PERIOD (600 B.C. TO 400 A.D.)

The *Book of Mormon* recounts that even before the final destruction of the Jaredites, God had already led a new group to the Americas shortly after 600 B.C. These were the people of Lehi. Before leaving the Old World, God told Lehi's son, Nephi, that they would be led to a "land of promise:"

> And inasmuch as ye shall keep my commandments, ye shall prosper, and shall be led to a land of promise; yea, even a land which I have prepared for you; yea, a land which is choice above all other lands (1 Nephi 2:20).

The phrase "if ye shall keep my commandments" was repeated over and over to each generation of Nephites. After the Nephites separated themselves from their combative brothers, the Lamanites, they moved to an area which they called the Land of Nephi. Like the Jaredites, the Nephites did not live in the New World for many years before problems began to plague their society because of their behavior. Jacob, Lehi's son who was born during their journey to the "land of promise," had to admonish his fellow Nephites for their fixation with enriching themselves with precious metals and for practicing polygamy and other sexual sins. Jacob, his son Enos, and other prophets worked to keep the people in line with the Law of Moses, while at the same time looking forward to the coming of the Messiah.

Sometime between 279 B.C. and 130 B.C., the Nephites were warned by the Lord to flee the Land of Nephi to avoid being destroyed by the more numerous Lamanites. During this migration into a new area, they discovered the Land of Zarahemla. The Nephites united with the people of Zarahemla and taught them the language of the Nephites. In the process, they learned that the people of Zarahemla were descendants of Mulek, the son of King Zedekiah, the Jewish King who was captured and killed by the Babylonians in Jerusalem in 588 B.C.

The *Book of Mormon* does not indicate the distance between the Land of Zarahemla and the Land of Nephi, but apparently it was sufficiently far that the Nephites enjoyed some respite from the wars, but close enough that eventually the wars between the Lamanites and the Nephites resumed. The prophets recorded that when the Nephites kept God's commandments, they prospered and were able to repel the more numerous Lamanites, but when they became wicked or proud, they were more likely to be beaten by the Lamanites.

In 92 B.C., the Nephites made a significant change in their form of government from a monarchy to a form of a democratic government in which the people elected judges to rule over them. The last king, Mosiah, promoted democracy:

> Now I say unto you, that because all men are not just it is not expedient that ye should have a king or kings to rule over you.
>
> For behold, how much iniquity doth one wicked king cause to be committed, yea, and what great destruction!
>
> And behold, now I say unto you, ye cannot dethrone an iniquitous king save it be through much contention, and the shedding of much blood.
>
> For behold, he has his friends in iniquity, and he keepeth his guards about him; and he teareth up the laws of those who have reigned in righteousness before him; and he trampleth under his feet the commandments of God.
>
> And he enacteth laws, and sendeth them forth among his people, yea, laws after the manner of his own wickedness; and whosoever doth not obey his laws he causeth to be destroyed; and whosoever doth rebel against him he will send his armies against them to war, and if he can he will destroy them; and thus an unrighteous king doth pervert the ways of all righteousness.
>
> Therefore, choose you by the voice of this people, judges, that ye may be judged according to the laws which have been given you by our fathers, which are correct, and which were given them by the hand of the Lord.
>
> Now it is not common that the voice of the people desireth anything contrary to that which is right; but it is common for the lesser part of the people to desire that which is not right; therefore this shall ye observe and make it your law–to do your business by the voice of the people (Mosiah 29:16-17, 21-23, 25-26).

Two of the larger books within the *Book of Mormon*, the Book of Alma and the Book of Helaman, cover the ninety two years of the reign of the judges and enumerate many battles between the Nephites and the Lamanites. When the Nephites kept God's commandments they consistently prevailed, but periodically they transgressed the commandments and were defeated by the Lamanites. Many Nephite dissenters joined the Lamanites and were usually given command of the Lamanite army units because of their superior military skills and their implacable hatred towards their fellow Nephites.

Alma formally established a church among the Nephites and baptized many into it. Frequently those Nephites who transgressed became careless in defending themselves and were killed and captured by the Lamanites. In addition, a few of the Nephites attempted to reestablish a monarchy which led to serious dissension and weakening of the Nephite armies torn by civil wars.

It is significant that the *Book of Mormon* makes note of a change in government from one of kings to one of judges in a period not many years before the birth of Jesus Christ. The chronicler Fernando de Montesinos recorded in his book that the people living in Peru, at about the time of the birth of Christ, also changed their government from one of kings to judges. Montesinos recorded the existence of a second Peruvian dynasty which started when the "dynasty of the *Piruas* [or kings]" ended about 100 B.C.[1] During this second dynasty, the country was governed by the *amautas* or wise men and judges. According to Montesinos, the Amauta Manco Cápac taught his people to worship Illatici Yachachic Huira Cocha [Ticci Viracocha]. Montesinos dated the period of Manco Cápac at about the time of the birth of Jesus Christ.[2] He wrote that the ancient judges knew how to read and write.

In addition to the comparison of governmental systems, the *Book of Mormon* and chronicle accounts compare favorably on other points. According to the *Book of Mormon* in about 52 B.C., a group of Nephites led by an ambitious man named Kishkumen and later by another man named Gadianton formed a band of robbers and murders, similar to the "secret combinations" formed among the Jaredites. Like the Jaredite group, the "Gadianton robbers" followed a dark order of secret oaths under which the

---

[1] Montesinos seemed to refer to the *piruas* as a title or as a king somewhat like the other Spanish chroniclers referred to the Lord Inca or Inca as the title of king.

[2] Montesinos, 50.

members pledged to keep each other's identity secret while committing murder, robbery, and other crimes.

The existence of the Gadianton robbers was eventually discovered when they attempted to murder Helaman, the Nephite Chief Judge. After their discovery, the Gadianton robbers fled into a wilderness. They eventually gained control over large areas from where they mounted their operations. This band of robbers caused great havoc among both the Nephites and the Lamanites for many years.

In 46 B.C., there was so much civil strife among the Nephites, that many of them went north to inhabit a new land. They traveled a great distance, crossing many rivers and large bodies of water. Helaman wrote that they spread out over the north land:

> Yea, and even they did spread forth into all parts of the land, into whatever parts it had not been rendered desolate and without timber, because of the many inhabitants who had before inherited the land.
>
> And now no part of the land was desolate, save it were for timber; but because of the greatness of the destruction of the people who had before inhabited the land it was called desolate.
>
> And there being but little timber upon the face of the land, nevertheless the people who went forth became exceedingly expert in the working of cement; therefore they did build houses of cement, in the which they did dwell (Helaman 3:5-7).[3]

Helaman added that the Nephites would not cut down trees, but left them to grow wherever possible.

The Andean chronicler Felipe Guaman Poma de Ayala noted that during a period not many years before the birth of Jesus Christ, a Changa Indian by the name of Ancauallo came out of the Lake Choclococha region in north-central Peru with

---

[3]It would appear that the Jaredites in their wars had destroyed most of the forests.

fifty thousand warriors. Ancauallo wanted to make himself the Lord Inca during the time of Mango Cápac Inca, the First. During the fighting, Ancauallo was killed. After his death, Ancauallo's people went into the mountains and passed over to the other part of what they called the *"North Sea"* [In the time of the chronicle writers, the "North Sea" was understood to be the Atlantic Ocean and the "South Sea" was understood to be the Pacific Ocean].

Poma de Ayala described the area as having a cold and rugged terrain where the Changas remained. Poma de Ayala narrated that according to the history recorded in the quipos, these Changas were disloyal to the government at Cuzco and established a new government.[4]

In a separate account, Poma de Ayala stated that the Lord Inca Topa Inca Yupanqui emitted a decree that no one was allowed to burn down or cut down any fruit tree or any tree used for wood products without the expressed permission of the Lord Inca or one of his representatives. Those who disobeyed this decree would be killed.[5]

The *Book of Mormon* records that in 38 B.C., numerous rebellious Nephites joined with the Lamanites and fomented war against the Nephite nation. During the next two years, the Lamanites and the Nephite dissenters took over the land of Zarahemla and pushed the Nephite army north to an area known as the Land of Bountiful.[6] Helaman explained that the

[4]Poma de Ayala, 62.
[5]Ibid., 131.
[6]In one of the few geographical descriptions provided in the *Book of Mormon*, Helaman stated that there was a narrow neck of land between Zarahemla on the south and Bountiful on the north and a Nephite could travel from the west sea to the east sea in one day. Some Latter-day Saints have speculated that this narrow neck of land is the Isthmus of Panama; however, the *Book of Mormon* narrates that the destruction at the time of the crucifixion of Jesus Christ was so great that some valleys were made mountains and some mountains were made valleys and many cities were swallowed up in the depths of the sea. Consequently, it is uncertain where the "narrow neck of land" might have been located before that upheaval.

Prosperity and Decline (600 B.C. to 400 A.D.)

Nephite armies were defeated because they did not merit God's help. He allowed them to be overrun. Helaman wrote:

> And it was because of the pride of their hearts, because of their exceeding riches, yea, it was because of their oppression to the poor, withholding their food from the hungry, withholding their clothing from the naked, and smiting their humble brethren upon the cheek, making a mock of that which was sacred, denying the spirit of prophecy and of revelation, murdering, plundering, lying, stealing, committing adultery, rising up in great contentions, and deserting away into the land of Nephi, among the Lamanites.
> And because of this their great wickedness, and their boasting in their own strength, they were left in their own strength; therefore they did not prosper, but were afflicted and smitten, and driven before the Lamanites, until they had lost possession of almost all their lands (Helaman 4:12-13).

At this time, the sons of Helaman, Nephi and Lehi, began to preach the gospel to both the Nephites, the Nephite dissenters, and to the Lamanites. They were so successful in converting Lamanites that the Lamanites restored the land of Zarahemla, which they had taken during the wars, to the Nephites. This caused peace to spread over most of their common territory and the Nephites and Lamanites traveled wherever they wanted throughout all of the land and they mingled and engaged in commercial trade. In the Book of Helaman, it was recorded:

> And it came to pass that they became exceedingly rich, both the Lamanites and the Nephites; and they did have an exceeding plenty of gold, and of silver, and of all manner of precious metals, both in the land south and in the land north.
> They did raise grain in abundance, both in the north and in the south; and they did flourish exceedingly, both in the north and in the south. And they did multiply and wax exceedingly strong in the land. And they did raise many flocks and herds, yea, many fatlings.
> Behold their women did toil and spin, and did make all manner of cloth, of fine-twined linen and cloth of every kind, to clothe their nakedness... (Helaman 6:9, 12-13).

Guaman Poma de Ayala wrote that the Purunruna Indians began to weave cloth with veins or stripes of color and to dye wool in many colors and to raise many llamas and alpacas. They began to mine gold and silver and incorporate precious metals into their clothing. They also mined for copper, lead, and tin.[7]

The period of prosperity shared by the Nephites and Lamanites did not last long. In the words of Helaman, "Satan did stir up the hearts of the more part of the Nephites, insomuch that they did unite with the bands of robbers and did enter into their covenants and their oaths (Helaman 6:21)." In a role reversal, the Lamanites began to gain more knowledge of God and lived closer to God's laws than the Nephites. The Lamanites, who had suffered at the hands of the Gadianton robbers, found a unique solution to that crime problem. They preached the gospel to the Gadianton robbers, many of whom repented. Thus the robber bands were eliminated in those areas controlled by the Lamanites.

Guaman Poma de Ayala recorded that the *amautas* or ancient philosophers among the Incas had a great understanding of the stars, the comets, and the eclipses of the sun and moon.[8] Fernando de Montesinos wrote that during the time of Manco Cápac, the second king with this name (according to Montesinos's time table, it would be a period shortly before the beginning of the Christian era), two comets were seen in the heavens. One of them was said to have the form of a lion and the other the form of a snake. There were also two eclipses of the sun and of the moon. Manco Cápac called together his astrologers and wise men and questioned them as to what the signs in the heavens meant. His astrologers consulted their "idols," and the "Devil" (Montesinos's description of the idol) made them understand that Illatici Huira Cocha [Ticci Viracocha] wanted to

---

[7] Poma de Ayala, 45.
[8] Ibid., 53.

destroy them because of their wickedness. Thus Ticci Viracocha sent a lion and a serpent.⁹

Montesinos also wrote that during the period of the *Amauta* Sinchi Ayar, who was the sixty first Peruvian king, there were many comets and other unusual phenomena in the sky. He noted that there were also great earthquakes with tremors that lasted many months. These occurrences were so frightening that the Indians made sacrifices to Ticci Viracocha and to the earth which they called Pachamama (mother earth).¹⁰

From the writings of several chroniclers, it is apparent that the ancient natives carefully watched the heavens. They had astrologers who constantly kept an eye on the celestial happenings. In Mexico, Durán narrated that during the reign of Motecuhzoma, the Second, about 1500 A.D., there was observed a strange comet in the sky. The comet was described as coming from the east with a large tail and it seemed to go in the direction of Mexico-Tenochtitlan (the name that the Spaniards gave to Mexico City after the conquest). Motecuhzoma reportedly called together his priests, sorcerers, presagers, soothsayers, and astrologers to ask them the meaning of the comet. They said they had not seen it. So Motecuhzoma went to his friend, the King of Tezcoco, who verified that the comet had appeared in the heavens. He stated that it came out of the east and went toward Mexico-Tenochtitlan and was an ill-omen for the whole region. (See Chapter 15.)

The signs of the birth of Christ prompted the Nephites to begin reckoning time from that event. Nephi wrote that in spite of the signs that attended the birth of Christ and validated the warnings of Samuel, the Lamanite prophet, the Nephites intensified their wicked behavior and the Gadianton robbers returned in force to plague the people. This time the Nephites and the

---

⁹Montesinos, 41.
¹⁰Ibid., 62.

Lamanites united to fight back. In 30 A.D., the Nephite chief judge was murdered and his government was overthrown. Nephi wrote:

> And the people were divided one against another; and they did separate one from another into tribes, every man according to his family and his kindred and friends; and thus they did destroy the government of the land.
> And every tribe did appoint a chief or a leader over them; and thus they became tribes and leaders of tribes (3 Nephi 7: 2-3).

So for the first time in six hundred years, there were no longer two great nations from the descendants of Lehi.

With the visit of Jesus Christ to the Americas, the survivors became one people again and were completely converted to Jesus Christ. He ordained twelve men as his primary disciples and commissioned them to travel throughout the land teaching the gospel and baptizing the newly converted. By 36 A.D., the *Book of Mormon* records that "everyone" had been converted to Christ and there were no contentions among them.

Mormon, who abridged the writings of the Nephites during this period of harmony, skipped decades without much detail of what this era was like. He mentioned that the disciples of Christ continued to perform many miracles and when the original disciples called by Christ died, they were replaced with others. He also mentioned that the people had greatly multiplied and spread out across the land. After nearly two hundred years of peace and prosperity, a few dissenters broke away, calling themselves Lamanites.

In 210 A.D., many churches began to appear which professed to teach the gospel of Jesus Christ, but rejected much of his teachings. Mormon condemned them because they administered sacred ordinances to those who were unworthy to receive such ordinances and they began to persecute the true followers

Prosperity and Decline (600 B.C. to 400 A.D.)

of Christ. The wicked also began to persecute the disciples of Jesus and tried in vain to kill them.

By 230 A.D., there was a great division among the people and they split into two main groups–those who believed in Jesus Christ and called themselves Nephites and those who rejected the gospel and called themselves Lamanites. Mormon pointed out that the latter did not gradually lose faith through neglect, but deliberately rebelled against the gospel of Christ. They taught their children to hate the Nephites. They dredged up the old oaths and criminal pacts of Gadianton, thus forming new gangs of robbers.

By 300 A.D., both the Lamanites and the greater part of the Nephites had become corrupt. In 320 A.D., Ammaron, who was in charge of the Nephite records, resolved to hide them so their history would not fall into the hands of unbelievers and be destroyed. Later Ammaron went to Mormon, who was only ten years old at the time, and told Mormon that, since he was "a sober child and was quick to observe," he would some day take custody of the hidden plates. Mormon was told to retrieve the plates of Nephi when he was 24 and to write the things that he had observed among the people. Following his instructions, Mormon recorded that renewed warfare between the Nephites and the Lamanites began in 322 A.D. at the borders of Zarahemla.

Mormon was obviously more than just a sober or serious child by nature. He wrote that when he was 15 years old, he "was visited by the Lord, and tasted and knew of the goodness of Jesus (Mormon 1:15)." He wrote that he tried to preach to the people and call them to repentance, but Jesus Christ forbade him. Christ explained that the people had wilfully rebelled against their God and, consequently, he had taken the Nephite disciples out of the land. When Mormon was 16 years old, he was given the command of the army of the Nephites and led them into battle against the Lamanites. Mormon wrote that his armies won back a few cities, but were generally overpowered by the more numerous Lamanites. Mormon tried to gather as many Nephites as possible to strengthen his army. He recorded:

> But behold, the land was filled with robbers and with Lamanites; and notwithstanding the great destruction which hung over my people, they did not repent of their evil doings; therefore there was blood and carnage spread throughout all the face of the land, both on the part of the Nephites and also on the part of the Lamanites; and it was one complete revolution throughout all the face of the land.
> ...for behold no man could keep that which was his own, for the thieves, and the robbers, and the murderers, and the magic art, and the witchcraft which was in the land.
> And they did not come unto Jesus with broken hearts and contrite spirits, but they did curse God, and wish to die. Nevertheless they would struggle with the sword for their lives.
> And it came to pass that my sorrow did return unto me again, and I saw that the day of grace was passed with them, both temporally and spiritually; for I saw thousands of them hewn down in open rebellion against their God, and heaped up as dung upon the face of the land. And thus three hundred and forty and four years had passed away (Mormon 2:8, 10, 14-15).

Mormon indicated that most of the Nephites were driven north of what he called a "narrow neck of land" in their territory. The Lamanites inhabited the land south of that narrow neck of land. Over the next few years the Nephites won several major engagements against the Lamanites, but instead of crediting God for their success, according to Mormon, they began to boast of their own strength, and swear that they would punish the Lamanites for spilling Nephite blood. When the Nephite army thus became the aggressor, Mormon refused to lead them into battle. In 364 A.D., the Nephite army attacked the Lamanites, but was badly beaten.

Prosperity and Decline (600 B.C. to 400 A.D.)

When it became apparent that the Nephites were close to being completely destroyed, Mormon offered to lead the Nephite armies again. Under Mormon, the Nephites were able to control a few of their cities, but those people who had not gathered into those protected cities were killed. In 380 A.D., the Lamanites again attacked and overpowered the Nephites, destroyed their cities, and caused the Nephites to flee for their lives. Those who could outrun the Lamanites escaped, but those who were slower were killed. The survivors gathered in a land called Cumorah.

Mormon wrote that in 385 A.D., the Lamanites, with overwhelming superiority, attacked the Nephite army there. Mormon had divided up his army into divisions of ten thousand men each, totaling at least 230,000 soldiers. During the ensuing battle, Mormon was so seriously wounded that the Lamanites passed him by thinking that he was dead. Only twenty four Nephite soldiers, including Mormon's son Moroni, survived the battle except for a few Nephites who escaped into the south countries and those Nephites who deserted to the Lamanites.

Moroni recorded in 400 A.D. that his father, Mormon and the others were eventually killed and that he, Moroni, was the last survivor. He lamented that he was alone and he had no friends nor kinsfolk and did not know where to go. He said that the Lamanites continued to hunt down and kill the remnants of the Nephite civilization. He also declared that the Lamanites were at war among themselves and the whole land was a battlefield. Moroni lived at least another twenty one years before he concluded his record. During that time, he abridged the record of Ether, occasionally including his own perspective of the events that had transpired among the Jaredites which were similar to the destruction of the Nephites. Moroni lived long enough to add a few verses of his own thoughts which he included on the gold plates before he buried his record.

...and I make not myself known to the Lamanites lest they should destroy me.

For behold, their wars are exceedingly fierce among themselves; and because of their hatred they put to death every Nephite that will not deny the Christ.

And I, Moroni, will not deny the Christ; wherefore, I wander whithersoever I can for the safety of mine own life (Moroni 1:1-3).

Chronicle Writings Concerning Great Wars

Montesinos narrated in his history that a few years before the birth of Jesus Christ, there were periods when the people in the New World suffered from great wars. At this time, during the end of the reign of Tupac Curi Amauta, the area of Cuzco was invaded by troops from Tucuman area, spanning parts of Argentina and Chile. Tupac Curi Amauta gathered his people and formed a great army. He sent his spies to learn about the invading army. He discovered that the invading army was divided into two parts. Tupac Curi Amauta placed his army on a high mountain covered with snow, approximately sixty miles from Cuzco. He fortified the area and waited there for the arrival of the enemy. Montesinos wrote that Tupac Curi Amauta and his troops fought the first army and defeated it easily. The second army, upon hearing of the destruction of the first, broke ranks and rushed into battle to help the first army, but it was also defeated. Tupac Curi Amauta and his army returned to Cuzco victorious.[11]

Montesinos also wrote that later during the reign of Manco Cápac, the third king with this name, after the beginning of the Christian Era in the Old World, other great armies of fierce warriors attacked the Cuzco area. Montesinos narrated that they

---

[11]Montesinos, 60-61.

came from the eastern slopes of the Andean mountains as well as from Brazil.[12]

Montesinos attempted to establish an accurate time line for these events. For example, he wrote that, according to the year-count of the *amautas*, the second year of the reign of Manco Cápac would coincide with the birth of Jesus Christ in the Old World. Manco Cápac reigned another 21 years and was succeeded by his son Cayo Manco Cápac, who reigned for twenty years. Cayo Manco Cápac was followed by his son, Sinchi Ayar Manco, who died after seven years on the throne. He was followed by Huaman Tacco Amauta, who was the 61st king of Peru. It was during the time of Huaman Tacco Amauta, that the Indians saw many signs in the sky such as comets and also experienced numerous earthquakes and tremors.[13] It would appear that the events recorded by Montesinos occurred within just a few years of the time frame recorded in the *Book of Mormon*.

Montesinos wrote that there was great tribulation among the people in the Cuzco area and the surrounding provinces because of the invasions as well as the astronomical phenomena that they observed and the earthquakes that destroyed many buildings. There were also many people who were announcing or prophesying about the destruction and expulsion of the inhabitants from Cuzco.

Huaman Tacco Amauta's successor, King Titu Yupanqui Pachacuti was filled with melancholy and occupied his time making sacrifices and praying to the gods. When Titu Yupanqui Pachacuti finally came out of his dark mood, it was just in time to fortify his armies for an attack by a large army coming from the Collao area in Bolivia around Lake Titicaca. The kings spies also discovered another army of fierce warriors was coming from the eastern slopes of the Andes. Montesinos noted that among

---

[12]Ibids, 63.
[13]Ibid., 62.

the two enemy armies some warriors had dark skins which implied that the Cuzco inhabitants had light skins.[14] These two huge armies began to overrun lands and cities. The rulers of the lands in the paths of these two armies could not defend their territory alone. Consequently, Titu Yupanqui Pachacuti decided to gather all of his forces to form a large enough army to resist the advancing forces.

He also divided his army into several combat forces sending one against the Collao army and another to fight the army from the Andes in the dangerous mountain passes and at key river and bridge sites. Titu Yupanqui Pachacuti also took the bulk of his army into the high mountains where he constructed fortifications including numerous platforms, deep pits, and trenches. He also built a series of walls, which were constructed in such a manner that each wall only had one entrance. When one was breeched by the invaders, they would then face another wall higher up which also had only one entrance. These walls continued in this fashion to the top of the mountain where Titu Pachacuti Yupanqui had his tent and headquarters.

When the invaders arrived at the fortified area, Titu Yupanqui Pachacuti gave them battle and was killed along with thousands of warriors and captains on both sides. At one point the Cuzco army sent a messenger to the invading forces requesting a pause in the battle so they could bury their dead. The invaders refused and within a short time, the stench from the decaying bodies became so strong that the smell was intolerable and the decay caused serious pestilence and illness. The fighting was so heavy that nearly all of the armies were destroyed. Titu Yupanqui Pachacuti's remaining forces destroyed all of the invaders who could not escape. The king's army then fled the area and went to a place known as Tamputocco, where the smell and the pestilence did not reach.

---

[14]Ibid., 64.

PROSPERITY AND DECLINE (600 B.C. TO 400 A.D.) 🕮 309

Montesinos added that with this great battle, the Peruvian monarchy was destroyed. The descendants of the former Cuzco natives did not return to the Cuzco area for more than four hundred years. Montesinos claims that the Inca Indians lost their ability to read and write during this exile period.[15]

The histories by the chroniclers in Mesoamerica did not cover a period as far back as those in South America. Those Mesoamerican chroniclers such as Diego Durán began their histories with the arrival of the Seven Nahuatl-speaking Tribes, who did not arrive in the area until about 800 A.D. In Yucatán, Father Diego de Landa burned most of the ancient books kept by the Maya and "thus was lost the knowledge of many ancient matters of that land which by them could have been known."[16]

Landa wrote that the earliest buildings constructed in Yucatán were larger and more elaborate than the buildings constructed by the fifteenth century Maya. As will be noted further in this chapter, the archaeologists have discovered several civilizations in Mesoamerica that date from after the Olmec (1500 B.C. to 400 B.C.) and disappear before the arrival of the Aztecs about 1100 A.D.

ARCHAEOLOGICAL EVIDENCE OF WARFARE

After the Chavín civilization had disappeared from the northern Peruvian coast at approximately 400 B.C., a new civilization known as Mochica or Moche appeared in the area approximately 200 B.C.. They were particularly adept at the manufacture of thousands of elaborately designed ceramic vessels. Christopher Donnan, Steve Bourget and other art histori-

---

[15]Montesinos, 64-65. (As indicated in the Introduction to the Chronicles, Fernando de Montesinos was discredited as a historian, however, his chronology and battle scenes coincide so closely with *Book of Mormon* narrative as well as recent archaeological discoveries that Montesinos's writings merit a closer examination.)

[16]Landa, 78, n340 (continued from page 77).

ans have provided a wealth of information concerning the Moche, who are generally believed to have existed from approximately 200 B.C. to 600 A.D. Warfare was an important element of everyday life among the Moche and many of the fine-line drawings on their ceramics depict battle scenes.

In her paper on "The Men Who Have Bags in Their Mouths," Elizabeth Benson drew attention to a 1984 roll-out drawing of a Moche IV stirrup-spout pot in the Museum Für Völkerkunde, Berlin, Germany. An article published by Gerdt Kutscher in 1954 noted the scene was typical of depictions of warriors commonly found in Moche art, but it was one of the few examples of Moche fighting against foreigners. These foreigners were identified thus because they carried bags in their mouths. It is believed that these bags were used to carry coca leaves, with lime to activate the coca. Kutscher also pointed out that another clue that the men were foreigners was the pendant-disk ear ornaments they wore.[17]

In his book, *Manual de Arqueologia Peruana*, Frederico Kauffmann Doig[18] showed a number of Moche ceramic pieces which he described as significantly different from the Chavín civilization (2500 B.C. to 400 B.C.), leaving little doubt that they were made by a different people. He portrayed three pictographic scenes on the pottery he analyzed which he ascribed as representative of mythological scenes of war. However, in light of the *Book of Mormon's* graphic descriptions of the final battles that took place roughly during the same time frame between the Nephites and the Lamanites, these scenes appear more real than mythological.

---

[17]Elizabeth Benson, "The Men Who Have Bags in Their Mouths," 1984. (A hand-out in a class on the Mochica, Department of Art History, University of Texas at Austin), 367-369.

[18]Federico Kauffmann Doig, *Manual de Arqueología Peruana*. Ediciones Peisa, Lima, Peru. Copyright: 1969.

PROSPERITY AND DECLINE (600 B.C. TO 400 A.D.) 311

A series of battle scenes taken from a Moche ceramic vessel that were included in Federico Kauffmann Doig's book <u>Manual de Arqueologia Peruana</u>. 1973 Edition.

The first scene shows two fully dressed warriors with an assortment of weapons and shields. One of the warriors is dark-skinned, the other warrior is light-skinned. The dark-skinned warrior shows a more aggressive posture. In the second scene, the white man is under attack by two darker warriors and one of the men is pulling the hair of the white man, which, according to art historian Dr. Steve Bourget, is a sign of great disrespect, while the other dark-skinned warrior has his spear thrust towards the throat of the white man.[19]

In the third scene, the white-skinned warrior has lost his weapons, shield and clothing, and is shown naked, either fleeing or sprawled on the ground. In this scene the white man is also shown for the first time with what appears to be a beard. The dark-skinned warrior holds the spear previously held by his opponent. There has also been added to this scene a bird lying on its back possibly dead.

Art historians who study the Moche civilization believe that the bird is a hummingbird and they claim the hummingbird is frequently represented in Moche iconography as the spirit of war. However, the symbolism of the hummingbird in ancient America is not that clear. In Mexico, the Aztecs used the symbol of the hummingbird to represent the renewal of life (per Durán) and the Guaraní in Paraguay and Brazil viewed the hummingbird as an important spiritual element in the creation of the world (per Cadogan).

The symbol of an apparently dead hummingbird may be the Moche way of indicating that peace between the two groups had been broken. The *Book of Mormon* account of the destruction of the Nephites by the Lamanite armies, at a time period shortly before the Moche made the ceramic vessel described above,

---

[19] It will be remembered from the *Book of Mormon* narrative that during the final battles between the Nephites and the Lamanites, the Lamanites greatly outnumbered the Nephites. In addition, the Nephites, who had traditionally been able to defeat the numerically superior Lamanites, had lost their advantage because God had abandoned them.

would suggest that the white-skinned warriors had lost the Spirit of the Lord and that God would no longer protect and aid them.

Art historians and archaeologists have uncovered numerous archaeological sites of pre-historic peoples in the New World who have flourished for a period and then disappeared. In Peru alone there are the Paracas ruins and culture that flourished about one hundred miles south of Lima around the beginning of the Christian era and further south are signs of the Nazca civilization. In Bolivia around Lake Titicaca is located the equally famous Tiwanaku or Tiahuanaco civilization that had flourished long before the Incas appeared in Cuzco.

In Mesoamerica, after the Olmec civilization essentially disappeared, there emerged other civilizations such as the Toltec, the Pre-Maya and the Classical Maya civilizations. There was the civilization that built Teotihuacan. There are numerous books and articles describing these ancient civilizations which mysteriously disappeared between about 400 A.D. and 600 A.D.

14

WHITE INDIANS IN THE NEW WORLD

In 1962, while studying for my undergraduate degree, I was assigned a report on Indians in the British West Indies for a class on the History of the Caribbean. In preparing my report, I acquired an English copy of Peter Martyr de Angleria's book, *The Syxte Booke of the Fyrste Decade, to Cardinall of Aragonie*, written in 1516, in which he described Columbus's third voyage to the Americas in 1498. During this voyage, Columbus sailed around the Island of Trinidad and along the coast of present day Venezuela. Martyr did not accompany the voyage, but debriefed Columbus on his return to Spain. Martyr wrote the following, which I included in my report:

> From their ships they could see that the country was inhabited and well cultivated; for they saw well-ordered gardens and shady orchards, while the sweet odors, exhaled by plants and trees bathed in the morning dew reached their nostrils. Following the shore somewhat farther, Columbus found a port sufficiently large to shel-

ter his ships, though no river flowed into it. . . . On the morrow a canoe was seen in the distance carrying twenty four men, all of whom were young, good looking, and lofty of stature...Besides their bows and arrows they were armed with shields which is not the custom among other islanders. They wore their hair long, parted in the middle and plastered down quite in the Spanish fashion. Save for their loin cloths of cotton in various colors, they were entirely naked. Columbus naively declared that he followed in this voyage the parallel of Ethiopia, but recognized that the people he found in Trinidad were not Ethiopians, for the "Ethiopians are black and have curly, woolly hair, while *these natives are, on the contrary, white and have long, straight blond hair* (emphasis added.)[1]

When I repeated this quote in my oral presentation to my history class, the professor interrupted me and told the class emphatically that "there were no white Indians in the Americas." Furthermore, he expressed his annoyance at the "Mormon belief" that there were "white Indians" in the New World. My protestations that I was only quoting from the 1516 writings of Peter Martyr earned the rebuttal that if there were any white-skinned natives in the Americas, they were the offspring of Spaniards and Indians. The professor overlooked that fact that Columbus's observations occurred in 1498, only six years after he made his initial contacts in the New World. Later research into other chronicle writings have amply demonstrated that my professor was misinformed. However, his understanding of the New World natives is universally shared by most university history professors.

The existence of white Indians in the New World has long been overlooked or ignored by historians focusing upon the pre-Columbian period. Such a finding goes against the "normative paradigm" proposed by the Independent Inventionists that all

---

[1] Pietro Martire de Anghiera, "The Syxte Booke of the Fyrste Decade, to Cardinall of Aragonie" as taken from the Third English Book on America.) First printed in 1516 later translated by Richard Eden in June 1555. In 1962, a copy of this translated book belonged to Dr. Campbell W. Pennington, Department of Geography, University of Utah.

New World natives were Tatars or Mongols. There are those who would explain away the reports of white Indians by claiming that early Spanish and Portuguese writers were color blind or were not sensitive to gradations in skin coloring and the chroniclers were mistaken in describing the natives as "white." An extensive examination of the chronicle writings does not support this allegation.

In the ensuing years, I obtained Columbus's *Diario a Bordo* and discovered that he encountered and described the dark-skinned Taino Indians living on Cuba and the surrounding islands. In his 12 October 1492 diary entry, Columbus claimed that the Indians were similar in color to the inhabitants of the Canary Islands, not white nor black. While exploring the island which he named Española (Hispaniola–the island which is now Dominican Republic and Haiti), Columbus sent three men with a native woman into the interior of the island. The men returned and reported that the people in the interior were the most beautiful and the best built (muscular) Indians that they had seen among the several islands that they explored.

Columbus wrote that he wondered how they could be any more beautiful than the other Indians because all of the natives he had seen had beautiful bodies and faces. The three Spaniards reported that the women in the interior of Hispaniola were much whiter than the women on the other islands and two of the women they saw were as white as any woman in Spain.[2] When Columbus went into the interior of Hispaniola and saw these natives for himself, he exclaimed that they were the most beautiful men and women that he had seen in the islands. He wrote that they were very white—"*harto blanco*"—and if the women were to wear clothing and keep out of the sun they would be almost as white as the Spaniards.[3]

---

[2]Ibid., 136.

[3]Ibid., 139. (The Spaniards seemed to have been more attracted to the light-skinned Indian women which may explain why they called the "white Indians" the "most beautiful" they had seen.)

In later writings both Columbus and Martyr provided excellent descriptions of the Indians of Trinidad. When he arrived at the Island of Trinidad, Columbus described these new natives as being very different than the Tainos. For one thing, the Indians of Trinidad spoke a different language. In Columbus's description of the event, the same event related by Martyr which I cited earlier, Columbus stated:

> The color of this people is whiter than any other people that have been seen in the Indies with nice manners and beautiful bodies. Their hair is long and straight, cut in a style similar to those of Castile [Spain]. Their hair was tied with a woven head scarves of bright colored cotton. They also wore cotton sashes around their waists instead of shorts.[4]

After leaving Trinidad, Columbus went ashore on the mainland of Venezuela in an area that the natives called Paria. Columbus mentioned that the natives of Paria were also white.[5] When Columbus discovered the mouth of the Orinoco River, he declared that he must have found the Garden of Eden, or the Earthly Paradise, and attributed the whiteness of the natives to the special climate enjoyed in this Earthly Paradise. In Peter Martyr's narrative, he wrote that the men and the women were white, except those who spent most of their life working in the sun, just as with the natives of Spain.[6]

During the exploration of the Lacuyas Islands (now called the Bahamas) during the early 1500's, Spaniards discovered another group of white natives. Peter Martyr wrote that he received this information from the Catholic Priest, Alvarez de Castro, who had traveled to the Lacuyas. Alvarez de Castro said "That race of men are white and they are taller than the normal height of the other men."[7] He also reported that many natives

---

[4]Colón, 271.
[5]Ibid., 274.
[6]Martyr, 68.
[7]Ibid., 505.

from the Lacuyas were enslaved by the Spaniards and taken to Cuba and other areas to work in the mines and the fields.

In his manuscript, the chronicler Francisco López de Gómara stated that the people of the Islands of Lucayas are much whiter and "better looking" than the natives of Cuba and Hispaniola, especially the women whose beauty attracted men from the mainland of Florida, Chicora (present day Georgia or the Carolinas), and the Yucatán, who went to live in Lucayas.[8]

López de Gómara also noted that the Spaniards depopulated the Lucayas and took the natives to Cuba and Hispaniola where they worked them to death. Martyr used one speculative estimate that 1,200,000 natives were killed on Cuba and Hispaniola by disease, excessive work, and famine. As the Indians on Cuba and Hispaniola died off, the Spaniards sought for new sources of slave labor, including the natives from the Lucayas.

In a separate account, Martyr observed that in 1526, Lucas Vázquez de Ayllón sailed north towards the mainland of what is now South Carolina and Georgia. Vázquez de Ayllón described a large bay on the mainland. On the north side of the bay, which he called Chicora, the Indians were quite dark-skinned. The men wore their black hair down to the waist and were beardless. On the other side of the gulf, the land was called Duhare by the natives. Here the Indians were white and blond. Their chief was an enormous white Indian named Datha. His wife was nearly as tall as her husband and they had five children.[9]

Pedro de Cieza de León was meticulous in his descriptions of the various Indian tribes that he encountered in Colombia, Ecuador, and Peru. In Colombia, he mentioned the Indians at Arma with the following comment:

---

[8]Francisco López de Gómara, *Historia General de las Indias*, (Initially written in 1552 in the city of Zaragoza.) Published by Espasa-Calpe, S.A., Barcelona, 1932. 87.
[9]Martyr, 506.

The Indians of the province of Arma are medium build, all are dark brown, so much so that the color of all the Indians of this area appear to be children of a single mother and father.[10]

Later while in Peru, Cieza de León observed that the "Indians of Tacunga were dark like the other Indians he had described before."[11] As he would encounter new Indian tribes, he would invariably describe them as dark brown. However, when Cieza de León arrived in the region of the Chachapoyas in northeastern Peru, he described the Chachapoyas as follows:

> These Chachapoya Indians are the whitest and most attractive I have seen anywhere I have been in the Indies, and their women were so beautiful that many of them were chosen to be wives of the Incas and vestals of the temples. Even today we see that the women of this lineage who are left are extremely beautiful, as they are very white and many of them very gracefully proportioned.[12]

Pedro Pizarro, who participated in the conquest of Peru, claimed that the people of the Inca Indians, at the time of the arrival of the Spaniards, were white or light-skinned. Pizarro described the Indians: "The people of this kingdom of Peru were white, a light brown color, and among the lords and ladies, they were even more white, like the Spaniards."[13] It would appear that he was referring only to the Inca nobility and not to all of the Indians in Peru. Pizarro further described them:

> There were some tall women, not among the daughters of the kings, but among those of the Orejones, their kinsmen. These women were very clean and dainty, and they wore their black hair long over their shoulders. They considered themselves beautiful, and almost all of the daughters of these Lords and Orejones were so. The

---

[10] Cieza de León, *La Cronica*, Chapter XIX, 63.
[11] Ibid., Chapter XLI, 116. (Von Hagen, 58-59.)
[12] Ibid., Chapter LXXVII, 191-192. (Von Hagen, 99.)
[13] Pizarro, Spanish Edition: 241.

Indian women of the Guancas, Chachapoyas, and Cañares were normally the most beautiful and refined. The rest of the women of Peru were thick, neither beautiful nor ugly.[14]

Felipe Guaman Poma de Ayala, the Peruvian native chronicler, also described at least some of the Inca nobility as being white. He specifically singled out Lord Inca Viracocha Yupanqui as being white in both his face and his body and having a sparse beard.[15]

Poma de Ayala named several important Inca noble women whom he described as white. He named the wife of the sixth Inca, Cusi Chinbo Mamamícay, as being white, very beautiful, gallant and generous.[16] He indicated that another female member of the Inca nobility, Cápac Mallquima, was tall, beautiful and whiter than any Spaniard.[17] Poma de Ayala also indicated that among other natives the men and women were dark-skinned.

In one of the first books written about Brazil, Pero Lopes de Souza, a Portuguese naval captain and brother of Admiral Martim Affonso de Souza,[18] stated in his diary that when the Portuguese fleet arrived at the Bahia de Todos Los Santos (today Baia do Salvador), the principal men of the local Indian tribe came to pay homage to Admiral Affonso de Souza and the Portuguese explorers. They brought to the fleet large quantities of food and organized great parties and dances to demonstrate their pleasure in seeing the Portuguese.

---

[14]Ibid., 242.
[15]Poma de Ayala, 77.
[16]Ibid., 96
[17]Ibid., 127.
[18]Admiral Martim Affonso de Souza was given the "captaincy" or land grant of São Vicente in Brazil which included all of the area that today belongs to São Paulo. Martim Affonso de Souza also became the governor of the Portuguese holdings in what is now India. The first Captaincy in Brazil was called Tamaracá, which took its name from a small island where the first settlement was situated, and was given to Captain Pero Lopez de Sousa, who first conquered it from the French and took possession of it in 1534.

In describing the Indians, Lopes de Souza declared: "The people of this land are all white; the men well-built and the women very beautiful; so beautiful that they did not have to be jealous of those on Rua Nova of Lisbon."[19] When the Portuguese Armada arrived at the bay of Rio de Janeiro, Lopes de Souza observed that the Indians of that river were the same as those of Bahia de Todos Los Santos, but of a more gentle nature.[20]

During this same voyage, Lopes de Souza encountered numerous different Indian tribes and groups such as Guaraní, Charrua, and Querandies along the Rio de la Plata as well as Indians in northern Brazil, all of which were described by others as dark brown. Lopes de Souza did not remark on their color as such, and the fact that he specifically described the Indians around Bahia el Salvador as white is a clear indication that the difference in skin coloring was striking.

John Hemming also related the account of Martím Affonso de Sousa, the Portuguese admiral who in 1531 sailed into the bay where is now located the city of Santos, Brazil. When de Sousa arrived, he encountered several Portuguese men living among the Indians of that area. These Portuguese narrated the story of the Spaniard, Alejo Garciá and several Spaniards, who were shipwrecked off the coast of Santa Catalina, Brazil, in about 1523. Garciá, together with a few Spaniards, made friends with the local Guaraní Indians and kept asking for gold or silver. The Indians told them about a white king wearing long robes and living in the mountains far to the west.

---

[19]Pero Lopes de Souza, *Diário da Navegação Da Armada Que Foi À Terra do Brasil Em 1530, Sob a Capitania-Mor de Martim Affonso de Souza* (Published by Francisco Adolfo de Varnhagen, Socio da Academia Real, Das Sciencias de Lisboa, Lisboa. 1839.) 17, 18.

[20]Ibid., 26. (It is unclear from Lopes de Souza's comment whether he was implying that the Indians seen at Rio de Janeiro were white or pale-skinned like the ones he described at Bahia de Todos Los Santos.)

In 1524, Garciá organized an expedition which traveled overland to the Paraná and Paraguay rivers and then with two thousand Guaraní Indians plunged across the Paraguayan Chaco region to the edges of the Inca empire near Cochabamba in modern Bolivia. Garciá's army sacked some Inca towns and returned with a booty of silver and copper objects. He was the first European to see the Inca Empire.[21]

Pero de Magalhães de Gandavo, reportedly the first Portuguese chronicler to live in Brazil and to write a description of the country and the Indians, observed that although the natives were much divided and had many different names for their tribes, they appeared to be as one in their appearance, their condition, their customs and their heathen rites. He described them as follows:

> These Indians are of a dark brown color with sleek hair; the face is flattened and some of their features resembled those of the Chinese; for the most part they are well set up, lusty and of good stature; a very brave people who esteemed death lightly, daring in war and of very little prudence. They are very ungrateful, inhuman and cruel, inclined to fight and extremely vindictive. They live at their ease, without any preoccupation save eating, drinking and killing people; and so they grow very fat, but with any vexation they immediately grow thin again... They are very fickle and changeable; they readily believe whatever they are urged to believe, however difficult or impossible it may be, and with a little dissuasion they as readily reject it. They are very dishonest and given to sensuality, giving themselves up to their vices as through they were without human reason: nevertheless in their congress, the males with the females, they have due reserve and show a certain modesty.[22]

In chapter twelve of *História da Província Sácta Cruz*, Magalhães mentioned the existence of white or light-skinned Indians in Brazil with the following account:

---

[21]Hemming, 242.
[22]Magalhães, 83-84.

> The *Aimorés* are whiter and of larger stature than the rest of the Indians of that land, and their language has no similarity or relationship to that of the others. They all live in the thick woods like brute beasts, without having villages or houses in which to gather. They are excessively strong, and carry very long bows which are thick in proportion to their strength with arrows to match. These brutes [*Aimorés*] have done much harm in the Captaincies from the time they descended on the coast and have killed some Portuguese and slaves, for they are very barbarous and hate everybody in the land.[23]

Magalhães said that there were also Indians on the banks of the Maranhão (Amazon) River, on the eastern shore, in latitude about two degrees, who were called *Tapuyas*, who said they were of the same race as the *Aimorés*, or at least brothers in arms, and hence they do not harm one another when they meet.

Menasseh Ben Israel, the Jewish writer in Amsterdam, Holland, who wrote about "white Israelites" in Colombia, provided additional arguments for the existence of white Israelites in the Americas. In particular, he mentioned a Spanish captain Pedro Hernandez de Quiroz, who spent most of his life in the Americas. While in Madrid preparing for a trip to the New World, he obtained some maps of areas that he wanted to explore in the New World. In addition, he was given letters to take to the governor of Panama urging him to outfit five sailing vessels for the trip.

From Panama, Hernandez de Quiroz sailed into the South Pacific and discovered some islands in the Pacific which Hernandez de Quiroz told Ben Israel he named "Selomoh" and "Ierusalem." Hernandez de Quiroz claimed to have discovered on one of the islands some dark-skinned natives, but on one of the larger islands he discovered some white Indians with blond hair. He claimed they wore long silk robes. He tried to anchor a

---

[23]Ibid., 108-111.

ship and put some soldiers onto the island where a large crowd of white Indians had gathered, but his ship hit a reef and sank.[24]

With the loss of one ship, Hernandez de Quiroz decided to make for the mainland of South America. After following the Pacific coast for some 900 miles, Hernandez de Quiroz found a river where he discovered "another multitude of large white people with blond hair and heavy beards who were extremely well dressed with tunic type clothing."[25] These white Indians sent two dark-skinned Indians with food out to the ships, but at the same time told Hernandez Quiroz and his ships to leave and not try to land. Hernandez Quiroz took the two dark-skinned men with him back to Madrid, but the Spaniards were not able to understand their language. The Indians frequently pointed to the beards of the Spaniards and seemed to be comparing them with the beards of their former masters.[26]

Ben Israel also mentioned the narrative of an unnamed Flemish ship captain, who explored the Atlantic coast area near the 7th degree north latitude between the Marañon (Amazon River) and the Gran Pará (the northern sector of Brazil). The Flemish captain was anchored in a large river where he encountered Indians who spoke some Spanish they had learned from their previous encounters with other explorers. He spent nearly six months exploring the area.

The captain learned from these Indians that if he sailed up river for another 60 miles to where the river divided into three tributaries and if he followed the left tributary for two days, he would discover a bearded white people wearing long robes who were extremely rich with an abundance of gold, silver and emer-

---

[24]Ben Israel, 37. (Note: These Islands of Selomoh and Jerusalem are not identifiable. Unfortunately, neither Hernandez de Quiroz nor Ben Israel provided any longitude and latitude information to mark the islands or the locations of the rivers on the mainland.)
[25]Ibid., 37.
[26]Ibid., 38.

alds. The Flemish captain was told that they lived in heavily populated, walled cities. He learned that some Indians from the Orinoco region in Venezuela, which lies just north of the sector the Flemish captain was exploring, had visited the area and returned with great riches. The captain sent some of his sailors to investigate, but they became lost and had to turn back when their Indian guide died about half way to their destination.[27]

In addition to accounts of bearded white Indians that Ben Israel heard about from several chroniclers and which Ben Israel implied were likely Israelites, still other chroniclers also noted the existence of bearded white natives in the Americas. Although the existence of "bearded white Indians" would tend to lend some credence to Ben Israel's theory, from the information provided, it cannot be stated with certainty that they were Israelites. From the reports of the chroniclers already cited, the presence of white- or light-skinned Indians was not confined to just one area nor is it known whether there was any relationship between these different groups or tribes of white Indians.

Tribes of white people also apparently inhabited the New World at different times and the natives reported to Spanish writers that many of them had disappeared. For example, Cieza de León wrote the following about bearded white Indians near the old Inca city of Huamanga (currently Ayacucho, Peru):

> The largest of those streams is called the Viñaque, where there are some large and very old buildings which, judging by the state of ruin and decay into which they have fallen, must have been there for many ages. When I asked the Indians of the vicinity who had built that antiquity, they replied that other bearded, white people like ourselves, who, long before the Incas reigned, they say came to these parts and took up their abode there.[28]

---

[27] Ibid., 40.
[28] Cieza de León as recorded in *The Incas*, 123.

Martín de Murúa, the Mercedarian priest, also mentioned the ancient ruins near the city of Huamanga described by Cieza de León. It was evident to the Spaniards that these ancient ruins were very sumptuous and very different from any that the Incas built. Murúa stated that when the Spaniards tried to find out the origin of those ancient ruins, their Indian informants replied that they had been told by their forefathers that an ancient people, very similar to the Spaniards in that they were both bearded and white, had built the buildings at Huamanga.[29]

Cieza de León was informed by the Indians about another group that anciently inhabited an island in Lake Titicaca:

> Many of these Colla Indians tell that before the rule of the Incas there were two great lords in their province, one called Zapana and the other Cari, and that they won many pucarás, which are their fortresses. And that one of them entered the lake of Titicaca, and found on the largest island of that body of water bearded white men with whom he fought until he had killed all of them.[30]

Concerning the origin of the Inca kings who reigned over the great Inca empire when the Spaniards arrived, all indications suggest that they were probably remnants of the Tiwanakan society who eventually migrated to Cuzco sometime after Tiwanaku fell approximately 600 A.D. Pedro Sarmiento de Gamboa is one of the chroniclers who suggested that the Incas arrived at Cuzco in approximately 600 A.D., close to the time that archaeologists, studying Tiwanaku, have suggested that Tiwanaku collapsed.

The assemblage of reports from various sources provide a substantial base to believe that the Inca royalty were "white" people with a strong technical culture. Both Pedro Pizarro and Felipe Guaman Poma de Ayala described the Inca nobility as being white. Some of the Incas had beards.

---
[29]Murúa, 553.
[30]Cieza de León, 273.

From the description of the Andean Indians, those who built the ancient buildings at Huamanga (Ayacucho, Peru) not far from Cuzco, were constructed by bearded white men who predated the Incas' reign in Cuzco. Huamanga was likely part of the Tiwanakan empire. The Incas worshiped the same deity that was worshiped by the Tiwanakans, Ticci Viracocha, whose statue was erected in the main plaza at Tiwanaku, near modern La Paz, Bolivia, hundreds of years before the Inca kings settled at Cuzco. They likely took a knowledge of Ticci Viracocha, their creator god, with them to Cuzco.[31]

WHITE INDIANS IN MESOAMERICA AND YUCATÁN

According to Henry B. Nicholson, who made an exhaustive study of all the chronicle writings covering Mexico and Mesoamerica as well as the findings of the art historians, it was Fray Andrés de Olmos, the Franciscan missionary-linguist-ethnographer to Mexico, who was the first Spaniard to report on the Toltec high priest, Topiltzin Quetzalcoatl, who reportedly lived in Mexico about 900 A.D. Topiltzin Quetzalcoatl was described by the Indians in Mexico as a bearded white man.[32] (Topiltzin, the Toltec high priest, followed the cult of the god Quetzalcoatl and took the name Topiltzin Quetzalcoatl.) Another Franciscan priest Gerónimo de Mendieta wrote the following about Topiltzin Quetzalcoatl:

---

[31]Tiwanaku is close to Lake Titicaca on the Bolivian side. After crossing the lake to Puno, Peru, there is a semi-modern railroad from Puno to Cuzco, perhaps located about 300 miles from Puno. The original Incas could have crossed the lake and followed a path similar to the railway route. I made that same trip in October 1959 after crossing Lake Titicaca from Tiwanaku.

[32]H. B. Nicholson, *Topiltzin Quetzalcoatl, The Once and Future Lord of the Toltecs*. Published by the University of Colorado Press, Boulder, Colorado, 2001. lvii.

He was a white man, large of body, with a broad forehead, large eyes, long black hair, and wore a large round beard. They canonized him as their "sumo dios," and rendered him great love, reverence, and devotion, offering him gentle, very devoted, and voluntary sacrifices for three reasons: (1) because he taught them the art of metallurgy, which before his coming had been completely unknown and of which the natives of Cholollan greatly boasted; (2) because he never desired or permitted sacrifices of the blood of men or animals, but only of bread, flowers, and sweet odors; and (3) because he prohibited, with considerable success, war, robbery, murders, and other harmful activities.[33]

In the *Book of the Gods and Rites*, Durán described Topiltzin Quetzalcoatl as a great man who came to Mexico, apparently from the north, and established a religious life and cult. He was called Papa by the Indians and was a venerable and devout person. Durán claimed to have seen a picture of him on an ancient drawing. The drawing showed Topiltzin Quetzalcoatl as an old man with a long red beard turning white. He was a tall man with long, straight hair, sitting in great dignity. His disciples were known as Toltecs, which means masters, or men wise in some craft. In her introduction to the *Book of the Gods and Rites,* Doris Heyden stated the following about Topiltzin-Quetzalcoatl:

> In Durán's time there was utter confusion about Topiltzin-Quetzalcoatl, the great Toltec priest-king and holy man. The mystery of this man has not been completely clarified in our own times; there are controversial theories about his identity, history, and birth and death dates. Archaeological work carried out since 1940 in the ancient city of Tula, in the State of Hidalgo, north of Mexico City, confirms Durán's statement that Tula was the city of Quetzalcoatl, ruler of the Toltecs. Archaeological discoveries have confirmed that the Toltecs formed a great civilization which reached its peak in central Mexico around the year 1000 A.D. They spoke the Nahuatl language and also introduced metallurgy in the central highlands of Mexico. They left the impressive ruins of Tula.

---

[33]Ibid., 57.

When the youth became a man, he was made high priest of this cult and adopted the name of Quetzalcoatl, their god. He spent most of his life in the city of Tula, or Tollan, where he acquired fame as a holy man. Despite the reverence in which he was held, a conflict between two rival religious sects—one of which urged him to offer human sacrifice—led to a plot against him. Certain sorcerers offered him strong wine, made him drunk and led him to commit incest with his sister. Disgraced, the priest abandoned Tula and went eastward toward present day Veracruz. Before his final departure, however, he left various signs of his passing throughout the countryside and promised to return one day.[34]

Apparently there were two Quetzalcoatls. There is the figure of Quetzalcoatl, who was revered in ancient Mexico as a creator God, and Quetzalcoatl, who Heyden described above as a high Priest of Tollan or Tula. Many chroniclers have confused the two. Some of the confusion is clarified by Nicholson. He clarified that there was the Quetzalcoatl, who appeared initially as one of the first gods and who the early inhabitants of Mexico believed participated actively in the creation of the earth and man.[36] Nicholson refers to this god Quetzalcoatl as Ehecatl Quetzalcoatl or the Deity 9 Wind. He was also known as the "feathered serpent." The "plumed serpent" idols seen at the Teotihuacan ruins near Mexico City and in various locations in Yucatán are in honor of Ehecatl Quetzalcoatl. (The Teotihuacan society—200 B.C. to 600 A.D.—had disappeared before the legendary high priest of Topiltzin Quetzalcoatl had lived among the Toltec.) His name has been linked with Ticci Viracocha in Peru and, in this regard, can be linked to Jesus Christ, who, according to the *Book of Mormon* account, appeared in the New World after his crucifixion.

Bishop Diego de Landa wrote that Quetzalcoatl (understood to mean Topiltzin Quetzalcoatl) built the Yucatán city of

---

[34]Durán, 57.
[35]Nicholson, 5.

Mayapan about 900 A.D. In Yucatán he was called Kukulcan. In Alfred M. Tozzer's notes accompanying Diego de Landa's *Relación de las Cosas* de Yucatán, Tozzer mentioned the founding of the city of Mayapan in Yucatán and referred to a man named "Sac mutal" which meant "white man." It was generally accepted that the great Lord of Mayapan, Quetzalcoatl or Kukulcan, was also a bearded white man.[37]

EXISTENCE OF WHITE INDIANS IN MODERN TIMES

In addition to the groups of white Indians discovered by the conquistadores, there are very small enclaves of white Indians in existence today. Perhaps the most visible of these groups are the Ache and Guayakí Indians in Paraguay. There have been several studies made of the Guayakís during the past one hundred years. One such study was carried out in the early 1970's by a team of Argentine scholars from the Instituto de Ciencia del Hombre (Scientific Institute of Man), located in Buenos Aires.[38] In the opening statement of their report, the team explained that the Guayakís's, threatened with extinction, constitute "an enigmatic ethnic enclave" in the jungles of Caaguazú, in eastern Paraguay. Not only is their origin and racial evolution completely unknown, but it is also difficult to define their scientific classification. The Argentine anthropologists were faced with a complex problem of defining the tribe's origin because of the Guayakís's white skin coloring, the shape of their heads, and the presence of heavy facial hair. According to the Argentine scientists, everything appears to indicate that the Guayakís come from a race whose characteristics are vastly different from the normal American Indian.

---

[37]Landa, 24.
[38]Instituto de Ciencia del Hombre. *El Orígin Étnico de los Indios Blancos Guayakis de Paraguay*. Director: Dr. Jaime María de Mahieu, (Buenos Aires. Circa 1970.)

Under the leadership of Dr. Jaime M. de Mahieu, the team of scientists put together an investigative plan to compare different physical characteristics of the group. The Guayakí men were determined to be white in color but showed evidences of being lightly tanned by the sun and wind. It was not possible to closely examine the women because of their timidity around foreigners. The women live naked in their natural jungle habitat but wear clothing in a camp setting. The investigators got only fleeting views of bare skin among the women and concluded that their coloring was "milky white."

The eye coloring of the men and women ranged from light hazel to dark brown. The hair coloring also ranged from light brown to dark brown and many of the men showed moderate baldness. The men had abundant facial hair, covering the chin, the upper lip and cheeks. They normally shaved with wooden knives, but their whiskers were still very evident and several wore heavy beards. The head size was unusually large for the body size suggesting to the team that in the not-so-distant past, the typical body had been larger.[39] The Argentine scientists theorized that because of their massive thorax capacity the Guayakís lived for an extended period in the Peruvian highlands where the air is thin.

The scientists concluded that the Guayakís were descendants of a group of white people such as is found in northern Europe, but who had lived many centuries in the Andean highlands where they developed greater lung capacity. They closely resemble other whites Indians who inhabited the Andean highlands centuries before the discovery of the Americas. Later, they migrated to tropical or semi-tropical regions where they underwent a degenerative process that brought about a reduction in

---

[39] The Cuna Indians in Panama are reported to have gone through the same stature reduction after the Spaniards took over Panama and the Indians were pushed onto the San Blas islands and suffered a significant change in diet. In 1963, while assigned to a U.S. military base, I worked closely with a group of Cuna (also called San Blas) Indians and was informed by the San Blas Indians that when the Spaniards arrived they were much taller.

their stature. The Argentine scholars theorized that the Guayakis probably left the Peruvian highlands, hundreds of years before the conquest.[40]

While I was serving at the American Embassy in Paramaribo, Suriname, in 1993, a pure-blooded Indian police captain told me of a small group of white Indians who came out of the jungles of Suriname in his lifetime. He said that these white Indians had been settled among a group of Amerindians (a term the Surinamese use when referring to native American Indians in order to distinguish them from the large population of Indians from India) near Paramaribo. The police captain had taken a great interest in the group and visited with them frequently.

BOOK OF MORMON ACCOUNTS OF WHITE INDIANS

The *Book of Mormon* provides additional information about the skin coloring and other physical characteristics of the native Americans. As previously indicated, the *Book of Mormon* relates the account of three migrations to the Americas: the Jaredites, the family of Lehi, and the Mulekites. There is no record in the *Book of Mormon* that the descendants of Lehi ever made contact with the Jaredites; however, the *Book of Mormon* is an account kept by only one branch of Lehi's family, the Nephites; the Lamanites may have had contact with the Jaredites independently.[41] The Lamanites apparently did not keep any records and lost their ability to read and write.

---

[40] Mahieu, 23.
[41] Because certain names found among the writings of both the Nephites and the Jaredites were the same or very similar, i.e., Abish-Akish, Corianton-Coriantum-Coriantor, Coriantumr-Coriantumr, Korihor-Corihor, Moroni-Moron, Nehor-Nehor, etc., some Latter-day Saint scholars believe that the Nephites had contact with the Jaredites and that not every Jaredite was killed in the last famous battle witnessed by the Prophet Ether and as they mixed with the Nephites some of their names were also shared.

There is no indication within the *Book of Mormon* of the skin color of the Jaredites. Both the people of Lehi and the Mulekites were Israelites; consequently, they would have been light-skinned and most of the men would likely have worn beards which was a custom among the Israelites under the Mosaic Law. The subject of skin coloring became an issue only after Lehi's death and his sons, Laman, Lemuel and their followers rebelled and refused to keep God's commandments. Nephi recorded the following:

> Wherefore, the word of the Lord was fulfilled which he spake unto me, saying that: Inasmuch as they will not hearken unto thy words they shall be cut off from the presence of the Lord. And behold, they were cut off from his presence.
> And he had caused the cursing to come upon them, yea, even a sore cursing, because of their iniquity. For behold, they had hardened their hearts against him, that they had become like unto a flint; wherefore, as they were white, and exceedingly fair and delightsome, that they might not be enticing unto my people the Lord God did cause a skin of blackness to come upon them.
> And thus saith the Lord God: I will cause that they shall be loathsome unto thy people, save they shall repent of their iniquities.
> And cursed shall be the seed of him that mixeth with their seed; for they shall be cursed even with the same cursing. And the Lord spake it, and it was done (2 Nephi 5:20-23).

A close reading of the *Book of Mormon* makes it clear that dark skin itself was not the curse, but only the mark of the curse to keep believers from mingling with non-believers. The real curse was the Lord's withdrawal of his spirit from among the Lamanites because they refused to receive and obey his commandments. The neutral value of skin color in God's eyes was clarified by Nephi a few years later, when he declared:

> ...for he doeth that which is good among the children of men; and he doeth nothing save it be plain unto the children of men; and he inviteth them all to come unto him and partake of his goodness;

and he denieth none that come unto him, black and white, bond and free, male and female; and he remembereth the heathen; and all are alike unto God, both Jew and Gentile (2 Nephi 26:33).

The change of skin coloring that the Lord brought upon the Lamanites appears to have happened very quickly–*And the Lord spake it and it was done* (2 Nephi 5:23). The direct effect of the cursing–separation from God—is revealed in the change of life styles experienced by the Nephites and the Lamanites. Nephi provided information concerning the lifestyle and behavior of the Nephites:

> And I did teach my people to build buildings, and to work in all manner of wood, and of iron, and of copper, and of brass, and of steel, and of gold, and of silver, and of precious ores, which were in great abundance.
> And I, Nephi, did build a temple; and I did construct it after the manner of the temple of Solomon save it were not built of so many precious things; for they were not to be found upon the land, wherefore, it could not be built like unto Solomon's temple. But the manner of the construction was like unto the temple of Solomon; and the workmanship thereof was exceedingly fine (2 Nephi 5:15-16).

Whereas the Nephites set about building up a new civilization in which they built houses and temples, established cities and farms, and engaged in numerous other crafts, the Lamanites pursued an entirely different course. Nephi described their condition after the Lord withdrew his spirit.

> And because of their cursing which was upon them they did become an idle people, full of mischief and subtlety, and did seek in the wilderness for beasts of prey.
> And the Lord God said unto me: They shall be a scourge unto thy seed, to stir them up in remembrance of me; and inasmuch as they will not remember me, and hearken unto my words, they shall scourge them even unto destruction (2 Nephi 5:24-25).

Enos, the son of Jacob and nephew of Nephi, was given the responsibility by his father to keep the small gold plates and to write of events in his day. He provided additional insight into the differences between the faithful Nephites and the rebellious Lamanites. He wrote about 500 B.C.:

> And I bear record that the people of Nephi did seek diligently to restore the Lamanites unto the true faith in God. But our labors were vain; their hatred was fixed, and they were led by their evil nature that they became wild, and ferocious, and a blood-thirsty people, full of idolatry and filthiness; feeding upon beasts of prey; dwelling in tents, and wandering about in the wilderness with a short skin girdle about their loins and their heads shaven; and their skill was in the bow, and in the cimeter, and the ax. And many of them did eat nothing save it was raw meat; and they were continually seeking to destroy us.
>
> And it came to pass that the people of Nephi did till the land, and raise all manner of grain, and of fruit, and flocks of herds, and flocks of all manner of cattle of every kind, and goats, and wild goats, and also many horses (Enos 1:20-21).

As far as can be ascertained within the *Book of Mormon* record, there was no inter-marriage between the Nephites and the Lamanites until about 145 B.C. when a group of wayward Nephite priests, living in the land of Nephi during the reign of a King Noah, abducted twenty four Lamanite women and married them. Subsequently, these priests joined up with the Lamanites and became known as Amulonites after Amulon, their leader and chief priest (Mosiah 23:30-35). The Amulonites were more wicked than the Lamanites.

About 87 B.C., another Nephite by the name of Amlici and his followers attempted to make Amlici a king over the Nephites even though the Nephites had changed their system of government from a monarchy to judges. When Amlici was rejected by the Nephites, he and his followers joined the Lamanites. Their combined forces attacked the Nephites, who were commanded by the high priest Alma. During the battle, Amlici and many of his followers were killed; however, those who were not killed remained living among the Lamanites and probably intermarried with them.

Alma observed that during the battle, the Amlicites marked their foreheads with red after the manner of the Lamanites and to distinguish themselves from the Nephite forces against whom they were fighting. Alma commented that when the Amlicites placed a mark upon their foreheads, they were fulfilling prophecy in that whosoever joined the Lamanites would have a mark set upon them (Alma 3:13-14).

The Amalekites were another group of Nephite defectors who joined the Lamanites. Being of a more murderous disposition than the Lamanites, the Amalekites were generally placed in key command positions over the Lamanite armies (Alma 43:13).

The migration of people was not always from the Nephites to the Lamanites. The *Book of Mormon* records several examples of colonies of Lamanites who accepted Jesus Christ and went to live among the Nephites. About 91 B.C., four of the sons of the Nephite king Mosiah went into the lands of the Lamanites as missionaries to preach the gospel. In fourteen years, they converted thousands of Lamanites, some of whom were forced out of Lamanite society and went to live among the Nephites.

These Lamanite exiles became known as the People of Ammon (Ammon was one of the four missionary brothers). Alma wrote that they became a very industrious people and were friendly with the Nephites and the curse of God was lifted from them. Later they were joined by a group of Zoramites, a rebellious group of Nephites, who had been reconverted to the church by Alma and other Nephite missionaries (Alma 35:5-14). Over a period of time, it is likely that the Lamanite converts intermarried with some of the Nephites.

The *Book of Mormon* account states that at the time of the crucifixion of Jesus Christ in Jerusalem, the massive destruction in the Western Hemisphere killed the unrighteous. Nephi, the author of 3 Nephi, wrote that many Nephites and Lamanites were spared and within a few short years all joined Christ's Church in the Americas (4 Nephi 1:2). The people ceased to identify themselves by tribal names. They all lived together and likely married others from different tribes. In the brief description of the events after the visit of Jesus Christ to the New World, the *Book of Mormon* writers did not clarify whether the mark of a dark skin was lifted from those who had been Lamanites even though the curse was lifted.

This righteous condition lasted for nearly two hundred years before a small group of people revolted from the Church and again took upon themselves the name of Lamanites (4 Nephi 1:20). Mormon did not clarify whether these new Lamanites were only descendants of the old Lamanite tribes.

After the final battle and destruction of the Nephites, Moroni recorded that only a few Nephites managed to survive and escape to the south. Other Nephites escaped death by deserting over to the Lamanite armies. For many years, the Lamanite armies ardently hunted down and killed many Nephites who had escaped into the south. After the Lamanites killed most of the Nephites they began to war among themselves. He observed that "the whole face of this land is one continual round of murder and bloodshed; and no one knoweth the end of the war" (Mormon 8:8).

About 421 A.D., Moroni, after abridging the account of the people of Jared, penned these words:

> . . .I had supposed not to have written more, but I have not as yet perished; and I make not myself known to the Lamanites lest they should destroy me.

For behold, their wars are exceedingly fierce among themselves; and because of their hatred they put to death every Nephite that will not deny the Christ (Moroni 1:1-2).

Although those few Nephites that escaped south were hunted constantly by the Lamanites, we must suppose that at least a few eluded the Lamanite armies. Moroni did not indicate how many Nephites managed to survive by denying the Christ, but under the circumstances there were probably many. There is no indication that the Lamanites killed the Nephites who "denied the Christ" and joined them.

THE CASE OF BEARDS AND WHITE-SKIN

Facial hair among the native Americans has long been an enigma. At the time of the European conquest most Indians did not have any facial hair. It is generally accepted by anthropologists that the average native American Indian does not have any facial hair. In Peru, Pedro de Cieza de León and other chroniclers who went to the Andes wrote about Indians with beards. Cieza de León provided a description of some of the inhabitants around the Guayaquil, Ecuador, area.

> The men of these regions are dark, of goodly aspect; they and their women go dressed in the fashion they learned from the Incas, their former rulers. In certain districts they wear their hair overly long; in others, short; and in some places, tightly braided. If any hairs of the beard grew, they cut them off, and throughout all the lands that he traveled, only exceptionally did he ever see a bearded Indian.[42]

Cieza de León also recorded Indian legends of bearded white men living on an island in Lake Titicaca as well as in the Ayacucho, Peru region. In 1615, Felipe Guaman Poma de Ayala

---

[42]Cieza de León, *La Cronica*, Chapter 56. (Von Hagen, *The Incas*, 93.)

described the Lord Inca Viracocha Yupanqui as having a beard or at least straggly facial hairs. As described earlier in this chapter, the Guayakí Indians in Paraguay have heavy beards.

In Mexico, Hernán Cortés and Bernal Díaz del Castillo described the Aztec king at the time of their arrival in Mexico, Motecuhzoma, the Second, as having a well kept, close-cropped beard.[43]

In his study of Topiltzin Quetzalcoatl, H.B. Nicholson cited the early writings of the Spanish missionary to Mexico, Fray Andrés de Olmos, who was the earliest chronicler to describe Topiltzin Quetzalcoatl as being a "bearded white man."[44] In Bishop Diego de Landa's Book, Tozzer noted that Topiltzin Quetzalcoatl or Kukulcan and some of his male followers had beards.[45]

In the Yucatán, Landa wrote that the males did not grow beards, and the Maya told him that their mothers burned their faces with hot cloths while they were still very young to keep a beard from growing. After the arrival of the Spaniards, some of the Maya men let their beards grow, but the beards were very coarse like "horse hair."[46] Landa also wrote that the Mayas were very light-skinned (not white), but became darker by constant exposure to the sun.[47]

Pero de Magalhães de Gandavo also noted in Brazil that some of the natives would not shave. He wrote that they were also accustomed to pulling out their beards, and they did not allow hair to grow on any part of the body except the head.[48] In their English translation of Alonso de Ercilla y Zuñiga's book, *La Araucana*, Charles Lancaster and Paul Manchester provided

---

[43]Díaz del Castillo, 224.
[44]Nicholson, xxxvii.
[45]Landa, 22, N124.
[46]Ibid., 88.
[47]Ibid., 125
[48]Magalhães de Gandavo, 88.

the following description of the Araucanos, "Hair on a man's face was a disgraceful mark of effeminacy. They plucked the hair from their faces in order to preserve their manhood. Their greatest contemptuous term for the European was "long beard."[49]

Apparently, some of the male natives went to considerable effort to eliminate any signs of a beard. For some the beard may have singled them out as a different ethnicity. Any dark-skinned Indians with facial hair perhaps could have been the offspring of a mixture of Nephite and Lamanite.

Cieza de León noted that the Indian chief in the Titicaca area of Bolivia killed the bearded white people.[50] Cieza de León's informants emphasized that they were both bearded and white. This ethnicity difference may have been the sole reason for killing them. Other white Indians became extremely secretive and aggressive to protect themselves such as the Aimorés and the Tapuyas in Brazil as recorded by Magalhães de Gandavo. The Guayakí Indians secreted themselves for centuries in the jungles of Paraguay.

In light of the *Book of Mormon* writer Moroni's narrative that the Lamanites endeavored to hunt down the white or light-skinned, bearded Nephites in order to kill them in an extremely cruel fashion, it is logical that the surviving Nephites would resort to any measures to avoid death. These efforts undoubtedly included measures to reduce the dissimilarities with the Lamanites.

Archaeologists and art historians working Olmec and Moche sites have uncovered a wide array of statues, pottery and line drawings which show some individuals with beards. The refer-

---

[49]Charles Maxwell Lancaster and Paul Thomas Manchester, *The Araucaniad*, (A version in English Poetry of Alonso de Ercilla y Zuñiga's *La Araucana*), Published for Scarritt College, Peabody College and Vanderbilt University by Vanderbilt University Press, Nashville, Tennessee, 1945. 18.
[50]Cieza de León, *The Incas*, 273.
[51]Ben Israel, 11. (See Chapter 3 above.)

ences to white and dark-skinned natives in North, Central and South America in both ancient, conquest and modern times should be sufficient evidence that not all Pre-Columbians were homogenous Mongols or Tatars. It would appear that the theory of the Independent Inventionists concerning one migration 15 to 20 thousand years ago needs to be reevaluated and modified or discarded. There is just too much evidence to the contrary.

15

FATALISM OR PROPHECIES AMONG THE INDIANS

The ease with which a handful of Spaniards were able to enter great kingdoms in the New World and quickly dominate and subdue millions of Indians has long been a source of controversy among scholars. In almost every conquest there has been "a native legend or prophecy" that foreigners from across the seas would arrive in their lands, dominate the Indians, and establish a new form of government.

Some historians, during the last one hundred years, argue that these "native legends" are inventions of the Spaniards to justify their brutal treatment of the Indians. However, the wide-spread, independent reporting, in great detail, by numerous chroniclers lends credence to the theory that the Indians expected conquerors. Some of the reports may be exaggerated or embellished with a touch of mythology and witchcraft, but the underlying reports are consistent. In addition, there are numerous prophecies and accounts in the *Book of Mormon* of the destruction that would occur among the descendants of Lehi by Old World conquerors. These will be discussed later in this chapter.

Peter Martyr wrote that sometime in the 15th Century before Columbus arrived on Hispaniola, there were two great Indian chiefs on the Island of Hispaniola. One of the leaders was a forefather of Guarionex, one of the five kings that Columbus encountered when he arrived on Hispaniola. These two early chiefs fasted for five days to prepare themselves spiritually so their *Zemes* (priests or spiritual leaders) could tell them about future events. Martyr recorded that after the native priests were satisfied with the fasting performed by the chiefs, they told the chiefs that men wearing clothing would come to their islands and these men would destroy their ceremonies and rites. These foreigners would also kill their children and would destroy their freedoms.[1]

Andean Prophecies of Destruction

The early chroniclers recorded numerous prophecies in the Andean regions. Martín de Murúa provided information about a prophecy that reportedly occurred during the reign of the Lord Inca Topa Inca Yupanqui (in the late 15th Century). According to Murúa's informants, Topa Inca Yupanqui, after consulting with his *huacas* or idols, claimed that there would arrive a bearded people to the coast of Peru who would be invincible. These bearded strangers would bring about the destruction of the Indian kingdoms in the Andean area and would subject the natives to perpetual servitude. The destruction of the Incas would be so great that they would be lost to memory. Murúa did not elaborate on the prophecy.[2]

---

[1] Martyr, 102-103.
[2] Murúa, 321.

Fatalism or Prophecies Among the Indians 345

Juan de Betanzos wrote that before the Lord Inca Pachacuti Inca Yupanqui died, he prophesied that after the days of his grandson, Huayna Cápac, the Incas would experience a "pachacuti" which meant "a change of the world." The prophecy specified that tall, bearded white men would come into their kingdom and that in the end these men would subjugate them. Pachacuti Inca Yupanqui said that after the white men came, there would be no more Inca kings and that the people should enjoy the good life as long as they could because few people would survive after the reign of Huayna Cápac.[3]

Fernando de Montesinos wrote that Lord Inca Viracocha conquered the coastal tribes of Peru and also repaired the temple at Pachacamac, where he made sacrifices. He requested that the priests of the temple pray to ascertain the future of his grandson, Topa Yupanqui. The priests at Pachacamac foretold that Topa Inca Yupanqui and Huayna Cápac would reign happily and would conquer many lands, but after Huayna Cápac's reign, new rulers who had never been seen before would conquer and rule over their kingdom. The priests said that these strangers would be a white people with beards and would be extremely severe in their treatment of the Indians.[4]

Cieza de León stated that when Huayna Cápac was in Quito, Ecuador, he received information concerning the appearance of a strange ship and the arrival of bearded men at Paita, Peru.[5] After Francisco Pizarro and his men sailed away, Huayna Cápac reportedly prophesied that the men who had been seen in the ship would return with great power and would conquer the land. Cieza de León opined that this "prophecy" could have been a fable or the work of the devil because how else would the Incas

---
[3]Betanzos, 128.
[4]Montesinos, 116.
[5]It was 1527, when Francisco Pizarro and the thirteen men of Gallo arrived at Paita.

know that the Spaniards would return. He wrote that shortly after this, Huayna Cápac was stricken with smallpox and died.[6]

Mesoamerican Prophecies of Destruction

This fatalism or premonition that the Indians would be conquered by foreigners was not just confined to the Caribbean or the Andes. Father Diego Durán, who wrote the history of the Aztecs, noted a prophecy uttered during the reign of Motecuhzoma, the First.[7] Durán stated that he received the following information from his native informants:

> Motecuhzoma, the First, acquired such glorious fame, became so powerful, and the people were so content with his rulership, evidenced by such prudent laws and ordinances that the people held him to be more divine than human. Once Motecuhzoma had acquired great fame, he proposed to send soldiers laden with gifts back to the Aztec's original homeland, the Seven Caves area to see if any of their people remained behind.
>
> Motecuhzoma called together the sorcerers and wise men to provide insights to its location. These sorcerers were sent to find the place of their origin. They allegedly found the original inhabitants still there and they also encountered Coatlicue, mother of Huitzilopochtli, with whom they spoke. The sorcerers claimed that she uttered a prophecy in which Huitzilopochtli would be cast down from his temple at Tenochtitlan by strangers. The sorcerers left their gifts with Coatlicue and returned to Tenochtitlan loaded with gifts for Huitzilopochtli. They repeated the prophecy that after a certain time, Huitzilopochtli would be expelled from the city of Mexico-Tenochtitlan and would have to return to his original home in the Seven Caves area because, in the same way he had subjected other nations and controlled them, the strangers would wrest control from him.[8]

---

[6]Cieza de León, *Señorio*, 231.
[7]Durán, Chapter XXVII
[8]Ibid., 221. (The destruction of the Temple of Huitzilopochtli occurred in early August 1521 when Bernal Díaz del Castillo and a small group of Spaniards fought their way to the top of the Temple of Huitzilopochtli, located in the district of Tlaltelolco, and destroyed the idols and burned the shrine.)

Fatalism or Prophecies Among the Indians 347

Durán narrated a separate account which happened during the reign of Motecuhzoma, the Second, grandson of Motecuhzoma, the First. When peace had returned to Tenochtitlan, Motecuhzoma was surprised to learn that the king of the neighboring city of Tezcoco, Nezahualpilli had arrived unannounced at his palace. King Nezahualpilli, who was described by Durán as a sorcerer as well as king, told Motecuhzoma that he had received a vision of an event that was to take place during the time of Motecuhzoma, the Second. He reported the following prophecy to Motecuhzoma:

> You must be on guard, you must be warned, because I have discovered that in a very few years our cities will be ravaged and destroyed. We and our children shall be killed, our subjects humbled. Of all these things you must not doubt. In order to prove to you that I speak the truth, you will see that whenever you wage war on Huexotzinco, Tlaxcala, or Cholula, you will be defeated. You will always be overcome by the enemy and will suffer great losses of your officers and soldiers. I shall add this: before many days have passed you will see signs in the sky that will appear as an omen of what I am saying. But do not be cast down because of these things, since one cannot turn one's face from that which must be. One consolation is that I shall not see these calamities and afflictions because my days are numbered. That is why I wished to warn you before my death, O my most cherished son.[9]

According to Durán, Motecuhzoma, the Second, soon wished to test this prophecy and sent a large army against Tlaxcala, located east of Tenochtitlan, but it was soundly defeated and his commanders were taken prisoner by the Tlaxcalans. Motecuhzoma was so enraged by their defeat that he greatly chastised his army for losing the war and gave orders that his soldiers should not be received back in Tenochtitlan with gladness nor with sadness. A strange silence spread over the entire city and the streets were empty when the defeated army returned.

[9]Ibid., 452.

As further punishment, Motecuhzoma stripped his soldiers of many of the privileges that he had previously accorded them. Under pain of death, they were forbidden to wear fine cotton mantles, but had to wear cloaks of maguey fiber like those of the common man. They were not allowed to wear the sandals of nobility and were banned from the palace for one year. After the year of punishment, King Motecuhzoma again declared war upon Tlaxcala and this time, his soldiers performed better. When the battle ended the Tlaxcalans had lost as many soldiers as the Aztecs. Motecuhzoma was pleased with the performance of his troops and restored their former privileges.

Durán narrated that soon after the battle with the Tlaxcalans, Motecuhzoma, the Second, saw a strange comet in the eastern sky that seemed to advance in the direction of Tenochtitlan. He was greatly astonished and remembered the words of King Nezahualpilli. He called upon Nezahualpilli, who responded that the comet had been seen in the sky for quite some time and that it was an ill omen for all of their kingdoms as terrible things would soon come upon all of them.

Nezahualpilli stated that great calamities and misfortunes would come upon all the provinces. Death would dominate the land and all the individual kingdoms would be lost. He told Motecuhzoma that all these things would transpire during his reign. Nezahaulpilli predicted that when he left Tenochtitlan and returned to Tezcoco he would die and would not see Motecuhzoma again. He reportedly exhorted Motecuhzoma to not faint, but meet the predestined troubles with courage. Motecuhzoma reportedly wept bitterly, saying:

> O Lord of All Created Things! O mighty gods who give life and death! Why have you decreed that many kings, many powerful lords, shall have ruled proudly but that my fate is to witness the unhappy destruction of our city? Why should I be the one to see the death of my wives and children and my subjects, and the loss of my powerful

kingdoms and dominions and of all the Aztecs have conquered with their mighty arms and the strength of their chests? What shall I do? Where shall I hide?

Durán reported that as the days passed, there were numerous other omens and prophecies foretelling the destruction that would come upon the Aztecs. According to the information Durán received from his native informants, a series of mysterious or mythical events transpired, all foretelling of the destruction of Motecuhzoma, the Second, and Tenochtitlan.

One such event occurred when Motecuhzoma ordered that a huge rock be transported to Tenochtitlan to be used as the sacrificial rock during the ceremony of the "flaying of men." The laborers, moving the rock, reported that a voice from within the rock spoke to them and told them that it was too late to transport the rock as it would not be needed in Tenochtitlan. The voice urged them to tell Motecuhzoma that a terrible event was about to take place and since the event came from divine will, he could not fight it. The voice said to let him know that his reign, his power, had ended.[10] Motecuhzoma, the Second, reportedly became so disturbed with the tale of the rock that he fled into the mountains to hide.

Later Motecuhzoma, the Second, attempted to flee to the mountain of the god Huemac, but a priest sought him out and shamed him into returning to his palace. Other dreams and omens were given to different people including the elderly with instructions to transmit these messages to Motecuhzoma. Motecuhzoma inevitably searched out and destroyed the families of those sent to warn him. He also killed most of the sorcerers and wizards who could not give him good news. Durán stated that Motecuhzoma gradually retreated from public life.

---

[10] Ibid., 479.

Durán also narrated that during this time frame, a man appeared at the palace who stated that while walking along the beach he had seen a mountain or a large house floating upon the water. Motecuhzoma quickly sent one of his officers to investigate.[11] The officer returned with the verification of the arrival in a ship of bearded white men dressed in multi-colored clothing. Motecuhzoma sent a delegation with fine jewelry and cloth to present to the strangers and to see whether the strangers were Topiltzin Quetzalcoatl himself, who had promised to return. Motecuhzoma reportedly said that if it were Topiltzin Quetzalcoatl, he would turn his kingdom over to the strangers because Motecuhzoma was aware that he was only guarding the domain for Topiltzin Quetzalcoatl until his return.[12]

The high priest Topilzin Quetzalcoatl, who lived approximately 900 A.D., fled Tula into Yucatán and then disappeared. Topilzin Quetzalcoatl had promised to return and reclaim his throne. It was the legend of the return of Topilzin Quetzalcoatl that was later used so effectively by Hernán Cortés during the initial conquest of Mexico. Cortés convinced Motecuhzoma, the Second, that he represented a powerful king to the east.

Motecuhzoma, the Second, in his desire to know more about Cortés, sent his ambassador, Tlillancalqui, with presents to offer to Cortés. He also sent a group of artists to make paintings of the Spaniards, their ships, horses, and weapons. Motecuhzoma compared these artists renderings of the Spaniards with some paintings of an old man from Xochimilco, who was well versed in

---

[11]Ibid., 495. (Heyden suggests that this particular report lay in the realm of mythology, but conceded that perhaps it could have been the 1518 expedition of Juan de Grijalva which traveled along the coast until the island which the Spaniards named San Juan de Ulúa. It was there that the first contact between the Aztecs and the Spaniards took place. Hernán Cortés arrived at Ulúa on 21 April 1519.)

[12]Diego Durán, *Book of the Gods and Rites* (1574-76) as well as *The Ancient Calendar* (1579). (Translated and edited by Fernando Horcasitas and Doris Heyden with Forward by Miguel León-Portilla.) University of Oklahoma Press, Norman, Oklahoma, 1971.

ancient history and art. Motecuhzoma observed that the details in the old man's paintings were nearly identical to those produced of the Spaniards in regard to beards, clothing and headdresses.

The old man had previously predicted that men would come on beasts similar to deer and others on eagles that would fly like the wind. These men were to conquer the country, settle in all its cities, multiply in great numbers, and become the owners of the gold, silver, and precious stones. Motecuhzoma reportedly was so impressed with the old man that he kept him close by and relied heavily upon his advice when dealing with the Spaniards.

Durán had high praise for Motecuhzoma, the Second, and stated that he was a man of peace who surrendered himself willingly to Cortés as the "representative" of the Great King who had promised to return. Motecuhzoma also reportedly predicted his own demise at the hands of the Spaniards and requested that Tlillancalqui, his ambassador to Cortés, take care of his children. Durán's record of these various prophecies painted an excellent picture of Motecuhzoma's frame of mind when the Spaniards arrived.[13]

Both Hernán Cortés and Bernal Díaz del Castillo made mention of a belief by the Aztecs about the return of a white god who would conquer them. During conversations with Aztec leaders after the conquest, the Indians related that among the Aztecs there existed a story that their ancestors had prophesied that men with beards would come from the direction of the sunrise and rule over them; consequently, there were many Indians watching for the arrival of the Spaniards. The audacity of the Spaniards against overwhelming odds surprised the Indians and may have contributed to the Indian belief that the Spaniards were divinely protected.

---

[13]See Hernán Cortés' *Cartas de la Relación* and Bernal Díaz del Castillo's *La Verdadera Historia de la Conquista de Nueva España* to read about the conquest itself. Durán describes the conquest, but it follows basically the same chain of events in these other two books.

Díaz del Castillo provided an example of this apparent invincibility when he narrated the events that transpired when Cortés arrived at the river that the earlier Grijalva expedition named the Grijalva River.[14] There Cortés met considerable resistence from thousands of heavily armed Indians who were inhabitants of the native city Tabasco. Through his interpreter Aguilar, Cortés made several appeals to the Indians to let him land and obtain water and food, but they steadfastly refused. He finally opted for force. After considerable fighting, but no deaths among the Spaniards, Cortés drove the Indians back and, in the presence of Diego de Godoy, the Spanish royal notary, Cortés took possession of that land for the king of Spain.

Díaz del Castillo also described a great battle the following day during which the Spaniards took on and defeated thousands of Indians. The use of horses and the extremely sharp Spanish swords brought real fear to the Indians. This was the first significant battle by Cortés in the New World and the site was named Santa Maria de la Victoria. All of the Spaniards humbly acknowledged that only by the help of God were they able to defeat a numerically overwhelming and determined army of Indians.[15] According to Cortés, the Indians later told him they had opposed him with an army of more than 40,000 warriors.

After leaving the Tabasco area, the fleet sailed to San Juan de Ulúa where Cortés encountered a delegation of Motecuhzoma's governors and personal representatives. Cortés exchanged gifts with Motecuhzoma's representatives and they, in turn, had their artists paint portraits of Cortés, his captains and soldiers, the horses, ships and sails, cannons and cannon-balls, and even two greyhound dogs.

---

[14]J. M. Cohen, who wrote the Introduction to Díaz del Castillo's book, stated that these Indians would have been Tzendals, a branch of the Mayas, and their language would have been Mayan.

[15]Díaz del Castillo, 75–77.

Fatalism or Prophecies Among the Indians 353

According to Díaz del Castillo, Motecuhzoma was convinced that the Spaniards were of that race which, according to the prophesies of their ancestors, would come to rule the land.[16] The Aztecs continued to be friendly with the Spaniards and exchanged gold and silver for beads and trinkets. They also supplied large quantities of food to the Spaniards; however, suddenly without any explanation, the Indian trading party disappeared taking with them the supplies Cortés relied on. The Spaniards soon learned that Motecuhzoma had ordered the withdrawal of Aztec support.

Continuing with his voyage, Cortés landed near what is now modern Veracruz, Mexico, where he encountered a tribe of Totonac-speaking Indians who had been subjugated for years by the Aztecs. Cortés treated these Indians very well and soon gained their confidence. He discovered that the Spaniards's reputation as courageous and skillful warriors preceded them and the Totonac-speaking Indians begged Cortés to help free them from Aztec rule.

While Cortés was meeting with the Totonac chiefs from Quiahuitzlan and neighboring villages, five tax collectors for Motecuhzoma arrived and demanded to know why the Indians were fraternizing with the Spaniards after Motecuhzoma had given orders to have no further contact with them. The tax collectors demanded twenty prisoners for a sacrifice. Cortés interceded and prompted the Totonacs to capture the tax collectors. The Totonacs were so surprised at Cortés's audacity and apparent lack of fear of Motecuhzoma that they referred to the Spaniards as *Teules*, which in their language meant gods or demons.

Cortés would later play up the idea that he had been sent by God. He subsequently freed two of the five tax collectors with instructions that they return to Motecuhzoma and inform him that the Spaniards had come in peace and wanted to meet with

---

[16] Ibid., 92.

him.[17] The two freed prisoners appeased Motecuhzoma's anger over the detention of his tax collectors, and piqued his curiosity; consequently, he initially constrained his warriors from attacking the intruding Spaniards who had landed in his empire.

Díaz del Castillo wrote that as time went on Motecuhzoma became more certain that the Spaniards were those people whose coming had been foretold by their ancestors, and must therefore be of their own race.

In a letter to King Charles V, Cortés described the ceremonial arrival of the great King Motecuhzoma with an entourage of two hundred lords and noblemen from Tenochtitlan. After the reception ceremony and an exchange of gifts, Cortés recounted Motecuhzoma's narrative of a great legend:

> Long ago we learned from a study of our scriptures, which were preserved by our ancestors and given to us, that neither I nor any of those who currently inhabit this land are natives of this area. We are all strangers here and we came from far away places. At the same time, we have information that our people were vassals of a great lord who brought them here and who later returned from where he had come. After a long time, he returned to lead our people back, but found that our ancestors had married native women of the area and several generations had already passed and our ancestors had built up towns and cities throughout the area. Our ancestors not only did not want to return with the great lord, but did not even want to receive him. Consequently this great lord went back to his own land and we have always believed that his descendants would one day come and conquer and rule this land and all of us as his vassals.
>
> From what you tell us that you have come from where the sun rises and what you have told us about this great king or lord who sent you here, we believe and are certain that your King might also be our natural king or lord. You have also told us that for many days your great king has known about us; therefore, you can be sure that we will obey you and your king about whom you have told us. We will not falter nor deceive you and you can go wherever you would like to go and do whatever you would like to do in the land where I am lord.

---

[17]Díaz del Castillo, 110-113.

Fatalism or Prophecies Among the Indians 355

You only need to ask and you will be obeyed and all that is ours will be given to you to do with as you would like. You can relax because you are now in your own land and you can rest from all of your travels and wars.[18]

Cortés readily played upon this ancient myth of Quetzalcoatl and the "great Lord of the East" to gain the confidence of Motecuhzoma and many of the Aztecs by pretending that King Charles V was, indeed, the great lord about whom the Aztecs had legends.

Diego de Landa wrote that in the same way that the Aztecs had signs and prophecies of the coming of the Spaniards, and of the destruction of Aztec power and religion, so did the Mayas have their prophecies. He said that an Indian named Ah Cambal, who held the office of *Chilam* (soothsayer or prophet), declared publically that the Maya would soon be subjected by a foreign race, and that the foreign race would preach to them one God and the "power of a tree."[19]

In the writing of Herrera, which Tozzer added as Appendix A to Landa's book, Herrera cited the prophecy of the Cocom tribe, one of the three main tribes of Yucatán. Don Juan Cocom showed the Spaniards a book, written years before the arrival of the Spaniards, which had a painting of an unusual deer. According to Don Juan Cocom, the Cocom religious leaders prophesied that when the great deer, which the Maya now realized from the artists rendition were cows, entered the land, the worship of their gods would be changed, which Don Juan Cocom had seen fulfilled with the arrival of the Spaniards and with them the cows.[20]

---

[18]Cortés, 116-117.

[19]Landa, 43. (Tozzer added the note that the Catholic Priests interpreted this to mean the coming of the Christians with the "tree" as referring to the cross.

[20]Ibid., 217. Appendix A. Antonio de Herrera de Tordesillas, *Historia General de los Hechos de los Castellanos en las Islas y Tierra Firme del Mar Océano* (1601). (Herrera, who had never been to the Americas, was named Historiographer Royal and was commissioned to write a history of the Indies.)

Concerning the prophecies that were reportedly given to the Indians about the coming of the Spaniards, it would be worthwhile revisiting the account of Aharon Levi which he shared with Menasseh Ben Israel, the Jewish Rabbi in Amsterdam, about the prophecy narrated by the Indian chief Francisco after Francisco and Levi allegedly visited a group of Israelites living deep in the Colombian or Venezuelan jungle. As stated in Chapter 3, Francisco provided the following account related by their tribal priests (mohanes) which his people believed to be true. According to Francisco, his tribal priests told his tribe:

> The God of these Sons of Israel is the true God. All that is written on their stones is true. At the end of time, they will be Lords over all the people in the world. There will come into this land a people who will bring with them many things and, after this land is completely filled up, these Sons of Israel will come out from where they are, and will dominate the whole land as they did before. Those of you who wish to be venturesome, remain close to them.

Francisco proclaimed that during his conversation with the Israelites who came to visit with Levi, the Israelites mentioned that the three most notable events, observed by the Israelites and which caused great celebration, had been the arrival of the Spaniards, the arrival of the ships in the South Sea [Pacific], and the visit of Aharon Levi. According to Francisco, the Israelites claimed that these three events were in fulfilment of their prophesies.[21] Ben Israel apparently tied these prophecies of the "American" Israelites with a general gathering of Israel and the return of the Ten Lost Tribes of Israel.

---

[21] Ben Israel, 14-15.

Book of Mormon Prophecies Concerning the Americas

According to the *Book of Mormon* narrative, about 592 B.C., the young prophet Nephi was visited by an angel who showed him in a vision the land of promise to which his family would sail. Nephi also saw the eventual downfall of his people. He foresaw numerous wars between his descendants, the Nephites, and the descendants of his brother, the Lamanites. He saw the end of the Nephite civilization and the centuries of warfare among the Lamanites (1 Nephi 13). The angel also showed him the oceans and how they would divide the "Gentiles" from the Lamanites.[22] The angel also told Nephi that the wrath of God would come upon the Lamanites and that eventually the Gentiles would be led to the Americas. Nephi recorded:

> And I looked and beheld a man among the Gentiles, who was separated from the seed of my brethren by the many waters; and I beheld the Spirit of God, that it came down and wrought upon the man; and he went forth upon the many waters, even unto the seed of my brethren, who were in the promised land.
>
> And it came to pass that I beheld the Spirit of God, that it wrought upon other Gentiles; and they went forth out of captivity, upon the many waters.
>
> And it came to pass that I beheld many multitudes of the Gentiles upon the land of promise; and I beheld the wrath of god, that it was upon the seed of my brethren; and they were scattered before the Gentiles and were smitten.
>
> And I beheld the Spirit of the Lord, that it was upon the Gentiles, and they did prosper and obtain the land for their inheritance; and I beheld that they were white, and exceedingly fair and beautiful, like unto my people before they were slain.
>
> ... wherefore, thou seest that the Lord God will not suffer that the Gentiles will utterly destroy the mixture of thy seed, which are among thy brethren.

---

[22] Gentile in this case is any person who is not of the house of Israel.

Neither will he suffer that the Gentiles shall destroy the seed of thy brethren.

... I will be merciful unto the Gentiles in that day, insomuch that I will bring forth unto them, in mine own power, much of my gospel, which shall be plain and precious, saith the Lamb.

For, behold, saith the Lamb: I will manifest myself unto thy seed, that they shall write many things which I shall minister unto them, which shall be plain and precious; and after thy seed shall be destroyed, and dwindle in unbelief, and also the seed of thy brethren, behold, these things shall be hid up, to come forth unto the Gentiles, by the gift and power of the Lamb.

And at that day shall the remnant of our seed know that they are of the house of Israel, and that they are the covenant people of the Lord; and then shall they know and come to the knowledge of their forefathers, and also to the knowledge of the gospel of their Redeemer, which was ministered unto their fathers by him. . . (1 Nephi 13:10-15, 30-31, 34-35; 15:14).

Nephi wrote that this record of his people would be preserved and would be given to the Gentiles who would come to the Americas and from them unto the descendants of Lehi. The Angel told Nephi that their record and history would testify of the veracity of the Bible and that both records together would testify that Jesus Christ is the son of God and the Savior of the world.

Before Lehi died in the New World, he gathered his family around him and told them that he had seen in a vision that Jerusalem had indeed been destroyed as he had prophesied when he left the city. (Jerusalem was sacked by the Babylonians between 586 B.C. and 590 B.C. as recorded in the Bible in 2 Kings 25, approximately ten years after the *Book of Mormon* records that Lehi and his family fled.) Lehi reminded his children that if they had remained in Jerusalem they would have died too. He then told them:

> But, said he, notwithstanding our afflictions, we have obtained a land of promise, a land which is choice above all other lands; a land

Fatalism or Prophecies Among the Indians 359

which the Lord God hath covenanted with me should be a land for the inheritance of my seed. Yea, the Lord hath covenanted this land unto me, and to my children forever, and also all those who should be led out of other countries by the hand of the Lord.

Wherefore, I, Lehi, prophesy according to the workings of the Spirit which is in me, that there shall none come into this land save they shall be brought by the hand of the Lord.

Wherefore, this land is consecrated unto him whom he shall bring. And if it so be that they shall serve him according to the commandments which he hath given, it shall be a land of liberty unto them; wherefore, they shall never be brought down into captivity; if so, it shall be because of iniquity; for if iniquity shall abound cursed shall be the land for their sakes, but unto the righteous it shall be blessed forever.

And behold, it is wisdom that this land should be kept as yet from the knowledge of other nations; for behold, many nations would overrun the land, that there would be no place for an inheritance.

Wherefore, I, Lehi, have obtained a promise, that inasmuch as those whom the Lord God shall bring out of the land of Jerusalem shall keep his commandments, they shall prosper upon the face of this land; and they shall be kept from all other nations, that they may possess this land unto themselves. And if it so be that they shall keep his commandments they shall be blessed upon the face of this land, and there shall be none to molest them, nor to take away the land of their inheritance; and they shall dwell safely forever.

But behold, when the time cometh that they shall dwindle in unbelief, after they have received so great blessings from the hand of the Lord—having a knowledge of the creation of the earth, and all men, knowing the great and marvelous works of the Lord from the creation of the world; having power given them to do all things by faith; having all the commandments from the beginning, and having been brought by his infinite goodness into this precious land of promise—behold, I say, if the day shall come that they will reject the Holy One of Israel, the true Messiah, their Redeemer and their God, behold, the judgments of him that is just shall rest upon them.

Yea, he will bring other nations unto them, and he will give unto them power, and he will take away from them the lands of their possessions, and he will cause them to be scattered and smitten (2 Nephi 1:4–11).

Lehi's comment about a book that would be written by his descendants which would eventually be translated and taken back to his descendants by the Gentiles (the *Book of Mormon*) adds new light to the words of those presumed Israelites who were discovered by Aharon Levi circa 1650 and subsequently published in Ben Israel's book, *Sobre El Origen de los Americanos*. These New World "Israelites" stated that "Joseph lives in the middle of the ocean (holding up two fingers together and then opening them) in two parts." Once Lehi arrived in the Americas, viewed as an island in the middle of the ocean, his family, descendants of Joseph, soon divided into two distinct groups or nations.

There is a Biblical prophecy that appears to indicate that the descendants of Joseph would be spread far:

> Joseph is a fruitful bough, even a fruitful bough by a well; whose branches run over the wall.
> The blessings of thy father have prevailed above the blessings of my progenitors unto the utmost bound of the everlasting hills; they shall be on the head of Joseph, and on the crown of the head of him that was separated from his brethren (Genesis 49:22, 26).

However, Aharon Levi would likely not have understood such a complicated prophecy to have been able to predict this division of Joseph's descendants which only becomes evident with the insights provided by the *Book of Mormon*. In a similar fashion, the statement by these New World Israelites that "Some day we will all speak and we shall come out as if the earth gave us birth." begins to have meaning once it is compared to the prophecy of Lehi and the words of Isaiah. It appears that these Israelites, visited by Aharon Levi, foresaw ancient writings coming out of the ground or out of the dust "as if the earth gave us birth."

Six years before the birth of Jesus Christ in Jerusalem, Samuel, a Lamanite prophet, in addition to providing signs concerning the birth and death of the Savior, also mentioned the state of the Lamanites in the "latter times."

> Yea, I say unto you, that in the latter times the promises of the Lord have been extended to our brethren, the Lamanites; and notwithstanding the many afflictions which they shall have, and notwithstanding they shall be driven to and fro upon the face of the earth, and be hunted, and shall be smitten and scattered abroad, having no place for refuge, the Lord shall be merciful unto them.
>
> And this according to the prophecy, that they shall again be brought to the true knowledge which is the knowledge of their Redeemer, and their great and true shepherd, and be numbered among his sheep.
>
> Therefore, saith the Lord: I will not utterly destroy them, but I will cause that in the day of my wisdom they shall return again unto me, saith the Lord (Helaman 15:12-13,16).

During the visit of Jesus Christ to the Americas as recorded in the *Book of Mormon*, he told the surviving Nephites and Lamanites about the "last days," the scattering of his covenant people the house of Israel, and the subsequent signs that would appear when God would begin to gather scattered Israel. Jesus Christ stated:

> And verily I say unto you, I give unto you a sign, that ye may know the time when these things shall be about to take place—that I shall gather in, from their long dispersion, my people, O house of Israel, and shall establish again among them my Zion;
>
> And behold, this is the thing which I will give unto you for a sign—for verily I say unto you that when these things which I declare unto you, and which I shall declare unto you hereafter of myself, and by the power of the Holy Ghost which shall be given unto you of the Father, shall be made known unto the Gentiles that they may know concerning this people who are a remnant of the house of Jacob, and concerning this my people who shall be scattered by them;
>
> Verily, verily, I say unto you, when these things shall be made known unto them of the Father, and shall come forth of the Father from them unto you;

For it is wisdom in the Father that they should be established in this land, and be set up as a free people by the power of the Father, that these things might come forth from them unto a remnant of your seed, that the covenant of the Father may be fulfilled which he hath covenanted with his people, O house of Israel;

And when these things come to pass that thy seed shall begin to know these things—it shall be a sign unto them, that they may know that the work of the Father had already commenced unto the fulfilling of the covenant which he hath made unto the people who are of the house of Israel (3 Nephi 21:1-4, 7).

Once again, the account of Francisco to Aharon Levi portends the scenes and events described in these chapters of the *Book of Mormon*. In an overview of Levi's report, Levi was told that foreigners would come into the land and essentially populate most of the New World. After this was accomplished, these "Sons of Israel" would come out from where they were hiding and would dominate the land as they did previously. His "Israelite" informants welcomed all "those of you who wish to be venturesome, remain close to them."[23]

It would appear that these New World "Israelites" are talking about a gathering of remnants of the house of Israel on this continent in the last days. The phrase in the last sentence of the quotation *Those of you who wish to be venturesome* seems to be referring to the Gentiles upon the land and this appears to be an invitation to them to remain close to the "Remnant of Jacob" living in the New World and participate in whatever activities and blessings the Lord has for these "scattered Israelites."

Mormon, who wrote about 385 A.D., continued to admonish both the Lamanites who survived the wars as well as the "gentiles" that both groups needed to believe in Jesus Christ. Moroni, the same Moroni who appeared to Joseph Smith fourteen hundred years later, inserted himself into the narrative and explained that his father, Mormon, had been killed in the fight-

---

[23]Ben Israel, 13.

ing and that he, Moroni, had been given the records from his father and would describe the final destruction of his people. Apparently Moroni was given the privilege of seeing hundreds of years into the future because he spoke of the last days. He even went so far as to say, "Behold, I speak unto you as if ye were present, and yet ye are not. But behold, Jesus Christ hath shown you unto me, and I know your doings" (Mormon 8:35).

Moroni claimed that he lived another thirty five years after the death of his father and the destruction of his people. In 421 A.D., Moroni finished his writings and buried the plates. Moroni included one final exhortation and a most unusual promise to his brethren, the Lamanites as well as the Gentiles. He urged everyone to read the record of his people as recorded in the *Book of Mormon* and then to ask God whether it was true:

> Behold, I would exhort you that when ye shall read these things, if it be wisdom in God that ye should read them, that ye would remember how merciful the Lord hath been unto the children of men, from the creation of Adam even down until the time that ye shall receive these things, and ponder it in your hearts.
>
> And when ye shall receive these things, I would exhort you that ye would ask God, the Eternal Father, in the name of Christ, if these things are not true; and if ye shall ask with a sincere heart, with real intent, having faith in Christ, he will manifest the truth of it unto you, by the power of the Holy Ghost.
>
> And by the power of the Holy Ghost ye may know the truth of all things (Moroni 10:3-5).

16

PRE-COLUMBIAN TECHNICAL SKILLS

When Columbus and the Spaniards first encountered the native Americans, they thought they had discovered a backward and simple people. As the Spaniards, subsequently, explored farther into Mexico and Peru, they were amazed by the vast array of technical and manual skills exhibited by many of the natives. One of the main objectives of the Europeans was to find gold and they soon discovered that the Indians were some of the finest, if not the finest, goldsmiths in the world. Many natives were extolled for their ability to work with stone especially in building unique pyramids, palaces, fortresses, roads, and complex irrigation systems. They also exhibited extensive knowledge in working with cement and cloth.

It is true that the Spaniards and Portuguese saw only skills demonstrated by the natives living in the early 1500's. The skills of earlier civilizations were not so evident to the untrained eye by the time the European conquest of the Americas began. The Olmec, Chavín, Tiwanakan, Teotihuacan, early Mayan, Toltec and Moche civilizations had long disappeared by the time the Europeans arrived and their handiwork would not be fully appreciated until archaeologists and art historians discovered it in the 20th Century. The Aztec, classical Mayan, Tezcocan, Tlaxcalan, Inca, Chimor and other civilizations encountered by the Europeans were of a more recent vintage. These later civilizations built upon old technologies and developed new ones in the years leading up to the arrival of the Spaniards.

Mormon, the ancient warrior and prophet who abridged many volumes of records, accumulated by the Nephites over their thousand year existence (600 B.C. to 400 A.D.), repeatedly stated that he could not include a hundredth part of their recorded history. He included very little information about their day-to-day living conditions or technical proficiencies. Whatever skills were identified in the *Book of Mormon* were only discussed peripherally. Most of the *Book of Mormon* material inserted by Mormon (Mosiah through 3 Nephi) covers the brief period from 130 B.C. to 34 A.D. Aside from the *Book of Mormon*, only sketchy information from this pre-Christian era endured through the centuries and appears in 16th Century folklore, hieroglyphs or quipos and observations made by the Spaniards.

Mormon covered the next three hundred years in the 49 verses of 4 Nephi. Both Mormon and Moroni, his son, provided limited historical information concerning the wars and final destruction of the Nephites and they dedicated their final verses to rendering strong admonitions and insights to the readers of the future about the factors that contributed to the destruction of such a mighty people. They did not delve into the technical skills that were used in the Americas. Moroni buried their record, engraved on gold plates, in 421 A.D., 600 to 800 years before the construction of Tenochtitlan, Chichen Itzá, or Cuzco.

The botanist, cartographer, and explorer, Alexander Von Humboldt arrived in the New World in 1799 and spent the next five years exploring and mapping the Orinoco River in Venezuela and traveling through Cuba, Ecuador, Colombia, and Mexico. Much of his work was dedicated to the naming of the thousands of plant species found in the New World as well as charting the oceanographic currents. He returned to Europe where he wrote about his findings and delivered numerous lectures. His most famous work *Cosmos: Sketch of a physical world description*, was published in five volumes. The first four were published between 1845 and 1858 and the fifth was published after his death in 1859.

As mentioned in Chapter 1, John Lloyd Stephens and Frederick Catherwood, traveled into Yucatán in 1839 to explore ancient ruins discovered there. Stephens wrote *Incidents of Travel in Central America, Chiapas and Yucatan*, which was published in June 1841. His descriptions of the Maya ruins coupled with Catherwood's drawings were the first modern attempts to describe the ancient Mayan buildings and cities. Intrigued by the possibilities of exploring these ancient ruins, other archaeologists followed Stephen's footsteps into Mexico. Peru has also attracted numerous archaeologists and art historians who have explored a wide variety of early civilizations.

In 1852 to 1854, Sir Clements Robert Markham traveled throughout Peru. He eventually published a book *The Incas of Peru* in 1910. In 1911, Hiram Bingham accidentally discovered Machu Pichu. Today universities are training hundreds of archaeologists and art historians who, in turn, are searching and excavating pre-Columbian sites throughout the New World. They have already contributed valuable information concerning the technological skills of these ancient American inhabitants. The chroniclers also recorded information concerning a wide array of skills before the Spaniards and other Europeans destroyed many of the pre-Columbian civilizations.

I will begin this chapter by exploring the navigational skills displayed by the Indians who lived close to oceans, rivers, and lakes.

Navigational Skills

Most modern scientists and historians discard the idea that the original Americans came to the New World through a boat migration from Europe or Asia. Early peoples did not have the compass nor were they thought to possess adequate navigational skills for such a journey. However, the first Spaniards to arrive in the New World discovered that many Indians were adept at navigating the ocean and traveled hundreds of miles over relatively open seas without the benefit of compasses.

Columbus recorded in his diary on 13 October 1492 that the Indians came to his three ships in dugouts which were built like long ships. He described these dugouts as extremely well made and observed that the length varied by the length of the trees from which they were made. Some of the dugouts were large enough to accommodate forty or fifty men. Columbus described their oars as skillfully and artistically made, resembling a long baker's stick. He noted that the dugouts were extremely fast in the water.[1] On 30 November, Columbus recorded seeing a dugout along the Cuban coast that was 95 hand spans long (approximately 65 feet) and could hold 150 people. He soon discovered that the Indians called their dugouts "canoes," which is a term that he subsequently employed in his diary.

The Indians of Cuba and Hispaniola told Columbus and his companions that they were frequently attacked by fierce Carib Indians who lived on far away islands and who raided other

---

[1] Colón, 67.

islands looking for Indians to cannibalize or take as slaves. Martyr claimed that according to Columbus's narrative, the Caribs would frequently travel by canoe over one thousand miles to hunt for new victims.² Much of this distance would be over open seas. The Tainos told Columbus about the existence of other islands and the kinds of people who lived there. It became obvious to the Spaniards that most of the Indians were accustomed to inter-island navigation.³

During Columbus's third voyage when he discovered the island of Trinidad and the north Venezuelan coast, including the mouth of the Orinoco River, he saw the natives using hundreds of canoes of various sizes. He observed that the canoes along the coast of Venezuela and Trinidad were larger and better made than the canoes of Cuba, Hispaniola and the Antilles. Some of the canoes were large enough that the Indians could construct a cabin in the center where tribal leaders and their wives could relax.⁴

Bishop Diego de Landa wrote that the Maya were accomplished traders, carrying salt, cloth and slaves to distant lands in exchange for cacao and stone beads, which they used as money. In a footnote to Landa's book, Tozzer wrote that much of this bartering took place by sea with Honduras and Nicaragua. He quoted Juan de Torquemada, who wrote, "Other nations traded in this province (Nicaragua) and especially those of Yucatán who came by the sea in canoes and brought mantas, feathers and other things and returned with cacao." Tozzer also mentioned that metal objects dredged from the natural well (Cenote of Sacrifice) at Chichen Itzá come from as far away as Colombia on the south and central Mexico on the north.⁵

---

[2] Martyr de Angleria, 17.
[3] Ibid., 192.
[4] Colón, 275.
[5] Landa, 94, n415.

According to the narrative of Peter Martyr, when Vasco Nuñez de Balboa was exploring the Bay of Urabá in Colombia and the Darién in Panama in 1513, he was told by the son of the Indian chief, Comogro, about another ocean on the other side of the mountains to the south.[6] The chief's son stated that from the tops of the mountains Nuñez de Balboa would be able to see native ships as large as the Spanish caravels, the standard size sailing vessel used by the Spaniards during this exploration period. These native ships were moved by both sails and oars. He was also told that if he sailed south on the "Mar del Sur" (Pacific Ocean), he would find a land filled with gold.[7]

According to Martyr, the chief's son related that the Indians from the south would frequently bring an assortment of gold and silver jewelry, beautifully-made pottery, blankets, and furniture to their area, which they exchanged for slaves or food products that the natives in the south lacked. The chief's son pointed out that the golden utensils and other trinkets which the Spaniards had seen among the Indians of the Darién came from those lands to the south.

Martyr wrote that the Spaniards encountered Aztec maps that included the lands of the Aztecs as well as placement and lands of their enemies. One map, discovered by the Spaniards, was painted on a large (30 ft. x 25 ft.) cotton cloth. This map accurately located the placement of mountains and the Mexican coast lines as well as some of the offshore islands.[8] From numerous conversations with the Indians, the Spaniards were convinced that the Indians had excellent navigational and direction finding skills both on the land and on the seas.

---

[6]In this area of Panama, the Isthmus of Panama runs east and west. The Pacific ocean was known as the "Mar del Sur" or South Sea. Interestingly, the Pacific Ocean entrance to the Panama Canal is further east than the Atlantic Ocean entrance.
[7]Martyr de Angleria, 145.
[8]Ibid., 465.

In the *Crónica del Perú, Tercera Parte* (*Chronicles of Peru, Third Part*), Cieza de León described the initial efforts of Francisco Pizarro to reach Peru. In 1523, Pizarro and a group of Spaniards sailed south along the coast of Colombia, but they soon ran out of food and water. While Pizarro and some of his men explored inland for food, Bartolomé Ruyz, the ship's pilot, sailed farther south and west. As they traveled south they spied a huge sail just appearing on the horizon coming towards them. Ruyz described the sail as being as large as the sail on a caravel. Not believing that there could be another European ship in the Pacific, they considered the presence of any sailing ship in the Pacific to be extremely strange. As the ship got closer, they recognized that it was not a European vessel, but was a large barge with five Indians on board. Ruyz treated the Indians well and welcomed them to board the Spanish vessel. Through sign language, Ruyz learned that the five natives came from Tumbez far to the south and they were going further north with a load of cloth, wool, and other merchandise to trade. The Indians also mentioned the words Huayna Cápac and Cuzco. They spoke of gold and other riches in that country.[9]

In Peru, Martín de Murúa wrote that in the late 1400s, the Lord Inca Tupa Inca Yupanqui [also spelled Topa Inca Yupanqui], father of Inca Huayna Cápac, finished the great fortress at Sacsahuamán near Cuzco, which his father Pachacuti Inca Yupanqui had begun many years earlier. After this project was finished, according to several elderly Indians who served as informants for Murúa, Tupa Inca Yupanqui went north overland to the mouth of the Guayas River [the modern city of Guayaquil, Ecuador, is located at the mouth of the Guayas River] and embarked by raft or barge and sailed into the Pacific

---

[9]Pedro de Cieza de Leon, *Crónica del Perú, Tercera Parte*. Originally written in manuscript form in 1553-54. (Manuscript discovered in the Biblioteca Apostólica Vaticana and published for the first time by Pontificia Universidad Católica del Perú, 1987.) 31.

Ocean for more than one year. Murúa did not describe the vessel, but it must have been similar in size and shape as the one encountered by Ruyz.

According to Murúa's informants, Tupa Inca Yupanqui claimed to have reached some islands which he called *Hahua Chumpi* and *Nina Chumpi*.[10] Tupa Inca Yupanqui reportedly brought back with him a few people described as being black, a large amount of gold and silver, a brass chair, and what Murúa described as horse hides, horse heads, and bones.[11] According to Murúa, years later during the civil war between Huayna Cápac's sons, Huascar and Atahualpa, Atahualpa's military commanders destroyed the trophies that Tupa Inca Yupanqui brought back so that these things would not fall into the hands of the Spaniards.[12]

Manuel Ballasteros Gambrois, who edited and annotated the 1987 edition of Murúa's book, wrote that in Quechua *Chumpi* means a belt or a ring and *Nina* means fire. Ballasteros suggests that Tupa Inca Yupanqui may have discovered some islands surrounded by fire or where there was an active volcano. The similarity in the sounds between *Hahua* or *Hawa* and Hawaii cannot be overlooked nor considered mere coincidence especially when coupled with the description of a ring of fire, possibly in reference to a volcano. Captain Cook did not discover the Sandwich

---

[10] Murúa, 92.

[11] Manuel Ballesteros, who edited Murúa's book in 1987, pointed out that there were no horses on any islands of the Pacific east of the Philippines. Since the Incas would not have called them horses either, it is unclear what kind of hides they may have been. Murúa did not claim that he personally saw the hides, heads and bones so it is unclear how he arrived at that conclusion.

[12] After the death of Lord Inca Huayna Capac, his sons Huascar, in Cuzco, and Atahualpa, in Quito, embarked on a bloody civil war that distracted them just at the time that Francisco Pizarro arrived in Peru in 1531. Atahualpa, in the process of marching on Cuzco, took a small military force to the Inca fortress at Cajamarca to see the Spaniards. The Spaniards managed to capture Atahualpa at Cajamarca and ransom him for gold and silver. They eventually killed Atahualpa. In the meantime, Atahualpa's military commanders had captured and killed Huascar. The chaos that resulted during this civil war greatly benefitted the Spaniards in their conquest of Peru.

Islands (Hawaiian Islands) until 1778, many years after Murúa wrote his manuscript in 1611; consequently, Murúa could not have known the name. From Murúa's description, it is possible that Tupa Inca Yupanqui reached the Hawaiian Islands.

The chronicler Pedro Sarmiento de Gamboa provided a similar description of the voyage of Lord Inca Tupa Inca Yupanqui into the Pacific. Sarmiento wrote that all along the coast of Peru, the natives believed that there were many islands in the Mar del Sur.[13] Sarmiento wrote that, while Tupa Inca Yupanqui was conquering the coast of Peru and Ecuador, some strangers arrived on the coast near Tumbez by large sail-powered rafts. They reportedly told the Lord Inca that they came from some islands called *Auachumbi* and *Niñachumbe*.

The natives reported that Tupa Inca Yupanqui built a large number of rafts and sailed towards the west with a 20,000 man army. Tupa Inca Yupanqui found the two Islands and he returned bringing with him a few people from those islands who were described as black. He also brought back considerable gold, a large brass chair, and the hide and jawbone of a horse. According to Sarmiento, these trophies were kept at the fort in Cuzco until the Spaniards arrived. Sarmiento added that the skin and the jawbone subsequently were entrusted to an Inca nobleman by the name of Urco Guaranga, who was still living in Cuzco at the time Sarmiento wrote his manuscript and from whom Sarmiento learned the details of the account.[14] Sarmiento did not claim to have personally seen the jawbone and horse hide.

---

[13] The Galápagos Islands were discovered by the Spaniards in 1535. In 1567, the provisional Governor of Peru, Lope García de Castro, outfitted two ships with provisions and 150 men to explore the Pacific. Sarmiento was invited to participate in this expedition, and was appointed captain of the main ship. On 15 January 1568, they discovered an island which they named Nombre de Jesús. During the next few weeks, Sarmiento discovered several other islands which are believed to be the Solomon Islands. On the island, now believed to be Guadalcanal, the natives rose up and killed nine Spaniards.

[14] Sarmiento, 217.

Murúa was also told that anciently, dark-skinned people arrived on the coast of Peru in large canoes or rafts. He was told that these dark-skinned people came from certain islands and they arrived at different sites along the Peruvian coast seeking gold, pearls and large snails. They were described as being very wealthy and were dressed in cotton clothing.

Cabello Valboa related the legend of the arrival on the north coast of Peru of numerous boats or rafts many years before the reign of the Incas. According to this legend, these rafts landed near Lambayeque in northern Peru. The foreigners were led by a man named Naymlap, who along with his family lived many years in Peru.

Unlike the dugouts or canoes seen by Columbus, many of the rafts along the coast of Peru were made from tightly woven reeds. Even today, these reed ships, called "Totoras" are seen along the northern Peruvian coast and particularly on Lake Titicaca where the Indians use them for fishing and transportation. When Cieza de León explored the Lake Titicaca area and the ancient ruins of Tiahuanaco, he mentioned the Inca bridge at Desaguadero which was made of reeds and was constructed in such a way that horses and men could pass over it.

In his book *The Incas*, Von Hagen inserted a picture of one of the totora boats that was lashed to other boats and supported the bridge (Figure 4, comes from Von Hagen's book *The Incas*). Reportedly it was necessary to replace each raft or barge every two years because the reeds began to rot after an extended period in the water. The use of these woven reed rafts or boats date back hundreds of years.[15] Ceramic vases discovered during excavations of the Moche ruins near Trujillo, Peru, show iconograph-

---

[15] Photo shown in Victor Wolfgang Von Hagen's book, *The Incas*. 209 Picture is courtesy of the University of Oklahoma Press. (When I visited the Lake Titicaca area in 1959 and again 1973, the Indians were still making a wide variety of totoras boats. I also rode a small totora canoe in the Pacific ocean near Trujillo in 1974.)

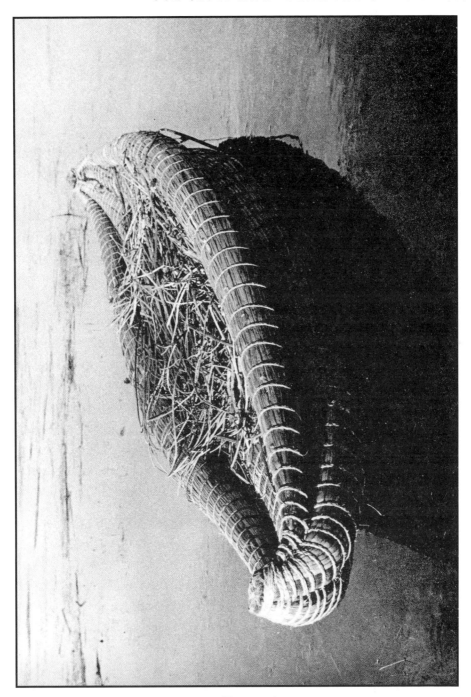

Figure 4

ic scenes of manned reed rafts or boats used by the Moche on the ocean along the northern Peruvian coast.[16]

As noted in Chapter 4, Cabello Valboa claimed that Ophir and his group traveled east from the legendary Tower of Babel, believed to be located in modern Iraq, passing through India and reaching the islands of South East Asia. He said that Ophir and his group spent considerable time around the islands until they lost their fear of the sea and gained knowledge of boat making and navigation. Subsequently, they sailed east until they arrived in "our Indies."[17] Cabello Valboa seems to imply that descendants of Ophir and his followers would have retained their navigational skills in the New World.

Lake Titicaca, to the west of La Paz, Bolivia, is the world's highest navigable lake (approximately 13,000 feet), and covers more than 3,140 square miles. Floating reed islands enable descendants of the Uru Indians to maintain floating villages. Inhabitants of the lake use the reeds growing around the lake to build the distinctive reed boats for which the lake is known. Contemporary adventurer Thor Heyerdahl had Uru Indian artisans from Lake Titicaca build both the 'Ra II' and 'Tigris' for his transoceanic expeditions in 1970. The Uru Indians, who live on man-made reed islands on Lake Titicaca, are descendants of people who lived in the area many years prior to the Christian era.

BOOK OF MORMON ACCOUNT OF BOATS AND NAVIGATION

The *Book of Mormon* mentions the use of barges by the Jaredites which they built at first to cross rivers and lakes in the Old World. In the Book of Ether it is recorded:

---

[16] See roll-out drawings of Moche pottery by Alana Cordy-Collins and Christopher B. Donnan. "Studies in Pre-Columbian Art & Archaeology Number Twenty-one, Dunbarton Oaks, Trustees for Harvard University, Washington, D.C. 1979.

[17] Cabello, 6.

Pre-Columbian Technical Skills 377

And it came to pass that they did travel in the wilderness, and did build barges, in which they did cross many waters, being directed continually by the hand of the Lord.

And the Lord would not suffer that they should stop beyond the sea in the wilderness, but he would that they should come forth even unto the land of promise, which was choice above all other lands, which the Lord God had preserved for a righteous people (Ether 2:6-7).

Later as the Jaredites were preparing to cross the ocean, a man known only as "the Brother of Jared" was given precise instructions on how to build a barge which could be an ocean-going vessel:

For behold, it came to pass that the Lord did bring Jared and his brethren forth even to that great sea which divideth the lands. And as they came to the sea they pitched their tents; and they called the name of the place Moriancumer; and they dwelt in tents, and dwelt in tents upon the seashore for the space of four years.

And the Lord said: Go to work and build, after the manner of barges which ye have hitherto built. And it came to pass that the brother of Jared did go to work, and also his brethren, and built barges after the manner which they had built, according to the instructions of the Lord. *And they were small, and they were light upon the water, even like unto the lightness of a fowl upon the water (emphasis added).*

And they were built after a manner that they were exceedingly tight, even that they would hold water like unto a dish; and the bottom thereof was tight like unto a dish; and the sides thereof were tight like unto a dish; and the ends thereof were peaked; and the top thereof was tight like unto a dish; and the length thereof was the length of a tree; and the door thereof, when it was shut, was tight like unto a dish (Ether 2:13, 16-17).

Since the Jaredites already had some experience building rafts or barges which they used to cross the rivers and lakes before arriving at the ocean, it would appear that God instructed them to expand their already existing skill by teaching them how to enclose the vessels, submarine-like. They were also told that they could not have a fire on board. There could be several reasons why a fire would be impractical. One reason would be the rapid consumption of oxygen within a closed space. A fire would also be a danger if the vessels were made of something flammable, such as reeds or wood.

The Jaredites had no need for a compass or for celestial navigational skills because the Lord told them that he would cause the winds to blow them in the course they should travel. Once the Jaredites were established in the "land of promise" there is no indication in the *Book of Mormon* that they ever built ships or barges again; however, it is mentioned on several occasions that they lived on the borders of the sea and it can be presumed that they built some kind of boats for fishing or coastal travel.

The case of the family of Lehi is somewhat different. As noted in Chapter 5, the sons of Lehi built a more "conventional" ship. Nephi remarked that they worked with timbers, but not after the "manner of men." Nephi's only description was that the ship was built after the manner the Lord had showed him and that when it was finished the travelers conceded that the "workmanship was exceedingly fine." Nephi remarked that they went "down into the ship" and they were driven by the wind. Nephi never mentioned whether they had rigged a sail for the ship; however, apparently the ship had a mechanical device which enabled the crew to steer it. Nephi claimed that the Liahona, the directional device that had served to guide Lehi and his family during their voyage across the Saudi desert, was used in a similar capacity during their sea voyage.

After Lehi and his family arrived in the Americas, there was no further mention of ship building or ocean travel until 57 B.C., more than five hundred years later. In the book of Alma, we read that a man named Hagoth built a large ship on the border of the land Bountiful, believed to be somewhere along the Pacific coast because the ship was launched into the "west sea." Hagoth built another ship which carried many Nephites north. When the first ship returned, it was loaded with many provisions and was sent north again. It was never heard from again and the Nephites feared that everyone aboard had been drowned in the sea. A third ship of Hagoth's also sailed away and was not heard from again.[18]

Over the next few years, many Nephites continued to go north to avoid the wars and contentions that continued in the south. Helaman wrote that the Nephites spread throughout all of the north land and the only thing they lacked in their new settlement was adequate timber. Helaman wrote that because of the scarcity of trees, the Nephites began to ship large quantities of timber to the settlers in the north. Helaman does not describe the size or the shape of their ships, but in order to ship large quantities of timber to build houses, they would need many large ships. Helaman later observed that he could not record a hundredth part of their activities at that time, but he specifically singled out the building of ships as an ongoing activity.

Metallurgical Skills

According to the record of Ether, the Jaredites were not in the New World long before they began to fight among themselves. The first use of metals appears in one of these family feuds as recorded in Ether 7:9. A young man named Shule was born to an ousted king and, becoming angry with his elder brother who had dethroned the king, he made himself and his followers swords of "steel." Ether recorded the following:

---

[18] Many Latter-day Saints believe these errant ships probably ended up in the Polynesian Islands. Although outside of the scope of this book, there are numerous legends recorded by the Hawaiians and the Polynesians that their ancestors arrived from the east.

Wherefore, he came to the hill Ephraim, and he did molten out of the hill, and made swords out of steel for those whom he had drawn away with him; and after he had armed them with swords he returned to the city Nehor, and gave battle unto his brother Corihor, by which means he obtained the kingdom and restored it unto his father Kib (Ether 7:9).

Apparently, the steel sword was a principal weapon used by the Jaredites during many of their battles. Ether narrated:

And they [the Jaredites] did work in all manner of ore, and they did make gold, and silver, and iron, and brass, and all manner of metals; and they did dig it out of the earth; wherefore, they did cast up mighty heaps of earth to get ore, of gold, and of silver, and of iron, and of copper. And they did work all manner of fine work (Ether 10:23).

As noted earlier, the Jaredites arrived in the New World between 2500 and 2200 B.C., depending upon the time frame for the dispersion of languages and the building of the Tower of Babel.

Metals Discovered among the Chavín

In his book, *Chavín, and the Origins of Andean Civilization*, Richard L. Burger stated that the first New World evidence of metallurgy appeared during excavations at Waywaka, an Initial Period (1900 B.C. to 1450 B.C.) village in the south-central highlands of Andahuaylas, Peru. Dozens of sheets of thin gold foil were recovered in association with early Muyu Moqo style ceramics that date to between 1900 and 1450 B.C.[19]

Burger provides additional insights to the advancement of metallurgy in the Formative Period (2500 B.C. to 600 B.C.) of Peru. He wrote:

---

[19]Burger, 127.

Technological advances occurred in metallurgy during the Early Horizon Period (about 1000 B.C.). Only small sheets of hammered gold and copper are known from the Initial Period, but during the Early Horizon large objects of forged and annealed gold and silver with complex Chavín-style motifs were produced by a number of techniques which have no known antecedents. According to Heather Lechtman, the production of three-dimensional forms by metallurgically joining pieces of pre-shaped metal sheets is one of the important traditions in Peruvian metallurgy, and it appears for the first time during the Early Horizon. Soldering, sweat welding, repoussé decoration, and the creation of silver-gold alloys were all utilized in the production of Chavín-style objects. Analysis of the solder in a gold artifact from Chavín de Huántar revealed that its melting point was 70 degrees lower than the pieces of metal being joined, due to a higher proportion of copper in the predominantly gold-silver alloy. An understandings of alloying and soldering, as well as the ability to control temperature, is implied by a metallurgical join of this kind.[20]

Concerning copper, Burger wrote:

The small-scale societies of the Initial Period offered stable conditions in which technological experimentation was possible, and recent excavations at Mina Perdida suggest that the initial stage of copper metallurgy may have been initiated before 1000 B.C. Small pieces of hammered copper sheets were discovered at Mina Perdida in 1991 in the western platform of the late Initial Period public complex. The foil never exceeded a few centimeters on a side and none had been shaped into finished artifacts. Nevertheless, the creation of the thin sheets of copper implies basic metallurgical knowledge as well as an interest in the development of this technology. At Mina Perdida, archaeological investigations recovered pieces of clay and stone that had been modified by high temperatures, as well as isolated chunks of copper ore. These finds suggest that copper may have been smelted rather than obtained as native copper.[21]

---

[20]Ibid., 201.
[21]Ibid., 98-99.

Burger was unsure as to what motivated this burst of innovative expansion during the Early Horizon period (1000 B.C.), but the inventions from that period enabled the natives to manufacture metal and stone objects. Many of these objects were buried in tombs of the period. Some of the first tombs discovered, pertaining to this Early Horizon period, were discovered along the northern Peruvian coast in 1928-1929. Two brothers, digging a water reservoir in the Department of Lambayeque, encountered a large undisturbed grave of three individuals who had been buried with many precious objects. The grave included a gold headband, 66 hollow gold beads, two pottery beads encased in gold, 19 gold snail shells, two large gold ornaments or gorgets, three gold finger rings, four gold pins, a gold and silver pin, and many other precious objects.[22]

There is no indication that the archaeologists ever found evidence of steel among the grave sites in Peru. Does this mean that the Chavín inhabitants did not know anything about iron or steel? They may not have found iron ores within the boundaries of the Chavín civilization.[23] Because of the high propensity of iron and steel to rust, it is unlikely that the native Americans would bury steel or iron artifacts with the bodies of their ancestors. Furthermore, iron or steel were not considered precious metals by the pre-Columbians and, consequently, would not be worthy of being buried with their dead. Gold, silver and copper were considered by the Indians to be more valuable. Also bodies of iron ore are not as plentiful in the Andean region of Peru and Ecuador as are veins of copper, silver and gold.

In his book *Historiales y Politicas del Perú*, Fernando de Montesinos records the legend that "giants" came to Peru and

---

[22]Ibid., 204.

[23]Peru has one large open-pit iron ore mine currently being worked which is located at San Juan de Marcona, several hundred miles south of Lima and almost directly west of the City of Nazca; however, there is insufficient evidence to indicate that the Chavín civilization extended as far south as Nazca.

built enormous buildings such as Pachacamac, located on the coast 15 miles south of Lima. He claimed that the giants had instruments of steel. Citing E. Nordenskjold's book, *The Copper and Bronze Ages in South America*, Horacio H. Urteaga, who wrote the notes in the 1930 edition of Montesinos's book, claimed that this was an incorrect statement by Montesinos because iron and steel were not known in pre-Columbian America.[24]

In his literary epic, *La Araucana*, Alonso de Ercilla y Zuñiga wrote that the Araucano warriors, located south of the Maule River in Chile had weapons of steel. According to Ercilla y Zuñiga, who fought against the Araucano Indians for many months during the Spanish efforts to subdue them, the Araucanos made heavy spears, pikes of iron, sharpened axes, steel-tipped maces, horn-shaped arms, swords, lances, clubs pointed with iron, and deadly missiles. He observed that the iron used by the Araucanos was not iron that the Indians scavenged from the Spaniards and retooled into new types of weapons. In their English translation of *La Araucana*, Lancaster and Manchester acknowledged in their introduction that the Araucanos made axes, hatchets, primitive weapons from gold, silver, copper, and lead which they dug from the Andes, but they did not single out iron.[25]

Ethan Smith wrote in his book, *View of the Hebrews or Tribes of Israel in America*, that investigators found no iron tools or weapons in the Mound Builder's fortifications in the United States. According to Ethan Smith, the investigators attributed the lack of iron to the likelihood that it would have rusted away. He indicated that some evidence of iron was found. In one particular Mound Builder area near Circleville, Ohio, investigators

---

[24]Montesinos, 44, n62.

[25]Although iron was not mentioned by Lancaster and Manchester in the introduction to their book, they wrote that the weapons were made of iron in their translation of Ercilla y Zuñiga's verses. They may not have believed him, but faithfully rendered his verses as he wrote them.

encountered the handle of a small sword or large knife, made of an elk's horn. The blade was missing, but in the hole of the handle there was left a trace of iron oxide or rust.[26]

Metallurgy in the Book of Mormon Continued

Almost immediately after arriving in the New World, Nephi wrote that his people found a wide variety of ores. He specifically mentioned gold, silver and copper. One of the first things that Nephi did was to make the gold plates on which he engraved the Nephite history. Within a few years after the Nephites arrived in the "promised land," Nephi's brother Jacob accused his people of acquiring gold and silver to enrich themselves:

> And now behold, my brethren, this is the word which I declare unto you, that many of you have begun to search for gold, and for silver, and for all manner of precious ores, in the which this land, which is a land of promise unto you and to your seed, doth abound most plentifully (Jacob 2:12).

Burger and many other archaeologists and art historians seem perplexed by the Indian fascination with gold. Burger suggested that perhaps gold had a religious value. However, Jacob's speech to his fellow Nephites is an acknowledgment that they sought gold because of its monetary value—a concept they brought from the Old World. They seemed to believe that he who had more gold than his neighbor was richer and, consequently, better than his neighbor. Lehi was a fairly wealthy man in Jerusalem and his sons understood the value of gold, silver and precious stones. Some of the later Nephite kings imposed heavy taxes upon their people to accumulate wealth and to build many elegant and ornate buildings, as well as surround themselves with

---

[26]Ethan Smith, 193-194.

Pre-Columbian Technical Skills

sycophant priests and concubines. One such ruler was King Noah who laid a heavy tax upon his subjects:

> And he laid a tax of one fifth part of all they possessed, a fifth part of their gold and of their silver, and a fifth part of their ziff, and of their copper, and of their brass and their iron; and a fifth part of their fatlings; and also a fifth part of all their grain (Mosiah 11:5).

Since the initial publication of the *Book of Mormon*, Mormon Church members have pondered about the nature of *ziff*. Mosiah's placement of ziff within a list of known metals seems to indicate that it was a metal. The *Book of Mormon* index notes that ziff was probably a metal used by the Nephites. It appears that Mosiah recorded these metals in their descending order of value. Gold is known to be more valuable than silver; and silver is apparently more valuable that ziff. If this is true, then ziff would appear to be more valuable than copper.

Modern archaeologists through their excavations might be able to shed new light on the nature of ziff. Burger wrote that the Chavín metallurgists were able to make an alloy using gold, silver and copper and the value of the alloy depended upon the amount of copper present.[27]

During modern excavations of the Moche culture (200 B.C.- 600 A.D.), Christopher B. Donnan and his fellow art historians have discovered, in several burial sites, face masks and breastplates made of a gold and copper alloy as well as face masks of a silver and copper alloy. In a paper Donnan and Luis Jaime Castillo wrote entitled "Finding the Tomb of a Moche Priestess," they described a silver-copper alloy mask that was found near the priestess's skull. It appears feasible that either the gold-copper alloy or the silver-copper alloy, discovered by these modern art historians, may be the metal ziff spoken of in Mosiah.

---

[27]Burger, 201.

In other *Book of Mormon* accounts, both Alma and Helaman indicate that the descendants of Lehi had large quantities of gold, silver and other precious metals.

> And it came to pass that they became exceedingly rich, both the Lamanites and the Nephites; and they did have an exceeding plenty of gold, and of silver, and of all manner of precious metals, both in the land south and in the land north.
> And behold, there was all manner of gold in both these lands, and of silver, and of precious ore of every kind; and there were also curious workmen, who did work all kinds of ore and did refine it; and thus they did become rich (Helaman 6:9,11).

In their book *Royal Tombs of Sipán*, Donnan and Walter Alva observed that the Moche did not use bellows to create a forced draft of air for their furnaces, but instead blew into the coals with long tubes:

> Moche metalworkers were extremely sophisticated in the alloying of metals, using gold, silver, and copper in various combinations. With faceted stone hammers they then flattened and smoothed the metal into even sheets, which they shaped into low relief and three-dimensional sculpture. They used solid metal forms over which sheet metal could be hammered to create sophisticated sculpture. Moche metalworkers excelled at joining metal pieces by edge-welding, soldering, crimping, and the use of tabs that projected through slits on adjacent pieces. Metalworkers were also skilled at lost wax casting. With this technique, they created complex three-dimensional sculptures, some of which have interlocking moveable parts.
> These artisans developed ingenious techniques for making metal objects appear to be pure gold. One method was to fabricate the object from an alloy of gold and copper, or gold, copper, and silver, and then treat the surface chemically to remove the copper and silver, leaving the gold in place. Subsequent heating of the object would cause the surface gold to smooth out over the whole exterior, giving the object the appearance of solid gold.
> Moche metalworkers also developed a means of gilding copper objects by electrochemical plating. Their procedure was to dissolve

gold in a solution of water and corrosive minerals such as ordinary salt and potassium nitrate. To this solution they added a compound such as bicarbonate of soda to achieve a pH of about nine. A clean copper object, dipped into this solution when it was gently boiling, served as both anode and cathode, and a thin coating of gold formed on its surface. Then the object was heated to a temperature between 500 and 800 C (932 to 1472 F) to bond the gold permanently to the copper.[28]

In a footnote to *The Incas*, Von Hagen noted that the Peruvian mountain settlement of Curamba, located at 12,500 feet, was a very important ore smelting center for the Incas. According to the writings of Pedro Sancho in 1534, the Incas used Curamba for "wind ovens" to smelt gold, silver, and copper ore. At the highest part of the crest, overlooking Curamba, there are numerous oval-shaped wind ovens eight feet in diameter with walls two feet thick; the openings face northeast in the direction of the winds from the Amazon. This is one of the few Inca manufacturing centers that have been found where the wind was strong enough to serve as a bellows to smelt metals.[29]

Cieza de León observed that gold was washed from the rivers in many provinces, and silver was found in the mountains throughout the kingdom; and all this wealth belonged to the Lord Inca. Each incoming Inca king was obliged to leave the wealth and possessions of his predecessor untouched and was forced to accumulate his own fortune. In the palaces and lodgings of the Inca kings there were bars of precious metals, and their royal garments were covered with ornaments of silver, gold, emeralds and other precious stones of great value. The dead were buried with great amount of treasure.

---

[28]Donnan, 19-22. (Donnan sites Heather Lechtman, Antonieta Erly, and Edward J. Barry, Jr. *New Perspectives on Moche Metallurgy: Techniques of Gilding Copper at Loma Negra, Northern Peru*, American Antiquity. Vol 47(1):3-30.)

[29]Cieza de León, *The Incas*, 133.

Cieza de León noted that once gold, silver and other precious jewels were brought to Cuzco, the Inca capitol, it was against the law to remove any of it. He wrote that when the Spaniards entered Peru, if they would have acted prudently and behaved differently, they would have been able to obtain much more gold and silver than they did. They ransomed the Lord-Inca Atahualpa for a large room full of gold and silver; however, after the metals had been delivered, the Spaniards killed Atahualpa anyway. Cieza de León said the Indians responded by burying much of their accumulated treasures so Spain could not take more.[30]

Metallurgical Discoveries in Mesoamerica

When Hernán Cortés arrived in the Americas, he marveled at the metallurgical skills of the natives. He believed the Aztecs to be the finest goldsmiths in the world. Fray Diego Durán frequently mentioned the existence of gold within the Aztec world. At one point he wrote:

> The king was surrounded by an enormous amount of gold jewelry, a variety of precious stones, a great pile of feathers of many colors and worked in different fashions, bracelets and leg ornaments of gold, and diadems of gold and fine stones made in the style they used. There were many vessels, plates and bowls, all of gold, for in this land silver was unknown and gold was the only metal worked.[31]

Durán also wrote that during a particular ceremony, Motecuhzoma, the First, and his great military leader, Tlacaelel, placed crowns of fine feathers, adorned with gold and precious stones, upon their heads, and on each arm was worn a sheath of gold reaching from the elbow to the shoulder. On their feet were

---

[30]Ibid., 157.
[31]Dúran, 385.

richly worked jaguar skin sandals, adorned with gold and gems.[32] When Cortés arrived in the New World, he received many gifts of gold, precious stones, feathers, splendid armbands, blouses, and ornate skirts.[33]

Durán wrote that when Cortés arrived in Tenochtitlan, he and his soldiers were housed in the palace that previously belonged to the father of Motecuhzoma, the Second. While exploring the palace, a few Spaniards discovered a small door that had only recently been plastered over and decided to find out what the room contained. When they reopened the door, the Spaniards discovered the great treasure storehouse of previous Aztec monarchs. Durán described the treasure as follows:

> They found a spacious chamber in the middle of which stood a pile of gold, jewelry, and rich stones, the whole pile as high as the tallest man. . . . The treasure did not consist of things acquired by the current king, nor were they objects for his own use. This was the treasure that had belonged to all the kings who were his ancestors, which they had deposited there but which could not be used by the present ruler. When a king died, on that very day all his wealth in gold, gems, feathers, and weapons and his entire wardrobe were placed in that room and guarded as if they were sacred or divine things. The king who was about to reign would then begin to acquire wealth so that it could not be said he used the treasures of his ancestors. So it was that the treasure was guarded as a testimony to the greatness of the city of Mexico-Tenochtitlan.
>
> In this room there were also heaps of fine mantles as well as clothing for women. On the walls hung many shields, weapons, and insignia of fine workmanship and colors. There were piles of golden vessels, of plates and dishes, made in the style of these people, which the kings used to eat from. The most remarkable were four large platters made to represent fountains, all beautifully worked in gold, as big as shields and so covered with dust that it was plain that they had not been used for a long time. There were also golden vessels for drinking chocolate, made in the shape of gourds, some with supports

---
[32]Ibid., 190.
[33]Ibid., 524.

and others without. In sum, this chamber contained the most amazing wealth ever seen, and the bewildered Spaniards took the gold platters to Cortés as proof of these great riches.[34]

In a footnote in Durán's book, Doris Heyden quotes Ross Hassig as stating that in Mexico: "Goods were sold by count and measure, not by weight, and although the Aztecs lacked a unitary system of money, cacao beans, mantas [blankets], quills filled with gold dust, and small copper axes had standardized values and augmented the prevalent barter system."[35]

In Alma, Chapter 11, the prophet Alma described the value of Nephite money and compared the value of gold or silver with the wages of a judge or a measure of barley.

> And the judge received for his wages according to his time—a senine of gold for a day, or a senum of silver, which is equal to a senine of gold; and this is according to the law which was given.
>
> Now these are the names of the different pieces of their gold, and of their silver, according to their value. And the names are given by the Nephites, for they did not reckon after the manner of the Jews who were at Jerusalem; neither did they measure after the manner of the Jews; but they altered their reckoning and their measure, according to the minds and the circumstances of the people, in every generation, until the reign of the judges, they having been established by king Mosiah (Alma 11:3-4).

Alma then named each different measure of gold and of silver and compared their values to each other and to a measure of barley or other grains.

From the writings of numerous chroniclers and from the findings of art historians and archaeologists, it is evident that the pre-Columbian Americans were experts in the use of a wide

---

[34]Ibid., 532.

[35]Ibid., 86n. (Ross Hassig, *Trade, Tribute and Transportation: The Sixteenth Century Political Economy of the Valley of Mexico*. Norman: University of Oklahoma Press.)

variety of metals and were excellent metallurgists. These ancient inhabitants were able to manufacture a copper that was much harder than any copper that is made today. Modern museums in Peru have on display copper tools of an excellent quality. Some of the tools were used in medical surgery. There are on display ancient skulls showing healed incisions where brain surgery had taken place. According to Peruvian authorities the pre-Columbian doctors used hardened copper tools.

When Joseph Smith announced that Moroni had shown him plates of gold, scoffers denounced the idea that Indians in ancient America could make plates or sheets of gold. Archaeologists have demonstrated that making plates of gold would be a simple task for early Americans and their understanding of the non-corrosive nature of gold would make the use of gold an excellent way to keep a historical record. The unschooled Smith would not have known the extent of their metallurgical capabilities.

Weavers of Cloth

Unlike the Indians that Columbus discovered throughout the Caribbean who were usually naked or wore a small loin cloth, most of the Indians in Peru or Mexico wore more clothing. The quality usually depended upon the status of the individual. The cultivation of cotton in the Andes dates back nearly 5,000 years. As pointed out by Burger, examples of cloth discovered in the ancient Chavín civilization ruins considerably predate the cloth used by the Incas and the other Andean natives. Burger wrote:

> By far the most developed visual art in these early coastal cultures was that of cotton textiles. . . The most popular technique for producing fabric was *twining*, in which weft yarns turn about the warps instead of interweaving between them. . . At Huaca Prieta, 71 percent of the textiles were twined, while only 5 percent were woven;

the remainder were made by looping or netting. Most of the decorated Pre-ceramic textiles from this site were made by twining, probably using a stationary frame or loom. Designs were highlighted by manipulating the variations of color in natural cotton and, more dramatically, by the use of colored pigments, including red, blue, yellow, and green.[36]

Cieza de León noted that the Indians raised a great deal of cotton which they used for making their clothing. They also used the wool or fleece of the cameloids (llama, alpaca, vicuña, and guanaco) from which they made some of their clothing and blankets. Although the Indians made a wide variety of clothing using only cotton fibers, they were expert at mixing the cameloid fleece with cotton fibers, or using the cameloid fleece by itself.[37]

Cieza de León stated that the Indians could weave as good a tapestry as any woven in Flanders from the wool of their flocks, and so fine a weave that it seemed of silk rather than of wool. Of the white Chachapoya Indians, who lived in northeast Peru, Cieza de León noted: "The women made fine and highly prized clothing for the Incas, and they still make excellent garments, and tapestry so fine and handsome that it is greatly esteemed for its quality."[38]

Cieza de León noted later that the wool of the guanaco was so fine that it resembled silken serge and was used to make the clothing for the Inca king. He provided a brief description of the vicuñas, a wild cameloid that lives in the high Andes. He said that the wool of the vicuña was so fine that it surpassed that of the Merino sheep of Spain.

Cieza de León included fine fabrics as part of the wealth of Inca royalty, and stated that the woolen clothing in the storehouses was so numerous and so fine that it would have been

---

[36]Burger, 34-35.
[37]Cieza de León, *The Incas*, 44.
[38]Ibid., 99.

worth a great fortune.[39] The clothing of the Inca kings were shirts of the vicuña or guanaco wool, some of them adorned with gold embroidery, others with emeralds and precious stones, and others with feathers; some were plain. Cieza de León also observed that the dyes excelled those of Spain.[40]

Betanzos noted that the common Indians used a maguey plant fiber for blankets and also for sacks to haul heavy objects.[41] Although maguey fiber was used in Peru, it appears to have been used more extensively in Mexico. The fibers were beaten and used to make paper products, clothing, and slings for weapons. Clothing made from maguey fibers were reserved for use by the common people. Durán wrote that from the time that Motecuhzoma, the First, came to power, the commoners were not allowed to wear cotton clothing, under pain of death. Commoners could use only garments of maguey fiber.[42]

Durán noted that cotton was grown extensively in Mexico. He wrote:

> A bewildering amount of cloth: lengths twenty, ten, five, four, or two *brazos* (arm span) long, according to the ability of each province.
> Fine mantles for the lords, of different weave and design, all richly worked. Some of them had beautiful fringes done in colors and feather-work. Others had insignia on them, others serpent heads, or jaguars, and some were adorned with the image of the sun. And yet others had skulls or blowguns or figures of the gods—all of them embroidered in many colored threads and enriched with feathers of duck and geese, those tiny feathers that are like down. All were beautifully and skillfully worked. Even though silk was unknown in this country, the people were extremely skilled in weaving, embroidering, and painting cotton cloth.
> Also mantles of maguey fiber given in large quantities as tribute by the Chichimecs, most delicately worked and painted in different

---

[39]Ibid., 70.
[40]Ibid., 177.
[41]Betanzos, 56.
[42]Durán, 209.

colors, some of them adorned with gilded eagles, a variety of weapons and insignia. . . .

Women's clothing was contributed: loose blouses, also skirts, all of them enriched with wide borders embroidered in different colors and designs, with feather-work on the front; insignia done in colored thread; and on the back some of them bore embroidered flowers; others, imperial eagles. Still others were covered with flowers that were not only embroidered but were combined with feather-work, and these were a splendid thing to see. Beautiful skirts of great price were richly woven, with excellent skill. All of these clothes were used by the ladies who were wives and concubines of the lords and great chieftains. Another type of female dress arrived through tribute. This was entirely white and was worn by the young women and the old women who served in the temples. There was yet another kind of clothing for women, made of maguey fiber, and this was worn by the servant girls in the homes, where it was allotted to them.[43]

Durán mentioned that the Indians were adept at making cotton armor. The armor was stuffed and quilted and was so thick that a dart or arrow could not penetrate it. Bishop Diego de Landa also wrote about these armor jackets made of twisted cotton. The Spaniards adopted these quilted cotton jackets into their own defensive armor.[44]

In Yucatán, Landa noted that the Mayan men wore for clothing, "a band of cloth the width of the hand, which served them for drawers and breeches. They wound it several times around the waist, so that one end fell in front and one end behind, and these ends the women made with a great deal of care and with feather-work. They wore large square blankets and they tied them over the shoulders. They wore sandals of hemp or of the dry, untanned skin of the deer, and they wore no other garments."[45]

---

[43]Ibid., 203-204.
[44]Landa, 35, n174.
[45]Ibid., 89.

Reference to Textiles in the *Book of Mormon*

In the *Book of Mormon*, the prophet Ether, in his narrative about the Jaredites, noted that the Jaredites had silks, fine-twined linen, and all manner of cloth to cover their nakedness (Ether 10:24). It is only in recent years, through archaeological excavations, that art historians have discovered that the ancients not only had weaving, but also used a form of twining in making their cloth. It is unlikely that Joseph Smith would have known about twining or known that twining was a method utilized in ancient America to manufacture cloth.

The *Book of Mormon* never refers specifically to cotton nor to cloth made from cotton fibers. *Book of Mormon* writers frequently mentioned silks, linens, fine-twined linens and "cloth of every kind." Since there was no known industry in the New World involving silk worms, perhaps the *Book of Mormon* writers were referring to the silky texture of their cloth and called it silk rather than the material used to spin the threads. The Spaniards frequently referred to the silky texture of native cloth.

About 178 B.C., Zeniff stated that he ordered the women to spin and work "all manner of fine linen" and "cloth of every kind"(Mosiah 10:5). Helaman uses nearly identical language a 150 years later:

> Behold their women did toil and spin, and did make all manner of cloth, of fine-twined linen and cloth of every kind, to clothe their nakedness. . . (Helaman 6:13).

Alma narrated that the Nephites enjoyed an abundance of silk and fine-twined linen, and "all manner of good homely cloth" (Alma 1:29). Considering the abundance of cotton used in both the Andes and in Mesoamerica, it is likely that "cloth of every kind" and "good homely cloth" was referring to cotton cloth.

Although the Nephites had a variety of fibers to "clothe their nakedness," Nephite prophets indicated that the Lamanites dressed more primitively. About 500 B.C., the prophet Enos described the situation of the Lamanites:

> And I bear record that the people of Nephi did seek diligently to restore the Lamanites unto the true faith in God. But our labors were vain; their hatred was fixed and they were led by their evil nature that they became wild, and ferocious, and a blood-thirsty people, full of idolatry and filthiness; feeding upon beast of prey; dwelling in tents, and wandering about in the wilderness with a short skin girdle about their loins and their heads shaven; and their skill was in the bow, and in the cimeter and the ax. And many of them did eat nothing save it was raw meat; and they were continually seeking to destroy us (Enos 1:20).

Apparently over the years the wardrobe of the Lamanites did not change significantly. About 178 B.C., Zeniff wrote that his small band of Nephites were attacked by the Lamanites who had taken over the land of Lehi-Nephi "...and they were girded with a leathern girdle about their loins" (Mosiah 10:8). About 21 A.D., a prophet named Nephi wrote about the dress of the Gadianton robbers ". . .and they were girded about after the manner of robbers; and they had a lamb-skin about their loins, and they were dyed in blood" (3 Nephi 4:7).

In 1530, when Pero Lopes de Souza went up the Paraná River in Argentina, he encountered several different Indian groups along the river. Lopes de Souza described the Indians as being covered with skins and many had some type of a hat or head covering; frequently it was the head of an animal.[46] Most of the Indians that Lopes de Souza found along the river lived in tents. Near the site of modern Montevideo, Uruguay, Lopes de

---

[46] Lopes de Souza, 47-48.

Souza encountered a band of Charrúa Indians who were also covered with skins. They did not appear to have any fixed home, but camped wherever the night found them.

It is apparent from the accounts of the chroniclers, the art historians and the *Book of Mormon* prophets that many of the natives in the New World were extremely adept at making textiles and clothing, and that their styles varied from intricate to primitive.

Stone Masons in the Andes

As Cieza de León rode south with the Spanish Royalist Army, he described many of the buildings that he encountered along the way. For example, in northern Ecuador, he encountered the buildings of the Caranqui Indians. He observed that the lodgings of the Caranqui were in a small town square; inside was a beautifully built stone pool. After arriving in Cuzco, Cieza de León described the palaces and houses of the Incas, which were made of fine great stones skillfully joined, without mortar, which he claimed "was a sight to see."[47] He provided glowing reports of many buildings which he encountered during his travels, including buildings that were built long before the Incas arrived in Cuzco.

In southern Ecuador was located the great city of Tomebamba (near the modern day city of Cuenca) which Cieza de León described as one of the finest and richest cities to be found in all the Andes. The Temple of the Sun in Tomebamba was of stones put together with the subtlest skill. Some of the Indians claimed that most of the stones used in the construction of these lodgings and the temple of the sun had been brought from the city of Cuzco—several hundred miles away—by order of Lord Inca Huayna Cápac and his father, Tupa Inca Yupanqui. The stones

---

[47]Cieza de León, *The Incas*, 21.

An early morning picture of Machupichu, Peru, complex with Huaynapichu mountain in the background. The vertical slope of the right face of Huaynapichu is clearly visible. Picture taken by the Author in 1973.

An early morning view of the Machupichu, Peru, complex reveals elaborate terracing and rock building formations. Picture taken by the Author in 1973.

The Machupichu, Peru, complex shows various buildings and staircases. Several staircases were cut out of solid rock. Picture taken by the Author in 1959.

The walls of several buildings at the Machupichu, Peru, complex are seen without roofs. The winding road, leading up from the Urabamba River can be seen in the upper right hand corner. Picture taken by the Author in 1959.

were pulled to the site with great cables, a feat which Cieza de León considered to be amazing considering the size of the stones and the distance involved. He also said that the fronts of the buildings were beautiful and highly decorative, some of them set with emeralds and other precious stones. Inside, the walls of the Temple of the Sun and the palaces of the Inca kings were covered with sheets of gold and incrusted with many gold statues.[48]

The Inca kings thought nothing of building an entire city out of stone. Cieza de León described the ancient city of Huánuco, located at 12,156 feet above sea level in the Peruvian Andes. He said that there was a beautiful royal palace, made of very large stones artfully joined. This palace was the center of power for the Incas in all that area and the Lord Inca always kept more than 30,000 Indians in Huánuco to serve it. In a footnote, Von Hagen wrote that the ruins of old Huánuco are immense. The plaza alone, which holds more than eight buildings, measures 675 feet by 950 feet and is approached by three flights of steps. It is surrounded on all sides by buildings. There were more than 1,000 stone structures in Huánuco in its pre-Columbian heyday.

One of the most incredible structures in the New World for stone work is the famous fortress of Sacsahuamán, which overlooks Cuzco. Sacsahuamán was started during the reign of Lord Inca Pachacuti Inca Yupanqui and finished during the reign of Lord Inca Huayna Cápac, some 80 years later. By the time, Cieza de León saw the fortress in 1548, it had been destroyed except for the foundation which he described as impressive. The native historians told Cieza de León that more than 20,000 workmen had been used in the construction of Sacsahuamán. He was told that 4,000 men quarried and cut the stones; 6,000 hauled them with great cables of leather and hemp; others dug the ditch for the foundation which was cut into solid rock. Cieza de León calculated that the fortress was 330 feet long and 200 feet wide. The

---

[48] Ibid., 70.

Walls in three tiers were curved in such a manner that each wall provided defenders with the ability to protect each other during an attack. The Sacsahuaman fortress near Cuzco, Peru, was impregnable against a frontal assault. Picture taken by the Author in 1959.

A typical doorway at the Sacsahuaman fortress near Cuzco, Peru. The trapezoid design reportedly protected the doorway during an earthquake. Picture taken by the Author in 1959.

Massive rock wall at Sacsahuaman near Cuzco, Peru, showing numerous angles and circular cuts as each rock is placed so tight against the other rocks that not even a knife blade can be inserted in the seams. Picture taken by the Author in 1959.

Massive rock wall at Sacsahuaman near Cuzco, Peru, has rocks that are more than 12 feet tall and weights more than 50 tons. How the rocks were moved several miles remains a mystery. Picture taken by the Author in 1959.

fortress had so many rock walls that none of the Spanish artillery was powerful enough to break the walls during a Spanish attack on the fortress.

There are stones set in the walls so large with both circular and angular cuts that it boggles the mind to think how they could have been brought up, shaped, and set in place. Some of the stones are about twelve feet wide and more than twenty feet long; others are three and four feet thick, and all so exactly set that a coin (or a knife blade) could not be inserted between them.[49]

Cieza de León was the first chronicler to describe the archaeological site of Tiahuanaco (also spelled Tiwanaku) near the city of La Paz, Bolivia. He wrote:

> Tiahuanacu is famous for its great buildings which, without question, are a remarkable thing to behold. Near the main dwellings is a man-made hill, built on great stone foundations. Beyond this hill there are two stone idols of human size and shape, with the features beautifully carved, so much so that they seem the work of great artists or masters. They are so large that they seem small giants, and they are wearing long robes, different from the attire of the natives of these provinces. They seem to have an ornament on their heads. Close by these stone statues there is another building, whose antiquity and this people's lack of writing is the reason there is no knowledge of who the people that built these great foundations and strongholds were, or how much time has gone by since then, for at present all one sees is a finely built wall which must have been constructed many ages ago. Some of the stones are very worn and wasted, and there are others so large that one wonders how human hands could have brought them to where they now stand. Many of these stones are carved in different ways, and some of them are in the form of human bodies, and these must have been their idols.
>
> Along the wall there are many underground hollows and cavities. In another spot farther to the west there are other still greater antiquities, for there are many large gates with jambs, thresholds, and door all of a single stone. What struck me most when I was observing and setting down these things was that from these huge gate-

---

[49]Ibid., 154.

ways other still larger stones project on which they were set, some of which were as much as thirty feet wide, fifteen or more long, and six thick, and this and the door, jamb, and threshold were one single stone, which was a tremendous thing. When one considers the work, I cannot understand or fathom what kind of instruments or tools were used to work them, for it is evident that before these huge stones were dressed and brought to perfection, they must have been much larger to have been left as we see them.

In conclusion, I would say that I consider this the oldest antiquity in all Peru.[50] It is believed that before the Incas reigned, long before, certain of these buildings existed, and I have heard Indians say that the Incas built their great edifices at Cuzco along the lines of the wall to be seen in this place. They even go further and say that the first Incas talked of setting up their court and capital here in Tiahuanacu.

Another strange thing is that in much of this region neither rocks, quarries, nor stones are to be seen from which they could have brought the many we see, and no small number of people must have been needed to transport them. The Indians state that they heard from their forefathers that all that are there appeared overnight. Because of this, and because they also say that bearded men were seen on the island of Titicaca and that these people constructed the building of Viñaque, I say that it might have been that before the Incas ruled, there were people of parts in these kingdoms, come from no one knows where, who did these things, and who, being few and the natives many, perished in the wars.[51]

One of the commanding stone elements at Tiahuanaco is the ten ton Gateway of the Sun, a monolith carved from a single block of granite. Its upper portion is deeply carved with intricate designs, including a human figure, condors, and other hiero-

---

[50]Carlos Ponce Sangines in his book, *Tiwanaku*, claims the Tiwanaku civilization lasted from approximately 237 B.C. to 667 A.D. The initial periods of the Chavín civilization is much older and predates Tiwanaku by perhaps as much as 2,000 years. Considering that Chavín disappeared about 400 B.C., then Tiwanaku followed by only about 150 years. Carlos Ponce Sangines was the Director of the Center for Archaeological Investigations in Tiwanaku and Titular Fellow of Archaeology of the National Academy of Sciences of Bolivia. (Carlos Ponce Sangines, *Tiwanaku Espacio, Tiempo y Cultura*, (Academia Nacional de Ciencias de Bolivia, Publicación No. 20, La Paz, 1972.)

[51]Cieza de León, *The Incas*, 282-284.

The famous Gateway of the Sun at Tiwanaku, Bolivia, is sculpted from one solid rock which stands more than 12 feet high. Courtesy of Rodney Dial who took the picture in 1980.

A close up of the "Weeping God" because of tears sculptured on its cheeks, which is located on the Gateway of the Sun at Tiwanaku, Bolivia. Archaeologists surmise it is symbolic of Ticci Viracocha. Courtesy of Rodney Dial who took the picture in 1980.

Two huge sculptured rock statues of the Tiwanakan god, Ticci Viracocha, located at Tiwanaku, Bolivia. After hearing the legend of Ticci Viracocha, Thor Heyerdahl made his famous Kon-Tiki voyage. Courtesy of Rodney Dial who took the picture in 1980.

glyph-type symbols. Directly in the center of the gate is the so-called "Sun God," whom the archaeologists studying Tiahuanaco call Viracocha [Ticci Viracocha]. Viracocha has rays shooting from his face in all directions. He is also holding a stylized staff in each hand. The "Sun God" is sometimes referred to as the "weeping god" because tears are on his cheeks.

Tiahuanaco is still relatively young compared to the ancient buildings and cities of the Chavín civilization. Their early Pre-ceramic sites in Peru at Aspero, El Paraíso in the Chillón Valley, Rio Seco in the Chancay Valley, Salinas de Chao, and several other large platform mounds were built perhaps as early as 2,700 B.C. making them contemporary with the royal pyramids of Egypt. The pyramids of the Olmec and other Pre-classic cultures of Mesoamerica did not appear until more than 1,000 years later.[52]

Burger provided descriptions of numerous Chavín Pre-ceramic cities one of which is described below:

> *El* Paraíso: Located on the central coast of Peru, this is the largest known Pre-ceramic period site. Radiocarbon dates indicate that it was built during the final centuries of the Pre-ceramic period (circa 2000 B.C.). El Paraíso covers approximately 58 hectares [143 acres], and 100,000 tons of stones were utilized in building its complexes. Archaeologist Thomas Patterson estimates that it would have taken a minimum of almost 2,000,000 person-days to construct these platforms. Two of the largest buildings, each over 400 meters in length, are located parallel to each other on opposite ends of a 7 hectare [17 acres] plaza.[53]

A religious emblem is seen in the tradition of a U-shaped pyramid complex that was first identified in 1971 by Peruvian architect Carlos Williams. Burger wrote:

> Thus far approximately 20 U-shaped pyramid complexes have been identified, though only a small number have been studied. The scale of this public architecture is substantially greater than that of

---
[52]Burger, 28.
[53]Ibid., 38, 40.

The front of the New Temple at Chavín de Huántar, including the main entrance and the two round pillars with iconographic carvings of a supernatural Harpy Eagle and a supernatural hawk. Picture taken by the Author in 1973.

One of the two round pillars at the New Temple at Chavín de Huántar, Peru. The pillar is an excellent example of Chavín iconography. Picture taken by the Author in 1973.

Archaeologists had discovered various entrances to two levels containing numerous rooms, chambers, and passageways within the Old Temple at Chavín de Huántar. One of the rooms contained the 14 ft. high sculptured granite rock, known as the "Lanzon," believed by many art historians to be a representation of Ticci Viracocha, the Andean Creator God. Picture taken by the Author in 1973.

A view of the Old Temple at Chavín de Huántar, Peru, taken from the top of the temple. The Chavín site was completely covered with a large mud slide during the 1940's and archaeologists are just now removing the debris from that slide. Picture taken by the Author in 1973.

the late Pre-ceramic. San Jacinto, in the Chancay Valley, would have required almost 2 million cubic meters of material just to level its 30-hectare [74 acres] plaza. The U-shaped monuments have a number of formal features in common. They comprise massive terraced platform mounds flanking three sides of a large rectangular plaza. The central mount is frequently the largest, but the layout does not display exact axial symmetry since the two lateral arms are always different in size, and a single opening invariably exists between the central pyramid and one of the lateral arms.[54]

Burger noted that features once thought to originate in Mesoamerica, such as pyramid construction, are now known to have emerged in the central Andes centuries before their appearance in Mesoamerica.[55]

The Moche is another north coast Peruvian civilization that existed from approximately 200 B.C. to 600 A.D. that specialized in massive building projects. In an article done by Drs. Steve Bourget and Margaret E. Newman entitled "A Toast to the Ancestors: Ritual Warfare and Sacrificial Blood in Moche Culture," the two art historians describe the massive structure known as the Huaca de la Luna (Temple of the Moon), built not far from the modern Peruvian city of Trujillo:

> The Huaca de la Luna, constructed alongside the massive Huaca del Sol in the Moche valley, probably represents one of the most impressive ceremonial temples of the Moche Culture. This complex structure is formed of three platforms connected together by four plazas and a number of corridors. Most of these features are still buried under windblown sand. The temple, measuring about 290 meters long by 210 meters wide, has been constructed at the base of a conical hill, the Cerro Blanco (White Mountain). They did not identify the height which is over several hundred feet.[56]

---

[54]Ibid., 60-61.
[55]Ibid., 221.
[56]Steve Bourget and Margaret E. Newman, "A Toast to the Ancestors: Ritual Warfare and Sacrificial Blood in Moche Culture," published in 1998. (During a class on Moche Art, Dr. Bourget, who has worked many years at the Huaca de la Luna site, indicated that the platforms were constructed with mud (adobe) bricks and it is estimated that millions of bricks were required to construct the massive complex.)

Stone Work in Mesoamerica

As indicated in the book, *The Olmec World, Ritual and Rulership*, the earliest evidence of significant human occupation in Mesoamerica is 1500 B.C. to 1200 B.C. Those occupants, the Olmec, left behind colossal stone heads, basalt thrones, stone monuments and highly polished jade statuary. According to Diehl and Coe, the site at San Lorenzo, located in the Isthmus of Tehuantepec, Veracruz State, Mexico, has yielded more than 70 stone monuments, among them some of the finest sculptures ever created in ancient Mesoamerica.[57]

La Venta, located farther east in Tabasco State was one of the earliest Olmec sites and it features a one-hundred foot high Great Pyramid. The Great Pyramid at La Venta appeared to be an effort to construct an artificial mountain. La Venta includes many features not found anywhere else in the Mesoamerican world.

Not many years after the disappearance of the Olmec civilization, another new civilization took root and began to expand in a valley about 30 miles northeast of the Valley of Mexico, the present site of Mexico City. This new group built the ancient city of Teotihuacan (a name assigned to the area by the Aztecs). The original name is unknown. Teotihuacan was initiated perhaps as early as 200 B.C. and was built up and declined in five phases. By 100 B.C. it was situated in two hamlets with a population that may have reached 5,000 people (Phase I). By 150 A.D., the great Pyramid of the Sun and the Avenue of the Dead had been built. This growing urban complex may have reached 50,000 inhabitants which would make it one of the largest urban areas in the world at that time (Phase II).

The Pyramid of the Sun has been described as the third largest pyramid in the world and is slightly smaller than the Great Pyramid of Egypt. The Pyramid of the Sun stands approx-

---
[57]Abrams, 15.

imately 210 feet high with a 650-foot-square base. Unlike the pyramids of Egypt, the Pyramid of the Sun had a temple constructed on the top. In 1971, archaeologists discovered a large cave directly underneath the Pyramid of the Sun which may explain why the pyramid was developed on that site. There are legends in both Mesoamerica and the Andes that the earliest inhabitants surfaced from a cave.

The Pyramid of the Sun was built of jagged stones, adobe mud and earth, and was faced with rock. The pyramid is a succession of pyramids built one on top of the other. According to modern archaeologists, the Pyramid of the Sun contains thick layers of mica, which was brought from Brazil, more than two thousand miles away. How the mica was transported and why it was placed in layers within the pyramid, remains a great mystery. The Pyramid of the Sun and other pyramids at Teotihuacan were all painted a bright red.

From 150 A.D. to 300 A.D., Teotihuacan was laid out in a grid format and covered roughly 20 square kilometers. Much of the construction took place during this phase including the Pyramid of the Moon, a smaller pyramid that stands at one end of the Avenue of the Dead and faces a beautiful plaza that was surrounded by ornate palaces. The buildings were brightly colored with enormous paintings on the walls. The complex of 12 smaller pyramids known as the Ciudadela may have been built during this period. La Ciudadela, an enormous plaza also houses the Pyramid of Quetzalcoatl and two other smaller pyramids making a total of 15 pyramids in the Ciudalela complex (phase III).[58]

From 300 A.D. to 650 A.D., Teotihuacan reportedly reached its pinnacle and dominated an area as large as the great Aztec

---

[58]When I visited Teotihuacan in 1959, I heard of a legend that the twelve smaller pyramids represented an ancient ancestor who had twelve sons. I heard of another legend in which the twelve pyramids represented twelve individuals chosen as teachers in the Americas by [Ehecatl] Quetzalcoatl, whose much larger pyramid dominated the plaza.

The massive Pyramid of the Sun, located at Teotihuacan, Mexico, is considered by archaeologists as the third largest pyramid in the world. Picture taken by the Author in 1966.

The Pyramid of the Moon, located at Teotihuacan, Mexico, is much smaller than the Pyramid of the Sun and situated at the head of the Avenue of the Dead and faces a large plaza with numerous smaller pyramids and buildings. Picture taken by the Author in 1966.

A view of the Avenue of the Dead at Teotihuacan, Mexico. The Avenue of the Dead begins at the Pyramid of the Moon and continues past the Ciudadela where the Pyramid of Quetzalcoatl or "feathered serpent" is located. Picture taken by the Author in 1966.

View of the Teotihuacan, Mexico, complex with the Ciudadela pyramids in the middle forground. Picture was taken from the top of the Pyramid of the Sun. Picture taken by the Author in 1959.

A close up of the "feathered serpent" on the Pyramid of Ehecatl Quetzalcoatl, located in the Ciudadela complex at Teotihuacan, Mexico. Picture taken by the Author in 1959.

The three small pyramids located within the Ciudadela complex at Teotihuacan, Mexico. Picture taken by the Author in 1966.

empire several centuries later. Archaeologists believe that Teotihuacan had a population during this period of nearly 200,000 people and was probably the third most populace urban area in the world at that time, exceeded perhaps only by Rome and the ancient Chinese Imperial city Tang, now Beijing. In addition to being a great commercial center, Teotihuacan was also a great religious center (Phase IV). Between 650 A.D. and 750 A.D., Teotihuacan was abandoned.

Elsewhere, in Yucatán, Landa described the numerous buildings that he found there. He considered the buildings to be the most remarkable feature of the New World. They are all of stone very well hewn. He also made note of a certain "white earth" which appeared to be suitable for building.[59] In a footnote by Alfred M. Tozzer, he mentioned that E. H. Thompson referred to this white earth as "of peculiar character and served the ancient builders, as it does those of the present day, as a building material to mix with lime in the place of siliceous sand which is practically unknown in Yucatán."[60]

Landa described a number of cities and buildings which were all made of hewn stone. In Landa's day, the Spaniards were already beginning to dismantle the Maya buildings to use the stone for their own buildings. In a footnote, Tozzer made the following comment:

> The greater part of early Merida and many of the other Spanish towns [in Yucatán] were built of worked stones taken from the ruined structures of the Mayas. Landa writes, "And we gave to the Spaniards a great deal of stone for their houses, and especially for their doors and windows, so great was the abundance of it." To this day worked and carved stones appear in the walls of structures dating back to early Spanish times.[61]

---

[59]Landa, 18.
[60]Ibid., 18, n106.
[61]Ibid., 176. n922.

The main pyramid at Chichen Itzá, Yucatán, Mexico. Picture taken by Author in 1959.

The complex known as the Temple of the Thousand Warriors as seen from the top of the main pyramid at Chichen Itzá, Yucatán, Mexico. Picture taken by Author in 1959.

The Mayan version of the "feathered serpent" at Chichen Itzá, Yucatán, Mexico. The "feathered serpent" is located at the base of the Pyramid at Chichen Itzá. Picture taken by Author in 1959.

The famous ball court located at Chichen Itzá, Yucatán, Mexico. Notice the rock rings mounted on each sidewall through which a player had to pass the ball apparently without touching it with his hands. Picture taken by Author in 1959.

In describing the buildings in and around Tenochtitlan (now Mexico City), Cortés reportedly stated that the finest palaces, castles and other buildings in Spain could not equal in beauty or quality some of the buildings in Mexico. He described the buildings as being built of stone and marble with many terraces. The buildings had columns of jasper and transparent marble; the flooring was highly decorative. The buildings also had huge doors carved with great architectural skill.[62]

STONE WORK IN THE BOOK OF MORMON

In general, the *Book of Mormon* does not elaborate about the cities and the buildings erected by the Jaredites or the descendants of Lehi. Ether recorded that King Coriantum built many mighty cities and ruled with integrity (Ether 9:23). However, after several generations of alternating benign and corrupt kings, Ether pointed out that during the reign of Riplakish, he imposed a heavy tax upon the people and with these taxes he built many "spacious buildings." Many years later, Morianton, a descendant of Riplakish, built many more cities. Ether stated that the people under Morianton became exceedingly rich both in buildings as well as in gold and silver (Ether 10: 5, 9, 12).

It is difficult to visualize what constituted a "spacious building" hundreds of years before the birth of Jesus Christ. Art historians working both the Chavín as well as the Olmec civilizations have found many huge temples and palaces, and enormous pyramids that were larger than many of the great pyramids of Egypt. Archaeologists and art historians have speculated that these great cities were built with slave labor. Ether implied in his writings that they were built by construction crews who were paid from the heavy taxes that were imposed upon the people. This does not discount the use of slave labor as well.

---

[62]Martyr, 399.

After the split between the Nephites and the Lamanites, Nephi wrote between 588 B.C. and 570 B.C. that he taught his people how to build buildings. He indicated that they even built a temple. Nephi recorded:

> And I, Nephi, did build a temple; and I did construct it after the manner of the temple of Solomon save it were not built of so many precious things; for they were not to be found upon the land, wherefore, it could not be built like unto Solomon's temple. But the manner of the construction was like unto the temple of Solomon; and the workmanship thereof was exceedingly fine (2 Nephi 5: 15, 16).

Several hundred years later when Zeniff and a group of Nephites returned to the land of Lehi-Nephi, where Nephi first settled after fleeing from his brothers, Zeniff wrote that he began to build new buildings and to repair the walls of the city of Lehi-Nephi and the city of Shilom (Mosiah 9:9). Before Zeniff died, he handed power over to his son Noah, who became an extremely wicked man. Noah imposed a 20 percent tax upon his people to support himself and his friends. The following account is recorded in Mosiah:

> And it came to pass that king Noah built many elegant and spacious buildings; and he ornamented them with fine work of wood, and of all manner of precious things, of gold, and of silver, and of iron, and of brass, and of ziff, and of copper;
> And he also built him a spacious palace, and a throne in the midst thereof, all of which was of fine wood and was ornamented with gold and silver and with precious things.
> And he also caused that his workmen should work all manner of fine work within the walls of the temple, of fine wood, and of copper, and of brass.
> And the seats which were set apart for the high priests, which were above all the other seats, he did ornament with pure gold; and he caused a breastwork to be built before them, that they might rest their bodies and their arms upon while they should speak lying and vain words to his people.

> And it came to pass that he built a tower near the temple; yea, a very high tower, even so high that he could stand upon the top thereof and overlook the land of Shilom, and also the land of Shemlon, which was possessed by the Lamanites; and he could even look over all the land round about.
>
> And it came to pass that he caused many buildings to be built in the land Shilom; and he caused a great tower to be built on the hill north of the land Shilom, which had been a resort for the children of Nephi at the time they fled out of the land; and thus he did do with the riches which he obtained by the taxation of his people (Mosiah 11:8-13).

From these few remarks, it would appear that the most elegant and spacious buildings were built during the period of religious and moral decline of the *Book of Mormon* people. In the ancient Peruvian civilization at Chavín de Huantar, the temple was greatly enlarged during a period when it would appear that the natives were in a moral decline judging from the proliferation of psychotropic substances, the increase in human sacrifice, and the apparent abandoning of the worship of their creator god, Ticci Viracocha. Cuzco was greatly enlarged while the Incas were in an expansionist mode.

Defense became another factor in the placement and construction of great cities as well as strategic fortifications in the *Book of Mormon*. About 72 B.C., the prophet Alma narrated an account of a series of wars between the Nephites and the Lamanites. At this time, the Nephites fortified many of their cities as well as built new ones in strategic areas to control access into their lands. Alma wrote:

> And now it came to pass that Moroni did not stop making preparations for war, or to defend his people against the Lamanites; for he caused that his armies should commence in the commencement of the twentieth year of the reign of the judges, that they should commence in digging up heaps of earth round about all the cities, throughout all the land which was possessed by the Nephites.

And upon the top of these ridges of earth he caused that there should be timbers, yea, works of timbers built up to the height of a man, round about the cities.

And he caused that upon those works of timbers there should be a frame of pickets built upon the timbers round about; and they were strong and high.

And he caused towers to be erected that overlooked those works of pickets, and he caused places of security to be built upon those towers, that the stones and the arrows of the Lamanites could not hurt them (Alma 50:1-4).

In his book, *View of the Hebrews*, Ethan Smith described some Mound builders fortifications that appeared to be similar to those described by Alma. Ethan Smith wrote:

Near Newark in Licking County, Ohio, between two branches of the Licking River, at their junction, is one of the most notable remains of the ancient works. There is a fort including forty acres, whose walls are ten feet high. It has eight gateways, each of the width of about fifteen feet. Each gateway is guarded by a fragment of a wall, placed before, and about nine feet within the gate of the bigness of the walls of the fort, and about four feet longer than the width of the gateway. The walls are as nearly perpendicular as they could be made with earth. Near this fort is another round fort contained twenty-two acres, and connected with the first fort by two parallel walls of earth about the size of the other walls. At the remotest part of this circular fort, and just without a gateway, is an observatory so high as to command a view of the region to some distance. A secret passage was made under this observatory to an ancient watercourse. At some distance from this fort (but connected by a chain of internal works, and parallel walls) is another circular fort of about twenty six acres, with walls from twenty five to thirty feet in height, with a ditch just under them. Connected with these forts is another square fort of about twenty acres, whose walls are similar to those of the fort first described.

These forts were not only connected with each other (though considerable distance apart) by communications made by parallel walls of five or six rods apart; but a number of similar communications were made from them by parallel walls, down to the waters of the river. All these works stand on a large plain, the top of which is almost level, but is high land by a regular ascent from near the two branches of the river, to a height of forty or fifty feet above the branches of the river. At four different places at the ends of these internal communications between the forts and down to the river are watch towers on elevated ground, and surrounded by circular walls. And the points selected for these watch towers, were evidently chosen with great skill, to answer their design.[63]

Archaeologists have found that it was not unusual for a city in ancient America to be abandoned for many years and then resettled by the same people or by another group. As the Lamanites increased in power and numbers, they frequently pushed the Nephites out of their land and took over their cities. In 1973, an archaeologist working the ancient site at Chavín de Huantar stated that this particular site had been abandoned and then re-inhabited on three different occasions. Montesinos claimed that Cuzco was abandoned for 400 years before it was resettled several hundred years before the arrival of the Spaniards.

CEMENT WORKS

Cortés left Cempoala, on the Mexican Gulf coast, in mid August 1519 and traveled towards Tenochtitlan via Jalapa, Mexico. Bernal Díaz del Castillo, who accompanied Cortés, said they came upon a fortress made of stone, mortar and something like cement which was so hard that it was difficult to demolish with iron pickaxes.[64]

Another area where cement is evidenced is in the ancient Mexican city of Cacaxtla. The archaeological site at Cacaxtla, located 113 kilometers east of Mexico City on federal highway 150, was discovered by archaeologists in 1976 when a painted

---

[63] Ethan Smith, *View of the Hebrews or Tribes of Israel in America* (Second Edition, Published and Printed in Poultney, Vt. 1825. 190-191.

[64] Díaz del Castillo, 142.

mural was exposed at the entrance of a looter's shaft in a hillside. The first significant excavations into the site were carried out by a group of Mexican Archaeologists and Art Historians. They published their findings in 1986 in the book, *CACAXTLA, El Lugar Donde Muere la Lluvia en la Tierra* (*CACAXTLA, The Place Where the Rain Dies on the Earth.*) [65]

Within the perimeter of the Cacaxtla site, the archaeologists have found artifacts and buildings dating from as early as 1200 to 800 B.C. Archaeologist Diana López de Molina believed the Cacaxtlans reached their greatest political/cultural height around 250 AD. to 600 A.D. when they felt the strongest influence from Teotihuacan.[66]

All of the spaces between the buildings as well as the courtyards were covered anciently with an excellent grade of cement.

Diego de Landa also wrote about the use of cement in Yucatán. In describing the Palace of Kukulcan at Chichen Itzá, Landa wrote:

> This building has around it many other well built and large buildings and the ground between it and them is covered with cement, so that there are even traces of the cemented places today, so hard is the mortar of which they make them there.[67]

In the *Book of Mormon*, Helaman mentioned the use of cement in the construction of houses while describing the activities of those Nephites who went north. Helaman wrote:

> And there being but little timber upon the face of the land, nevertheless the people who went forth became exceedingly expert in the working of cement; therefore they did build houses of cement, in the which they did dwell.

---

[65]Sonia Lombardo de Ruiz, Diana López de Molina, Daniel Molina Feal, Carolyn Baus de Czitrom, and Oscar J. Polaco: *CACAXTLA, El Lugar Done Muere la Lluvia en la Tierra*. Published under the auspices of the Mexican Instituto Nacional de Antropologia e Historia and the Government of the State of Tlaxcala. 1986.

[66]Ibid.,18.

[67]Landa, 179.

And the people who were in the land northward did dwell in tents, and in houses of cement, and they did suffer whatsoever tree should spring up upon the face of the land that it should grow up, that in time they might have timber to build their houses, yea, their cities, and their temples, and their synagogues, and their sanctuaries, and all manner of their buildings.

And thus they did enable the people in the land northward that they might build many cities, both of wood and of cement (Helaman 3:7, 9, 11).

Highways and Irrigation Canals

Pedro de Cieza de León traveled by horse from Popayán, Colombia, through Cuzco on to Bolivia. Normally, the Spaniards traversed the extremely mountainous terrain over roads built by the Incas. Cieza de León marveled at these great highways that stretched for thousands of miles. He observed that the great Andean highway extended for 1,100 leagues or roughly 3,300 miles. There was also a coastal highway that was not as long, but connected all the provinces along the Pacific coast from Tumbes, Peru, near the Ecuadorian border to the Maule River in Chile. Periodically the Incas had built connecting highways between the Andean highway and the coastal highway.

In most areas these highways were all-weather, hard surface roads that were carefully maintained throughout the year. Cieza de León commented that the Spaniards could travel with six horses abreast over most of the coastal and Andean highways. These highways were about 25 feet wide. Naturally, the highways connecting the Andean route with the coastal highway narrowed considerably when passing through difficult mountain terrain. He noted that the great Inca highway was as famous in the New World as the highway Hannibal built across the Alps when he marched into Italy.[68] He also noted that every three or four

---

[68]Cieza de León, *The Incas*, 20.

leagues (9 to 12 miles) along the highway, the Indians built very fine lodgings or palaces which were richly adorned for the Inca king to lodge while traveling.[69]

Cieza de León wrote the following about Inca road building technology:

> One of the things that most took my attention when I was observing and setting down the things of this kingdom was how and in what way the great, splendid highways we see throughout it could be built, and the number of men that must have been required, and what tools and instruments they used to level the mountains and cut through the rock to make them as broad and good as they are. For it seems to me that if the Emperor [Spanish] were to desire another highway built like the one from Quito to Cuzco, or that which goes from Cuzco to Chile, truly I do not believe he could do it, with all his power and the men at his disposal, unless he followed the method the Incas employed. These highways stretched more than 1,100 leagues [3,300 miles] over mountains so rough and dismaying that in certain places one could not see bottom, and some of the sierras so sheer and barren that the road had to be cut through the living rock to keep it level and the right width. All this they did with fire and picks. In other places the incline was so steep and rough that they built steps from the bottom to ascend to the top, with platforms every so often so that the people could rest. In other places there were piles of snow, and this was the most dangerous, and not just in one spot but in many places.
>
> When the Lord-Inca had decided on the building of one of these famous highways, no great provisioning or levies or anything else was needed except for the Lord-Inca to say, let this be done. The inspectors then went through the provinces, laying out the route and assigning Indians from one end to the other to the building of the road. In this way, from one boundary of the province to the other, at its expense and with its Indians, it was built as laid out, in a short time; and each province did the same, and, if necessary, a great stretch of the road was built at the same time, or all of it. When they came to the barren places, the Indians of the lands nearest by came with victuals and tools to do the work, and all was done with little

---

[69]Ibid., 45.

effort and joyfully, because they were not oppressed in any way, nor did the Incas put overseers to watch them.⁷⁰

In a footnote, Victor Wolfgang Von Hagen noted that the distance of the Royal Road from Angasmayo, Colombia, to the Maule River in Chile is 3,250 miles; the coastal road, beginning at Tumbes, Peru, extends 2,520 miles to Santiago, Chile. There were many other radials and laterals which totaled more than 10,000 miles of all-weather roads. The coastal road had a uniform width of 24 feet; the mountain road varied, depending on terrain, from 15 to 24 feet; the laterals which joined coastal and Andean roads were of varying widths, three to 10 feet, since they were built into canyon walls.

Not only were the Incas extremely adept at road building, but they also built incredible bridges to span numerous rivers. Cieza de León described one of the bridges at Vilcas, not far from Cuzco, Peru. He stated that from one side of the river to the other there are two high rows of stone piles, stout and deeply buried, on which to lay the bridge, which was made of twisted vines, like ropes for drawing up water from a well with a pulley. Cieza de León said the bridges, made in this way, were so strong that horses could gallop over them as though they were crossing the bridge of Córdoba, Spain. He noted that when he crossed the bridge at Vilcas, the bridge was 166 "pasos" (approximately 400 feet long.)⁷¹

When Cieza de León passed through the Peruvian Province of Cajamarca, he noted the numerous irrigation canals built by

---

⁷⁰Ibid., *The Incas*, 136-138. (I have driven from Lima to Huancayo over passes reaching 16,000 feet, from Lima to the Callejón de Huaylas and then over the "White Mountains," Cordillera Blanca, to Chavín de Huantar on the eastern slopes. In Ecuador, I have traveled on the old road from Quito to Otavalo on roads reaching over 17,000 feet and from there north through Ibarra to the Colombian border. The drop-offs were so steep and deep that clouds and birds could be seen far below in valleys. The terrain is rugged with high mountains on all sides.)
⁷¹Cieza de León, *La Cronica del Perú*, 210.

the Indians of that region. They were excellent farmers and raised a wide variety of edibles.[72] In the days of the Incas, there was very little arable land that was not under cultivation or heavily populated. Cieza de León lamented that it was a sad thing to reflect that the idol-worshiping Incas should have had such wisdom in knowing how to govern and preserve their far-flung lands, and that the Christians had destroyed so many kingdoms.[73]

Cieza de León observed that whenever the Incas conquered new lands and people, they treated the newly conquered foes as friends. If the fallen enemy lacked food, the Lord Inca supplied food for them from other areas. If they did not know how to farm and raise adequate food, he taught them how to farm and showed them how to build irrigation canals. Cieza de León believed that there had never been a nation or a people in the world who had constructed irrigation canals over such rough and difficult terrain. The Incas also built canals and aqueducts to transport water into their villages. Many cities in Peru still obtain their water from the old Inca aqueducts. As Cieza de León crossed the many valleys along the coastal route, he wrote:

> As the rivers flow from the highlands through these valleys, and some of the latter are broad and all are cultivated, or where they were thickly settled, they built irrigation ditches at intervals, and, strange though it seems, both in upland and low-lying regions and on the sides of the hills and the foothills descending to the valleys, and these were connected to others, running in different directions. All this makes it a pleasure to cross these valleys, because it is as though one were walking amidst gardens and cool groves. The Indians took and still take great care in bringing the water through these ditches. There have been occasions when I have stopped beside one of these canals, and before I have had time to pitch my tent, the ditch was dry and the water had been diverted elsewhere. For, as the rivers never dry up, the Indians can conduct the water where they will. There is

---

[72]Cieza de León, *The Incas*, 96.
[73]Ibid., 62.

always verdure along these ditches, and grass grows beside many of them, where the horses graze, and among the trees and bushes there is a multitude of birds, doves, wild turkey, pheasants, partridge, and also deer.[74]

When the Spaniards, under the leadership of Hernán Cortés, arrived near Tenochtitlan in Mexico, Díaz del Castillo described his amazement at the opulence and beauty of the cities. He briefly described the city of Iztapalapa, located on the lake not far from Tenochtitlan. He marveled at how spacious and well built were the palaces where they were lodged. The palaces were made of beautiful stone work, cedar wood and other sweet-scented woods, with awnings of cotton cloth. The orchards and gardens had a wide variety of beautiful plants and flowers including native roses and fruit trees, and ponds of fresh water. Díaz del Castillo noticed hundreds of canoes moving around on the Tenochtitlan lake engaged in commerce and other activities. The canoes were able to pass from the lake into the ponds through a series of locks. There were many varieties of birds on the ponds and near by. He said that as he looked over the panorama, he was sure that nowhere else in the world could they find lands that could equal in beauty the scenes around the lake of Tenochtitlan. He also lamented that within a few years after the arrival of the Spaniards everything had disappeared.[75]

Diego de Landa briefly described the roads connecting the various cities in Yucatán. In a footnote, Tozzer wrote

> There are remains of paved highways which traverse all this kingdom and they say they ended in the east on the seashore where it crosses an arm of the sea for the distance of four leagues [12 miles]

---

[74]Ibid., 318.

[75]Díaz del Castillo, 214-215. (The Aztec city of Tenochtitlan was built in the center of the lake with causeways connecting Tenochtitlan with other cities around the lake coast. Over time, Lake Tenochtitlan disappeared along with the canals and ponds. Modern Mexico City covers the area that was formerly Lake Tenochtitlan and the city.)

which divides the mainland from that island [Cozumel]. These highways were like the "caminos reales," which guided them with no fear of going astray so that they might arrive at Cozumel for the fulfillment of their vows, to offer their sacrifices, to ask for help in their needs, and for the mistaken adoration of their false gods.[76]

Later in his book, Landa again referred to the road system in Yucatán. He wrote:

> The second buildings, of those which are the chief ones in this country, and so old that there is no memory of their founders, are those of Tihoo. They lie at thirteen leagues from Izamal and eight from the sea, as do the others, and there are signs today of there having been a very beautiful road from one (set of buildings) to the other.[77]

In his footnotes, Tozzer stated that several of the early Spanish governing authorities mention these roadways ("sac beob," or white roads) connecting various cities. For example, Lacandone has four trails or roads leading to it, corresponding to the four cardinal points and the roads running to the four directions as shown by Lizana, who wrote, "They made pilgrimages from all parts, for which reason there have been made four roads or causeways to the four cardinal points, which reach to all the ends of the land, and passed to Tabasco, Guatemala and Chiapas." Tozzer wrote that the most notable system of ancient roads center around the ruined group at Coba in northeast Yucatán. The earliest known mention of this road is found in a land survey, dated 1820, given and noted by Roys in 1932, who stated that "the south line ran along a raised road, about the height of a man, dating from ancient times."[78]

---

[76]Landa, 109, n500.

[77]Ibid., 174.

[78]Ibid., 174, n908. (Modern archaeologists have discovered that more than 50 unusual 4 foot high and 30 foot wide roads (sac beob) with ramps and intersections, run in straight lines from the farthest points of the Mayan's realm to converge in Coba's temple square. The Maya are not believed to have the wheel or draft animals and the use of these roads has remained a mystery to modern science.)

The *Book of Mormon* contains only limited information about the building of roads in the New World. In 3 Nephi is recorded:

> And there were many highways cast up, and many roads made which led from city to city, and from land to land, and from place to place (3 Nephi 6:8).

In summary, archaeologists, chroniclers, and *Book of Mormon* writers respectively describe great technological skills among many of the native American groups particularly those in the Andes and Mesoamerica. The fact that so many Europeans refused to recognize or associate these technical skills with the Indians' sophistication eventually led to the near destruction of these New World inhabitants.

In his book, *Short Account of the Destruction of the Indies*, Bartolomé de las Casas repeatedly condemned the Spaniards for destroying the Indies. He said it was they who had laid to waste vast and fertile lands, territories at once richer and grander than anything his readers in Europe could hope to imagine. Anthony Pagden, who wrote an introduction to the 1992 edition of Las Casas's writings, said that Las Casas hoped to be able to reverse the destruction of this earthly paradise, but by the time his writings were originally published the destruction of the Indies was virtually complete.[79] The Indians, their culture all but eradicated or forgotten, were already faced with the need either to become a lowly, marginal part of the European colonial system or, as they continued to do in increasing numbers, to perish altogether.

---

[79] Las Casas, xli.

17

WARFARE AND WEAPONRY

If Joseph Smith were an imposter and the *Book of Mormon* were a work of fiction, one area of his narrative that would have been challenging for him to fabricate would be in the descriptions of warfare and weaponry in the Pre-Christian era. Joseph Smith received no training in military tactics. Manuals or books on Pre-Columbian American weaponry or military tactics did not exist at that time. The numerous battle scenes, weapons and fighting tactics, described in the *Book of Mormon*, particularly the books of Ether, Alma, and Helaman, would reveal an imposter if they did not harmonize with later findings.

Nevertheless, without benefit of research or scholarship, Smith persevered, and the *Book of Mormon* includes considerable information concerning weaponry and warfare in ancient America. The various *Book of Mormon* recorders often went into great detail concerning complicated military tactics during the wars between the Nephites and the Lamanites. Their description of Jaredite weapons and tactics were more limited, but that is in keeping with the brief description of the Jaredite history.

In the book of Ether, it is recorded that Shule obtained ore from the hill of Ephraim and smelt the ore from which he made swords out of steel. Ether did not elaborate on how Shule obtained the ore or the process he used to smelt the iron. As we have seen previously, these ancient Jaredites had considerable metallurgical technology and mined a wide variety of minerals and metals. Apparently the sword was the main weapon used by the Jaredites and it also influenced the type of defensive armor that they used. Interestingly there is no indication that the Jaredites used the bow and arrow. During the final battles, Ether wrote:

> And it came to pass that when they were all gathered together, everyone to the army which he would, with the wives and their children—both men, women and children being armed with weapons of war, having shields, and breastplates, and head-plates, and being clothed after the manner of war—they did march forth one against another to battle; and they fought all that day, and conquered not.
>
> And it came to pass that they fought all that day, and when the night came they slept upon their swords.
>
> And on the morrow they fought again; and when the night came they had all fallen by the sword save it were fifty and two of the people of Coriantumr, and sixty and nine of the people of Shiz (Ether 15:15, 20, 23).

Ether gave the impression that the swords used by the Jaredites were fairly long. He stated that in the very last battle scene when the enemy commander Shiz had fainted from loss of blood, Coriantumr leaned upon his sword to rest before cutting off Shiz's head. The sword may have been four feet long or more and, in fact, may have been close to the length of the wooden swords, described as being as long as broadswords, that were used by some of the natives when the Spaniards arrived.

This final Jaredite battle was waged sometime between 588 B.C. and 300 B.C. Art historians studying the Chavín and Olmec civilizations agree that both civilizations disappeared about 400 B.C. Approximately 200 years after this final battle of the Jaredites, Limhi, a Nephite who had returned to the original land of Nephi, sent an expedition of 43 men to attempt to locate again the land of Zarahemla. This troop of warriors became lost and wandered north. When they returned to Limhi in the land of Nephi, they related the following account:

> And they were lost in the wilderness for the space of many days, yet they were diligent, and found not the land of Zarahemla but returned to this land, having traveled in a land among many waters, having discovered a land which was covered with bones of men, and beasts, and was also covered with ruins of buildings of every kind, having discovered a land which had been peopled with a people who were as numerous as the hosts of Israel.
>
> And for a testimony that the things that they had said are true they have brought twenty-four plates which are filled with engravings, and they are of pure gold.
>
> And behold, also, they have brought breastplates, which are large, and they are of brass and of copper, and are perfectly sound.
>
> And again, they have brought swords, the hilts thereof have perished, and the blades thereof were cankered with rust . . . (Mosiah 8:8-11).

ARCHAEOLOGICAL EVIDENCE OF FORMATIVE PERIOD

During the 1937 excavation of the ruins at Cerro Sechín, located on the Pacific coast of Peru approximately 200 miles north of Lima, the Peruvian archaeologist, Julio C. Tello, discovered a three-tiered platform. The pyramidal construction was quadrangular with rounded corners and measured 53 meters on a side. Its outer wall was adorned with approximately 400 stone sculptures. According to a joint Peruvian-German team of art historians, the construction of the pyramid and the stone sculptures predate a radio carbon date of 1519 B. C. Burger wrote:

> The hundreds of individual sculptures were arranged in the platform wall to portray a single mythological or historical scene in which two columns of warriors approach each other from opposing sides amidst the carnage of their adversaries. The military procession is depicted as though it were advancing towards the central staircase from the rear of the building. At the head of each column is a banner, probably emblematic of the victorious group. The two sculptures of banners flank the main staircase, and their original height has been estimated at 4 meters.
>
> The representations on the sculptures are of humans, and there is a conspicuous lack of animal attributes or other features that might suggest that supernaturals were being represented. The victorious warriors, which constitute about seven percent of the carvings, appear exclusively on the large slabs and are easily identifiable from the pillbox headdresses, flowing loincloths, and the staffs and darts they hold. One is shown with decapitated heads hanging as trophies from his waist. The defeated are portrayed as naked, in positions that graphically express their agony. Nude bodies are shown with eyes bulging and hands flailing, their torsos sliced in two by transverse cuts. Sometimes the body lacks its head or, in other cases, blood or entrails gush from the victim. Other sculptures depict severed body parts, such as arms, legs, rows of eyes, and stacks of vertebrae.
>
> This stone frieze is vivid evidence that small-scale raiding existed in the Initial Period, and suggests the degree to which violence played an integral role in the religious and political ideology of these early societies, if not their daily lives.[1]

Although swords or knives are not mentioned as being part of their weaponry, the description of the transverse cuts and severed heads would indicate that the weapons were more than clubs, spears or rocks[2]. The pillbox hats also could have provided some protection. Undoubtably, weaponry and defensive armor would have developed even further during the more than one

---

[1]Burger, 78-79.
[2]Ibid., 78-79.

WARFARE AND WEAPONRY

The terraced platform at Cerro Sechín was decorated with hundreds of stone sculptures depicting a procession of victorious warriors and their mutilated victims. Wearing spotted pillbox hats and holding staffs of authority, two guards flank the rear stairway of the site. Photo courtesy of Chavin and the Origins of Andean Civilization by Richard L. Burger, published by Thames and Hudson Ltd, London.

Cerro Sechín sculpture of a victim writhing in agony while his intestines spill from his body. Height c. 1.7 m. Photo courtesy of Chavin and the Origins of Andean Civilization *by Richard L. Burger, published by Thames and Hudson Ltd, London.*

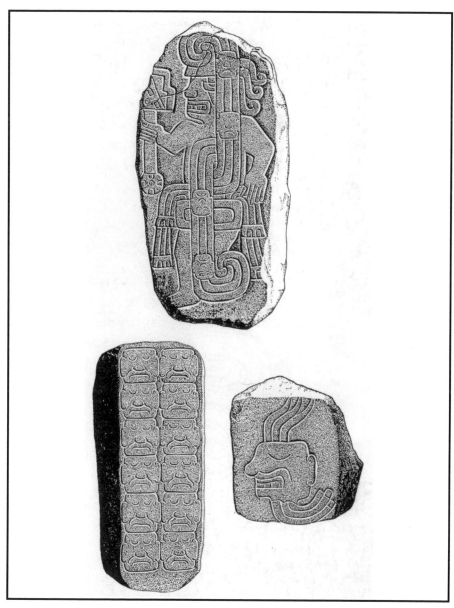

These gruesome Cerro Sechín sculptures depict: (above) a successful warrior adorned with severed heads (28 cm high); (below) a large pile of decapitated heads (2.74 m high) and the bleeding head of a defeated soldier (41 cm high). Photo courtesy of Chavin and the Origins of Andean Civilization by Richard L. Burger, published by Thames and Hudson Ltd, London.

thousand years between the battles depicted at Cerro Sechín and the final battles of the Jaredites.

Information concerning the types of weapons used by the Olmec is very sparse. Some iconographic scenes reveal individuals killing a human sacrifice with large paddle-shaped clubs. They also had an array of blood-letting instruments that could have been used in warfare as well. Art historians have focused more attention on the fascinating Olmec art. Later groups used spears, and swords, but these have not appeared in Olmec iconography nor have other types of weapons.

NEPHITE AND LAMANITE WEAPONS

The record keepers of the accounts of the Nephites and the Lamanites wars were explicit in describing the kinds of weapons used during their battles. Even before leaving Jerusalem, Lehi and his sons were acquainted with the use of the bow and arrow. Old Testament prophets made various references to the use of the bow and arrow including the use of steel bows which was one of the primary weapons of war in ancient Israel.[3] Nephi recorded:

> And it came to pass that as I, Nephi, went forth to slay food, behold, I did break my bow, which was made of fine steel; and after I did break my bow, behold, my brethren were angry with me because of the loss of my bow, for we did obtain no food.
>
> Now it came to pass that I, Nephi, having been afflicted with my brethren because of the loss of my bow, and their bows having lost their springs, it began to be exceedingly difficult, yea, insomuch that we could obtain no food.
>
> And it came to pass that I, Nephi, did make out of wood a bow, and out of a straight stick, an arrow; wherefore, I did arm myself with a bow and an arrow, with a sling and with stones (1 Nephi 16:18, 21, 23).

---

[3] I Samuel 2:4–The bows of the mighty men are broken, and they that stumbled are girded with strength. Psalm 18:34–He teacheth my hands to war, so that a bow of steel is broken by mine arms.

WARFARE AND WEAPONRY

Nephi also mentioned that he kept with him the sword of Laban, that he had taken from the Israelite elder before leaving Jerusalem. When the Lord commanded Nephi and his followers to separate themselves from their angry brothers, Laman and Lemuel, Nephi took the records of brass he got from Laban, the compass (Liahona) and the sword of Laban. Using the sword of Laban as a pattern, Nephi made many swords for his family to protect themselves against the Lamanites.

Jacob's son, Enos, wrote that the Lamanites were skilled in the bow, the cimeter,[4] and the ax.

The book of Mosiah contains the separate record of Zeniff and a group of Nephites who had returned to the original land of Nephi to live among the Lamanites. After approximately 13 years, the Lamanites began to harass this small band of Nephites and Zeniff was forced to arm his followers. Zeniff recorded that he armed his followers with "bows, and with arrows, with swords, and with cimeters, and with clubs, and with slings, and with all manner of weapons which we could invent" (Mosiah 9:15). Zeniff pointed out that the Lamanites had similar weapons (Mosiah 10:8).

About 74 B.C., the Lamanites attacked the main population of Nephites, who were led by a new military commander, Moroni, the chief captain over all the Nephite armies. (This is a predecessor of the Moroni, who was the last record-keeper in the *Book of Mormon*.) During this same period of wars, the Nephite military leader Teancum killed two opposing commanders with his javelin (Alma 51:34 and Alma 52:36). There are several references to the use of spears. In addition to the usual array of weapons, Moroni introduced defensive armor. Alma described the situation as follows:

---

[4]The English dictionary provides the definition of a scimitar, which is a short, curved, single-edge sword used among the Orientals, particularly the Turks and Persians. This may have been similar to the cimeter spoken of by the Nephite writers.

> And it came to pass that he met the Lamanites in the borders of Jershon, and his people were armed with swords, and with cimeters, and all manner of weapons of war.
>
> And when the armies of the Lamanites saw that the people of Nephi, or that Moroni, had prepared his people with breastplates and with arm-shields, yea, and also shields to defend their heads, and also they were dressed with thick clothing–
>
> Now the army of Zerahemnah was not prepared with any such thing; they had only their swords and their cimeters, their bows and their arrows, their stones and their slings; and they were naked, save it were a skin which was girded about their loins; yea, all were naked, save it were the Zoramites and the Amalekites;
>
> But they were not armed with breastplates, nor shields–therefore, they were exceedingly afraid of the armies of the Nephites because of their armor, notwithstanding their number being so much greater than the Nephites (Alma 43:18-21).

Not only did Captain Moroni provide body armor to protect the warriors, he went to great efforts to fortify his cities by erecting high walls around the cities so that the arrows and the stones cast at them by the Lamanites would be less effective. Alma wrote:

> And behold, the city had been rebuilt, and Moroni had stationed an army by the borders of the city, and they had cast up dirt round about to shield them from the arrows and the stones of the Lamanites; for behold, they fought with stones and with arrows.
>
> But behold, how great was their disappointment; for behold, the Nephites had dug up a ridge of earth round about them, which was so high that the Lamanites could not cast their stones and their arrows at them that they might take effect, neither could they come upon them save it was by their place of entrance (Alma 49:2, 4).
>
> And upon the top of these ridges of earth he caused that there should be timbers, yea, works of timbers built up to the height of a man, round about the cities.
>
> And he caused that upon these works of timbers there should be a frame of pickets built upon the timbers round about; and they were strong and high.

And he caused towers to be erected that overlooked those works of pickets, and he caused places of security to be built upon those towers, that the stones and the arrows of the Lamanites could not hurt them.

And they were prepared that they could cast stones from the top thereof, according to their pleasure and their strength, and slay him who should attempt to approach near the walls of the city.

Thus Moroni did prepare strongholds against the coming of their enemies, round about every city in all the land (Alma 50:2-6).

Weapons Encountered by Conquistadores

During Columbus's several trips to the New World, Peter Martyr wrote that Columbus discovered Indians on Hispaniola, who were expert in the use of bows and arrows, clubs, spears or lances as well as poisonous darts.[5] The Carib Indians were similarly armed. When Columbus discovered the Island of Trinidad and the coast of Venezuela, he also observed that the Indians had shields as well as their bows and arrows.[6]

After Columbus's death, the King of Spain sent Diego Nicuesa and Alfonso Hojeda to explore further along the Venezuelan and Colombian coasts. Near the area of modern Cartagena, Colombia, Hojeda encountered a group of Indians who were heavily armed with swords made of wood, bows and arrows, poisonous darts, and shields. The Indians killed more than 70 Spaniards, mainly with poison-tipped darts and arrows.[7]

Martyr pointed out that Indians from different regions often used different types of weapons. In the Darién, Panama, Nuñez de Balboa found a group who fought hand-to-hand with long wooden swords called *Macanas* which had been hardened by fire. They also used spears and darts. In another area in the Darién,

---
[5]Martyr, 23.
[6]Ibid., 65.
[7]Ibid., 121.

Nuñez de Balboa fought natives who armed themselves with bows and arrows, wooden swords, which looked like broadswords, javelins, and lances with they threw with excellent marksmanship.[8]

Diego Muñoz Camargo, a mestizo born in Tlaxcala shortly after the conquest, wrote a manuscript entitled the *History of Tlaxcala* (*Historia de Tlaxcala*) in approximately 1576, but it was not published until 1892.[9] He dedicated an entire chapter in his manuscript to offensive and defensive weapons used by the Tlaxcalans and the Nahuatl speaking tribes. He wrote:

> The primary weapon used by the Tlaxcalans was the bow and the arrow which they used to hunt animals for food. They also used slings and lances that were about eight feet long which were thrown with great force by a spear propeller (*atlatl*). The points of the lance were made of obsidian or flint, copper, or fish bone. The arrows and the darts had the same kind of points. In addition, they used heavy clubs and wooden swords edged with obsidian. For defense, they made heavy shields and used a padded armor of woven cotton cords. They dug pits in the ground and inserted sharpened stakes into the ground within the pits. These pits were covered over with camouflage. On their heads, they wore helmets of the head of a fierce animal such as a jaguar, a wolf, an eagle, etc. These head pieces were highly decorated to make the warrior appear more fierce. The warrior also painted himself with bright colors.[10]

Díaz del Castillo narrated that the Tlaxcalans were armed with two-handed swords, shields, and lances. Díaz del Castillo claimed the swords were as long as broadswords and the edges were of sharpened flint or obsidian that cut worse than a knife.[11]

---

[8]Ibid., 199.

[9]Diego Muñoz Camargo, *Historia de Tlaxcala*, original manuscript finished in approximately 1576. (First published with notations by Alfredo Chavero in 1892.) Current edition published by Editorial Innovación, S. A., Mexico D.F., Mexico 1978.

[10]Muñoz Camargo, 13-14.

[11]Díez del Castillo, 142-143.

Durán frequently referred to a wide variety of weapons used by the Aztecs and their allies. In a footnote Doris Heyden described these weapons in the following terms:

> *Atlatl*: "propelled spear," a weapon that propels projectile points.
> *Bow and Arrow*: though introduced in late times by the Chichimecs, these also were used by the Aztecs but were not known by some earlier groups.
> *Chimalli*: a shield of reeds and leather.
> *Macuahuitl*: a wooden sword or club edged on both sides with blades of obsidian, or flint.
> *Tepoztopilli*: a lance almost ten feet long tipped by a flint point.
> The sling was also an important weapon and was made of woven maguey fiber. The ball cast was of finely rounded stone or clay.
> The blowgun, which shot marble-size clay balls, also played a prominent part in ancient Mexican warfare.
> The armor of the Aztec warrior was a fitted, heavily padded, quilted cotton suit surmounted by a helmet that could have the form of an eagle, a jaguar, or figures that served as insignia of rank as well as identifications of group and provenance. One aim of the warrior's costume was to terrify the enemy–thus the extravagant decoration.[12]

Heyden and art historians have noted that earlier groups did not use the bow and the arrow. There is no record in the Book of Ether that the Jaredites used the bow and the arrow nor have I found any indication that the Chavín or the Olmec were acquainted with the bow and the arrow. It would appear that these ancient Formative Period civilizations lived and fought for nearly 2,000 years without developing this extremely useful hunting and fighting tool.

The *Book of Mormon* narrates that Lehi and his family brought the bow and arrow with them from Jerusalem about 600 B.C. Heyden indicates that suddenly the Chichimecs introduced this weapon into the Mesoamerican area sometime before the Christian era. From the general description of the

---

[12]Durán. 34, n5.

Chichimecs, they sound very much like the Lamanites described by Enos. (It is interesting that Joseph Smith put the bow and the arrow into the hands of his later migratory group, but made no mention of the Jaredites having such a weapon.)

In Yucatán, Landa stated that the Maya learned from the Mexicans the use of the bow and arrow, the lance and the axe, their shields and jackets (armor) made strong with twisted cotton cords. Tozzer stated in a footnote that this cotton cord armor was so strong that arrows did not go through it. This type of cotton armor was subsequently adopted by the Spaniards under the name of *escaupil*. Sometimes the legs were enclosed in such quilted armor.[13]

In the Andean region, Cieza de León provided excellent descriptions of the weapons used by different Indian groups. For example, when he passed through the area of Tacunga, located about forty miles south of Quito, Ecuador, he noted that the natives of Tacunga "employed for arms, palm lances and javelins and darts and slings."[14] In a separate chapter, Cieza de León wrote that the Inca warriors carried slings, axes, clubs, *ayllos* (boleadoras–bolos), darts, and some lances.[15] Betanzos described the *ayllos* (sometimes spelled *aillos*) as three lines knotted together in the center. A ball the size of a small orange is tied at each end. The balls are usually made of metal or stones. The Indians grasp one ball, twirling the other two in the air the way one throws a sling. When they throw the balls, they throw them at the legs, entangling the victim and preventing him from taking a step. A man who is caught in this fashion cannot cut the cord

---

[13]Landa, 35, n174.

[14]Cieza de León, *The Incas*, 58. (During a 1964 assignment in Ecuador, I was given a ten foot long, black palm spear that appeared to be perfectly balanced. It had been thrown from the bushes by an Auca Indian. Black palm is an extremely hard wood and, in this case, the pointed end of the wooden shaft was serrated so that it could not be pulled back out of the wound. It did not require a separate flint or metal point.)

[15]Ibid. 117. (Modern gauchos in South America still use the boleadoras.)

quickly enough to prevent the enemy from overtaking him and killing him.[16]

In a separate narrative, Martín de Murúa described weapons that he encountered in Peru that were used by the Incas, including black palm lances which were frequently tipped with a poisonous substance. They used bows and arrows, darts, clubs (also made from black palm), slings, and another weapon which Murúa called a *champis* which had a point of hardened copper shaped like a star. They carried shields and wore helmets of woven fibers that would protect against the blow of a sword or club. Before entering into battle, the Incas painted themselves to appear more fierce.[17]

Pedro Pizarro noted that in addition to the above named weapons, the Incas used a large blanket-like shield which they held over their heads and could cover as many as one hundred soldiers. They used these shields when attacking forts and fortified cities. He also mentioned the Inca helmets which were made of intertwined cane strips that were so effective that a thrown rock or a blow from a club would not injure the wearer.[18]

Montesinos wrote that the natives used sharpened copper as the main metal for their weapons. They also used backplates and breastplates to provide additional protection as well as heavy cotton armor for their legs and arms.[19]

In Brazil, Pero de Magalhães de Gandavo, declared that the Indians fought with great courage without shields or armor. They were experts with the bow and the arrow and seldom if ever missed their mark no matter how difficult the shot. Magalhães de Gandavo said it was a very strange sight to see two or three thousand naked men on opposing sides shooting with bows and arrows at one another while emitting loud shouts and cries, all

---

[16]Betanzos, 135.
[17]Murúa, 410.
[18]Pizarro, 104.
[19]Montesinos, 50-51.

the time hopping about with great agility from one spot to another, so that the enemy could not hit them.

Magalhães de Gandavo said the Aimorés, the extremely large white Indians of Brazil, were so strong that they carried very long bows which were thick in proportion to the strength of the bearer with long arrows to match. He observed that the Aimoré women also carried heavy clubs like maces and joined the fighting when necessary.

The Araucano Indians in Chile employed a variety of lethal weapons which they used effectively against the Incas as well as the Spaniards. Alonso de Ercilla y Zuñiga provided an account of their weapons in his epic poem, *La Araucana*. He wrote that the Araucanos used many different weapons such as the bow and arrow, bludgeons, truncheons, armor, pikestaffs, swords, lances of dense grained timbers, scimitars and bucklers.[20] From Ercilla y Zuñiga's numerous travels throughout Spain and Europe with Prince Phillip, he would have become acquainted with a scimitar. It is not usually mentioned by the chroniclers as a weapon in other areas of South America or Mexico.

Ercilla y Zuñiga claimed that the Araucano warrior wore no uniform, but had a leather breastplate, helmet, sword, lance, pike or club pointed with iron. In addition to wooden weapons, the Araucanos also made heavy spears and pikes of iron, sharpened axes, steel-tipped maces, horn-shaped arms and hand-thrown missiles. Ercilla y Zuñiga lauded the abilities of the Araucanos in the use of weapons by describing the exploits of the Indian warrior, Tucapel, who leaped into a Spanish fort and fought single-handedly against numerous Spanish soldiers. He narrated in poetic style the forgoing battle scene:

> Scarcely had the headstrong savage
> Landed firmly in the plaza
> When he swung his bulky cudgel

---

[20]Ercilla, 200.

And dispersed his lurking foemen.
Fine-meshed mail, stout armor-plating,
Helmets were not worth a copper.
Raining blows they could not suffer;
Skulls and brains were mashed and mangled.

Some fell, bruised and badly crippled;
Others swooned from life-long damage;
Through their chests he drove their neck-bones,
And their ribs and backs he fractured.
As if all their bones were beeswax,
They were twisted, crushed, and mauled,
As he forced his way, unflinching,
Through the armored human thicket.[21]

MILITARY TACTICS DURING FORMATIVE PERIOD

Neither Ether nor Moroni provide many details of the military tactics used by the Jaredites during their wars. As was noted in Chapter 12, frequently a son of a king, eager for power, would rebel against his father and flee to another area where he could build up an army and return with sufficient forces to capture the throne from his father. This tactic was repeated for many generations. After the introduction of the "secret combinations" among the Jaredites, these groups of robbers and murderers moved into the wilderness area where they built up strongholds from which to plunder the cities or they fought among themselves. Toward the end of the Jaredite reign, war apparently became more generalized and involved millions of warriors on each side. These great armies came together on vast open plains to fight. Ether, who witnessed some of the battles, wrote:

---

[21]Ibid., 104.

> And it came to pass that the brother of Shared did give battle unto him in the wilderness of Akish; and the battle became exceedingly sore, and many thousands fell by the sword.
>
> Coriantumr did lay siege to the wilderness; and the brother of Shared did march forth out of the wilderness by night, and slew a part of the army of Coriantumr, as they were drunken (Ether 14:4-5).
>
> Coriantumr saw that there had been slain by the sword already nearly two millions of his people, and he began to sorrow in his heart; yea, there had been slain two millions of mighty men, and also their wives and their children (Ether 15:2).

These armies set up camps and took their wives and their children with them. After battling all day, each side would leave the battle field to obtain food and to rest. In the final battles, even the women and the children were pressed into battle.

Ancient Fortifications

In his book on the Chavín civilization, Burger noted that Early Horizon (about 1000 B.C.) citadels had been found on both sides of the Santa River, just south of Trujillo and north of Lima, and similar complexes were built at roughly the same time in the Casma and Nepeña valleys north of Lima. He observed that the citadels on the north-central Peruvian coastal area are the first convincing indications of intersocietal warfare, as opposed to small-scale raiding parties. It is significant that the construction of these fortresses in Nepeña and Santa was roughly contemporaneous with a shift in the settlement pattern to less vulnerable locations, away from the valley floor.[22] Burger concluded that the construction of fortresses in the mountains was the beginning of conflicts between sizeable armies. Burger wrote that the Chavín society entered a period (approximately 500 B.C.) of total disintegration that art historians viewed as being caused by a massive social upheaval which occurred throughout central and northern Peru.[23]

---

[22]Burger, 188.
[23]Ibid., 228.

It is much more difficult to track Olmec weaponry and military tactics. Many of the scientists who work on Olmec sites cannot agree among themselves about why some villages disappeared and new settlements emerged. Archaeologists from the University of Veracruz's Institute of Anthropological Investigations have collected a few masks, axes and ritual implements from a river bottom where local fishermen discovered a cache.[24] According to archaeologists, the highly acidic nature of the soil in Mesoamerica destroys organic and metallic matter rapidly. Like the Chavín civilization in Peru, the Olmec also disappeared around 300 to 400 B.C.[25]

MILITARY TACTICS DURING THE NEPHITE PERIOD

Concerning the ongoing conflicts between the Nephites and Lamanites, the *Book of Mormon* touches on numerous military battles and prolonged conflicts in the first 600 plus years of their existence in the New World (600 B.C. to 34 A.D.). The prophet Mormon, who abridged the larger, historical records of the Nephites, described in greater detail many of the military campaigns during the 100 year period prior to the birth of Jesus Christ. Mormon, who was also the commander of the Nephite armies during the final destruction of the Nephites approximately 380 years after Christ, obviously understood military tactics. He paid particular attention to the warfare tactics of the great military tactician, Captain Moroni (not to be confused with Moroni, the son of Mormon, who buried the records approximately 421 A.D.). This earlier Moroni was put in charge of the Nephite forces about 74 B.C. and was appointed chief captain over all of the Nephite armies when he was 25 years old.

---

[24]Abrams, 19.
[25]Ibid., 11.

Captain Moroni armed his soldiers with a variety of weapons and protective armor. Anticipating a Lamanite invasion, Moroni had especially fortified the cities nearest the borders of the Lamanite territory and then placed sufficient troops to defend these heavily fortified cities. He placed the bulk of his army so he could defend the less fortified cities. As anticipated, the Lamanite armies did not attempt to attack the heavily fortified cities along the border area and pushed into Nephite territory looking for targets that were more vulnerable. Moroni sent his spies to watch the Lamanite movements. Moroni also sent a few soldiers to Alma, the high priest and leader of the church, with a request that Alma ask God where Moroni should place his armies to better defend their lands.

Alma told the messengers that God had revealed that the Lamanite armies had gone into the area near Manti. With this insight, Moroni split his army into several "brigades," and moved them into strategic locations in the land of Manti. He hid one brigade in the valley west of a river the Nephites called Sidon. He also placed his forces in the wilderness near a strategic mountain where Moroni knew the Lamanite armies would have to pass before reaching the Sidon River. After the Lamanite armies had passed, Moroni's army began to attack them from the rear. Alma wrote that the combat was heavy with loss of life on both sides, but more Lamanites were killed because they did not have as good a protective armor as the Nephites and they began to retreat towards the river Sidon. As they crossed the Sidon River, the Nephite army in hiding there attacked the fleeing Lamanite army. Even though the Lamanites fought back with great effort, they were surrounded and suffered the loss of thousands of warriors (Alma 43:24-54).

During this period of Nephite history, the Nephites were ruled by a series of elected judges, but a few ambitious Nephites, led by Amalickiah, decided they wanted to return to the system of kings. They became known as "Kingmen." These Kingmen caused a civil war to break out among the Nephites at a time when they were busy fighting the Lamanites, which greatly weakened the Nephite defensive efforts. Moroni's armies were forced to fight the Nephite Kingmen until they were defeated.

During the period while Moroni and the defenders of liberty were defeating the Kingmen, the Lamanite armies began to capture many Nephite cities that had been strongly fortified, but undermanned. Once the Lamanites had gained control of these fortified cities it was very difficult for the Nephites to attack them in their newly acquired strongholds. The Nephites were greatly outnumbered, but had a distinct advantage against the Lamanites in open areas. They tried many ways to entice the Lamanites to come out of their fortified cities and onto the field of battle. When this failed, Moroni devised a plan to lure them out of the cities.

Captain Moroni instructed one of his commanders, Teancum, to take a few men and march into an area where they could be seen by the Lamanites. In the meantime, Moroni marched a large army by night into a strategic location near the Lamanite stronghold where they would not be discovered by the Lamanite army. He also had another commander, Lehi, place his army "brigade" in the neighboring city, Bountiful.

When the Lamanites saw Teancum and his few soldiers near their stronghold, they sent a large army out to capture them, but Teancum and his men fled towards Bountiful with the Lamanite army in pursuit. Moroni and his army quickly captured the nearly undefended fortress, killing all the Lamanites who would not give up their weapons. Then, leaving a small force behind to protect the city, Moroni and the rest of his army began to pursue the Lamanite army that was racing after Teancum.

When Teancum and his men arrived near Bountiful, Lehi's forces came out to attack the Lamanites, who, realizing they had been caught in the open, retreated. Moroni and his army caught the retreating Lamanite army in the open and attacked them. Although the Lamanite army fought valiantly against Moroni and his army, they were soon attacked in the rear by Lehi and Teancum's forces. When the Lamanites again realized they were surrounded and were being slaughtered, they accepted Moroni's surrender terms (Alma 52:21-40).

Helaman, who described these battles, had great praise for Captain Moroni, not because of his conquests, but because of his great defense and leadership. Helaman wrote:

> And Moroni was a strong and a mighty man; he was a man of a perfect understanding; yea, a man that did not delight in bloodshed; a man whose soul did joy in the liberty and the freedom of his country, and his brethren from bondage and slavery;
>
> Yea, a man whose heart did swell with thanksgiving to his God, for the many privileges and blessings which he bestowed upon his people; a man who did labor exceedingly for the welfare and safety of his people.
>
> Yea, and he was a man who was firm in the faith of Christ, and he had sworn with an oath to defend his people, his rights, and his country, and his religion, even to the loss of his blood.
>
> Yea, verily, verily I say unto you, if all men had been, and were, and ever would be, like unto Moroni, behold, the very powers of hell would have been shaken forever; yea, the devil would never have power over the hearts of the children of men (Alma 48:11-13, 17).

One of the problems that the armies faced at the end of the conflict was what to do with the dead. Normally the victorious army collected its dead and brought them home, but dealing with enemy dead was a different matter. Alma stated that the Nephites threw the enemy dead into rivers.

A study of the chronicles reveal that many of the battle tactics and strategies, described in the *Book of Mormon* continued, down through the centuries and were employed by later kingdoms. Both the Incas and the Aztecs had great military strategists and inspiring leaders.

BATTLE TACTICS AMONG INDIANS RECORDED BY CHRONICLERS

Montesinos wrote that during the period of the *amautas* (wisemen or judges) about 100 B.C., the Peruvians were beset by large armies that came from both the north and the south. The soldiers in outlying areas were no match for the host of invaders. During this period there was numerous incursions from Tucuman, a region in Argentina, and Chile in the south. Montesinos also mentioned that the people of Cuzco also fought many battles with the Chimus who lived along the coast of Peru. The Peruvian king at Cuzco, Titu Yupanqui, worked hard to fortify his defenses against the attacking armies. He also sent out spies to learn the size of their armies and their intentions. The battle was so great that the armies for both sides were nearly wiped out.

In a description of another battle, Montesinos wrote about an attack that the Inca Roca made upon the Andahuaylas Indians in northern Peru. Inca Roca built a strong fort which was located about three miles from a site identified as Guancarrama. He left part of his army in the fort to protect it and proceeded with the bulk of his army towards Andahuaylas. However, en route he encountered an army which controlled a narrow passage through the mountains. Inca Roca sent a third of his army to stealthily go over the mountains and come up behind the enemy. In a closely coordinated attack, Inca Roca rushed the enemy forces while his force that had gone over the mountain attacked from behind. Inca Roca caught the

Andahuaylas army between his two armies and slaughtered the Andahuaylas forces until they sued for peace.[26]

Juan de Betanzos and other chroniclers record that during the reign of Lord Inca Viracocha, who is believed to have ruled during the early 1400s, Cuzco was threatened by the Chanca Indians from northern Peru under the leadership of Uscovilca. In Betanzos's narrative, a younger son, Pachacuti Inca Yupanqui and three friends refused to leave Cuzco and set about to organize resistance forces. Betanzos wrote that Pachacuti Inca Yupanqui told Uscovilca that he had been born free and was ready to die fighting. Pachacuti Inca Yupanqui attempted to organize neighboring tribes, but they only offered help if Pachacuti Inca Yupanqui could put together an army on his own.

Betanzos claimed that Pachacuti Inca Yupanqui then fasted and prayed to his god, Ticci Viracocha with these words:

> Lord God who created me and gave me the form of a man, come to my aid in this difficulty in which I find myself. You are my father who created me and gave me the form of a man. Do not allow me to be killed by my enemies. Give me help against them. Do not allow them to make me their subject. You made me free and your subject only. Do not allow me to be a subject of these people who want to subdue me this way and put me in bondage. Lord, give me the strength to resist them. Make of me whatever you will, for I am yours.[27]

Betanzos wrote that Pachacuti Inca Yupanqui prayed with all his heart and while praying, he fell asleep. The next morning, he claimed that during his sleep, Ticci Viracocha came to him in the form of a man and spoke to him: "My son, do not be distressed. The day that you go into battle with your enemies, I will send soldiers to you with whom you will defeat your enemies, and you will enjoy victory." On the night before the battle, Viracocha

---

[26]Montesinos, 82.
[27]Betanzos, English edition, 29.

again came to him and warned him that the battle would commence the next day. Betanzos wrote that on the following day when Uscovilca and his army initiated their attack on Cuzco, 20 squadrons of soldiers never seen or known to Pachacuti Inca Yupanqui or his followers appeared. They defeated the Chancas and killed Uscovilca. Shortly after the defeat of the Chancas, the mysterious army disappeared and Pachacuti Inca Yupanqui could find only the soldiers sent to his aid by the neighboring tribes.

Fray Martín de Murúa provided information concerning Inca war preparations, weapons and tactics. When the Inca decided to send troops into battle, he selected the bravest and most qualified men as captains. The king also used patrols of scouts to probe the enemies defenses and spy out the best approach routes and battle fields before committing his forces into battle. Battle tactics were carefully planned to the last detail.

Most of the soldiers were hardened veterans, but for training purposes, the Lord Inca always mixed into his army a judicious number of raw recruits ranging between the ages of 18 and 25. Men of this age were still considered youths by the Incas. Each soldier received training in the use of a particular weapon. The weapons generally used by the Incas were fire-hardened black palm lances, bows and arrows, darts, clubs, and sling shots. As noted previously, the Incas protected themselves with quilted cotton armor and wore helmets that could resist the hit of a sword. They generally were divided into squadrons.

Cieza de León stated that Tupa Inca Yupanqui led a large army south into the Colla-suyu region (now Bolivia) and defeated the natives in a heavy battle at the fortress Pucará.[28] Once the Colla-suyu was conquered, Tupa Inca Yupanqui turned his

---

[28]Von Hagen described Pucará as an immense Gibralter-like massif (4,380 meters high) close to the Lake Titicaca basin. It was a natural stronghold rising 1,200 feet above the valley. After the victory, the Incas rebuilt it as one of their most strategic fortresses. He pointed out that *pucará* means fortress and there were hundreds of pucarás scattered throughout the Inca world.

attention to expanding his kingdom and, with an army of over 200,000 men, he started north from Cuzco. Cieza de León described in detail the logistical supply system organized by the Inca kings to feed, cloth and shelter such a large army. Tupa Inca Yupanqui built the city of Huánuco high in the Andes and settled 40,000 people there. It became his garrison city and the finest city in the Inca Empire north of Cuzco. From there he marched his troops 500 miles northeast into the land of the Chachapoyas, in north east Peru. His troops clashed with the Aguarunas, head-hunters in the jungles of the eastern slopes of the Andes, but quickly retreated when the Incas realized they were not adept at jungle fighting

Tupa Inca Yupanqui then entered the region of modern Ecuador and fought with the Paltas and the Cañaris in southern Ecuador. From there, he advanced to an area that is now Quito, which he also conquered. From Quito, he turned west towards the coastal areas where he made a peaceful conquest of the Huancavilca Indians, centered around the Guayas River. At each site Tupa Inca Yupanqui left *mitimaes* (resettled people from other areas in the Inca Kingdom who knew how to govern and were loyal to the Lord Inca).[29]

Murúa also wrote that after Huayna Cápac, son of Tupa Inca Yupanqui, became the Lord Inca in the early 1500s, following in the tradition of former Inca kings, he carried out numerous wars of expansion. He also sent an army against the Chiriguanos (near Cochabamba, Bolivia) and fortified his south eastern holdings by stationing a large army at Cochabamba in modern eastern Bolivia.

---

[29]Von Hagen described the resettlement Indians or *Mitimaes*. These were Quechua-speaking colonists, sent out by the Inca administration after the conquest of a new territory to resettle the area or to instruct those living in the area how to run their affairs by Inca standards. By moving out unruly or politically suspect people and repopulating a region with Quechuas, this made the entire Inca realm a homogenous nation. There were three kinds of *Mitimaes*: political, economic and military. Cieza de León, *The Incas*, 232n.

Huayna Cápac eventually moved his court north to Tomebamba (now part of Ecuador, near Cuenca). Huayna Cápac sent his armies north of Quito to conquer the Cayambes and other Indian tribes near what is now the southern Colombia border. During one of those wars, there were so many Cayambes Indians killed that the Incas threw their bodies into a lake which turned red because of the quantity of blood that stained the water. This lake became known, and is still known today, as Yaguar Cocha or Lake of Blood, which is located at Ibarra, Ecuador, a few miles from the Colombian border.

The Catholic Priest Bernabé Cobo, in his book, *History of the Inca Empire*, published in 1890 by Marcos Jiménez de la Espada, narrated an interesting account of this series of battles between the Incas and the Cayambes, north of Quito. When the Cayambes discovered that they could not defeat the Inca forces on the open battlefield, they retreated to a very large fortress that they had built. Huayna Cápac had his forces mount a siege against the fortress, but the Cayambes resisted so effectively that the Incas lost many men. Huayna Cápac withdrew and set into motion a strategy in which he hoped to lure the Cayambes out of their fortress. He divided his army into three groups. Cobo narrated the attack as follows:

> Many men came to Huayna Cápac's aid from Cuzco and the highland provinces; with these men and with those that he had before, the Inca formed a powerful army, and he divided it into three parts in the following way. The regiment of the *orejones* [literally "big ears–the Inca nobility] was entrusted to the commander Apu Mihi, and the Inca ordered him to go quietly past the fortress of the Cayambes on one side without being seen by the enemies and to continue on ahead a few leagues. The regiment of Chinchaysuyu was to go past on the other side in the same way, continuing on a few leagues also. From there both groups of soldiers were to swing back at a certain time.

The Inca, who stayed with the main body of the army to lay siege to the fortress, finally attacked the fortress through the place that best suited his purposes. The combat lasted a few days, and, according to the plan that the Inca had made with his captains, he gave the signal for the army to retreat, pretending to flee. When the besieged soldiers saw this, they came out of the fortress, and, chanting victory, they went after their enemies, thinking that they could catch them and destroy the Inca's army as they had done previously.

When the Cayambes had almost caught up with the retreating Inca soldiers, the Incas turned to face them, and those who were lying in ambush attacked the fortress, and they entered it without resistance and set fire to it. Upon seeing this, the Cayambes lost their courage and, throwing down their weapons, they sought refuge in clumps of rushes growing along the edge of a large lake nearby. The Inca's men surrounded them on all sides. Huayna Cápac ordered his soldiers to cut the throats of the Cayambe soldiers in retaliation for how the Cayambes had treated his soldiers earlier. As they caught them and, after killing them, threw their bodies into the lake which became so darkened with blood that it was given the name of Yahuar Cocha, which means "lake of blood"[30]

WAR TACTICS IN MESOAMERICA

The battle tactics employed in Mesoamerica by the various Nahuatl speaking nations were not so dissimilar to those employed in the Andes. Fray Diego Durán provided probably the best description of these tactics in his book, *The History of the Indies of New Spain.* Initially when the Aztec tribe arrived in the vicinity of the Lake Tenochtitlan (the area that is now the modern day Mexico City), there was no unclaimed land in the immediate vicinity. The other six Nahuatl speaking tribes, which had arrived from the north earlier, had already settled the surrounding areas. One of these tribes, the Tepanecs, finally gave the

---

[30]Father Bernabé Cobo, *History of the Inca Empire*, Written in manuscript form in 1653. (First published in Spanish by Marcos Jimenez de la Espada between 1890-1893.) Translated and edited by Roland Hamilton from the holograph manuscript in the Biblioteca Capitular y Colombina de Sevilla. Foreword by John Howland Rowe. University of Texas Press, Austin, 1979. 158.

Aztecs an area considered worthless. From these humble beginnings the Aztecs grew into a mighty kingdom which dominated the entire area.

Durán reported that the Aztecs suffered through difficult times under several of their own kings who were dominated, humiliated, and, at times, assassinated by their more powerful neighbors. In 1424, Itzcoatl, the son of an Aztec king and a slave girl, was chosen by "common accord" to be the next Aztec king. Durán wrote that up to that time the Aztecs had been intimidated and had little experience in the arts of war. Durán claimed that his informants described King Itzcoatl as leader of great valor and good sense. Itzcoatl selected his nephew, Tlacaelel, to command his armies. Concerning Tlacaelel, Durán wrote:

> Tlacaelel was to become the greatest warrior, the bravest and the mightiest, that the Aztec nation ever had. He was the wisest, the most cunning, man in the arts and science of war ever found in Mexico-Tenochtitlan.[31]

Unlike the Nephite military leader Captain Moroni, who always defended the Nephites against outside invasion, Tlacaelel formed a large offensive army and gradually dominated his closest neighbors, beginning with the Tepanec tribe that had subjugated and humiliated the Aztecs for so many years. Eventually the Aztecs formed a close military and political alliance with the Tepanecs and the Colhuas (the tribe living at Tezcoco, just east of modern Mexico City).

When Itzcoatl died, he was succeeded by his nephew, Motecuhzoma, the First, who was a brother to Tlacaelel. Tlacaelel continued to function as the commander of the Aztec armies. Motecuhzoma and the combined armies fought numerous battles and subdued rebellious tribes and city-states in the

---

[31]Durán, 72. (Tlacaelel's military daring is reminiscent of the daring displayed by Captain Moroni hundreds of years earlier.)

area. (They were never able to completely dominate the Tlaxcalans, who later joined the Spanish forces and played a key role in the defeat of the Aztec army in 1522.)

As the Aztecs were expanding their influence throughout Mexico, they came into the Huaxtec territory (Oaxaca, Mexico). The Aztec King Ahuitzotl sent his explorers and spies into the area to locate the enemy strengths and weaknesses. In a battle tactic, common to the Nephites and the Inca armies, King Ahuitzotl chose 200 men and sent them in advance to engage in a skirmish with the Huaxtecs. At the same time, King Ahuitzotl sent the bulk of his forces into the woods and brush to set up an ambush. The Huaxtec army quickly gained the advantage as they engaged the 200 advance forces. The Aztecs began an orderly retreat and as they retired, the Huaxtecs followed them shouting, whistling, and crying out in hoarse wails. Durán wrote that the Huaxtecs were howling ecstatically until they reached the ambush site. The Aztecs came out suddenly and surrounded them. This was done so quickly that the Huaxtecs did not know which way to turn, and many were killed or were taken prisoner.[32]

Because Tlacaelel often had soldiers from several different regions fighting with his combined army, he had each group make up a flag identifying the army so friendly forces would not mistakenly fight each other. *Book of Mormon* writers noted that at one time, dissident Nephites painted their bodies to distinguish themselves as they battled other Nephites.

There are numerous examples of warfare in the chronicles that resemble tactics used hundreds of years earlier by *Book of Mormon* commanders. Joseph Smith would not have known about the weapons and battle tactics of American civilization thousands of years prior to his publication of the *Book of Mormon*.

---

[32]Durán, 325-326.

18

THE MESSIAH BEN JOSEPH[1]

Menasseh Ben Israel was born in Lisbon in 1604 or 1605. The members of his family, who were considered to be marrano[2] Jews, fled Portugal for Amsterdam shortly after Menasseh was born. Ben Israel was a brilliant student and he joined an academic circle when he was very young. There he studied the *Talmud* and the *Torah*. He quickly became a gifted orator and by the age of 15 was giving speeches that were greatly admired and applauded. By the time he was 17, he had written his first book on Hebrew grammar. Ben Israel became the Chief Rabbi of a small congregation by the time he was 18. His linguistic ability was phenomenal. He reportedly mastered Spanish, Portuguese, Latin, Hebrew, Dutch and English. Shortly after his appointment as a rabbi, he was

---

[1]The title Messiah Ben Joseph means the Messiah, son of Joseph.

[2]Marrano is a name applied in Medieval Spain to the Jews and Moors who had converted to Catholicism and particularly to those Jews who had not truly converted, but made a pretense in order to avoid the effects of the inquisition.

awarded the title of "maestro" or professor of the *Talmud*. Pérez Junquera, who wrote the introduction to the 1881 re-edition of Ben Israel's *The Hope of Israel*, stated that Ben Israel delivered more than 450 sermons in the synagogues of Amsterdam. Hugo Grotius, considered the father of international law, and Rembrandt were among his admirers and Rembrandt painted and engraved a portrait of Ben Israel.

Ben Israel founded the first Hebrew printing press in Amsterdam in 1626, where he published works in Hebrew, Spanish and Portuguese. He wrote several books including *Conciliador* in which he attempted to reconcile discordant passages in the *Old Testament*. He also wrote a book in 1636 on death and resurrection entitled *De Resurrectione Mortuorum*. His most famous book was *The Hope of Israel, About the Origin of the Americans* (*Es Esperança de Israel, Sobre el Origen de Los Americanos*), which he dedicated to the British Parliament in an effort to obtain the good will of the British government.

After Ben Israel received Aharon Levi's report of Levi's professed discovery of Israelites in the New World (See Chapter 3), he sensed that the time was soon coming for the redemption of the Jews and the gathering of Israel. In Ben Israel's mind, that would also require the return of the Jews to England from where they had been expelled in 1290. Ben Israel initiated a dialogue with Oliver Cromwell, Lord Protector of England, and he subsequently met with Cromwell at Westminster Abbey in 1655. Although Ben Israel did not succeed in persuading Cromwell to open England to the Jews, he was influential in getting permission for a group of marrano Jews to practice openly in England.

Ben Israel was an accomplished teacher of the *Talmud* and, in *The Hope of Israel*, he referred to various Talmudic passages. Ben Israel analyzed extensively the scattering of Israel by the Assyrians and the Babylonians, citing numerous passages of scripture from the *Old Testament* as well as Talmudic writings.

His main focus, however, was on the eventual gathering of Israel and in this regard he cited several Old Testament prophets. He specifically mentioned Isaiah 11:12-13:

> And he shall set up an ensign for the nations, and shall assemble the outcasts of Israel, and gather together the dispersed of Judah from the four corners of the earth.
> The envy also of Ephraim shall depart, and the adversaries of Judah shall be cut off: Ephraim shall not envy Judah, and Judah shall not vex Ephraim.

Ben Israel observed that when the twelve tribes of Israel are gathered again they will be under the rulership of "Messiah Ben David," who will be their shepherd.[3] Messiah Ben David will remain the prince over the twelve tribes of Israel forever. He stated that in the day of redemption the ten lost tribes of Israel will come to the Holy Land, led by a prince and a leader who was spoken of in the *Talmud* and the *Chaldean Paraphrases* as Messiah Ben Joseph.[4] The Talmudic writings claim that Messiah Ben David (also known as Messiah Ben Judah) will reveal himself to Messiah Ben Joseph.[5] Ben Israel also claimed that Messiah Ben Joseph has been mentioned by the ancient sages in many places, particularly the *Babylonian Talmud*, tractate Suca, Chapter 5.[6]

---

[3] Ben Israel, 87 (Mormons believe Messiah Ben David is Jesus Christ.)

[4] Chaldean Paraphrases are also known as "Targums" which are Aramaic translation of ancient Biblical scripture.

[5] Ben Israel, 88.

[6] The Babylonian Talmud is a commentary on the *Mishnah*, whose order it follows. The *Mishnah* is the study of the oral traditions of the Torah and is organized independently of scripture. The Babylonian Talmud was composed over several generations, from the early third century A.D. to about the sixth century A.D.. As a commentary, it deals with many aspects of the *Mishnah*, often going far beyond any explanation given in the *Mishnah*. The Babylonian Talmud covers 36 of the 60 tractates (general orders or divisions) that comprise the *Mishnah*. The Hebrew root word of *Mishnah* is ShNH which means "to repeat" and refers to memorization by repetition. *Mishnah* has the sense of that which is memorized by rote rather than what is read and recited from the written text.

Ben Israel stated that this future leader in the house of Israel would be known as Messiah Ben Joseph not only because he would descend from Joseph but also because Joseph was a true "type" or symbol of all Israel. Ben Israel referred to Joseph's imprisonment in Egypt after his brothers sold him, his subsequent rise to power there, and how he was hidden from his brothers for many years. This was seen as a symbol of how the ten tribes are "hidden" or lost from the rest of the house of Israel at the present time. In this example, Ben Israel indicated his belief that the ten lost tribes will be redeemed or reinstated and rise in glory even as Joseph was redeemed and rose to glory in Egypt.

Ben Israel added that the future Messiah Ben Joseph will die in the war of Gog and Magog (sometimes known as the war between good and evil or Armageddon) and afterward, he will be resurrected and receive his glory; not as the king, but as the vice-king, as did Joseph in Egypt (alluding to the fact that Joseph became the second most powerful man in Egypt after the Pharaoh). The king will be Messiah Ben David from the Tribe of Judah.[7]

Ben Israel clarified that sometimes Messiah Ben Joseph was also called Messiah Ben Ephraim because he would be born of the tribe of Ephraim (son of Joseph who was one of the 12 sons of the patriarch Jacob or "Israel.")[8] The tribe of Ephraim became the most prominent tribe within the ten northern tribes in Israel when Jeroboam, a leader in the tribe of Ephraim, caused the ten tribes to break away from Judah and part of the tribe of Benjamin during the reign of Rehoboam, King Solomon's son.

---

[7]Ben Israel, 89-90.

[8]Joseph received the blessing of the first-born or blessing of the birthright of Jacob, which was passed to Joseph's sons and particularly Ephraim (1 Chronicles 5:1 and Genesis 48:17-20). When the twelve tribes of Israel left Egypt and settled in Palestine, the descendants of Joseph were given two areas for the tribes named after Ephraim and Manasseh.

Book of Mormon Teachings about Joseph

According to the *Book of Mormon* narrative, Lehi also referred to Joseph, who was sold into Egypt. During the final blessing which Lehi gave to his youngest son, Joseph, he told Joseph that he, Lehi, was a descendant of that Joseph, the son of Patriarch Jacob, who was sold into Egypt. Lehi said that God made great covenants and promised many blessings to Joseph, Jacob's son:

> Wherefore, Joseph truly saw our day. And he obtained a promise of the Lord, that out of the fruit of his loins the Lord God would raise up a righteous branch unto the house of Israel; not the Messiah, but a branch which was to be broken off, nevertheless, to be remembered in the covenants of the Lord that the Messiah should be made manifest unto them in the latter days, in the spirit of power, unto the bringing of them out of darkness unto light–yea, out of hidden darkness and out of captivity unto freedom.
>
> For Joseph truly testified, saying: A seer shall the Lord my God raise up, who shall be a choice seer unto the fruit of my loins.
>
> Yea, Joseph truly said: Thus saith the Lord unto me: a choice seer will I raise up out of the fruit of thy loins; and he shall be esteemed highly among the fruit of thy loins. And unto him will I give commandment that he shall do a work for the fruit of thy loins, his brethren, which shall be of great worth unto them, even to the bringing of them to the knowledge of the covenants which I have made with thy fathers.
>
> And I will give unto him a commandment that he shall do none other work, save the work which I shall command him. And I will make him great in mine eyes; for he shall do my work.
>
> And he shall be great like unto Moses, whom I have said I would raise up unto you, to deliver my people, O house of Israel.
>
> And Moses will I raise up, to deliver thy people out of the land of Egypt.
>
> But a seer will I raise up out of the fruit of thy loins; and unto him will I give power to bring forth my word unto the seed of thy loins–and not to the bringing forth my word only, saith the Lord, but

to the convincing them of my word, which shall have already gone forth among them.

Wherefore, the fruit of thy loins shall write; and the fruit of the loins of Judah shall write; and that which shall be written by the fruit of thy loins, and also that which shall be written by the fruit of the loins of Judah, shall grow together, unto the confounding of false doctrines and laying down of contentions, and establishing peace among the fruit of thy loins, and bringing them to the knowledge of their fathers in the latter days, and also to the knowledge of my covenants, saith the Lord.[9]

And out of weakness he shall be made strong, in that day when my work shall commence among all my people, unto the restoring thee, O house of Israel, saith the Lord.

And thus prophesied Joseph, saying: Behold, that seer will the Lord bless; and they that seek to destroy him shall be confounded; for this promise, which I have obtained of the Lord, of the fruit of my loins, shall be fulfilled. Behold, I am sure of the fulfilling of this promise;

And his name shall be called after me; and it shall be after the name of his father (emphasis added). And he shall be like unto me; for the thing, which the Lord shall bring forth by his hand, by the power of the Lord shall bring my people unto salvation (2 Nephi 3:4-15).

It would appear from the above prophecy that the Joseph, who was sold into Egypt, saw the migration of some of his descendants to the New World and witnessed their subsequent rise and decline. But more importantly, he beheld their historical record and the great value that it would have for future generations of his descendants, the rest of the house of Israel and the "Gentiles" as well. On the first page of the *Book of Mormon*, Moroni stated that this record was "Written to the Lamanites, who are a remnant of the house of Israel; and also to Jew and Gentile. . . And also to the convincing of the Jew and Gentile that Jesus is the Christ, the Eternal God, manifesting himself to all nations."

---

[9] See Ezekiel 37:15-20 also Ben Israel's *Hope of Israel*, 87.

JOSEPH SMITH, A DIRECT DESCENDANT OF JOSEPH

From the translation of the Nephite history as recorded on the gold plates and subsequently published as the *Book of Mormon*, Mormons believe that Joseph Smith, Jr., who is named after his father, Joseph Smith, Sr., is the seer foreseen by Joseph anciently. Although Chapter 4 delved into Joseph Smith's role in connection with the translation and publication of the *Book of Mormon*, that chapter did not address other spiritual manifestations and heavenly visitations that Joseph Smith claims to have received in the establishment and expansion of The Church of Jesus Christ of Latter-day Saints. With the exception of the First Vision and the various visits by Moroni in which Joseph was alone, he was usually accompanied by at least one other individual during other visitations by heavenly beings.

Ben Israel mentioned the conflict of Gog and Magog or the battle between good and evil that would be initiated in the "last days." In a speech delivered in June 2001, Elder Jeffery R. Holland, former president of Brigham Young University and subsequently a member of the Quorum of the Twelve Apostles of The Church of Jesus Christ of Latter-day Saints, stated:

> All of heaven and all of hell knew that Joseph Smith was the man that God had chosen to restore the gospel. Only the boy Joseph was unaware of the transcendental events that he would initiate with his humble petition to know what church was right. . . . If Satan could have killed Joseph, he would have done so. . . The Savior wanted to leave no doubt in Joseph's mind where the truth was and what was about to occur.[10]

---

[10] Talk delivered by Elder Jeffery R. Holland to the Round Rock Texas Stake Conference on 2 June 2001 in Round Rock, Texas.

This will become apparent through a more detailed examination of the First Vision. Joseph Smith's narrative of that event is as follows:

> After I had retired to the place where I had previously designed to go, having looked around me, and finding myself alone, I kneeled down and began to offer up the desires of my heart to God. I had scarcely done so, when immediately I was seized upon by some power which entirely overcame me, and had such an astonishing influence over me as to bind my tongue so that I could not speak. Thick darkness gathered around me, and it seemed to me for a time as if I were doomed to sudden destruction.
>
> But, exerting all my powers to call upon God to deliver me out of the power of this enemy which had seized upon me, and at the very moment when I was ready to sink into despair and abandon myself to destruction–not to an imaginary ruin, but to the power of some actual being from the unseen world, who had such marvelous power as I had never before felt in any being–just at this moment of great alarm, I saw a pillar of light exactly over my head, above the brightness of the sun, which descended gradually until it fell upon me.
>
> It no sooner appeared than I found myself delivered from the enemy which held me bound. When the light rested upon me I saw two Personages, whose brightness and glory defy all description, standing above me in the air. One of them spake unto me, calling me by name and said, pointing to the other–*This is My Beloved Son. Hear Him!*
>
> My object in going to inquire of the Lord was to know which of all the sects was right, that I might know which to join. No sooner, therefore, did I get possession of myself, so as to be able to speak, than I asked the Personages who stood above me in the light, which of all the sects was right (for at this time it had never entered into my heart that all were wrong)–and which I should join.
>
> I was answered that I must join none of them, for they were all wrong; and the Personage who addressed me said that all their creeds were an abomination in his sight; that those professors were all corrupt; that: "they draw near to me with their lips, but their hearts are far from me, they teach for doctrines the commandments of men, having a form of godliness, but they deny the power thereof."
>
> He again forbade me to join with any of them; and many other things did he say unto me, which I cannot write at this time. When

I came to myself again, I found myself lying on my back, looking up into heaven. When the light had departed, I had no strength; but soon recovering in some degree, I went home....It seems as though the adversary was aware, at a very early period of my life, that I was destined to prove a disturber and an annoyer of his kingdom; else why should the powers of darkness combine against me? Why the opposition and persecution that arose against me, almost in my infancy (Joseph Smith History 1:15-20).

Although the appearance of God, the Father, and his son, Jesus Christ, were by far the most significant of the divine visitors to Joseph Smith, there were numerous other notable visits by celestial beings. Chapter 4 described the various visits by the Angel Moroni to not only Joseph Smith, but to at least three other individuals, and will not be further elaborated in this chapter.

Joseph Smith and his scribe Oliver Cowdery also claimed to have received other visions. In their history of events, they state that while they were translating the *Book of Mormon* in May 1829, they encountered important scriptures concerning baptism. Recognizing that they had never been baptized, the two men went to an isolated area along the banks of the Susquehanna River near Harmony, Pennsylvania, to ask the Lord about baptism. Joseph recorded the event as follows:

> We still continued the work of translation, when, in the ensuing month (May, 1829), we on a certain day went into the woods to pray and inquire of the Lord respecting baptism for the remission of sins, that we found mentioned in the translation of the plates. While we were thus employed, praying and calling upon the Lord, a messenger from heaven descended in a cloud of light, and having laid his hands upon us, he ordained us, saying:
>
> *Upon you my fellow servants, in the name of Messiah, I confer the Priesthood of Aaron, which holds the keys of the ministering of angels, and of the gospel of repentance, and of baptism by immersion for the remission of sins; and this shall never be taken again from the earth until the sons of Levi do offer again an offering unto the Lord in righteousness.*

He said this Aaronic Priesthood had not the power of laying on hands for the gift of the Holy Ghost, but that this should be conferred on us hereafter; and he commanded us to go and be baptized, and gave us directions that I should baptize Oliver Cowdery, and that afterwards he should baptize me.

Accordingly we went and were baptized. I baptized him first, and afterwards he baptized me–after which I laid my hands upon his head and ordained him to the Aaronic Priesthood, and afterwards he laid his hands on me and ordained me to the same Priesthood–for so we were commanded.

The messenger who visited us on this occasion and conferred this Priesthood upon us, said that his name was John, the same that is called John the Baptist in the New Testament, and that he acted under the direction of Peter, James and John, who held the keys of the Priesthood of Melchizedek, which Priesthood, he said, would in due time be conferred on us, and that I should be called the first Elder of the Church, and he (Oliver Cowdery) the second. It was on the fifteenth day of May, 1829, that we were ordained under the hand of this messenger, and baptized (Joseph Smith–History 1:68-72).

John the Baptist told Joseph and Oliver that they would later receive a higher priesthood, the Melchizedek Priesthood, and the power to lay on hands for the gift of the Holy Ghost. At some unspecified later date, Peter, James and John appeared to Joseph Smith and Oliver Cowdery and conferred upon them the Melchizedek Priesthood.[11] Joseph never cited a date when this occurred. It is assumed that it happened sometime between the appearance of John the Baptist on 15 May 1829 and the organization of the newly founded Church of Jesus Christ on 6 April 1830.

---

[11] The Melchizedek Priesthood, named after the great high priest, Melchizedek, the King of Salem, to whom Abraham paid his tithing and from whom he received a blessing, is the same priesthood that Jesus Christ conferred upon his twelve apostles. Mormons believe Peter, James and John were the last ones to hold all the keys of the Melchizedek Priesthood during the early Christian era; consequently, it was appropriate that they confer the keys or authority upon Joseph Smith and, in this case, Oliver Cowdery. Adam, Enoch, Noah, Abraham, Isaac, Jacob, Moses and a few other Old Testament prophets such as Samuel and Elijah possessed this high priesthood as did Lehi, Nephi and their descendants in the New World.

THE MESSIAH BEN JOSEPH 473

The heavenly manifestations did not cease with the restoration of the priesthood. According to Joseph Smith, on 16 February 1832, less than two years after the Church was restored to the earth, he and Sidney Rigdon were involved in the "translation of the Scriptures."[12] Joseph noted that from sundry revelations which had been received, it was apparent that many important doctrines had been taken from the *Bible*, or lost before it was compiled. Joseph recorded that while he and Sidney Rigdon were translating The Gospel According to St. John, they beheld the following vision.

> And while we meditated upon these things, the Lord touched the eyes of our understandings and they were opened, and the glory of the Lord shone round about.
>
> And we beheld the *glory of the Son, on the right hand of the Father, and received of his fulness*. (emphasis added)
>
> And saw the holy angels, and them who are sanctified before his throne, worshiping God, and the Lamb, who worship him forever and ever.
>
> And now, after the many testimonies which have been given of him, this is the testimony, last of all, which we give of him: *That he lives*! (emphasis added)
>
> For we saw him, even on the right hand of God: and we heard the voice bearing record that he is the Only Begotten of the Father—
>
> That by him, and through him, and of him, the worlds are and were created, and the inhabitants thereof are begotten sons and daughters unto God (D&C 76:19-24).

On this occasion it was Sidney Rigdon, not Oliver Cowdery, who accompanied the Prophet Joseph and professed to be a witness of this heavenly scene. The circle of individuals around Joseph Smith, who were reported to have seen heavenly manifestations, appeared to be expanding with the addition of Sidney Rigdon to the growing number. This vision is highly significant

---

[12]On 7 March 1831, Joseph was instructed to begin a translation of the New Testament from which important information would be made known (D&C 45:60-62).

because the heavens were open and two men were privileged, once again, to see both God the Father and his son, Jesus Christ. Students of the Bible will notice similarities to the vision received by Stephen before he was stoned to death as recorded in the Book of Acts:

> But he, being full of the Holy Ghost, looked up stedfastly into heaven, and saw the glory of God and Jesus standing on the right hand of God, and said, Behold, I see the heavens opened, and the Son of man standing on the right hand of God (Acts 7: 55-56).

In the *Doctrine and Covenants*, Joseph Smith recorded that he received instructions in May 1833 to build a temple where the Lord could provide additional instructions to his new Church. With great hardship and sacrifice, the impoverished Mormons built the Kirtland Temple which was completed and dedicated to the Lord on 27 March 1836. The Prophet Joseph and others, who attended the dedication, testified of viewing and participating in great spiritual manifestations during and shortly after the dedication ceremony.

Frederick G. Williams claimed that while Sidney Rigdon was offering a prayer, an angel entered the window and took his seat between Joseph Smith, Sr., and himself. Joseph recorded in his journal that when George A. Smith rose and began to prophesy, a noise was heard like the sound of a mighty rushing wind, which filled the temple, and all the congregation simultaneously arose, being moved upon by an invisible power; many began to speak in tongues and prophesy; others saw visions; and Joseph Smith claimed to see the temple filled with angels.

According to the historical account, the people of the neighborhood came running towards the temple when they heard the unusual sounds and saw a bright light like a "pillar of fire" resting upon the temple.[13] Joseph also noted that on 30 March 1836,

---

[13] *History of the Church*, Vol II, 427-428.

the Twelve Apostles of the Church met in the temple, exhorting, prophesying and speaking in tongues. They declared that the Savior appeared to some of them while angels administered to others. Joseph proclaimed it to be a time of Pentecost.[14]

Joseph again recorded that on 3 April 1836, there was a "great outpouring of the spirit" within the temple and that he and Oliver Cowdery saw four heavenly beings, who "committed to them important keys (authority and power)" to carry out God's work upon the earth. This unique event, as recorded in *Doctrine and Covenants*, Section 110, describes perhaps the greatest outpouring of Priesthood keys that had ever been received on earth at any one time.

Joseph wrote that the first heavenly visitor on that occasion was Jesus Christ himself. Joseph and Oliver recorded his appearance in the following language:

> The veil was taken from our minds, and the eyes of our understanding were opened.
> We saw the Lord standing upon the breastwork of the pulpit, before us; and under his feet was a paved work of pure gold, in color like amber.
> His eyes were as a flame of fire; the hair of his head was white like the pure snow; his countenance shone above the brightness of the sun; and his voice was as the sound of the rushing of great waters, even the voice of Jehovah, saying:
> I am the first and the last; I am he who liveth, I am he who was slain; I am your advocate with the Father.
> For behold, I have accepted this house, and my name shall be here; and I will manifest myself to my people in mercy in this house.
> Yea, I will appear unto my servants, and speak unto them with mine own voice, if my people will keep my commandments, and do not pollute this holy house.
> Yea the hearts of thousands and tens of thousands shall greatly rejoice in consequence of the blessings which shall be poured out, and the endowment with which my servants have been endowed in this house.

---

[14]Ibid., 432.

And the fame of this house shall spread to foreign lands; and this is the beginning of the blessings which shall be poured out upon the heads of my people. Even so. Amen (D&C 110:1-10).

Immediately after the appearance of the Savior in the Kirtland Temple, Joseph and Oliver stated that the great Israelite lawgiver, Moses, appeared to them. Their entry of this account in the *Doctrine and Covenants* was short, but significant. Joseph wrote:

> After this vision closed, the heavens were again opened unto us; and Moses appeared before us, and committed unto us the keys of the gathering of Israel from the four parts of the earth, and the leading of the ten tribes from the land of the north (D&C 110:11).

Earlier in this chapter, it was noted that Ben Israel stated that the Messiah Ben Joseph, would be a great leader and prince who would lead the ten lost tribes back to the Holy Land. Moses, who was given the responsibility to lead the twelve tribes out of Egypt, obviously held the keys or authority for such an important mission. In the above verse, Joseph Smith and Oliver Cowdery claimed that Moses appeared to them in the Kirtland Temple and conferred upon them the keys to commence that gathering of Israel.[15]

As soon as Moses had disappeared, an individual known only as "Elias" appeared in the Temple to Joseph and Oliver:

---

[15] On 30 October 1831, Orson Hyde, then a Jew, was baptized into the Church. Shortly after his baptism, he received a blessing from Joseph Smith in which Joseph promised him that "In due time thou shalt go to Jerusalem, the land of thy fathers, and be a watchman unto the house of Israel; and by thy hands shall the Most High do a great work, which shall prepare the way and greatly facilitate the gathering together of that people (History of the Church 4:375). In 1840, Joseph Smith sent Orson Hyde, a member of the Quorum of the Twelve Apostles, to Palestine to dedicate that land for the return of the Jews. On 24 October 1841, Orson Hyde stood upon the Mount of Olives where he dedicated Palestine for the return of the Jews and in his prayer, he asked the Lord to inspire "kings and the powers of the earth" to help "restore the kingdom unto Israel" (History of the Church 4:457).

> After this, Elias appeared, and committed the dispensation of the gospel of Abraham, saying that in us and our seed all generations after us should be blessed (D&C 110:12).

Little is known about this Elias. He is not mentioned in Genesis in connection with Abraham, however this heavenly messenger restored the keys necessary to establish the Abrahamic covenant.[16] Elias restored the patriarchal order, the power by which eternal families are organized through the new and everlasting covenant of marriage.[17]

Joseph Smith and Oliver Cowdery then described the next highly significant visitation in the following verses:

> After this vision had closed, another great and glorious vision burst upon us; for Elijah the prophet, who was taken to heaven without tasting death, stood before us, and said:
> Behold the time has fully come, which was spoken of by the mouth of Malachi–testifying that he [Elijah] should be sent, before the great and dreadful day of the Lord come–
> To turn the hearts of the fathers to the children, and the children to the fathers, lest the whole earth be smitten with a curse–
> Therefore, the keys of this dispensation are committed into your hands; and by this ye may know that the great and dreadful day of the Lord is near, even at the doors (D&C 110:13-16).

Robert Millet, professor of ancient scripture at Brigham Young University, wrote in an official Latter-day Saint magazine,

---

[16] According to the Bible Dictionary, the Covenant of Abraham consisted of several important steps. Abraham first received the gospel by baptism. Then he received the Melchizedek Priesthood and entered into celestial marriage with the promise that he and his wife would be together forever. Included in the Abrahamic Covenant was the promise that the Christ would come through his lineage, and that his descendants would receive certain lands as an eternal inheritance. This covenant was renewed with Isaac and with Jacob.

[17] Additional information about Elias and the Abrahamic covenant can be found in an article written by Robert L. Millet entitled *The Ancient Covenant Restored*, printed in the Mormon Church magazine, *ENSIGN*, March 1998 edition. Robert L. Millet is dean of religious education and professor of ancient scripture at Brigham Young University.

ENSIGN, that it was precisely on 3 April 1836, the day when Elijah's appearance took place, that Jews throughout the world were engaged in the celebration of the Passover. Since the time of Malachi, four centuries before Christ's mortal birth, Jews, worldwide, have awaited Elijah's coming at Passover.[18] Elijah came to a temple of the Latter-day Saints and to his legal administrator on earth, a descendant of Joseph and of Ephraim (Joseph Smith, Jr.).

In the same March 1988 *ENSIGN* article, Millet explained that Elijah was sent in 1836 to reveal keys of priesthood and heavenly powers to seal or join in heaven marriages and families that were together on earth. The use of such powers on earth were not operational in Joseph Smith's day until they were brought back by Elijah. Elijah restored the keys or authority whereby families, organized in the patriarchal order through the powers just delivered by Elias, could be sealed together for eternity. Furthermore, Elijah added that the hearts of the children would turn to their ancient fathers because the children are now participants in and recipients of the blessings and covenants God made with their ancient forefathers. With these powers, the living children do everything possible (through family history research and sacred temple ordinances) to ensure that the blessings of Abraham, Isaac, Jacob, and Joseph are enjoyed by ancestry as well as posterity.

During his 38 years of life, Joseph claimed to have received numerous revelations and visions from the Lord providing him with instructions on how to organize the Church, clarify gospel principles, and provide new information for the Church as a whole as well as instructions for specific members. These "reve-

---

[18]In the early 1970's while living in Peru, I was an honorary member of the Hebrew Club in Lima and each year at Passover time, my family and I were invited to the Passover meal. There was always a place set at the table for Elijah to come and participate with them during the Passover meal in remembrance of the promise of the eventual coming of Elijah.

lations and inspired declarations" were eventually published in Missouri in 1833, under the title *A Book of Commandments for the Government of the Church of Christ* (D&C 1:6). The title was later changed to *The Doctrine and Covenants of The Church of Jesus Christ of Latter-day Saints*. Of the 138 sections in the Doctrine and Covenants, 135 are attributed to Joseph Smith. The Explanatory Introduction to the Doctrine and Covenants states the following:

> The Doctrine and Covenants is a collection of divine revelations and inspired declarations given for the establishment and regulation of the kingdom of God on the earth in the last days. Although most of the sections are directed to members of The Church of Jesus Christ of Latter-day Saints, the messages, warnings and exhortations are for the benefit of all mankind, and contain an invitation to all people everywhere to hear the voice of the Lord Jesus Christ, speaking to them for their temporal well-being and their everlasting salvation.
>
> These sacred revelations were received in answer to prayer, in times of need, and came out of real-life situations involving real people. The Prophet and his associates sought for divine guidance, and these revelations certify that they received it. In the revelations one sees the restoration and unfolding of the gospel of Jesus Christ and the ushering in of the dispensation of the fulness of times. The westward movement of the Church from New York and Pennsylvania, to Ohio, to Missouri, to Illinois, and finally to the Great Basin of western America, and the mighty struggles of the saints in attempting to build Zion on the earth in modern times, are also shown forth in these revelations.
>
> In the revelations the doctrines of the gospel are set forth with explanations about such fundamental matters as the nature of the Godhead, necessity for obedience, the need for repentance, the workings of the Holy Spirit, the ordinances and performances that pertain to salvation, the destiny of the earth, the future conditions of man after the resurrection and the judgment, the eternity of the marriage relationship, and the eternal nature of the family. Likewise the gradual unfolding of the administrative structure of the Church is shown with the calling of bishops, the First Presidency, the Council of the Twelve, and the Seventy, and the establishment of

other presiding offices and quorums. Finally, the testimony that is given of Jesus Christ—his divinity, his majesty, his perfection, his love, and his redeeming power—makes the Doctrine and Covenants of great value to the human family and of more worth than the riches of the whole earth.

In one revelation, given in February 1833, known as the "Word of Wisdom," the Lord warned members of the Church to avoid alcoholic beverages, tobacco, and hot drinks which has been interpreted to mean coffee and tea. Foods, deemed healthy for people and animals, were identified. This revelation was given with a promise to those who follow its instructions. In modern times, scientific and medical discoveries have verified what Joseph Smith proclaimed more than 170 years ago.

Another prophecy that received attention was the revelation in December 1832 in which Joseph Smith foresaw a war in which the southern states would declare war on the northern states, beginning with a rebellion in South Carolina that would terminate with the "death and misery of many souls." This revelation also alludes to the First and Second World Wars as well as the eventual overthrow of communism and other wars to take place before the second coming of Christ.

Most of Joseph Smith's initial education came from reading the Bible and he frequently turned to the Bible for solace and comfort. As indicated above, Joseph recognized from the vision that he received in 1820 in the sacred grove that the Bible was not complete and that many important scriptures were missing or not sufficiently clear to render a correct understanding. On one occasion, he informed church members, "I believe the Bible as it read when it came from the pen of the original writers. Ignorant translators, careless transcribers, or designing and corrupt priests have committed many errors." By June, 1830, responding to divine direction, Joseph Smith began a revision of the Book of Genesis. Part of his revision of Genesis was published as *The Book of Moses* and is considered by Latter-day Saints to be scripture.

In a revelation given on 19 January 1841, the Lord called this revision of the Bible a new translation (D&C 124:89). In the August 1997 publication of the *ENSIGN*, David Rolph Seely noted that the prophet Joseph took his task of revising the Bible very seriously, referring to it as a "branch" of his prophetic calling.[19] Seely noted that Joseph Smith did not "translate" the Bible in the traditional sense of the word–that is, go back to the earliest Hebrew and Greek manuscripts to make a new rendering into English. Rather he went through the biblical text of the King James Version and made corrections, revisions, and additions as he felt inspired by God.

Joseph Smith never recorded exactly how he did this work, but it appears that he and a scribe would sit at a table with the prophet having the King James Version of the Bible open before him. During the years 1830 to 1833, Joseph, assisted by various scribes, worked his way completely through the Bible. Sidney Rigdon wrote on 2 July 1833 that they had "finished" the "translation of the scriptures." These changes were not published at that time; however, and throughout his life, when time permitted, Joseph continued to work on the manuscripts, editing, and making further changes, preparing them for publication. He was killed before the revisions were published. Seely noted that the manuscripts of the Joseph Smith Translation were preserved by his widow, Emma Smith, and eventually became the property of the Reorganized Church of Jesus Christ of Latter Day Saints, which published various editions of the translation.[20]

---

[19] *History of the Church*, Vol 1:238.

[20] The Reorganized Church of Jesus Christ of Latter Day Saints was organized a few years after the death of Joseph Smith by church members who did not accept Brigham Young as the new leader of the church. They eventually chose Joseph Smith's son, Joseph Smith, III, as the head of the Reorganized Church and established their headquarters in Independence, Missouri. In 2001, the Reorganized Church of Jesus Christ of Latter Day Saints officially changed the church name to the Community of Christ.

In 1968, Robert J. Matthews, a professor at Brigham Young University, was given permission by the Reorganized Church to examine the original manuscripts. He published a book in 1975 entitled *A Plainer Translation: Joseph Smith's Translation of the Bible, a History and Commentary*. Many significant Joseph Smith changes were incorporated as footnotes and appendices into the 1979 Latter-day Saint edition of the King James Version of the Bible.

During the winter of 1832-1833, Joseph Smith organized a "School of the Prophets" in which many of the leading men in the Church studied foreign languages and gospel doctrine. Joseph became somewhat fluent in Hebrew, Egyptian, and German. He once proclaimed that the most correct translation of the Bible was the German translation.

In July 1835, Joseph Smith was studying both Hebrew and Egyptian. At that time he received a visit from Michael H. Chandler, who brought with him four mummies and several scrolls of papyri discovered in Egypt in 1831 by Chandler's uncle, the French explorer Antonio Sebolo. Donna Hill narrated in her history of Joseph Smith that little was known about Egyptian hieroglyphics at that time. Although the French linguist Jean François Champollion had worked out the principles for deciphering hieroglyphics with the aid of the Rosetta stone and had published several works on that subject, his Egyptian grammar would not be published until 1836 and his Egyptian dictionary until 1841.

Hill explained that Chandler had little hope of finding someone who could translate his scrolls of papyri; consequently, he was pleased to learn later about how Joseph Smith claimed to have found and translated ancient plates with similar characteristics. Chandler traveled to Kirtland, Ohio, to show his mummies and papyri to Joseph. Chandler found that Joseph and the

Mormons were very interested in the scrolls and the mummies and he sold them to the Latter-day Saints.[21]

Joseph started to work on the scrolls immediately. He wrote in his journal entry for July 1835 the following:

> ... with W. W. Phelps and Oliver Cowdery as scribes, I commenced the translation of some of the characters or hieroglyphics, and much to our joy found that one of the rolls contained the writing of Abraham, another the writings of Joseph of Egypt, etc.–a more full account of which will appear in its place, as I proceed to examine or unfold them. Truly we can say, the Lord is beginning to reveal the abundance of peace and truth.[22]

Joseph's translation of the scroll of Abraham was first published in Nauvoo in 1842 and eventually was included in the *Pearl of Great Price*. There is no record that Joseph ever translated the scroll or papyri of Joseph. These ancient scrolls remained in the possession of the church for many years after Joseph's death. Hill stated that eventually the scrolls disappeared. In 1966, some of the papyri were discovered in the Metropolitan Museum of New York, where they were recognized by a University of Utah professor of Middle Eastern Studies, Dr. Aziz S. Atiya. Atiya subsequently identified some 22 separate papyri fragments which were believed to have been part of the original collection purchased by the Church in 1835.

Critics of Joseph Smith claim that the partial translation of these rediscovered fragments do not match the *Book of Abraham* as translated by Joseph in the 1830's time frame. In a July 1988 article that appeared in the *ENSIGN*, Michael D. Rhodes, a researcher of ancient scriptures at Brigham Young University pointed out that the 22 papyri fragments, which are now in the possession of Brigham Young University, are not the same scrolls that Joseph used in his translation. Joseph described the

---
[21]Hill, 192-193.
[22]*History of the Church*, Vol. II, 236.

papyrus he used in translation in these words: "The record of Abraham and Joseph, found with the mummies, is beautifully written on papyrus, with black, and small part red, ink or paint, in perfect preservation."[23] The papyri found in New York do not have any writing in red ink and are in an extremely poor state of preservation.[24]

The *Book of Abraham* is divided into five chapters and provides supplementary information about Abraham that is not available in the Bible. In a March 1997 *ENSIGN* article entitled "The Book of Abraham–A Most Remarkable Book," Andrew Skinner, an associate professor of ancient scripture at Brigham Young University, declared the following:

> Truly, it is a most remarkable book–an authentic ancient record that immediately plunges us back into a specific time and place in the Near East, and yet, at the same time, opens to us the wide expanse of the physical universe. It is so dynamic that it can reveal the historical and cultural origins of ancient Egyptian civilization, and yet, in the turn of a phrase, teach us profound truths about eternity. The great power of the book is sometimes overlooked precisely because its five chapters offer tantalizing tidbits about subjects that may seem mysterious or forbidding–Egypt and the universe. But the *Book of Abraham* is a powerful, Christ-centered text that has as its main themes the eternal nature of the Abrahamic covenant, the pre-eminence of Jesus Christ as represented even in the vast scheme of planets and stars, and the role of Jesus Christ in the three great events of the plan of salvation–the Creation, the Fall, and the Atonement.[25]

On 27 April 1838, Joseph Smith recorded in his journal that he began to write a formal history of The Church of Jesus Christ of Latter-day Saints from the earliest period of its existence, up to this date.[26] This is not to suppose, as some critics have alleged,

---

[23] *History of the Church*, 2:348.

[24] Michael D. Rhodes, "I have a Question," *ENSIGN*, July 1988. 51.

[25] Andrew Skinner, "The Book of Abraham–A most Remarkable Book," *ENSIGN*, March 1997. 16.

[26] *History of the Church*, Vol. 3:25.

that Joseph only then began to write his history relying completely upon memory. In a revelation received on 6 April 1830, Joseph was told that there should be a record kept in the newly organized Church (D&C 21:1). By 26 April 1838, Joseph had already received one hundred fifteen revelations which were published in the Doctrine and Covenants. Each of these revelations were recorded and dated at the time they were received. Joseph not only recorded the dates when the revelation was received, but provided background information surrounding the circumstances of the revelation.

In the initial years prior to the organization of the Church, it is unclear whether he kept a personal journal or just made notes of events as they transpired. Early on, he frequently referred to dates in a vague manner such as in the early spring or in the month of May, etc.; however, he provided exact dates for some of the events that transpired in the development and organization of the new Church before he began his formal history. Joseph utilized a scribe or a secretary to make notes and keep a record of their events or transactions. Oliver Cowdery, who wrote down the narrative of the *Book of Mormon* as Joseph translated the passages, kept the minutes of important meetings and conferences as they occurred. John Whitmer was also formally appointed to be the Church historian and took notes of important meetings and events.

Starting with the entry of 12 February 1833 in Volume One, Joseph changed the format of his historical narrative and began recording dates with accompanying notes that appear to be more like journal entries.[27] He continued with this journal entry format from that date throughout the six volumes of his version of the history of the Church which contained approximately 3000 pages. The role of the clerk or secretary became more formalized and individuals were specifically assigned or employed to accom-

---
[27] Ibid., Vol. 1:326.

pany the Prophet and record his pronouncements, prophecies, letters, and other events of importance. These historians also became key witnesses of the progress and development of the Church.

Joseph Smith included not only his activities, but he included the activities of many of those around him in his history. He recorded the text of letters either written by him or written to him by other Church leaders, State government, or United States government leaders. He included the expansion of the Church into Missouri and the conflicts that occurred there as well as the subsequent conflicts that occurred in Illinois. He incorporated details of the great missionary proselyting work in the United States, Canada, and particularly the British Islands.

In addition to the one hundred thirty five revelations received by the Prophet Joseph, published in the Doctrine and Covenants, Joseph also included numerous other prophetic statements about events or individuals. In extensive footnotes, B. H. Roberts included comments covering the fulfilment of most of these prophecies. He included doctrinal instruction and the organizational evolution within the Church. Even in the final hours of his life while confined in the Carthage jail, Joseph Smith was accompanied by a scribe who recorded the final events leading up to and including the martyrdom of the Prophet Joseph and his brother, Hyrum Smith.

From the moment that Joseph Smith received his first vision, he began to gain a greater appreciation of his responsibilities. As he received additional heavenly visitations, priesthood authority, and new information concerning the restoration of the gospel, Joseph became increasingly aware of his unique position both within the Church as well as within the world. Joseph considered this new and fledgling Church to be the literal Kingdom of God upon the earth. In D&C 65:2, the Lord revealed that the keys of the Kingdom of God were committed unto man on the earth, and would roll forth throughout the world as was foreseen by the Prophet Daniel anciently (Daniel 2:34-45).

Joseph also recognized in the writings of Nephi that he, Joseph Smith, was foreordained to establish this great kingdom. It was through the power of this unique vision that he was able to prevail upon newly baptized men to leave their homes, even in times of poverty or sickness, and travel extensively to preach the gospel at their own expense. Initially, the missionaries remained in the United States and Canada, but by July 1837 they arrived in England.[28]

As early as August 1830, the Lord indicated to Joseph that he was establishing his Church on the earth for the last time. He referred to this era as the Dispensation of the Fullness of Times (D&C 27:13, 112:30).[29] A representative from each of the earlier Dispensations brought to Joseph Smith the keys of his particular dispensation so that the Prophet Joseph received all keys thus fulfilling the scripture found in Ephesians 1:10: "That in the dispensation of the fullness of times he might gather together in one all things in Christ, both which are in heaven, and which are on earth; even in him."

---

[28] By the end of December 2002, there were 61,638 full time missionaries working in over 160 nations of the world. These missionaries pay for their own living expenses. The Church transports them to and from their fields of labor. Unlike the early missionaries who were fathers with families, most of today's missionaries are single young men and women; however, there is an increasing number of older, retired couples who also serve.

[29] Bruce R. McConkie, a former member of the Quorum of the Twelve, stated that a *dispensation* is a period of time when the gospel of Jesus Christ or His Plan of Salvation–the Father's eternal plan to save his children–was taught upon the earth. McConkie stated that we do not know how many dispensations there have been on the earth. We have received all of the "keys, and powers, and glories," possessed by them of old. Angelic ministrants have come from those Biblical dispensations which had distinctive keys and powers. (Bruce R McConkie, "This final Glorious gospel Dispensation, *ENSIGN Apr*, 1980, 21.) The known *Dispensations* or periods when the gospel was taught to God's children are the *Dispensations* of Adam, Enoch, Noah, Abraham, Moses, Jesus Christ, and the "Dispensation of the Fullness of Times."

In August 1840, Joseph sent a letter throughout the Church urging the members to gather to Nauvoo, Illinois. One paragraph in this letter typified Joseph Smith's vision of the work in which he was engaged:

> The work of the Lord in these last days, is one of vast magnitude and almost beyond the comprehension of mortals. Its glories are past description, and its grandeur unsurpassable. It is the theme which has animated the bosom of prophets and righteous men from the creation of the world down through every succeeding generation to the present time; and it is truly the dispensation of the fullness of times, when all things which are in Christ Jesus, whether in heaven or on the earth, shall be gathered together in Him, and when all things shall be restored, as spoken of by all the holy prophets since the world began; for in it will take place the glorious fulfilment of the promises made to the fathers, while the manifestations of the power of the Most High will be great, glorious, and sublime.[30]

In August 1842, Joseph told the Church members that God would continue to preserve him, by their united faith and prayers, until he had fully accomplished his mission, and had firmly established the dispensation of the fullness of the priesthood in the last days, that all the powers of earth and hell can never prevail against it.[31]

At that time, Joseph apparently felt there was still considerable work to be done. For one thing, in January 1841, the Lord instructed the impoverished Saints at Nauvoo to build another temple. Joseph urged the gathering of the saints so that they could build this temple to the Lord so the Lord could reveal new temple ordinances that had been revealed to him.

In a letter to the Quorum of the Twelve, he hinted at one such ordinance to be performed in a temple—"baptism for the dead." Joseph pointed out that baptism by proxy for dead ancestors was practiced in the early Church and he referred the Twelve

---

[30] *History of the Church*, Vol 4:184-187.
[31] Ibid., Vol 5:140.

Apostles to the writings of Paul to the Corinthians in which Paul asked, "Else what shall they do which are baptized for the dead, if the dead rise not at all? Why are they then baptized for the dead?" (I Corinthians 15:29).

Later Joseph Smith provided extensive information concerning "baptism for the dead" and he tied it closely with the keys received from Elijah in which the hearts of the fathers would turn to the children and the hearts of the children would turn to their fathers. He also taught about other sacred ordinances that could only be performed within a temple. He introduced the concept of eternal marriage wherein a man and woman could be married for eternity and children could be "sealed" or united to their parents for eternity so that the family organization extended beyond the grave. By November 1841, the Nauvoo Temple had progressed to the point where the baptismal font could be dedicated to perform baptisms for the dead.

On 6 August 1842, while visiting the Saints in Montrose, Iowa, Joseph Smith reflected upon the continuing harassment the church suffered from Missouri and was beginning to experience in Illinois. He declared:

> I prophesied that the Saints would continue to suffer much affliction and would be driven to the Rocky Mountains, many would apostatize, others would be put to death by our persecutors or lose their lives in consequence of exposure or disease, and some of you will live to go and assist in making settlements and build cities and see the Saints become a mighty people in the midst of the Rocky Mountains.[32]

This prophetic pronouncement is just one of many recorded by Joseph Smith during the 24 years that he lived after his first

---

[32] *History of the Church*, Vol. 5:85. In 1846, the Latter-day Saints were driven from Nauvoo, Illinois, in the middle of winter. During the sojourn across Iowa and subsequently across the plains to the Salt Lake Valley, it is estimated that more than 5,000 saints died along the way. Many of the Nauvoo exiles were instrumental in settling and developing the valleys in the Rocky Mountains.

vision. One frequently overlooked prediction is recorded as the words of Moroni when he appeared to Joseph Smith during the evening of 21 September 1823. As indicated earlier, Moroni told Joseph that God had a work for him to do and that *his name should be had for good and evil among all nations, kindreds, and tongues, or that it should be both good and evil spoken of among all people* (emphasis added). If Joseph Smith were an imposter, as many people have suggested, that was a bold statement to be uttered by a 17 year old, uneducated boy. Many years after Moroni informed Joseph of his future, millions of devout members worldwide publically declare that Joseph Smith is a prophet.

From the time that the boy Joseph told his Methodist minister friend of his vision of God, he was hounded, beaten, abused, and arrested unjustly. Although the Palmyra neighbors did not believe Joseph's story of the gold plates, they made every effort conceivable to steal those plates from him. In March 1832, while Joseph was living in Hiram, Ohio, a mob descended on his home, pulled him out of bed and dragged him outside where they tore his clothes off, scratched his skin, attempted to pour poison down his throat–chipping a tooth in the process–and covered him with hot tar. One of his children, sick with the measles, died of exposure when the mob left the doors open during the assault on the Prophet. While confined to the Liberty Jail in 1838, Joseph and his companions were extremely ill-treated and were frequently fed rotten food.[33]

Although Joseph Smith was arrested many times, he always predicted that he would not be killed and would be released unharmed until he had finished his work. However, he sensed, when he was arrested in June 1844, that he had finished his work and would finally be killed by his enemies. On the road to jail in Carthage, Illinois, he announced prophetically:

---

[33]See Appendix B.

> *I am going like a lamb to the slaughter, but I am calm as a summer's morning. I have a conscience void of offense toward God and toward all men. If they take my life I shall die an innocent man, and my blood shall cry from the ground for vengeance, and it shall be said of me "He was murdered in cold blood!"*

Joseph and his brother Hyrum were shot while in jail at 5:00 p.m. on 27 June 1844, by a mob with blackened faces. John Taylor, one of the two apostles who was with them during the attack, subsequently wrote the following:

> Joseph Smith, the Prophet and Seer of the Lord, has done more, save Jesus only, for the salvation of men in this world, than any other man that ever lived in it. In the short space of twenty years, he has brought forth the *Book of Mormon*, which he translated by the gift and power of God, and has been the means of publishing it on two continents; has sent the fulness of the everlasting gospel, which it contained, to the four quarters of the earth; has brought forth the revelations and commandments which compose this book of *Doctrine and Covenants*, and many other wise documents and instructions for the benefit of the children of men; gathered many thousands of the Latter-day Saints, founded a great city, and left a fame and name that cannot be slain. He lived great, and he died great in the eyes of God and his people; and like most of the Lord's anointed in ancient times, has sealed his mission and his works with his own blood; and so has his brother Hyrum. In life they were not divided, and in death they were not separated! (D&C 135:3)

19

A Marvelous Work and a Wonder

In the preceding chapters, considerable details, gleaned from the writings of the Spanish and Portuguese chroniclers and modern art historians and archaeologists, working in Mexico, Central America and the Andean countries, have been presented which strongly support the accounts, events, and claims set forth in the *Book of Mormon*. It should be evident by now to investigators of the *Book of Mormon* that neither Joseph Smith nor anyone in 1830 could have written such a complex book which contains so many details of ancient America, details that were unavailable to historians in the United States in the early 1800s.

As noted, most of the Spanish and Portuguese chronicles were not published until at least 50 years after the *Book of Mormon* was published and did not begin to appear in the United States until the early 1900s. The relevant findings of art historians and archaeologists have only been discovered in the 1900s as well. Information gained from these two diverse sources should lay to rest the many unfounded criticisms of the *Book of Mormon*.

Referring to Historian Jan Shipps's observations, cited earlier, that judging whether the *Book of Mormon* is interesting, informative, or worthwhile is not enough; the issue is much more fundamental. Shipps pondered a significant question for truth-seekers:

> Is the *Book of Mormon* a Hebraic record once "hid up," but now "brought forth" to show the Indians that they are a "remnant of the House of Israel" and "brought forth," in order to demonstrate to "Jew and Gentile" that Jesus is the Christ, the Eternal God manifesting himself to all nations? In other words, is the *Book of Mormon* "another testament of Jesus Christ?"[1]

Shipps remarked that the *Book of Mormon* has never lent itself to the same process of verification that historians use to verify ordinary accounts of past histories. She made reference to the words of Moroni wherein Moroni exhorts the readers of the *Book of Mormon* to pray to God to receive an answer concerning the veracity of the book (Moroni 10:4-5). She suggests that this method of verification is not very scientific and is usually not an accepted method of proving the truthfulness of a work.

Shipps noted that from the standpoint of archaeology, the *Book of Mormon* accounts of settlements and peoples makes sense and could have happened. She rightfully observed that such accounts point, finally, only to plausibility. Proof is a different matter.

Readers of the *Book of Mormon* soon discover that its central theme is spiritual in nature and temporal details are secondary. A reading of the scriptures shows that spiritual truths must be verified by the Holy Ghost, who has the capability and responsibility to speak and testify directly to our souls—Spirit to spirit. The revelation given to Peter of the divinity of Jesus Christ is an excellent example of this:

---

[1] Shipp, 27.

> When Jesus came into the coasts of Caesarea Philippi, he asked his disciples, saying, Whom do men say that I the Son of Man am?
>
> And they said, Some say that thou art John the Baptist: some, Elias; and others, Jeremias, or one of the prophets.
>
> He saith unto them, But whom say ye that I am?
>
> And Simon Peter answered and said, Thou art the Christ, the Son of the living God.
>
> And Jesus answered and said unto him, Blessed art thou, Simon Bar-jona: for flesh and blood hath not revealed it unto thee, but my Father which is in heaven (Matthew 16:13-17).

As Jesus Christ neared the end of his mortal ministry, he knew that in spite of the fact that Peter and the rest of the Apostles had been associated with him for three years their testimonies were not yet firm. They had not yet received the gift of the Holy Ghost. In the Gospel according to St. John, Jesus promised to send them the Holy Ghost. John recorded the Savior's instructions to them:

> But the Comforter, which is the Holy Ghost, whom the Father will send in my name, he shall teach you all things, and bring all things to your remembrance, whatsoever I have said unto you (John 14:26).

The reception of the testimony of the Holy Ghost requires faith and a desire to know the truth. The ultimate witness to the truthfulness of the *Book of Mormon* is the spiritual witness from the Holy Ghost as Moroni promised. Consequently, the lack of empirical evidence "proving" the *Book of Mormon* has not stopped millions of people around the world from accepting this unusual book as scripture.

Although Joseph Smith urged everyone who inquired after the *Book of Mormon* to read the book and to pray about its message, he was equally convinced that God would eventually "prove" the *Book of Mormon*. Joseph predicated in 1842 that "It will be as it ever has been, the world will prove Joseph Smith a true prophet by circumstantial evidence." In 1830 there was no outside evidence to support the claims and accounts narrated in the *Book of Mormon* and any such outside evidence did not begin to appear for many years.

As future events began to unfold, it would appear to Mormon faithful that God again intervened in the affairs of his children. For hundreds of years the manuscripts of the New World chroniclers had remained in obscurity—unpublished, unread, and unappreciated. After this extended hiatus, Spanish and Portuguese historians became obsessed with a sudden interest in these "eye-witness" accounts of the native Americans.

Towards the end of the 19th Century, historians in Spain, Mexico and Peru, evidencing this newly acquired interest, began searching through libraries, museums, monasteries and private collections in an effort to locate and publish the lost manuscripts of these early chroniclers. The written accounts of the searchers revealed unusual excitement on their part as they discovered, one by one, the original manuscripts of Pedro de Cieza de León, Felipe Guaman Poma de Ayala, Miguel Cabello Valboa, Martín de Murúa, Juan de Betanzos, Diego de Landa, Diego Durán and a host of other chronicle accounts.

After the initial high interest in the chronicle manuscripts in the late 1800s and early 1900s, historians seemed to lose interest in them and the chronicles were frequently relegated to dusty library shelves once again. The sudden loss of interest in these 16th and 17th Century books may be explained by the burgeoning advances in archaeology and art history. About the time historians were searching out the chronicles, archaeologists and art historians were becoming increasingly interested in the ancient American cultures and civilizations. Studies of the newly discovered ruins in Mexico, Mesoamerica, and the Andes were enhanced by scientific innovations such as Carbon-14 testing which enabled scientists to more accurately date the ancient ruins. This enabled the scientists to separate the different cultures into recognizable time-lines. The excavations by hundreds of archaeologists and art historians have enabled scientists to assemble a wealth of information about these ancient American inhabitants. The more spectacular advances have been made in the last fifty years. Scientists have become more confident that science can provide all the answers to the origin and culture of these ancient Americans.

One of the by-products of these scientific advances is the unfortunate loss of interest in the chronicle writings, which were regarded as irrelevant to the scientific approach. In an attempt to explain this lack of interest in the chronicles, modern historians emphasized that the early chroniclers were not trained historians, did not follow evidentiary procedures, and were believed to be biased by their religious backgrounds.

Increasingly, members of the scientific and historical communities began to accept, as fact, the theory that the native Americans were Mongols or Tatars who crossed the northern land bridge 15,000 to 20,000 years ago, a period thousands of years before the Biblical timetable for a Moses, or a Noah, or even before the Biblical appearance of the first humans, Adam and Eve. Theories of evolution negated the idea of a divine creation. The diffusionist ideas of many of the chroniclers and their tales of encountering Hebrew or Christian traditions in the New World do not coincide with the prevailing Independent Inventionist hypotheses.

Although modern scientific theories would appear to negate *Book of Mormon* and chronicle accounts, it is precisely the findings of the archaeologists and art historians that frequently support the claims of both the chronicles and the *Book of Mormon*, as has been demonstrated in previous chapters. Details, gleaned from the writing of the Spanish and Portuguese chroniclers as well as new scientific discoveries often support the claims and accounts set forth in the *Book of Mormon*.

If Joseph Smith invented the *Book of Mormon* and fraudulently portrayed it as a "translation" of ancient records, his unsubstantiated descriptions of events, customs, native skills and religious practices recorded in the *Book of Mormon* would have to withstand future historical and scientific discoveries. A careful study of Chapters 6 through 17 in this book demonstrate how many of Joseph Smith's descriptions in the *Book of Mormon* are similar to findings of the chroniclers or art historians and archaeologists. Joseph Smith obviously could not have known about these future discoveries when he "translated" the gold plates and published the *Book of Mormon*.

Book of Mormon critics such as Fawn McKay Brodie and Dan Vogel have argued that Joseph may have used existing books such as Ethan Smith's *View of the Hebrew* to describe the evidence of ancient Hebrew (Mosaic) rites in the New World. In their efforts to find a "logical" explanation for the *Book of Mormon*, they ignore the fact that the *Book of Mormon* is almost totally focused on Jesus Christ.

Other critics such as Eder D. Howe, editor of the Painesville Telegraph in 1830, have suggested that the uneducated Joseph Smith could not have written the *Book of Mormon* and it must have been written by a more scholarly individual such as Sidney Rigdon. However, Rigdon and any early 19th Century scholar would have had to face the same dilemma–include hundreds of details and descriptions that would only come to light 50 to100 years in the future.

Dr. Hugh W. Nibley described the difficulties a fiction writer would face. Reiterating Dr. Nibley's comment cited earlier:

> There is no point at all to the question: Who wrote the *Book of Mormon*? It would have been quite as impossible for the most

learned man alive in 1830 as it was for Joseph Smith. And whoever would account for the *Book of Mormon* by any theory suggested so far—save one—must completely rule out the first forty pages.

To write a history of what could have happened at the very beginning of recorded history would have been as far beyond the scope of any scholar living in 1830 as the construction of an atom bomb would have been.[2]

Nibley's observations are magnified many fold, when the information presented in this book are included. The new archaeological discoveries in recent years as well as the discovery and publication of numerous sixteenth and seventeenth century chronicles in the last 150 years highlight what a remarkable book the *Book of Mormon* is.

The more ingenious may argue that Joseph Smith made a few lucky guesses. Guesswork introduces laws of probability. One has a 50 percent chance of guessing on the flip of a coin or one in six on the roll of a die. As you add dice the probabilities become exponential. When the critics realize that Joseph Smith accurately described hundreds of events and accounts that parallel or appear very similar to events and accounts discovered by the scientists or brought to light in the chronicles, as has been narrated in the previous chapters, probabilities become astronomical.

The following is a brief synopsis of a few of the major similarities:

A. A period of time when the sun did not shine which was accompanied by massive destruction in the Americas, brought on by earthquakes, storms, fires in which numerous cities were completely destroyed and the inhabitants killed. These catastrophic events were followed by the appearance of a bearded white man who healed the sick and taught the natives "gospel" principles. The *Book of Mormon* identified the individual as the resurrected

---

[2]Nibley, xiv.

Jesus Christ. The surviving inhabitants gave him various names, but generally each name indicated that he was the "Creator of the World." Art historians studying Moche iconography have identified an individual whom the scientists call a "rayed deity" who quelled an apparent "revolt of the objects." (See Chapters 6 and 7.)

B. Writers in the *Book of Mormon* taught the people about the immortality of the soul and the eventual resurrection of the body. These American prophets taught Christian principles while practicing the law of Moses. The chroniclers saw evidence of religious practices that caused many chroniclers to believe the Indians were descendants of Jews, but at the same time they encountered Christian rites. (See Chapter 8 through 11.)

C. The *Book of Mormon* described the migrations of three groups to the Americas after the universal flood. The first group existed from approximately 2500 B.C. to a period between 588 B.C. and 279 B.C. before it self destructed. Archaeologists identified the Chavín civilization in the 1930s and subsequent investigation reveals that the Chavín civilization in Peru lasted from approximately 2500 B.C. to 400 B.C. and the Olmec in Mexico from approximately 1500 B.C. to 400 B.C. Lehi and his followers arrive about 588 B.C. and the Mulekites within just a few years. These two new groups brought a culture quite different from the culture of Chavín or Olmec. These new societies began to spread out in the Americas. Archaeologists have discovered new societies exhibiting very different cultures than those exhibited by the Chavín and Olmec societies. These new societies became sufficiently established by 200 B.C. to 300 B.C. that the scientists have been able to gather sufficient data to identify them as Tiwanakan and Moche in the Andes and Mayan and Teotihuacan in Mesoamerica and Mexico. (See Chapters 12 and 13.)

D. While historians and scientists teach of the homogeneity of the American Indians, Joseph Smith narrated that there were migrations of different groups and that there were both dark and light-skinned peoples living in the Americas. The Spaniards and Portuguese discovered a wide variety of natives in the Americas. They encountered both white (light-skinned) as well as dark-skinned peoples. They encountered tribes where the men wore beards. Art historians have found painted murals revealing people of different skin coloring such as at Cacaxtla and among the Maya. They have discovered statues and iconography showing men with beards. (See Chapter 14.)

E. The writers in the *Book of Mormon* frequently cautioned the people to keep God's commandments or their "land of promise" would be given to "gentiles" and they would be scattered and destroyed. Legends about how the native American would be conquered by "bearded white men" were encountered throughout the Caribbean, Mexico and the Andes. How could Joseph Smith have known about these prophetic legends? (See Chapter 15.)

F. The *Book of Mormon* writers mention and frequently describe some of the technical skills enjoyed by the Pre-Columbian Americans. Boat making and navigational skills, metallurgy, textile manufacturing, stone masonry, road building and the use of cement were all analyzed. With the eventual publication of the chronicle manuscripts, it was discovered that each technical skill described in the *Book of Mormon* had been discovered by the chroniclers. Archaeologists and art historians have described many of the technical skills used by the various ancient American civilizations. The reader must ask, "How could Joseph Smith have known about the use of cement in ancient America or had knowledge of the depth of their metallurgical skills?" (See Chapter 16.)

G. Descriptions of warfare, weaponry and military tactics comprise many verses in the *Book of Mormon*. How could Joseph

Smith have known that over 3,000 years ago, the warriors in the Americas at that time wore metal backplates and breastplates and had metal helmets as described by art historians digging through the ruins of the Chavín civilization? How could he have known that the sword and the sling were important weapons in Pre-Columbia America? The Spanish conquistadores discovered that the Indians used military tactics that were similar to tactics used hundreds of years earlier. Although scientists have discounted the use of steel or iron in their weaponry, chroniclers discovered that at least in Chile, the Araucano Indians were skilled in the use of a variety of weapons made with iron. (See Chapter 17.)

Modern archaeologists and art historians can routinely provide good answers to *what*, *where*, *when*, and *how* societies developed in the New World; but they have considerable difficulty identifying the origin of these American natives and *why* they demonstrated so many Hebrew and Christian characteristics. I believe that many archaeologists and art historians have unduly complicated their findings by adhering steadfastly to unproven theories about evolution and to the *Independent Inventionist* hypothesis that all Indians are descendants of Tatars or Mongols who came to the Americas 15,000 or 20,000 years ago and had no subsequent contact with the outside world.

Many reputable scientists simply ignore any evidence that suggests there have been several migrations from different areas of the Old World. The Indians themselves demonstrate numerous physical characteristic which indicate that they are not just from one gene pool. One example highlighting the exclusion of important information is the fact that the existence of bearded white natives in the Americas is not generally taught in the history books. Why the silence about white Indians in the face of numerous chronicle reports of direct encounters with white Indians and the Indian narratives themselves? There are still pockets of white Indians living in isolation in diverse, often remote, areas from as far north as the United States to as far south as Paraguay. When high school and university professors adhere blindly to unproven theories concerning native Americans, they limit themselves to teaching a "make believe" history about ancient America.

The narrative contained in the *Book of Mormon* often provides us with answers concerning the *who* and *why* of a particular custom or history. The histories, folklore and legends gleaned by the chroniclers also help fill in the gaps. A study of the chroniclers, whether they were Catholic priests, soldiers, or government officials, suggests that they were guided by an honest effort to inform their fellow Europeans about the New World and the native Americans. Most wrote at considerable sacrifice of time, money, and comfort. They were often highly dedicated and highly motivated men who gathered their information and wrote under difficult circumstances. Unlike many of their contemporaries, they appeared to care more for knowledge than for wealth. Many expressed the desire that they wanted future generations to know what they had discovered in the New World.

The chroniclers were not without flaws and they struggled with language difficulties, political problems, and inadequate information. Within their limited capacities, they faithfully recorded the folklore, legends, teachings, and accounts passed down over hundreds of years by native historians. Many of the legends had no meaning to the writers at the time, but were included because the chroniclers sensed that these accounts were important to the natives.

As has been demonstrated repeatedly, the *Book of Mormon* substantiates many of the chronicle writings and often adds a dimension to them that makes them relevant and provides additional meaning. The New World writers could not have known about the plates that Moroni buried more than 1,000 years before Columbus arrived in the Americas. They could only record the stories that had been passed down over hundreds of years. As historian Rolena Adorno wrote:

> The problem was not a failure in intellectual and creative endeavors during those centuries, but rather the much more recent failure to appreciate the learned and original contributions of early New World writers.[3]

Since the *Book of Mormon* narrative has been discovered to frequently support many of the findings of the chronicle writers and has demonstrated that these eye-witnesses were, in fact, reliable reporters of native folklore and events, should not historians take a renewed interest in the chronicles? Also since archaeologists and art historians are uncovering information that frequently supports *Book of Mormon* claims, conversely, could the *Book of Mormon* be an effective tool in their scientific research as well? After analyzing the wealth of details provided in the preceding chapters, the unbiased reader should be able to declare that combining information obtained from these three separate *voices from the dust* provides a more complete picture of ancient America.

Several of the New World writers, such as Columbus and Cieza de León, declared that they felt God's influence compelling them to pursue their lofty activities. It is noteworthy that most of these 16th and 17th Century manuscripts were discovered and published many years after the publication of the *Book of Mormon*. If the libraries of the 1820's had been replete with these early American chronicles, the critics of the *Book of Mormon* could have argued that Joseph Smith simply used these early chronicle accounts to write an historical fiction novel. In the absence of concrete outside evidence, the followers of Jesus Christ have always relied upon faith to sustain their beliefs.

---

[3] Leonard, xxvii.

The need for a book like the *Book of Mormon* should not come as a surprise to Bible students. The Bible contains numerous prophecies concerning an eventual "falling away" or an apostasy after the Savior's resurrection. Isaiah spoke of this future falling away in several of his revelations. During Joseph Smith's First Vision, Jesus Christ quoted Isaiah: "Forasmuch as this people draw near me with their mouth, and with their lips do honour me, but have removed their heart far from me, and their fear toward me is taught by the precept of men"(Isaiah 29:13). Amos also prophesied:

> Behold, the days come, saith the Lord God, that I will send a famine in the land, not a famine of bread, nor a thirst for water, but of hearing the words of the Lord:
> And they shall wander from sea to sea, and from the north even to the east, they shall run to and fro to seek the word of the Lord, and shall not find it (Amos 8:11-12).

In several of his epistles to the saints, Paul warned the early saints that there would be a falling away or an apostasy within the Church that the Savior had established. Paul instructed the Church leaders at Ephesus that they should take care of themselves and their "flocks" over which they had been given stewardship:

> For I know this, that after my departing shall grievous wolves enter in among you, not sparing the flock. Also of your own selves shall men arise, speaking perverse things, to draw away disciples after them (Acts 20:29-30).

Paul also told the Thessalonians, who were waiting for Christ's return, that Christ would not come immediately. He wrote:

> Let no man deceive you by any means: for that day shall not come, except there come a falling away first, and that man of sin be revealed, the son of perdition (2 Thessalonians 2:3).

Before, Lehi and his family left the Old World, Nephi saw in a vision that many important parts of the Bible would be lost or changed:

> Wherefore, thou seest that after the book hath gone forth through the hands of the great and abominable church, that there are many plain and precious things taken away from the book, which is the book of the Lamb of God.
>
> And after these plain and precious things were taken away it goeth forth unto all the nations of the Gentiles; and after it goeth forth unto all the nations of the Gentiles, yea, even across the many waters which thou hast seen with the Gentiles which have gone forth out of captivity, thou seest–because of the many plain and precious things which have been taken out of the book, which were plain unto the understanding of the children of men, according to the plainness which is in the Lamb of God–because of these things which are taken away out of the gospel of the Lamb, an exceedingly great many do stumble, yea, insomuch that Satan hath great power over them (1 Nephi 13:28-29).

The prophets in the Americas foresaw how the Christians would begin to interpret the *Bible* in diverse ways which would ultimately lead to the formation of numerous churches, all proclaiming that they had the truth. They prophesied how the followers of Jesus Christ would gradually misunderstand his mission and the atonement, and their misunderstanding would lead to numerous false doctrines. Such simple ordinances as baptism would be changed. Mormon wrote an epistle to his son Moroni warning him that men would misunderstand the atonement of Jesus Christ and would begin to baptize little children even though little children were incapable of repentance and were not in need of baptism (Moroni chapter 8).

Even before leaving the Old World, Nephi foresaw the apostasy that would befall his people after the visit of the Savior to the Americas. Years later, Nephi spoke again of this eventual falling away among his people:

> But the Son of righteousness shall appear unto them; and he shall heal them, and they shall have peace with him, until three generations shall have passed away, and many of the fourth generation shall have passed away in righteousness.
>
> And when these things have passed away a speedy destruction cometh unto my people; for, not withstanding the pains of my soul, I have seen it; wherefore, I know that it shall come to pass; and they sell themselves for naught; for, for the reward of their pride and their foolishness they shall reap destruction; for because they yield unto the devil and choose works of darkness rather than light, therefore they must go down to hell (2 Nephi 26:9-10).

Although signs of the apostasy apparently began somewhat earlier in the Church established by the Savior in the Old World, it is interesting to note that by 400 A.D. a general apostasy had destroyed Christ's Church throughout the world. Not only did prophets foresee the "falling away," but they were also privileged to see in vision the future restoration of the Church of Jesus Christ in the last days. Isaiah referred to the restoration of the gospel as a "marvellous work among this people, even a marvellous work and a wonder" (Isaiah 29:14).

In the famous dream of King Nebuchadnezzar, Daniel revealed how the many kingdoms of the earth would eventually fall to be replaced by a single kingdom in the last days. Daniel wrote:

> And in the days of these kings shall the God of heaven set up a kingdom, which shall never be destroyed: And the kingdom shall not be left to other people, but it shall break in pieces and consume all these kingdoms, and it shall stand for ever (Daniel 2:44).

The prophecy of Malachi, concerning the eventual return of Elijah, the Prophet, "before the coming of the great and dreadful day of the Lord" has already been quoted several times.

Luke recorded the words of Peter to the early saints concerning the restoration of the gospel in the last days. Peter stated:

> Repent ye therefore, and be converted, that your sins may be blotted out, when the times of refreshing shall come from the presence of the Lord;
> And he shall send Jesus Christ, which before was preached unto you:
> Whom the heaven must receive until the times of restitution of all things, which God hath spoken by the mouth of all his holy prophets since the world began (Acts 3:19-21).

Finally, John, the Revelator, also described the restoration of the gospel which was to be brought back by an angelic visitation:

> And I saw another angel fly in the midst of heaven, having the everlasting gospel to preach unto them that dwell on the earth, and to every nation, and kindred, and tongue, and people (Revelation 14:6).

Mormons believe that John saw the eventual coming of Moroni to Joseph Smith and the translation of the *Book of Mormon* which is believed to contain the everlasting gospel.

Nephi, the son of Lehi, was privileged to see the restoration of the gospel and more importantly, the role that the *Book of Mormon* would play in this great spiritual drama:

> And it came to pass that the angel of the Lord spake unto me, saying: Behold, saith the Lamb of God, after I have visited the remnant of the house of Israel–and this remnant of whom I speak is the seed of thy father–wherefore, after I have visited them in judgment, and smitten them by the hand of the Gentiles, and after the Gentiles do stumble exceedingly, because of the most plain and precious parts of the gospel of the Lamb–I will be merciful unto the Gentiles in that day, insomuch that I will bring forth unto them, in mine own power, much of my gospel, which shall be plain and precious, saith the Lamb.

For, behold, saith the Lamb: I will manifest myself unto thy seed, that they shall write many things which I shall minister unto them, which shall be plain and precious; and after thy seed shall be destroyed, and dwindle in unbelief, and also the seed of thy brethren, behold, these things shall be hid up, to come forth unto the Gentiles, by the gift and power of the Lamb.

And in them shall be written my gospel, saith the Lamb, and my rock and my salvation.

And blessed are they who shall seek to bring forth my Zion at that day, for they shall have the gift and the power of the Holy Ghost; and if they endure unto the end they shall be lifted up at the last day, and shall be saved in the everlasting kingdom of the Lamb; and whoso shall publish peace, yea, tidings of great joy, how beautiful upon the mountains shall they be (1 Nephi 13:34-37).

Before turning the records over to his brother, Jacob, Nephi again prophesied concerning how the remnants of his people would receive the gospel from the Gentiles:

For behold, I say unto you that as many of the Gentiles as will repent are the covenant people of the Lord; and as many of the Jews as will not repent shall be cast off; for the Lord covenanteth with none save it be with them that repent and believe in his Son, who is the Holy One of Israel.

And now, I would prophesy somewhat more concerning the Jews and the Gentiles. For after the book of which I have spoken shall come forth, and be written unto the Gentiles, and sealed up again unto the Lord, there shall be many which shall believe the words which are written; and they shall carry them forth unto the remnant of our seed.

And then shall the remnant of our seed know concerning us, how that we came out from Jerusalem, and that they are descendants of the Jews.

And the gospel of Jesus Christ shall be declared among them; wherefore, they shall be restored unto the knowledge of their fathers, and also to the knowledge of Jesus Christ, which was had among their fathers.

And then shall they rejoice; for they shall know that it is a blessing unto them from the hand of God; and their scales of darkness shall begin to fall from their eyes; and many generations shall not pass away among them, save they shall be a pure and a delightsome people.

And it shall come to pass that the Jews which are scattered also shall begin to believe in Christ; and they shall begin to gather in upon the face of the land; and as many as shall believe in Christ shall also become a delightsome people.

And it shall come to pass that the Lord God shall commence his work among all nations, kindreds, tongues, and people, to bring about the restoration of his people upon the earth (2 Nephi 30:2-8).

The testimony of the *Book of Mormon* has immense religious implications for the entire world. The knowledge that all mankind will resurrect and will eventually appear before Jesus Christ and will be judged by him should cause all men to rejoice and repent. Biblical scholars should be pleased to know that there is "another witness" that complements the *Bible* and provides additional insights to scriptural meanings. Moroni wrote in his introductory page that the *Book of Mormon* was written to convince the House of Israel that Jesus is the Christ, the Eternal God, who manifests himself to all nations.

Some religions teach that Jesus Christ, the son of Mary, was a great prophet, but he was only one "messenger" of many messengers and was not the son of God. They teach that the Biblical narratives which claim that Jesus raised the dead should be interpreted in such a fashion that he did not literally raise the dead, but only awakened those who were spiritually dead. They assert that God promised Jesus that he would die a natural death. The followers of these religious beliefs teach that although Jesus was placed upon the cross at Calvary, he was taken down from the cross while still alive.

Such teachings negate the infinite atonement and deny the literal resurrection of Jesus Christ. The *Book of Mormon* and the *Bible* both testify that Jesus Christ, the Creator of the world, died upon the cross and was literally resurrected. The implication of this great message is eternal and eventually every man, women and child "shall bow the knee, and every tongue shall confess" that Jesus is the Christ, the Son of the Living God.

Not only does the *Book of Mormon* testify of Jesus Christ, but it also provides specific warnings to the inhabitants of the earth, and more particularly the inhabitants of the Western Hemisphere during the "last days" (the "last days" being defined as those days from the time of the coming forth of the *Book of Mormon* until the Savior comes in his glory). The book warns that everyone needs to learn sound gospel principles and keep God's commandments. Nephi prophesied:

> And as I spake concerning the convincing of the Jews, that Jesus is the very Christ, it must needs be that the Gentiles be convinced also that Jesus is the Christ, the Eternal God.
>
> And that he manifesteth himself unto all those who believe in him, by the power of the Holy Ghost; yea, unto every nation, kindred, tongue, and people, working mighty miracles, signs, and wonders, among the children of men according to their faith.
>
> But behold, I prophesy unto you concerning the last days; concerning the days when the Lord God shall bring these things forth unto the children of men.
>
> And the Gentiles are lifted up in the pride of their eyes, and have stumbled, because of the greatness of their stumbling block, that they have built up many churches; nevertheless, they put down the power and miracles of God, and preach up unto themselves their own wisdom and their own learning, that they may get gain and grind upon the face of the poor. (2 Nephi 26:12-14, 20).
>
> But, behold, in the last days, or in the days of the Gentiles–yea, behold all the nations of the Gentiles and also the Jews, both those who shall come upon this land and those who shall be upon other lands, yea, even upon all the lands of the earth, behold, they will be drunken with iniquity and all manner of abominations (2 Nephi 27:1).

God again interceded in the affairs of nations to ensure that the site that he chose for the restoration of the gospel and the establishment of his Church would be in a free nation. The colonizers who came to what is now the United States came initially from northern Europe and were seeking refuge for religious freedom. Although the Spanish and Portuguese monarchies had been given almost free rein throughout the Caribbean, Mexico, Central America and South America, they were never able to establish a foothold in the eastern portion of what is now the United States where they might have imposed their religion. It is not that they did not try. The chronicles record several major efforts to establish settlements in eastern North America, which ended in failure.

In his *Decadas*, Peter Martyr stated that Juan Ponce de León was the first to discover Florida in 1513, but was rejected by the Indians.[4] Inca Garcilaso de la Vega provided better details of this event in his book, *The Florida of the Inca*. He narrated that the first Spaniard to explore the land of Florida was Juan Ponce de León, who was the governor of the island of San Juan de Puerto Rico. Ponce de León was searching for an island named Bimini (also called Buyoca) where, according to fables of the Indians, there was a fountain that rejuvenated the aged.

Ponce de León wandered for many days searching for this island and was eventually blown by a storm to a coast that lay north of Cuba. He named it Florida. Without taking the pains to determine whether Florida was an island or the mainland, he immediately sailed to Spain to petition for the right to govern and conquer this new land. Queen Isabella and King Fernando granted him this favor. Ponce de León sailed for Florida in 1515 with three ships. When he landed, he was attacked by Indians who killed nearly all of his men. He managed to escape with only six of his companions. They returned to Cuba, where they all died from the wounds they received.[5]

---

[4]Martyr, 322, 355.
[5]Inca Garcilaso de la Vega, *The Florida of the Inca*, 8.

As previously noted, Peter Martyr described the 1526 voyage of Lucas Vázquez de Ayllón towards the mainland of North America where he explored parts of what is now South Carolina and Georgia. Martyr indicated that Vázquez de Ayllón wanted to establish a colony probably in Chicora (believed to be somewhere along the South Carolina coast).[6] Garcilaso de la Vega wrote that Vázquez de Ayllón, who was a high court judge, also went to Spain where he petitioned for the right to conquer and govern Chicora, considered to be one of many provinces in Florida. Not only did the King grant his request, but he also honored him with knighthood in the Order of Santiago.

Vázquez de Ayllón, traveled to Santo Domingo where he outfitted three large vessels and sailed north. He eventually landed on the coast of a "peaceful and delightful region near Chicora where the natives initially received him with praise and festivity. Once the Spaniards had relaxed, sensing that they were welcome in this new land, the Indians attacked and killed most of the men. Vázquez de Ayllón and a few others barely escaped and returned to Santo Domingo.[7]

In 1537, Pamphilo de Narváez made an ill-fated venture into Florida. Accompanying him was Alvar Núñez Cabeza de Vaca, who, along with only four others, managed to escape death. They gradually made it overland back to Mexico. Núñez Cabeza de Vaca wrote about his adventures in his book, *Naufragios* (*Disasters*).

The next ambitious adventure into Florida was organized and led by Hernando de Soto, who had become rich and famous during the conquest of Peru. In 1538, De Soto petitioned Charles V for permission to conquer and settle Florida.. Charles was so pleased to grant the request that he also made De Soto, the governor of Cuba as well as Florida. On 12 May 1539, De

---

[6]Martyr, 506.
[7]Garcilaso de la Vega, *La Florida,*10-11.

Soto sailed from Havana with more than 1,000 fighting men and 350 horses, in eight ships. He is believed to have landed near what is now Tampa Bay. After he unloaded his men and supplies, he literally had to fight his way inland. He also sent several vessels farther north along the west coast of the Florida peninsula to scout out a possible settlement site. A site was located, but never established, in what is now believed to be Pensacola Bay.

De Soto and his force fought across Florida and Georgia. It appears that the Spaniards went as far north as present-day Greenville, South Carolina, before turning west and crossing the Appalachians into modern Tennessee. They then turned back south with the idea of going to the coast and establishing a colony in the Pensacola area. When they reached about the area of Selma, Alabama, they had a terrible battle with the Indians.

For some reason, instead of proceeding on to Pensacola as planned, De Soto turned northwest and traveled across the Mississippi River. Although he and his men encountered a few friendly Indian tribes, they were harassed in most areas which cost the lives of many Spaniards and many horses. After crossing the Mississippi, De Soto traveled into Texas, reaching what is believed to be the Trinity River, before he returned to the Mississippi River. After reaching the Mississippi again, he came down with a mysterious fever and died while encamped on the Mississippi River.

Garcilaso de la Vega claimed that De Soto put together the largest and best equipped armada that had been assembled up to that time by the Spaniards, but it completely failed because of the dissension among the Spaniards and the harassment by the Indians.

The first successful Spanish colony in the eastern United States was the Presidio of San Augustin established by Pedro Menéndez de Avilés in 1565. Later the colony was named St. Augustine, Florida. The fortress served to protect the primary trade routes to Europe and to defend the Spanish-claimed land against invasion. The fort was ruled by the Spanish for 256 years, but they apparently did not expand outside the local area and certainly not towards the north.

The first English colony was established at Jamestown, Virginia, in 1607 and the Pilgrims, founders of Plymouth, Massachusetts, arrived in 1620. By 1650, the English had established a dominant presence on the Atlantic coast.

One only needs to contemplate the plight of the Jews in Spain and Portugal, who suffered under the inquisition, to realize that an independent church would not survive in a land controlled by a heavy-handed government in which church and state were not separated. God was preserving an area where "wise" leaders would ensure they enjoyed the separation of Church and State.

The Lord revealed to Joseph Smith that he had inspired men to write the Constitution of the United States. Joseph recorded this revelation in the Doctrine and Covenants:

> According to the laws and constitution of the people, which I have suffered to be established, and should be maintained for the rights and protection of all flesh, according to just and holy principles;
>
> That every man may act in doctrine and principle pertaining to futurity, according to the moral agency which I have given unto him, that every man may be accountable for his own sins in the day of judgment.
>
> Therefore, it is not right that any man should be in bondage one to another.
>
> And for this purpose have I established the Constitution of this land, by the hands of wise men whom I raised up unto this very purpose, and redeemed the land by the shedding of blood (D&C 101:77-80).

Even with these constitutional guarantees and the freedom of religion, The Church of Jesus Christ of Latter-day Saints barely managed to survive the intense hostility and persecution by fellow Christians.

Before Jesus Christ left the American Continent, he had one final word of warning to the people who would establish many churches in the New World:

> Turn, all ye Gentiles, from your wicked ways; and repent of your evil doings, of your lyings and deceivings, and of your whoredoms and of your secret abominations and your idolatries, and of your murders, and your priestcrafts and your envyings, and your strifes and from all your wickedness and abominations, and come unto me and be baptized in my name, that ye may receive a remission of your sins and be filled with the Holy Ghost that ye may be numbered with my people who are of the house of Israel (3 Nephi 30:2).

Several hundred years later as Mormon was viewing the destruction of his people and knowing that their record would eventually be given to a prophet in the latter-day, he wrote a warning to the Gentiles that they should not be so foolish as to reject the gospel and the record which the Nephites had been so careful to preserve:

> Therefore I write unto you, Gentiles, and also unto you, house of Israel, when the work shall commence, that ye shall be about to prepare to return to the land of your inheritance;
>
> Yea, behold, I write unto all the ends of the earth; yea, unto you, twelve tribes of Israel, who shall be judged according to your works by the twelve whom Jesus chose to be his disciples in the land of Jerusalem.
>
> And I write also unto the remnant of this people, who shall also be judged by the twelve whom Jesus chose in this land; and they shall be judged by the other twelve whom Jesus chose in the land of Jerusalem.
>
> And these things doth the Spirit manifest unto me; therefore I write unto you all. And for this cause I write unto you, that ye may know that ye must all stand before the judgment–seat of Christ, yea, every soul who belongs to the whole human family of Adam; and ye must stand to be judged of your works, whether they be good or evil;

A Marvelous Work and a Wonder 517

And also that ye may believe the gospel of Jesus Christ, which ye shall have among you; and also that the Jews, the covenant people of the Lord, shall have other witness besides him whom they saw and heard, that Jesus, whom they slew, was the very Christ and the very God.

And I would that I could persuade all ye ends of the earth to repent and prepare to stand before the judgment-seat of Christ (Mormon 3:17 -22).

As Moroni was finalizing the record of his father, Mormon, who had been killed by the Lamanites, Moroni, with an obviously heavy heart, looked forward to the time when their record would again be upon the earth. He remembered the great prophets who had gone before as well as the saints who had lived righteous lives. He saw the record being revealed in the last days. Perhaps remembering the words of the Prophet Isaiah concerning a voice speaking from the dust, he reminded the remnant of his people, the house of Israel, and the Gentiles that the former saints will speak to them as if from the dust:

Yea, behold I say unto you, that those saints who have gone before me, who have possessed this land, *shall cry, yea, even from the dust* (*emphasis added*) will they cry unto the Lord; and as the Lord liveth he will remember the covenant which he has made with them (Mormon 8:23).

He spoke very openly, almost familiarly, to our generation. Moroni narrated that he speaks "unto you as if ye were present, and yet ye are not. But behold, Jesus Christ hath shown you unto me, and I know your doings" (Mormon 8:35). Moroni prophesied that the gold plates would be revealed and translated.

And no one need say they shall not come, for they surely shall, for the Lord hath spoken it; for out of the earth shall they come, by the hand of the Lord, and none can stay it; and it shall come in a day when it shall be said that miracles are done away; and it shall come even as if one should speak from the dead.

> And it shall come in a day when the blood of saints shall cry unto the Lord, because of secret combinations and the works of darkness.
>
> Yea, it shall come in a day when the power of God shall be denied, and churches become defiled and be lifted up in the pride of their hearts; yea, even in a day when leaders of churches and teachers shall rise in the pride of their hearts, even to the envying of them who belong to their churches.
>
> Yea, it shall come in a day when there shall be heard of fires, and tempests, and vapors of smoke in foreign lands;
>
> And there shall also be heard of wars, rumors of wars, and earthquakes in divers places.
>
> Yea, it shall come in a day when there shall be great pollutions upon the face of the earth; there shall be murders, and robbing, and lying, and deceivings, and whoredoms, and all manner of abominations; when there shall be many who will say, Do this, or do that, and it mattereth not, for the Lord will uphold such at the last day. But wo unto such, for they are in the gall of bitterness and in the bonds of iniquity.
>
> Yea, it shall come in a day when there shall be churches built up that shall say: Come unto me, and for your money you shall be forgiven of your sins (Mormon 8:26-32).

I have touched extensively upon the prophecies of the last days mainly because we are living in the last days. The prophecies of these ancient American prophets of the conditions that will exist at this time are very exact.

Archaeologists, art historians, the chronicle writings, and the *Book of Mormon* indicate that for thousands of years great civilizations have thrived for a period in the Americas and then disappeared. These include the Chavín and the Olmec, Teotihuacan and Tiwanaku, Moche and Toltec just to name a few. Later with the arrival of the Spaniards and the Portuguese, the Aztec, Maya, and Inca civilizations as well as millions of native Americans scattered throughout the New World were destroyed. The *Book of Mormon* reveals that these civilizations disappeared because of the wickedness of their people.

Throughout this book, in accordance with standard nomenclature used by the conquistadores, I have referred to the Americas as the New World and to Europe, the Middle East, etc., as the Old World. If we accept Joseph Smith as a prophet and accept his "revelations" as God's word, then, viewed in the light of modern revelation, this nomenclature may be incorrect. The Prophet Joseph Smith revealed that the Garden of Eden was located where Jackson County, Missouri, now sits.[8] After Adam and Eve left the Garden of Eden, they dwelt for some time at a place called Adam-ondi-Ahman. In a revelation given to Joseph Smith, Adam-ondi-Ahman is near Spring Hill, Daviess County, Missouri (D&C 116). According to another revelation given to Joseph Smith, a singular event occurred at Adam-ondi-Ahman.

> Three years previous to the death of Adam, he called Seth, Enos, Cainan, Mahalaleel, Jared, Enoch, and Methuselah, who were all high priests, with the residue of his posterity who were righteous, into the valley of Adam-ondi-Ahman, and there bestowed upon them his last blessing.
> And the Lord appeared unto them, and they rose up and blessed Adam, and called him Michael, the prince, the archangel.
> And the Lord administered comfort unto Adam, and said unto him: I have set thee to be at the head; a multitude of nations shall come of thee, and thou art a prince over them forever.
> And Adam stood up in the midst of the congregation; and, notwithstanding he was bowed down with age, being full of the Holy Ghost, predicted whatsoever should befall his posterity unto the latest generation (D&C 107:53-56).

The belief that Adam and his family were in the Americas prior to the flood might be useful to scientists as they examine ancient civilizations. La Peyrère and a few other early writers expressed their views that men seemed to have been in the

---

[8] See *Journal of Discourses*, 10:235; Matthias F. Cowley, *Wilford Woodruff: History of His Life and Labors* (1964), 481, 545-546.

Americas before the flood. Noah's ark apparently landed in the Middle East; however, and his descendants began to spread out from that area.

Once again we see the hand of the Lord involved with his children as he guided the righteous Jaredites back to the Americas, which he repeatedly described as a "promised land, a land choice above all other lands." One of the Lord's stipulations was that the Americas be free from earthly kings. Jesus Christ would be the king. He warned each group that if they did not keep his commandments they would be destroyed. This has been borne out with the flood, the destruction of the Jaredites, the destruction of the wicked at the time of the crucifixion of the Savior and with the subsequent destruction of the Nephites at the hands of the Lamanites, and finally the destruction of the great Indian nations, tribes and kingdoms after their discovery by the Europeans. Scientists have estimated that within the first 150 years of the conquest more than 90 percent of the native Americans disappeared through wars, disease, famine, relocation, excessive forced labor, and melancholy.

It is also important to note that there were similar signs of wickedness prevalent in each civilization before it was destroyed. Pride, idolatry, immorality, and violence were the prime sins that plagued each civilization. The existence of idolatry was a clear indication that men had forgotten their true God and creator. They sought out and worshiped false gods, often degenerating into sacrificing other humans to these false gods. All three of our "voices from the dust" indicate that human sacrifice and frequently cannibalism was practiced by the groups before they disappeared. Pride and accumulation of great riches caused the societies to develop social classes. They were plagued by "secret combinations."

Archaeologists have discovered the use of a wide variety of narcotic substances and drug paraphernalia present at most archaeological digs. These seemed to have been used to create visions and revelations perhaps as substitutes for true visions and revelations received from Deity. The chroniclers were also scandalized by the amount of homosexual behavior they discovered and generally made a point of identifying which groups had deteriorated into "sodomy" or other forms of deviant sexual behavior.

How many of these "indicators which lead to destruction" do we have in our own societies? It is true that we do not have great stone altars, where men and women are thrown on their backs and their hearts cut out to satisfy our idol gods nor do we openly sacrifice children. However, thousands, perhaps millions, of children, God's children, are aborted each year because of our ignorance of God's purposes and our irresponsibility.

For many years the United States has been waging a losing war on drugs and spending billions of tax dollars to combat the effects of drugs, alcohol, and tobacco. The use or need for drugs today does not appear to be very different than it was 3,000 years ago. People still use drugs to have that false experience, to lose oneself, to convert oneself into that "jaguar that can leap high buildings or swim great rivers." It was a substitute for a true spiritual experience in ancient America and it is a substitute for a true spiritual experience now.

According to the Lord, violence destroyed the antediluvian civilizations. Will violence and terrorism destroy our current civilization? We see an increase of violence in our streets and we also see an increase in violence on an international level fomented by "secret combinations." In the *Book of Mormon*, Ether claimed that these "secret combinations," that were allowed to develop because the Jaredites forgot true gospel principles, essentially destroyed the great Jaredite civilization.

Mormon claimed that the Nephites had drifted so far away from living gospel principles that these "secret combinations" also greatly weakened the Nephite civilization so it could not withstand the onslaught of Lamanites. There are many kinds of "secret combinations" abroad in the world today. Certainly international terrorism is one form of a "secret combination." Organized crime and large narco-trafficking organizations are other forms of "secret combinations" that will have a serious impact upon the well-being of the world.

Jesus Christ repeatedly said that the nations which rise up in the Americas must be Christian nations and have as their king, the Savior himself, Jesus Christ. Our early forefathers recognized this and, as they created the United States of America, they frequently turned to the Lord for guidance and direction. Our motto became "In God We Trust." However, there are numerous movements within the United States to take God out of our culture. Do God-fearing people have the courage, the understanding, and the conviction to withstand the forces of atheism and agnosticism that threaten to undermine our reliance upon a loving Heavenly Father?

The *Book of Mormon* was preserved for hundreds of years to provide our generation with the understanding of and a testimony of Jesus Christ. This *"Second Witness of Jesus Christ,"* that was seen by many prophets, has been published for just this purpose. The *Book of Mormon* is meant to support, bolster and testify of the *Bible*. The primary role of the early-American chronicles and the findings of the archaeologists and art historians, the two other *"Voices from the Dust"* is to testify of the *Book of Mormon*. The day will come, when all men will realize, as Joseph Smith emphatically stated, "The *Book of Mormon* is the most correct of any book on earth, the keystone of our religion, and a man would get nearer to God by abiding by its precepts, than by any other book."[9]

---

[9] Smith, *History of the Church*, Vol. 4:451.

Appendix A

For many years, Church archaeologists and historians have attempted to retrace the footsteps of Lehi through what is believed to be the Arabian desert. It is generally accepted that Lehi's family traveled from Jerusalem down the east side of the Red Sea. Dr. Hugh Nibley traced the approximate route based on geography and clues in the text of the *Book of Mormon* and decided that when Lehi's group turned east they followed approximately along the 19th parallel which would have taken them across some of the worst desert in Arabia. On that route they would have avoided the heavily traveled and dangerous spice routes as well as the densely populated Kingdom of Saba (now Yemen). An easterly direction would have brought them into the Qara Mountain region of the south Arabian desert.

The most serious investigation to date to follow Lehi's route and to discover the legendary Bountiful has been the efforts carried out by two Australians: Warren P. Aston and Michaela Knoth Aston in connection with the Foundation for Ancient Research and Mormon Studies (F.A.R.M.S.), at Brigham Young University in Provo, Utah.[1]

Using a 1763 German map of southern Arabia, they discovered a site called Nehhm which sounds similar to the site Nahom, where Ishmael was buried and where Lehi turned eastward. A modern Yemeni map identified the site as Nehem. They

---

[1] Warren P. Aston & Michaela Knoth Aston, *In the Footsteps of Lehi, New Evidence for Lehi's Journey across Arabia to Bountiful*, (Deseret Book company, Salt Lake City, Utah, 1994.)

soon discovered that the Hebrew word NHM with variants Nehem, Nihm, Nahm is not found as a place name anywhere else in Arabia. They learned that in the Hebrew language NHM or Nahom means to comfort or console.

During their investigation, the Astors learned that the area in question belonged to the Nihm tribe which had been in that area since ancient times. An ancient burial ground was found in the hills of Nehem by a French archaeological team that has worked in the area many years and the archaeologists informed the Astons that the circular rock tombs there may date to 3000 B.C. or earlier.[2] The Astons also discovered that the great spice trade route which anciently passed within a few miles of Nehem also turned east there heading towards the Hadhramaut coast and the ancient port of Qana.

Using Nehem as the pivotal point, the Astons turned their attention to the Arabic coastal region, directly east of Nehem, which would likely place the valley Bountiful where Lehi's family launched its ship in Oman not far from the Yemeni border. The Astors soon discovered that very little is known even today about the history of the Arabian coast. Most of the coastal areas in Yemen and southern Oman have never been visited by scientists of any discipline.

The Astors explored several possible sites along the Arabian coast, but discarded each because the site did not meet the criteria described by Nephi. They finally discovered a site virtually unknown to the outside world for more than 160 years after the Book of Mormon was published. It is the Wadi Sayq (River Valley) in Oman. The Wadi Sayq is a valley some 16 miles long leading from the desert to the ocean on the Qamar coast. The coastal mouth of this valley, Khor Kharfot, is the most fertile coastal location on the Arabian Peninsula with abundant freshwater, large trees, fruit, and vegetation.

---

[2]Ibid., 19. Interview with Remy Audoin, centre Français d'Etudes Yemenites, Sana'a, October 1987.

This area has been hidden from the outside world and little is known about the area within Oman today. They found large timber trees such as sycamore and tamarind along the sides of the valley almost to the present shoreline. There is also an abundance of date palms which may be the fruit found in the valley mentioned by Nephi. The high mountains which surround the valley effectively isolate it from surrounding areas. The Astors discovered the remains of ancient ruins of a small settlement which they intend to investigate with a team of archaeologists once permission is given by the Omani government. The only access anciently was by boat or a long tortuous trip overland to the mouth of the Wadi.

Appendix B

Although space will not permit a full historical treatment of Joseph Smith and the development and expansion of The Church of Jesus Christ of Latter-day Saints, a brief synopsis of the early history is needful to better understand the role of the Prophet Joseph.

The Church was officially organized on 6 April 1830 in Fayette, New York. By this time, there were ardent followers of Joseph in the Palmyra and Colesville, New York, areas. Missionaries were soon dispatched to various other areas in the eastern United States.

In September 1830, Joseph received revelations in which Oliver Cowdery and Peter Whitmer, Jr. were instructed to go on a mission to teach the "Lamanites" (Indians) in the west.

Before these two men started west, the Prophet Joseph received a revelation that Parley P. Pratt and Ziba Peterson were to accompany them. The four men preached the "restored gospel" along the way. Near Kirtland, Ohio, they encountered numerous members of the Campbellite Church, followers of Alexander Campbell. Many of those people, including a few Campbellite ministers, joined The Church of Jesus Christ of Latter-day Saints at that time. One of the more notable converts was Sidney Rigdon. Before continuing their journey west, Cowdery and the others organized a small branch of the Church in the Kirtland area.

By December 1830, the opposition to Joseph Smith and the newly organized Church had increased substantially in New

York and the Lord instructed Joseph that he should stop the translation of the Bible until after he had moved to Ohio (D&C 37). On 2 January 1831, in another revelation (D&C 38), the Lord commanded Joseph to move to Ohio where the Lord would give Joseph "my law; and there you will be endowed with power from on high." Joseph, Emma and a few followers transferred to Kirtland in late January 1831. There were already 100 members of the Church there.

Even while some of the Church members began to assemble at or near Kirtland, Joseph Smith was sending pairs of missionaries into the south and toward the western frontier. Joseph Smith, Sidney Rigdon, Martin Harris and several other members traveled to Missouri and met at Independence, Jackson County, Missouri, in mid-July 1831 with the missionaries and members who had also arrived at Independence.

On 20 July 1831, the Prophet Joseph received a revelation (D&C 57) in which the Lord designated Independence, Missouri, as the Biblically promised "City of Zion" and the land that the Lord had "appointed and consecrated" for the gathering of the saints or members of his Church. The members were commanded to begin to purchase land in Independence and the surrounding regions for their needs. God also instructed that a store and a printing office be established. Newly converted Mormons began to assemble at both Kirtland and Jackson County.[1] The site for the future "Temple of Zion" was selected at Independence.

Joseph Smith returned to Jackson County again in July 1832 to instruct the members who were gathering by the hundreds into that area. He remarked that he "transacted considerable

---

[1] B. H. Roberts and other historians have noted that in 1831 western Missouri was the western frontier of the United States. The Indian Nation was just across the Missouri River and outlaws and other riff-raff had assembled in the area because of its closeness to the Indian Nation that would enable the bandits to avoid the law by crossing the river.

business for the salvation of the Saints, who were settling among a ferocious set of mobbers, like lambs among wolves." The prophet admonished the Church members in Missouri to faithfully keep all of the commandments which they had received and to live up to all of the covenants they had made to support one another. He warned them that they would be severely chastened if they failed to be obedient.

Joseph returned to Kirtland in May 1832 where he remained overseeing the Church and translating the *Bible*. On 8 November 1832, Brigham Young and his brother Joseph Young arrived in Kirtland. Brigham Young was baptized into the Church in Mendon, New York, in March 1832. Upon arriving in Kirtland, Brigham Young sought out the prophet. In his own words, Brigham wrote in his journal:

> Here my joy was full at the privilege of shaking the hand of the Prophet of God, and receiving the sure testimony, by the spirit of prophecy, that he was all that any man could believe him to be as a true prophet.

Brigham Young became one of Joseph Smith's staunchest supporters and eventually became the president of the Quorum of the Twelve Apostles and three years after the martyrdom of Joseph, he became the second president of the Church. Brigham Young gained fame by leading the Latter-day Saints to the Rocky Mountains in 1847.

In May 1833, Joseph Smith received a revelation (D&C 94) in which the Lord commanded the Saints in Kirtland to begin building a temple. The cornerstones for the temple were laid on 23 July 1833 and after great sacrifice the Kirtland Temple was completed and dedicated on 27 March 1836. It was a magnificent structure at that time, considering the impoverished nature of the Mormons.

In early April 1833, the anti-Mormon forces, which Joseph described as a mob, met to plan the destruction of the Mormons in Jackson County, Missouri. In July, the anti-Mormon forces published a "Manifesto" or Secret Constitution in which they bound themselves together to carry out their objective of ridding their community of Mormons. A few excerpts from the "Manifesto" will suffice to present the general flavor of their feelings towards the Mormons:

> We, the undersigned, citizens of Jackson county, believing that an important crisis is at hand, as regards our civil society, in consequence of a pretended religious sect of people that have settled, and are still settling in our county, styling themselves "Mormons;" and intending, as we do, to rid our society, "peacefully if we can, forcibly if we must," and believing as we do, that the arm of the civil law does not afford us a guarantee, or at least a sufficient one, against the evils which are now inflicted upon us, and seem to be increasing, by the said religious sect, deem it expedient, and of the highest importance, to form ourselves into a company for the better and easier accomplishments of our purpose—a purpose which we deem it almost superfluous to say, is justified as well by the law of nature as by the law of self-preservation.[2]

There are many factors which caused friction between the Missourians and the Mormons. The Mormons were gathering in Missouri in ever increasing numbers and began buying up all the available land. The Missourians feared that soon the Mormons would outnumber the Missourians and, if they voted as a block, would soon control many of the local offices. They were seen as religious fanatics who proclaimed that God had given them the area around Jackson County as a "New Zion." Their industrious ways were quickly making them more prosperous than the less industrious Missourians.

Most of the Mormons were from the northeast United States and were opposed to slavery. At that time, most of the

---

[2]See the entire Manifesto in *History of the Church*, Vol. 1:374-376.

APPENDIX B 531

Missourians were from the southern states who favored slavery. The Missourians feared that Mormons were abolitionists and would exercise their power to eliminate slavery in Missouri. Greed and religious bigotry were also important factors as ministers from other churches urged the Missourians to attack the Mormons and drive the "heretics" from the state.

On 20 July 1833, the mob attacked the Mormon leaders in Jackson County. The office of the printing press was demolished with the press, type and important papers destroyed. Several of the Church leaders were beaten, tarred and feathered.[3] The Lieutenant Governor of the State of Missouri, Lilburn W. Boggs, was present and secretly aided the mobsters. Further destruction was averted when the Mormons agreed to relocate out of Jackson County at the first opportunity, which was considered to be the spring of 1834; however, they refused to sell their property which they believed the Lord had commanded them to purchase for the city of Zion.

The Mormons quickly sent appeals to the governor of Missouri that their freedom of religion and the freedom to hold property, which they had bought from the United States Government, be respected. On 1 November 1833, mob elements again struck isolated settlements of Church members. Men, women and children were driven from their homes into freezing weather and forced to walk more than 20 miles to find shelter in a neighboring county. The exiles lost most of their furniture, clothing, and farm animals, and their crops were destroyed. Joseph recorded that Lieutenant Governor Boggs was the main force behind the mob attacks.[4]

On 16 December 1833, Joseph Smith received a revelation (D&C 101) in which the Lord explained that he had allowed the abuse of the Mormons in Missouri because of their disobedi-

---

[3] The practice of applying hot tar to the naked skin and then covering it with feathers was a popular form of injuring and humiliating one's foes in the 19th Century.
[4] *History of the Church*, Vol. 1:437.

ence. The Lord promised that his indignation would eventually fall upon the persecutors and that Zion would eventually be redeemed. He reminded the Mormons that he had inspired the framers of the Constitution of the United States to establish fair laws that would protect his people and the Lord instructed Joseph Smith to have the Church members in Missouri appeal to the governor of Missouri and if that was insufficient to appeal to the Federal government to obtain redress.

In spite of the numerous difficulties with the Missourians, Mormons continued to move into that state in areas other than Jackson County. The Jackson County mob elements were not content to drive the Mormons from just their county. Disgruntled Jackson County residents began to stir up trouble among the somewhat sympathetic Missourians in neighboring counties. In February 1834, Joseph Smith received a revelation from the Lord directing him to organize a large force from Kirtland and the eastern states to travel to Missouri and help the beleaguered Church members there. This body of volunteers became known as Zion's Camp. They departed Kirtland on 5 May 1834, carrying food, clothing, seeds and other provisions.

Zion's Camp traveled about 900 miles. Approximately 180 men arrived in western Missouri on 23 June 1834. Zion's Camp was not successful in restoring the impoverished saints back on their lands in Jackson County nor in redeeming Zion; however, the willingness of most of the men in Zion's Camp to obey the Lord received his approbation. Zion's Camp was disbanded on 25 June 1834 and the men split into small groups and returned to Kirtland by different routes, preaching and baptizing along the way.

On 14 February 1835, the Quorum of the Twelve Apostles was organized. Most of the individual members of the Quorum were selected and ordained Apostles by the three Special Witnesses of the Book of Mormon. The Quorum of the

Seventies was also organized. Most of the Twelve and most of the Seventy had been part of Zion's Camp. In D&C 107:24, the Lord revealed that the Twelve Apostles would hold equal authority with the First Presidency of the Church. Consequently, when the President of the Church dies, the Quorum of the Twelve Apostles then assumes control of the Church and oversees the Church until the First Presidency is reorganized.[5]

On 2 November 1836, the members in Kirtland attempted to organize a banking institution, to be called the Kirtland Safety Society. Although many members put their money into the Kirtland Safety Society, it could not obtain a banking charter from the state of Ohio and ultimately failed.

Joseph observed in his history in late May 1837 the following:

> At this time the spirit of speculation in lands and property of all kinds, which was so prevalent throughout the whole nation, was taking deep root in the Church. As the fruits of this spirit, evil surmisings, fault-finding, disunion, dissension, and apostasy followed in quick succession, and it seemed as though all the powers of earth and hell were combining their influence in an especial manner to overthrow the Church at once, and make a final end.[6]

Some Church members, even high ranking ones, blamed Joseph Smith for the bank failure, believing that as a prophet he should have foreseen the financial crisis and warned them.

---

[5] In the Church government, when the President of the Church dies, the senior Apostle is then selected to become the President of the Church and a new Apostle is chosen to ensure that there are always twelve men in the Quorum of the Twelve.

[6] B. H. Roberts added a footnote to Joseph Smith's *History* in which he pointed out that the financial maelstrom in which the Kirtland Safety Society met disaster was national and not merely local. There was a wide-spread financial panic of 1837. Soon after Martin Van Buren became President there was a great commercial crisis. This was in April 1837 and was occasioned by a reckless spirit of speculation, which had, for two or three preceding years, been fostered and encouraged by excessive banking, and the consequent expansion of paper currency beyond all the legitimate wants of the country.

Joseph claimed that he had strenuously cautioned the Church members to avoid the schemes that proved their undoing.

During the next two years, opposition to the Church in the Kirtland area began to grow. Some of this was brought about by non-members, but most of the problems were created by members who had left the Church for sundry reasons. Joseph claimed that he repeatedly warned the leaders as well as the members to discern between the evil spirit prevalent during that time and the righteous spirit that they had experienced during the days leading up to the Temple dedication and at the dedication itself.

Joseph reported that many Church leaders began taking sides and secretly met with the enemies of the Church. Martin Harris became embittered over the financial problems that beset the saints in Kirtland and he left the Church. Oliver Cowdery and David Whitmer were both excommunicated from the Church in Missouri for disobedience. Although these three witnesses of the *Book of Mormon* left the church, they never renounced their testimony of seeing the Angel Moroni nor of handling the gold plates.

During this time of great upheaval within the Church, Joseph Smith sent the first missionaries to the British Isles under the leadership of Heber C. Kimball. These newly arrived missionaries experienced great success as literally thousands of new converts joined the Church in England, Scotland and Wales. In the meantime, the members in Missouri were looking for more suitable areas to purchase land north of the Missouri River. They purchased land in Caldwell, Daviess and Ray Counties. Far West in Caldwell County became the center where most of the members settled.

Under an increase of mob violence, Joseph Smith, Sidney Rigdon and their families left Kirtland on 12 January 1838 for Far West, Missouri. Joseph began dictating his *History of the Church* on 27 April 1838. Joseph Smith was not in Missouri for many months before problems erupted. When a few Church members, living near Gallatin, Daviess County, went to vote, they were prevented from voting and a fight broke out between the members and the Missourians. Many ministers of other churches supported and encouraged the anti-Mormon forces. The ministers argued that the Missourians could recover the lands they had previously sold to the Mormons and keep the money already received by driving the Mormons out of the state. The ministers and other leaders of the mobs assured their followers that the government would not interfere.

The situation deteriorated between the Mormons and many of the old Missouri settlers. Not only did the state government refuse to help the Mormons, but on 28 October 1838, the newly elected Governor Lilburn Boggs issued his infamous Extermination Orders. Governor Boggs stated, "The Mormons must be treated as enemies and must be exterminated or driven from the state, if necessary for the public good." Local militia commanders were authorized to include the mob elements as members of the militias. The Mormon villages were raided by hundreds of mob/militia forces. Their homes and crops were destroyed, women raped, and many men, women, and children killed.

The worst incident occurred at Haun's Mill on 30 Oct 1838 when 240 heavily armed men attacked this small village of about 60 Mormons. The women and children attempted to flee into the woods, but most of the men stayed to defend the village from inside a blacksmith shop. The logs were too far apart to provide adequate protection and about 20 men were killed by gunfire through the gaps between the logs. Two 10-year old boys were also killed. One of the boys was alive when he was discovered by an attacker who fired into the boy's head at close range.[7] After

---

[7] *History of the Church*, Vol. 3:182-186. Joseph Smith used the signed affidavit of Joseph Young, the brother of Brigham Young and a member of the First Presidency of the Seventies, for the historical narrative of the events at Haun's Mill. There are numerous accounts of the massacre of Haun's Mill written by the survivors.

this attack, most of the Latter-day Saints assembled at Far West for protection.

On 31 October 1838, Missouri state militia forces amassed to attack Far West. Under a flag of truce, Joseph Smith, his brother Hyrum and several Church leaders were induced by the head of the Mormon militia, Lt. Colonel George M. Hinkle, to meet with the commanding officer of the Missouri state militia. As soon as Joseph and his party were in the hands of the state militia, they were arrested. Major General Samuel D. Lucas, commander of the militia forces opposing the Mormons, ordered Brig. General A.W. Doniphan to publically execute Joseph and the other captured leaders. General Doniphan refused the order and told Lucas that he would hold Lucas legally responsible if Lucas murdered Joseph and the others.[8]

On 3 November 1838, Joseph Smith and his companions were marched towards Richmond for trial. Parley P. Pratt recorded that at the beginning of this march, Joseph Smith cheerfully whispered to his companions the following words of consolation: "Be of good cheer, brethren; the word of the Lord came to me last night that our lives should be given us, and that, whatever we may suffer during this captivity, not one of our lives shall be taken."[9] The militia also gathered up all the weapons of the Mormon settlers. Once there was no danger of a retaliation, the mobs were then let loose on Far West. During their rampage, about 30 Mormon men were killed, nearly all of the animals were slaughtered or stolen and approximately 60 men were arrested and taken to Richmond.

---

[8] Flagrantly insubordinate as was General Doniphan's refusal, he was never called to account for it. The Mormons have always remembered General Doniphan's humanity on this occasion as well as on others and when, in 1873, he went to Salt Lake City, he was received warmly by Brigham Young and other authorities of the Church and State. *History of Caldwell County*, 137 as recorded in *History of the Church*, Vol 3:191.

[9] *History of the Church*, Vol 3:200. (*Autobiography of Parley P. Pratt*, 210.)

Appendix B

While the Prophet Joseph, Sidney Rigdon, Parley P. Pratt and other Mormon leaders were imprisoned at Richmond, Missouri, awaiting a trial or execution, the prison guards constantly heaped abuse upon them and spoke in a vulgar and foul language. Parley P. Pratt related an incident that occurred in the jail which provided insights to Joseph Smith under duress:

> In one of those tedious nights, we had lain as if in sleep till the hour of midnight had passed, and our ears and hearts had been pained, while we had listened for hours to the obscene jests, the horrid oaths, the dreadful blasphemies and filthy language of our guards, Colonel Price at their head, as they recounted to each other their deeds of rapine, murder, robbery, etc., which they had committed among the "Mormons" while at Far West and vicinity. They even boasted of defiling by force wives, daughters and virgins, and of shooting or dashing out the brains of men, women and children. I had listened till I became so disgusted, shocked, and horrified, and so filled with the spirit of indignant justice that I could scarcely refrain from rising upon my feet and rebuking the guards; but had said nothing to Joseph, or anyone else, although I lay next to him and knew he was awake. On a sudden he arose to his feet, and spoke in a voice of thunder, or as the roaring lion, uttering, as nearly as I can recollect, the following words:
>
> "Silence, ye fiends of the infernal pit! In the name of Jesus Christ I rebuke you, and command you to be still; I will not live another minute and hear such language. Cease such talk, or you or I die this instant!"
>
> He ceased to speak. He stood erect in terrible majesty. Chained, and without a weapon; calm, unruffled and dignified as an angel, he looked upon the quailing guards, whose weapons were lowered or dropped to the ground; whose knees smote together, and who, shrinking into a corner, or crouching at his feet, begged his pardon, and remained quiet till a change of guards.
>
> I have seen the ministers of justice, clothed in magisterial robes, and criminals arraigned before them, while life was suspended on a breath, in the courts of England; I have witnessed a Congress in solemn session to give laws to nations; I have tried to conceive of kings, of royal courts, of thrones and crowns; and of emperors assembled to decide the fate of kingdoms; but dignity and majesty have I seen but once, as it stood in chains, at midnight in a dungeon, in an obscure village in Missouri.[10]

---

[10] *History of the Church*, 208. (Autobiography of Parley P. Pratt, 228-230.)

Joseph and the others were charged with treason and murder. During the trial in Richmond, the state paraded a wide list of non-Mormons and a few former Mormons before the judge. No active Church members were allowed to testify. All of the prisoners except Joseph and his brother Hyrum, Sidney Rigdon, Parley P. Pratt and seven others were released. Joseph, Hyrum, Sidney, and three others were transferred to the jail in Liberty, Missouri. Parley and five others were kept in a jail in Richmond.

In the meantime, Brigham Young and other Church leaders began to arrange the departure of the Mormons from Missouri during the cold winter months. The initial group, including Emma Smith and her children, left Far West on 6 February 1839. The exiles escaped Missouri, crossing the Mississippi River near the city of Quincy, Illinois, where they were kindly received. It is estimated that between 12,000 and 14,000 Mormons were expelled from Missouri under the "Extermination Order."

After languishing months in prison under extremely adverse conditions and without being convicted of any charges, Joseph Smith and his fellow prisoners in Liberty Jail were transferred to Daviess County. On 16 April 1839, during a subsequent transfer to Boone County, the sheriff and the guards provided horses for the prisoners and then proceeded to get drunk, thus enabling the prophet and his companions to escape.

On 22 April 1839, Joseph and his party arrived safely in Quincy. While in Liberty Jail, Joseph received and recorded two significant revelations on coping with adversity and on the righteous use of Priesthood powers. Joseph also narrated that he was sentenced to die on at least three different occasions, but was spared by the providential hand of God.[11]

---

[11]On 4 July 1839, Parley P. Pratt made his escape from his Missouri jail and finally the Missourians released all the other Mormons. None of the captured men perished as predicted by Joseph Smith.

Appendix B

In May 1839, Joseph and his family moved to a small settlement known as Commerce, Illinois, which was nestled in a broad curve of the Mississippi River. He counseled the other members to move there as well. Although Commerce was located on a beautiful bend in the Mississippi River, the swamps on the river bank posed a health hazard and there were few buildings or homes in the area. Most of the Mormons lived in the open or in tents when they initially arrived. Joseph subsequently renamed Commerce and the immediate vicinity as Nauvoo, which he explained was a Hebrew word which meant "a beautiful place." Joseph also sent some of the members to live at Montrose on the Iowa side of the river.

The area around Nauvoo was infested with mosquitos. Because of extreme poverty and extended exposure to the elements during the flight from Missouri, hundreds of Mormons fell victim to a variety of illnesses. Wilford Woodruff wrote in his autobiography:

> In consequence of the persecutions of the Saints in Missouri, and the exposures in which they were subjected, many of them were taken sick soon after their arrival at Commerce; and as there was but a small number of dwellings for them to occupy, Joseph had filled his house and tent with them, and through constantly attending to their wants, he soon fell sick himself. After being confined to his house several days, and while meditating upon his situation, he had a great desire to attend to the duties of his office. On the morning of 22 July 1839, he arose from his bed and commenced to administer to the sick in his own house and door-yard, and he commanded them in the name of the Lord Jesus Christ to arise and be made whole; and the sick were healed upon every side of him.
>
> Many lay sick along the bank of the river; Joseph walked along up to the lower stone house, occupied by Sidney Rigdon, and he healed all the sick that lay in his path. Among the number was Henry G. Sherwood, who was nigh unto death. Joseph stood in the door of his tent and commanded him in the name of Jesus Christ to arise and come out of his tent, and he obeyed him and was healed. After healing all that were sick along side of the river, he called Elder Kimball and some others to accompany him across the river to visit

the sick at Montrose. Many of the saints were living at the old military barracks. Among the number were several of the Twelve. On his arrival, the first house he visited was that occupied by Elder Brigham Young, who lay sick. Joseph healed him, then Brigham arose and accompanied the Prophet on his visit to others who were in the same condition. They visited Elder Wilford Woodruff, Elder Orson Pratt, and Elder John Taylor.

The next place they visited was the home of Elijah Fordham, who was supposed to be about breathing his last. When the company entered the room, the Prophet of God walked up to the dying man and took hold of his right hand and spoke to him; but Brother Fordham was unable to speak, his eyes were set in his head like glass, and he seemed entirely unconscious of all around him. Joseph held his hand and looked into his eyes in silence for a length of time. A change in the countenance of Brother Fordham was soon perceptible to all present. His sight returned, and upon Joseph asking him if he knew him, he, in a low whisper, answered "Yes." Joseph asked him if he had faith to be healed. He answered, "I fear it is too late; if you had come sooner I think I would have been healed." The Prophet said "Do you believe in Jesus Christ?" He answered in a feeble voice, "I do." Joseph then stood erect, still holding his hand in silence several moments; then he spoke in a very loud voice, saying, "Brother Fordham, I command you, in the name of Jesus Christ, to arise from this bed and be made whole." His voice was like the voice of God and not man. It seemed as though the house shook to its very foundations. Brother Fordham arose from his bed, and was immediately made whole.[12]

The Mormons soon began to dig ditches in an effort to drain the swamps.[13] The Church purchased large tracts of land in and

---

[12] *History of the Church*, Vol 4, 4. (Initially included in Wilfred Woodruff's book, *Leaves from my Journal*, Ch X!X.)

[13] Medical science had not yet linked the mosquito to the spread of malaria, dengue, and yellow fever which were some of the diseases that plagued the Mormons. (In the late 1800's, the Frenchman, Count Fernando de Lesseps, who previously built the Suez Canal, attempted to build a canal across Panama, but mosquito related sicknesses killed so many workers that their efforts ended in failure after 20 years. In the early 1900's the U.S. Army Corps of Engineers, under the capable medical instruction of Colonel William Crawford Gorgas, a medical doctor who recognized that mosquitos were the carriers, dug ditches and drained the swamps in Panama. With the use of newly discovered pesticides, Gorgas was able to eradicate or lessen the mosquito-borne plagues thus enabling the U.S. forces to complete the construction of the canal in 1914. *El Canal de Panama, 50 Aniversario–1914-1964*.)

around Nauvoo and Joseph laid out a city plan. As thousands of Mormons moved into the city and surrounding areas, western Illinois became a hive of activity. In September 1839, Brigham Young and other members of the Quorum of the Twelve Apostles left for missions to the British Isles where thousands more were converted to the Church. On 29 October 1839, Joseph Smith and Sidney Rigdon left for Washington, D. C. in a futile effort to gain the support of the President and Congress to obtain redress for their losses in Missouri. Joseph wrote disparagingly of his interview with President Martin Van Buren in these words:

> During my stay, I had an interview with Martin Van Buren, the President, who treated me very insolently, and it was with great reluctance he listened to our message, which, when he had heard, he said: *'Gentlemen, your cause is just, but I can do nothing for you. If I take up for you I shall lose the vote of Missouri.'* His whole course went to show that he was an office-seeker, that self-aggrandizement was his ruling passion, and that justice and righteousness were not part of his composition."[14]

After the experiences in Missouri, Joseph Smith wanted greater governmental protection for the gathering Church members. Taking advantage of existing laws of Illinois, he applied for a generous city charter that would give Nauvoo all powers not reserved for state and federal governments. On 16 December 1840, Illinois Governor Thomas Carlin signed perhaps the most powerful city charter that had been granted in Illinois. In addition to ample powers delegated to the city government, the Nauvoo Charter also allowed the city to organize its own militia and to establish a university. Governor Carlin also commissioned Joseph Smith as a Lt. General in the Nauvoo Legion. There was no military officer in Illinois who held a higher rank. By 1843,

---

[14]Smith, *History of the Church*, Vol 4:40, 80.

the Nauvoo Legion had 3,000 members under arms. Also by 1843, Nauvoo was one of the largest cities in Illinois, rivaling Chicago in population.

During the Nauvoo period, Joseph Smith was continually plagued by efforts of the Missourians to get him back into Missouri to execute him. In June 1841, the governor of Missouri sent a request to the governor of Illinois requesting that Joseph Smith be arrested and sent to Missouri to stand trial. Upon his arrest, Joseph obtained a *writ of habeas corpus* and appeared before Judge Stephen A. Douglas, who had been appointed as a justice of the Illinois Supreme Court and a judge of the Fifth Judicial Circuit Court of Illinois. After hearing the prosecutor and the defense, Judge Douglas concluded that the writ was invalid. The governor of Missouri would have to issue a new one.

In spite of the adversity, new members flocked to the Church. In one four month period in the British Isles more than 1,300 new converts were baptized. Branches were organized throughout the United States. Every month the newly baptized converts from England arrived at New Orleans and proceeded up the Mississippi to Nauvoo.

On one occasion, Joseph Smith told a gathering of Mormon women that,

> Insomuch as the Lord Almighty has preserved me until today, he will continue to preserve me, by the united faith and prayers of the Saints, until I have fully accomplished my mission in this life, and so firmly established the dispensation of the fullness of the priesthood in the last days, that all the powers of earth and hell could never prevail against it.[15]

Joseph Smith had reason to be concerned about his welfare as no less than the governor of Missouri, Thomas Reynolds, again sent a petition in early January 1843 to Thomas Ford, the

---
[15] Ibid., Vol 5:139-140.

APPENDIX B 543

governor of Illinois, to have Joseph arrested and delivered to Missouri to stand trial for conspiracy in the attempted murder of Lilburn W. Boggs, the former governor. Although Boggs never saw his assailant, he assumed that Joseph Smith was somehow involved. Governor Reynolds accused Joseph of being a fugitive from justice in Missouri. Once again, the Circuit Court at Springfield, Illinois, found in favor of the prophet.

Thwarted in his attempts to get his hands on Joseph, Governor Reynolds arranged to have Joseph arrested and forcefully taken to Missouri. When the sheriff of Jackson County, Missouri, in company with a constable from Carthage, Illinois, managed to arrest Joseph in Dixon, Illinois, in June 1843, Joseph prophesied that they would not be successful in taking him illegally to Missouri. As the events played out, Joseph was taken before a judge in Illinois and released once again. Joseph later commented that he had been the target of 38 law suits because of his religion and all of the law suits against him had been in vain.[16]

Josiah Quincy, who later became the mayor of Boston and was a member of the noted Massachusetts family that produced John Quincy Adams, visited Nauvoo in 1844 where he interviewed the prophet and observed Nauvoo society. He took copious notes and in 1883 published a book entitled *Figures of the Past* in which he dedicated a chapter to Joseph Smith. Quincy began this chapter with a prophecy of sorts which must have surprised his readers of the day:

> It is by no means improbable that some future text-book, for the use of generations yet unborn, will contain a question some like this: What historical American of the nineteenth century has exerted the most powerful influence upon the destinies of his countrymen? And it is by no means impossible that the answer to that interrogatory may be thus written: *Joseph Smith, the Mormon Prophet*. And the

---

[16]Ibid. Vol 5:518.

reply, absurd as it doubtless seems to most men now living, may be an obvious commonplace to their descendants.

Born in the lowest ranks of poverty, without book learning and with the homeliest of all human names, he had made himself at the age of thirty-nine a power upon earth. Of the multitudinous family of Smith ... none had so won human hearts and shaped human lives as this Joseph. His influence, whether for good or for evil, is potent today, and the end is not yet.[17]

As the United States contemplated the presidential elections of 1844, Joseph Smith wrote to the leading presidential candidates to ascertain their feelings towards righting the wrongs committed by Missouri against the Mormons. J. C. Calhoun, Senator from South Carolina, replied that "candor compels me to repeat what I said to you at Washington, that, according to my views, the case does not come within the jurisdiction of the Federal Government, which is one of limited and specific powers."[18] Joseph wrote a scathing rebuttal demonstrating what he believed was the folly of Calhoun's assertion that the government of the United States had less power than the individual states.

When no candidate presented a viable option to obtain justice for the Mormons, Church members drafted Joseph Smith as their candidate for president. Joseph's candidacy created considerable stir. The *Illinois Springfield Register* applauded his forthright support for a national bank and a protective tariff and deplored presidential candidate Henry Clay's vacillation. The *Iowa Democrat* stated: "if superior talent, genius, and intelligence, combined with virtue, integrity, and enlarged views, are any guarantee to General Smith's being elected, we think that he will be a 'full team of himself'." The *Missouri Republican* expressed its view that Joseph Smith's candidacy would be the death of Martin Van Buren, and all agreed that it would be injurious to the

---

[17]Ibid., Vol 6:3, footnote only.
[18]Ibid., Vol 6:156.

Democratic ranks. In June 1844, the Democrats dropped Van Buren as a candidate and substituted James K. Polk.

In addition to the problems in Missouri, there was increasing opposition within Illinois to Joseph Smith and the Mormons. The rapid growth of the Church in and around Nauvoo, with its apparent prosperity, created envy and a certain political fear that the Mormons would vote as a block and totally dominate the local political scene. The non-Mormon sentiment was compounded with the overt threats from former Mormons. On 10 June 1844, as the mayor of Nauvoo, Joseph attended a Nauvoo City Council meeting during which the City Council investigated the merits of a new anti-Mormon newspaper, *The Nauvoo Expositor*, published by apostate Church members. The City Council declared the newspaper to be a nuisance because of its slanderous verbiage and ordered it to be destroyed.

The destruction of the *Nauvoo Expositor* gave Joseph's enemies the ammunition they needed to rally the anti-Mormon forces both in Illinois and Missouri and to mount one final campaign against the prophet. Joseph alleged that Governor Ford accepted unquestioningly the version of the events from the anti-Mormon forces and refused to meet with or hear the version of the Nauvoo City Council.

Ford sent a letter to Joseph denouncing the activities of the Nauvoo City Council and informing him that he was sending a posse to arrest and escort him to Carthage, Illinois, the county seat. After reading the letter, Joseph said that the governor would offer no mercy. Hyrum pessimistically concluded that if they fell into the hands of the mob, they would be killed. Joseph concluded that the mob and the governor were only seeking Joseph and Hyrum and that the rest should go about their business because none of them would be bothered. He decided that he and Hyrum would flee west into Iowa or even farther.

On Saturday 22 June 1844, Joseph and Hyrum crossed the Mississippi River into Iowa. On 23 June several friends implored them not to leave. Others, not so friendly, accused Joseph of cowardice and of fleeing the area, leaving the members to contend with the mob. After studying the situation, the prophet announced that if he returned, they would be butchered. Nevertheless, he and Hyrum returned to Nauvoo and prepared to travel onto Carthage. As Joseph passed the not-yet-completed Nauvoo Temple, he remarked, "This is the loveliest place and the best people under the heavens; little do they know the trials that await them." Although Joseph and the Mormon leaders had been given Governor Ford's word of honor that they would not be jailed or mistreated, Joseph, Hyrum and several other Church leaders were illegally jailed in Carthage. Joseph Smith was charged with treason and arrested on 25 June 1844.

Joseph Smith argued that as a Lt. General in the Nauvoo Legion, he should only be tried by his peers; consequently, he noted that his arrest was illegal. When he was taken before Governor Ford, he requested permission to speak privately with Ford, but Ford refused to meet with him alone. Ford then dismissed all of the troops in and around Carthage who were there to protect Joseph and replaced them with militia known as the Carthage Greys, the group most violently opposed to Joseph and the Mormons.

While the opposition laid their plans to kill the prophet, Governor Ford traveled to Nauvoo on 27 June to chastise the Mormons. He took with him the troops who had been assigned to protect the prophet. At 5:00 p.m., a mob with faces covered with mud, stormed the Carthage Jail and shot and killed first Hyrum and then Joseph. John Taylor was also wounded with four balls. The other occupant of the jail, Willard Richards, was miraculously not hit.

After the death of Joseph Smith, the opponents to the Church fully expected the Church to fold and dismantle without the leadership of the charismatic Joseph. There was a brief period of confusion because many of the senior apostles were away from Nauvoo. Sidney Rigdon, who had been a counselor in the First Presidency of the Church, attempted to gain control, but when Brigham Young returned to Nauvoo, as the President of the Quorum of the Twelve Apostles, he was accepted as the leader of the Church. Brigham Young accelerated finishing the construction of the Nauvoo Temple.

When opponents realized that the Church was not going to disband, but continued to increase in size as new members arrived from other states, Canada and Europe, persecution and harassment continued throughout the rest of 1844 and 1845. Mobs stepped up their attacks against small settlements outside Nauvoo and Church members and their animals were killed. Brigham Young proved to be a very effective organizer and during 1845, he urged the members to obtain wagons, oxen, food and seeds in order to leave for the west in the summer of 1846.

The persecution and threats to the members became so intense that in February 1846, the members began to leave Nauvoo and transfer to the Iowa side of the river. In what was described as a miraculous "deep freeze," the Mississippi River froze to the point that wagons and their teams could safely cross over the river on the ice.

Under the worst of circumstances, hundreds of member families departed Nauvoo and struggled across Iowa. The wagons finally reached the Missouri River at what is now Council Bluffs, near present Omaha, Nebraska, where they were forced to spend the winter of 1846-47. Exhaustion, exposure and disease killed hundreds of members. Brigham Young organized several temporary settlements across Iowa where a few members remained behind to help those leaving Nauvoo at later times. They had the foresight to plant crops that could be harvested by others coming behind.

In June 1846, representatives of the United States army arrived at Council Bluffs and requested 500 Mormon volunteers to join the army in the fight against Mexico. Although many voices among the members were raised in opposition to the departure of such a large contingency of men leaving behind families, Brigham Young counseled that it would be to the Mormons' favor to support the Federal Government. He promised the departing members of the "Mormon Battalion" that none of them would be killed in combat. The Mormon Battalion marched from Council Bluff back to Fort Leavensworth, Kansas, where the members were provided military equipment. It then marched across the territories of the south to Mexico and eventually on to San Diego, California. This march of the Mormon Battalion is considered to be one of the longest military marches in history.

Brigham Young and the rest of the exiles remained in the Omaha area and established a settlement, which they named Winter Quarters, until the spring of 1847 when Young and an advance group began the long march toward the Great Salt Lake Basin area more than 1,000 miles west. The Mormon pioneers entered the Salt Lake valley on 24 July 1847. Within days, the pioneers planted crops, laid out a city and selected a new temple site in Salt Lake City. As members poured into the Salt Lake valley from the east, he sent them on to build settlements throughout the area. He envisioned a mighty inland empire and sent settlers as far north as Canada and as far south as Mexico. Today historians consider Brigham Young as one of the greatest colonizers that ever lived.

For nearly three and a half years, Brigham Young presided over the Church in his capacity as the senior Apostle. It was not until 5 December 1847 that he was finally sustained as the

President of the Church. He also served as the Governor of the territory of Utah until once again the Federal Government intervened and insisted that Utah have a governor who was not also the President of the Church. He continued to send missionaries to other states as well as to foreign countries. These new converts trekked across the plains in long wagon trains or in hand-cart companies. When Brigham Young died on 29 August 1877, there were thousands of Church members located mainly in the Rocky Mountains.

During the ensuing years the Church continued to grow in both size as well as acceptance as a world recognized Church. As of 31 December 2004, there were more than 12 million members scattered throughout the world. Members are no longer encouraged to gather to a central place, but are encouraged to remain in their own countries and build the Church locally. Missionary work is still an important force contributing to the growth of the Church and at the end of 2004 there were more than 56,000 missionaries serving in more than 150 countries around the world.

The prophetic utterance of the Angel Moroni to Joseph Smith that "God had a work for him to do and that his name should be had for good and evil among all nations, kindreds, and tongues, or that it should be both good and evil spoken of among all people" has certainly come to pass (Joseph Smith–History. 1:33).

BIBLIOGRAPHY

ABRAMS, Harry N. *The Olmec World*, Published by the Art Museum, Princeton University with essays by Michael D. Coe, Richard A. Diehl, David A. Freidel, Peter T. Furst, F. Kent Reilly, III, Linda Schele, Carolyn E. Tate, Karl A. Taube. Forward and Acknowledgments by Allen Rosenbaum, Princeton, 1995.

ACOSTA, Joseph de. *Historia Natural y Moral de las Indias,* Initially written and published in 1590 in Seville. (Edition Prepared by Edmundo O'Gorman, professor in the College of Letters and Sciences in the National Autonomous University of Mexico. 1940, Mexico D.F.)

ALVA IXTLILXOCHITL, Fernando de. *Historia de la Nación Chichimeca*, (Original manuscript reportedly written between 1610 and 1640, but disappeared. Brought to light by Edmundo O'Gorman in 1975.) Current edition with Introduction and Notes by Germán Vázquez was published in Madrid by Historia 16, 1985.

ALVA, Walter and Christopher B. Donnan, *Royal Tombs of Sipán*, Fowler Museum of Cultural History, University of California, Los Angeles, 1993. 119-123.

ASTON, Warren P. & Aston, Michaela Knoth. *In the Footsteps of Lehi, New Evidence for Lehi's Journey across Arabia to Bountiful*, (Deseret Book Company, Salt Lake City, Utah, 1994.)

AVILA, Father Francisco de. *The Huarochiri Manuscript, A Testament of Ancient and Colonial Andean Religion*. (Reportedly compiled from information obtained while assigned to the Curate at Huarochirí in 1598.) This version was translated from Quechua by Frank Salomon and George L. Urioste. (Published by the University of Texas Press, Austin. 1991.)

BENAVENTURA DE SALINAS Y CORDOVA, Fray. *Memorial de las Historias del Nuevo Mundo, Lima.* Printed in Lima in 1630 by Geronymo de Contreras. (Current edition with Introduction by Luis E. Valcarcel and a study of the author by Warren L. Cook. Printed by Universidad Nacional Major de San Marcos, Lima. 1957.)

BEN ISRAEL, Menasseh. *Sobre el Orígen de los Americanos.* Published in Amsterdam in 1650. (Reprinted in Madrid in 1881. Reprinted by Editorial Plata S.A. 1974.)

BETANZOS, Juan de. *Suma y Narración de los Incas,* original manuscript completed in 1557, but not published until 1880. (Prologue, transcription, y notes by Maria del Carmen Martin Rubio; preliminary studies by Horacio Villanueva Urteaga, Demetrio Ramos and Maria del Carmen Martin Rubio). Madrid. 1987.

BETANZOS, Juan de. *Narrative of the Incas,* original manuscript completed in 1557, but not published until 1880. (Translated and edited by Roland Hamilton and Dana Buchanan), University of Texas Press, Austin. 1996.

BIBLE, Authorized King James Version with explanatory notes and cross reference to the Standard Works of The Church of Jesus Christ of Latter-day Saints. Published by The Church of Jesus Christ of Latter-day Saints. 1979.

BOLETIN MENSUAL DE LA ASOCIACIÓN ISRAELITA DE VENEZUELA. October 1972 Tishri - Jeshvan 5.733 - No. 29.

BOOK OF MORMON, Translated by Joseph Smith in 1829 and published on E. B. Grandin Press in 1830. Published by The Church of Jesus Christ of Latter-day Saints.

BRODIE, Fawn M. *No Man Knows My History, The Life of Joseph Smith,* (Copyright and published by Adolph A. Knopf, Inc., New York,1945) Revised and published by Adolph A. Knopf, Inc. in New York, 1971.

BURGER, Richard L. *Chavín and the Origins of Andean Civilization.* (Thames and Hudson Ltd, London. 1992.)

BUSH, Lester E. Jr. *The Spalding Theory, Then and Now.* Mormon Miscellaneous, Reprint Series. Originally appeared in *Dialogue: A Journal of Mormon Thought.* (Vol X, No. 4 Autumn 1977.)

BUSHMAN, Richard L. *Joseph Smith and the Beginnings of Mormonism.* (University of Illinois Press, Urbana and Chicago. 1988.)

CABELLO VALBOA, Miguel. *Miscelánea Antártica, Una Historia del Peru Antiguo.* Written in manuscript form in 1586. (Introduction and Notes by Luis E. Valcarcel. Published by the Universidad Nacional Mayor de San Marcos, Facultad de Letras, Instituto de Etnología, Lima 1951.)

CADOGAN, Leon. *Ayvu Rapyta—Textos Míticos de los Mbyá Guaraní del Guaira.* Boletim No. 227 - Antropologia, No. 5, São Paulo, Faculdade de Filosofia, Ciencias e Letras, 1959. (Second edition was edited by Bartomeu Melià and published by the Biblioteca Paraguaya de Antropología, Asunción, 1992.)

CIEZA DE LEON, Pedro de. *La Crónica del Peru.* Madrid, 1553. (Reprinted by Promoción Editorial Inca S.A. 1973.)

CIEZA DE LEON, Pedro de. *El Señorio de los Incas.* Madrid Circa 1553. Original manuscript was lost until 1880 when it was published by Marcos Jimenez de la Espada, Madrid. (Republished by the Instituto de Estudios Peruanos, Lima, 1967.)

CIEZA DE LEON, Pedro de. *Crónica del Perú, Tercera Parte.* Originally written in manuscript form in 1553-54. (Manuscript discovered in the Biblioteca Apostólica Vaticana and published by Pontificia Universidad Católica del Perú, 1987. Editing, prologue and notes by Francesca Cantù.)

Cobo, Father Bernabé. *History of the Inca Empire*, Written in manuscript form in 1653. First published in Spanish by Marcos Jimenez de la Espada between 1890-1893. (Translated and edited by Roland Hamilton from the holograph manuscript in the Biblioteca Capitular y Colombina de Sevilla. Foreword by John Howland Rowe. University of Texas Press, Austin, 1979.)

Colón, Cristóbal. *Diario de a Bordo*. Introduction, Appendix y Notes de Vicente Muñoz Puelles. (This Edition by El Grupo Anaya, S.A., Madrid, 1985.)

Cortés, Hernán. *Cartas de la Relación*, written between 1519 and 1526. (Edition of Mario Hernandez Sanchez-Barba, Professor of Contemporary History at the Universidad Complutense de Madrid, Printed by NILO, Industria Gráfica, Madrid, 1985.)

Díaz del Castillo, Bernal. *The Conquest of New Spain*, Written in the 1560's, but not published until 1632. (Translated with an Introduction by J. M. Cohen, Penguin Books, Great Britain, 1963.)

Diaz de Guzman, Ruy. *La Argentina*. Published in 1612 in Charcas, Argentina. Edition of Enrique de Gandia. (Reprinted by Hermanos Garcia Noblejas, Madrid. Historia 16)

Doctrine and Covenants, The. (Containing revelations given to Joseph Smith, the Prophet with some additions by his successors in the Presidency of the Church.) Partially published in Independence Missouri in 1833 under the title of *A Book of Commandments for the Government of the Church of Christ*. Later published in 1835 in Kirtland, Ohio, with current title.) Republished by The Church of Jesus Christ of Latter-day Saints in Salt Lake City, Utah, USA, 1981.

Donnan, Christopher B. and Donna McClelland, *The Burial Theme in Moche Iconography*, Dunbarton Oaks, Washington, D.C. 1979.

DURÁN, Diego. *The History of the Indies of New Spain*, originally written in 1581 but not found until 1850 and partially published in 1867. (Translated, Annotated, and with an Introduction by Doris Heyden. Published by University of Oklahoma Press. 1994.)

EDMONSON, Munro S. *The Ancient Future of the Itza, The Book of Chilam Balam of Tizimin,*. (Translated and annotated by Munro S. Edmonson, published by University of Texas Press, Austin, Texas. 1982.)

ERCILLA Y ZUÑIGA, Alonso de. *La Araucana*, published in parts between 1569 and 1589. Introduction by Ofelia Garza de Del Castillo. (Published by Editorial Porrua, S.A. in Mexico City, 1968.)

GARCIA COOK, Angel; Merino Carrion, Beatriz Leonor. *Antología de Cacaxtla*. Published under the auspices of the Mexican Instituto Nacional de Antropologia e Historia, Volumes I and II, Mexico, D.F. 1995.

GARCÍA, Fray Gregorio. *Origen del Nuevo Mundo e Indias Occidentales*, (First Edition 1607, Valencia). Preliminary study and notes by Franklin Pease, G. Y., Reedited by Fondo de Cultura Económica, México, 1981.

GARCILASO DE LA VEGA, Inca. *Comentarios Reales*. Volumes I, II, and III. Printed in Portugal in 1609. (Printed by Editorial Litografica, La Confianza S.A. Lima, Peru.)

GARCILASO DE LA VEGA, Inca. *The Florida of the Inca*, initial manuscript finished in 1599 and, subsequently, published in 1605 in Portugal under title *La Florida del Ynca. Historia del Adelantado Hernando de Soto, Governador y capitan general del Reyno de la Florida, y de otros heroicos cavalleros Españoles è Indios*. (Translated and Edited by John Grier Varner and Jeannette Johnson Varner from the 1723 Spanish edition published by Andrés González Barcia Carballido.) University of Texas Press, Austin. 1996.

HANSEN, L. Taylor. *He Walked the Americas.* (Amherst Press, Amherst, Wisconsin. 1963.)

HEMMING, John. *Red Gold, The Conquest of the Brazilian Indians,* (first published by Macmillan London, 1978)

HERNANDEZ, Francisco. *Antigüedades de la Nueva España,* written in manuscript form in 38 notebooks in 1576. Part of manuscript was published in Italy in 1648; part in 1790. (Current edition with Introduction and Notes by Ascención H. de León-Portilla was printed by Heroes, S.A. Madrid, 1986.)

HILL, Donna. *Joseph Smith, The First Mormon.* (Doubleday & Company, Garden City, New York. 1977.)

HUDDLESTON, Lee Eldridge. *Origins of the American Indians, European Concepts, 1492- 1729.* Published for the Institute of Latin American Studies by the University of Texas Press, Austin and London, 1967.

INSTITUTO DE CIENCIA DEL HOMBRE. *El Orígin Étnico de los Indios Blancos Guayakis de Paraguay.* (Buenos Aires. Circa 1960.)

KAUFFMANN DOIG, Federico. *Manual de Arqueología Peruana.* (Ediciones Peisa, Lima, Peru. 1969.)

LANCASTER, Charles Maxwell and Manchester, Paul Thomas. *The Araucaniad,* A version in English Poetry of Alonso de Ercilla y Zuñiga's *La Araucana.* (Published for Scarritt College, Peabody College and Vanderbilt University by Vanderbilt University Press, Nashville, Tennessee, 1945.)

LANDA, Father Diego de. *Relación de las Cosas de Yucatán,* Originally written in 1566. Manuscript discovered in 1864 by Abbé Brasseur de Bourbourg in the Academia de la Historia de Madrid. First published in 1864. Eighth Edition, translated and edited with notes by Alfred M. Tozzer. (Published by the Peabody Museum of American Archaeology and Ethnology, Harvard University, Published by the Museum. 1941.)

LAS CASAS, Bartolome de. *Brevísima Relación de la Destrucción de las Indias.* Originally published in 1542. (Republished by Información y Revistas, S.A. -Cambios 16, Hermanos García Noblejas, 41 - 28037 Madrid. 1992.)

LAS CASAS, Bartolomé de. *A Short Account of the Destruction of the Indies,* (Edited and Translated by Nigel Griffin with an Introduction by Anthony Pagden.) Published by Penguin Group, London, England, 1992.

LEONARD, Irving A. *Books of the Brave.* Originally published at Cambridge, Harvard University press, 1949. (Republished with a new Introduction by Rolena Adorno at University of California Press, Berkeley and Los Angeles. 1992.)

LOMBARDO DE RUIZ, Sonia, López de Molina, Diana, Molina Feal, Daniel, Baus de Czitrom, Carolyn, and Polaco, Oscar J. : *CACAXTLA, El Lugar Done Muere la Lluvia en la Tierra.* (Published under the auspices of the Mexican Instituto Nacional de Antropologia e Historia and the Government of the State of Tlaxcala. 1986.)

LÓPEZ DE GÓMARA, Francisco. *Historia General de las Indias,* (Initially written in 1552 in the city of Zaragoza.) Published by Espasa-Calpe, S.A., Barcelona, 1932.

LUMBRERAS, Luis Guillermo. *Los Templos de Chavín.* (Edited by the Corporación Peruana del Santa, 1970.)

MACCORMACK, Sabine. *Religion in the Andes, Vision and Imagination in Early Colonial Peru.* (Princeton University Press, Princeton, New Jersey, 1991.)

MAGALHÃES DE GANDAVO, Pero de. *The Histories of Brazil.* Translated into English and annotated by John B. Stetson, Jr. in 1921. (Published from the unabridged edition of 1922 by Longwood Press Ltd, Boston, 1978.)

MÁRTIR DE ANGLERIA, Pedro. *Décadas del Nuevo Mundo* (First published in partial form in 1516, First complete edition in Latin in 1530. The first Spanish Edition published in 1892.) Published in Buenos Aires, Argentina by Editorial Bajel with the Latin to Spanish translation of Dr. Joaquín Torres Asensio in 1944. Republished in Mexico City with Introduction and Notes by Edmundo O'Gorman by Jose Porrua e Hijos in 1964.

MARTIRE DE ANGHIERA, Pietro. *The Syxte Booke of the Fyrste Decade, to Cardinall of Aragonie.* Taken from the Third English Book on America. First printed in 1511 later translated into English by Richard Eden in June 1585.

MILLS, Kenneth. *Idolatry and Its Enemies: Colonial Andean Religion and Extirpation, 1640-1750.* (Princeton University Press, Princeton, New Jersey, 1997.)

MONTESINOS, Fernando de. *Memorias Antiguas Historiales y Políticas del Perú. Crónica del Siglo XVII,* Manuscript finished in 1642. First published in 1909. Notes and reconciliation with other Chronicles of the Indies by Horacio H. Urteaga, written 6 March 1930, Lima. (Published by Libreria e Imprenta Gil in Lima, 1930.)

MUÑOZ CAMARGO, Diego. *Historia de Tlaxcala,* original manuscript finished in approximately 1576. (First published with notations by Alfredo Chavero in 1892.) Current edition published by Editorial Innovación, S. A., Mexico D.F., Mexico 1978.

MURÚA, Martin de. *Historia General del Perú de los Orígenes al Último Inca.* Originally written in 1611 in Peru, but the manuscript was lost until 1950 when it was discovered in the collection of the Duke of Wellington. (Edited and annotated by Manuel Ballasteros Gabrois, Published by Informaciòn y Revistas, S.A., Hermanos García Noblejas, 41 - 28037 Madrid. Historia 16, 1986.)

NIBLEY, Hugh. *Lehi in the Desert; The World of the Jaredites; There Were Jaredites.* (Current edition published by Deseret Book Company, Salt Lake City, Utah, 1988.)

NICHOLSON, H. B. *Topilzin Quetzalcoatl, The Once and Future Lord of the Toltecs*. Published by the University of Colorado Press, Boulder, Colorado, 2001.

PAGDEN, Anthony. *The Fall of Natural Man, the American Indian and the Origins of Comparative Ethnology*. (Cambridge University Press, 1982. Printed in great Britain at the University press, Cambridge, 1982.)

PAGDEN, Anthony. *European Encounters with the New World, From Renaissance to Romanticism*. (Yale University Press, New Haven & London, 1993.)

PASTOR BODMER, Beatriz. *The Armature of Conquest, Spanish Accounts of the Discovery of America, 1492-1589*. (Published by Casa de Cuba, Havana, Cuba., 1983. Translated by Lydia Longstreth Hunt and republished by Stanford University Press, Stanford, California. 1992.)

PEARL OF GREAT PRICE, The. Contains the *Selections from the Book of Moses, The Book of Abraham*, and *Extracts from the History of Joseph Smith, The Prophet*. (First published in 1851 in England. Presented as Scripture by the First Presidency of the Church to the October 1880 General Conference) Published by The Church of Jesus Christ of Latter-day Saints in Salt Lake City, Utah, USA, 1981.

PHELAN, John Leddy. *The Millennial Kingdom of the Franciscans in the New World. A Study of the Writings of Gerónimo de Mendieta (1524-1604)*. (University of California Press, Berkeley and Los Angeles. 1956.)

PIZARRO, Pedro. *Relación del Descubrimiento y Conquista de Los Reinos del Perú*. Original manuscript presented in Arequipa, Peru on 28 March 1572. First printed in the late 1870's. (Current edition with notes and preliminary considerations by Guillermo Lohmann Villena and Pierre Duviols by Pontificia Universidad Catolica del Peru. 1986.)

POLO DE ONDEGARDO, Juan. *Informaciones Acerca de la Religión y Gobierno de los Incas, Volume III,* written in 1571 under instructions from the Council of Lima. (Biographic Notes and Concordance of the Text by Horacio H. Urteaga, Dean of The History of Civilization at the University of San Marcos, Lima, Peru. Printed in Lima, Peru 1916.)

POMA DE AYALA, Felipe Guaman. *Nueva Corónica y Buen Gobierno.* Original manuscript finished in 1615, but not discovered until 1908 by Richard Pietschmann and published in 1936. Transcription, Prologue, Notes y Chronology by Franklin Pease. (This edition was printed in Venezuela by Biblioteca Ayacucho Caracas, Venezuela. 1978.)

PONCE SANGINÉS, Carlos. *Tiwanaku Espacio, Tiempo y Cultura,* (Academia Nacional de Ciencias de Bolivia, Publicación No. 20, La Paz, 1972.)

PONCE SANGINÉS, Carlos. *Procedencia de las Areniscas Utilizadas en el Templo Precolombina de Puma-Punka (Tiwanaku),* Academia Nacional de Ciencias de Bolivia, Publicación No. 22, La Paz, 1971.

POPOL VUH. An ancient Maya Codex (Edition of Carmelo Saenz de Santa Maria, Historia 16, - Información y Revistas, S.A., Hermanos Garcia Noblejas, Madrid, 1988.)

POPOL VUH, (translated and edited by Allen J. Christenson.) Published by The Foundation for Ancient Research and Mormon Studies (FARMS), Provo, Utah, 2000.

PRESCOTT, William H. *Historia de la Conquista del Peru.* With preliminary observations about the civilization of the Incas. Originally written and published on 2 April 1847 in Boston. Translated from English by Nemesio Fernández Cuesta. (Ediciones Imán, Buenos Aires. 1943.)

QURAN, The. Arabic text with a new translation by Muhammad Zafrulla Khan. (Olive Branch Press, New York. 1991.)

BIBLIOGRAPHY 561

Rowe, John H. *CHAVIN ART—An Inquiry into Its Form and Meaning*, The Museum of Primitive Art, New York. (Distributed by University Publishers Inc., New York 1962)

Ruiz de Montoya, Antonio. *La Conquista Espiritual de Paraguay*. Edited in Madrid in 1639. (New Edition by the Equipo Disfusor de Estudios de Historia Iberoamericana, Entre Rios, Argentina. 1989.)

Sahagún, Fray Bernardino de. *A History of Ancient Mexico—The Religion and the Ceremonies of the Aztec Indians—1547-1577*. Translated by Fanny R. Bandelier from the Spanish version of Carlos Maria de Bustamante. (The Rio Grande Press, Inc., Glorieta, New Mexico. 1976.)

Sarmiento de Gamboa, Pedro. *Historia de los Incas*. Edition and Introduction by Angel Rosenblat. Manuscript finished in 1572. (First Spanish edition printed in 1942 by EMECÉ, S. A., Buenos Aires.)

Sarmiento de Gamboa, Pedro. *Viajes al Estrecho de Magallanes*. Collection of two documents: Document I written 17 Aug 1580 narrates Sarmiento de Gamboa's first trip; Document II was finished on 15 September 1590 and relates his adventures in setting up the colonies in the Straits of Magallanes. Introduction, transcription and notes by Maria Justina Sarabia Viejo. (Published by Alianza Editorial, Madrid 1988.)

Schele, Linda and Mathews, Peter. *The Code of Kings, the Language of Seven Sacred Maya Temples and Tombs*. (Scribner, New York, Copyright 1998.)

Schele, Linda and David Freidel, *A Forest of Kings, The Untold Story of the Ancient Maya*, Published by William Morrow and Cia, Inc. New York 1990

Shipps, Jan. *Mormonism, The Story of a New Religious Tradition*. (University of Illinois Press. 1987.)

SMITH, Ethan. *View of the Hebrews or Tribes of Israel in America* (Second Edition, Published and Printed in Poultney, Vt.) 1825.

SMITH, Joseph. *History of The Church of Jesus Christ of Latter-day Saints.* (A six volume work dictated by Joseph Smith to scribes from 1838 to 1844.) Copyrighted by George Albert Smith for The Church of Jesus Christ of Latter-day Saints 1951. An introduction and Notes by B. H. Roberts. Second Edition Revised and Published by the Deseret Book Company, Salt Lake City, Utah 1973.

SMITH, Joseph. *Teachings of the Prophet Joseph Smith*, Comp. Joseph Fielding Smith (Salt Lake City, Deseret Book, 1976)

SMITH, Lucy Mack. *History of Joseph Smith by His Mother*, was dictated to Martha Jane Knowlton Coray, who acted as her amanuensis. It was first published by Apostle Orson Pratt in Liverpool, England 1853 without the consent of Brigham Young. The original was revised somewhat and then republished in Salt Lake City in 1901 by her grandson, Joseph F. Smith (Hyrum's son and the sixth President of The Church of Jesus Christ of Latter-day Saints.)

SORENSON, John L. *An Ancient American Setting for the Book of Mormon.* Foreword by Leonard J. Arrington, Truman G. Madsen, and John W. Welch. (Published by Deseret Book Company, Salt Lake City, Utah. 1985.)

SOUZA, Pero Lopes de. *Diario da Navegaçâo Da Armada Que Foi Á Terra do Brasil Em 1530, Sob a Capitania-Mor de Martim Affonso de Souza.* (Published by Francisco Adolfo de Varnhagen, Socio da Academia R. Das Sciencias de Lisboa, 1839.)

SULLIVAN, Lawrence E. *Icanchu's Drum, An Orientation to Meaning in South American Religions.* (Macmillan Publishing Company, New York, 1988.)

TAYLOR, William B., *Magistrates of the Sacred, Priests and Parishioners in Eighteenth-Century Mexico.* (Stanford University Press, Stanford, California. 1996.)

VOGEL, Dan. *Indian Origins and the Book of Mormon* (Signature Books, Inc. United States of America, 1986.)

VON HAGEN, Victor Wolfgang. *The Incas of Pedro de Cieza de Leon.* Translated by Harriet de Onis. (Published by the University of Oklahoma Press, Norman, Oklahoma. 1959.)

WELCH, John W. *Reexploring the Book of Mormon.* Updates of the Foundation for Ancient Research and Mormon Studies (FARMS), Provo, Utah. Edited by Welch. (Published by Deseret Book Company, Salt Lake City, Utah. 1992.)

INDEX

Aaronic Priesthood 235, 471, 472
abandoned 142, 245, 281
Abinadi 170, 171, 234, 236, 239
abolitionists 531
abomination 219, 470
Abraham 48, 64, 65, 158, 160, 210, 212, 235, 237, 251, 252, 472, 477, 478, 483, 484, 487
Abrams, Harry N. 13
abridged 302, 305, 366
abridgement 115, 116, 119
accounts 68, 88, 494, 499, 503
Acosta theory 13
Acosta, Joseph de 6, 11, 43, 225, 244
Adair, James 10, 91, 92, 93, 203, 204, 210
Adam 3, 9, 30, 78, 115, 150, 157, 211, 212, 213, 226, 227, 235, 472, 487, 497, 516, 519
Adam-ondi-Ahman 519
admonitions 77, 366
Adonay 64
Adorno, Rolena 39, 40, 504
adultery 85, 207, 210, 243, 244, 245, 246, 247, 248, 299
adversary 114, 471
adversity 244
afflictions 358, 361
afterlife 180, 181, 184

agriculture 42, 49
Aimorés 324, 341, 448
Aizenberg, Isidoro 205
Alderete, Gerónimo de 32
alloy 385
Alma 105, 162, 170, 171, 235, 236, 237, 266, 295, 296, 337, 378, 386, 390, 395, 421, 433, 441, 452
alpaca 392
Alva Ixtlilxochitl, Fernando de 45, 61, 62
Alva, Walter 182, 218, 386
Alvarado, Pedro 46
Alvarez de Castro 318
Amalekites 337
Amauta Manco Cápac 296
Amauta Sinchi Ayar 301
amautas 51, 246, 250, 288, 296, 300, 307, 455
Amazon River 69
American Bible Society 10
Americas 1, 2, 118, 271, 274, 361, 366, 499, 519
Amlici 336, 337
Ammaron 303
Ammon 254
Ammonihah 149
Amos 505
Amsterdam, Holland 63, 67, 324, 356, 463, 464
Amulek 149
Amulonites 336

ancestors 59, 173, 184, 204, 353, 354, 382, 389, 488
ancestry 478
Andahuaylas Indians 455
Andahuaylas, Peru 380, 456
Andean Indians x, xiv, 29, 198, 222, 230, 244, 263, 286, 297, 307, 328, 332, 344, 391, 493
Andean region x, xiv, 198, 222, 263, 344, 493
Andes 45, 53, 54, 69, 127, 134, 190, 215, 249, 250, 291, 307, 308, 339, 346, 391, 396, 412, 431, 458, 460, 496, 500, 501
Angasmayo, Colombia 427
angel 11, 80, 81, 89, 103, 111, 128, 130, 133, 159, 160, 161, 162, 167, 169, 171, 212, 357, 358, 471, 473, 474, 475, 508, 534, 537, 549
Anian 6
anointed 224, 229
Anthon, Charles 78
Anthropological Investigations 451
anthropologists 185, 190, 197, 289, 331, 339
anthropology 11, 14
anthropomorphized 149
Antilles 369
Apocryphal 5
apostasy xiv, 120, 213, 214, 489, 505, 506, 507, 533
apostles xiv, 5, 32, 75, 112, 159, 161, 163, 187, 189, 225, 495, 547, 548

Arabian desert 523
Arabian Peninsula 524
Arabic 79
Araucano Indians 33, 341, 383, 448, 502
Archaeological x, xii, xvi, 16, 96, 287, 329, 395, 499, 524
archaeologists xii, xvii, xviii, 31, 53, 55, 56, 57, 58, 95, 96, 152, 153, 185, 189, 197, 215, 216, 269, 275, 280, 281, 287, 289, 309, 313, 327, 341, 366, 367, 382, 384, 385, 390, 391, 412, 416, 419, 423, 424, 430, 431, 451, 493, 497, 498, 500, 501, 502, 504, 518, 520, 522, 523, 525
archaeology x, 11, 12, 14, 15, 148, 494, 496
architecture 277, 278, 281
Arequipa, Peru 29
Argentina xv, 32, 136, 306, 396, 455
Argentine 331, 332, 333
Arias de Avila, Pedro 20, 23
Ark of the Covenant 208
Armenia 137
armor 441, 444, 445, 446, 448, 452
arm-shields 442
arrows 434, 440, 442, 448, 457

art historians xii, xvii, xviii, 3, 12, 15, 53, 56, 68, 148, 153, 184, 185, 197, 215, 216, 230, 269, 275, 284, 287, 290, 309, 312, 313, 328, 341, 366, 367, 384, 385, 390, 395, 397, 410, 419, 424, 435, 440, 445, 450, 493, 497, 498, 500, 501, 502, 504, 518, 522
art history x, 156, 496
artifacts 16, 275
artillery 403
ascension 112
assassination 11, 72, 75, 461
Assyriac 79
Assyrians 214, 464
Aston, Michaela Knoth 523
Aston, Warren P. 523
astrologers 301
astronomical 307
Atahualpa 264, 372, 388
atheism 522
Atlantic Ocean 5, 13, 18, 23, 62, 298, 325
Atlantis 4, 6
atlatl 444, 445
atom bomb 95
atonement 150, 153, 170, 205, 207, 213, 226, 227, 231, 236, 484, 506, 510
authority 281, 478
Avila, Francisco de 125
ax 336, 396, 441
Axayacatl 230

axe 446
axes 383, 448, 451
Ayacucho, Peru 326, 339
Ayar Cachi 52
Ayar Cachi Awga 52
Ayar Manco 52
Ayar Oco 52
Ayarauca 44
Ayarcache 44
Ayarhuchu 44
ayllos 446
Aymara 44
Aztecs 3, 10, 22, 24, 25, 42, 55, 58, 59, 60, 68, 127, 132, 176, 177, 188, 202, 220, 230, 239, 243, 246, 248, 254, 255, 259, 262, 264, 266, 312, 340, 346, 349, 351, 353, 355, 366, 370, 388, 389, 390, 411, 445, 455, 460, 461, 462, 518
Aztlan 59

B

Babylon 49, 100
Babylonians 109, 214, 294, 358, 464
backplates 447, 502
Bahamas 20, 318
Bahia de Todos Los Santos 321, 322
Ballasteros Gambrois, Manuel 372
bands of death 150
Baptism 5, 111, 238, 242, 302, 471, 477, 506, 532,

baptism for the dead 488, 489
baptized 225, 243, 296, 472, 516, 529, 542
Barcelona 17
barges 99, 116, 117, 157, 371, 376, 377, 378
Battle tactics 457, 460
Bay of Urabá 370
bearded white Indians 69, 325, 341, 326, 404, 502
bearded white men 327, 328, 331, 339, 340, 345, 350, 499, 501
beards 68, 69, 285, 321, 325, 327, 329, 334, 339, 340, 341, 344, 351, 501
Bedouins 95
Beijing 416
Belize 55
Beloved Son 133, 165, 470
Ben Israel, Menasseh 62, 63, 67, 68, 69, 202, 324, 325, 326, 356, 360, 463, 464, 465, 466, 469, 476
Benson, Elizabeth 148, 180, 310
Bering Straits 6, 13, 14, 290
Bering, Vitus 6
Berlin Vase 142, 147
Berlin, Germany 310
Betanzos, Juan de 125, 126, 132, 180, 222, 248, 259, 265, 393, 345, 446, 456, 457, 496
Bible 3, 13, 73, 75, 87, 134, 150, 157, 158, 160, 163, 166, 190, 195, 234, 239, 252, 261, 358, 360, 465, 473, 480, 484, 497, 505, 506, 510, 528

bigotry 531
Bingham, Hiram 367
bishops 240
black palm lances 457
blemish 221, 222
blond hair 285, 316, 319, 324, 325
blood 70, 207, 213, 216, 220, 224, 237, 295, 304
bloodletting 230, 231, 243
bludgeons 448
Boggs, Lilburn W. 531, 535, 543
Bolivia xii, 54, 121, 286, 287, 307, 313, 323, 425, 457
Book of Acts 474
Book of Deuteronomy 64
Book of Ether 115, 118, 119, 157, 376
Book of Lehi 80
Book of Moses 201, 211, 235, 272
Book of Mosiah 235
Botchia 42, 58
Boudinot, Elias 9, 10
Bountiful 105, 110, 133, 378, 453, 524
Bourget, Steve 141, 181, 216, 218, 309, 312, 410
bows and arrows 316, 324, 336, 396, 434, 440, 441, 442, 443, 444, 445, 446, 447, 457
Bradley, Joshua 76
Brahmans 136
brass 108, 119, 236, 335, 380, 385, 420, 435
brass plates 101, 102, 105, 109, 252
Brasseur de Bourbourg, Abbé 27

Brazil 18, 19, 32, 136, 190, 255, 307, 312, 321, 323, 325, 412, 447, 448
breastplates 77, 274, 278, 434, 435, 442, 447, 448, 502
bridges 427
Brigham Young University 37
British 91
British government 464
British Islands 486, 534, 541
broadswords 434, 444
Brodie, Fawn McKay 87, 88, 89, 90, 91, 92, 93, 498
brother of Jared 116, 117, 118, 156, 157, 158, 270, 271, 377
bucklers 448
Buenos Aires 331
Burger, Richard L. 56, 57, 215, 275, 277, 278, 280, 281, 282, 290, 291, 380, 382, 384, 385, 391, 407, 410, 450
Bush, Lester E., Jr 86
Bushman, Richard L. 73, 79, 82, 83, 94
Bustamante, Carlos Maria de 26

Caamaño, Jijón 249
Cabello Valboa, Miguel 4, 48, 49, 56, 69, 70, 124, 134, 135, 136, 137, 190, 198, 199, 374, 376, 496

Cabral, Pedro Alvarez de Gouvea 18, 19
cacao 369, 390
Cacaxtla 423, 424, 501
Cacha 135, 136, 137
Cadogan, León 190, 199, 312, 210
Cain 272
Cajamarca 264
calamities 348
Cali, Colombia 29
Campbell, Alexander 84
Campbell, Thomas 84
Campbellite Church 527
Canada 73, 486, 487, 547, 548
cannibalism 42, 168, 215, 250, 267, 369
canoes 316, 368, 369, 374, 429
capabilities 51
Cape Catoche 24
Cape of Good Hope 18
Captain Moroni 253, 441, 442, 443, 451, 452, 453, 454, 461
captaincy 321, 324
Caranqui 397
caravels 370, 371
Carbon-14 277, 496
Carib Indians 368, 369, 443
Caribbean 315, 346, 391, 501, 512
Carlin, Thomas 541
carnivores 6
Cartagena, Colombia 63, 66, 443
Carthage Greys 546

Carthage jail 486, 546
Carthage, Illinois 490, 543, 545, 546
Casma, Peru 278, 281
Castillo, Luis Jaime 385
castles 419
catastrophe 45
Catawba 91
Catherwood, Frederick 12, 367
Catholics 3, 15, 32, 40, 49, 63, 225, 463
cattle 336
Cayambes 459
celestial marriage 477
cement 365, 423, 424, 425, 501
Central America 58, 60, 493, 512
century cycle 127
ceramic pottery vessels 43, 139, 146, 181, 218, 309, 310, 312, 374, 380
ceremonies 25, 70, 187, 207, 220, 223, 225, 230, 241, 265, 266, 344
Cerro Sechín 278, 435, 440
Chachapoyas 320, 321, 392, 458
Chalcas 59
Chaldaic 79
champis 447
Chanca Indians 456, 457
Chandler, Michael H. 482
Chardon, Ohio 85
Charrúa Indians 322, 397
chasquis 288
chastity 219

Chavín civilization 53, 56, 122, 139, 215, 216, 275, 277, 280, 281, 287, 290, 291, 309, 366, 381, 382, 391, 404, 407, 419, 435, 445, 450, 451, 500, 502, 518
Chavín de Huántar 56, 215, 278, 282, 291, 421, 423
Chavín metallurgists 385
Cherokee 10, 91
Chi, Gaspar Antonio 49
Chiapas 55
Chichen Itzá 366, 369, 424
Chichimecs 445, 446
Chickasaw 10, 91
Chiclayo 54
Chicora 319, 513
Chilam 355
Chile 33, 50, 175, 287, 306, 383, 427, 448, 455, 502
Chimalli 445
Chimor 122, 139, 366, 455
China 56, 73
Chinese 13, 14, 92, 203, 323
Chiriguanos 458
Choctaw 10
choice land 116, 270
Cholula 24, 347
Christ 93, 151, 211, 229, 260, 301, 306, 339, 363, 454, 468, 477, 478, 484, 488
christening 243
Christenson, Allen J. 46, 191, 193, 194, 195, 196, 197

Christian ordinance 242, 243, 500
Christian Science Church 87
Christianity xiv, 5, 19, 32, 46, 47, 48, 70, 82, 93, 128, 150, 157, 172, 185, 187, 188, 190, 191, 198, 220, 223, 225, 244, 251, 256, 260, 264, 266, 300, 445, 497, 500, 502, 506, 516
chroniclers x, xi, xiii, xvi, xvii, xviii, 2, 4, 5, 14, 15, 22, 23, 25, 27, 29, 30, 31, 33, 35, 36, 40, 45, 48, 49, 50, 57, 113, 132, 134, 147, 174, 179, 185, 187, 199, 220, 222, 223, 230, 239, 244, 246, 248, 262, 269, 285, 297, 301, 309, 317, 321, 326, 339, 340, 343, 344, 367, 373, 390, 397, 431, 448, 456, 493, 496, 497, 498, 500, 503, 521
Chronicles ix, xi, xii, xvi, xvii, 2, 9, 18, 36, 38, 42, 51, 71, 94, 96, 136, 137, 147, 148, 149, 156, 163, 184, 189, 254, 263, 282, 454, 462, 497, 499, 504, 512, 518, 522
chronological period 289
Cieza de León, Pedro de ix, 27, 28, 29, 35, 40, 43, 51, 58, 113, 121, 122, 123, 124, 132, 133, 135, 137, 168, 173, 190, 241, 248, 257, 259, 264, 265, 282, 319, 320, 326, 327, 339, 341, 345, 371, 374, 387, 388, 392, 393, 397, 400, 403, 425, 426, 427, 428, 446, 457, 458, 496
cimeters 336, 396, 441, 442
Circleville, Ohio 383
citadels 450

Cities of Refuge 208
City of Moroni 131
City of Zion 528, 531
Ciudadela 412
civilizations xiv, 12, 53, 68, 70, 96, 262, 269, 270, 282, 289, 291, 313, 335, 365, 366, 367, 410, 411, 462, 518, 519, 521
Classical Period x
clergymen 34
cloth 264, 350, 365, 369, 371, 395, 396
clothing 284, 392, 393
clubs 383, 443, 447, 448, 457
Coba 430
Cobo, Bernabé 459
coca leaf 122
Cochabamba, Bolivia 54, 323, 458
Cocom tribe 355
codices 3, 184
Coe, Michael D. 13, 14, 58, 216, 289, 290, 411
Coelho, Duarte 19
Cole, Abner 84
Colesville, New York 77
Colhuas 59, 60, 461
Colla 44
Collao 307
Colombia 23, 27, 42, 54, 63, 67, 121, 319, 324, 356, 367, 369, 370, 371, 425, 443, 459
colonial 32, 40
colonization 22, 23, 29

colonizers 1, 2, 512

colossal heads 290

Columbia College 78

Columbus x, 1, 2, 7, 13, 15, 17, 18, 20, 21, 37, 38, 41, 104, 172, 315, 316, 317, 318, 344, 365, 368, 369, 374, 391, 443, 504

comets 300, 301, 348

commandments 49, 50, 106, 116, 118, 127, 162, 212, 214, 233, 235, 237, 267, 270, 283, 287, 293, 294, 295, 334, 359, 467, 470, 475, 491, 501, 520, 529

communications 163

compass 5, 105, 106, 368, 378

computers 94

condemnation 240

confession 5, 229, 242, 244

confiscation 36

conflict 109

confounding of tongues 48, 99, 272

Conneaut, Ohio 85

conquest 2, 22, 23, 24, 25, 27, 29, 34, 47, 55, 320, 333, 342, 345, 351

conquistadores ix, xiii, 1, 2, 21, 22, 23, 31, 38, 39, 41, 42, 43, 49, 122, 172, 229, 269, 502, 519

Constitution of the United States 515, 532

contentions 260, 295, 302

continent 18, 76, 362

contradictions 281

controversy 71, 343

Cook, Captain 372

copper 108, 119, 182, 183, 236, 285, 286, 300, 323, 335, 381, 382, 383, 384, 385, 387, 390, 391, 420, 435, 444, 447

Cordy-Collins, Alana 376

Corianton 171

Coriantumr 109, 110, 115, 274, 434, 450

Corinthians 489

Cortés, Hernán 21, 22, 23, 24, 220, 251, 340, 350, 351, 352, 353, 354, 355, 388, 389, 390, 419, 423, 429

cotton 56, 263, 318, 348, 374, 391, 394, 395, 396, 429

cotton armor 394, 446, 457

Council Bluffs 547, 548

Council of the Indies 34

Covarrubias, Miguel 290

covenants 251, 252, 300, 358, 359, 361, 362, 467, 468, 477, 478, 509, 517, 529

Cowdery, Oliver 81, 82, 84, 89, 105, 471, 472, 473, 475, 476, 477, 483, 485, 527, 534

creation 13, 45, 47, 68, 102, 115, 159, 166, 190, 194, 195, 196, 202, 231, 312, 359, 484, 488, 497

Creator 38, 45, 50, 51, 52, 57, 133, 152, 162, 199, 201, 224, 226, 283, 284, 288, 328, 330, 500, 510, 520

creeds 470

critics xvii, 86, 87

critiques 72
Cromwell, Oliver 464
crucifixion of Jesus Christ 103, 118, 119, 124, 147, 152, 212, 330, 338, 520
Cuba 23, 24, 172, 317, 319, 367, 369, 368, 512, 513
Cuenca 122, 397, 459
cultures xii, xiv, 2, 16, 23, 33, 40, 56, 70, 140, 148, 189, 215, 282, 287, 289, 496, 497, 522
Cumorah xiv, 77, 305
Cuna Indians 261
Curamba 387
curse 334, 337
customs 26, 27, 31, 42, 43, 70, 96, 177, 203, 209, 210, 240, 334, 498, 503
Cuzco 30, 51, 52, 57, 122, 174, 180, 249, 251, 288, 306, 307, 308, 309, 313, 328, 366, 371, 373, 388, 397, 400, 404, 421, 423, 427, 455, 458

D

Daniel 487, 507
Darién, Panama 20, 23, 173, 370, 443
darkness 127, 129, 149, 470, 471, 509, 518
dark-skinned 308, 312, 317, 319, 321, 325, 334, 338, 341, 342, 374, 501
darts 334, 443, 446, 447, 457
Darwin, Charles 12
daylight 126
de Laet, Joannes 8
De Soto, Hernando 255, 513, 514
deacon 240
death 168, 175, 348, 361
Deity 37, 42, 51, 204, 235, 521
Deloria, Dr. Vine, Jr., 15
democratic government 294
descendants 51, 103, 104, 105, 238, 284, 288, 302, 309, 338, 354, 357, 358, 360, 386, 468, 500
descriptions 27, 132, 319, 498
desolate 297
destruction 45, 100, 114, 131, 133, 137, 294, 295, 305, 335, 338, 344, 347, 349, 358, 363, 366, 470, 499, 507, 520, 521, 530, 531
devil 5, 75
diabolical 225
Díaz del Castillo, Bernal 23, 24, 251, 340, 346, 351, 352, 353, 354, 423, 429, 444
Diehl, Richard A. 13, 14, 58, 216, 289, 290, 411
Diffusionists 7, 13, 189, 497
disappeared 330, 366
disciples 225, 226, 239, 302, 303
discoveries xvii, 7, 17, 18, 20, 34, 37, 87, 480, 494, 498, 499, 504
disintegrate 280, 282, 450
disobedience 534
dispensation 477, 487, 542

Dispensation of the Fullness of Times 487, 488
dissension 273, 296, 514, 533
dissenters 295, 298
Divine Faith 7
divine intervention 33
division 303
doctrines 96, 468, 473, 479
Dom Manuel 18, 19
dominate 362
Dominican Republic 317
Doniphan, Brig. General A.W. 536
Donnan, Christopher B. 146, 181, 182, 218, 309, 376, 385, 386
Douglas, Stephen A. 542
dugouts 368, 374
Duhare 319
Duke René II 19
Dumbarton Oaks Museum 140
Durán, Diego 24, 25, 49, 55, 58, 59, 60, 61, 127, 128, 132, 168, 175, 188, 189, 220, 221, 223, 225, 226, 230, 246, 255, 262, 301, 309, 312, 329, 331, 340, 346, 347, 348, 349, 350, 351, 388, 389, 390, 393, 394, 445, 460, 461, 462, 496
Dutch 2, 8, 36, 463
Dutch West India Company 8
dyes 393

E

Early and Middle Formative 289
Early Horizon Period 56, 381, 382, 450
earthquakes xi, 45, 127, 134, 147, 169, 188, 301, 307, 499, 518
East Asia 203
Ecuador 50, 53, 69, 275, 291, 319, 367, 373, 382, 397, 458, 459
Eden, Richard 20
Egypt 9, 13, 56, 78, 79, 158, 205, 407, 411, 412, 466, 467, 468, 476, 482, 484
Ehecatl Quetzalcoatl 198, 330
El Lanzón 57
El Salvador 55
Elias 160, 476, 477
Elijah, the Prophet 97, 160, 472, 477, 478, 489, 507
Emer 273
emeralds 325, 387, 393, 400
endowment 475
England 35, 92, 464, 487, 534
English 2, 8, 28, 36, 463, 481
Enoch 472, 487
Enos 294, 336, 396, 441
Ensign 37, 477, 478, 481, 483
Ephraim 380, 465, 466, 478
Ercilla y Zuñiga, Alonso de 32, 33, 340, 383, 448

establishment 72, 469
Eternal God 468, 494, 510
eternal marriage 489
Ether 115, 116, 119, 120, 270, 271, 272, 273, 274, 305, 379, 380, 395, 419, 433, 434, 449, 521
ethnicity 341
ethnographer 24
ethnology 11, 92
Europe 18, 36, 448, 512, 515, 519, 547
Europeans 1, 2, 8, 9, 17, 35, 39, 46, 172, 234, 261, 323, 339, 341, 366, 368, 371, 431, 503, 520
Eve 3, 150, 163, 167, 213, 497, 519
evidence 496
evolution 12, 14, 16, 48, 502
excavations 381
excommunicated 85, 534
expedition 23, 24, 29, 33, 323
expeditions 18, 21, 376
expiation 206
exploration 20, 22, 41, 42, 45, 370
explorers 1, 17, 18, 367
Extermination Orders 535, 538
eye-witness 15, 24, 29, 504
Ezekiel 235

F

fables 44, 345, 512
Fairchild, James 86
famine 273, 319, 520
fanatics 530
Far West 534, 536, 538
fasting 204, 208, 222, 243, 264, 265, 267, 282, 344, 456
fatalism 346
Father of heaven and earth 162
Father of the sun 123
Fayette, New York 81, 83
feathered Serpent 62, 330
feats of endurance 39
fiction 72, 433
fine-twined linen 119, 299, 395
fire 45, 117, 131, 132, 136, 205, 378, 475, 499, 518
firelight 126
firepits 215
First Vision 75, 76, 469, 470, 505
fish 145, 444
flint 444, 445
flood 9, 44, 45, 46, 48, 50, 134, 202, 319, 519
Florida 20, 255, 512, 513
folk tales 283
folklore x, xi, xvii, 15, 25, 39, 42, 87, 153, 210, 366, 503, 504
Ford, Thomas 542, 545, 546

foreigners 310, 343, 346, 362
foreordained 487
Formative Period x, 380, 445
fornication 245, 247
Fort Leavensworth, Kansas 548
fortifications 10, 285, 308, 421, 452
fortresses 280, 285, 365, 423, 447, 450, 460
Foundation for Ancient Research and Mormon Studies 523
Framer and Shaper 47, 48, 197
France 35
Francisco 63, 64, 65, 66, 67, 68, 356, 362
Freidel, David A. 148, 184, 185
French 2, 36, 91, 92

Gadianton robbers 286, 296, 297, 300, 301, 303, 396
García, Alejo 322
García, Gregorio 6, 7
Garcilaso de la Vega, Inca 30, 43, 179, 255, 256, 512, 513, 514
Garden of Eden 60, 150, 157, 163, 318, 519
Gateway of the Sun 404
gathering of Israel 476
genealogy 101, 102, 109, 288
generations 293, 503
Genesis 3, 190, 194, 197, 211, 477

gentiles 84, 103, 104, 271, 335, 357, 360, 361, 362, 468, 494, 501, 506, 508, 509, 516, 517
geography xiv, 24, 118, 523
geological upheaval 103
Georgia 20, 319, 513
ginseng 72, 73
glyphs 26, 231
God xvii, 37, 38, 45, 47, 48, 49, 50, 51, 52, 56, 61, 64, 66, 74, 75, 76, 105, 113, 118, 126, 150, 157, 159, 163, 166, 167, 169, 170, 171, 198, 200, 202, 204, 211, 212, 213, 214, 221, 225, 228, 233, 235, 238, 239, 240, 243, 252, 254, 257, 265, 270, 283, 284, 287, 291, 293, 299, 300, 303, 304, 313, 335, 352, 353, 355, 356, 359, 361, 396, 452, 467, 470, 473, 474, 475, 478, 488, 494, 495, 496, 501, 504, 507, 509, 511, 515, 519, 520, 521, 522
God, the Eternal Father 198, 361, 362, 363, 471, 475
Godhead 198, 479
Godoy, Diego de 352
gods 47, 123, 194, 197, 247, 393
gold 29, 101, 102, 106, 108, 111, 119, 156, 182, 236, 257, 258, 261, 262, 273, 285, 286, 299, 300, 325, 335, 351, 353, 365, 370, 371, 372, 373, 374, 380, 381, 382, 383, 384, 385, 386, 387, 388, 389, 390, 393, 400, 420, 475
gold bible 83

gold plates x, xii, xv, xvii, 11, 76, 77, 78, 79, 81, 82, 88, 89, 90, 105, 111, 115, 120, 193, 305, 336, 384, 469, 490, 517, 534
goldsmiths 365
González, Gil 45, 46
gospel 9, 11, 21, 76, 234, 236, 302, 487
government 272, 294, 296, 302, 343
Governor Reynolds 543
Grandin Press 84
Grandin, Egbert B. 82
graves 124, 130, 209
Great Salt Lake Basin 548
great waters 157
greed 50, 261, 531
Greenville, South Carolina 514
Grieder, Dr. Terrence 291
Grijalva, Juan de 24, 352
Grotius, Hugo 8, 464
Guaman Chawa 283
guanaco 392, 393
Guaraní Indians 32, 178, 179, 312, 322, 323
Guariaga River 69
Guarionex 344
Guatemala 46, 54, 55, 58, 203
Guatemala City 46
Guatemalan 231
Guayakí Indians 331, 332, 333, 340, 341
Guayaquil, Ecuador 248, 339, 371
Guayas River 371

guidance xvii
Gulf of Mexico 54, 55, 290

H

Hagar 160
Hagoth 378, 379
Hahua Chumpi 372
Haiti 317
hallucinogenic drugs 281, 282
Harmony, Pennsylvania 77, 78, 81, 471
Harris, Martin 78, 79, 80, 81, 89, 105, 107, 118, 528, 534
Haun's Mill 535
Havana 514
Hawaiian Islands 372, 373
Hawaiians 379
head-plates 274, 434
healed 499
Heart of Sky 197
heaven 61, 177, 284
Heber 48, 49, 50, 287
Hebraic record 84, 91, 494
Hebrew laws 193, 247
Hebrews 5, 11, 49, 62, 63, 64, 78, 92, 107, 109, 185, 187, 188, 189, 194, 196, 202, 205, 206, 208, 209, 210, 220, 227, 463, 464, 481, 482, 497, 498, 502, 524, 539
Helaman 228, 295, 297, 298, 299, 300, 379, 386, 433, 454

hell 150, 168, 170, 177, 284, 507, 542
helmets 278, 447, 448, 457, 502
Hemming, John 14, 322
Henry VIII 32
heresy 72, 83
Hernández de Córdoba, Francisco 24
Hernandez de Quiroz, Pedro 324
Hernandez Sanchez-Barba, Mario 22
Heyden, Doris 188, 329, 390, 445
Heyerdahl, Thor 126, 376
hieroglyphs 3, 16, 25, 26, 47, 68, 78, 205, 241, 366, 407, 482, 483
High Priest 205, 235, 241, 266, 330, 452
highways 130, 425, 426, 429, 430, 431
Hill, Donna 75, 482
Hinkle, Lt. Colonel George M. 536
Hiram, Ohio 490
Hispaniola 173, 203, 317, 319, 344, 368, 443
historians x, xvii, 5, 15, 22, 24, 31, 36, 37, 40, 92, 96, 189, 190, 343, 368, 400, 485, 486, 493, 494, 496, 497, 501, 523
historical 17, 44, 96, 193, 366, 391, 436, 498
historiography 40
history 25, 26, 28, 30, 31, 46, 61, 74, 95, 99, 101, 107, 108, 110, 115, 188, 309
hoax 76, 79
Hocquenghem, Anna Maria 140, 145
Hojeda, Alfonso 443

Holland 63, 65, 202
Holland, Jeffery R. 469
holy ark 204
Holy Ghost 161, 198, 237, 239, 361, 363, 472, 474, 494, 495, 509, 511, 516, 519
Holy Land 465
Holy Office of the Inquisition 34
Holy One of Israel 170, 359, 509
Holy Spirit 204, 266, 479
homicide 246
homosexual 245, 246, 248, 249, 250, 251, 521
Honduras 55, 58, 231, 369
horses 8, 336, 352, 372, 373, 514
hostility 75
House of Israel 111, 158, 358, 361, 466, 467, 468, 494, 510, 516
Howe, Eder D. 85, 498
Hrdlicka, Aleš 14
Huaca de la Luna 218, 410
Huamanga 326, 327, 328
Huancavilca 458
Huánuco 173, 400, 458
Huarochiri Manuscript 146
Huarochirí, Peru 125
Huascar 372
Huayna Cápac 345, 346, 371, 372, 458, 459
Huddleston, Lee Eldridge 8
Huexotzinco 188, 347
Huguenot 8

Huitlapalan 61
Huitzilopochtli xi, 42, 59, 61, 198, 223, 224, 225, 230, 265, 346
Huixachtlan 128
Human Faith 7
hummingbird 177, 200, 223, 224, 312
Hunt, Lydia Longsteth 37
Huracán 194, 197
Hurlburt, Philastus 85, 86
Hurtado de Mendoza, Andrés 33
Hurtado de Mendoza, Don García 33
Huxley, Thomas Henry 12
Hyde, Orson 476
hypothesis 4, 14, 153, 497, 502

I

I AM 158, 198, 475
Ibarra 459
Ice Age 13
iconography x, xi, 3, 15, 57, 96, 139, 140, 147, 148, 152, 181, 278, 312, 374, 440, 500, 501
idolatry 3, 191, 192, 236, 246, 249, 251, 271, 286, 291, 336, 396, 516, 520
idols 42, 220, 221, 224, 229, 239, 240, 251, 284, 300, 344, 346, 521
Illinois 486, 541, 545
immigrants 87
immorality 171, 168, 246, 520
immortality of the soul 42, 155, 169, 170, 172, 173, 174, 175, 178, 180, 185, 227, 500
imperfections 221
imposter 72, 433, 490
Inca Roca 250, 251, 286, 455
Inca Viracocha Yupanqui 198, 321, 340, 345, 456
Incas 10, 29, 30, 42, 57, 123, 139, 174, 175, 180, 199, 222, 230, 241, 244, 248, 259, 283, 309, 313, 323, 366, 387, 388, 391, 392, 397, 404, 421, 425, 426, 428, 447, 455, 457, 458, 459, 460, 462, 518
Independence, Jackson County, Missouri 528
Independent Inventionist 7, 13, 14, 290, 316, 342, 497, 502
India 49
Indus Valley 56
inhabitants x, xiii, 22, 76, 153, 282, 297, 352, 376, 499, 511
iniquity 295
Initial Olmec Period 58
Initial Period 278, 280, 281, 380, 381, 436
Inquisition 63, 191, 192, 515
inter-marriage 9, 336
Inti Capác 288
inventions 382
investigations xvii, 191
investigators 493
Iowa 547

Iraq 49
iron 108, 119, 236, 335, 380, 382, 383, 384, 385, 420, 448, 502
irrigation 284, 285, 427, 428
Isaac 48, 64, 65, 212, 252, 472, 477, 478
Isabella 17, 21
Isaiah xii, 235, 360, 465, 505, 507, 517
Ishmael 100, 102, 104, 105, 106, 108, 160, 523
Israel 5, 9, 65, 210, 213, 252, 440, 464, 465, 466
Israelites xiv, 4, 5, 62, 63, 64, 66, 67, 68, 70, 92, 100, 108, 133, 158, 185, 188, 190, 202, 203, 204, 205, 206, 207, 208, 210, 214, 221, 223, 227, 233, 235, 251, 324, 326, 334, 356, 360, 362, 441, 464, 476
Isthmus of Panama 23
Isthmus of Tehuantepec 54, 55
Italians 2
Itzcoatl 461

J

Jackson County, Missouri 530, 532, 543
Jacob 48, 64, 65, 82, 89, 105, 106, 169, 210, 234, 252, 266, 294, 336, 361, 441, 466, 467, 472, 477, 478, 509
Jalisco 60
James 160
Jamestown, Virginia 515
Jared 99, 116, 271, 338
Jaredites 99, 110, 115, 116, 117, 118, 120, 156, 157, 234, 270, 271, 272, 273, 274, 282, 286, 287, 289, 291, 293, 294, 296, 305, 333, 334, 376, 377, 378, 379, 380, 395, 419, 434, 435, 440, 445, 446, 449, 520, 521
Jarom 234
Jauja 122
javelin 441, 444, 446
Jehovah 42, 64, 157, 158, 204, 475
Jensen, Dr. De Lamar 37
Jeremiah 11, 100, 235
Jerusalem 5, 11, 63, 85, 95, 99, 100, 101, 102, 103, 107, 109, 111, 112, 152, 161, 172, 214, 233, 238, 252, 286, 294, 338, 358, 359, 360, 440, 441, 445, 476, 509, 516, 523
Jesuit Priests 32, 136
Jesus Christ xi, xviii, 11, 42, 51, 75, 84, 93, 111, 112, 113, 115, 125, 127, 128, 129, 130, 133, 134, 137, 148, 150, 152, 157, 158, 159, 160, 161, 162, 166, 171, 172, 194, 198, 200, 201, 212, 213, 225, 226, 227, 228, 231, 235, 236, 238, 253, 266, 270, 271, 275, 286, 296, 297, 302, 303, 304, 306, 307, 330, 337, 338, 358, 360, 361, 362, 419, 451, 465, 468, 471, 472, 474, 475, 479, 480, 484, 487, 491, 494, 495, 498, 500, 504, 505, 506, 507, 508, 509, 510, 516, 517, 520, 522, 537, 539, 540

jewelry 350, 389
Jewish 65, 93, 206, 324
Jews 5, 62, 70, 84, 100, 103, 107, 111, 115, 161, 188, 205, 207, 285, 335, 463, 464, 468, 476, 478, 494, 500, 509, 511, 515, 517
Jimenez de la Espada, Marcos 27, 459, 460
John 82, 160, 166, 194, 508
John the apostle 112, 160, 163, 227
John the Baptist 160, 472, 495
Joktan 4, 48, 49, 64
Joseph (son of Lehi) 105, 106, 234, 467
Joseph, the son of Jacob 65, 102, 360, 463, 465, 466, 467, 468, 469, 478, 483
Josephus 48
Joshua 235
journey 101, 104, 368
Judah 109, 465, 468
Judaism 188
Judeo-Christian 13, 156, 245, 258
judges 294, 295, 296, 336, 452, 455

K´iche´-Maya 46, 47, 193, 196, 200
Kauffmann Doig, Frederico 310
keystone 522
Kimball, Heber C. 534
King Ahuitzotl 462

King Benjamin 161, 257, 258
King Charles V 22, 32, 35, 220, 354, 355, 513
King Coriantum 419
King Coriantumr's 273
King David 213
King Fernando 17, 21, 443, 512
King Louis XI 20
King Nezahualpilli 348
King Nicoragua 45
King Noah 170, 234, 235, 236, 336, 385
King Phillip II 31, 36, 121
King Shalmaneser IV 5
King Solomon 4, 48, 466
King Zedekiah 100, 294
King's Council 34
kingdom of God 479, 486
Kingdom of Israel 214
Kingdom of Judah 214
kingdoms 42, 343, 428
Kingmen 453
kings 30, 44, 62, 296, 389
Kirkham, Francis W. 84
Kirtland Temple 474, 476
Kirtland, Ohio 86, 482, 527, 528, 529, 533, 534
Kishkumen 296
Koran 87
Kukulcan 62, 331, 340
Kutscher, Gerdt 310

L

La Florida 59
La Gasca, Pedro de 122
La Paz, Bolivia 54, 328, 376, 403
La Venta 58, 290, 411
Laban 101, 102, 161, 252
Lacuyas Islands 318, 319
Lake Tenochtitlan 59, 60, 460
Lake Titicaca 44, 54, 286, 287, 307, 313, 327, 339, 376
Laman 101, 102, 103, 104, 106, 151, 161, 334, 441
Lamanites 104, 106, 108, 109, 110, 113, 114, 115, 130, 168, 172, 218, 219, 233, 238, 239, 253, 254, 260, 262, 267, 284, 286, 294, 295, 296, 298, 299, 300, 302, 303, 304, 305, 306, 310, 333, 334, 335, 336, 337, 338, 339, 341, 357, 361, 362, 386, 396, 420, 421, 423, 433, 440, 441, 442, 443, 446, 451, 452, 453, 454, 468, 517, 520, 522, 527
Lambayeque 182, 374, 382
Lancaster, Charles 340
lance 383, 443, 444, 445, 446, 447, 448
Land of Nephi 109, 294
land of promise 103, 106, 270, 293, 294, 357, 377, 378
Land of Zarahemla 294

Landa, Diego de 26, 62, 177, 189, 191, 192, 229, 241, 242, 245, 246, 309, 330, 355, 369, 394, 416, 424, 429, 430, 446, 496
languages 2, 26, 107
Lanzón 280
Las Casas, Bartolomé de 17, 22, 35, 46, 431
Las Haldas 281
Late Pre-ceramic 277
Latin 34, 85, 463
Law of Moses 190, 213, 214, 234, 285, 294, 500
law of sacrifice 213
lead 300
Lechtman, Heather 381
legends ix, xi, xii, xvi, xvii, 2, 15, 23, 25, 27, 40, 42, 43, 126, 127, 146, 147, 153, 210, 343, 350, 354, 355, 382, 501, 503
Lehi 85, 99, 100, 101, 103, 104, 105, 106, 108, 111, 151, 152, 166, 167, 169, 233, 234, 235, 238, 256, 284, 289, 293, 294, 299, 302, 333, 334, 344, 358, 359, 360, 378, 384, 419, 440, 445, 453, 454, 467, 472, 500, 506, 508, 523, 524
Lemuel 101, 102, 103, 104, 106, 151, 161, 334, 441
Leonard, Irving A. 38, 39
Levi, Aharon 63, 64, 65, 67, 356, 360, 362, 464
Levitical Priesthood 235

Liahona xv, 105, 106, 378, 441
Liberty Jail 490
Liberty, Missouri 538
light 123, 129, 131, 200, 202, 471, 507
Light of Christ 202
light-skinned 108, 308, 312, 320, 323, 334, 340, 341, 501
Lima, Peru ix, 54, 122, 181, 277, 278, 383, 435, 450
Limhi 435
lineage 248
Lisbon 18, 62, 463
Liverpool, England 74
Lizana, Bernardo de 192
llamas 125, 183, 222, 300, 392
Lopez de Gomara, Francisco 180, 319
Lord 78, 97, 100, 101, 106, 120, 157, 162, 164, 165, 201, 212, 214, 235, 236, 237, 239, 252, 266, 270, 273, 282, 303, 313, 334, 335, 358, 359, 361, 441, 456, 470, 473, 475, 480, 491, 509, 515, 517, 520, 521, 528, 532, 533
Lord Inca 241, 244, 251, 257, 259, 298, 387, 457
Lord Kingsborough 45
Lucas, Major General Samuel D. 536
Luke 261, 508
Lumbreras, Luis Guillermo 57
lying histories 38
Lyon, Patricia J. 140, 145

Machu Pichu 367
Macuahuitl 445
Madrid 324, 325
Maeder, Dr. Ernesto J. A. 32
Magalhães de Gandavo, Pero de 18, 19, 36, 255, 261, 323, 324, 340, 341, 447, 448
Magellan, Ferdinand 4, 6
maguey 263, 348, 393, 445
Mahieu, Dr. Jaime M. de 332
Maize Gods 231
Malachi 477, 478, 507
Manasseh 102
Manchester, New York 73
Manchester, Paul 340
Manco Cápac 44, 52, 286, 298, 300, 306, 307
Mani, Yucatán 191
Manifesto 530
manuscript x, xii, xvii, 2, 25, 27, 29, 30, 31, 34, 35, 46, 50, 80, 85, 86, 87, 373, 481, 482, 496, 501, 504
Mar del Sur 370, 373
Marañon River 69, 324, 325
Markham, Clements Robert 367
marrano Jew 63, 463
Martin Rubio, Maria del Carmen 125

Martyr of Angleria, Peter 3, 20, 21, 41, 172, 173, 315, 316, 319, 344, 369, 370, 443, 486, 512, 513
Mary Tudor 32, 35
Mary, the mother of Jesus Christ 160, 162
Mather, Cotton 9
Mathews, Peter 68, 230
Matthews, Robert J. 482
Maule River 27, 383, 425
Mayas 3, 10, 12, 27, 42, 47, 48, 62, 68, 177, 184, 185, 191, 192, 220, 241, 242, 245, 246, 248, 309, 355, 366, 367, 369, 394, 446, 500, 501, 518
Mbyá-Guaraní Indians 190, 199, 200, 201, 210
McClelland, Donna 181
McConkie, Bruce R. 487
McKay, David O. 87
Means, Philip Ainsworth 29
Melchizedek 235, 237
Melchizedek Priesthood 235, 236, 472, 477
Mendieta, Gerónimo de 328
Menéndez de Avilés, Pedro 514
Mesoamerica x, xiv, 3, 49, 53, 56, 58, 132, 184, 189, 198, 216, 230, 275, 277, 290, 291, 309, 313, 328, 396, 407, 410, 411, 412, 431, 445, 451, 460, 496, 500
Mesopotamia 9, 56, 277
Messiah 103, 111, 198, 228, 234, 294, 359, 463, 467, 471

Messiah Ben David 465, 466
Messiah Ben Joseph 465, 466, 476
Mester, A. M. 149
mestizo 9, 45
metallurgy 329, 381, 434, 501
metals 108, 380, 502
metalworkers 386
Methodist 74, 75, 490
Metnal 178
Mexicans 24, 60, 188, 202, 289, 446
Mexico City 55, 301, 329, 330, 460, 461
Mexico xiv, 21, 26, 31, 45, 58, 59, 62, 68, 127, 175, 189, 203, 220, 223, 225, 251, 254, 259, 264, 301, 312, 328, 329, 340, 350, 365, 367, 369, 391, 393, 448, 462, 493, 496, 500, 501, 512, 513, 548
Mexico-Tenochtitlan 127, 301, 389, 461
mica 412
Middle East 11, 519, 520
Middle Formative 58, 230
migrations xiii, xiv, 11, 48, 70, 95, 99, 108, 332, 333, 337, 468, 500
military skills 295
military tactics 433, 501
millennialism 87
Millet, Robert 477
ministering of angels 471
Ministers 531, 535
miracles 105, 111, 112, 118, 133, 137, 148, 162, 239, 302, 511, 517

missionaries 47, 87, 337, 487, 527, 528, 534, 549

Mississippi River 10, 547

Missouri 486, 489, 519, 529, 534, 545

Missourians 530, 531, 532, 535, 542

mitimaes 458

Moche xi, 54, 139, 140, 145, 147, 148, 149, 150, 151, 152, 180, 181, 182, 185, 216, 218, 219, 287, 309, 310, 312, 341, 366, 374, 376, 385, 386, 410, 500, 518

Mohanes 66, 67, 242, 356

Molina, Diana López de 424

monarchy 294, 296

Mongols 8, 13, 14, 92, 189, 203, 317, 342, 497, 502

Montesinos, Fernando de 31, 49, 50, 51, 52, 249, 250, 251, 282, 287, 288, 289, 296, 300, 301, 306, 309, 345, 382, 383, 423, 447, 455

Montevideo, Uruguay 396

Montezinos, Antonio 63

Morianton 419

Mormon 112, 114, 115, 137, 218, 219, 238, 260, 262, 302, 303, 304, 305, 362, 366, 451, 506, 516, 517, 521

Mormon Battalion 548

Mormonism 83, 87

Mormons 85, 316, 469, 474, 496, 530, 531

Moroni x, xii, 76, 77, 81, 85, 107, 115, 116, 118, 119, 120, 157, 162, 163, 219, 228, 305, 306, 338, 339, 341, 362, 366, 421, 449, 468, 469, 490, 494, 495, 503, 506, 508, 510, 517

Moronihah 131

Mosaic Law 93, 207, 209, 244, 334, 498

Moses 97, 102, 158, 159, 160, 163, 164, 165, 227, 233, 235, 252, 467, 472, 487, 497

Mosiah 214, 253, 257, 294, 337, 385, 441

Moslem world 160

Motecuhzoma, the First 246, 262, 346, 347, 388, 393, 461

Motecuhzoma, the Second 251, 259, 301, 340, 347, 348, 349, 350, 351, 352, 353, 354, 355, 389

Mound Builders 10, 383, 422

Mount Horeb 158

Mulek 100, 109, 294

Mulekites 100, 109, 110, 333, 334, 500

Munich vase 145, 150

Muñoz Camargo, Diego 444

murder 207, 244, 245, 272, 297, 329, 449, 516, 518

murderer 246, 304

Murphy, John 89

Murúa, Martín de 44, 222, 244, 247, 263, 327, 344, 371, 372, 373, 374, 447, 457, 458, 496

mythology 155, 190, 191, 193, 200, 278, 310, 343, 436
myths 37, 48, 58, 88, 124, 140, 156, 199, 355

N

Nahom 105, 523, 524
Nahuatl 3, 25, 26, 58, 60, 61, 62, 128, 132, 184, 220, 309, 329, 444, 460
Ñamandui 200
narcotics 52, 168
Narváez, Pamphilo de 255, 513
Native Americans xvi, 29, 63, 283, 496, 497, 503
native books 3, 192
Nauvoo Charter 541
Nauvoo Legion 542, 546
Nauvoo Temple 489, 547
Nauvoo, Illinois 488, 539, 541, 542, 543, 545, 546, 547
navigation xv, 49, 61, 368, 369, 370, 378, 501
Naymlap 374
Nazca 54, 287
Nebuchadnezzar 11, 100

Nephi 85, 93, 95, 101, 102, 103, 104, 105, 106, 111, 112, 113, 130, 151, 152, 161, 167, 214, 225, 227, 233, 238, 252, 262, 271, 293, 294, 299, 302, 334, 336, 338, 357, 378, 384, 396, 420, 435, 441, 442, 472, 487, 506, 508, 509, 525
Nephite disciples 303
Nephites 106, 107, 108, 109, 110, 113, 114, 115, 120, 128, 130, 157, 162, 167, 168, 169, 171, 172, 218, 219, 228, 233, 234, 235, 237, 238, 239, 253, 254, 256, 257, 260, 266, 272, 284, 286, 293, 294, 295, 296, 298, 299, 300, 301, 302, 303, 304, 305, 306, 310, 335, 336, 337, 338, 339, 341, 357, 361, 366, 379, 384, 385, 386, 395, 396, 420, 421, 423, 433, 440, 441, 451, 452, 453, 454, 461, 462, 469, 516, 520, 521
New Fire ceremony 128, 221
New Laws 35, 121
New Spain 24, 175, 188
New Temple 282
New Testament 157, 190, 194, 227, 239, 240, 472

New World xvi, xvii, 1, 2, 3, 6, 7, 11, 15, 16, 17, 18, 19, 21, 22, 24, 25, 28, 29, 32, 33, 35, 36, 39, 41, 42, 49, 50, 53, 56, 62, 66, 68, 70, 85, 96, 99, 100, 103, 104, 106, 108, 111, 118, 120, 128, 137, 153, 168, 169, 172, 175, 185, 187, 188, 189, 190, 191, 210, 216, 220, 225, 226, 228, 234, 235, 238, 239, 246, 248, 260, 262, 264, 267, 271, 275, 277, 283, 284, 286, 287, 290, 294, 306, 313, 316, 317, 324, 326, 330, 343, 352, 360, 362, 367, 368, 376, 379, 380, 384, 389, 400, 443, 451, 464, 468, 472, 496, 497, 498, 502, 503, 504, 516, 518, 519

New York 71, 80, 84, 483, 527

New York City 78

Newman, Margaret E. 216, 410

Nezahualcoyotzin, King of Tetzcuco 45

Nibley, Hugh W. xvi, 90, 94, 95, 105, 117, 498, 499, 523

Nicaragua 203, 369

Nicholson, Henry B. 328, 330, 340

Nicuesa, Diego 443

Nina Chumpi 372

Noah 3, 30, 44, 48, 50, 51, 115, 158, 212, 472, 487, 497, 520

Nordenskjold, E. 383

normative paradigm 14, 16, 189, 316

North Sea 298

northern Asia 290

Núñez Cabeza de Vaca, Alvar 513

Nuñez de Balboa, Vasco 20, 23, 48, 173, 370, 443, 444

O'Gorman, Edmundo 6, 45

oaths 245, 251, 253, 254, 255, 272, 296, 300, 303, 454

Oaxaca, Mexico 60, 61, 462

Oberlin College 86

obsidian 444, 445

ocean 106, 377, 524

Ohio 528, 533

Old Temple 57, 215, 278

Old Testament 100, 157, 160, 188, 213, 223, 233, 235, 251, 464, 465, 472

Old Testament prophets 440

Old World 5, 6, 11, 13, 68, 70, 99, 118, 128, 156, 185, 188, 272, 277, 293, 306, 307, 344, 376, 384, 502, 506, 507, 519

Olmec civilization 13, 53, 54, 58, 61, 216, 230, 275, 277, 289, 290, 291, 341, 366, 407, 411, 419, 435, 440, 445, 451, 500, 518

Olmos, Andrés de 328, 340

Omaha, Nebraska 547

Oman 95

Only Begotten Son of God 212, 226, 473

Ophir 4, 48, 49, 50, 56, 287, 376

Opinion 7
opposition 78, 527
ordained 225, 235, 237
ordinances 226, 247, 302, 346, 489
Orejones 122, 459
origin xiv, 5, 6, 7, 16, 40, 42, 44, 48, 71, 174, 190, 210, 502
Orinoco River 318, 326, 367, 369
other sheep 111
Owl 150, 200
Owl Deity 145, 146, 148

P

Pacarimoc Runa 51, 284
Pacaritambo 44
Pacha Cámac 50, 51
Pachacamac xi, 42, 122, 198, 283, 345, 383
Pachacuti Inca Yupanqui 223, 265, 371, 456, 457
Pacific Ocean 5, 13, 20, 23, 53, 54, 55, 67, 118, 275, 298, 325, 356, 370, 371, 373, 378, 435
Pagden, Anthony 431
Page, Hiram 82, 89
Painesville Telegraph 85
Painesville, Ohio 84
paintings 2, 3, 350, 351
Paita 122, 345
palaces 419, 420, 426, 429

paleontology 12, 14
palm lances 446
Palmyra Reflector 84
Palmyra, New York 10, 71, 73, 74, 78, 79, 80, 81, 84, 99, 490
Panama 20, 23, 24, 173, 249, 261, 324
paper 393
papyrus 482, 483, 484
Paracas 54, 287, 313
Paracelsus 8, 9
Paraguay xi, xv, 32, 136, 178, 179, 190, 312, 323, 331, 340, 341, 503
parallel xiv, 499
Paramaribo, Suriname 333
Paraná 323
Parana River 396
Paria 318
Passover 69, 133, 478
Pasto, Colombia 27, 54
Pastor Bodmer, Beatriz 36, 38, 39
patriarchal order 477, 478
Paul 227, 489, 505
pearls 374
Pease, Franklin 29
Peleg 48, 64
penitence 229, 230
People of Ammon 337
Perkins, Keith W. 89
Pernambuco, Brazil 67, 69
persecution 75, 81, 271, 471
Personages 470

Peru xii, 27, 30, 31, 33, 44, 49, 50, 51, 52, 53, 54, 69, 121, 122, 123, 126, 132, 139, 175, 182, 203, 215, 225, 244, 246, 250, 263, 265, 275, 277, 287, 289, 290, 291, 296, 297, 313, 319, 320, 328, 344, 365, 367, 371, 373, 374, 382, 388, 391, 393, 435, 447, 450, 451, 458, 496, 513
Peruvian 54, 57, 203, 277, 291, 296, 309, 321, 332, 333, 376, 382, 400, 450, 455
pestilence 119, 127, 308
Peter 160, 494, 495, 508
Peterson, Ziba 527
Peyrère, Isaac de la 8, 9, 519
Pharaoh 466
Phelps, W. W. 483
Phoenicians 4, 13
pikestaffs 448
pillar of fire 474
pillar of light 470
pillbox hats 436
Pirua Pacari Manco 52, 53
Pizarro, Francisco 29, 126, 264, 345, 371
Pizarro, Gonzalo 29, 121, 122
Pizarro, Pedro 29, 265, 320, 327, 447
plagues 119, 127
plates of brass 161, 214, 233, 441
Plato 3
Pliny 3
Plymouth, Massachusetts 515
poisonous darts 443

poisonous snakes 119, 273
Polk, James K. 545
pollutions 518
Polo de Ondegardo, Juan 174, 175
Polynesians 14, 379
Poma de Ayala, Felipe Guaman 20, 30, 50, 51, 108, 126, 136, 127, 147, 149, 190, 246, 247, 282, 284, 285, 286, 287, 297, 298, 300, 321, 327, 339, 496
Ponce de León, Juan 20, 512
Popol Vuh 146
Portugal 2, 18, 19, 36, 463, 515
Portuguese ix, x, xii, xiii, xiv, 19, 21, 68, 69, 70, 156, 168, 188, 220, 234, 260, 261, 269, 317, 321, 323, 324, 463, 464, 493, 496, 501, 512, 518
post-diluvial 48
pottery 16, 341, 370
Poultney, Vermont 91
Pratt, Orson 74, 540
Pratt, Parley P. 527, 536, 538
Pre-ceramic 392
pre-Christian 366, 433
precious fruit 102
precious jewels 102, 261, 388
precious metals 285, 294, 299, 300, 386
precious ores 335
precious stones 351, 393, 400
Pre-classic period 55, 58, 277, 289

pre-Columbian xiii, 12, 13, 15, 16, 30, 31, 33, 34, 40, 42, 53, 93, 96, 148, 153, 155, 156, 184, 185, 187, 260, 269, 287, 316, 342, 367, 368, 382, 383, 390, 391, 433, 501, 502

prediction 351, 490

pre-historic 313

pre-Inca 27

prejudice 16

Pre-Maya 313

premonition 346

Presbyterian 74

Presidio of San Augustin 514

pride 114, 256, 262, 299

priestcrafts 516

priesthood 20, 169, 202, 213, 234, 235, 238, 239, 240, 241, 242, 473, 478, 486, 538, 542

Priesthood keys 475

priests 1, 2, 5, 22, 24, 25, 26, 31, 33, 38, 42, 45, 120, 128, 170, 177, 188, 190, 191, 192, 206, 210, 221, 234, 235, 236, 237, 238, 240, 241, 242, 244, 248, 301, 336, 344, 345, 355, 356, 385, 459, 480, 503, 519

Prince Phillip 32, 34, 35, 448

pristine civilizations 56

promised land 59, 100, 102, 116, 118, 256, 357, 520

Proof 96, 494

prophecies 66, 67, 102, 110, 241, 299, 337, 343, 344, 345, 346, 347, 349, 351, 355, 356, 360, 361, 486, 505, 507, 518

prophesy 128, 134, 271, 345, 353, 359, 468, 474, 489, 506, 509

prophet x, xii, 11, 71, 100, 102, 111, 114, 134, 157, 168, 185, 204, 205, 206, 207, 208, 214, 233, 234, 256, 262, 271, 291, 294, 355, 366, 395, 451, 474, 482, 486, 488, 490, 491, 496, 506, 507, 510, 516, 518, 519, 527, 529, 533, 546

prosperity 269, 300

Provincia da Sancta Cruz 19

psychotropic drugs 291, 421

Ptolemy 3, 48

publication 34, 36, 39, 72, 104, 469, 481, 499, 504

published xvii, 31, 32, 48, 50, 174, 493

Pucarás 285, 327

punishment 50, 207, 247, 283, 348

purify 206, 207, 208, 221, 229

Purunruna 284, 285, 300

puzzle 16

pyramids 140, 188, 224, 280, 281, 290, 365, 407, 410, 411, 412, 419, 435, 436

pyramids of Egypt 277

Q

Quechua 44, 50, 69, 125, 126, 205
Queen Isabella 20, 512
Querandíes 322
Quetzal Serpent 194
Quetzalcoatl xi, 42, 45, 58, 62, 152, 220, 240, 329, 330, 331, 355, 412
Quijada, Diego 192
Quilter, Jeffrey 140, 145, 146, 147
Quincy, Illinois 538
Quincy, Josiah 543
quipocamayoc 30
quipos 2, 30, 43, 51, 283, 288, 366
Quito, Ecuador 49, 63, 122, 345, 446, 458, 459
Quorum of the Twelve Apostles 487, 488, 529, 532, 541

R

rabbi 202, 463
radiocarbon 275, 277
rainbow 44
Ramírez, José Fernando 25
Rayed Deity xi, 146, 148, 150, 151, 152, 500
records 101, 102, 104, 106, 109, 303, 358, 363, 382, 456, 468, 485, 498, 504, 516
Red Sea 95, 101, 102, 523
Redeemer of Israel 124, 166, 198, 358, 359, 361
redemption 464, 465
Reilly, F. Kent, III 216, 230
Relación 22, 68
religions xiii, xiv, 2, 3, 25, 40, 42, 70, 74, 75, 174, 188, 241
religious beliefs 11, 23, 42, 43, 70, 76, 92, 156, 206, 210, 215, 244, 281, 355, 384, 510, 512
religious ceremonies 215, 224, 277
Religious revivals 74
Rembrandt 464
Remnant of Jacob 362
research 6, 16, 88, 433
restitution 508
restoration 163, 473, 479, 486, 507, 511
resurrection xi, 42, 103, 110, 111, 134, 135, 148, 150, 152, 156, 159, 160, 169, 170, 171, 172, 175, 179, 180, 181, 228, 231, 464, 466, 479, 499, 500, 505, 510
revelations 75, 76, 78, 81, 158, 159, 233, 282, 299, 473, 479, 481, 485, 486, 494, 495, 505, 521, 528, 531, 538
revelator 71
Revolt of the Objects 145
Reynolds, Thomas 542
Rhodes, Michael D. 483
Rice, L. L. 86

Richards, Willard 546
Richmond Conservator 89
Richmond, Missouri 89, 536, 538
Rigdon, Sidney 84, 86, 473, 474, 481, 498, 527, 528, 534, 536, 538, 539, 541, 547
righteous 273, 338
righteousness 295, 507
Rimac River 122
Rio de Janeiro 322
Rio de la Plata 175, 322
Riplakish 419
rites 25, 31, 174, 187, 223, 242, 344, 498
rituals 96, 149, 187, 211, 215, 218, 230, 278, 281, 451
Roberts, B. H. 486, 528
Rochester, New York 10, 86
Román y Zamora, Jerónimo 5
Romances of Chivalry 38
Rome 416
Rowe, John H. 56
Royal Decree 35
Roys, Ralph L. 192
Ruiz de Montoya, Antonio 136, 178
Runacamac Viracocha 50
Ruyz, Bartolomé 371

S

sacerdotal 221
sacrament 111, 213, 223, 226, 241
sacrifice 42, 61, 70, 128, 149, 168, 174, 175, 180, 185, 206, 211, 212, 214, 216, 218, 219, 220, 221, 222, 223, 224, 226, 228, 229, 230, 251, 256, 265, 267, 291, 307, 329, 330, 345, 349, 353, 440, 520
Sacsayhuamán 371, 400
Saenz de Santa Maria, Carmelo 46
Sahagún, Bernardino de 25, 26, 36, 176, 177, 189, 229, 230, 239, 240, 242, 243, 254, 264, 265
Saint Bartholomew 136
Saint Jerome 48
Saint Thomas 136, 137
saintly preachers 5
Salomon, Frank 125
salt 369
Salt Lake City 548
Sam 101, 106, 151, 161
Samuel the Lamanite 128, 130, 134, 171, 239, 301, 360
San Blas Islands 261
San Diego, California 548
San Juan de Puerto Rico 512
San Juan de Ulúa 352
San Lorenzo 58, 289, 290, 411
Sancho, Pedro 387
sanctified 206, 227, 229, 237

Santa Catalina, Brazil 322
Santiago, Chile 27, 54
Santo Domingo 513
Santos, Brazil 322
São Vicente in Brazil 321
Sariah 101, 151
Sarmiento de Gamboa, Pedro 327, 373
Satan 149, 151, 163, 164, 165, 166, 167, 168, 187, 225, 300, 469
Savior 76, 111, 213, 358, 361, 469, 475, 476, 505, 506, 507, 520
Schele, Linda 68, 184, 185, 193, 230, 231
Scherzer, Carl 46
Scholes, Frances V. 192
Science 7, 15, 68, 87, 96, 494, 498, 504
scientists 12, 14, 15, 16, 189, 190, 368, 451, 497, 500, 501, 519
scimitars 448
Scotland 534
scripture 64, 71
sculptures 278
sea lions 145
Sebolo, Antonio 482
secret combinations 120, 272, 286, 296, 449, 520, 521
Seely, David Rolph 481
seer 71, 78, 467, 469, 491
Selma, Alabama 514
serpents 231
Seven Caves 59

Seville, Spain 27
sexual relations 206
shamans 149, 234, 242, 291
Sharon, Windsor County, Vermont 72, 73
Shelem 117
Shem 48
shields 183, 274, 312, 316, 389, 434, 442, 443, 444, 446, 447
Shiloh 206
ship 105, 106
Shipps, Jan 73, 83, 96, 494
Shule 434
Sidon 452
signs 120, 129, 243, 301, 307, 330, 347, 355, 360, 361, 511
silks 37, 119, 264, 273, 324, 392, 393, 395
silver 77, 101, 102, 108, 119, 156, 182, 236, 257, 258, 261, 262, 273, 285, 286, 299, 300, 323, 325, 335, 351, 353, 370, 372, 380, 381, 382, 383, 384, 385, 386, 387, 388, 390, 420
silver-gold alloys 381
similitudines hominis 9
Sinche Roca Inca 127
Sipán 182
sixteen small stones 117, 156
Skinner, Andrew 484
slings 440, 445, 446, 447, 457, 502
smallpox 346
Smith, Emma 77, 78, 481, 528, 538

Smith, Ethan 10, 91, 93, 383, 422, 498
Smith, George A. 474
Smith, George Albert 85
Smith, Hyrum 74, 75, 82, 486, 491, 536, 538
Smith, Joseph F. 74
Smith, Joseph x, xiv, xv, 71, 72, 74, 78, 80, 81, 82, 84, 85, 86, 87, 88, 90, 91, 92, 93, 94, 95, 97, 105, 107, 118, 137, 158, 163, 193, 235, 362, 391, 395, 433, 446, 462, 469, 470, 471, 472, 473, 474, 475, 476, 477, 478, 479, 480, 481, 482, 483, 484, 485, 486, 487, 488, 489, 490, 491, 493, 495, 498, 499, 501, 504, 505, 508, 515, 519, 522, 527, 528, 529, 531, 532, 533, 534, 535, 536, 537, 538, 539, 541, 542, 543, 544, 545, 546, 547, 549
Smith, Joseph, Sr. 72, 73, 474
Smith, Lucy Mack 72, 80
snake 176, 300
societies 155, 502
sociologist 87
socio-political 148
Son of God 129, 133, 162, 164, 198, 214, 235, 273, 358, 495, 507
sons of Israel 66, 67, 356, 362
sorcerers 177, 239, 346, 347, 349
South America 309, 512
South American 155
South Carolina 20, 91, 319, 513
South East Asia 49
South Pacific 324
South Sea 67, 298, 356
Souza, Admiral Martim Affonso de 321, 322
Souza, Pero Lopes de 321, 322, 396
Sovereign and Quetzal Serpent 197
Spain 2, 17, 18, 20, 25, 27, 35, 36, 121, 315, 317, 388, 392, 393, 419, 448, 496, 512, 515
Spalding theory 87
Spalding, Solomon 85, 86, 87
Spaniards ix, xiv, 3, 9, 21, 25, 32, 35, 36, 40, 41, 46, 60, 66, 67, 69, 122, 125, 168, 180, 188, 198, 220, 226, 242, 246, 255, 256, 260, 264, 301, 316, 318, 319, 320, 322, 327, 328, 340, 343, 346, 350, 351, 352, 353, 354, 355, 356, 365, 366, 368, 369, 370, 371, 383, 388, 389, 390, 395, 416, 423, 425, 429, 431, 434, 446, 448, 501, 513, 518
Spanish x, xii, xiii, 34, 39, 47, 68, 70, 156, 234, 269, 317, 383, 403, 463, 464, 493, 496, 502, 512, 514
spears 312, 440, 441, 443
spirit 156, 166, 174, 179, 198, 204, 207, 242, 267, 313, 359, 475, 494, 516, 533
spirit of God 103, 130, 357
spirit of war 312
spirit world 181
spirits of the dead 149

spiritual 258, 282, 494
spiritual death 150, 170
St. John 495
steel 108, 335, 380, 383, 434, 502
stench 308
Stephens, John Lloyd 12, 367
Stetson, John B. 34, 36
stone heads 411
stone masonry 501
stone monuments 290
stones 66, 403, 404, 440
storehouses 259
Stowell, Josiah 77
Sullivan, Lawrence E. 155
Sun 42, 45, 123, 127, 132, 147, 200, 202, 300, 393, 475, 499
sun worshiper 52
Supay 169
supernaturals 57, 145, 216, 282, 436
superstitions 36
supplication 151, 152
Supreme Council of the Indies 21
Susquehanna River 471
sword of Laban 105, 441
swords 304, 352, 379, 380, 383, 434, 435, 436, 440, 441, 442, 443, 448, 450, 457, 502
symbolism 148, 312
symbols 3, 148, 244, 466
synergism 40
synopsis 527

T

Tabasco 58, 352, 411, 430
tactics 434, 451, 454, 457
Tacuba 60
Tainos 41, 317, 318, 369
Talmud 62, 463, 464, 465
Tamaulipas 59
Tampa Bay 514
Tapuyas 324, 341
Tatars 8, 13, 14, 92, 317, 342, 497, 502
taxes, 257
Taylor, John 491, 540, 546
Teancum 441, 453, 454
technical skills 96
technological 367, 381, 431
Tello, Julio C. 56, 57, 275, 435
temples 42, 49, 56, 57, 69, 110, 111, 120, 123, 128, 139, 174, 203, 215, 218, 221, 222, 223, 224, 234, 241, 247, 335, 345, 346, 400, 420, 421, 474, 488, 489, 529, 548
temporal death 150
Ten Commandments 5, 190, 234, 246
Ten Lost Tribes 4, 5, 92, 187, 189, 356, 465, 466, 476
Tennessee 514
Tenochtitlan 24, 188, 251, 262, 263, 346, 347, 348, 349, 354, 366, 389, 419, 423, 429

Teotihuacan 55, 313, 330, 366, 411, 412, 416, 424, 500, 518
Tepanecs 59, 60, 461
Terrazas, Captain Bartolomé de 135
terrestrial paradise 177
testify 522
testimony 89, 248
Texas 514
textile manufacturing 501
Tezcoco 60, 220, 347, 348, 366, 461
theology 46
theories 4, 5, 7, 10, 12, 15, 48, 53, 71, 86, 88, 90, 91, 95, 187, 190, 287, 332, 333, 342, 343, 497, 499, 502, 503
theses 50
Thompson, E. H. 416
three Nephites 137
thunderings and lightnings 129, 130, 131
Tiahuanaco 44, 54, 126, 286, 313, 374, 403, 407
Ticci Viracocha xi, 42, 52, 57, 58, 123, 124, 126, 133, 135, 152, 198, 250, 265, 273, 280, 283, 284, 288, 296, 300, 301, 328, 330, 407, 421, 456
tidal waves 127
Tikal 184
tin 300
Titicaca 123, 341, 374
Tiwanaku 44, 54, 287, 313, 327, 328, 366, 403, 404, 500, 518
Tlacaelel 255, 388, 461, 462

Tlalhuicas 59, 60
Tlalocan 177
Tlaxcalans 24, 59, 60, 220, 347, 348, 366, 444, 462
Tocay 44
Tollan 55, 62, 330
Toltecs 55, 61, 62, 188, 189, 202, 313, 328, 329, 366, 518
Tomebamba 122, 459
Topa Inca Yupanqui 298, 345, 371, 372, 397, 457, 458
Topiltzin Quetzalcoatl 62, 188, 189, 328, 329, 330, 340, 350
topography 2, 118
Torah 463, 465
Torquemada, Juan de 369
torture 191, 192
total darkness 110
Totoras 374
Tower of Babel 11, 48, 99, 110, 115, 116, 188, 270, 376, 380
Tozzer, Alfred M. 27, 49, 168, 169, 192, 241, 331, 355, 369, 416, 429, 430, 446
traditions xiv, 2, 7, 193, 203, 497
transformation 181, 282
transgression 169, 213, 258
translation x, 11, 78, 81, 360, 469, 471, 481, 482, 483, 498, 508, 528, 529
translators 480
Tree of Life 151, 152, 167
Tribe of Judah 63, 100, 466

Tribe of Levi 63, 64
tribulation 38, 307
Trinidad 41, 315, 318, 369, 443
Trinity 198
Trinity River 514
Trujillo, Peru xi, 54, 122, 141, 287, 374, 410, 450
truncheons 448
Tsohar 117
Tucuman, Argentina 54, 455
Tula 55, 62, 193, 329, 330
Tumbes, Peru 371, 373, 425, 427
Tupac Cauri Pachacuti 249
Tupac Curi Amauta 306
twelve apostles 235, 238, 469, 472, 475, 533, 540
twelve disciples 103, 111, 112, 113, 137, 238, 302
twelve tribes of Israel 465, 516
twenty four gold plates 110, 115, 435
twining 391, 392, 395

U

Uhle, Max 249
United States 88, 486, 487
Urim and Thummim 77, 78, 80, 81, 82, 105, 109, 193
Urioste, George L. 125
Uru Indians 376
Uruguay xi

V

Vaca de Viega, Diego 68
Valley of Mexico 60, 128
Van Buren, Martin 12, 541, 544
vapor of darkness 131
Vari Runa 30
Vari Viracocha Runa 30, 50, 283, 284
Vasquez, Guinaldo 288, 289
Vaz de Caminha, Pero 19
Vázquez de Ayllón, Lucas 20, 319, 513
Velázquez, Diego 24
Venezuela 315, 318, 326, 367, 443
Venezuelan 42, 356, 369, 443
Veracruz, Mexico 24, 61, 251, 289, 330, 353
verification 96, 494
Vespucci, Amérigo 18, 19
viceregal period 40
viceroy 36
vicuña 392, 393
Villar, Leonardo 57
violence 520, 521
vision 37, 75, 76, 79, 100, 101, 102, 103, 151, 282, 347, 357, 471, 473, 474, 480, 486, 488, 490, 506, 521
Vogel, Dan 91, 92, 93, 94, 498
volcanos 127, 372
Von Buchwald, Otto 249

Von Hagen, Victor Wolfgang 27, 28, 34, 35, 57, 123, 241, 387, 400, 427
Von Humboldt, Alexander 367
voyages 21, 369

Wadi Sayq 524
Waldseemüller, Martin 19
Wales 534
Wallace, Henry A. 88
warclubs 183
warfare 96, 114, 280, 291, 310, 433, 450, 501
warriors x, 353, 366, 436, 461, 502
wars 520
Washington, D. C. 140, 541
weapons 96, 102, 278, 312, 380, 383, 389, 393, 433, 434, 436, 440, 442, 446, 448, 452, 457, 501
West Indies 4
Western hemisphere 137, 338, 511
white god xi, xiv, 351
white Indians xv, 42, 63, 68, 69, 313, 316, 317, 319, 321, 322, 325, 332, 333, 334, 342, 345, 448, 503
white llamas 222
white man 69, 123, 133, 329, 331, 345, 357
Whitmer, David 81, 89, 105, 534
Whitmer, John 82, 89, 485
Whitmer, Peter, Jr. 81, 82, 84, 527
whoredoms 518

wickedness 113, 114, 236, 239, 271, 273, 291, 295, 299, 301, 518, 520
wilderness 101
Willers, Diedrich 72
Williams, Carlos 407
Williams, Frederick G. 474
Winter Quarters 548
witchcraft 177, 239, 246, 304, 343
witness 495
witnesses 88, 89
woman 140, 145, 149, 150, 207, 209, 219, 245, 264, 286, 332, 395
wooden swords 444, 445
Woodruff, Wilford 539, 540
World Tree 152, 231
wrath of God 357
writings 25, 283, 288

Xibalba 169, 231
Xicalancas 61
Ximénez, Francisco 46
Xmucane (She Who Has Born Children) 197
Xochimilcas 59
Xochimilco 350
Xpiyacoc (He Who Has Begotten Sons) 197

Y

Yaguar Cocha 459, 460
Yemen 523
Young, Brigham 74, 82, 481, 529, 535, 536, 538, 540, 541, 547, 548, 549
Young, Joseph 529, 535
Yucatán 8, 12, 20, 24, 27, 49, 55, 62, 177, 191, 192, 193, 202, 241, 242, 246, 309, 319, 330, 331, 340, 350, 355, 367, 369, 394, 416, 429, 430, 446

Z

Zapana 327
Zarahemla 109, 110, 128, 130, 131, 236, 294, 298, 299, 303, 435
Zemes 344
Zeniff 395, 420, 441
ziff 236, 385, 420
Zion 479, 509, 530, 532
Zion's Camp 532, 533
Zoram 102, 106, 252, 253
Zoramites 337